A History
of WAGR
Passenger Carriages

Researched and written by
Andrew May and Bill Gray

ISBN: 0-646-45902-3
First Published 2006 by Bill Gray
© Copyright 2006 Bill Gray
Cover Design & Layout by Red Kettle Designs
www.redkettledesigns.com
Printed by Asia Pacific

This book is dedicated to my wife Colleen and my children David and Nicole who lived with it for 20 years.

INTRODUCTION and ACKNOWLEDGEMENTS

"This book was born on a cold winter's night in 1980. I was travelling home by bus from a friend's place in one of Perth's northern suburbs. The route took me past the old Perth carriage sheds next to the bus station. At that time I had only a casual interest in Westrail (being a parochial pommie), but the old coach which I saw that night changed everything. AM 313 was quite unlike anything I had seen before. It looked very old. I was hooked. I had to find out more.

That encounter led me to try and unravel the story of W.A.G.R's carriages. With the help of Laurie White, Jeff Della Bosca and Jeff Austin the tale has been unravelled. It remains only to be told."

This was the introduction which appeared at the beginning of a 55 page manuscript Andrew May researched and wrote during the early 1980's. Soon after producing the manuscript Andrew, having also completed his university studies, returned to the UK to work and the manuscript was left with Graham Watson, who set about finding someone to complete it.

Graham lent me a copy the manuscript in the late 1980's, and in it I found a wealth of information "remaining only to be told", but felt that it needed to be reformatted so the histories of individual classes and individual carriages could be followed more easily. This resulted in an almost total rewrite based on Andrew's original information, but with the addition of new material which came to light as the research continued. I hope I have done his original work justice.

While Andrew and I appear on the title page of this book as its authors, it would be less than honest of either of us to accept sole credit for the project. I am certain that anybody who has ever attempted a work of this magnitude would agree that the end product is actually the result of the input of many people in various ways. There are a number of people without whom this book would never have been completed, and in no real order of preference I wish to acknowledge them:

Graham Watson, who encouraged, cajoled, criticized, and spent many hours discussing the project as well as keeping an eye out in the Australian Railway Historical Society (WA Division) archives for relevant material;
Likewise, Jeff Austin provided continual encouragement over the years, freely gave of any information he had, helped resolve issues with some of the earlier carriages and patiently re-answered questions I had already asked him;
Murray Rowe, who unselfishly allowed me access to the Geoff Blee collection of slides and photographs and, in so doing, gave me the final impetus and encouragement to finish the project off;
Rob Clark, who assisted early on with sorting out the various classes of carriage and their histories, and who came with me on a number of field trips to look at old coaches stored in and around Perth;
Joe Moir, who also encouraged the work and offered me his slides and extensive knowledge of the workings of the railways in Western Australia;
Roger Palmer, who assisted with many photographs, drawings and his expertise with computers;

There are also many others who I'd rather not try and name for fear of forgetting someone. There are many people who gave me permission to use their photographs, offered information, answered questions and generally supported the project in a myriad of ways. My thanks to them all.

The story to date has now been told, even though it has not yet ended. People will continue to travel by rail and passenger cars will be needed to carry them. As you read the following pages it is my hope that you enjoy the journey.

Bill Gray
31 March, 2006.

A Note to the Reader

No project the size of this one will be without it's errors and ommissions. If any reader can add further information, particularly the whereabouts of any surviving carriages not already detailed herein, the authors would be pleased to hear about it at www.wacarriages.com.

Purchasing Further Copies

Further copies can be purchased at our website: www.wacarriages.com.

CONTENTS

CHAPTER ONE
THE EARLY YEARS 1877 - 1890.

Around the end of August 1871, following a period of typical blustery winter weather, the brigantine "Nightingale" arrived in Geographe Bay in the colony of Western Australia. Included in the cargo unloaded from the ship was a small, black steam locomotive, the first seen in the colony, for the Western Australian Timber Co. A short time later this little locomotive, with the name "Ballaarat" emblazoned down the side of its timber boiler lagging, puffed out of Lockeville bound for the forests of Yokonup some 12 miles (18 km) away, and so began the history of railways in Western Australia. The WA Timber Co. did not intend the line to convey passengers, but there can be little doubt that, over the years, the occasional individual made use of the empty wagons going up to the forests, or perched precariously atop the stacks of sawn timber travelling down, in order to avoid the long and arduous journey by foot or other less comfortable means of transport.

By 1872 the railways in the other colonies of Australia were an obvious success, as was the Lockeville to Yokonup line, along with two other timber carrying lines located closer to Perth, and it became apparent that the government was going to have to involve itself in this revolutionary form of transport. However, the West Australian administrators found themselves in a dilemma over the issue with a lack of funds on one hand (the economy had slumped since the transportation of convicts ceased in 1868) and the newspapers (and hence the public) providing pressure on the other. Arguments over the siting of the proposed railway flew back and forth, till the decision was taken to build it from Geraldton, some 250 miles (400 km) North of Perth, to Northampton, another 34 miles (54 km) further on. Lead and copper were being mined at Northampton and the theory was that the cost savings in the transport of these commodities to the coast at Geraldton would offset the cost of the railway. The surveys were done, contracts let, the first sod turned to mark the start of construction of the Northern Railway on 22 October, 1874, and late that year an order was placed with the Metropolitan Railway Carriage and Wagon Co. of Birmingham in England for two 4 wheeled passenger carriages. These vehicles, Western Australia's first passenger cars, arrived in Geraldton on 7 November, 1875 aboard the barque "Fitzroy" and by April, 1876 had been assembled and were ready for traffic.[1] However, several engineering problems, including the death of the Construction Engineer, and the resulting politics, caused considerable delays to the construction of the new railway. The first section was finally opened on 25 September, 1877 and by the time the full length of the line was officially opened on 26 July, 1879, the railway had cost twice as much as originally planned. To make matters even worse, the price of lead had halved, so causing the line to be a financial disaster.[2]

While the two Northern Railway cars trundled back and forth between Geraldton and Northampton, the politicians turned their attention to an area where there were more people (and more money) for the next railway in the colony. On 3 June, 1879 contractor John Robb began work on a line from Fremantle to Perth and on to Guildford, which places were, at that time, quite distinct and separate centres. This line became known as the Eastern Railway.

In April, 1880, three more 4 wheeled cars (1-3), nearly identical to those operating on the Northern Railway, were ordered from the Metropolitan Railway Carriage and Wagon Co. for the Eastern Railway. They were not available for the opening of the first section of the line between Fremantle and North Fremantle on 31 August, 1880, but arrived at Fremantle on 11 January, 1881 aboard the "Fitzroy".[3] The new cars were ready for service in February, two were used on a special train from Perth to Guildford on 14 February, 1881[4] and all three were used on the opening day of the line to Guildford on 1 March, 1881.

The 4 wheeled carriages set the standard for the design of most of the WAGR's passenger cars for the rest of the decade, with their side loading compartments, panelled timber bodies and peanut oil lamps mounted in the roof.

Hard on the heels of the Eastern Railway's 4 wheeled cars came the first of two 6 wheeled carriages. One car was in service by June, 1881. It had its padded seats slashed by a vandal on 16 June.[5] The second car entered service during the latter half of that year. These cars were composite saloons, numbered 4 and 5. They rode on a Cleminson chassis, which consisted of three axles, each carried on its own truck. The front and rear trucks could pivot while the centre one was able to move sideways, and the trucks were linked together in such a way that when one was moved by a curve in the rails the others followed suit, so allowing the carriage to negotiate sharp curves more readily than it could have done with a rigid wheel base.[6] As a result they were known as "Cleminson" cars. Like the first 4-wheeled cars, the "Cleminson" carriages had sunshades over their windows, a fixture deleted on later cars because of its uselessness. Two second class "Cleminson" cars (6 and 7) were ordered in 1882. These were delivered to Fremantle aboard the barque "West Australian" on 28 February, 1883[7] and entered traffic in March.

The Eastern Railway proved itself to be a great success and it quickly became obvious that the demand for services was far greater than could be provided, leading to the acquisition of larger coaches. Western Australia's first bogie carriages arrived at Fremantle aboard the "SS Kennett" on 9 February, 1884[8] from the Metropolitan Railway Carriage and Wagon Co. They entered traffic in March. The new cars were composite saloons with end platforms and, because of their appearance, they were known as "American" cars. The first batch of four (8-11) went into traffic on the Eastern Railway which had reached Chidlow's Well in March, 1884 and was heading for York, reaching that town, then the centre of the agricultural area, in June, 1885.

1885 proved to be a busy year for the fledgling WAGR. Soon after the arrival of a second batch of six "American" cars (12, 14-18), the first withdrawal of a carriage from passenger service took place when 4-wheeled car No. 1 was fitted with a clerestory roof and converted into Western Australia's first State saloon. This conversion was completed in June, 1885 and the car was used for the first time in its new role on the opening of the railway to York on 29 June, 1885. Another 4 wheeler, car No. 13, arrived from England to replace it, going into service about July 1885. About 1885 the two "Cleminson" cars (4 and 5) were converted to first class saloons, and in 1886 one of them (possibly No. 5) was fitted with a new body, for reasons not now known.[9] In 1889 No. 5 was rebuilt again, this time into a bogie State saloon, and it replaced the 4 wheeler, No. 1. In 1890 No. 5 was replaced by "Cleminson" car BC 6, which had also been rebuilt and fitted with bogies. Car 6 was replaced in 1901 by AN 206. Meanwhile, car No. 1 rejoined the passenger fleet as a first class saloon in 1889, being reclassified as a composite car again in 1890.

During 1886 a system of classification for the Government's locomotives was introduced[10] and the five different types then in service on the Eastern Railway were put into separate classes. (The Kitson built locos on the Northern Railway remained unclassified till 1891.) The coaches also appear to have been placed in classes around 1886 as follows, but the classifications were a little less distinct:-

»	Northern Railway 4 wheelers	- unclassed till 1899;
»	Eastern Railway 4 wheelers	- Class AB;
»	Composite "Cleminson" cars	- Class ABC;
»	Second class "Cleminson" cars	- Class BC;
»	"American" cars	- Class AB, but they were reclassified ABA soon afterwards.
»	4 wheeled State saloon (VIP cars)	- Class A.

Despite the new classifications these carriages were still referred to by type in official documentation, rather than class letter, a practice which continued right up to the reclassification of 1900.

Late in the evening of 8 December, 1885 locomotive C.1 (now preserved at the Rail Transport Museum at Bassendean) shunted eight loaded ballast wagons out of Smith's Mill siding, located east of Darlington, onto the mainline where the intention was to stop and back up to the brake van. However, the line at that point was on a downgrade and the locomotive's brakes were unable to hold the train against its load, causing it to start moving down the hill. The guard was apparently on the engine, so was unable to pin down the wagon brakes and, despite the crew's desperate attempts to stop the runaway, it continued to gather speed. They finally gave up hope and abandoned it to its fate. Further down the hill, between Darlington and Greenmount, was a sharp curve around the spur of a hill known to enginemen as "Cape Horn", for reason of it being as treacherous as its better known namesake, and it was here that the train came to grief, causing itself considerable damage in the process. As a result of this accident it was decided to fit all passenger coaches and brake vans with automatic vacuum brakes as soon as the equipment became available. By the end of 1888 all the carriages on the Eastern Railway had been so fitted, but the Northern Railway cars appear not to have been done. In later years the 4 wheelers had the braking equipment removed again, retaining a through pipe to allow their use in passenger trains.[11]

Five more 4 wheeled cars (19-23) went into traffic on the

Eastern Railway about March, 1886,[12] and in early 1891 two more (NR 3 and 4) entered service on the Northern Railway, making thirteen of the type in traffic. The last of the type was NR 5 for the Northern Railway, this car entering service in 1894.

In late 1887 the isolated railway between Bunbury and Boyanup was opened. It was owned by the WAGR, but operated by a private contractor using horses as the motive power, six 4 wheeled tramcars with end platforms for passenger carriages, and two 4 wheeled brake vans. In July, 1890 the WAGR took over the operation of the line, but the cars, apparently two second class and two composites, were never allocated numbers in the passenger stock list, being deleted before the combined list was introduced. The horses were replaced by the first of two H class 0-6-0T steam engines soon after the takeover. The Bunbury to Boyanup line was connected to the main system in 1893 via the Southwest Railway, and the Bunbury Tram Cars appear to have lasted till about 1897.

In 1886 two branch lines were completed, one from Spencer's Brook to Northam and the other from York to Beverley, the completion of the Beverley branch more readily allowing work to begin on the privately owned Great Southern Railway. The Great Southern was a land grant railway, under which scheme a company undertaking the construction of a line was granted tracts of land along its route, thus saving the Government large sums of money, but still satisfying the ever growing demand for rail transport. Construction of the Great Southern Railway began in October, 1886 simultaneously at Beverley and Albany and, in anticipation of the extra traffic the Great Southern line would generate over its own tracks, the WAGR placed an order with the Metropolitan Railway Carriage and Wagon Co. for four more 6 wheeled composite "Cleminson" cars, but with side door compartments. These cars were ordered rather than the more modern and comfortable bogie cars because Mr. W. Mather, the Locomotive Superintendent at the time, considered them to be more economical.[13] They entered service as numbers 24-27 in 1888, classed ABC, and were followed by another two (28 and 29) in 1891. The Great Southern Railway was opened to traffic on 1 June, 1889.

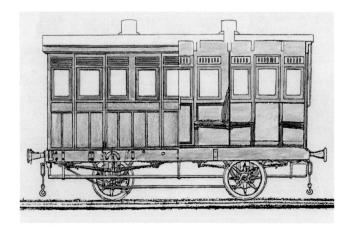

Newly restored AI 258 at the Midland Workshops, June 1990.   *Photo courtesy Nick Pusenjak*

The WAGR's first two carriages were 4 wheelers, ordered from the Metropolitan Railway Carriage and Wagon Co. of Birmingham in England. They arrived in Geraldton aboard the barque "Fitzroy" on 7 November, 1875 and were assembled by April, 1876,[14] entering service on the Northern Railway in 1877.

The underframes and bodies of these cars were made of teak, the interiors red pine, and the roofs Bavarian pine. They were fitted with three compartments, the centre one being first class because it was the biggest of the three, and the other two were designated second class. Each carriage seated 22 passengers, 6 first class and 16 second. The first class seats were padded and upholstered while the second class were only varnished timber. Lighting was by oil lamps, two of which lit all three compartments.

It would appear that the new 4-wheeled cars were not popular with the Railway's administration almost from the outset, being described by Mr. James H. Thomas, Engineer (Civil) Public Works Department and Railways from 1878 to 1881 (and later the first Commissioner of Railways), as "reduced models of old English stock, and totally unsuited for this climate, and not of the class generally employed on successfully worked narrow gauge lines."[15] The two cars were presumably numbered Northern Railway (NR) 1 and 2.

On 1 March, 1881 three more almost identical 4-wheeled cars entered service on the newly opened Eastern Railway. Mr Thomas' criticisms of 1876 had been handled by the addition of sunshades over the windows, apparently to improve the suitability of the cars to the local climate. These vehicles were numbered 1-3.

In 1885 car No. 1 was fitted with a clerestory roof and converted into Western Australia's first State saloon.[16] A new 4-wheeler (13) arrived from the Metropolitan Railway Carriage and Wagon Co. on 13 June, 1885 aboard the "SS Delcomyn" to replace it,[17] going into service about July. About this time the 4-wheelers were classified AB, and car No. 1 was classed A, but in 1889 it rejoined the passenger fleet as a first class saloon and was reclassified AB. In 1890 it was redesignated as a composite car again, apparently being refitted with compartments, and it retained its clerestory roof throughout the rest of its working life.

About March, 1886 five more 4-wheelers (19-23) went into traffic on the Eastern Railway, despite the apparent obsolescence of the design. The reason given for their purchase was that their light weight made them "very convenient for adding to a train if required, or to a goods train to accommodate passengers".[18] On 29 April, 1891 two more 4-wheelers (NR 3 and 4) were delivered to Geraldton aboard the "SS Flinders" and entered service on the Northern Railway on the 14 May.[19] The class reached its numerical peak of fourteen cars when one more AB was put into service in 1894, this being NR 5 on the Northern Railway. This vehicle was a former Bunbury car, whereas all the others were from the Metropolitan Railway Carriage and Wagon Co.

As the 1890's progressed and greater numbers of the bigger and more comfortable bogie cars appeared on the WAGR, passenger dissatisfaction with the now ageing 4-wheelers began to increase, and complaints from the railway patrons who were forced to ride in their cramped and uncomfortable compartments reached the point where something had to be

The much published, but historically significant photograph of the first three AI cars with Robb's engine and a brakevan at Perth station on the opening day of the Eastern Railway. Note the sunshades over the windows.

Photo courtesy Battye Library Ref: 3467B

done about them.[20] As a stopgap measure the accommodation in them was reduced to 18 by putting 6 passengers in each of the second class compartments instead of 8.[21] One plan was to put the bodies of two 4-wheeled cars onto a bogie underframe and to "build a brakevan at the end. One such coach would form a train in itself on lines where passenger traffic is small."[22] Although drawings were prepared, the proposal was deemed to be too expensive. In 1899 AB 21 and 23 were converted to louvred meat vans, but the WAGR Mechanical Branch claimed that "this created a non-standard and difficult to maintain vehicle",[23] so no more conversions were done.

That same year the Northern Railway cars were included in the AB classification and were renumbered (in order) 258-262. NR 4 (AB 261), which had been transferred to the Eastern Railway in 1895, did not carry its new classification for long, if at all, as it was condemned later in 1899. A 4-wheeled car reportedly caught fire at Mingenew about 15 August, 1898 and was burnt out, despite the valiant efforts of the locomotive crew to save it.[24] While no positive record has been found, AB 261 seems to have been this car.

In September, 1900 the WAGR reclassified its rolling stock and the remaining 4-wheelers became class AI, but the writing was on the wall for these vehicles as they had outlived their usefulness. In 1901 AI 3 was converted into a P class travelling workman's van and AI 259 followed suit the next year. In 1902 AI 262 was sold to the Canning Jarrah Timber Co. for use on the Kalamunda Zig Zag line between Midland Junction and Canning Mills. Its eventual fate is not known. In 1903-04 another four cars were disposed of, AI 258 being sold to the Goldfields Water Supply Administration for use on their Mundaring to Mundaring Weir line, AI 1 was sold to Millars Karri and Jarrah Co. in 1903, and AI 19 and 20 were condemned in 1904, possibly also having gone to Millars the previous year. AI 1 was demolished at Jarrahdale about 1960.

At the beginning of 1905 only four AI class cars were left, but in 1906 AI 260 followed AI 258 to Mundaring and in 1907 AI 13 was sold, its fate remaining unknown. In 1909 it was found that the Goldfields Water Supply Administration's line was operating in breach of the Government Railways Act[25] and on 15 September, 1909 the line and stock were sold to the WAGR. Included in the sale were AI 258 and 260. It is doubtful that any of the remaining AI's saw much use, probably spending most of their time idle. In March, 1912 AI 258 was sold to the Public Works Department and converted to a "tramcar" by having its doors and compartment walls removed. It was sent to Carnarvon in June, 1912. In 1914 AI 2 and 260 were transferred to the WAGR's "Working Railway Timber Mill" at Banksiadale. They both arrived there on 20 June, 1914, but only ten days later AI 2 was destroyed by fire. AI 260 lasted longer, finally being demolished.

AI 22 was the last to go, being sold to the Department of the Northwest at Carnarvon and it headed north in 1925 to join AI 258 as a "tramcar". Both these vehicles ran till the 1960's, with AI 258 being noted intact at Carnarvon in 1965. It was separated from its frame at about that time and its body was placed in a nursery in Carnarvon. The frame, along with a number of other old flat wagons and underframes found their way to the Recreation Ground where they were apparently used as seats. AI 22, in the meantime, was destroyed. The relics at Carnarvon were all but forgotten till 1988 when they were rediscovered and the body of AI 258 went into the care of the Gascoyne Historical Society in May that year. It was placed on an H wagon at Carnarvon jetty, but was subjected to some vandalism there and on 20 October, 1989 both body and frame were returned to Midland. Here the historic little carriage was returned to running condition by Westrail, being outshopped in June, 1990. It is currently on display at East Perth Terminal.

AI 258 as a tram car at Carnarvon in 1965. *Photo courtesy Dr. I. Cutter*

A derelict AI 1 stands next to a Millars coach at Yarloop, both awaiting their fate.
Photo courtesy Len Purcell

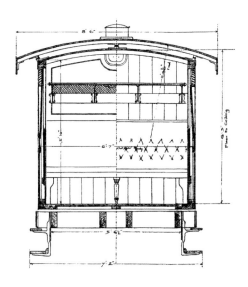

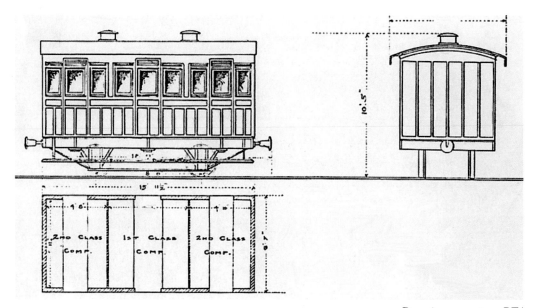

Drawings courtesy PTA

AI 22 (closest to the camera) & AI 258 in service at Carnarvon as tram cars. Note the different roof overhang between the two cars.

Photo late E. Woodland, ARHS Collection.

1881   6-Wheeled Composite Saloon   4 & 5
AC class (1886)
AH class (1900)
1883   6-wheeled Second Class saloon   6 & 7
BC class (1886)

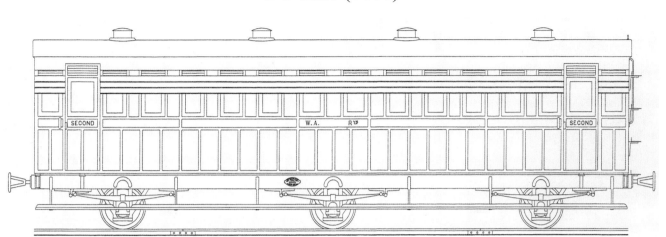

This drawing by Jeff Austin depicts the Cleminson saloon in its original condition, as no photographs have come to light.

By June, 1881 the first of two 6 wheeled "Cleminson" carriages had entered service.[26] It is believed both cars arrived in the colony on 22 April, 1881 aboard the barque "Daylight",[27] having been built by the Metropolitan Railway Carriage and Wagon Co. They were, in effect, two four wheeled coaches joined in the middle, without compartments and with a 6-wheeled Cleminson underframe to support them. The second car entered service sometime after July that year.

Their bodies were of timber, painted Indian red and carried on a steel underframe. The cars were delivered as composite loose seat saloons, (although the builder's drawing designated them as first class cars with longitudinal seating), but in May, 1885 they were fitted with longitudinal seats. The First Class seats were padded and upholstered, while the hapless Second Class passengers made themselves as comfortable as they could on the varnished timber benches. Passenger capacity in this configuration is not known. The cars were provided with four oil lamps for lighting, but this proved to be insufficient, so two more were added later. The cars were built with plain 12' radius curved roofs, but were fitted with clerestory roofs by 1900. The new cars were numbered 4 and 5.

In March, 1882 two more "Cleminson" cars, this time second class saloons, were ordered from the Metropolitan Railway Carriage and Wagon Co.[28] and these went into service in March, 1883. They were numbered 6 and 7 and were identical in every respect to "Cleminson" cars 4 and 5, except that they were second class throughout.

Cars 4 and 5 were classified AC in 1886 having recently been converted to first class saloons, probably by the expedient method of padding the second class seats. In his Annual Report in 1885, Mr. Mather wrote that the alteration in the seating of the "First Class carriages alone cost £180, the advantage gained however, by this being a gain of double the seating accommodation."[29] They had become composites again by May, 1887.[30] The second class cars (6 and 7) were classified BC. It had been reported in October, 1882 that one of the then two cars in service (4 and 5) was performing

splendidly, while the other had a number of serious problems which had remained unresolved, despite several visits to the workshops.[31] It is thought that this car was No. 5. In 1886 one of the AC's, also thought to be No. 5, was rebuilt, being fitted with "a new body and internal fittings of a more comfortable kind".[32] It has been suggested that its old body was in very poor condition, but the reason for a carriage body only four years old to be so bad as to need replacing is not known. Perhaps its earlier problems and subsequent body condition were linked. In any event, after its rebuild it was used on the special train to the opening of the Beverley railway on 5 August, 1886, the local media reporting it as "...a car which was built at the Fremantle Railway Workshops...being faithfully constructed and very handsomely upholstered..."[33] Thus it became the first passenger car body to be built by the WAGR. In 1889 No. 5 underwent further major reconstruction, which included the replacement of its 6 wheeled underframe with bogies, to become the State saloon.[34] It was classified A 5 and its underframe was utilised in the construction of the first Post Office van for service between Fremantle and Albany.[35] In 1890 A 5 was redesignated as the Commissioner's saloon, having had its role taken over the year before by another former 6-wheeler, BC 6, which had also been placed on a bogie underframe and presumably fitted with better and more comfortable facilities. Car 6 was also placed in the A class and remained in VIP service till 1901 when it was replaced by AN 206. It was then converted into a Z class brake van. The responsibility for the utilisation of No. 5 was placed in the hands of the Minister for Railways in 1895 and it finally became an AL class inspection car in 1901, being written off in 1953. It was scrapped three years later.

Meanwhile, BC 7 was converted to a brake composite car for use on the Newcastle branch, entering service on 13 February, 1889 and reclassified AC. It had its brake compartment located in the centre of the car and was fitted with lookouts and end platforms. It was later redesignated first class and reclassified A (when is not known), before being converted into a funeral car in 1899.

Of the four "Cleminson" saloon cars AC 4 led the quietest life. It arrived at the Fremantle Workshops for repairs on 16 May, 1898 and for a while it looked like it might be converted into a breakdown van, but nothing appears to have been done.[36] It was put into the AH class in 1900 with the other passenger carrying 6 wheeled cars (see 1888) and was rebuilt with bogies around 1906-07. At the same time it was redesignated second class and appears to have been retired and stored in 1920. In 1927 it was converted into a Z class brakevan.

None of the first four "Cleminson" cars survive.

Cleminson car AH 4 at Perth Station, 1897.
Photo courtesy Battye Library 225440P

AL 5 at Kalgoorlie c.1896.   Photo courtesy ARHS Archives

AN 6 at Kalgoorlie c.1896.   Photo ARHS Archives

Car No. 7 as a brake car with platforms.
Drawing courtesy PTA.

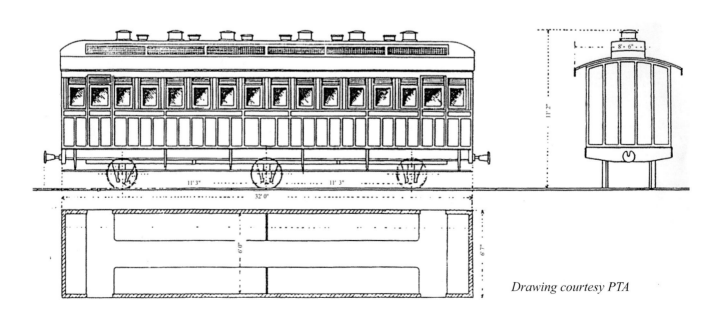

Drawing courtesy PTA

1884

Bogie Composite Saloon - "American" cars
AB class (1886)
ABA class
AG class (1900)

8-12

14-18

AG 14 as displayed at Bassendean till removed for restoration in September, 2002. Photo taken 15 May, 1993.

Photo: Bill Gray

Western Australia's first four bogie carriages (8-11) were ordered from England on 15 March, 1883[37] and went into traffic on the Eastern Railway early the following year.[38] They were called "American" cars by the WAGR, owing to their perceived similarity to the contemporary American carriages of the day, even though they had been built by the Metropolitan Railway Carriage and Wagon Co. of Birmingham in England. With their steel underframes and timber panelled bodies they were much heavier and longer than the earlier carriages. They were painted Indian red, but it is believed that the underframes were painted to give the appearance of timber. The "American" cars carried 20 first class passengers and 26 second class in two compartments fitted with longitudinal seating. They were the first cars on the WAGR to have gangways between the end platforms allow passengers to move from one carriage to the next. Six oil lamps set in the roof of the carriage provided lighting.

In 1885 another six "American" cars (12, 14-18) went into service.[39] About the same time they were classified AB, but soon afterwards this was altered to ABA,[40] presumably to avoid confusion with the 4 wheeled cars. In the 1900 reclassifications they were grouped together with the American built "Gilbert" cars as the AG class.

In 1905 three (AG 9, 12 and 17) had brake compartments fitted and were transferred to Kalgoorlie to operate as brake cars on local trains in the Goldfields, replacing the ageing P class 4 wheeled brake vans. By 1921 they had been returned to Perth, owing to the loss of passenger traffic to the Kalgoorlie electric tram system. All three cars entered the workshops where they received completely new buffet car bodies, which were similar in style to the latest AQ and AR class corridor coaches. They were classified AGB.

In 1925 AG 15 was fitted with a lavatory and sent to do to a two year stint on the isolated Esperance Railway, returning to the main system when the Esperance line was linked up in 1927. In 1933 four of the "American" cars were stored, but two years later these vehicles, plus one other (AG 8, 10, 14, 16 and 18) were converted to AGV class brake vans for use on suburban goods trains. Two (AGV 10 and 14) were fitted with double doors into the guard's compartment during their conversion and another (AGV 18) retained its seats. They were reclassified ZAG in 1936, and were joined by AG 11 and 15 as ZAG's in 1938. The external appearance of these cars was altered very little by this conversion.

All seven ZAG's were reclassified ZG in 1940, however they began to disappear soon afterwards with ZG 15 being scrapped in 1941. (Another brakevan numbered Z 15 was built on the frame of brakevan Z 111 to replace it). ZG 10 and 16 were written off in 1947, while ZG 14 was converted to a breakdown van (VC 1441) the same year. It spent its last years at Geraldton before being written off in 1972 and preserved at Bassendean by the ARHS. ZG 18 was rebuilt with a new body in 1949 to become a workman's van (VW 6790). It was converted to a scale adjustor's van (VS 6790) in 1950 and remained so till it was scrapped in 1980. ZG 8 was demolished in 1950 (written off in 1951), and the last car, ZG 11, was written off in 1960.

AG 15 near Salmon Gums, enroute to Esperance, 1925.　　　　　　　　*Photo: ARHS Collection*

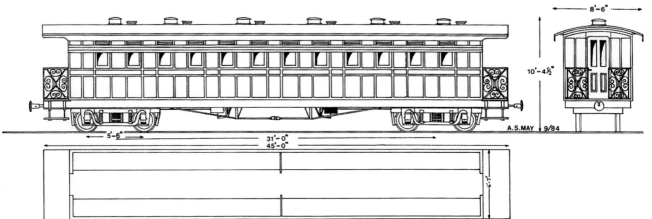

Drawing by Andrew May

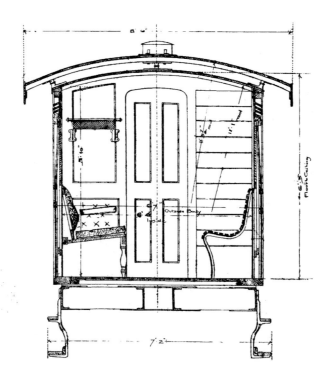

Drawing courtesy PTA

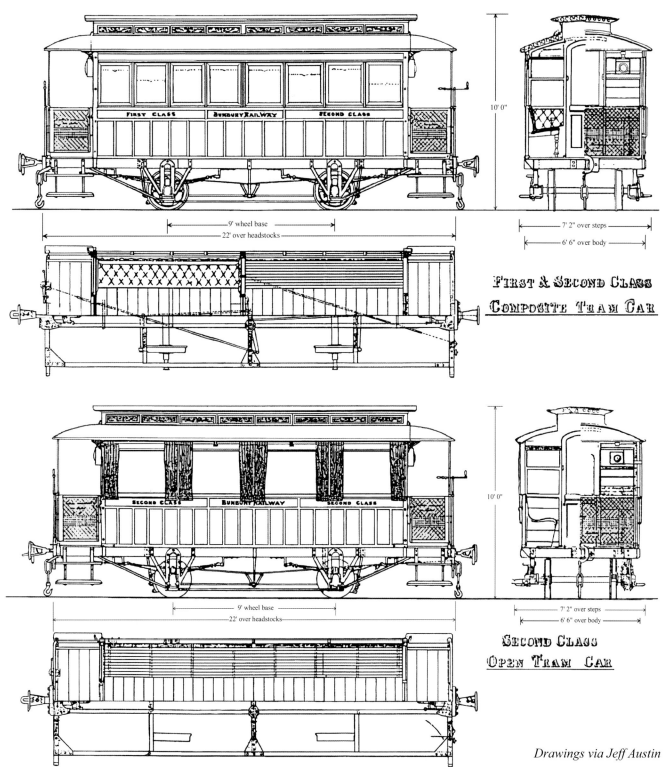

First & Second Class
Composite Tram Car

10' 0"

7' 2" over steps
6' 6" over body

9' wheel base
22' over headstocks

Second Class
Open Tram Car

Drawings via Jeff Austin

Eight small 4-wheeled tram cars were purchased from the Metropolitan Railway Carriage and Wagon Co. in 1887 for use on the isolated Bunbury to Boyanup Railway. They arrived in Bunbury aboard the barque "Rewa" on 24 December, 1887.[41] Two of the eight cars were brakevans and the other six consisted of two composite and four second class vehicles.[42] The composite cars had two compartments with longitudinal seating, the First Class compartment seated 8 passengers and the Second Class accommodated 12. The Second Class carriages carried 24 passengers in a single saloon on plain varnished seats. There was no internal lighting provided. The brakevans were of a similar design, but shorter in length.

Two cars were shipped separately to Fremantle in 1891 (much to the disgust of the people of Bunbury). The first was a Second Class car which was damaged in transit and appears never to have been used. The second car was a Composite, which was shipped twelve days later and entered service on the Eastern Railway as Car No. 30. It carried 6 First class passengers and 12 Second class.

A private contractor originally operated the Bunbury Railway, and horses hauled the cars. The line was connected to the main system in 1893 via the Southwest Railway, and the Bunbury Tram Cars appear to have lasted till about 1897, being locomotive drawn after the WAGR assumed responsibility for the operation of the line in July, 1890.[43] They were never numbered.

The remaining Composite car from Bunbury was also shipped away, in 1894, this time to the Northern Railway where it became (NR) 5. It was renumbered AB 262 in 1899, but it may have never carried the number, having been hired to the Canning Jarrah Timber Co. It was sold to them in March, 1902

There is some doubt as to the final disposal of the remaining Bunbury cars. On 4 February, 1898 six Bunbury cars were reported as stored at North Fremantle.[44] This may have included the damaged Second class car. Mr. R.B. Campbell, the Locomotive Superintendent, asked for details of "conversion of old 4 wheeled carriages (Bunbury stock)"[45] and a few days later received the reply that the "average cost of converting six old carriages into employee cabins will be from □25 to □30."[46] Further correspondence in July, 1898 indicated that the cost of dismantling the "saloons old Bunbury 4 wheeled" was □9/10/- .[47] In October, 1898 it was stated that the cost of conversion of these vehicles to "lamp rooms" was too high and it was decided to scrap them[48]. Then, only two weeks after that it decided instead to sell their bodies by public auction with the ironwork being retained by the WAGR for re-use[49]. The final fates of these cars remains unknown.

Few photographs exist of Bunbury cars. Above is a Composite car 262 at Wellington Mills.

Photo courtesy Janice Calcei, via Jeff Austin

AI 1 flanked by two 6-wheeled cars, with 2 Bunbury tram cars behind.

Photo ARHS Archives

ABC class
AH class(1900)

An anonymous AH class Cleminson car in original condition.   *Photo courtesy Battye Library Ref: 303996P*

Four new 6-wheeled "Cleminson" coaches, classified ABC (24-27), arrived in 1888 from the Metropolitan Railway Carriage and Wagon Co. in England, in anticipation of an increase in traffic with the opening of the Great Southern Railway. Unlike the earlier 6-wheelers, these were compartment cars rather than saloons. Externally they looked similar to the older cars, but were slightly wider and had more windows with six doors along each side for access to the individual compartments. Seating was provided for 44 passengers, 12 first class and 32 second. As originally built, four roof mounted oil lamps lit the interior of the carriages, but this was later changed to six lamps, one serving each compartment. Sunshades were fitted above the outside windows and the vehicles were painted Indian red.

The first four compartment "Cleminson" cars were found to be satisfactory, and another two arrived in 1891,[50] numbered 28 and 29. These were also built by the Metropolitan Railway Carriage and Wagon Co. In 1900 they were all classified AH, being joined in this class by AC 4, the only other 6 wheeler still in regular passenger service. AH 27 suffered premature retirement after being badly damaged in an accident about 1904.

Two AH class cars, 24 and 25, were sent to provide passenger accommodation on the isolated Ravensthorpe to Hopetoun railway on the south coast of WA in April, 1909. The copper mine at Ravensthorpe was something of a stop-start affair and consequently the two "Cleminson" cars were not often used.[51] Even though the line lingered till 1936, the two cars had been abandoned in 1930, having run relatively few miles on the line.

AH 25 was separated from its frame and sold to a buyer in Newdegate in 1939 and AH 24 lost its frame before being sold to Mr. F.E. Daw in 1940. Both were written off as abandoned in 1943 and their frames were sold for scrap in 1947. One (AH 24) has since found a place in the Ravensthorpe Museum, while the other (AH 25) forms part of a private house at Hopetoun.

Meanwhile, the three remaining cars on the Eastern Railway (AH 26, 28 and 29) were used to provide suburban services in Perth and were written off as a group in 1924, although AH 29 was re-issued to traffic in 1925 as a DW class workman's van, finishing up as a mobile school room before being written off in 1950. It is thought to have been scrapped at Lakeside about 1964.

AH 29 out of use at Lakewood in 1964, having been previously used as a school room.   *Photo courtesy Guido Rinaldi*

Interior of AH 29 at Lakewood, 1964.
Photo courtesy Guido Rinaldi

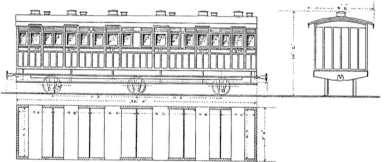

Drawing courtesy PTA

AH 25 incorporated into a holiday house at Hopetoun, photographed 5 April, 1980.   *Photo courtesy Jeff Austin*

CHAPTER TWO
GOLD & THE BOOM YEARS 1891 - 1900

In 1884 gold was discovered at Hall's Creek in the north of Western Australia, causing a minor gold rush to that part of the colony. The gold soon ran out, but the prospectors, some of whom had been on the goldfields in New South Wales and Victoria, drifted south in search of more of the precious metal, their paths roughly following what is now the Great Northern Highway. Gold finds were made down through the Murchison and these could have sparked off more rapid development of the railway in that area, were it not for the enormously rich finds further south. Gold was discovered at Southern Cross in 1888 and as the prospectors moved slowly eastward from there the demands for rail services began to increase. The government employed Mr. Charles Yelverton O'Connor as Engineer in Chief of the colony and in May, 1891 he was given the added responsibility of Acting General Manager of Railways.[1] He found the WAGR in a very poor state, barely coping with things as they existed, let alone being able to handle the rapidly increasing demand, so he set about refurbishing the railway system.

In 1892 the WAGR acquired the first of its bogie composite carriages fitted with compartments, the ubiquitous "dog box" style of car which appeared on the WAGR in large numbers over the next decade to become the backbone of the passenger fleet. They were purchased from the Midland Railway Co. of WA (MRWA) which, in anticipation of the opening of its railway between Midland Junction and Walkaway, had ordered ten cars from the Lancaster Wagon Co. in England. These arrived in Fremantle in 1892.[2] The company's stop-start construction of the Midland Railway and the delays incurred meant that a great deal of rolling stock was locked up at Fremantle, adding to the company's financial woes, so five of the brand new passenger cars, which would have been numbered K 6-10, were sold to the WAGR by late 1892 without ever entering service on the Midland line.[3] They became AB 31-35 with the WAGR.

In 1892 gold was discovered at Coolgardie, and then at Kalgoorlie in 1893. Work had begun on the Eastern Goldfields Railway, heading to Southern Cross from the end of the branch at Northam, and the Southwest Railway from Perth to Bunbury was completed. The dilemma of meeting the ever increasing demand for rail travel with only limited funds led to the WAGR purchasing ten new bogie cars, five First Class and five composite, from the Gilbert Car Manufacturing Co. of the USA. They arrived in Fremantle in 1892 and caused immediate uproar. To many people the very idea of a railway in one of Her Majesty's colonies purchasing rolling stock from America was something akin to treason, and these vehicles, which became known on the WAGR as "Gilbert" cars, were the subject of considerable controversy at the time. Questions were asked in Parliament as to why they had not been bought from Britain[4] and, even though it was pointed out that they were considerably cheaper than the comparable British built vehicles, the message hit home - no more carriages were ever purchased from America.

The gold discoveries at Kalgoorlie and the subsequent establishment of the associated goldfields caused Western Australia's population and economy to boom and, while the rest of Australia dragged itself through a severe recession after the gold and land booms had ended, the Western colony wallowed in some new found prosperity. During 1894 the Northern Railway was opened between Geraldton and Mullewa on the first stage of its extension into the gold producing areas of the Murchison, and on 1 November, 1894 the Midland Railway Co. opened their line, so linking the WAGR's Eastern and Northern Railways. On that same date the Eastern Goldfields Railway was completed to Southern Cross, and although no new carriages arrived that year, a large number had been ordered.

The Southwest line was extended from Bunbury to Busselton during 1895 and Mr. Robert Buchanan Campbell, the new Locomotive Superintendent, found himself confronted with some enormous problems, among which was the introduction of no less than forty new carriages during the year, effectively doubling the passenger fleet. The first of these were ten brake composite cars (46-55), classed AB (later AD), which were similar to the brake carriages used on the GSR. These were followed by another ten bogie composite cars of the same type as those acquired from the MRWA in 1892. They, too, were classified AB, (later AC), receiving the numbers 56-65 and were built by the Oldbury Carriage & Wagon Co. in England.

Twenty composite cars arrived late in the year (66-85), these being the first carriages in Western Australia to be equipped with a lavatory compartment. Strangely, this was at one end of the car and there was no access to it for the unfortunate passengers in the other compartments. Quite possibly it was never intended that the lavatories be used on the move, but instead were a way of ensuring that lavatory facilities were available wherever the train went. These cars were also classed AB (later ACE), and one of them, AB 70, was the first WAGR passenger carriage to be destroyed in an accident [see 1895, Bogie Composite cars fitted with lavatory)][5].

In addition to all these deliveries, one of the Northern Railway cars (NR 4) was transferred to the Eastern Railway in 1895, the Commissioner lost his saloon (A 5) to the Minister for Railways, with the title "Commissioner's Saloon" being abolished, and another 4 wheeler, one of the more unusual carriages to be operated by the WAGR, went into service in 1895/96. Very little is known about this vehicle, but it is believed to have been converted to a passenger car from breakdown van No. 201 as a stop gap measure at a time when passenger cars were in short supply. Van No. 201 was built at the Fremantle Workshops in 1888. Presumably it was classed AB, but there is no record of its road number other than 201, so it is assumed that it retained this while it was in passenger service.

In 1895 a unique carriage went into service. This was a new Ministerial saloon supplied by the Birmingham Railway Carriage & Wagon Co. It was the first VIP carriage built for that purpose and remained un-numbered till 1899.

Steam loco N73 at Perth station with an AD class brake car and a train of AF second class cars.   *Photo courtesy ARHS*

In 1896 O'Connor's Parkerville deviation was opened, halving the grades up the Darling Range just east of Midland Junction, and the Eastern Goldfields Railway was opened to Coolgardie, reaching Kalgoorlie later in the year. More carriage deliveries were made during the year, starting with the arrival from the Metropolitan Railway Carriage & Wagon Co. of Western Australia's first sleeping cars, considered necessary due to the imminent opening of the Eastern Goldfields Railway. There were eight vehicles in this batch (86-93, classed A, and later AP), and the type ran on the first train to Coolgardie, and also the first train to Kalgoorlie, a Ministerial special on 8 September, 1896.[6] Not only were these the first carriages on the WAGR with sleeping accommodation, they were also the first to have a lavatory for each compartment, although night time use of this facility meant that two passengers had to get out of bed and stow their bunks so that the poor soul wanting to use the lavatory could gain access to it. Despite these facilities it was still to be many more years before sleeping cars were provided for second class passengers. A third batch of twelve AB class (later AC) bogie composite cars (94-105) arrived from the Metropolitan Railway Carriage & Wagon Co. at about the same time as the sleeping cars.

On 1 December, 1896 the WAGR took over the Great Southern Railway from the WA Land Co., and with it acquired the GSR's locomotive, carriage and wagon stock, including ten composite bogie brake cars, four composite bogie cars, and one rather unique little 6 wheeled inspection saloon, used by the GSR's General Manager.[7] The ten composite bogie brake cars had been built in 1887 by the Metropolitan Railway Carriage & Wagon Co., and the WAGR's composite bogie brake cars (later AD class) were almost identical to them, except that the GSR cars had seven compartments (one extra second class) and no luggage area.[8]

The GSR cars went into WAGR service, the composite

brake cars became AB 176-180 and AB 185-189, the four 49' (14.94m) composite cars were allocated the numbers 181-184, also in the AB class and the inspection car was classified A, with the number 190. The takeover of the GSR merely added to Campbell's problems, as did the state of the Fremantle Workshops. They were proving to be totally inadequate, being both cramped and stretched to the limit assembling new stock, while the queue of locomotives and rolling stock awaiting repairs grew longer and longer.

In 1896 Mr. Mather left the WAGR after eleven years of service, during which time the carriage stock had expanded from 20 coaches to 115, with many more on order, and the growth continued unabated. The years 1897 and 1898 must have become a nightmare for those charged with the task of ensuring the efficient utilisation of the WAGR's passenger stock. Construction of new lines continued apace with a branch line from Kalgoorlie, through Boulder, to Lakeside, while the Southwest Railway extended from Brunswick Junction to Collie, both in 1897. Another branch line northwest from Kalgoorlie to Kanowna, and one from York east to Greenhills were opened, the old Bunbury Railway was extended from Boyanup through Donnybrook and on to Bridgetown, and the Northern Railway was completed from Mullewa to Cue, with the Midland Railway providing the connection to Perth, all in 1898. C.Y. O'Connor left the railways in 1897, handing the position of General Manager over to Mr. John Davies.[10] The first regular train ran into Kalgoorlie on 1 January, 1897, this event marking the opening of the Eastern Goldfields Railway along its full length. Early in 1897 twenty more brake composite cars (106-125, later AD) went into service, the first twelve coming from the Bristol Carriage & Wagon Co. and the other eight from Brown Marshall & Co., both of England. A first class version of the lavatory compartment cars appeared in 1897 with five carriages (126-130, later AE), and fifteen examples of a similar second class car (131-145, later AF) also went into traffic, all built by the Gloucester

G50 and another G class at the head of the Ministerial Special at the opening of the Eastern Goldfields Railway to Coolgardie in 1896. The photograph was taken at Hines Hill. Trailing the train engine are a van, two AC or ACE class cars and four of the brand new AP class sleeping cars.   *Photo courtesy Battye Library Ref: 8066B*

Railway Carriage & Wagon Co. in England. The only loss to the carriage stock during 1897 were the Bunbury Railway Tram Cars, which were retired after the connection of that line to the main system.

Despite the arrival of the sleeping cars and the twelve bogie composite cars in 1896, the shortage of carriage stock was still so severe that a number of covered goods wagons were converted into temporary carriages and brakevans. In his report dated 30 June, 1897, Mr. John T. Short, the Chief Traffic Manager, reported. "now that carriage stock has been and is daily arriving, the goods wagons gave been returned to their legitimate traffic."

In August, 1897 an application was made requesting £300 to fit internal door handles to all the WAGR's carriages, except the sleeping cars. The number of cars involved was 150. Up until the time this work was done, the doors had to be opened by lowering the window and reaching out to the external door handle.[11]

To reinforce the small fleet of first class sleeping cars, a second batch of ten cars (146-155, later AP) arrived in 1898 and were quickly pressed into service on the overnight trains to Kalgoorlie and Albany. Ten more first class lavatory compartment cars (191-200, later AE) also went into service that year, so completing the order commenced in 1897. A second batch of the second class lavatory cars arrived and was placed in traffic in the second half of 1898. They were numbered 164-175 (later AF), making a total of twenty seven carriages of the type.

Late in 1898 a final batch of eight more first class lavatory compartment cars numbered 156-163 (later AE) arrived. In

1898, two "Gilbert" cars (37 & 39) were converted into A class inspection cars, and at about the same time, the other eight were sent to work the Kalgoorlie suburban services.[12] Perhaps it was a case of sight and therefore out of mind.

In 1899 yet another goldfields branch from Kalgoorlie to Menzies was opened and in the three years from mid 1896 to mid 1899 the length of railway in the colony rose from 588 to 1355 miles (941 to 2169 km).[13] It was becoming obvious that, as the rails stretched across the colony, train journeys would become longer, and so a large batch of carriages intended specifically for long distance journeys was ordered. These were probably the only cars which Campbell had a hand in designing during his brief reign as Locomotive Superintendent between 1896 and 1903, and was the largest group of carriages ever purchased by the WAGR at any one time. There were fifty carriages in the batch, twenty first class cars and thirty second class, and they were a great improvement over the earlier vehicles. The first class cars (201-220, later AA) were delivered from the Oldbury Carriage & Wagon Co. of England in 1899 and were not dissimilar in general appearance to the bogie composite cars acquired from the GSR. A new innovation was the provision of lavatories such that all the passengers in the coach, for the first time in a WAGR sit up car, had access to a lavatory during their journey. The second class cars (221-250, later AB) were also built by Oldbury and were almost identical to the first class vehicles, but were fitted with an extra compartment. Both first and second class cars were classified A.

The inaccessible lavatory compartment in the older first and second class cars (later AE and AF classes) was a fairly useless arrangement, and with the arrival of the first specifically designed long distance cars with lavatory access for all the passengers, the lavatory cubicles in the older cars were removed and the compartment converted for the accommodation of passengers.[14] Due to the fact that the compartment in the Second Class cars was much bigger than normal passenger compartments, the conversion included a peculiar U shaped seat. The work was completed by 1903 and the carriages settled down on suburban and short haul services.[15]

Early in 1899 the carriages taken over with the GSR were numbered in the WAGR lists, the brake composite cars becoming AB 176-180 and 185-189, the 49' (14.94m) bogie composites AB 181-184, and the old General Manager's saloon, now an inspection car, A 190. Later that year the Northern Railway stock was also integrated into the WAGR numbering system and so the four cars on that line, plus NR 4 on the Eastern Railway, became AB 258-262. The Ministerial car delivered in 1895 was numbered A 261 and also included in the passenger stock list and numbered at the same time were three 6 wheeled mail vans (251-253) and four bogie mail vans (254-257).

During the late 1890's the old 4 wheeled cars began to fall out of favour, so passenger accommodation in them was reduced to 18 to try and make them more comfortable.[16] In 1899 two (AB 21 and 23) were converted to louvred meat vans, and one, AB 261 (formerly NR 4) was condemned.

Another unique carriage went into service in 1899. This was a funeral car, rebuilt from the old 6 wheeled "Cleminson" carriage AC 7. This vehicle had begun life in 1883 as a second class "Cleminson" saloon, classified BC, and in 1889 it was rebuilt as a brake car. As a funeral car it was classified AO. It retained its number and was used to transport coffins and mourners to the Karrakatta cemetery, adjacent to the Eastern Railway between Fremantle and Perth.

Electric lighting was introduced into WAGR carriages in 1899. The first car so fitted was the Ministerial saloon A 261, and twenty cars used on express trains, namely A (AA), A (AB), and A (AP) class vehicles, were fitted with electric lighting equipment in place of the old peanut oil lamps on a trial basis, beginning with AA 207. By May, 1900 these cars had run a total of some 900,000 miles (1.44m km) between them with the new equipment, and the trial was declared a success. The decision was taken to fit all the WAGR's passenger cars with electric lights and the conversions went ahead. Further sets of equipment were ordered and the use of electric lighting spread through the fleet in the years before the First World War, all new coaches built after 1900 being fitted with it as standard. Passenger carrying freight stock, however, retained oil lighting. Most of the AA's, AB's and AP's received the new equipment at an early date, as these were the cars used on the principal expresses at this time.[17]

In 1899 the delivery of passenger carriages came to an abrupt halt. Despite the fact that O'Connor had done a great deal to rejuvenate the railway system, by 1900 it was still in a mess, and an Inquiry (called a Royal Commission by the newspapers of the day, even though it wasn't) was held to investigate the running of the WAGR. Campbell had resigned in January, 1900,[18] partially due to his poor relationship with Davies, and Davies himself was suspended in August, 1901[19] for alleged mismanagement. He was cleared of any wrong doing, but resigned soon after the Inquiry and left for England in early 1902.[20] It is interesting to speculate on whether or

not he was made a political scapegoat when it is considered that he had to follow in the footsteps of a man later regarded as a genius in the engineering field, at a point in time when the WAGR was going through one of its most difficult and chaotic periods ever. The post of Locomotive Superintendent went with Campbell and was replaced by the position of Chief Mechanical Engineer (CME), the first being Mr. Thomas Firth Rotheram.[21]

The second important result of the Royal Commission was a complete reclassification of the entire carriage and wagon stock, with all brake and accident vans being transferred out of the carriage lists.[22] This event took place in September, 1900, and from then on the passenger carriages had (or should have had) their class and number painted in large characters on their sole bars. They were reclassified as follows:-

Type & Date Introduced		Pre 1900	Post 1900
4 w. composite car	1876	AB	AI
6 w. composite saloon	1881	ABC	AH
6 w. 2nd class saloon	1883	BC	-
Bogie composite saloon ("American" cars)	1884	AB, ABA	AG
6 w composite car	1888	ABC	AH
Vice Regal car	1890	A	AN
Bogie composite car	1892	AB	AC
Bogie cars (1st & comp.) ("Gilbert" cars)	1893	AB	AG
4 w. car	1895	AB	-
Bogie comp brake car	1895	AB	AD
Bogie comp car with lav.	1895	AB	AC, ACE
1st class sleeping car	1896	A	AP
Ex GSR bogie comp car	1896	AB	AC
Ex GSR inspection car	1896	A	AL
1st class car with lav	1897	AB	AE
2nd class car with lav.	1897	AB	AF
Inspection car ("Gilbert")	1898	A	AL
1st class long dist. Car	1899	A	AA
2nd class long dist. Car	1899	A	AB
Funeral car	1899	-	AO
Ministerial car	1899	A	AM

These reclassifications were not without problems. The ex GSR cars caused some confusion at first, with the composite brake cars initially being classed AC, while one of the 49' (14.94m) cars was classified AC and the other three as AD's. This was obviously a mistake and the cars were reclassified in their correct classes by the end of 1901. The second class long distance cars were, in the main, classified AB, but very early in their lives some of them had been converted into composite cars, and it is possible that four never saw service as second class cars at all. These vehicles were in the group numbered 231-240, but the four cars involved have not yet been identified. Having been converted into composites prior to 1900, they were reclassified from A to AC, rather than AB. By 1901 a total of twelve AB's had been converted into composites and reclassified AC, as had another four by June, 1902.[23] The AC classification wound up in a terrible mess, with several types of carriage having been classed AC, as follows:-

- the 42' (12.81m) bogie composite cars (1892);
- the bogie composite cars with a single lavatory compartment (1895);
- four long distance cars with lavatories in the batch 231-240 (1898) which had been converted from second class cars to composites by 1900, plus another eleven identical cars from the AB class which were converted to composites and reclassified around 1901.

By 1902 things had become so confused that it was decided to split the AC class into three separate groups. The cars with the single lavatory compartment became ACE, the long distance cars became class ACL, while those without lavatories remained as AC's. This latter group included the twenty 42' (12.81m) bogie composite cars and the four ex GSR 49' (14.94m) bogie composite cars. These vehicles did not receive their new designations till 1906-1908.

By 1900 two of the composite "Gilbert" cars had been converted to second class, enabling them to carry more passengers. Interestingly, at the time of the 1900 reclassifications the AG class "Gilbert" and "American" cars were the only two types of carriage in service with interconnecting gangways allowing passenger access from one car to the next.

Perth station in the mid 1890's   *Photo courtesy ARHS Archives*

An AC class car at Midland *Photo courtesy ARHS*

Five bogie composite cars were purchased from the MRWA in 1892. They were part of a group of ten cars the MRWA had imported from the Lancaster Wagon Co. in England, but were unable to use. They were classed AB by the WAGR, numbered 31-35. These cars had 42' (12.81m) long wrought iron underframes and their bodies were built of "best Moulmein teak", sealed with a coat of linseed oil and gold size (a thin gelatinous substance made from glue or wax) and then coated in varnish, with gold lettering.[25] They must have made a magnificent sight, but unfortunately the WAGR chose to paint them in unrelieved Indian red. The cars contained seven compartments, three first class located in the central part of the carriage, and a pair of second class at each end. The first class compartments accommodated 6 passengers each and were panelled with sycamore and banded with teak. These timbers were french polished and finished with gilt moulding, while the seat cushions were covered with American buffalo hide. The floor was covered with plain linoleum.[26] The second class compartments were smaller and, like those in the earlier cars, somewhat less ornate. The walls were grained and varnished and the seats were "of red pine, shaped to as to form as comfortable a seat as possible".[27] These seats were smaller than the first class, and each compartment carried 8 passengers.

In 1895 the WAGR purchased ten new bogie composite cars which were similar, if not identical, to the ex MRWA carriages. They too were classified AB, receiving the numbers

56-65 and were built by the Oldbury Carriage & Wagon Co. in England. The next batch of AB class bogie composite cars was built by the Metropolitan Railway Carriage & Wagon Co. and went into service in 1896. There were twelve carriages in this order, numbered AB 94-105.

In September, 1900 all twenty seven cars of the 42' (12.81m), seven compartment AB class were reclassified AC, along with a large group of other carriages, most of which were reclassified again soon afterwards because of confusion between the types.

As a result of a Parliamentary Select Committee enquiry into the running of the MRWA, an exchange of coaches was arranged with the WAGR in 1903.[28] The Midland Railway received four AB class cars in exchange for four of its K class composite cars, these four cars becoming AC 273-276. They were part of the original MRWA order for ten carriages from the Lancaster Wagon Co., of which the WAGR now owned nine.

Between 1910 and 1913 seventeen 42' (12.81m) AC class cars were converted to AF second class suburban cars, as follows:-

1910 - 31, 34;
1911 - 33, 35, 56, 58, 95, 274, 276;
1912 - 57, 62, 275;
1913 - 32, 64, 100, 102, 273.

The conversion apparently involved little more than the alteration of the seating in the First Class compartments from 6 passengers to 8, a change of class designator, restriction of the cars to suburban services, and only allowing holders of Second Class tickets to ride in them.

The remaining fourteen AC class carriages were left unmolested till late in 1922 when AC 59 was rebuilt into an AF second class suburban car. Unlike the other cars reclassified as AF's, AC 59 was completely rebuilt with a new AT style body.

Between 1923 and 1925 nineteen ACE class cars were converted for suburban use and joined the AC class, even though they differed slightly to the existing AC class cars. These were 66-69 and 71-85 (see 1895).

In 1934 and '35 falling demand for First Class travel led to fifteen AC class cars (including six of the original AC's) being reduced to second class suburban status and reclassified AF. These were:-

1934 - 99, 101, 105, and 183 (ex GSR);
1935 - 61, 63, 66, 69, 74, 75, 78, 79, 81, 85 & 94.

This meant that by the end of 1935 there were only seven of the original AC class carriages left, with twenty three converted to AF's and one totally rebuilt to AF.

In 1942 AC 60 was rebuilt to become the first and only member of class AK, a new type of suburban car. The wooden body of the old car was demolished and replaced with a new steel body on a lengthened underframe. The conversion was such that it is doubtful if much more than the bogies and parts of the frame were re-used. (See 1942).

AC 103 was one of several cars replaced by new AY/AYB class suburban carriages in 1945, leaving only five AC's in traffic. When the decision was made to repaint the WAGR's coaching stock Larch green, only two of these cars received the new livery, AC 96 in 1953 and AC 97 in 1956. By this time the class was in use on suburban services and the other three Indian red cars were replaced by the ADG class diesel railcars introduced in 1954. In 1955 AC 65, 98 and 104 were written off and in 1960 the two Larch green AC's met the same fate.

None appear to have survived, although the last of the ten MRWA K class composites is preserved, much modified, as inspection car AL 17 at the ARHS Rail Transport Museum at Bassendean.

An N class steam loco with an early train at Chidlows Well. The first car in the train is an AC. Note the window shades.
Photo courtesy ARHS (2787)

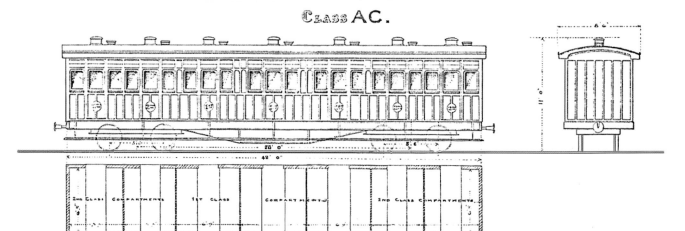

CLASS AC.

Drawing courtesy of PTA.

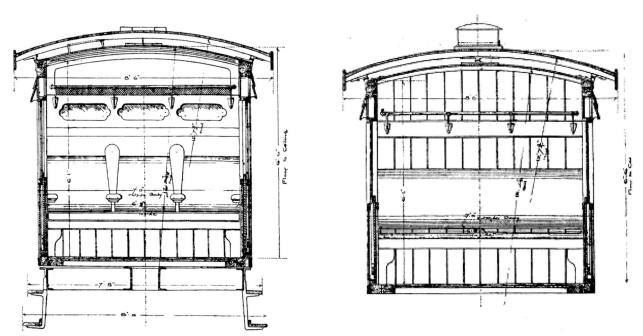

Cross section of an AC class car showing First and Second Class compartment layouts.

Drawing courtesy of PTA.

AB class
AG class (1900)

Gilbert Car No. 38 taken at Kalgoorlie about 1896   *Photo courtesy ARHS Archives*

The "Gilbert" cars were the only carriages the WAGR ever purchased from America, and their non English origins caused no small amount of controversy at the time. They arrived at Fremantle aboard the "S.S. Nairnshire" on 13 February, 1892, and were impressive vehicles, typically American with their clerestory roofs sweeping down over the two end platforms and their large windows giving them an air of importance. Their bodies and underframes were of timber, with the body sides of tongue and groove panelling painted Indian red. Gangways on the end platforms allowed passage between the cars.

First Class cars 36 and 39 carried 37 passengers, while cars 37, 38 and 40 carried 41 people in seats which were also typically American with their iron frames and scroll work on the ends. The cars were lit by oil lamps fitted in the clerestory roof. The external appearance of the composite "Gilbert" cars 41-45 was identical to the first class vehicles, but the seating capacity in them differed. Cars 41 and 42 accommodated 15 first class passengers and 18 second class, while cars 43 - 45 carried 18 first class passengers and 20 second class.[29] The lighting was the same as the First class cars. All ten were classed AB.

It could almost be believed that the American origins of the "Gilbert" cars was a continuing source of embarrassment to those responsible for their acquisition for, in 1898, two of them (AB 37 and 39) were fitted with an observation compartment, a kitchen, sleeping and bathing facilities, and were redesignated A class inspection cars, while the other eight were sent to work the burgeoning Kalgoorlie suburban services at about the same time. By 1900 two of the composite cars had been converted to second class, as had another two by 1902, allowing room for 41 passengers. This had been achieved by removing the seats from the first class compartments and replacing them with longitudinal seats running down both sides of the carriage. The reason for

these conversions is not now apparent, but may have been to improve the passenger capacity on the Kalgoorlie suburban trains, upon which the "Gilbert" cars were a familiar sight for many years. In every other respect the second class cars were identical to their brethren. In the 1900 reclassifications the "Gilbert" cars became AG, along with the "American" cars. The two "Gilbert" inspection cars were reclassified AL.

By 1902 all eight AG class "Gilbert" cars were in the Eastern Goldfields, being hauled around the Kalgoorlie area by N class 4-4-4T steam locomotives, but AG 36 did not stay long, being converted into an AL class inspection car in 1903. With the arrival in Kalgoorlie of the three AG class "American" cars in 1907, the last of the first class "Gilbert" cars, AG 40, was released and returned to Perth where it underwent conversion into an AM class Ministerial car to work with AM 261. By the middle of 1907 there was only one second class "Gilbert" car left, the other having apparently been reconverted into a composite car about 1906. As the Kalgoorlie tramway system made inroads into the railway services and train numbers were reduced, the "Gilbert" cars became redundant. In 1922 AG 38 was removed from passenger service and converted into an exhibition car. It carried the words "Westralian Industries League" above the windows, and "SUPPORT YOUR OWN INDUSTRIES" on the body sides below in large white letters.[30] This car was quite a success in this role till it was replaced in 1928 by the Reso (short for "resources") trains, and converted into an AL class inspection car. That same year AG 45 became the Reso train bath car, so that the passengers travelling on these trains could keep clean. Its career as a bath car came to an end in 1935 when it was replaced by the shower car AGS 17. It is then noted as having been placed in the hands of the District Engineer in Geraldton, but its role there is not recorded.

By 1933 the Kalgoorlie suburban patronage had fallen off to the point where four of the AG class cars were withdrawn and stored. In 1938 five composite "Gilbert" cars (AG 41-45) were converted for use with the ADE ("Governor") class diesel railcars. There were few external changes made, but internally the carriages were fitted with a guard's compartment which also carried the luggage, a lavatory compartment in the centre section of the car, and electric lighting. Prior to the conversions only two of these carriages were still in passenger configuration, these being AG 42 and 44. AG 41 and 43 were converted from survey cars and AG 45 (the former RESO Bath Car) was returned from Geraldton. AG 43 lasted only a short time as a "Governor" trailer because it was destroyed when it derailed and overturned at Wooroloo in October, 1938. It was written off the following December. The remaining four cars were replaced by the purpose built ADT class "Governor" trailers in 1939-40.

The start of World War Two almost certainly gave the last of the passenger carrying "Gilbert" cars a reprieve from the scrap yards, as they were used from 28 July, 1940 to provide a recruiting train for the RAAF.[31] In this role they toured around Western Australia enticing recruits to join the air force, but by 1941 the shortage of rolling stock was so acute that all four cars returned to passenger work. However, their age was starting to catch up with them. Two (AG 41 and 44) were written off in 1944 after being wrecked in an accident at Robb's Jetty, and in 1945 AG 45 was one of nine cars written off after the entry into service of a new set of AY/AYB class suburban cars. Despite being removed from the records on 22 December, 1945, AG 45 was fitted out as a sleeping van and sent to Pinjarra in 1946. In 1949 it went to Northam, and ended its days at Toodyay where it was demolished in 1963. AG 42 was the next to go in 1951, being sold to the Albany Harbour Board[32] as a mobile office and it languished there for many years before being burnt. AL 36 was written off in 1959 and AL 37 followed it two years later, being replaced by the old Ministerial car AM 40 which was simply reclassified AL. In 1962 AL 38 was converted to a workman's van, and in 1965 AL 39 was one of forty carriages which were written off. AL 38, as VW 5080 was sold to the Castledare Miniature Railway at Ferndale in Perth, but was burnt by vandals. This left only AL 40 in service, and it lasted till 1971, finishing its days at Bunbury before being preserved at the ARHS Rail Transport Museum at Bassendean in Perth. It is the only survivor.

A poor quality, but nonetheless interesting shot of AL 38 in later years, showing the roof detail.

Photo courtesy ARHS Archives

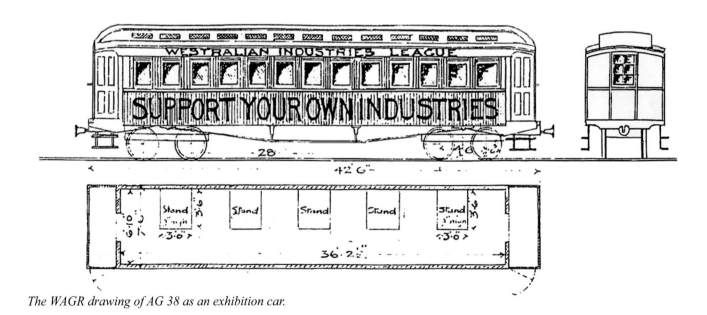

The WAGR drawing of AG 38 as an exhibition car.

The RAAF recruiting train at the Midland Workshops during the handover inspection on 25 July, 1940. The car nearest the camera is AG 41.   *Photo courtesy WA Newspapers*

AL 39 stands at Midland awaiting its final fate, 4 July, 1966   *Photo Geoff Blee Collection, courtesy Murray Rowe*

AG 42 partially dismantled at Albany   *Photo courtesy Graham Watson*

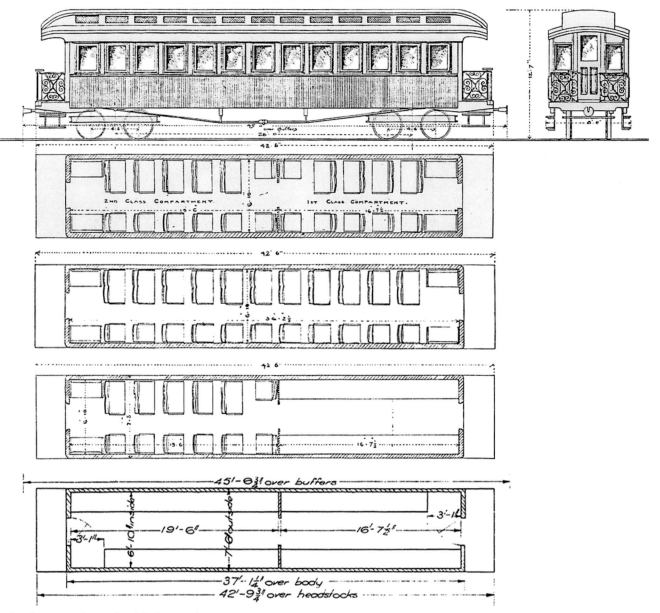

The drawings depict the AG class and its interior layout in its various forms, Composite (top), First class (second) and Second class (third), and as converted to passenger work during the Second World War (bottom)   *Drawings courtesy PTA*

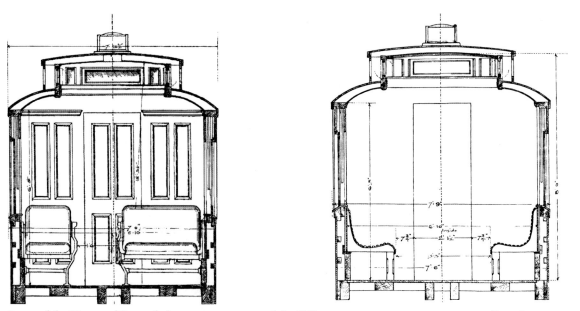

Cross section s of the First and Second class compartments of the Gilbert cars.   *Drawings courtesy PTA*

An unidentified AD class car in original condition at York   *Photo courtesy Battye Library Ref:5240B/22*

Up until the mid 1980's train crews traditionally consisted of three men, the driver and fireman whose job it was to operate the locomotive, and the guard who was responsible for the overall running of the train. The guard was generally ensconced in his own van, but a guards (or brake compartment) at one end of a passenger carriage was much more efficient than trailing around an often empty brake van. Thus, brake cars came into being.

The WAGR purchased ten composite bogie brake cars in 1895 from the Metropolitan Railway Carriage & Wagon Co. and they were classed AB, (46-55), in style being very similar to the AB class composite bogie cars (later AC) which first appeared in 1892. They were identical in size to the bogie Composite cars, but were slightly heavier at 15 tons (15.15t) tare. The underframes were of wrought iron and the bodies of timber, the outside panels being painted in Indian red. The greatest external difference was that there were three fewer windows on each side at one end, with the guard's lookouts and large double doors marked "Luggage" in their place, reflecting the existence of the brake/luggage compartment inside. There was also access to this compartment via doors on each side at the very end of the car, with a circular plate on each of them inscribed with the word "Guard".

The interior of the cars consisted of five passenger compartments, three second class, two larger first class in the centre, and the guard's compartment, which was large enough to carry luggage. Six passengers were accommodated in each first class compartment and 8 in each second class, making a total capacity of 36 passengers.

On 1 December, 1896 the WAGR took over the Great

Southern Railway from the WA Land Co. and with it acquired the GSR's locomotive, carriage and wagon stock, including ten composite bogie brake cars. These vehicles had been built in 1887 by the Metropolitan Railway Carriage & Wagon Co. in England, and the WAGR's composite bogie brake cars were identical to them, except that the GSR cars contained seven compartments (one extra second class) and no luggage area. By 1898 eight of these cars had the second class compartment adjacent to the brake compartment converted into a luggage area to bring them into line with the WAGR cars.[33] In 1897 another large batch of identical carriages were been placed in service. These new cars were numbered AB 106-125, the first twelve coming from the Bristol Carriage & Wagon Co. and the other eight from Brown Marshall & Co., both of England. About 1899 the ex GSR Composite brake cars became AB 176-180 and AB 185-189. In September, 1900 all forty composite bogie brake cars were reclassified AD, although the ex GSR cars caused some confusion at first, initially being classed AC. However, the mistake was quickly corrected and the ten brake composites became AD's.

In 1905 the first of the AU first class suburban brake cars was delivered and, along with the similar first class AW suburban cars, produced a surplus of first class accommodation on the short distance and suburban trains.[34] As a result, several AD class cars were converted to second class throughout (AD 114, 118, 119, 121, 177 and 186), but initially retained their AD classification. This "conversion" was made by altering the seating to carry 2 extra passengers in each of the first class compartments, so bringing the accommodation to 40.

In 1906 AD 188 and 189 were rebuilt as AX class saloons

for use on express trains. Externally there were fewer doors, the guard's lookouts and double luggage compartment doors were removed, and the windows were re-spaced to take up the room, while on the inside they were completely rebuilt. In addition, the internal arrangements differed between the two cars (see 1906). Although ten were scheduled for conversion, only two were done.[35]

By June, 1907 two hundred and two WAGR coaches had been fitted with electric lighting and, despite the apparent success of this equipment, the decision was taken to fit AD 186 with acetylene lighting on a trial basis.[35] Either the trial lasted 23 years or AD 186 was forgotten because the acetylene equipment was not replaced with electric lights till 1930!

Two AD class carriages (AD 49 and 117) were damaged in a fire at the Midland Workshops paint shop on 10 December, 1909,[37] but it is difficult to determine how bad the damage was. The AD's, which could have been regarded as obsolete, were both rebuilt as AD's and this could indicate that they were not totally destroyed in the blaze. Both cars returned to service in February, 1912.

The continuing fall off of traffic which had begun in the 1920's, the decline of the Kalgoorlie suburban services, and the onset of the Depression, resulted in six more AD class cars (52, 55, 125, 178, 180 and 187) becoming second class in 1935, and in 1937 all twelve of the second class AD's were reclassified ADS. However, in 1943 ADS 125 was reclassified back to an AD class composite car again.

In 1945 AD 124 had its brake compartment enlarged to enable it to take prams, presumably because of the post war baby boom. This was done by removing the partition between the luggage area and the adjacent compartment, thus reducing the number of passenger compartments in this car to four.

The first of the class to be written off was AD 116 in 1947, after it had been involved in a head on collision between two suburban trains in Fremantle yard. ADS 178 was written off in 1951, and that same year the WAGR decided to repaint its stock Larch green. Of the AD/ADS class cars numbers 47-55, 106-112, 114, 115, 117, 118, 121-125, 176, 177, 179, 180 and 185-187 were altered to the new livery between 1952 and 1956.

The AD and ADS class largely finished its days on suburban and short distance trains, including suburban goods trains due to the brake van shortage during the early 1950's.[38] In 1955 three (AD 46, 113 and 120) were written off and demolished after the introduction of the ADG class diesel railcars, and ADS 119 had its body removed and scrapped, its frame being used to build an AYE class suburban car (AYE 701). AD 53 was written off in 1956 and AD 106 followed in 1958, these two being the first Larch green AD's to go. The combination of AYE suburban cars, ADX railcars, and ADA railcar trailers opened the floodgates on the destruction of the AD/ADS class and over the next few years they were written off as follows:-

1959 - AD 47, 54, ADS 55, 177;
1960 - AD 109, 111, 124, 185, ADS 52, 188;
1961 - AD 107 converted to a workman's van, ADS 186;
1962 - AD 49, 125, ADS 121;
1963 - AD 110, 122.

In 1964 a second batch of ADA class railcar trailers entered service, but the only AD to be written off that year was 123. In 1965 AD 176 had its doors screwed shut and the words "Suburban Goods Traffic Only" stencilled on the sides.[39] It was used as a brake car on suburban goods trains. That same year ADS 180 was written off. 1966 saw the demise of AD 48, 112 and 179, and in 1967 AD 176's brief career on suburban goods trains came to an end when it, too, was written off. Also in 1967 AD 50, 51, 114, 117 and ADS 187, the last of the ADS class and also the last survivor of the old GSR composite brake cars, were written off. The following year ten ADK/ADB class diesel railcars and trailers were delivered, spelling the end of the AD class when the last car, AD 108, was written off.

As far as is known, none have survived.

An AD brings up the rear of a train of suburban cars under cover at Fremantle station in the early 1950's.

Photo by MA Park, courtesy ARHS Archives

Two AD class cars bring up the rear of a short goods train in the Darling Ranges. Note the different sized guards lookouts between the two cars.

Photo Don Finlayson Collection

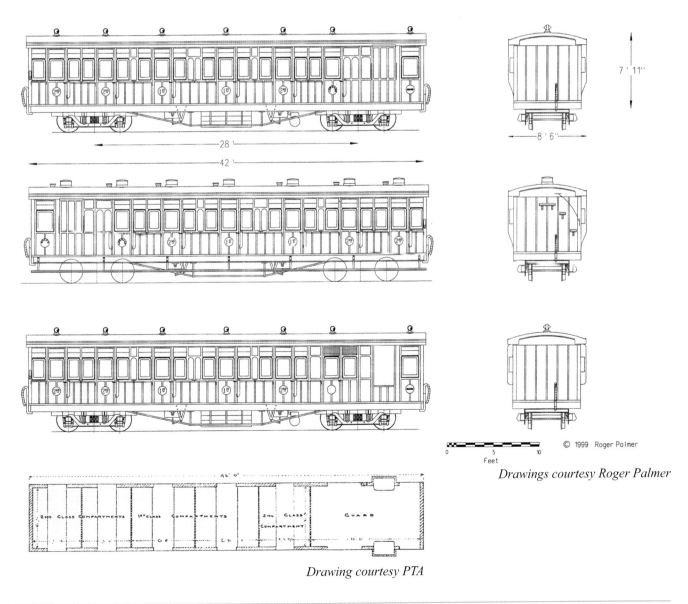

Drawings courtesy Roger Palmer

Drawing courtesy PTA

AD 123 in its natural habitat at Subiaco on 19 November, 1953.

Photo CC Singleton, courtesy ARHS Archives Ref: 1401

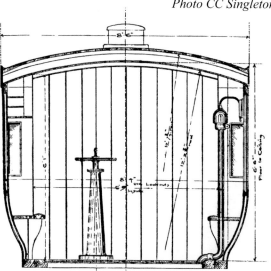

Cross section of the AD class guards compartment   *Drawing courtesy PTA*

AD 51, having been written off, awaits its final fate.

Photo courtesy ARHS Archives

AB class
AC (ACE) class (1900)

AC 80, formerly an ACE, in pristine condition   *Photo WAGR, courtesy ARHS.*

Late in 1895 the first cars fitted with lavatories arrived on the WAGR, the twenty vehicles involved being built by Brown Marshall & Co. in England. They were classified AB (Nos. 66-85) and externally were almost identical to the earlier 42' (12.81m) AB (later AC) class cars, the main differences being the spacing of the window dividers for the first class compartments and the absence of mouldings above those windows not incorporated in the doors.

The underframes of these cars were made of steel and the bodies of timber, with panelling on the outside painted in the usual Indian red colour scheme. They had six passenger compartments, two first class with a pair of second class either side of them, and a lavatory compartment at one end of the car. There was a seat across the lavatory compartment, facing the cubicles, so it seems likely that the compartment was also used to accommodate passengers. Six passengers were carried in each first class compartment and 8 in each second class. The compartments were isolated from each other, including the lavatory compartment, making life uncomfortable for the unfortunate passengers accommodated elsewhere in the carriage. At least, a train with one of these carriages in the consist had lavatory facilities available, no matter where it went.

AB 70 had only a very brief career on the WAGR. On 30 June, 1896 it was the only passenger car on a "mixed" train of 22 wagons and a brakevan when, at Lion's Mill on the Eastern Railway, a coupling snapped and twenty wagons, AB 70 and the brakevan started to roll back down the hill towards Perth. The guard screwed down his brake and managed to pin down several wagon brakes, but to no avail and the runaway got away from him. At Stoneville the vehicles left the rails at very high speed, completely destroying themselves and killing one of the two passengers in the AB.[40]

The Annual Report of 1900 made mention of the fact that

these carriages were being placed on mixed trains between Northam and Albany, Kalgoorlie and Menzies, and Geraldton and Cue.

In the 1900 reclassifications they were classed AC, along with the 42' (12.81m), 49' (14.94m) cars, and Composite long distance cars, but this arrangement caused considerable confusion and in 1902 the composite cars with the single lavatory compartment in them were reclassed ACE. It took some time before the individual carriages actually received their new class letters. AC's 66, 67, 69, 72, 73 and 76-85 became ACE's in 1906, AC's 68, 74 and 75 became ACE's in 1907, and AC 71 became an ACE in 1908.

Between 1923 and 1925 all nineteen ACE's were converted to suburban cars. This was done by removing the toilet cubicles and converting the lavatory compartment into a large passenger compartment with a peculiar U shaped seat in it.[41] The cars were then classified AC, even though they differed slightly to the other 42' (8.12m) AC class cars. The ACE's were converted as follows:-

1923 - 66, 68, 74, 79, 80;
1924 - 69, 73, 75, 77, 83, 85;
1925 - 67, 71, 72, 76, 78, 81, 82, 84.

Thus the rather odd lavatory equipped ACE's ceased to exist and the nineteen carriages led a similar history to the other AC's.

In 1935 eight of the former ACE's (AC 66, 69, 74, 75, 78, 79, 81 and 85) were converted to second class suburban cars, apparently by the alteration of their seating and redesignation of the first class compartments. They were reclassified AF.

When the WAGR livery was changed from Indian red to Larch green after 1951, three of the eleven remaining cars were repainted, AC 68 in August, 1953, AC 76 in May, 1956 and AC 83 in December, 1954. Seven of the other eight cars (AC 67, 71-73, 77, 82 and 84), plus one of the green ones (AC 76) were written off in 1955 after the arrival in service of the ADG class diesel railcars. One of these, AC 73, had its body broken up and the frame used to build a new AYE class suburban saloon for use as a railcar trailer, numbered AYE 702. In 1956 AC 76 received a reprieve when it was returned to traffic, and in 1960 AC 68 and 83 were written off. AC 76 was written off for the second time in 1962 and AC 80 went in 1964, possibly still in Indian red, as no record of its repainting has come to light. None have survived.

Thought to be AC 82 at Midland. This car was also once an ACE and is shown in a far less pristine condition than the heading shot of AC 80.
Photo courtesy ARHS Archives

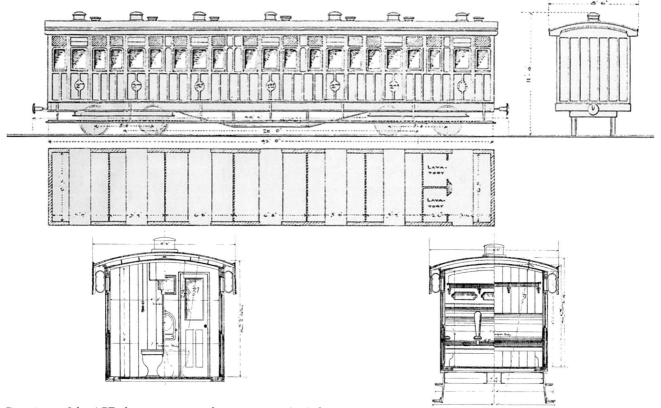

Drawings of the ACE class cars, general arrangement (top), lavatory compartment cross section (centre), & passenger compartments, First & Second class (bottom).
Drawings courtesy PTA

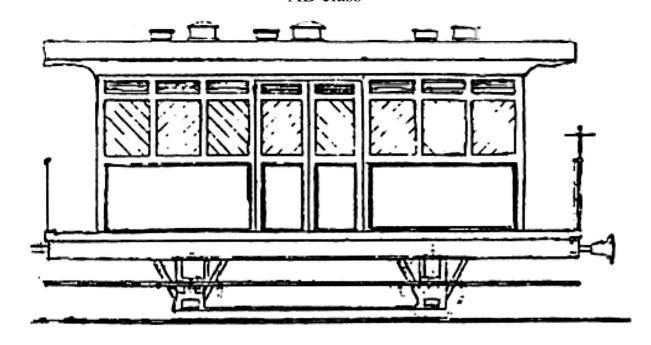

One of the more unusual carriages to be operated by the WAGR was a 4 wheeled car which went into service in 1895/96. Very little is known about this vehicle, but it is believed to have been converted to a passenger car from breakdown van No. 201 as a stop gap measure at a time when passenger cars were in short supply. Van No. 201 was built at the Fremantle Workshops and entered service on 1 August, 1888.[42].

It had a panelled timber body and at 20' (6.1m) long over the headstocks, it was a bit bigger than the other 4 wheeled passenger cars. It had two end platforms, with a door leading from each into the saloon and there were two double doors,

one on each side of the vehicle, but it is not known if these were used during its rather brief sojourn into the world of passenger traffic. Lighting was provided by three oil lamps set into the roof, but the details of the interior layout are not known.

Presumably it was classed AB, but there is no record of its road number other than 201, so it is assumed that it retained this while it was in passenger service. By 1899 its usefulness as a passenger car had declined and this unusual little vehicle was converted back to a breakdown van. Its was written off the WAGR's books on 7 March, 1954 as D.201.[43]

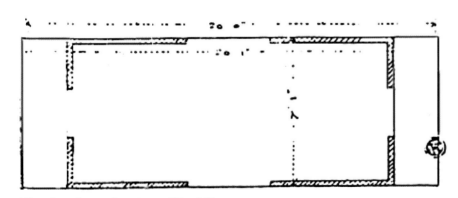
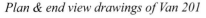
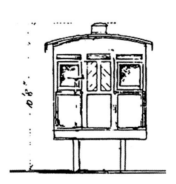

Plan & end view drawings of Van 201   *Drawings courtesy PTA*

AM 261 in original condition at Collie   *Photo courtesy Collie Mining Museum*

In 1894 the Birmingham Railway Carriage & Wagon Co. supplied the WAGR with a new Ministerial saloon classed A. It arrived at Fremantle on the "S.S. Gulf of Lions" on the 30 January, 1895. The new car was the first VIP carriage built for that purpose, and it is thought to have been built with at least one end platform, but this was very quickly closed in.[44] It was fitted with a clerestory roof and was constructed of timber on a steel underframe, with steel sheeting for side panelling, although it was similar in style to the other cars in WAGR service. It was painted Indian red. The side entry doors at the ends led into coupe compartments, each containing a small fold down table and three "cane seated revolving chairs, the seats fitted with springs."[45] These compartments had three windows across the ends, allowing panoramic views of the landscape through which the train had just passed. Furnishings in the car were blue in colour and the floor was covered with "linoleum laid on thick felt".[46] It was the first WAGR carriage

to be fitted with electric lighting, although this was not the Stone's lighting equipment used a few years later, but was a storage battery system which required recharging at regular intervals. It was examined for fitting of Stone's equipment in 1897. The car had eight light fittings mounted in the clerestory roof. In 1899 it was given the road number 261, formerly allocated to one of the old Northern Railway 4-wheeled cars, and in September, 1900 it was reclassified AM.

In 1920 the first class corridor sleeping car AQ 414 was converted into an AM class Ministerial car, replacing AM 261 which was removed from service. Two years later, in March, 1922, it was converted into an AF second class suburban car, and in 1965 it was converted again, this time into a VC class breakdown van numbered 2100.Initially it was painted yellow, then later, red/brown. It was finally written off in 1974 and placed on display in the ARHS Rail Transport Museum at Bassendean.

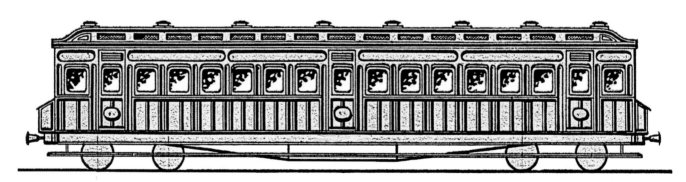

WAGR drawing of AM 261 showing the short lived extensions on the ends.

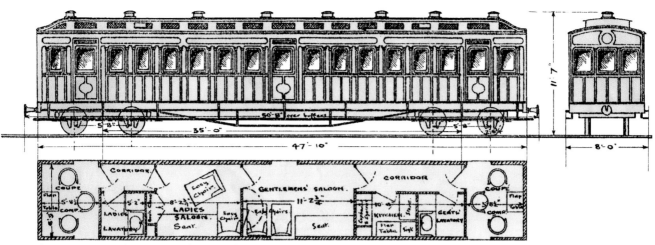

General arrangement of AM 261 without the box like arrangements on each end.   *Drawing courtesy PTA.*

Courtesy of The West Australian, via J. Austin

AM 261 posing as breakdown van VC 2100 at Bassendean yard, 14 September, 1974.

Photo courtesy Jeff Austin

Locomotive Instruction Van VI 7979 was converted from AP 86. This photo shows it in almost original condition, the only obvious things missing being the hand rails and door handles.

Photo L.G. Poole Collection, courtesy ARHS Archives

The initial batch of eight A class sleeping cars (the first sleeping car on the WAGR) arrived in the colony, four in February and four in March, 1896[47] from the Metropolitan Railway Carriage & Wagon Co. The first four cars (86-90) were placed into traffic on 9 March, 1896 to work the Eastern Goldfields Railway to Southern Cross, and all eight cars in this batch were in traffic in time for the first train, a Ministerial special, into Kalgoorlie on 8 September, 1896.

The sleeping cars had wooden bodies built on steel underframes, with timber panelled body sides painted Indian red. They were slightly larger and heavier than any of the earlier WAGR carriages, and the shape of their Mansard roof made them distinctive. There were five passenger compartments in the coach, each of which could accommodate 4 passengers if used as a sleeping car, or 6 passengers if employed as a day time sit up car. The passenger compartments, being first class, were relatively large, and these carriages were the first in WA in which every passenger had access to a lavatory. Ten more A class sleeping cars arrived in 1898 (A 146-155). The cars were used on the Eastern Goldfields Railway and the new batch also allowed sleeping car services to be provided on the Albany Express.[48]

Some members of the A class were among the twenty vehicles chosen to be fitted with the new electric lighting on a trial basis in 1899, and when this equipment had proved itself the remaining sleeping cars, which had been reclassified AP in September, 1900, had their oil lighting replaced by electric illumination within a very short time.

In 1904 four AP's (AP 86-88 and 93) were rebuilt as second class suburban day cars and reclassified AF, having been replaced by new AQ class corridor cars. They retained their AP bodies, but were altered internally for their new role.

In 1905 AP 89 was converted to an AA class long distance day car to replace AA 206 which had been rebuilt as a Vice Regal carriage. This conversion seems to have been nothing more than a change of seating and classification with the vehicle being employed only as a day time sit up car.

The Midland Railway provided first class sleeping accommodation on its services by hiring an AP from the WAGR. This arrangement came to an end in 1915 when AP 148 went to the Midland Railway as JB 22 in exchange for the Midland car JA 22, which became an ACL with the WAGR. AP 148 remained in Midland Railway service till at least 1938, but had been written off by 1940. Ten years later its body was removed and the frame used for the construction of a vehicle to carry a tractor and its driver. Since fitted with another underframe and a rebuilt body, this vehicle still exists.

In 1920 two surplus AP class cars (AP 147 and 149) were converted into second class sleeping cars and redesignated APS. This conversion did nothing to change the external appearance of the cars, but increased the capacity to 30 sleeping passengers by fitting two extra berths in each compartment, or 40 sitting day passengers. Another car (AP 146) was reclassified as an APC class composite sleeping car at the same time. In this case the compartments at either end were converted to second class while the three compartments between them remained first class.

During the 1920's two more AP's were converted to composite status and reclassified APC, AP 154 in 1923 and AP 151 in 1924. The type was then left alone to wander round the state on country trains till 1938. In that year APC 154 was sent north to operate on the isolated line between Port Hedland and Marble Bar. It had its electric lighting removed before it went[49] and, after 1945, carried the load, such as it was, on its own due to the other passenger car, ACL 385, being withdrawn from service and sent back to the main system. APC 154's fate is uncertain. It was written off in 1951 when the railway closed and never returned south. In May-June, 1973 the remaining rolling stock at Port Hedland was piled up and burnt,[50] but whether the remains of the sleeping car were still there then is not known.

Late in 1941 two APS class cars (APS 147 and 149) were converted to APC's and in 1948 these vehicles, plus two others (APC 146 and 151) were converted back to first class AP's again. This left car number 154 at Port Hedland as the only surviving APC.

During the early 1950's ten of the remaining AP's were repainted from Indian red to the new Larch green colour scheme, as follows:-

AP 91   November, 1954
AP 92   April, 1952
AP 146   June, 1953
AP 147   August, 1953
AP 149   June, 1952
AP 150   June, 1952
AP 151   August, 1955
AP 152   June, 1952
AP 153   March, 1952
AP 155   November, 1954

By the early 1960's many of the branch line passenger trains no longer existed, having been replaced by bus services, and large numbers of carriages were in store, waiting patiently to carry passengers who were no longer there. AP 90 had been converted to a workman's van in 1951 and that same year APC 154 was written off in Port Hedland, having been handed over to the Public Works Department.[51] The others disappeared very quickly after 1961. AP 151 was converted to a workman's van that year, AP 153 was written off in 1962 and in May, 1963 the remaining eight AP class sleeping cars (AP 91, 92, 146, 147, 149, 150, 152 and 155) were written off as a group, so causing the type, in its original form, to become extinct. Five (including two converted to AF and one to AA) served a little longer as workman's vans, as did AP 88/93 as an inspection car, and AP 86 as an instruction van. The frames of most of those written off were converted to QS class flat wagons.

Three AP class vehicles, (87, 88/93 and 89) still exist at Midland, Kalgoorlie and Esperance respectively, while a fourth is used as a holiday cabin near Ledge Point, north of Perth.

AP class cars on a train at Collie 5 August, 1898, soon after Collie Station was opened in 1897

Photo courtesy Battye Library Ref. 24902P

AP 153   *Photo Late Jack Stanbridge, courtesy Greg Hill*

Drawings courtesy PTA.

Blood Transfusion Car APT 87 at Pinjarra   *Photo R. Briggs, courtesy ARHS Archives*

AL 88   *Photo late Allan Hamilton Collection, courtesy Joe Moir*

Ex GSR Bogie Composite Cars
AB class
AC class (1900)

The only known photograph of the former GSR cars, AC/AF cars 181-184, taken at East Perth in 1954.

Photo courtesy ARHS Archives 0488

In December, 1896, the WAGR took over the Great Southern Railway, a private land grant railway which ran between Beverley and Albany. Included in the stock taken over were four bogie composite carriages which were very similar to the WAGR's 42' (12.81m) composite bogie cars (later AC class), but were 7' (2.13m) longer with an extra compartment in them. They contained four second class compartments and four first class, the latter being located in the centre of the car. The First Class compartments were bigger than the Second Class, with seating for 24 first class passengers and 32 second class. The cars had been built by the Metropolitan Railway Carriage & Wagon Co., and had steel underframes and timber bodies with panelled sides which, in WAGR service, were painted Indian red. The livery carried on the GSR is not known.

These cars had originally been delivered to Albany on the ship "Morialta", arriving on 2 October, 1888. One was erected especially for the last spike ceremony at Katanning on 14 February, 1889. Three cars were used for a trip from Albany to Mt. Barker and return for the local people on 13 April, 1889.

In WAGR service they were allocated the numbers 181-184 in 1897 and, at the same time, were classified AB. In the reclassification of September, 1900 one was classified AC and the other three were lumped in with the brake cars as AD's. This error was quickly rectified and the cars were reclassified AC by the end of 1901.

In 1907 AC 181 was downgraded to second class and reclassified as an AF class suburban car, followed by AC 184 in 1912 and AC 183 in 1934. This left only one ex GSR AC, No. 182. It was repainted Larch green in December, 1953 and of the original four cars it remained in service the longest, being written off in 1966.

One end of one of these cars was used as a "pie cart" after retirement, and subsequently found its way to Northam. In 1995 it was moved to Boyanup for restoration.

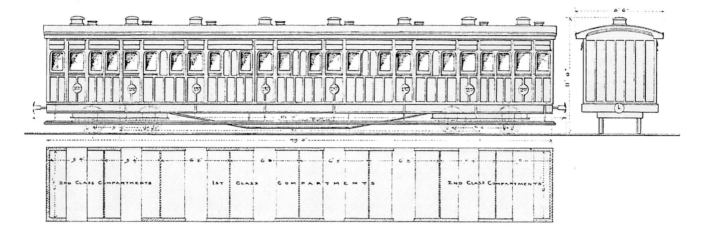

Drawing courtesy PTA

The surviving remains of one of the ex GSR cars when discovered at Northam. It was moved to Boyanup for refurbishment and preservation. Photographed on 29 June, 1991.

Photo Bill Gray

AL 190 as part of a goods train, thought to be at Nannine . *Photo courtesy ARHS Archives*

Among the fifteen passenger cars taken over with the Great Southern Railway on 1 December, 1896 was a rather unique little inspection car. This vehicle had been built by Craven Brothers of Sheffield in England as a 4 wheeler, fitted with a platform at one end, a small compartment for servants and a saloon with a toilet cubicle in it. It was first used in service on 22 November, 1888. During the early 1890's it was rebuilt at Albany, being given a longer rigid 6 wheeled underframe and fitted with another end platform. It had a steel underframe and timber body with panelling on the sides. Neither its livery or its number on the GSR are known, and when the rebuild

was completed the car became the Great Southern Railway General Manager's saloon.[52]

After it passed into the ownership of the WAGR in 1896 it was repainted Indian red and issued to traffic as an inspection car, being the only 6 wheeled car in the WAGR passenger stock not to have a Cleminson underframe. It was numbered 190 and about 1899 was classified A, then in the general reclassification in September, 1900 it was reclassed AL.

Its final years were spent as the inspection car at Geraldton, but it was damaged in an accident and written off on 6 June, 1916.

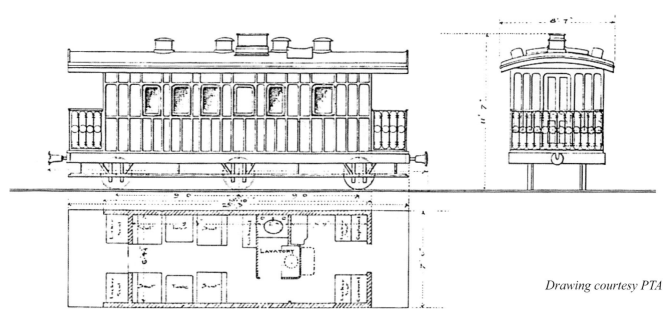

Drawing courtesy PTA

1897   First Class Car with lavatory   126-130
AB class   156-163
AE class (1900)   191-200

AE 197 in WAGR service   *Photo WAGR, Geoff Blee collection, courtesy Murray Rowe*

In 1897 a batch of five carriages arrived from the Gloucester Railway Carriage & Wagon Co. These were a first class version of the composite bogie cars of 1895 (later ACE class) fitted with a lavatory compartment, at one end. Their underframes were made of steel, with timber bodies and panelled body sides painted Indian red. When built they contained five passenger compartments and one lavatory compartment, but like the composite cars, this was not accessible from the rest of the car. The cars carried 30 passengers and the lighting was provided by the usual oil lamps. To complete the initial fifteen car order, the same builder supplied another ten cars of the same type in October, 1897. These cars entered service in March, 1898 and the entire group was classified AB, the first five carriages being numbered 126-130 and the second batch becoming 191-200. Later that year a final batch of eight more first class cars arrived which were numbered 156-163, and these probably entered service in 1899. Four of the cars delivered in 1898 aboard the "SS Andavia" had been water damaged during the voyage to Australia due to defective packing. Damage included sycamore ventilators and roof panels, and teak fascias. It was reported that the door panels and mouldings were so swollen that the doors could not be opened.[53] In the September, 1900 reclassification of the WAGR's rolling stock all these carriages were designated AE class.

The lavatory compartment arrangement was not ideal and, with the arrival of the first specifically designed long distance cars in 1899 in which each compartment had its own lavatory, it was converted into a sixth passenger compartment. This work was completed on all the AE class cars by 1903,[54] and they were then employed on short distance and suburban trains. One AE class car, No. 191, was destroyed in a fire at the Midland Workshops paint shop on 10 December, 1909.

Towards the end of the First World War there was a shortage of dynamos for the conversion of carriage lighting to electricity to continue, and in August, 1917 the following AE class cars were coupled together on a semi-permanent basis:-

AE 127 + 199
AE 128 + 160
AE 129 + 159.

In addition, around 1919, AE 156 was coupled to AD 115. By the Second World War most, if not all these carriages had been separated again.

In 1939 five AE class cars (126, 128, 158, 160 and 163) were reclassified AF, followed by another seven in 1940 (AE 156, 161, 192, 194 and 196-198). This was done by fitting second class seating and putting more people in each compartment, but it produced a temporary shortage of first class cars, so three (AF 128, 158 and 160) were converted back to AE class again later in 1940. Four more AE's (130, 157, 199 and 200) became AF's in 1941 and another two (AE 129 and 159) were reclassified AF in 1942. Curiously, AF 161 became an AE again at the same time. It was, perhaps, a case of reclassifying the best cars as AE's (first class) while those in poorer condition became AF's (second class). In any case, this spate of reclassifications came to an end in 1943 when AE 160 became an AF again.

In 1947 AE 193 was one of three cars written off after a head on collision between two suburban trains in Fremantle yard, and to replace it AF 196 was reclassified AE again. AE 127 was written off in 1951, and in 1953 the first of six AE's to be repainted in the new Larch green colour scheme was done. These were:-

AE 128   July, 1953   AE 162   April, 1953
AE 158 December, 1953
AE 195 September,1953   AE 161   March, 1954
AE 196   May, 1956.

In 1959 AE 158 was written off, followed by AE 161 in 1960

and AE 195 was converted into a workman's van in 1961. The last three AE's disappeared one at a time, quietly and without fuss, AE 128 in September, 1962, AE 162 in April, 1964 after the placing in traffic of a second batch of ADA class railcar trailers, and AE 196 in June, 1965. This car had been out of use for some time before write off. AE 162 was re-issued to traffic in April, 1969 as a workman's van, but as far as is known, no AE class carriages have survived.

Builders photo of an AE class car, carrying an incorrect road number. The car portrayed is thought to be AE 126.
Photo courtesy ARHS

AE 128 at Perth station with a Dd class steam locomotive, November, 1953.
Photo CC Singleton, courtesy ARHS.

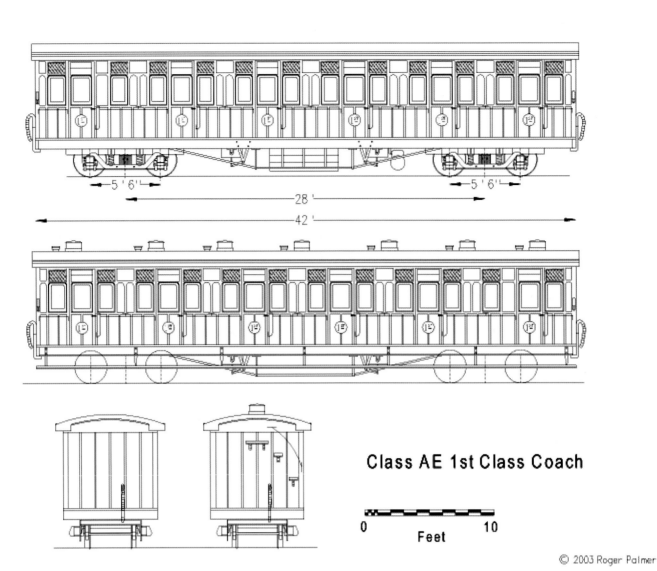

Class AE 1st Class Coach

0 — Feet — 10

© 2003 Roger Palmer

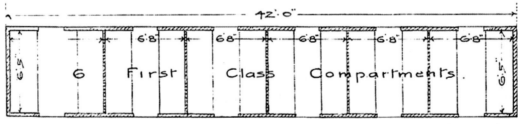

General arrangement drawings of the AE class cars. *Top courtesy Roger Palmer.*

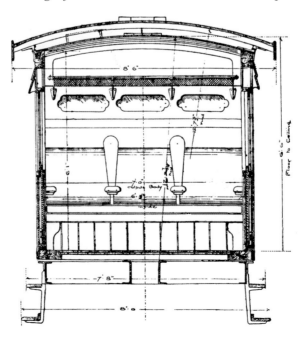

Interior drawings courtesy PTA.

Second Class Car with lavatory
AB class
AF class (1900)

AF 136 fresh out of the factory where it was built. Note the lavatory compartment at the right hand end.

Photo courtesy ARHS

The first of fifteen second class cars, each fitted with a single lavatory compartment, arrived in WA from the Gloucester Railway Carriage & Wagon Co. in 1897. The general overall appearance of the new cars followed the pattern of the earlier WAGR carriages, with panelled timber bodies painted Indian red, carried on steel underframes. They were fitted with seven compartments, one more than the first class cars, six of those being passenger compartments and the seventh the lavatory compartment. As in the previous single lavatory compartment cars, the toilet facilities were inaccessible to the majority of passengers on board. Each compartment carried 8 passengers. The second class cars were numbered 131-145 in the AB class, a classification which seemed to apply at the time to almost any passenger carrying vehicle. Another batch of these cars arrived and was placed in traffic in the second half of 1898 They were numbered 164-175, making a total of twenty seven carriages of the type. Six cars from this batch, including Car No. 169, suffered from salt water damage during the voyage to Australia, due to defective packaging, thus delaying their entry into service till mid to late August, 1898.[55] As with the first class cars the lavatory compartment proved to be fairly useless, and since new carriages designed for long distance services had arrived, the lavatory cubicles were removed and the compartment converted for the accommodation of passengers. Like the ACE class cars this conversion included a U shaped seat in the compartment because it was much bigger than the other compartments. By 1903 the conversion work had been completed and the carriages, classified AF in September, 1900, settled down on suburban and short haul services.[56] The AF classification very quickly became synonymous with second class suburban coaches in general, and finished up encompassing a remarkable variety of conversions, reclassifications, rebuilds, and new cars.

In 1903 four AP class sleeping cars (86-88 and 93), soon to be displaced by the new AQ class corridor cars then on order,

were converted to second class suburban status and classed AF. However, they retained their body shapes, the alterations being confined to their interiors.

Included in a group of cars downgraded to second class after the introduction of the AU and AW first class suburban cars was one of the ex Great Southern Railway AC class bogie composite cars, No. 181, which became second class throughout and was reclassified AF. This made thirty two AF class carriages of three different types.

In 1909 a new type of AF class car was built. This vehicle had body work similar to the newer suburban cars (classes AS and AT), but was only 37' (11.28m) long. Numbered 13, it could carry 60 passengers in its six compartments. It was possibly intended as a prototype for a new class of car, but no more were ever built and it remained a unique vehicle throughout its service life.

A fire in the paint shop at the Midland Workshops late in the evening on 10 December, 1909 claimed twenty one carriages and among them were three AF class cars, 134, 139 and 145.

They seem to have been totally destroyed in the blaze because none of them were ever rebuilt as AF's.

Continuing growth of passenger traffic on suburban services saw a number of AC class carriages reclassified to join the ranks of the AF class between 1910 and 1913. This seems to have involved little more than the alteration of the seating in the first class compartments from 6 passengers to 8. The reclassifications stopped when the First World War broke out. The carriages were reclassified as follows:-

1910 - AC 31, 34;
1911 - AC 33, 35, 56, 58, 95, 274, 276;
1912 - AC 57, 62, 184 (the ex GSR 49' (14.94m) AC), 275;
1913 - AC 32, 64, 100, 102, 273.

This brought the total number of AF's to forty eight, consisting of five different types of carriage.

AF 164 at Perth station about 1895.   Photo ARHS.

By 1917 a shortage of dynamos meant that some of the suburban cars had to be semi-permanently coupled together, with one carriage in each pair carrying a dynamo. Several of the cars so coupled were AF's, as follows:-

AF 32 + 165 - February, 1919
AF 33 + 135 - April, 1919
AF 35 + 171 - May, 1919
AF 56 + 167 - June, 1919
AF 57 + 144 - May, 1919
AF 58 + 132 - May, 1919
AF 68 + 138 - June, 1919
AF 100 + 131 - March, 1919
AF 134 + 252 - c.1919
AF 137 + 172 - March, 1919
AF 141 + 174 - February, 1919
AF 164 + 169 - April, 1917?
AF 275 + 276 - c.1920

These vehicles were progressively separated as dynamos became available, but some remained coupled till the Second World War.

In 1922 two more unique carriages joined the AF class, one a new car and the other a conversion. The new car was built on the frame of AC 59, with a new body similar in style to the AT class suburban cars, but only 42' (12.81m) long. This meant that AF 59 could have been regarded either as a shortened AT, or a stretched version of AF 13. It had seven compartments, each accommodating 10 passengers. Like AF 13, AF 59 may also have been intended as a prototype for a large rebodying programme, but no further cars were given the same treatment and it also remained a unique vehicle in the class.

The other carriage had been built in 1895 as a Ministerial car, later numbered AM 261, and it was converted to its second class suburban status in March, 1922. Its various partitions were removed, as were the kitchen and toilet facilities, and it

was fitted with a fixed full width seat at each end and fourteen rows of wooden tram car seats with an aisle down the middle. The seats had throw over backs, allowing the passengers to face the direction of travel if they chose to do so. The end windows were also filled in. In this configuration AF 261 could accommodate 66 passengers. The passenger saloon was just over 47' (14.33m) long and it must have given many regular a suburban traveller quite a surprise to open the door and step into an open style vehicle rather than the narrow compartments normally expected on suburban cars. In the late 1930's the regular WAGR worker's train which ran between Fremantle and the Midland Workshops consisted mostly of the older cars, and for this reason was known as the "Rattler". AF 261 was a regular vehicle on the train, its open and probably draughty saloon (especially in winter) earning it the nickname "The Freezer".

In 1934, with fewer people travelling first class, four more AC class cars (99, 101, 105 and ex GSR 183) were converted to second class throughout, followed by eleven more (AC 61, 63, 66, 69, 74, 75, 78, 79, 81, 85 and 94) in 1935, eight of these being former ACE's with the U shaped seat in the old lavatory compartment.

During World War Two the demand for rail journeys increased sharply and this was exacerbated by the introduction of petrol rationing during 1940. Five AE class cars (126, 128, 158, 160 and 163) were converted to AF's in 1939, by altering the seating to fit more passengers in each compartment, and another seven (AE 156, 161, 192, 194 and 196-198) were converted to AF the same way the following year.

It was at this point in time, albeit briefly, that the AF class reached its numerical peak of seventy eight carriages. The class was made up of:-

24 cars built as AB (AF from 1900);
 4 cars from AP;
 3 cars ex GSR AC;
 1 car built new on a 37' (11.28m) underframe
    (AF 13);
23 cars from 42' (12.81m) AC's;
 1 car built new on 42' (12.81m) underframe
    (AF 59);
 1 car converted from AM (AF 261);
 8 cars from ACE's; and
13 cars from AE.

War or no war, some people still wanted to travel first class, and the loss of thirteen first class cars in such a short space of time produced a temporary shortage of this type of accommodation so, in 1940, three of these cars (AF 128, 158 and 160) were classified back to AE again. That same year plans for a new steel bodied first class suburban car were put into effect and the AJ class was born. Four AF's (64, 69, 95 and 166) were taken out of service, their bodies removed and demolished, and the underframes used for the new cars. They retained the old numbers and went into service in 1941.

An AF in WAGR service.   *Photo courtesy Battye Library Ref 225752P*

or their underframes exchanged at some time, but this would seem to be unlikely, especially as there is no record of such an exchange taking place. A more likely scenario is that the two cars were stored together in 1951, with AF 93 being slated for conversion to the track recorder car, but when the time came to do the work, AF 88 was hauled into the workshops by mistake and the conversion carried out. Whichever case is correct, ALT 88 was reclassified as an AL in 1960 and lasted another twenty years before being written off and preserved by the Kalgoorlie-Boulder Loopline Preservation Society.

From 1951 a number of the AF class cars were repainted in the new Larch green colour scheme. The first was AF 168 in December, 1951 and the others were as follows:-

AF 13	December, 1956
AF 163	March, 1954
AF 33	August, 1956
AF 171	August, 1954
AF 35	? 195?
AF 172	April, 1956
AF 57	September, 1953
AF 175	December, 1954
AF 62	February, 1958
AF 181	May, 1954
AF 63	October, 1956
AF 183	November, 1953
AF 74	May, 1955
AF 184	August, 1954
AF 81	January, 1956
AF 261	February, 1958
AF 85	August, 1954
AF 274	October, 1954
AF 142	March, 1955

To replace some of these vehicles more AE first class cars were converted to AF in 1941. These were AE 130, 157, 199 and 200. In 1942 AF 161 was converted to an AE again at the same time as AE 129 and 159 became AF's. Why this swapping of carriages between first and second class took place is now hard to understand, but possibly had to do with the first class cars being those in better condition.

While one of the AE's converted to AF in 1941 replaced car 161, the other took the place of AF 66. This car, formerly an ACE, was written off in 1942 and the body removed and demolished in preparation for it to become the second AK class steel bodied suburban saloon, but a shortage of materials caused the project to be abandoned. AF 66, almost by default, ceased to exist. The constant reclassifying of these carriages finally came to an end with the conversion (for the second time) of AE 160 back to an AF in 1943.

In 1945 nine compartment cars, six of which were AF's (101, 105, 130, 174, 198 and 276) were replaced by a new AY/AYB class set of six suburban saloons, followed by another similar set of four cars in 1946, which replaced four more AF's (61, 86, 94 and 192). These losses in the AF ranks proved to be the beginning of the end of the class, and in 1947 AF 144 and 164 were written off after accidents. AF 144 was hit by a log truck at a level crossing at East Guildford,[57] and AF 164 was on a suburban train which collided head on with another in Fremantle yard.[58] AF 196 was reclassified AE again.

In 1948 AF 87 (formerly an AP class sleeping car) was converted into the only APT class blood transfusion car and in 1950 another six worn out AF class cars (88, 137, 170, 173, 194 and 199) were removed from the books. AF 88, 173, 194 and 199 were re-issued to traffic in 1952 as workman's vans.

In 1951 the slow trickle out of the class continued with the apparent conversion of AF 93 into a VT class track recorder car (VT 4998). However, after only three months it was returned to the carriage stock lists as ALT 88. Why the road number was changed is not certain, but there seem to be two possibilities. AF 88, although written off in 1950, is recorded as later returning to traffic as a VW class workman's van, carrying "Car No. 93" plates on its underframe. Therefore, it could be concluded that 88 and 93 had either their plates

By 1952 a serious shortage of goods brake vans had developed and to help ease the situation five AF class cars (143, 102, 78, 157 and 34) were converted into temporary brake vans, numbered ZAF 430-434 respectively. They retained their bodies in this change of role, but were repainted Larch green. In November that same year AF 59, the 42' (12.81m) car with the AT body, was converted into an AL class inspection car, also painted Larch green.

There was a bit of a lull before the storm in the writing off of AF class cars, but the introduction of the ADG class diesel railcars in 1954 made large inroads into the numbers of remaining carriages in the class. In 1955 no fewer than twenty two AF's were written off, with six of these cars having their frames re-used under AYE class suburban saloons. The carriages written off and scrapped were AF 56, 58, 75, 79, 100, 126, 129, 131-133, 136, 138, 156, 159, 165 and 169, while those involved in the AYE conversions were AF 99, 140, 160, 167, 197 and 200. These became AYE 703-708. In addition to these, ZAF 433 (formerly AF 157) also had its body removed and demolished, the underframe being used to build AYE 709.

In 1956 only AF 141 was written off, but in 1958 a second batch of AYE's was constructed on the frames of old AF class cars, these being AF 275, 57, 31, 32 and 273. Their frames went under AYE 710-714 respectively. In 1959 two more AF's met their end when AF 81 and 163 were written off. AF 163 was the last of those converted from the AE class cars.

In 1960 the Midland built ADX class diesel railcars were turned out, allowing the release of another group of wooden cars for demolition, and twenty one cars were written off that year, including AF 63, 74, 85, 183 and 184.

By 1960 only thirteen AF's still existed and these slowly disappeared over the next seven years. In 1961 new railcar trailers, classed ADA, were introduced into service to run with the ADG and ADX diesel railcars and among the carriages disposed of at that time were AF 33 and 135, both of which were converted to workman's vans.

In 1962 two of the ADH country railcars were converted for suburban work and this, combined with a drop in patronage,[59]

saw the demise of AF 35 and 175, followed by AF 181 in 1963 after the other two ADH class railcars were also converted for suburban use.

In 1965 a clearance of old carriages in storage was deemed necessary and forty one cars were written off, including AF 168 which was later re-instated as a workman's van, and the unique AF 261 which was converted to a VC class car (VC 2100) for crew accommodation on break down trains. In 1966 AF 62, 142, 171, 172 and 274 were all written off, and in 1967 the class finally became extinct on the WAGR with the writing off of the unique AF 13. This vehicle was converted into a workman's van and lasted in service till 1979.

Only six AF class cars still survive, but not in their original configuration. Three of those converted from AP class sleeping cars are preserved, AF 87 at Midland as a workman's van, AF 88/93 at Kalgoorlie and AF 89 at Esperance. AF 59 is preserved at the Old Northam Railway Station as an AL, AF 13 is preserved on the Bellarine Peninsular Railway in Victoria, and AF 261 survives at the ARHS Bassendean Rail Transport Museum.

The cars which were converted to the AF class from other classes were as follows:-
13, new car with AT style body; 59, new car with AT style body on AC frame;
From AC: 31-35, 56-58, 61-64, 94, 95, 99-102, 105, 273-276;
From AP: 86-88, 93;
From ACE: 66, 69, 74, 75, 78, 79, 81, 85;
From AE: 126, 128-130, 156-161, 163, 192, 194, 196-200;
From ex GSR AC: 181, 183, 184;
From AM: 261.

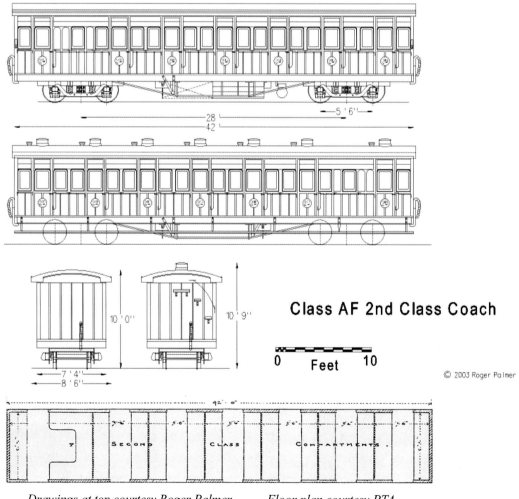

Drawings at top courtesy Roger Palmer,   *Floor plan courtesy PTA.*

AF 13

AF 13 at the Midland Workshops after it's conversion to a workmans van VW5112.   *Photo courtesy Joe Moir.*

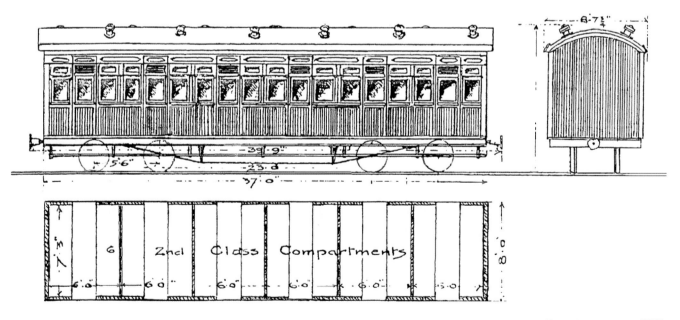

Drawing courtesy PTA.

AF 59

AF 59 at Avon Yard after it's conversion to Inspection Car AL 59.   *Photo Geoff Blee, courtesy Murray Rowe*

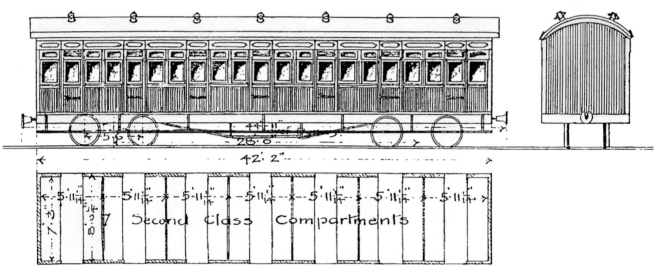

Drawing courtesy PTA.

This photograph of an N class steam loco hauling a suburban train illustrates the similarity of AF 13 & 59 to the AT class cars. The train consists of AF 59, AW, AT, AF 13, & AU.   *Photo late Alan Hamilton Collection, courtesy Joe Moir.*

Converted from AC/ACE

AF 274 stowed at Midland, 21 February, 1966

Photo courtesy Graeme Kirkby

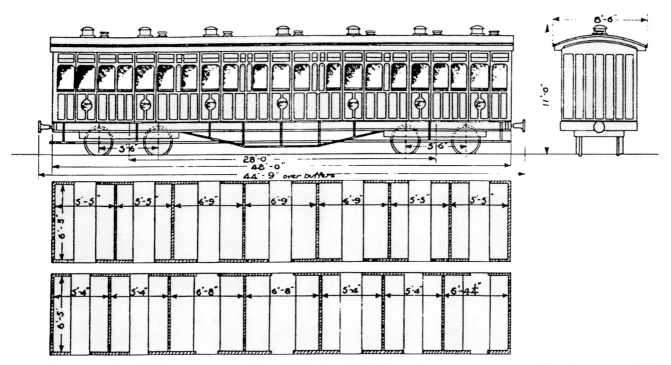

Drawings of an AF class car converted from AC (top) and ACE (bottom).

Drawing courtesy PTA.

Converted from AP

VW 5066, formerly AP 89, then AF 89, preserved in the Esperance Museum, 26 December, 1999.   *Photo Bill Gray.*

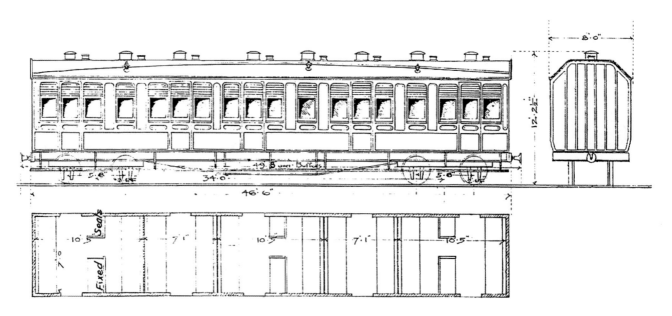

Drawing courtesy PTA.

Converted from AE

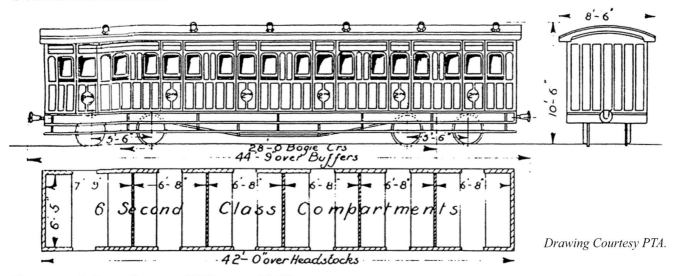

Drawing Courtesy PTA.

Converted from former GSR cars (AC)

A suburban train, photographed at East Perth in 1954. The lead car behind then locomotive is a former GSR AC, the second and fourth cars appear to be AF's, while the third car is an AE. The fifth vehicle is an AD brake car.

Photo courtesy ARHS 0488.

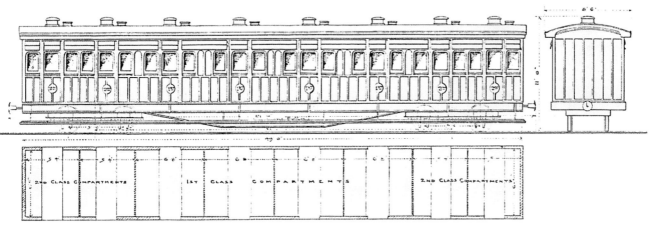

Drawing Courtesy PTA.

Converted from AM

AF 261 posing as VC 2100 at the Bassendean Rail Transport Museum, prior to it's restoration. Photographed on 28 December, 1991.   *Photo Bill Gray*

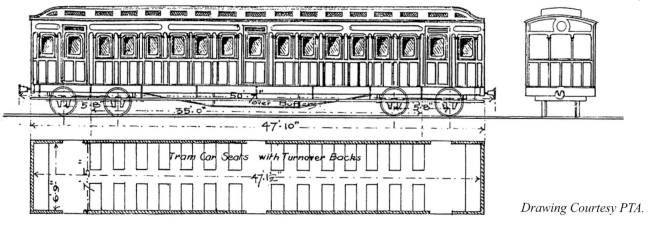

Drawing Courtesy PTA.

Dm 586 hauling a Royal Show train on 17 November, 1954. The first car is AF 261, followed by an AS, AW, AT & AS   *Photo RB McMillan courtesy ARHS Archives 2808.*

First Class Long Distance Car
A class
AA class (1900)

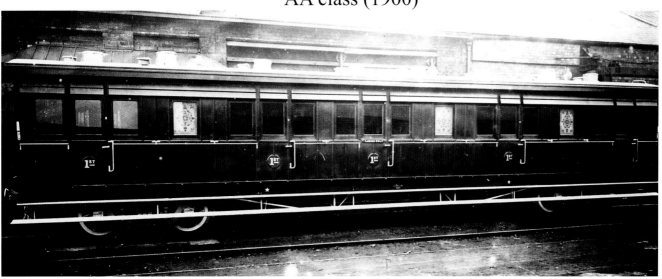

Builders photo of an unidentified AA class car   *Photo courtesy ARHS*

Twenty first class long distance cars (201-220) arrived from the Oldbury Carriage & Wagon Co. of England in 1899 as part of an order for fifty First and Second Class country cars, the largest order ever made by the WAGR at one time. Externally, these cars were not dissimilar in general appearance to the bogie composite cars acquired from the Great Southern Railway, being almost exactly the same size, with a timber panelled body, painted Indian red, on a steel underframe. The new cars were fitted with five passenger compartments, which were generally larger than those in the earlier cars, and each had its own adjacent lavatory compartment. Thus, all the passengers in the coach, for the first time in a WAGR sit up car, had access to a lavatory during their journey. The coach only accommodated 25 passengers and weighed 18 tons 15 cwt (18.94t), so while the provision of lavatories was no doubt appreciated by the long suffering passengers, the arrangement used was rather clumsy, producing a high tare weight per passenger.

The new long distance cars were classified A and remained a fairly stable group for many years. In 1899 some were fitted with electric lighting equipment in place of their oil lights and when this new form of illumination had proved itself a success, most of the first class long distance cars, being used on the main express trains of the day, were converted to it.

Following the Royal Commission into the running of the WAGR, the A class long distance cars were reclassified AA in September, 1900. In 1901 AA 206 was rebuilt as an AN class Vice Regal car, replacing AN 6, originally a 6 wheeler. To replace the AA, sleeping car AP 89 was reclassified AA in 1905, but apparently the alterations made for its new role were relatively minor.

A fire at the Midland Workshops which originated in the paint shop on 10 December, 1909 claimed only one AA class carriage, this being AA 218. It was not rebuilt or repaired and its number was allocated to a new AW class suburban car in 1911.

In 1920 an almost new AQ class sleeping car was removed from service and converted into an AN class Vice Regal car to take over the duties of AN 206, allowing this car to be re-converted back into an AA class long distance car in 1922.

During the early 1920's the demand for first class rail travel began to decline and this resulted in six AA class cars being reclassified as composites and classed ACL. Three (AA 202, 204 and 211) were converted in 1923 and another three (AA 203, 209 and 210) in 1924. By this time the AA's had been displaced from the main line trains, but gave the WAGR good service for many years on country branch line passenger trains till these services were wound down during the 1950's and '60's.

Several of the AA's were repainted Larch green during the 1950's, as follows:-

AA 201	September, 1952
AA 206	December, 1952
AA 216?	September, 1953
AA 205	March, 1954
AA 208	July, 1954
AA 214	September, 1955?
AA 207	October, 1955
AA 213	November, 1956
AA 212	December, 1956
AA 215	March, 1957
AA 217	? 195?
AA 220	? 195?

In 1956 AA 219 was written off the books and two years later the old AP (89), which had been masquerading as an AA for nearly five decades, was converted to a workman's van. AA 216 was written off in 1960, but 1965 was the year in which these cars almost completely disappeared. AA 201, 205-208, 212-215 and 217-220 were all written off, class AA becoming extinct in the process. This left only two of the original AA class cars, 202 and 210, both as ACL's, and in 1968 they were also written off.

The only car from the original twenty AA's to survive is 210, which was one of the two ACL class cars written off in 1968. It now saw occasional use on the Leschanault Preservation Society's Vintage Train as an ACM (an ACL with the lavatory doors screwed shut for use on suburban trains), and it is now housed at the Boyanup Transport Museum.

AA 206 on the Jarrahdale line during ARHS WA Division's second outing, 22 May, 1960.   *Photo courtesy ARHS Archives.*

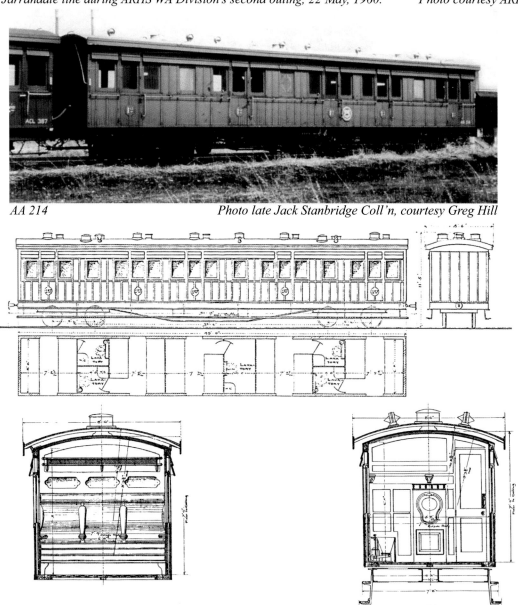

AA 214   *Photo late Jack Stanbridge Coll'n, courtesy Greg Hill*

WAGR drawings of the AA class car, general arrangement at top, a passenger compartment cross section at bottom left, and a view through the lavatory compartment bottom right.   *Drawings courtesy PTA.*

1899

Second Class Long Distance Car
A class
AB class (1900)

221-250
396-402

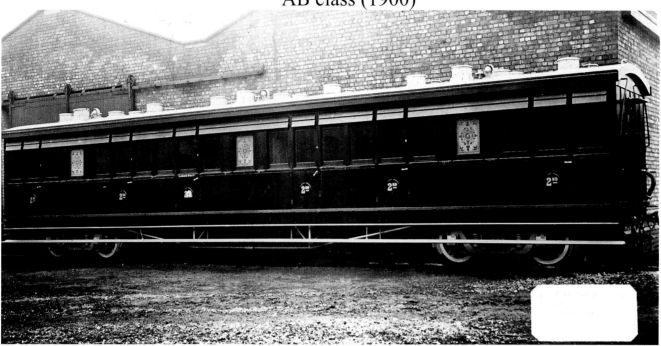

The builders photo of an unidentified AB class car   *Photo courtesy ARHS*

In 1898 the Oldbury Carriage & Wagon Co. received an order for fifty long distance cars, twenty first class (later AA), and thirty second class (later AB), this being the largest group of carriages ever purchased by the WAGR at any one time. The second class cars had one door and three windows more on each side than the first class, and two additional oil light fillers on the roof, evidence of an extra compartment within. They were built on steel underframes and had timber panelled bodies painted in the WAGR standard of Indian red. Seating was provided for 42 passengers, 7 in each of six compartments, and each compartment had its own adjacent lavatory compartment.

The second class cars went into traffic in 1899 and were numbered A 221-250. Later that year some of them were fitted with electric lighting on a trial basis and, being mainline cars, they were among the first converted to electricity once the viability of this new technology was proven.

In September, 1900 these vehicles, in the main, were classified AB, but very early in their lives some of them had been converted into composite cars, and it is possible that four never saw service as second class cars at all. These vehicles were in the group numbered 231-240, but the four cars involved have not yet been identified and, having been converted into composites prior to 1900, they were reclassified from A to AC, rather than AB. By 1901 a total of twelve AB's had been converted into composites and reclassified AC, these cars being 226, 229 and 231-240. By June, 1902 AB 225, 227, 228 and 230 had also been converted to composite cars and reclassified as AC.

The MRWA received four AB class cars (AB 222, 242, 249 and 250) from the WAGR in 1903, in exchange for four of its K class composite cars (see 1892 - Bogie Composite Cars). The AB's were converted to composites before they were handed over and upon arrival on the Midland Railway they were numbered J 1-4. This left only eleven of the original cars

as second class vehicles after a mere three years in service.

By 1902 the AC classification was in a terrible mess, and the resolution of the problem by further reclassifying the class saw the long distance AC's become ACL's. It took some time for the cars to receive their new designations, as follows:-

1906 - 225, 227, 228, 230-232, 234, 236, 237;
1907 - 226, 229, 233, 235, 239;
1908 - 238.

AC 240 may also have been reclassified during this period, but when is not certain.

In 1912 another small batch of AB's was built at Midland Workshops. These seven cars, numbered 396-402, entered service late in 1912 and early in 1913, making a total of eighteen carriages in the class. As a group they then led a fairly peaceful existence, mostly on country branch line trains, having been displaced from the more important expresses early in the twentieth century.

Between 1952 and 1958 all but two of the remaining AB class cars were repainted in the plain Larch green colour scheme, those two being AB 244 and 245.

AB 221 was written off in 1956 after the ADH class country railcars went into service, and in 1958 AB 244 became a workman's van, followed by AB 245 in 1959. During the 1960's the withdrawal of older branch line cars began to gather pace with the writing off of AB 240 in 1963 and AB 398 and 401 in 1964. That same year the WAGR took over the MRWA and among the carriages acquired in the takeover were two of the four old composite cars handed over in 1903. One, formerly AB 222 (MRWA J 1), had been converted to a workman's van in Midland Railway service, and was written off in 1964 and stored. In 1970 it was re-instated as workman's van VW 5121 and it still exists. The other was formerly AB 250 which served the MRWA as J 4, and after the WAGR takeover it became ACL 31.

By 1965 there was little work available for most of the old branch line cars and many were written off. Included among them were the last of the AB's, 223, 224, 241, 243, 246-248, 396, 397, 399, 400 and 402. Several of the old AB class cars still remain in their converted or reclassified forms and in various states of repair. AB 222 is preserved at Bassendean Rail Transport Museum as VW 5121, 232 is preserved at the Old Coolgardie Railway Station as an ACL, and 238 is with the Leschanault Railway Preservation Society at Boyanup as an ACM. The remains of AB 242 and 249 spent many years lying together on a property in the rural suburb of Hazelmere in Perth, having served the MRWA as J 2 and J 3, their bodies being sold privately after write off. They were finally destroyed early in 1994 to make way for a housing development.

The WAGR photographer's official shot of an AB class car in service.   *Photo Geoff Blee Coll'n, courtesy Murray Rowe*

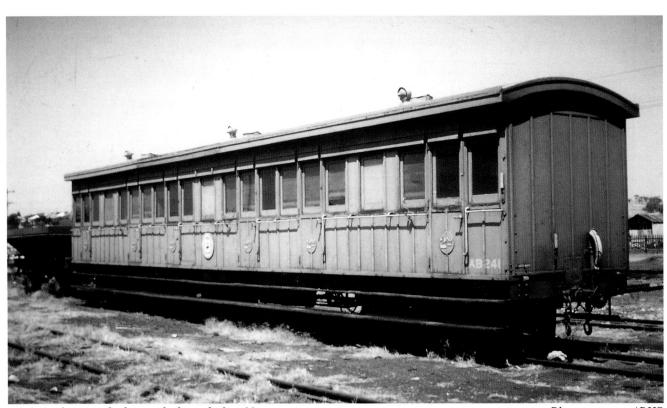

AB 241, photographed towards the end of its 66 year existence   *Photo courtesy ARHS*

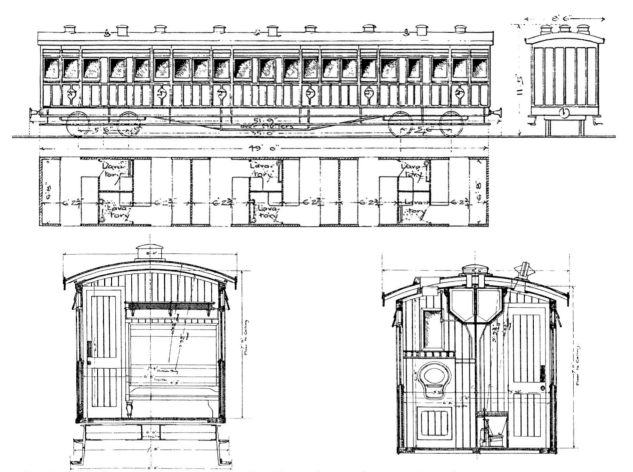

Drawings depicting then general arrangement of the AB cars (top), and cross sections of a passenger compartment (bottom left) and the lavatory compartment (bottom right).   *Drawings courtesy PTA.*

VW 5121, formerly AB 222 & MRWA's J.1, at Forrestfield, 16 February, 1991   *Photo Bill Gray*

Although the date this photograph was taken is not known, it would seem to have been shot in the days before motor vehicle ownership was a common thing, and the happy couple, whoever they may have been, were about to depart on their honeymoon by train, travelling in Second Class car AB 241. Note also the nowadays politically incorrect "Smoking" sign affixed to the compartment door.

Photo courtesy Philippa Rogers

AO 7 on its 6 wheel Cleminson underframe, at an unknown location.   *Photo courtesy Battye Library. Ref. BA888/4*

Prior to the advent and widespread use of motor vehicles, coffins containing the last mortal remains of Western Australian citizens were generally transported to the cemeteries for burial by horse drawn hearses. Relatives and friends of the deceased who wished to attend the funeral travelled by foot, horse, horse drawn vehicle or bicycle. In 1899 an obsolete 6 wheeled first class brake car, AC 7, was converted into the WAGR's one and only funeral car. This vehicle had begun life in 1883 as a second class "Cleminson" saloon, classified BC, and in 1889 it had been rebuilt as a brake composite car and reclassified AC. It had its brake compartment located in the centre of the car body and was fitted with lookouts and end platforms. It was later redesignated first class and reclassified A (when is not known), then became the funeral car in 1899. It was classified AO.

AO 7 was a unique vehicle in its role as a rail borne hearse. It retained its 6 wheeled Cleminson underframe and its panelled timber body, typical of the bodies on WAGR carriages then in service. It was painted Indian red.

Inside, there were two main compartments, a mourner's compartment with longitudinal seating on both sides for 12 passengers, and a combined guard/coffin compartment. One interesting feature about AO 7 was that the coffin compartment was fitted with roof mounted ventilators, perhaps absolutely necessary in those days with refrigeration still in its infancy!

The first person to have the doubtful privilege of using AO 7 was a Mr Creighton from Waroona, who was also the first of many to be interred at the Karrakatta cemetery. His funeral took place on 24 April, 1899.

The car was fitted with a bogie underframe prior to the First World War, but in every other way it retained its appearance. By 1930 there was little use for a funeral car, as road transport was coming of age, so AO 7 was withdrawn from service and converted into a Z class brakevan (Z 5006), being re-issued to traffic on 17 May, 1930. By 1940 it was renumbered Z 29 and it was later rebodied, being written off in November, 1973.

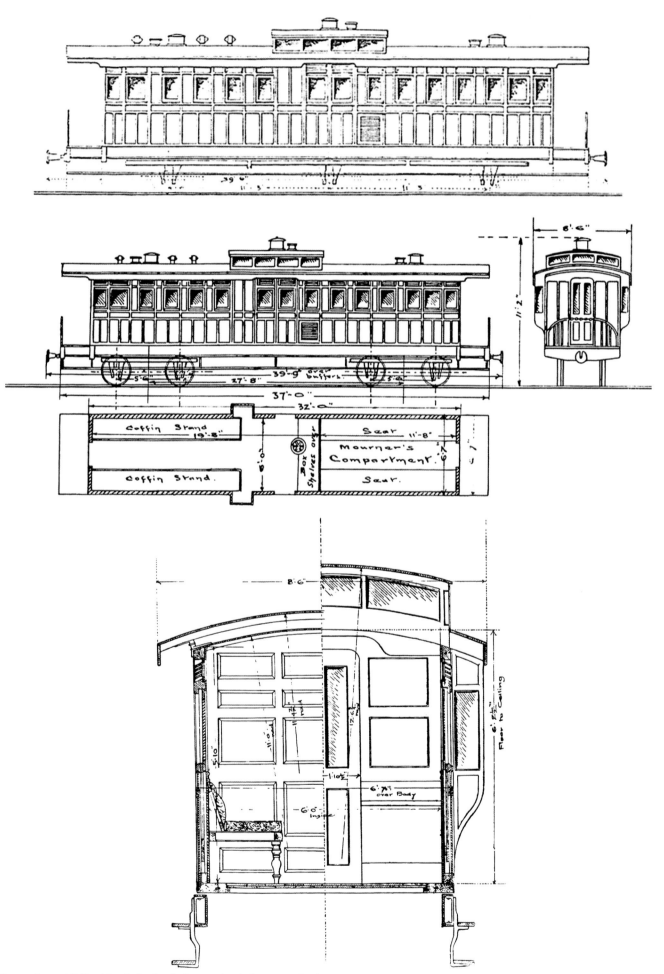

Funeral car AO 7 with it's 6 wheel chassis (top), bogie underframe (centre), & cross section through the mourners & coffin compartments.
Drawings courtesy PTA.

CHAPTER THREE
CONTINUED EXPANSION and CONSOLIDATION 1901 - 1910

The WAGR underwent a relatively quiet period between 1899 and 1902 while the administration problems, a reflection of both the personality clashes between some of the senior personnel and the massive expansion of the late 19th century, were sorted out. The only significant change to the carriage stock during this period of upheaval was the replacement of the Vice Regal car AN 6 by the bigger and better appointed AN 206, converted from an AA class long distance car in 1901. In 1905 sleeping car AP 89 was converted to an AA class car.

Construction of new lines was little affected by the disruption in Perth, and the Brown Hill Loop line, running from Kalgoorlie down through Brown Hill and back up through Boulder to Kalgoorlie again, was opened in March, 1902.[1] At this time the Kalgoorlie services were greater in number than those in suburban Perth, and it was around this loop that the remaining eight passenger carrying "Gilbert" cars and, later, the three "American" brake cars, hauled by N class 4-4-4T steam locomotives, were put to good use.[2]

In 1902 two new types of brakevan were introduced into service. The first of these, although not passenger carrying vehicles, were included in the passenger stock lists and were an integral part of passenger trains right to the end of their lives. These were the AJ class express passenger brakevans, built by the Ashbury Railway Carriage & Iron Co. of England, ten of which entered service during the year (AJ 263-272). They represented a change of direction in the appearance of the WAGR's carriages, with matchboard sides rather than flat panelling and a 6'(1.83m) radius roof in place of the older style, flatter, 12' (3.66m) radius roof. This made them taller than the older cars and they looked it. They were followed later in 1902 by another type of brakevan, the ZA class. These were fitted with two second class passenger compartments, but were never classified in the passenger stock, being listed as goods brakevans. The reason for this would seem to lie in the fact that they were designated as goods brakevans used to provide passenger accommodation on goods trains, while the express brakevans were intended for use on passenger trains, so it appears that these vehicles were classed according to their intended use rather than what they actually carried. The ZA's were similar in style to the AJ class vans, and thirty arrived in two batches, fifteen (ZA 5843-5837) from the Oldbury Carriage & Wagon Co., followed by fifteen more (ZA 6270-6284) built by the Ashbury Railway Carriage & Iron Co. While delivery of the ZA's commenced in 1902, the last two of the 5000 number series appear to have been placed in traffic after 30 June, 1903, along with the 6000 number series vans. These thirty vehicles were joined by another ZA class van (4992) built at Midland between 1905 and 1907 to replace a P class 4 wheeled brakevan which had been destroyed by fire. The new van was allocated the 4 wheeler's number.

During 1902 a Parliamentary Select Committee enquiry was held into the running of the Midland Railway, which was still using its K class coaches on the line, despite their not being equipped with toilets. This was apparently causing some discomfort, if not considerable embarrassment, to some of the passengers. One of the several recommendations made by the Committee was that "lavatory cars be provided at once, for the convenience of female passengers in particular"[3]. To comply with this recommendation plans were prepared for new lavatory compartment cars, but these were never built. Instead, the company arranged an exchange of coaches with the WAGR. In 1903 four AB class cars (222, 242, 249 & 250) went to the Midland Railway in exchange for four K class composite cars[4]. The AB's were converted to composites before they were handed over and upon arrival on the Midland Railway they were numbered J 1-4. This left only eleven of the original thirty cars as second class vehicles after a mere three years in service. The MRWA K class cars became AC 273-276 on the WAGR and, as a result, the WAGR now owned nine of the original ten composite cars ordered for the Midland Railway.

The Fremantle Workshops had become so cramped by the turn of the century that locomotives and rolling stock were being assembled in the open, and it was decided to move to a new location. Midland Junction was chosen and in 1902 work began on the new facilities there, with the move starting late the following year.[5] Railway construction continued in other parts of the system and in 1903 the Northern Railway from Cue to Nannine was opened, as was a branch in the Eastern Goldfields from Menzies to Leonora. Despite the large numbers of carriages placed in service during the 1890's the system still did not have enough capacity to satisfy the demand, and as a consequence, covered vans were used to carry passengers on Special Race Days and holiday excursions.[6]

T.F. Rotheram, the first CME, was an engineer of great experience, who had spent most of his career in New Zealand, but had originally been trained on the Manchester, Sheffield & Lincolnshire Railway in Britain.[7] He worked on the New Zealand Railways for over twenty years before he came to Western Australia and although he was only CME for three years (he died in 1903), he was responsible for the replacement of express trains made up of side loading "dog box" cars hauled by locomotives like the R class 4-4-0's, with 12 wheeled end platform AR and AQ class corridor cars led by E class 4-6-2's. The AR class cars were Western Australia's earliest 12 wheeled carriages and they first appeared in December, 1903. These nine second class sit up corridor cars were numbered 277-285 and were followed in mid 1904 by nine similar first class sleeping cars (AQ 286-294). All eighteen carriages were built by the Gloucester Railway Carriage & Wagon Co. in England. These cars introduced a radical change in design compared to the older WAGR passenger carriages, not being dissimilar to carriages being used in New Zealand. They were fitted with end platforms and gangways which allowed access through the train. The interiors of these cars were ornately decorated with mouldings and panels in contrasting timbers, acid etched crown light windows, and decorative plaster and pressed tin mouldings in ceilings and walls. These displayed a high quality of workmanship, and when compared with our modern rolling stock, indicate how much we have lost in the name of economy.

The AP's displaced from the principal expresses by the new AQ's found work on other country trains or, in the case of four of them (AP 86-66 & 91), as Perth suburban cars, converted to second class suburban status and classed AF. However,

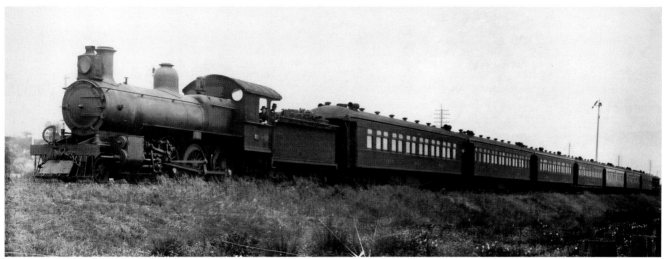

Steam loco E.323 on a train of new end platform cars. The photo is believed to have been taken near Bayswater before the First World War.   *Photo WAGR courtesy Lindsay Watson*

they retained their body shapes, the alterations being confined to their interiors. These were the first of many conversions from other classes into the AF class of suburban cars, a class which was eventually made up of large numbers of coaches of various types and styles. Rotheram was succeeded by Mr. Edward Shotton Hume, who had been the Workshops Manager since 1900. He was only 28 years old and proved to be the longest serving CME the WAGR ever had.[8]

The new mainline country cars were quickly followed by another classic series of WAGR carriages, the 58' (17.69m) suburban stock. These cars were built on the same type of chassis as the country cars, but their body style was more akin to the AJ class brakevans. Like the country cars which preceded them, they made full use of the loading gauge, and were rugged, fairly basic vehicles, intended to provide short distance stop-start travel, the first of a style of car which became the backbone of suburban services till the end of steam. The first of the type to be delivered were eight second class suburban cars (AT 295-302) from the Gloucester Railway Carriage & Wagon Co., which entered service at the end of 1904 and were followed in March, 1905 by the first Australian built carriages to appear on the WAGR in any number. These were twelve first class suburban cars of similar design to the AT's, classed AW (323-334), and built by Westralia Ironworks of Rocky Bay (now North Fremantle). They entered service in pairs over a two month period between the middle of March and the middle of May, 1905. During this time five similar first class suburban brake cars classified AU (307-311) were placed in service after their delivery from the Gloucester Railway Carriage & Wagon Co. in England, and a sixth car, AU 312 also arrived from England in 1906. After Westralia Ironworks had delivered the last of their AW class cars, they built six AU's, all of which entered service during July, 1905.

During this hectic period of suburban car deliveries, a small group of country cars entered service. These were four dining cars, officially known as "restaurant cars", classed AV (313-316) which, built by the Gloucester Railway Carriage & Wagon Co., were the last locomotive hauled cars to be imported by the WAGR. They were the first dining cars in Australia and operated exclusively on the Kalgoorlie trains till after the First World War. Visually they were very similar to the AQ and AR class cars, contributing enormously to the neat, uniform appearance of the WAGR expresses of this period.

The move into the Midland Workshops from Fremantle was completed on 5 January, 1905[9] and soon afterwards that establishment turned out its first passenger car, an AW which was given the number 20. The rash of suburban car deliveries finally ended with the arrival of another four AT's in August, 1905.

The placing in service of the new AU and AW first class suburban cars produced a surplus of first class accommodation on the short distance and suburban trains. As a result, several AD class brake cars were converted to second class throughout (AD 114, 118, 119, 121, 177 & 186), but initially retained their AD classification. This "conversion" was made by altering the seating to carry 2 extra passengers in each of the first class compartments, so bringing the accommodation to 40.

Construction of new lines continued with the opening of the Malcolm to Laverton branch in the Eastern Goldfields in 1905, while decisions being made back in Perth were destined to have a long term effect on the railways in Western Australia, ultimately being a factor in the demise of country passenger train services. Realising that the gold boom had peaked around 1900, the government set out to provide an alternative industry by encouraging farming, particularly wheat. A Royal Commission held on immigration in 1905 recommended that a railway be provided to within at least 15 miles (24km) of any farm and this idea was enthusiastically embraced by the government, which promptly set about having these lines built. However, they were constructed by the Public Works Department at minimum cost, with few earthworks, light rails, dirt ballast, poor drainage, crude sleepers, and only very basic station and loading facilities. As each of these lines, known as agricultural railways, were completed, they were handed over to the WAGR which had to operate and maintain them and, in some cases, upgrade them before they could be used at all.[10] The end result was that a large proportion of the WAGR's financial allocation in subsequent years was spent on their maintenance, which meant that there was much less money available for other projects, including new passenger cars.

In 1906 new lines were completed from Narrogin southwest to Darkan, so linking Bunbury and Collie to the Eastern Goldfields Railway. Little in the way of new carriages arrived during this period, but the first of the ACL class cars made

ZJ class brakevans being constructed` at the then new Midland Workshops   *Photo WAGR courtesy ARHS Archives*

its appearance on the WAGR in January, 1906. This class came into being as a result of the confusion created after the September, 1900 reclassifications when four different types of car were placed in the AC class. Among these were sixteen composite long distance cars, originally of the AB class, although a few of them probably never carried that classification, being converted to composites prior to 1900. To help sort out the confusion, the long distance carriages in the AC class were reclassified ACL, and by the end of 1908 all the cars in the group 225-240 had been reclassified.

In addition, two brake composite cars, AD 188 and 189, were withdrawn from service and converted into lavatory equipped composite saloons, classed AX, for use on long distance express trains. These were interesting conversions because the two AX class cars were not identical, differing considerably in their internal arrangements.[11] Although ten cars were scheduled for conversion, plans to build more AX class cars did not eventuate.

Delivery of a new batch of AJ class express brakevans commenced began in December, 1906, and continued into 1907. The first five of these vehicles (364-368) were built at the Midland Workshops, while the second five (359-363) came from Westralia Ironworks. These ten vans were identical to the first batch of AJ's, except that they were 3" (89mm) wider.[12]

Three AG class "American" cars (AG 9, 12 & 17) had had brake compartments fitted to them in 1905 and were transferred to Kalgoorlie where they replaced the P class 4 wheeled brakevans on the suburban trains. After their arrival, one of two remaining first class "Gilbert" cars, AG 40, was returned to Perth where it was converted into a Ministerial car in 1907.

By June, 1908 two hundred and two WAGR coaches had

been fitted with electric lighting and, despite the apparent success of this equipment, the decision was taken to fit composite brake car AD 186 with acetylene lighting on a trial basis.[13] Either the trial lasted 23 years or AD 186 was forgotten because the acetylene equipment was not replaced with electric lights till 1930! In 1907 the line from Northam to Goomalling was opened, being the first stage of the agricultural railways to the northern wheatbelt, and the WAGR purchased a short privately owned railway between Albany and Denmark.

Delivery of new carriages recommenced in 1908. Twelve AQ's (335-346) and twelve AR's (347-358), seven of each from Westralia Ironworks and five of each from the Midland Workshops arrived, these cars being slightly different to the earlier cars of the same classes. They were all built on timber underframes instead of steel, and in the AR's the crown lights were shorter, the corridor was altered by angling it at each end of the car to allow room for a relocated linen closet, while the AQ's differed in the arrangement of the lavatory compartments, and only accommodated 20 sleeping passengers. In addition, their crown lights were arranged differently. Delivered shortly after the new AQ's and AR's entered service were twelve AS second class suburban brake cars (369-380), also from Westralia Ironworks. These new cars were the only batch of AS class cars produced, and were, in effect, an AT with a brake compartment at one end. Their AS classification had been vacated by two 6 wheeled luggage vans which had been converted into Z class brakevans in 1906.

In 1909 a new type of AF class car was built. This vehicle had body work similar to the newer second class suburban cars (classes AS and AT), but was only 37' (11.28m) long. Numbered 13, it could carry 60 passengers in its six compartments. It was possibly intended as a prototype for a new class of car, but no more were ever built and it remained a unique vehicle throughout its service life.

Two AH class "Cleminson" cars, 24 and 25, were sent to the isolated railway between the copper mining town of Ravensthorpe and the port of Hopetoun on the south coast of WA in April, 1909. This line was opened on 3 June, 1909 with G class steam locomotives providing the motive power, and by 1911 the two AH's, two 6 wheeled ex Great Southern Railway brakevans and a ZA class passenger brakevan (ZA 6281) were in passenger service there.[14] The mining of copper at Ravensthorpe was, at best, spasmodic, finally ceasing after World War One, but the line stayed open till 1 April, 1931. After this date it operated seasonally till completely closed on 23 February, 1936. The "Cleminson" cars, however, had been abandoned in 1930, having run relatively few miles on the line.

In 1909 it was found that the Goldfields Water Supply Administration's line between Mundaring and Mundaring Wier in the hills near Perth was operating in breach of the Government Railways Act and on 15 September, 1909 the line and stock were sold to the WAGR. Included in the sale were two H class steam locomotives and the old 4 wheeled cars AI 258 and 260, which had been sold to the Goldfields Water Supply Administration in 1903-04 and 1906 respectively. This brought the number of AI class cars in WAGR ownership to four, but it is doubtful that any of them saw much use. The WAGR's earliest carriages finally became extinct on the system when the last of them, AI 22 was sold to the Department of the Northwest in 1925 to join AI 258 at Carnarvon as a "tramcar".

Around 1909 and 1910 the lung disease tuberculosis (consumption) was rampant and so that people suffering from this affliction could travel by train to the Sanatorium at Wooroloo for treatment, a compartment in some cars was set aside for them with a door in the corridor being marked accordingly. In this way consumptives were considered less likely to affect other passengers.[15] The cars with a compartment allocated for consumptives were AR 283 in 1909, and AR 284 and 285 in 1910.

Ten new ACL's were built at the Midland Workshops in December, 1909 and these were given the lowest available numbers in the stock list (1, 3, 6, 19, 21, 23, 27, 30, 70 & 222). However, the last five never entered service. Late in the evening of Friday 10 December, 1909, after a hot summer's day, the paint shop at the Midland Junction Workshops caught fire. The building was thirteen years old, made of galvanised iron and timber, with a floor of old packing case timber, no doubt deeply impregnated with the oils and other flammable materials used in the painting of railway rolling stock. Despite the valiant efforts made to extinguish the fire and an unsuccessful attempt to remove some of the carriages with a steam locomotive, twenty one cars were destroyed and five others damaged.[16] The cars destroyed were:-

ACL 23, 27, 30, 70, 222;
AD 49, 117;
AF 134, 139, 145;
AX 189;
AE 191;
AA 218;
AT 299, 306;
AU 309, 319;
AW 326, 332;
ZA 5846, 6283.

The five cars damaged, but known not to have been destroyed were ACL's which had their seat cushions burnt. A rebuilding programme was quickly implemented and it is now difficult to tell how much, if any, of the original carriages were used in the rebuilds. In the case of the AD's, by then obsolete cars, the fact that they were rebuilt as AD's could indicate that they were not totally destroyed in the blaze, but this is by no means certain. In any case, two AD's, either new cars or rebuilds of the burnt ones, and carrying the old numbers, entered service in February, 1912. It is presumed that the other cars were totally destroyed, being replaced over the next three years by new cars which were given the road numbers of the fire victims.

1910 was a fairly quiet year while the staff at Midland cleaned up after the fire and generally reconsolidated. There was also the small problem of the burnt coaches not being insured,[17] so money was scarce for any new projects. No new cars were built, but new railways were opened from Nannine to Meekatharra, so completing the line from Geraldton along its full length, and a branch from Pinjarra to Dwellingup was opened for traffic, largely to service the timber industry.

The first decade of the twentieth century had been one of continued and rapid growth in the WAGR, but without the frenzied activity of the late 1890's. One hundred and fifty six new passenger cars went into service, most of them of modern design, so complementing the large fleet of older compartment cars.

Kalgoorlie yard, with a train consisting of AG American cars, trailed by an AG Gilbert car.

Photo courtesy ARHS.

Express Brakevans
AJ class
ZJ class (1940)
(ZJA class (1960))

ZJ 266 at the former Midland Workshops, painted in the original Indian Red livery, 14 September, 2003.   *Photo Bill Gray.*

In 1902 a group of ten new express brakevans (263-272) arrived from the Ashbury Railway Carriage & Iron Co. of England, and entered service as the AJ class. Although not passenger vehicles, they were classified in the passenger stock list and they represented a change of direction in the appearance of the WAGR's carriages. The AJ's were fitted with a 6' (1.83m) radius roof and were similar in style to the small gold bullion van (VX 4999), delivered in 1898 (see App. 1). The AJ's had with tongue and groove body panelling painted Indian red on a 49' (14.94m) steel underframe. They had a tare weight of 10 tons (10.1t) and were rated to carry a 9 ton (9.09t) load. Lighting in the express vans was electric, although most of them lost their dynamos to the passenger cars after World War One and were converted to oil. This situation lasted till the mid 1930's, by which time the AJ's were electrically lit again.

Delivery of a second batch of five AJ class express brake vans (364-368) began in December, 1906, these vans being built at the Midland Workshops, and they were followed by another five (AJ 359-363) from Westralia Ironworks early in 1907. These vans were identical to the first batch, except that they were 3" (89mm) wider.[18]

The opening of the Trans Australia Railway in 1917 created an increase in the number of passengers carried and several new cars were built to cater for this, including three more AJ's. These went into service in 1919, numbered 427-429 and were identical to the 1906/07 batch except that they were fitted with a new design longer wheel base 4 wheel bogie. During the early 1920's most of the other AJ's were fitted with the new bogies as well, once they had proven to be satisfactory in service, and several AJ brakevans were fitted with shelves for

carrying milk at about the same time. The vehicles so treated were AJ 263, 267, 269, 272, 367 and 368.

In 1930 a "one off" AJ class van was put into service. It was built on the underframe of a ZA class brakevan (ZA 9346) which had been destroyed by fire late in 1928 and, as a result, the new van was only 42' (12.81m) long. It was numbered 260. During the latter half of the 1930's the WAGR's AZ class sleeping cars were fitted with new bogies to improve their riding qualities and their old bogies went under the express brakevans not yet fitted with the long wheel base undercarriage. These were:-

1938 - AJ 362, 363, 367;
1939 - AJ 364.

However, during the late 1940's these four vans were fitted with the same long wheel base bogies as the other AJ's to standardise the fleet.

In 1940 the AJ's were reclassified into freight stock as the ZJ class, but they retained their numbers. ZJ 427 was removed from normal service in 1941 and used as part of the Commonwealth Government's ambulance train. For this role it was painted white with large red crosses on the sides and roof. It was returned to the WAGR in 1945.

In 1944 ZJ 272 was equipped with a cool chamber for the carriage of perishable goods and in 1947 another five express brakevans (AJ 361, 363, 367, 368 & 428) were similarly treated. Two more (ZJ 359 & 364) received cool chambers in 1948 and the final conversion was ZJ 365 in 1949. One of these vans (ZJ 367) was fitted with end doors and gangways at the same time, allowing access from the vehicle into the rest

ZJ 260 after it's conversion into Bullion Van VY 5000.   *Photo courtesy ARHS Archives*

of the train.

In 1947 ZJ 427 was chosen to be used on the new "Australind" which ran between Perth and Bunbury. It was refurbished for its new role, being fitted with end doors and gangways and repainted green and cream to match the other cars on the train. The following year some of the other ZJ's were also repainted in the green and cream livery for use on the "Westland" consist.

The first ZJ to disappear from the system went in 1948. This was ZJ 260 which was withdrawn from service in September that year and converted into a VY class gold bullion van, replacing VY 4999. ZJ 260, numbered VY 5000, was fitted with the safe from the old bullion van. That same month (September) ZJ 360 was damaged in a collision at Mt. Kokeby on the Great Southern Railway, south of Beverley, when, at the rear of the "Albany" express, it was run into by a goods train.[19] It was written off early in 1949.

When the WAGR's standard colour scheme was altered from Indian red to Larch green after 1951, all the ZJ's still in service, with the exception of ZJ 264 and possibly 428, were repainted.

In 1954 ZJ 264 was the first ZJ class brakevan to be written off in the normal course of events, followed by ZJ 263 & 428 in 1957, the latter vehicle having been destroyed by fire between Malcom and Murrin Murrin. However, in 1960 five new express brakevans (430-434), of very similar design to the 1919 vintage vehicles. were built as part of a carriage refurbishment programme and were classified ZJA. That same year ZJ 272 was fitted with end doors and gangways.

The carriage refurbishment programme of the early 1960's included a new colour scheme of Larch green, with cream along the window line and all the ZJ class brakevans still in service were repainted, as were the ZJA's. These vans were ZJ 265-272, 359, 361-368, 427, 429 and ZJA 430-434.

One of the new ZJA's (434) was painted in a special red and ivory livery in 1964 for use on the "Midlander" after the WAGR took over the Midland Railway Co. in August that

year. The "Midlander" was a weekday service and ZJA 434 spent its weekends on the "Albany Weekender" trains. It was repainted green and cream in 1967. ZJ 363 was badly damaged in a collision in 1967. It was rebuilt with a new plywood body, but without the double roof, and three other ZJ's (269, 364 & 366) also lost their outer roofs at about the same time. However, the bodies of these three vans retained their matchboard sides.

ZJ 359 was the next one to be written off, this taking place in 1973 after the overnight passenger trains started to disappear, and ZJ 368 went the following year.

By 1978 most of the main passenger trains, including the Reso's had finished, leaving the "Australind" as WA's only locomotive hauled country passenger train, and the demise of the express brakevans began to gather momentum. They were written off as follows:-

1978 - ZJ 265, 268, 363, 366;
1979 - ZJ 272;
1980 - ZJ 269;
1981 - ZJ 271, 361, 364, 365, 367;
1982 - ZJ 427.

The writing off of ZJ 427 left the "Australind" without a brakevan but it was replaced by the ARA class brake cars and ZJA 431, which emerged from the workshops late in 1982 sporting a fresh coat of paint, plywood sides, and gangways.

From July, 1985 Westrail (as the WAGR had become) stopped using brakevans on most of its trains.[20] In 1984 ZJ 267 was written off and the following year most of the remaining express brakevans were removed from service. These were ZJ 270, 362, 429, ZJA 430 and 432-434. Most were stored for a while before being disposed of, with ZJ 266 and ZJA 431 being the last in Westrail service. Several still survive. ZJ 270 was purchased by the ARHS in 1987 and converted into a mobile museum van at their Rail

ZJA 433 brings up the rear of the "Midlander" at Geraldton station on 29 December, 1966.
Photo late Geoff Blee, courtesy Murray Rowe.

Transport Museum, being returned to service on 9 October, 1988. ZJ 266 and ZJA 431 have also found a home with the ARHS for use on tour trains. ZJ 359 is preserved at the old Coolgardie Railway Station, ZJ 363 found a home with the Hotham Valley Railway, but was demolished in December, 2002. ZJ 367 is retained in Hotham Valley Railway service, ZJ 427 is preserved at Kalamunda outside Perth, serving as an arts and crafts centre, the Leschanault Preservation Society has ZJA 432 and 434 stored at the Boyanup Transport Museum, and another ZJ survives at the Bullsbrook rodeo grounds. ZJ 429 serves as a shelter for live steam locomotives and rolling stock at Esperance. In addition to these, several others have been sold to private owners such as farmers for use as sheds and the like.

ZJ 270, in preservation, rests at Forrestfield, 11 April, 1992.   *Photo Bill Gray*

An anonymous & well used ZJ behind an F class diesel   *Photo courtesy Joe Moir*

ZJ 361, one of the wider vans built by Westralia Ironworks which entered service in early 1907. Photographed at Kalgoorlie, 30 December, 1967.   *Photo late Geoff Blee, courtesy Murray Rowe*

Australind brakevan ZJ 427 standing at Bunbury, 13 January, 1968.   *Photo late Geoff Blee, courtesy Murray Rowe*

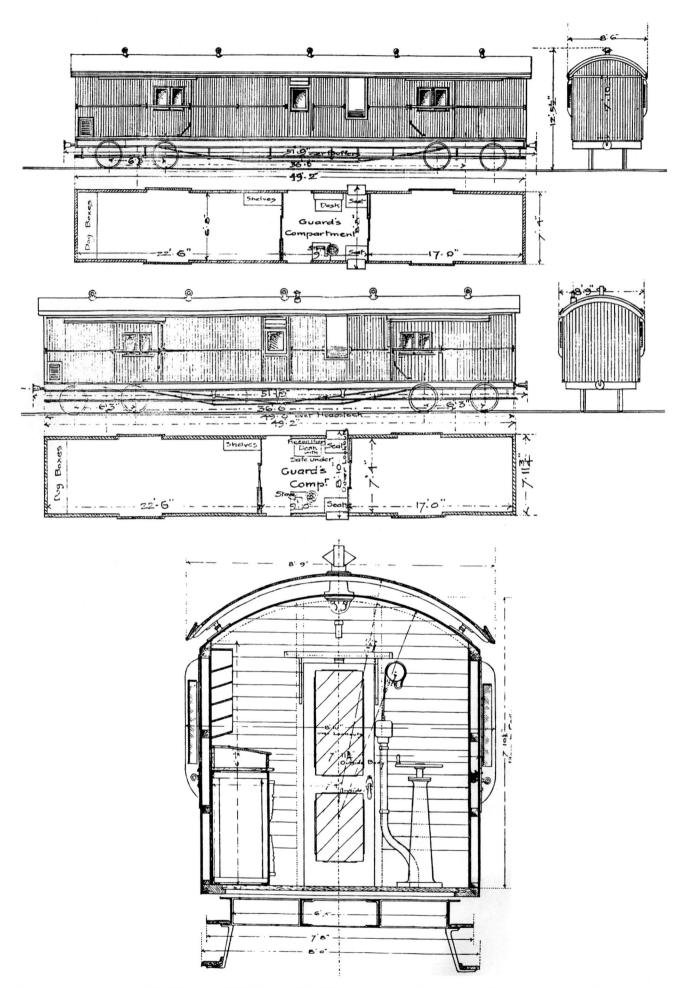

The drawings depict AJ 263-272 (top), AJ 359-368 & 427-429, these being wider (centre). The cross section of the brake compartment is representative of the wider vans. Drawings courtesy PTA.

ZJ 363 out of service at Pinjarra, 24 April, 1991. Note the single roof and plywood sides. Despite the protective pink undercoat, the van was demolished in late 2002.

Photo Bill Gray

ZJ 367 shows off it's cool room door and end access door in Perth Yard, 9 December, 1967

Photo late Geoff Blee, courtesy Murray Rowe

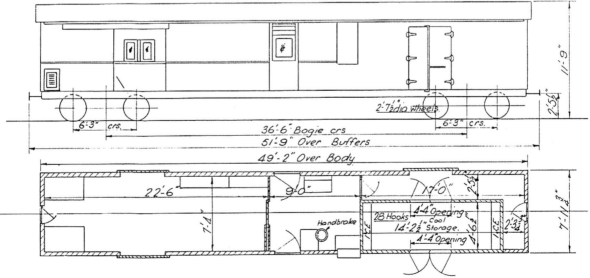

The WAGR drawing of ZJ 367 with the cool room and end access doors.   *Drawing courtesy PTA*

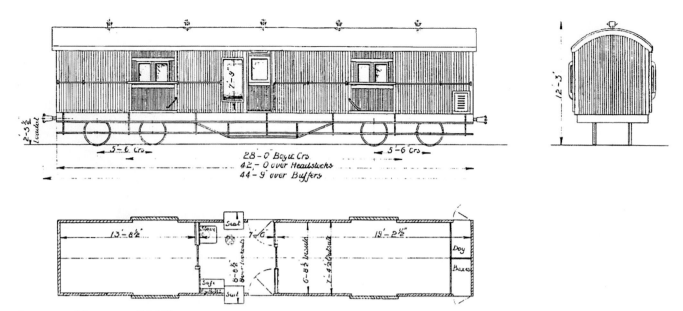

Drawing of the unique ZJ 260.   *Drawing courtesy PTA*

ZJA

ZJA 434 in the green and cream livery, Forrestfield.   *Photo late Geoff Blee, courtesy Murray Rowe*

ZJA 433 stands in the salvage yard at the Midland workshops awaiting it's fate. Note the steel door with round cornered window leading to the guard's compartment.   *Photo Bill Gray.*

ZJA 431 on the siding outside the Bassendean Rail Transport Museum, 27 May, 1991.   *Photo Bill Gray.*

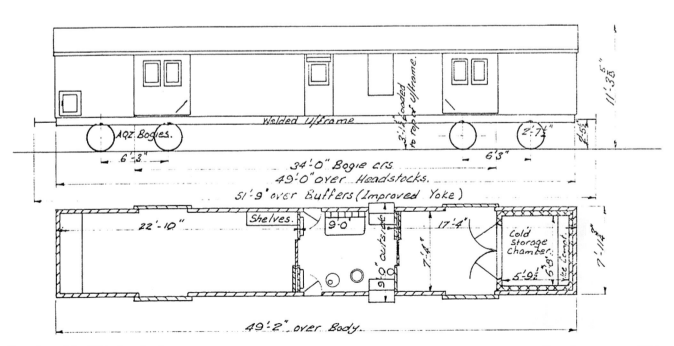

Drawing of the ZJA class brakevan.   *Drawing courtesy PTA.*

1902   Goods Brakevan with Second Class Compartments   4992,

ZA class   5843-5857,

6270-6284, 9336-9349, (Later 158, 159-173, 174-188, 189-201 respectively.)

An unidentified ZA class brakevan with end platform, at Collie,3 January, 1943.

Photo WRB Johnson, courtesy ARHS Archives.

1902 could have been regarded as the year of the brakevan, with the introduction into service of the AJ and ZA class vans. The ZA's were fitted with two second class passenger compartments, but were never classified in the passenger stock. Instead they were classified as goods brakevans, being intended to provide passenger accommodation on goods trains. The first batch of fifteen (ZA 5843-5857) arrived from the Oldbury Carriage & Wagon Co. in 1902, while a second batch of fifteen (ZA 6270-6284) built by the Ashbury Railway Carriage & Iron Co. went into traffic in 1903.

The ZA's were constructed on steel frames, and had bodies of timber with matchboard sides and ends. They were similar in style to the AJ class vans, but at one end they had a small platform. The passenger compartments were fairly typical of the WAGR passenger cars of the day, with seating for a total of 14 passengers. Because the ZA's were regarded as goods stock the lighting was by oil lamps, and they were painted Indian red.

While delivery of the ZA's commenced in 1902, the last two of the 5000 number series appear to have been placed in traffic after 30 June, 1903, along with the 6000 number series vans. These thirty vehicles were joined by another ZA class van (4992) built at Midland between 1905 and 1907 to replace a P class 4 wheeled brakevan which had been destroyed by fire. The ZA was allocated the 4 wheeler's number.

A fire at Midland Workshops in December, 1909 claimed two ZA class brakevans (5846 & 6283), and two new vans were built at Midland to replace them, these vehicles taking the numbers of the fire victims. It is not known how much, if any, of the original vehicle's components were used in the rebuilds, but both vans entered service in 1912.

Meanwhile, in 1909 the isolated Hopetoun to Ravensthorpe line was opened and the following year a ZA class brakevan was required there. Accordingly, ZA 6281 was sent to work the line with the 6 wheeled AH class passenger cars and a P class brakevan.

A new batch of ZA's (9336-9349) was built at Midland late in 1912, but they were slightly different to the earlier vans. The guard's compartment was in the centre of these vehicles and there was no end platform. One of these new vans (ZA 9346) was destroyed by fire in 1928, but the frame was salvaged, and in 1930 it was used for the construction of an AJ class express brakevan (see AJ class - 1902). This vehicle was, however, 7' (2.13m) shorter than the standard 49' (14.94m) long AJ's. Also in 1930 ZA 6281 on the Ravensthorpe to Hopetoun line was abandoned at Hopetoun, as passenger services had ceased. The frame was apparently sold for scrap, probably during the 1940's, but the body, written off in 1946, found use as a cabin in a holiday camp at Hopetoun. It was rescued sometime after 1966 and preserved in the Ravensthorpe Museum.

ZA 9337, one of the vans built sat Midland in 1912, with the guard's compartment in the centre and no end platform.
Photo WAGR, courtesy ARHS Archives.

In 1938 a decision was made to reclassify and renumber all the WAGR's brakevans in their own group,[21] and while the ZA's retained their classification, they were all renumbered. ZA 5843-5857, and 6270-6284 became ZA 159-188, including the Hopetoun van, its allocation of ZA 185 being a book entry only, ZA 4992 became ZA 158, and ZA 9336-9349 became ZA 189-201. The renumberings were complete by 1940.

In 1949 ZA 164 was written off after suffering a collision with locomotive G.46 at Geraldton, but it was another seven years before any more changes to the number of ZA's in service took place. In the meantime, the WAGR standard livery was changed from Indian red to plain Larch green and the entire class of ZA's was repainted. ZA 166 was written off in 1956 after being destroyed in a collision, and in 1961 ZA 175 and 179 were converted to workman's vans.

As country branchline passenger services were wound down, fewer of the ZA's were needed and from 1962 withdrawals began in earnest, although many found favour as workman's vans (VW) or breakdown vans (VC). They were written off as follows:-

1962 - ZA 167, 195, 198;
1963 - ZA 169, 184, 187;
1964 - ZA 182, 190;
1965 - ZA 158 (to VW), 159 (to VC), 165, 168 (to VW), 170 (to VW), 171 (to VW), 172, 174 (to VW), 178, 181 (to VW), 188 (to VW), 191 (to VC), 193 (to VW), 197;
1966 - ZA 163 (to VW), 176 (to VC), 186 (to VW), 189 (to VW), 194 (to VW);
1967 - ZA 162, 180 (to VW), 201 (to VW);
1968 - ZA 160 (to VW), 196 (to VW);
1969 - ZA 161 (to VC), 183 (to VC), 192;
1970 - ZA 173, 200;
1971 - Nil;
1972 - Nil;
1973 - ZA 199.

In 1975 the last ZA class brakevan, ZA 177, was written out of WAGR service. ZA 183, which became a VC class breakdown van in 1969, was later reconverted to a ZA for the Vintage Train at Bunbury and was returned to Westrail's books. It was written off again in 1985, but remained in Vintage Train service.

Several of these vans still exist. A number of them were stored at Midland and Forrestfield as workman's vans during the early 1990's, some eventually being sold as farm sheds and the like. Other known survivors are:-

ZA 191 as VC 5088, stored at Midland for the ARHS, then to Cannington Greyhound track in Perth;
ZA 173 preserved at the Rail Transport Museum, Bassendean;
ZA 183 is housed at Boyanup;
ZA 189 preserved on 2' gauge bogies at Whiteman Park;
ZA 200 at the Bellarine Peninsular Railway, Victoria.

Other survivors are the bodies of ZA 6281 at the Ravensthorpe Museum, and ZA 196 in use as the "Carriage Coffee Shop" in a park at South Beach, Fremantle.

VW 5140, formerly ZA 160, at Forrestfield.

Photo courtesy Graham Watson.

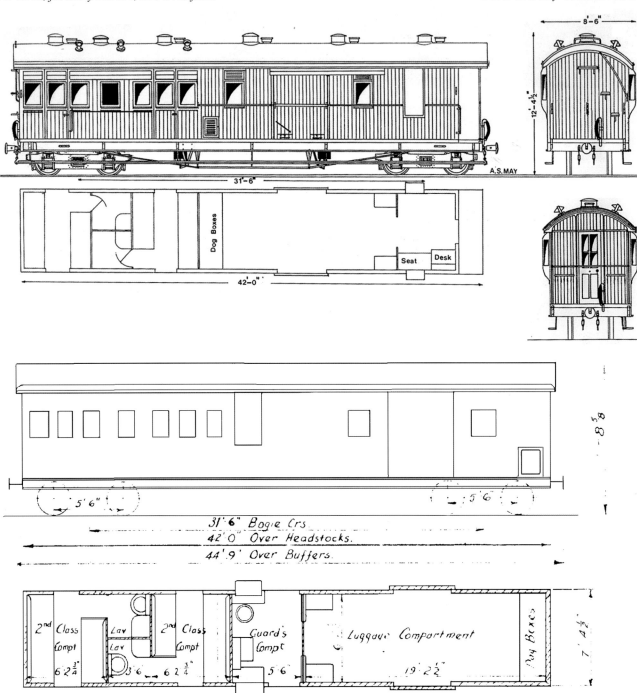

ZA drawings showing both types of van.

Top courtesy Andrew May, bottom courtesy PTA.

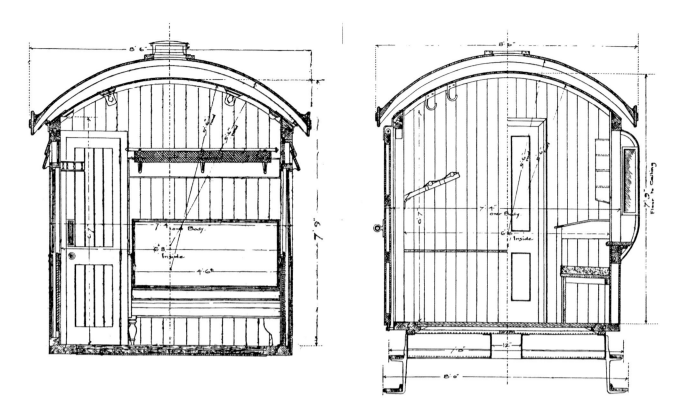

WAGR drawings showing the passenger compartment and guard's compartment.   *Drawings courtesy PTA*

ZA 194 at Bowelling.   *Photo courtesy ARHS Archives*

VW 277, formerly AR 277 & ARS 277, the first of its kind on the WAGR. It is currently a grounded body at Dongara, near Geraldton, used as accommodation units.   *Photographed at Forrestfield, 10 June, 1989, by Bill Gray.*

AR 357 in original condition at the Midland Workshops. This car is representative of the second batch of AR class cars built on timber underframes.   *Photo WAGR courtesy Lindsay Watson.*

The first group of nine of T.F. Rotheram's new AR class corridor cars (AR 277-285) entered service in December, 1903, heralding a radical change in design compared to the older WAGR passenger carriages. They were built by the Gloucester Railway Carriage & Wagon Co. as second class sit up corridor cars, being carried on a steel underframes with timber bodies and matchboard (tongue and groove) coachwork. The cars were fitted with 6 wheeled bogies and a bull nosed roof which curved down at both ends where it covered the end platforms, these being surrounded by steel scroll work fences and gates. Gangways were fitted, allowing passengers to move through the train, although notices on all WAGR end platform cars proclaimed that passengers were not permitted to ride on the platforms. Furthermore, ladies and children were not supposed to cross the gangways unaccompanied. Glazed doors on the end platforms opened into a corridor which ran down the side of the car and was so narrow (about 17" (432mm) wide) that two people walking in opposite directions had difficulty passing one another. However, the narrowness of the corridor also assisted in keeping upright any passenger

who might have lost his balance in the moving carriage, as there was a tendancy to simply bounce from wall to wall. The corridor led past six passenger compartments, each of which seated 8 passengers. The interiors of these cars were ornately decorated with acid-etched crown light windows, ceiling bows of dark varnished timber and contrasting walls of lighter varnished timber panelling or matchboard, carved and moulded timber panels, and decorative plaster and pressed tin mouldings in ceilings and walls. The AR's were painted Indian red, lined out in gold and black with the lettering in gold and red. They were fitted with electric lighting.

In 1908 Westralia Ironworks provided another seven AR class cars (347-353) and the Midland Workshops turned out five more (354-358), these twelve cars being slightly different to the earlier cars. They were built on timber underframes instead of steel, the etched crown light windows were shorter, and the corridor was altered by angling it at each end of the car to allow room for a relocated linen closet. In this way the entry door was located in the centre of the end of the car, in line with the gangway.

Around 1909 there was a tuberculosis (consumption) epidemic in Western Australia, and so that people with the affliction could travel by train to get treatment, a compartment in three AR class cars was set aside for them. In this way consumptives were considered less likely to affect other passengers. The AR's concerned were AR 283 in 1909, and AR 284 and 285 in 1910.

Late in 1911 two AR class cars (280 & 283) were converted into second class sleeping cars, but retained their AR classification (see 1911). These were the first sleeping cars provided for second class passengers and they proved to be so popular that another three (AR 277-279) were converted in 1912, another in 1913 (AR 284) and a final pair in 1914 (AR 281 & 285). Cars 283-285 probably lost their consumptive's compartments during this rebuild.

By 1924 the AR class day cars and the AR class sleeping cars were causing some confusion, so the sleepers were reclassified ARS. In December that year another AR day car (282) was converted into a second class sleeping car and reclassified ARS, which meant that the first group of AR class cars built were now all ARS sleeping cars.

The remaining AR class day cars (AR 347-358) continued to operate unmolested for many years. After 1951 several were repainted in the new Larch green colour scheme, these being AR 347, 351, 352 and 354-357, but none of them carried this livery as AR's for very long. The wooden chassis on these cars were worn out by the mid 1950's, so rather than scrap the vehicles they were rebuilt as ARS class sleeping cars and fitted with the steel underframes from old suburban cars, mostly AT's and AU's, which had been made redundant by the introduction of diesel railcars. The AR class cars so converted were:-

1955 - AR 353, 358;
1956 - AR 348-350, 352, 354, 355;
1957 - AR 347, 351, 356, 357.

The conversion of the last of these cars (AR 356 on 24 June, 1957) spelled the end of the second class AR sit up cars and, sadly, none have survived in their original condition, although a few still exist in much modified form as workman's vans, ARM's, ARS's and ARA's.

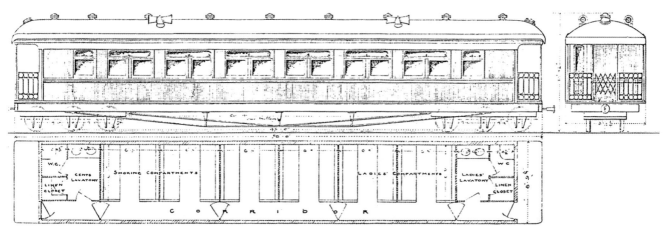

A WAGR drawing of an AR second class corridor car of the first series. The principle dimensions are:
Length over body 58', Length over buffers 60'9", Width over body 8'9½",Height from rail to top of ventilators 12'4¾",
Wheel base (centre wheel of one bogie to centre wheel of the other) 45',Axle box to axle box 4', Length of compartments 6'5",
Length of lavatory compartments 3'8½"

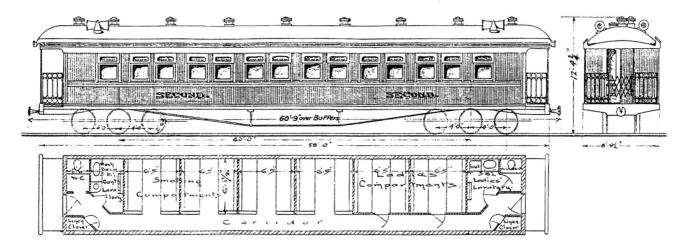

Second series AR class car. Note the wooden underframe. Principle dimensions were the same except that the bogies were
placed at 40' centres.   *Drawings this page courtesy PTA.*

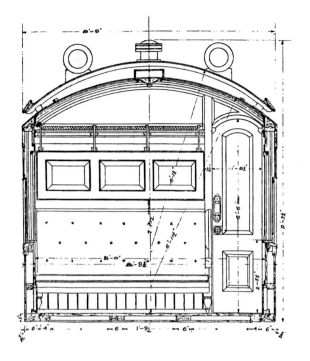
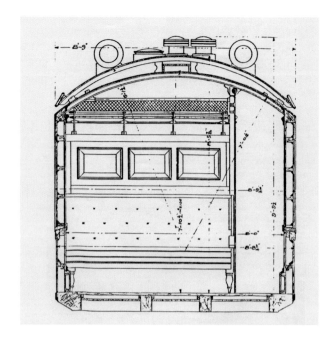

Cross section of the two types of AR class cars.

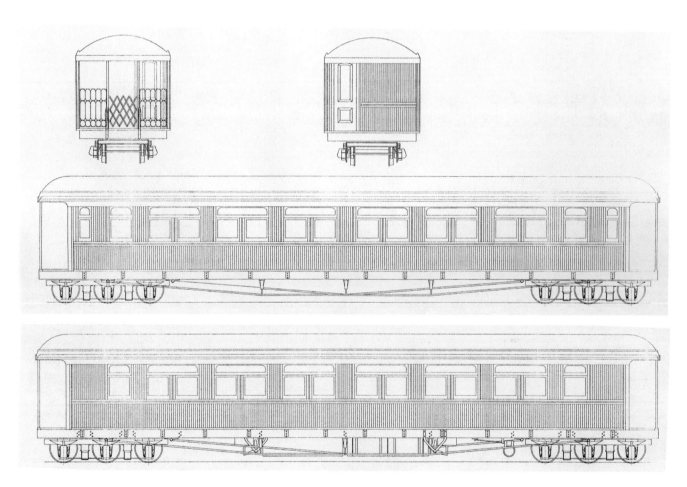

Roger Palmer's drawings showing both sides of the Gloucester Wagon & Carriage Co. built AR class cars.

1904   First Class Corridor Sleeping Cars   286-294
AQ class   335-346
       413-418

AQS 294, formerly AQ 294, at Mullewa on 31 December, 1966. This car was the last of the first batch of AQ class cars from the Gloucester Carriage & Wagon Co. in 1904.

Photo late Geoff Blee, courtesy Murray Rowe

In 1904 the first of the 12 wheeled first class corridor sleeping cars, similar in style to the AR's, arrived from the Gloucester Railway Carriage & Wagon Co., classed AQ (286-294). They were built on 58' (17.69m) steel underframes with timber bodies and matchboard sides and ends, painted Indian red and lined out in black and gold with red and gold lettering. Bull nosed roofs covered the end platforms, and gangways allowed passengers to move through the train. The AQ's carried 22 sleeping passengers or 33 day passengers in six compartments. Like the AR's, their interiors were highly decorated, with extensive use of varnished timber in contrasting shades and ornate mouldings on ceilings and some walls.

The AQ's initially displaced the older AP class sleeping cars from the main express trains, and a second batch arrived in service during 1908. Seven of these (AQ 335-341) were built by Westralia Ironworks and the other five (AQ 342-346) by the Midland Workshops. They were similar to the earlier AQ's, but differed in the bogie spacing, and arrangement of the lavatory compartments. They only accommodated 20 sleeping passengers. In addition, the etched crown light windows were arranged differently. Like the AR class cars in the same batch, these AQ's were built on timber underframes. The WAGR drawings of these cars also show a fold down table in each compartment.

In 1918, following the opening of the Trans Australia line the previous year, a final group of six AQ's (413-418) was put into traffic. These were built by Westralia Ironworks on 59' (17.99m) wooden frames (1' (305mm) longer than the earlier cars) and were fitted with new long wheel base 4 wheeled bogies. Despite an apparent shortage of carriage stock,[22] two of the brand new cars were converted into VIP carriages. AQ 413 became a Vice Regal car (AN), replacing AN 206, and AQ 414 was converted into a new Ministerial car (AM), replacing the unique AM 261. Neither car was ever returned to passenger service, AN 413 finally becoming AL 4 in 1958, and AM 414 became an inspection car in 1973, before being written off in 1980.

The introduction of the AZ first class sleeping cars in 1928 (replacing the AQ's on the Kalgoorlie trains[23]), followed by the Depression in the 1930's, rendered a number of passenger cars surplus and four AQ's (342-345) were converted into AQC class composite sleeping cars in 1932. As composite cars they were much more versatile and replaced older sleeping cars on other overnight trains. They could seat 39 day passengers, 15 first class and 24 second, but they still slept only 20. In 1935 a decision was made to convert all the ARS second class cars from six berths to four[24] and, to make up for the resulting loss of second class berths, four AQ's were reclassified as AQS second class cars. These cars were AQ 286, 291, 293 and 294. In this guise they could accommodate 44 day time passengers, but still only their original 22 sleeping passengers. No external physical alteration (other than the class designators) was made to the AQ class cars to make them AQC or AQS, but the AQC's had a door fitted in the corridor which separated 1st and 2nd classes.

1940 and 1941 were bad years for the AQ's and their derivatives. In 1940 AQS 293 was destroyed by fire at Paroo and written off, followed by AQS 291 in 1941, also as a result of a fire, this time at Pindar. That same year five AQ class cars (287-290 & 292) were "temporarily" reclassified as second class (AQS). This "temporary" reclassification became permanent in 1948.

In 1942 two AQ's (339 & 340) were provided for use on the ambulance train operated by the Commonwealth Government. They were not used very often and lasted on this train till December, 1944 when they were returned to the WAGR for normal service.[25]

In 1948 six new AH class sleeping cars entered service on the "Westland", replacing the AZ's. These then replaced the AQ's on other overnight trains and four more of the displaced AQ's (336, 338-340) were reclassified as AQC composite cars in 1949, themselves replacing four APC class cars.

In 1950 AQS 286 was converted into an AV class dining car to replace AV 316 after it had been destroyed by fire, and in 1954 four AQ's (415-418) were rebuilt with eight twin berth first class sleeping compartments. These cars were reclassified as AQZ's.

Most of the AQ/AQC/AQS class cars were repainted in the new Larch green colour scheme during the first half of the 1950's, in fact all those still in service at the time received the new livery, with the possible exception of AQ 346.

In 1955 a programme of rebuilding the AQ's and AQC's began in which their worn out wooden frames were replaced with the steel underframes from withdrawn suburban cars. The cars so treated were:-

1955 - AQC 344;
1956 - AQ 335, AQC 339, AQ 341.
AQC 343 was also reframed, but when is not known.

Withdrawals began in 1957, starting with the wooden framed cars. AQC 345 was written off in June that year, having been destroyed by fire between Murrin Murrin and Malcom the previous February, and AQ 346 was written off in October. AQ 337 went in 1958.

In 1960, suffering from a lack of money to build new carriages, the WAGR decided on a programme of refurbishment for the old ones and the AQ's were heavily involved. AQC 336 was written off in 1961 and AQC 343 was converted to an AQS to replace it. It was the only 3xx series AQ to ever become an AQS and it was subsequently used on the "Albany Progress". Two new buffet cars (AQL) were produced in 1961 by rebuilding AQS's 288 and 290,

the latter car being fitted with vestibule ends and gangways, while 288 retained its old fashioned end platforms. Two more AQS class cars (287 & 292) were rebuilt as twin berth second class sleeping cars (AQM) and, like the AQL's, one (292) was rebuilt with vestibules, while the other (287) retained its end platforms. The vestibuled cars were allocated to the "Mullewa" because of the dust problem in that area.. All the refurbished cars had an outer plywood skin added over the original matchboard sides when they were rebuilt, and most were also rebogied at the same time. The refurbishment programme also saw a few of the remaining AQ/AQC/AQS cars repainted Larch green and cream, including AQ 335, 341, AQC 339, 340, 342, 344 and AQS 289, 294 and 343.

In 1964 AQC 338 became a workman's van and in 1968 the writing off of these cars began in earnest with AQS 294 and AQC 342. In 1970 five AQ/AQC/AQS class cars were replaced by cars previously used on the "Westland", which had stopped running in 1969 after the standard gauge line between Perth and Kalgoorlie was opened. Four of the five (AQ 335, 341, AQC 340 & 344) were written off, while the fifth (AQS 343) was retained and rebuilt as a hospital car. It was reclassified AQA and repainted white with a red cross on both sides. AQC 344 was also retained and re-issued to traffic as a workman's van in 1973. AQ 335 and 341 were the last of the first class AQ's.

AQS 289 was written off in 1972, its body later destroyed in civil defence exersizes, and by 1975 country passenger services were almost finished. That year AQC 339, the last of the breed, was written off and converted to a workman's van four years later.

Fortunately several of these cars remain. AQ 286 survives as VW 286, AQ 287 and 292 remain as AQM's, AQ 288 and 290 survive as AQL's, AQS 294 is on display in original condition at the Rail Transport Museum at Bassendean. AQC 340 had its interior removed for placement in a shop in Perth city (since closed down), and the remains of it and AQC 338 lay on a dump at Bushmead in Perth for many years. AQC 340 was destroyed during 1993, and the remains of AQC 338 succumbed a few years later. AQ 339 is preserved at Northam as VW 339, AQ 343 survives at the ARHS Museum at Bassendean as the hospital car AQA 343, AQC 344 is in storage as VW 5146 at Kojonup(?), and AQ 415 survives as an AQZ at York, owned by the ARHS, complete with its wooden underframe.

AQ 342

Photo WAGR courtesy ARHS

An original WAGR photograph of AQ 339, taken when the car, built by Westralia Ironworks on a wooden underframe, was new. Note the indian red livery with black trim & gold scroll work.

Photo courtesy Mark Beard.

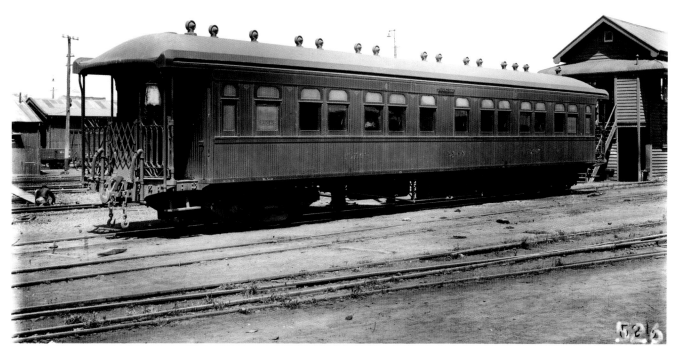

Another WAGR photo, this time of AQ 416, also built by Westralia Ironworks, but on a 59' wooden frame & fitted with 4 wheeled bogies. The car is painted indian red with the gold scroll work, but does not appear to have the black trim. Note the water bag on the end platform. The class number & class designator have been blotted out, possibly by a government censor, since the return date painted on the side of the car is 30-11-1918.

Photo courtesy Mark Beard.

AQS 289 at Midland Workshops in all over Larch Green, 10 March, 1967.   *Photo late Geoff Blee, courtesy Murray Rowe*

AQ 335 at Midland after a general overhaul , 25 May, 1967. This car was placed on a steel underframe in 1956.
Photo late Geoff Blee, courtesy Murray Rowe

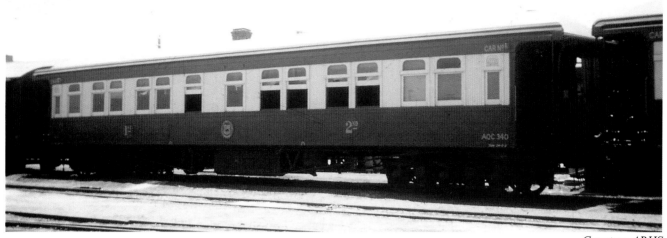

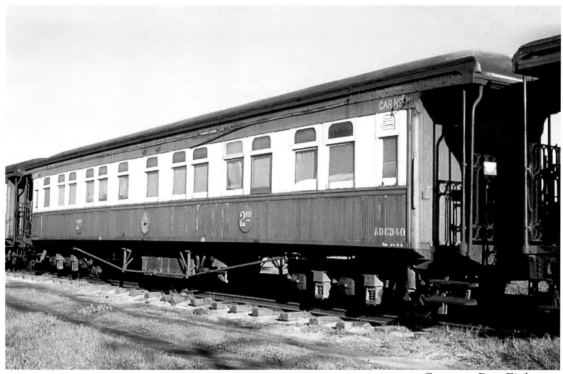

AQC 340 in service, in storage, & at the end of it's days in a rubbish dump at Bushmead.   Bill Gray

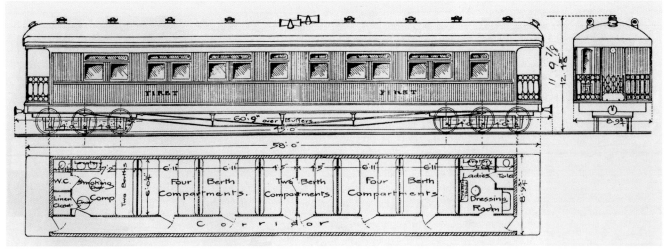

Drawing of the steel framed 58' AQ (286-294)   *Drawing courtesy PTA*

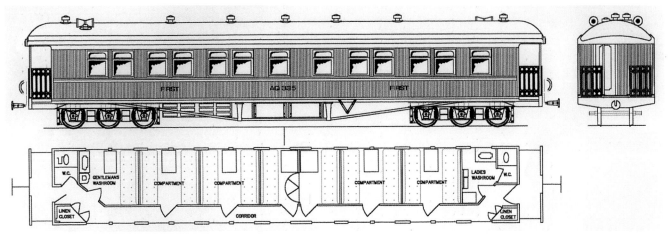

Drawing of the 58' wooden framed AQ class cars (335-346).   *Drawing courtesy Lindsay Watson.*

AQC 345 burning in 1957.   *Photo courtesy Philippa Rogers*

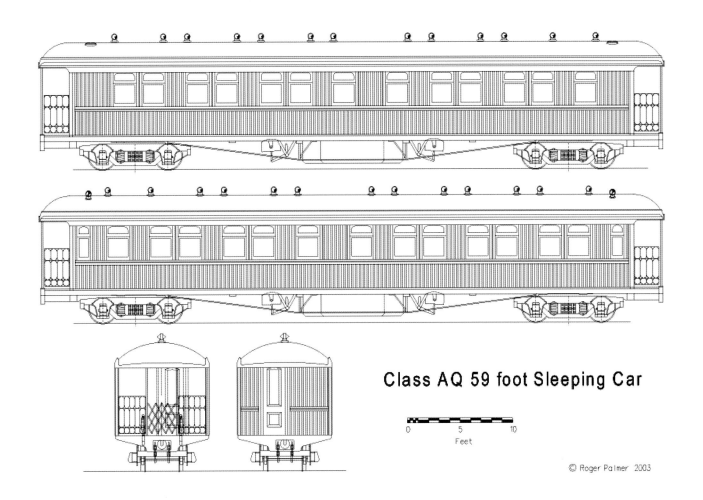

Class AQ 59 foot Sleeping Car

0   5   10
Feet

© Roger Palmer 2003

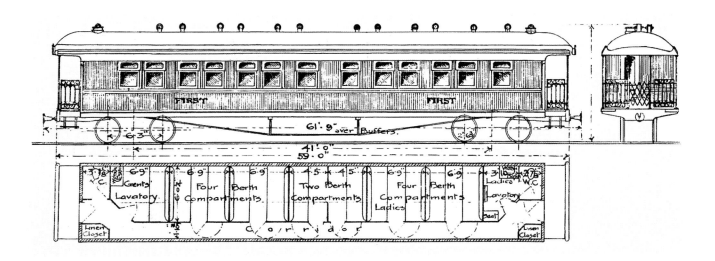

AQ class sleeping car.

Drawings courtesy Roger Palmer (top) & WAGR (bottom).

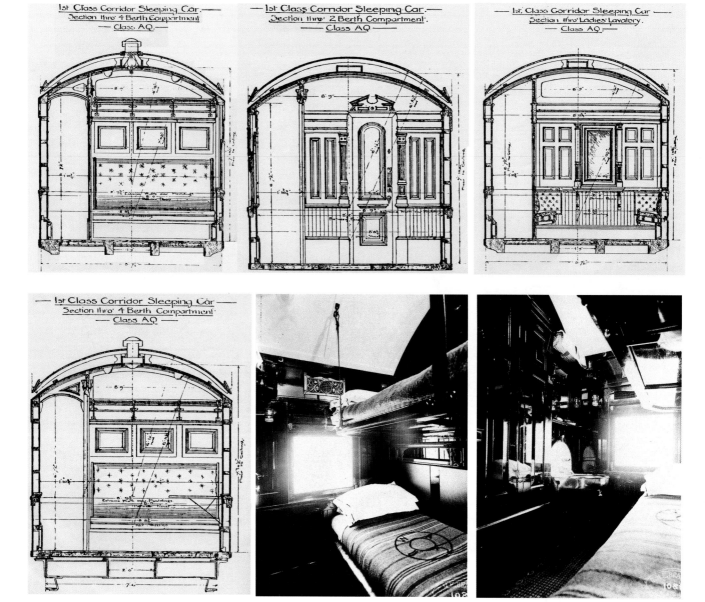

Cross section drawings of AQ class compartments (courtesy PTA), & a compartment made up for night use about 1910.
Photos PTA, courtesy ARHS.

An original AQ class compartment (left), & the corridor in AQS 294 at Bassendean Rail Museum.
Photos Rail Gazette (left) & Bill Gray (right).

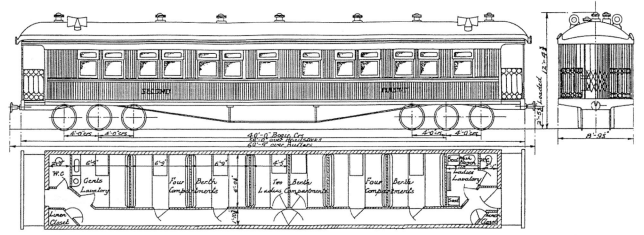

General arrangement drawing of an AQC class car.   *Drawing courtesy PTA*

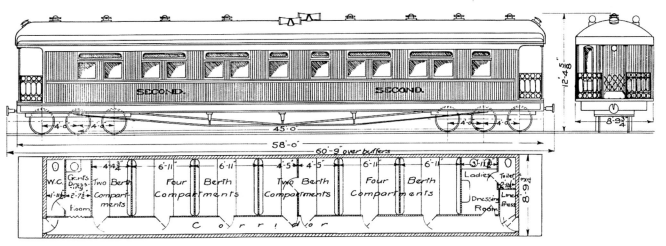

General arrangement drawing of an AQS class car.   *Drawing courtesy PTA*

Photo WAGR courtesy ARHS.

AQS 343 (top) at Perth, 17 January, 1967, & the same coach (bottom) as AQA 343 at Midland on 27 February, 1989.

Second Class Suburban Car
AT class
134, 139, 145, 242, 249, 252, 253, 259, 262, 20.

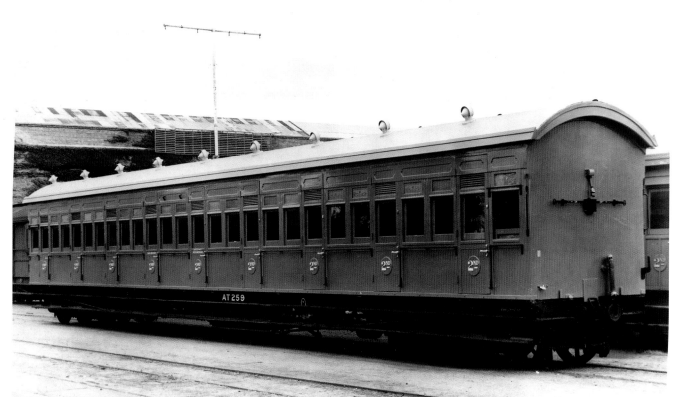

AT 259 outside the Midland workshops.

Photo Late Alan Hamilton collection, courtesy Joe Moir.

The AT class cars were the first of a new style of suburban car, bearing a family resemblance to the AJ and ZA classes of brakevan. In 1904 eight of these second class suburban cars (AT 295-302) were delivered from the Gloucester Railway Carriage & Wagon Co. in England, and went into traffic in suburban Perth, followed by another four cars (AT 303-306) from the same builder in 1905.

They were constructed on 58' (17.69m) steel underframes and had timber bodies with matchboard sides painted Indian red. The chassis' under these cars were the same as those under the AQ and AR class main line cars, including the 6 wheeled bogies. Accommodation was provided in nine passenger compartments, carrying 10 passengers each. As in the main line cars ornate acid etched crown lights adorned the area above the normal windows and the lighting was provided by electricity.

Two AT's were lost in a paint shop fire at the Midland Workshops in 1909, these being AT 299 and 306.[26] The building of replacements for the coaches lost in the fire began almost immediately and in the last two months of 1911 Westralia Ironworks produced five AT's (134, 139, 145, 242 & 249), three of which (AT 134, 139 & 145) replaced the AF second class suburban cars destroyed in the fire. Replacements for the two AT's (299 & 306) were part of a batch of ten cars (AT 252, 253, 259, 262, 299, 306 & 381-384) built by Westralia Ironworks early in 1912. The replacements were given the road numbers of those cars destroyed.

All twenty five AT class cars then spent the next four decades roaming back and forth along Perth's three suburban

lines, little affected by the deprivations of war or depression. Around 1919 the shortage of dynamos being experienced by the WAGR caused most of the AT's to be semi-permanently coupled together in pairs, with one car in each pair carrying a dynamo. The AT's so coupled were:-

AT 295 + 302	c.1920		AT 383 + 384	c.1920
AT 296 + 304	c.1920		AT 134 + 252	c.1919
AT 297 + 306	1921		AT 139 + 145	c. 1919
AT 300 + 303	1921		AT 242 + 249	c.1919
AT 301 + 305	c.1921		AT 253 + 299	1921
AT 381 + 382	c.1920		AT 259 + 262	1920

Most, if not all, these cars had been separated again by World War Two.

When the decision to alter the WAGR's standard colour scheme from Indian red to Larch green was made in 1951, the AT's were included, but it appears that only three had been done by 1955, the rest being repainted between then and 1958. Seven were destined never to carry the new livery at all because they were written off. AT 297 was the first to go in 1954, followed by AT 139, 242, 252, 295, 299 and 305 in 1956 after the successful introduction of the ADG class diesel railcars onto Perth's suburban services. However, these AT's did not entirely go to waste, as the steel frames from five of them were used to replace the timber frames under five ARS class cars, and AT 305 donated its body to AW 20, which then became AT 20 with a useful increase in seating capacity.

In 1961 AT 296 was written off as the number of diesel railcars on the system increased, and this was followed to the scrap yard in 1963 by AT 145. AT 382 was also written off that year, but was re-issued to traffic as a workman's van in 1964.

From 1956 the diesel railcars had been progressively given a new colour scheme of green lower body panels, white upper panels and a red band separating the two. Between 1963 and 1966 thirteen of the remaining AT's were also painted in this colour scheme, these being:-

1963 - AT 20, 303, 381;
1964 - AT 249, 253, 259, 262, 298, 301, 304, 306, 383;
1965 - Nil;
1966 - AT 300.

In 1965 AT 302 was written off and stored, returning to service as a workman's van in 1968, and AT 134 followed in 1966, being converted to a workman's van in 1967. Steam hauled suburban services finally ended in 1968 following the introduction of the ADK/ADB class railcar sets, after which the twelve wheeled suburban cars saw little use. Twelve AT's were written off in 1970, most of them in one group. AT 300 was the last to go, being written off in June, 1971, but about the same time AT 303 was re-issued to traffic as a workman's van.

At least two AT's survive, one (AT 306) as an accommodation unit (current whereabouts unknown), and AT 259 at the ARHS Rail Transport Museum at Bassendean.

A D class loco hauling a suburban train consisting of an AU, two AT's, an AS & possibly an AC/AF car bringing up the rear, photographed in March, 1941.   *Photo Late Alan Hamilton Collection, courtesy Joe Moir.*

AT 259 preserved at the Rail Transport Museum at Bassendean in the green, white & red livery, 9 April, 1988.

Photo Bill Gray.

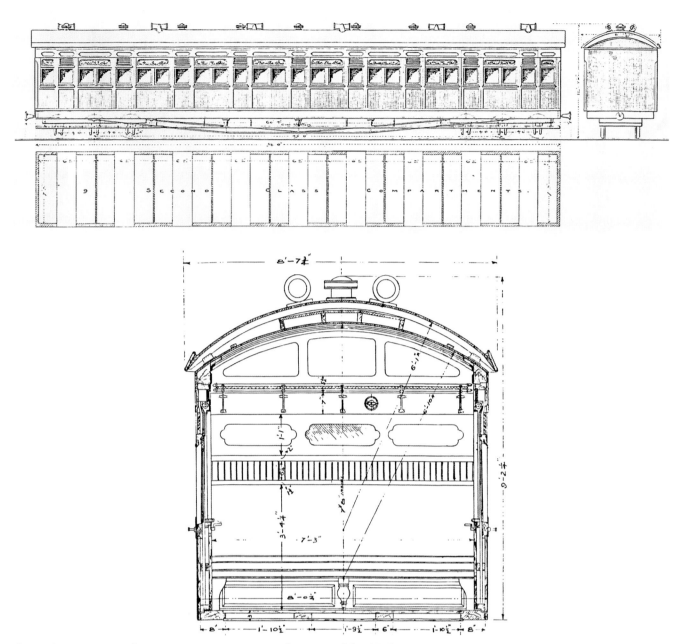

General arrangement & compartment cross section drawings of the AT class car.　　　　　*Courtesy PTA.*

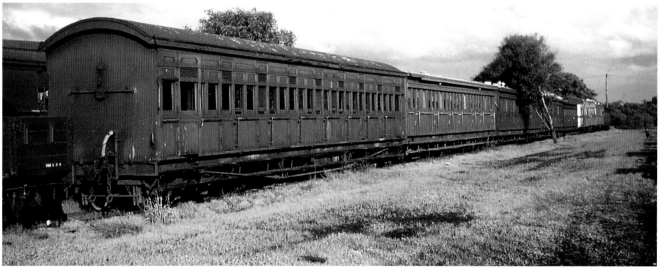

An unidentified AT in storage at Midland, 4 July, 1966.　　　　　*Photo Late Geoff Blee, courtesy Murray Rowe.*

Two new AW class cars, AW 323 nearest the camera.   *Photo courtesy ARHS*

In March, 1905 Westralia Ironworks handed over to the WAGR the first of the AW class suburban cars, a first class version of the AT. They were built on standard 58' (17.69m) steel underframes carried on 6 wheeled bogies, with timber bodies and tongue and groove sides painted Indian red with black and gold lining. Sixty four passengers were carried in eight compartments and the lighting was provided by electricity.

There were twelve of these cars in the first batch (AW 323-334) and after they had been delivered the Midland Workshops produced their very first carriage, also an AW, which was given the number 20, completely out of sequence with the rest of the fleet.

Two AW class cars (326 & 332) were destroyed in a fire at the Midland Workshops paint shop in December, 1909,[27] and in 1911 three new AW's were built by Westralia Ironworks (AW 218, 326 & 332) to replace them. All three cars took the numbers of coaches burned in the fire, 218 having formerly been an AA class long distance car.

The First World War caused a shortage of dynamos to power the lighting in Western Australia's carriages and a number of suburban cars were semi-permanently coupled together, sharing a single dynamo between them. This included most of the AW class cars, which were coupled to AU first class brake cars, as follows:-

AW 20 + AU 312	1921
AW 330 + AU 320	c.1920
AW 323 + AU 318	c.1920
AW 331 + AU 308	1918
AW 325 + AU 322	1921
AW 332 + AU 309	1921
AW 327 + AU 307	c.1921
AW 333 + AU 319	c.1920
AW 328 + AU 321	1921
AW 334 + AU 310	c.1920
AW 329 + AU 311	c.1920

Separation of these cars began during the 1930's, but some remained together till 1941.

During the 1920's the demand for first class travel in the suburbs fell to the point where the AW's were being used less and less, especially after the Depression hit in 1929. As a result, three cars were converted into AU class brake cars, AW 218 and 326 in 1932, and AW 324 in 1933. This was done by converting the passenger compartment at one end into a brake compartment. Then, to better utilise some of the other AW's, two more (327 & 330) underwent more drastic surgery in 1933, emerging from the workshops as ACW class long distance composite cars. Another four (AW 323, 325, 329 & 331) were similarly converted in 1934. This left only five AW class cars in service.

The Second World War created a severe shortage of passenger cars and the AW's were downgraded to second class so that more people could be carried in them. They never returned to first class status because the demand for it never rose, and classed travel on the suburban system was cut out in the early 1950's.[28] AW 328, 333, and 334 were downgraded in 1940, followed by AW 20 and 332 in 1941.

When the standard livery of the WAGR passenger cars became Larch green after 1951, four AW's were repainted:-

1952 - AW 328;
1953 - AW 334;
1957 - AW 332, 333.

The only car not repainted was AW 20 and, in 1956 the body from AT 305, recently written off, was placed on AW 20's frame, converting it to an AT with increased passenger capacity. It was the only AW so treated.

The introduction of the ADX class diesel railcars in 1960 spelt the end of the AW's. AW 334 was written off that year and AW 332 followed in 1961. However, it was discovered that AW 332 was in better condition than AW 333 which was still in service, so AW 332 was re-instated in 1962 as AW 333,

and the original AW 333 went to the scrap yard in its place.

The last two AW's were repainted in the green, red and white livery of the suburban diesel railcars, AW 328 in 1963 and AW 333 (originally 332) probably in 1966. However, the days of both cars were numbered and they were written off in 1970, with AW 328 being converted into a workman's van in 1971.

None of the AW's survive in their original form, but at least three still exist under different classifications. AW 323 (later ACW 323, then VW 2141 & still later AL 3) is preserved at Northampton, AW 330 became ACW 330, then VC 2143 & is preserved with the Hotham Valley Railway as such, and one other is understood to be preserved on private property at Wanneroo. In addition AW 218 is in use on the Vintage Train at Boyanup as an AU class brake car.

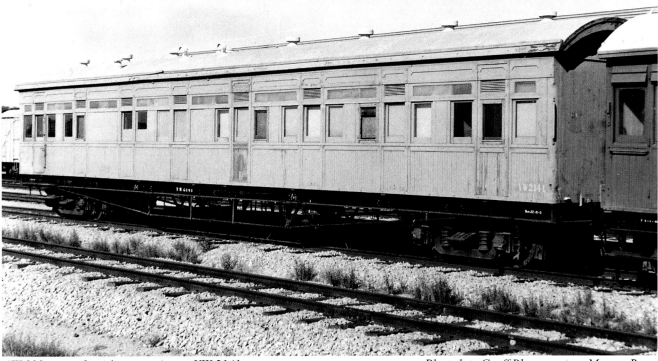

AW 323 soon after it's conversion to VW 2141.   *Photo late Geoff Blee, courtesy Murray Rowe*

VW 2141 at Kulja in the 1966-67 season.   *Photo courtesy Malcom Searle.*

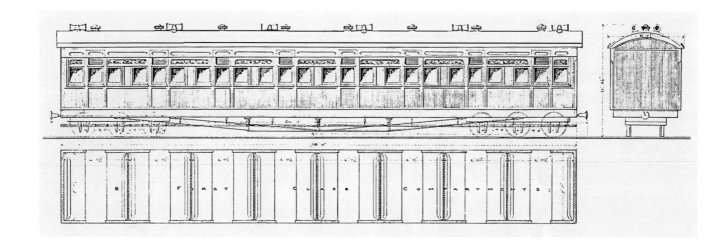

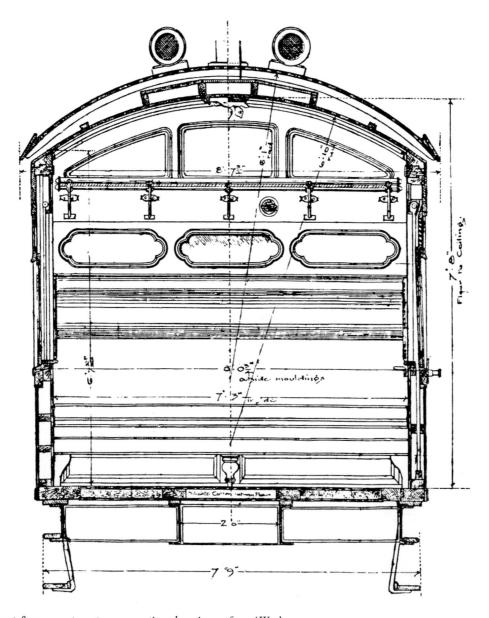

General arrangement & compartment cross section drawings of an AW class car.

Courtesy PTA

First Class Suburban Brake Car
AU class
218, 324, 326.

AU 321 in new condition. This car is painted in the Indian red, black & gold livery.   *Photo courtesy Mark Beard.*

Soon after the initial batch of AT's were delivered, and within four weeks of the first AW's, the first four AU class suburban cars went into traffic, these being first class brake cars, similar in style to the other new suburban cars. During 1905 the Gloucester Railway Carriage & Wagon Co. in England delivered AU 307-311, plus AU 312 in 1906, and Westralia Ironworks produced AU 317-322. These twelve cars were the sum total of the class.

The AU's were built of timber with matchboard panelling, on a steel underframe carried on 6 wheeled bogies. The underframes were identical to those used on the AQ and AR class main line cars and the AT and AW class suburban cars. They were painted Indian red, lined out in black and gold. The cars contained seven first class compartments accommodating 56 passengers, plus a guard's compartment at one end.

In 1909 two AU's (309 & 319) were burnt in a paint shop fire at Midland Workshops and two new cars were built by Westralia Ironworks in 1911 to replace them. The two new cars took the road numbers of those destroyed in the blaze.[29]

When the First World War created a shortage of dynamos and many of the suburban cars were semi-permanently coupled together, the AU's did not miss out. Being brake cars, they were coupled to AW first class suburban cars as follows:-

AU 307 + AW 327	c.1921	
AU 312 + AW 20	1921	
AU 308 + AW 331	1918	
AU 318 + AW 323	c.1920	
AU 309 + AW 332	1921	
AU 319 + AW 333	c.1920	
AU 310 + AW 334	c.1921	
AU 320 + AW 330	c.1920	
AU 311 + AW 329	c.1920	

AU 321 + AW 328	1921
AU 322 + AW 325	1921

At least five of these pairs remained coupled till 1941.

The onset of the Depression during the early 1930's saw a dramatic drop in demand for first class suburban travel and by 1932 this had become so bad that several AW First Class cars were little used.[30] To put them to some sort of use three were converted to AU class brake cars, two (218 & 326) in 1932 and the other (324) in 1933.

In 1945 and 1946 the brake compartments in the AU's were enlarged so that they had room for prams, presumably because of the post war baby boom. This was done by removing the partition between the guard's compartment and the adjoining passenger compartment. The cars converted were:-

1945 - AU 312, 317-319, 321, 324;
1946 - AU 218, 307-311, 320, 322, 326.

When the WAGR's livery for passenger cars was changed to plain Larch green, all but three AU's were repainted. The three not done were AU 310, 321 and 322 and there is some doubt about AU 309. Those cars repainted were done between 1951 and 1957.

In 1956 five AU class cars (309, 310, 312, 321, & 322) were written off after the ADG class diesel railcars settled into service. The bodies of these carriages were disposed of, but the underframes were all used to replace the wooden underframes of several country cars of the AQ, AR and ARS classes, so giving them a new lease of life.

In 1961 the first workman's van to be converted from an AU entered service (324) and over the next decade the AU's quietly disappeared, although six lasted long enough to be repainted in the new railcar livery of green lower panels and white upper panels with a red band in between. These cars (AU 218, 307, 308, 317, 320 & 326) were done between 1963 and 1965.

In 1965 AU 319 and 320 were written off, followed by AU 318 in 1966. This latter car was converted to a workman's van in 1967, as was AU 307. In 1968 AU 317 was written off after the introduction of the ADK/ADB class railcars, but two years later it and AU 326 were converted to workman's vans.

However, that year three more AU's were written off (218, 308 & 311), these being the last of the class. AU 308 was converted to a workman's van in 1971, and only three AU's are known to still exist, these being 218, housed at Boyanup with the Leschanault Railway Preservation Society, AU 307 as a workman's van at Northam, and AU 318 on a private property at Chidlow, outside Perth.

AU 218 at the Midland Workshops after it's conversion from an AW class car.   *Photo courtesy ARHS.*

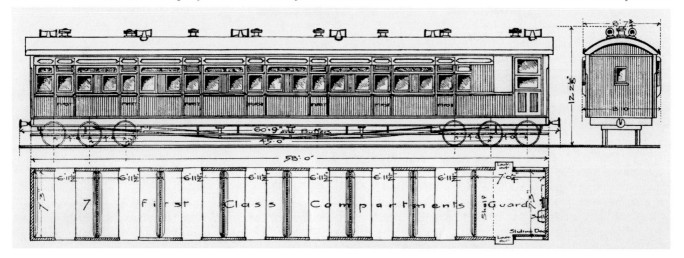

General arrangement drawing of the AU.   *Drawing courtesy PTA.*

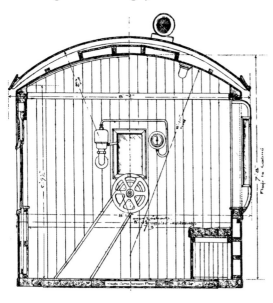

A standard AU brake compartment (left) & the brake compartment in AU 218.

Drawing courtesy PTA
Photo Bill Gray

AU 218 at Boyanup on 3 November, 1985.   *Photo Bill Gray*

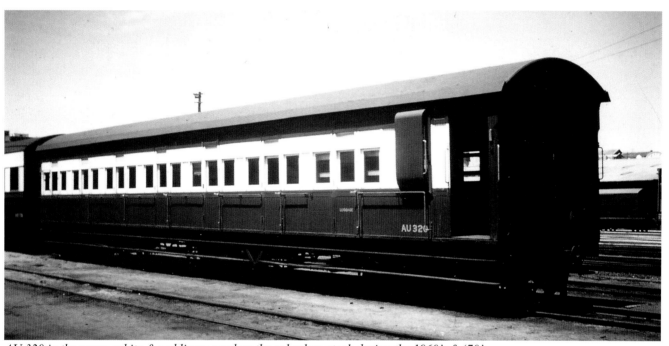

AU 320 in the green, white & red livery used on the suburban stock during the 1960's & '70's.

Photo courtesy ARHS Archives

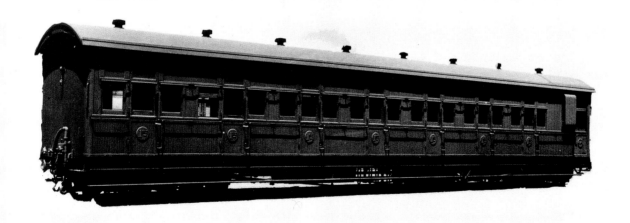

An unidentified AU.   *Photo courtesy ARHS.*

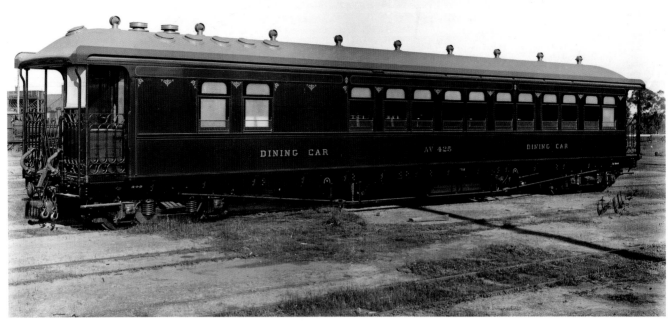

AV 425 captured by the WAGR photographer in new condition.   *Photo courtesy Mark Beard.*

The Gloucester Railway Carriage & Wagon Co. in England supplied four dining cars (AV 313-316) to the WAGR in 1905. These were the first dining cars in Australia and the last locomotive hauled passenger cars imported for the WAGR. The four new cars, classed AV, operated exclusively on the Kalgoorlie trains till after the First World War.

Externally, they were the same style and size as the AQ and AR class cars already in traffic, built on steel underframes with timber bodies and matchboard sides and ends painted Indian red, lined out in black and gold, with red and gold lettering. The dining saloon was decorated in the ornate varnished timber style of the AQ and AR class coaches, and tables and chairs for 24 passengers were placed down both sides of the saloon, those tables on the kitchen side accommodating 4 diners and those on the other side accommodating 2. The kitchen was totally self contained, being fitted with a wood fired stove, carving table, sinks, meat safe, cupboards and crockery racks. It must have been a hellish place to work in during the summer, particularly away from the relatively cooler coastal areas.

In 1919, as a result of the opening of the Trans Australia Railway two years earlier, several new cars were built, including two new AV's, 425 and 426, at the Midland Workshops. They were similar to the earlier dining cars in most respects, except that they were carried on new long wheel base 4 wheeled bogies, the position of some of the windows differed, the lavatory was replaced by a pantry, and the kitchen roof was fitted with five large vents with lids on them which could be opened by the staff to allow air in, or cooking smoke out. In addition to these changes the bottom part of each window had a wire mesh grille arrangement fitted to it, presumably to prevent items placed on the tables from falling out of open windows, as the table tops were at window sill height. However, this did not prevent plates, cups and the like from vanishing out the windows, and even today pieces of WAGR crockery can occasionally be found along the old

Eastern Railway formation.

The introduction of the two new dining cars allowed these services to be extended to the Southwest and Great Southern lines to Bunbury and York respectively in October, 1920. The provision of dining cars on these services was considered by the Commissioner of Railways to be an inducement to travel rather than being profitable in themselves, but dining services on the Bunbury trains proved to be so uneconomical that they were stopped soon after mid 1921.[31]

In the early 1920's, the older AV's, were fitted with long wheel base 4 wheeled bogies of the same type as the newer cars, in order to improve their riding qualities. The cars were altered as follows:-

1923 - AV 314;
1924 - AV 313, 315, 316.

The dining cars became an integral part of the Reso trains, first run in 1928, as the passengers often ate their meals on board the train. AV 426, which had been used on a Royal train during the visit to WA by the Prince of Wales in 1920, was again honoured by being part of the consist on the first Reso train, which conveyed a party of "gentlemen from Victoria" on a tour of the southern part of the state.[32]

In the late 1920's falling patronage on the WAGR caused the removal from service and storage of AV 313. The dining cars were really only economical on the Kalgoorlie services and this, plus the onset of the Depression, had rendered AV 313 surplus to requirements. In 1932 it was converted into an AM class Ministerial car, the corridor being the only vestige remaining of its dining car days.

The other dining cars saw much use on the "Westland", introduced in 1938 between Perth and Kalgoorlie, and it was on this train and the "Kalgoorlie" that they spent most of the rest of their working lives. In 1942 AV 314 was taken out of regular service and used on the Commonwealth Government's ambulance train for the duration of the Second World War. It was painted white with red crosses on the sides and roof and was returned to normal service in 1945.

All five dining cars, used on both "The Westland" and "The Kalgoorlie", were refurbished and modernised during the late 1940's, largely to increase their seating capacity to bring them closer into line with the Commonwealth Railways diners which could accommodate 48 passengers.[33] The refurbishment programme increased the length of the dining saloon, and the ornate woodwork and the timber panelling were removed or painted over. Tubular and laminated tables and chairs were fitted, along with lino squares on the floor, the overall effect being vaguely reminiscent of a 1950's milk bar. Each table now seated 4 passengers and in this configuration each meal sitting could accommodate 40 people. The kitchens were also altered, and after the refurbishment programme AV 315 differed from the other dining cars in that it was fitted with a gas fired stove, a feature not popular with the cooks because it couldn't provide the heat of the wood fired stoves.[34] With a crew of cook, kitchen hand, and four waitresses, things must have become crowded at times! The AV's were refurbished as follows:-

1947 - AV 316, 425, 426;
1948 - AV 314, 315.

The first three emerged from the workshops in the standard Indian red livery, but the two cars turned out in 1948 were painted Larch green, light green and cream as part of the new look "Westland" consist. By this time "The Westland" was the only WAGR train still to provide a dining car service.

Normally, two dining cars were based at Perth and two at Kalgoorlie, and between 1940 and 1954 the changeover point was Yellowdine where, for example, a Perth dining car would be detached from the train going to Kalgoorlie and replaced with a Kalgoorlie dining car. The Perth based car would then wait for the next train back to Perth. So it was that in September, 1950, AV 316, while being prepared for a return service, caught fire and was burned out. The story goes that the morning's breakfast caught fire, but the cook was not in attendance and the fire was first noticed by a passing motorist.[35] AV 316 was written off, but a replacement car was needed, so AQS 286 was rebuilt as an AV to replace it. No time was wasted, for the "new" dining car entered service only seven weeks after the loss of 316.

When the WAGR's standard colour scheme was altered from Indian red to Larch green, all five dining cars were repainted. AV 315 and 425 in 1951 and AV 286, 314 and 426 in 1953. At the same time, AV 286 was fitted with new 8' (2.44m) wheel base bogies, the same as those under the AH class cars of 1948. In 1958 AV 314 was withdrawn from service and converted into a lounge car for continued use on "The Westland". It was reclassified AVL.

In 1969 the last "Westland" ran, the old Eastern Railway being replaced by the new standard gauge line, so the four remaining AV's became redundant. AV 425 and 426 were withdrawn from use and stored, finally being written off in 1974, while the other two saw occasional use on Reso trains and other specials. The last one, (AV 286) ran in October, 1975 on an ARHS tour. AV 286 and 315 were both written off that year and in 1979 they were converted into workman's vans.

All except AV 316 still exist, AV 313 as an AM class car, AV 314 as an AVL at the Rail Transport Museum at Bassendean, AV 286 with the ARHS at Midland (as a workman's van), AV 315 at Cunderdin, AV 425 is preserved at Midland, and AV 426 is in use with the Hotham Valley Railway.

AV 315 in it's later days of service

Photo late Geoff Blee, courtesy Murray Rowe.

AV 426 rests at Perth 21 January, 1967.   *Photo late Geoff Blee, courtesy Murray Rowe.*

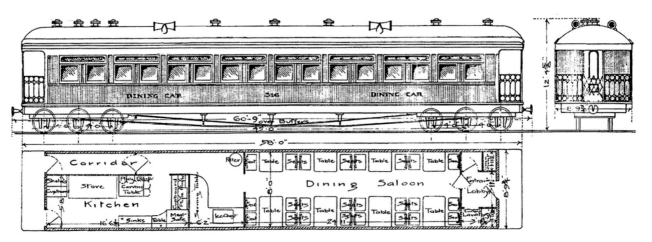

WAGR drawing of AV 316.   *Drawing courtesy PTA.*

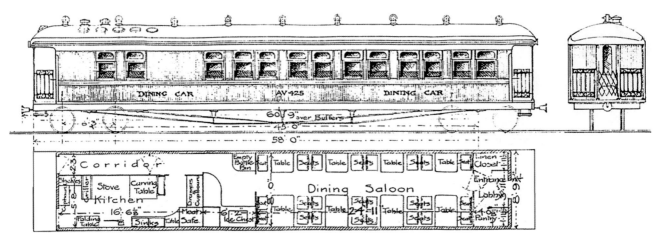

WAGR drawing of AV 425.

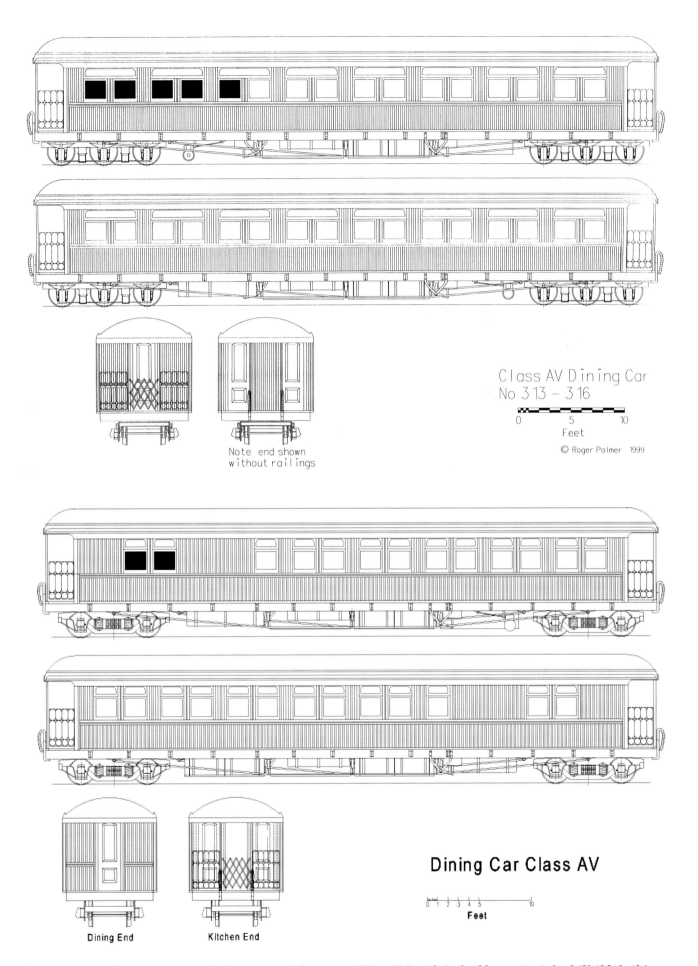

Class AV Dining Car
No 313 – 316

0   5   10
Feet

© Roger Palmer 1999

Note end shown
without railings

Dining Car Class AV

0 1 2 3 4 5   10
Feet

Dining End   Kitchen End

Roger Palmer's drawings showing the first series of dining car (313 – 316) with 6 wheel bogies (top) &.of AV 425 & 426
showing the different window arrangement as well as the 4 wheel bogies (bottom)   *Drawings courtesy Roger Palmer.*

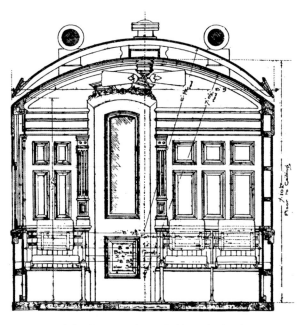 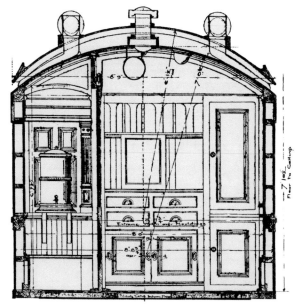

Cross section of the dining saloon (left) & the kitchen (right) in the AV.

Drawings courtesy PTA

Inside the dining saloon, looking towards the kitchen (left) & the entry door (right).

The dining saloon in AV 286 (left) & that of an AV dining car after the 1947/48 refurbishment (right).

Photos this page WAGR, courtesy ARHS Archives.

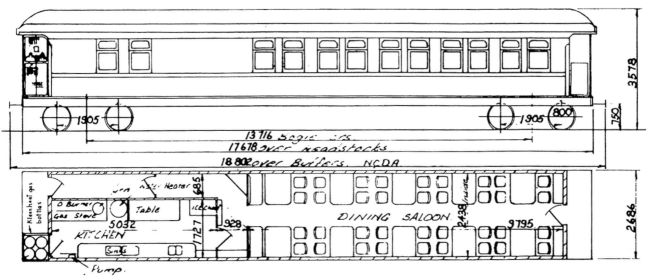

Drawing of AV 315 showing the gas bottle on the end platform & the 40 seat layout.

Drawing WAGR courtesy Lindsay Watson.

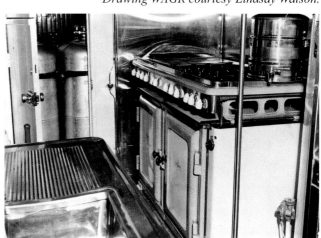

Two views of the kitchen in AV 315.

Photos courtesy ARHS.

AV 425 at Bassendean prior to its return to service, 25 May, 1991.

Photo Bill Gray.

Composite Long Distance Car
ACL class

70, 189, 191, 222, 385-395, 403-412.
From AA:202-204, 209-211,
From AB:225-240,
Ex MRWA:258.

ACL 226, a short bodied car reclassified from an AB in 1907 (top), & ACL 391, a long bodied 58' car, built new by the WAGR at Midland in 1912 (bottom).
Photos courtesy ARHS.

The ACL class came into being as a result of the confusion created after the September, 1900 reclassifications when four different types of car were placed in the AC class. Among these were sixteen composite long distance cars, originally of the AB class, although a few of them probably never carried that classification, being converted to composites prior to 1900. These cars were classified ACL as follows:-

1906 - 225, 227, 228, 230, 232, 234, 236, 237;
1907 - 226, 229, 233, 235, 239;
1908 - 238.

AC 240 is also believed to have been converted to an ACL by 1908, to bring the number of ACL's in service at that time to sixteen.

As a result of their originally being AB's, the ACL's were identical in most respects to their second class forebears, although their height has been given as 11' (3.35m) rather than 11'5" (3.48m) (see 1899)[36]. Of the six compartments inside, two at one end and one at the other remained second class, while the three compartments between them were redesignated first class, presumably being fitted with upgraded seating. The three first class compartments carried 5 passengers each, and the three second class compartments 7, making a total capacity of 36 passengers.

The Midland Workshops built ten new ACL's late in 1909, (1, 3, 6, 19, 21, 23, 30, 70 & 222), but only the first five were completed before the paint shop fire on 10 December, 1909, the second five being totally destroyed in the blaze. The first five (ACL 1, 3, 6, 19 & 21) did not escape damage, however, having their seat cushions burnt.[37]

Three more new ACL's (385-387) were built at Midland in 1911 before work started on the replacements for those burnt in the fire. Seven new cars were turned out in December, 1911 and took the numbers of the burnt ACL's (23, 27, 30, 70 & 222), as well as the numbers of an AX (189) and an AE (191) which were also destroyed in the Midland blaze. This made a total of twenty eight ACL class cars in service, and these were followed by eight more in 1912 (388-395). Cars 389-395 from this group were built on longer 58' (17.69m) underframes instead of the standard 49' (14.94m) chassis used on the earlier cars, and so they had an additional second class compartment, designated as a ladies' compartment.

Also in 1912, the near new ACL 385 was sent to the north of the state to provide passenger accommodation on the isolated Port Hedland to Marble Bar railway, having its electric lighting equipment removed before it went.

In 1915 the WAGR received a Midland Railway Ja class composite long distance car (JA 22) in exchange for an AP class sleeping car. Ja 22 had been constructed by the Metropolitan Railway Carriage & Wagon Co. in 1913 and was virtually identical to the WAGR's 49' ACL class cars. It was reclassified ACL and given the road number 258.

As the WAGR continued to expand, and the First World War brought about an increase in traffic, even more long distance cars were needed. The government would not approve finance for new corridor cars, but did allow enough for the construction of ten new composite compartment cars, ACL 403-412, which appeared late in 1915 and into the first half of 1916. These were also built on 58' (17.69m) frames and brought the number of ACL's in service to forty seven, the largest number of any one type of car to operate country services on the WAGR. However, there were more to come. A drop in demand for first class travel during the 1920's caused the reclassification of three AA first class cars to ACL in 1923 (202, 204, & 211), followed by another three (203, 209 & 210) in 1924. This conversion was accomplished by downgrading the appropriate compartments and putting more people (7) in them. The AA class cars were the same length as their AB class brethren [49' (14.94m)], but had only five compartments, so this conversion produced a "new" type of ACL, with larger than normal compartments. These were the last of the ACL's, making a class total of fifty three cars.

The ACL's went about their work for the next two decades in an efficient and business like manner, little affected by events like depressions and wars. In 1945 ACL 385 was returned south from Port Hedland, leaving an AP class sleeping car and ZB class brakevan there to carry the few passengers who would want to travel to Marble Bar, and in 1948 ACL 393 was written off after an accident at Mt. Kokeby, south of Beverley, in which a goods train ran into the rear of the "Albany" express.[38]

The decision made in the late 1940's to replace the country branch line mixed trains with buses[39] eventually caught up with he ACL's and as they became due for overhaul or repair they began, very slowly, to fall out of service and into storage, many not being written off till years after their retirement.

ACL 225 was the first to go in 1957 and it was the only ACL to be scrapped in its Indian red livery. The remainder of the fleet was painted in the plain Larch green colour scheme after that livery became the WAGR standard in 1951.

In 1959 ACL 211 was converted into a workman's van, and in 1960 a new Larch green and cream livery was introduced, but only five ACL's ever ran in these colours, these being 202, 232, 385 (possibly), 407 and 410. As the 1960's progressed the number of ACL's being written off increased, and they went as follows:-

1961 - ACL 230;
1962 - ACL 209, 387;
1963 - ACL 203, 231, 235, 237, 239, 240.

In August, 1964 the WAGR took over the Midland Railway Co., and with it acquired eight of their J/Ja class bogie composite cars (J 1, 4, Ja 6-8, 10 & 11). J 1 was, in fact, a workman's van, and four of these cars (J 1, and Ja 7, 8 and 11) were written off without entering service, while the others (J 4, & Ja 5, 6 & 10) became ACL 31-33 and 36. By 1965 there were large numbers of branch line cars, including ACL's, in store and that year seventeen (ACL 1, 3, 6, 19, 21, 23, 27, 30, 189, 191, 204, 227-229, 234, 388 & 389) were written off. In addition to these another fourteen cars still in good condition were converted for suburban use (the lavatory doors were screwed shut) and reclassified as ACM's. These were ACL 31-33, 36, 210, 238, 386, 391, 392, 395, 404, 408, 409 and 412.

The writing off of ACL's continued with the following:-

1966 - ACL 70;
1967 - ACL 258, 390, 411;
1968 - ACL 202, 226, 233, 236, 385, 394, 403, 406.

Two of these (ACL 236 & 403) were converted to workman's vans, and ACL 406 went to the Vintage Train, leaving only four ACL's on the books. Two more (ACL 232 & 405) were written off in 1973 after the overnight trains to Kalgoorlie were done away with, and the other two (ACL 407 & 410) went to the Vintage Train at Bunbury.

Several ACL's and their derivatives still survive. The Leschanault Railway Preservation Society at Boyanup, has preserved ACL 406, 407, 410, 210, 238 and 391. Two (ACL 232 & 405) are preserved at the old Coolgardie Station, at least one (ACL 403) has been sold as a farm shed, and ACL 31 is at Kojonup, although much modified as ablutions car VW 5149. In addition, ACM 33 has been restored as the Midland Railways Ja 6 and is on display at Bassendean.

ACL 405 at Mullewa, complete with water bags, 31 December, 1966.   Photo late Geoff Blee, courtesy Murray Rowe.

ACL 406 in Larch Green.   Photo late Geoff Blee, courtesy Murray Rowe.

This photograph shows the pressed metal ceiling in VW 5143, formerly ACL 404, on 21 July, 1989. The coach was damaged in an SES exercise at Midland & subsequently burnt.   Photo Bill Gray.

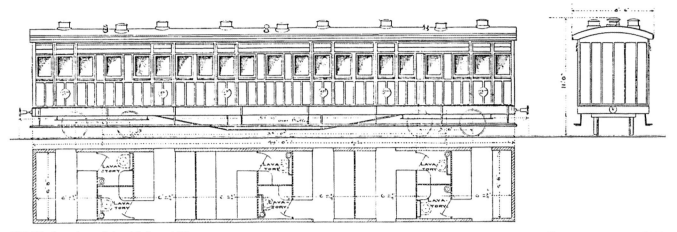

WAGR drawing of the 49 foot ACL

Drawing courtesy PTA.

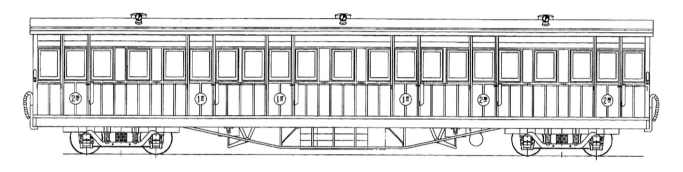

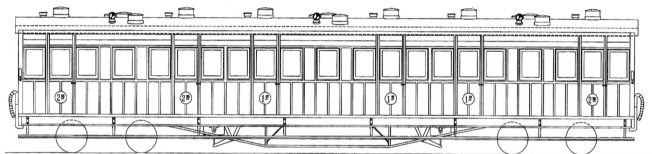

Roger Palmer's drawings of the 49 foot ACL.

ACM 210 near Bunbury on 12 May, 1991.

Photo Bill Gray

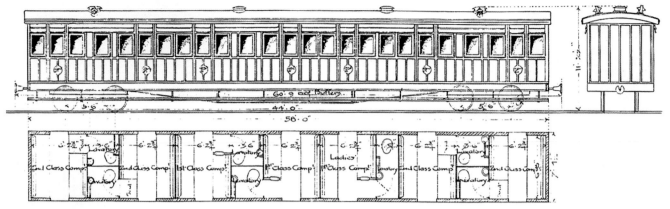

Drawing of the 58 foot ACL   *Drawing courtesy PTA.*

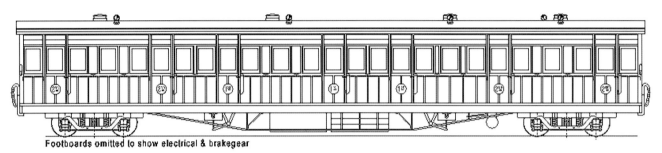

Footboards omitted to show electrical & brakegear

Long Distance Coach Class ACL
58' length

0 1 2 3 4 5   10

Drawing of the 58 foot ACL   *Drawing courtesy Roger Palmer.*

VW 5143, formerly ACL 404, at Northam, 21 July, 1989.   *Photo Bill Gray.*

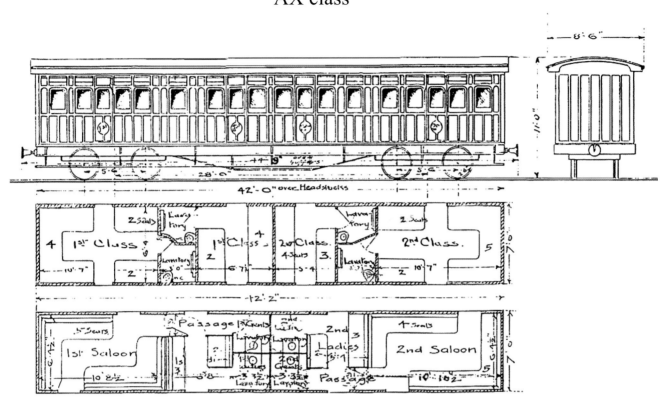

No photographs have been uncovered of either of the AX class cars. The drawing above depicts the class, the interior at the top depicting AX 189, & the one at the bottom showing the interior layout of AX 188.

Drawing courtesy PTA.

In 1906 two brake composite cars, AD 188 and 189, were withdrawn from service and converted into composite saloons, equipped with lavatories for use on long distance express trains. They were prototypes for more carriages of the same design, but for reasons not now apparent, no more were converted. The two cars differed considerably in their internal arrangements and the first to be turned out in March, 1906 was AX 188.

Externally, the most obvious difference between the AX's and the AD's from which they were derived was the removal of the guard's lookouts, with extra windows fitted in their place, and the spacing of the entry doors, of which there were four on each side. AX 188's interior consisted of first and second class sections, each able to carry 14 passengers. They were almost mirror images of each other, but the first class ladies compartment was longer than its second class counterpart, causing the first class saloon to be slightly shorter than the second class.

AX 189 was also divided into two halves, one first class and one second. The second class saloon seated 9 passengers, and the first class saloon seated 8, while the passenger compartment in both classes accommodated 6 people. Lighting in the AX's was electric, and they were painted Indian red.

The AX class cars led distinctly unspectacular lives after their entry into service. AX 189 was destroyed in the Midland paint shop fire in 1909 and was not rebuilt, while AX 188 soldiered on as a unique vehicle till August, 1950, when it was written off and converted for use as an office and store at Collie. Proposals to build ten more of these cars came to naught and AX 188 was, for many years, the sole member of the class.

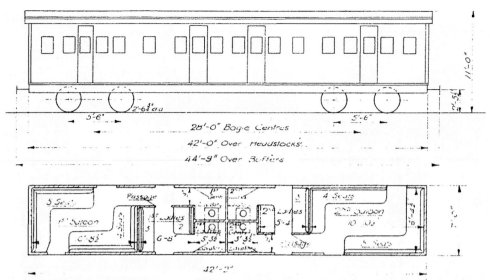

General arrangement drawing of AX 188.

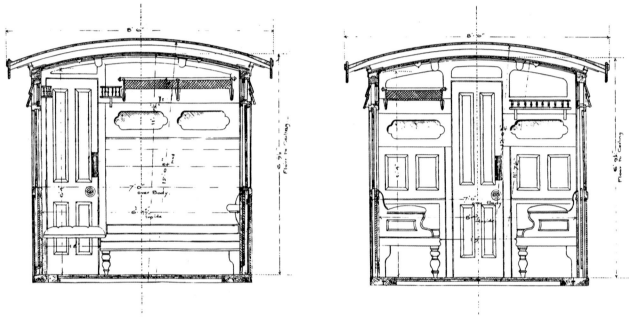

Cross section of 2nd class compartment in AX 188 left) & 2nd class saloon in AX 189 (right).

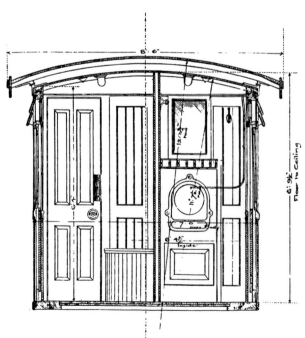

Cross section of the AX lavatory compartment.   *Drawings courtesy PTA.*

AS class

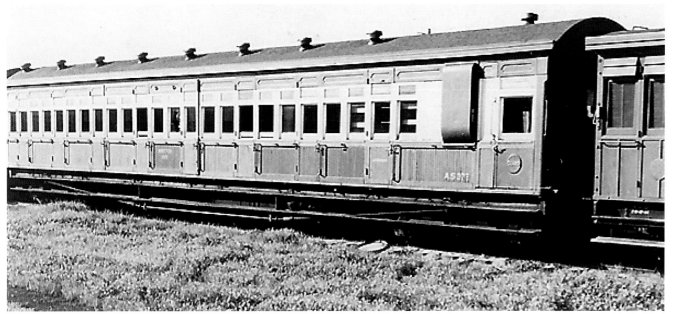

What appears to be AS 372 written off & awaiting its fate.   *Photo via G. Watson.*

The AS class, comprising twelve cars (369-380) built by Westralia Ironworks in 1908, were second class brake cars for use in the Perth suburban area and close lying regions. They were identical in style to the other post-1900 suburban cars and were, in effect, an AT with a brake compartment at one end. Their 58' (17.69m) steel frames rode on 6 wheeled bogies and the exterior body was built of tongue and groove (matchboard) timbers painted Indian red. They had eight passenger compartments in them, accommodating 10 passengers each.

The twelve cars built in 1908 were the only batch of AS class cars produced. Interestingly, they, were not coupled to each other or to any other suburban cars during the dynamo shortage after World War One, but after the end of World War Two they had their guard's compartments enlarged to enable them to carry prams more readily. This was achieved by removing the partition between the existing guard's compartment and the adjacent passenger compartment, converting the former passenger area to carry luggage. This work was carried out as follows:-

1945 - AS 369, 372, 377;
1946 - AS 370, 371, 373-376, 378-380.

The first to be written off was AS 370. It was on a suburban train being shunted across the main line at Midland Junction on 28 February, 1949, when it derailed and was hit by "The Westland" express.[40] However, it would be another eleven years before any more changes to the class took place, the AS's being little affected by the introduction of the diesel railcars in 1954.

Between 1955 and 1957 all eleven of the remaining AS class cars were repainted Larch green, and in 1960 AS 374 was converted into a trade and industries display saloon, reclassified ASD. In concept it was very similar to the conversion of AG 38 almost forty years before.

In 1963 and 1964 all ten cars were repainted again, this time into the green and white livery with the red band separating the two colours, and it was not until 1967 that the AS class began to disappear from Perth's suburban railway lines, following the delivery of a final batch of ADA class railcar trailers the year before. AS 372 and 380 went in 1967, 372 being converted into a workman's van in 1968. That year two more cars, ASD 374 and AS 375 were also converted into workman's vans, and AS 376 was written off, becoming a workman's van in 1970. The final AS class cars went quickly with the loss of AS 371 and 378 in 1969, followed by AS 369, 373, 377 and 379 in 1970.

One former AS class carriage, AS 374, spent many years at West Toodyay as workman's van VW 5118, but was sold during the early 1990's. Only one AS class carriage is known to still exist, that being AS 376 which survives as a workman's van with the Bellarine Peninsular Railway in Victoria.

VW 5118 at West Toodyay, 21 July, 1989. This car was formerly AS 374, then Trade & Industries Display saloon ASD 374, hence the large sliding door where the guard's compartment used to be.
                                                                                                                Photo Bill Gray

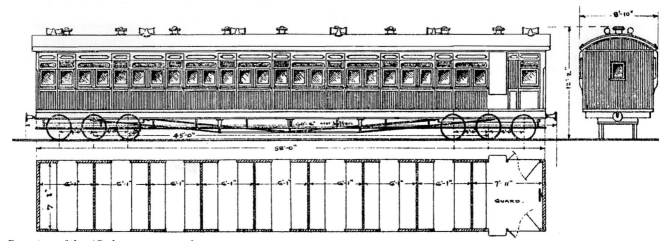

Drawing of the AS class car general arrangement.   *Drawing courtesy PTA.*

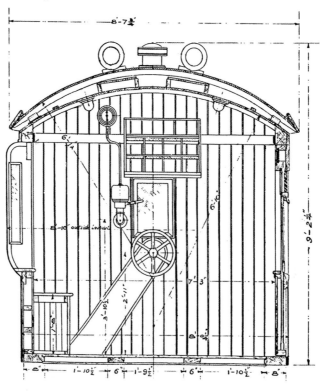

The WAGR drawing of the AS class brake compartment. The passenger compartment was identical to the AT class cars.
                                                                                                                Drawing courtesy PTA.

AS 376 in it's workmans van guise at Queenscliffe in Victoria, 24 July, 1991.   *Photo Bill Gray.*

Loco G 50 passes East Perth loco depot with an AS AT AT AS set.   *Photo Late Geoff Blee, courtesy Murray Rowe*

CHAPTER FOUR
WAR and DEPRESSION - 1911-1930

In 1911 three new ACL's (385-387) were turned out by the Midland Workshops, after which work began on the replacement of the cars destroyed in the paint shop fire. Seven new ACL's (23, 27, 30, 70, 189, 191 and 222) replaced the five destroyed in the fire, as well as the AX and the AE (189 and 191 respectively). Westralia Ironworks was also involved in carriage replacement and in 1911 produced two AU's (309 and 319), three AW's (218, 326 and 332), one of which took the place of an AA (218), and five AT's (134, 139, 145, 242 and 249), the first three of which replaced the burnt AF's. In 1912 Westralia Ironworks continued the building of AT's, producing another ten during the year (252, 253, 259, 262, 299, 306 and 381-384), including the last two replacement cars (AT 299 and 306). The replacement cars were all given the numbers of those destroyed in the blaze. The replacement ZA class brakevans and AD class cars were built at Midland, these vehicles also taking the numbers of the fire victims, and they entered service in 1912, so completing the rebuilding programme.

While the rebuilds were underway, continuing growth of passenger traffic on suburban services saw several cars, notably AC's, reclassified as second class suburban cars (AF). Between 1910 and 1913 seventeen 42' (12.81m) AC class cars were converted to AF. One of the ex Great Southern Railway AC class bogie composite cars, No. 181, had been similarly downgraded to second class in 1907, and this was followed by a second car, AC 184 in 1912. The reclassifications stopped when the First World War broke out.

In 1911 it was decided that sleeping facilities should be provided for second class passengers on overnight trains, so two AR class day time corridor cars (280 and 283) were taken into the workshops to have their seats removed and replaced by six sleeping berths which could be folded out of the way to provide seating for day time travellers. In this configuration there were berths for 36 sleeping passengers, while the sit up capacity remained unchanged at 48. These were the first sleeping cars in Western Australia for Second Class passengers and as a result of their introduction the passenger numbers in the First Class sleeping cars fell. Another six (AR 277-279, 281, 284 and 285) were also converted between 1912 and 1914. The newly converted sleeping cars initially retained their AR classification, but later became the ARS class.

Carriage construction continued apace through 1912 with the AT's previously mentioned, and eight ACL's (388-395), the last seven of which were built on 58' (17.69m) frames instead of the standard 49' (14.94m) chassis used on the earlier cars. These had an additional second class compartment, designated as a ladies' compartment. Also built in 1912 were four AB's (396-399) from Westralia Ironworks, and fourteen ZA brakevans (9336-9349), which appeared late in the year from the Midland Workshops. These differed from the earlier ZA's in that the guard's compartment was in the centre of the van instead of at one end and there was no end platform.

The Port Hedland to Marble Bar railway was opened in 1912, largely to provide transport for the large quantities of gold thought to be at Marble Bar[1]. The gold wasn't there, but the line survived another forty years and, to provide passenger services, ACL 385 was sent north in April, 1912 after having

its electric lighting equipment removed. That year new lines from Dwellingup to Holyoake were opened, as was the Yuna branch on the Northern Railway.

The construction of new carriages continued briefly into 1913 with the completion of the last batch of AB class cars (400-402) at the Midland Workshops. As a group the AB's led a fairly peaceful existence, mostly on country branch line trains, having been displaced from the more important expresses early in the twentieth century. After their delivery, carriage construction then stopped because the money ran out. This situation was aggravated by the onset of the 1914-1918 war which created shortages of both materials and man power because so many men went to enlist[2].

In 1915 the line from Perth through Northam to Wongan Hills and Mullewa was completed, linking the Northern and Eastern Railways with a WAGR operated line. The Midland Railway Co. had been providing first class sleeping accommodation on its services by hiring an AP class sleeping car from the WAGR, but this arrangement came to an end in 1915 when AP 148 went to the Midland Railway as Jb 22 in exchange for their long distance composite car Ja 22, which became an ACL with the WAGR. Thus, the Midland Railway Co. no longer needed to hire sleeping cars from the WAGR.

Hume had predicted that unless funds for new stock were provided by the government there would be a severe shortage of cars by 1915. He even went so far as to suggest that they would have to fit V class vans with seats unless something was done about the situation[3], so the government grudgingly gave him permission to build ten new long framed ACL's. These cars (403-412) appeared late in 1915 and early in 1916, and brought the number of ACL's in service to forty seven, the largest number of any one type of car to operate country services on the WAGR up to that time. However, Hume could still not get permission to build any new corridor cars. The tight-fistedness of this government and of every one which followed it, combined with other factors like the agricultural railways, wars and depression, crippled every CME after Hume and eventually brought about the demise of the country passenger train in Western Australia.

When the First World War broke out a shortage of dynamos for the electric lighting occurred, so many of the suburban cars of the AF, AE, AT, AU and AW classes were coupled together in pairs, with one car in each pair carrying a dynamo to power the lights in both cars. The first of these semi-permanently coupled pairs appeared in 1917 and more were joined together each year through to 1921. They were generally coupled together in classes, as follows:-

AE 127 + 199, AE 129 + 159, & AE 128 + 160 August, 1917
In addition, AE 156 was coupled to AD 115 around 1919.

AF 32 + 165, & AF 141 + 174 - February, 1919
AF 68 + 138, & AF 56 + 167 - June, 1919
AF 33 + 135 - April, 1919
AF 100 + 131, & AF 137 + 172 - March, 1919
AF 35 + 171, AF 58 + 132, & AF 57 + 144 - May, 1919
AF 164 + 169 - April, 1917?
AF 134 + 252 - c.1919

AF 275 + 276 - c.1920

AT 295 + 302, AT 383 + 384, AT 296 + 304, & AT 381 + 382 c.1920
AT 134 + 252, AT 139 + 145, & AT 242 + 249 - c.1919
AT 297 + 306, AT 300 + 303, & AT 253 + 299   1921
AT 301 + 305 c.1921
AT 259 + 262   1920

The AU brake cars were coupled to AW first class cars as follows:-

AU 307 + AW 327, & AU 310 + AW 334 - c.1921
AU 312 + AW 20, AU 309 + AW 332, AU 321 + AW 328, & AU 322 + AW 325 - 1921
AU 308 + AW 331 - 1918
AU 318 + AW 323, AU 319 + AW 333, & AU 320 + AW 330, & AU 311 + AW 329 - c.1920
At least five of these pairs remained coupled till 1941.

Interestingly the AS second class cars were not coupled to each other or to any other suburban cars during this time. The coupled coaches were progressively separated as dynamos became available, but some remained together till the Second World War. The shortage of dynamos was so acute that the AJ class brakevans lost their electric lighting equipment to the passenger carriages, and were converted to oil lighting. This situation lasted till the mid 1930's, by which time the AJ's were electrically lit again.

On 22 October, 1917, with relatively little fanfare (other than at Kalgoorlie) the Trans Australia Railway was opened. Serious surveys for this remarkable piece of railway engineering had begun in 1908 and construction started in 1911, moving inwards from both Kalgoorlie and Port Augusta to meet in the desert on 17 October, 1917. Western Australia was no longer isolated from the eastern states, but a change of train from the standard gauge (4'8"/1435mm) Commonwealth Railway to the narrower (3'6"/1067mm) gauge WAGR was required at Kalgoorlie for the completion of the journey to Perth. During 1919 Hume retired and was replaced by Mr. Ernest Alfred Evans[4]. Hume had carried on the modernisation of the WAGR which Rotheram had started, but the financial restrictions placed on him by his superiors in government had hobbled him. The same restrictions applied to Evans and, if anything, were even tighter. He moved into the position of CME at a time when the country was recovering financially from the war and money for new carriages was almost non existent. However, the extra traffic generated on the WAGR by the opening of the Trans Australia Railway finally loosened the purse strings a little and two sets of corridor cars were ordered, although they were not ready till late 1918/early 1919. Westralia Ironworks built six AQ class sleeping cars (413-418) and six AR second class sleeping cars (419-424) on 59' (17.99m) timber underframes (1' (305mm) longer than the earlier cars), while two AV class dining cars (425 and 426) and three AJ class brakevans (427-429) were built by the Midland Workshops on standard length steel underframes. All seventeen cars were carried on new long wheel base 4 wheel bogies. The new AR second class sleeping cars were almost identical to the earlier converted AR class sleepers.

The new AV's were similar to the earlier dining cars, with some improvements to their internal fittings. Their introduction allowed dining car services to be extended to the Southwest and Great Southern lines, but such services on the Bunbury trains were not uneconomical and were stopped soon after[5].

Enough money was also found for some conversions to be carried out. The introduction of the new AQ's created a surplus of first class sleeping accommodation, so two of the brand new cars were converted into VIP carriages in 1920. AQ 413 became a Vice Regal car (AN) and AQ 414 was converted into a new Ministerial car (AM). Both the new VIP carriages were issued to traffic on 28 June, 1920, in time for the visit to Western Australia of the Prince of Wales and his entourage. Exactly one week after the cars entered service they were being used to carry the Prince and his party on a tour through the south of the state, near Jardanup, between Pemberton and Bridgetown, when AM 414 and AN 413, which were at the rear of the seven car train, derailed and toppled over onto their sides. The accident was caused by heavy rain which washed away a low embankment, so allowing the track to spread. Fortunately, the train was crossing the embankment at low speed due to the inclement weather and no-one was badly hurt. Reports of the day indicated that the Prince was found in the overturned carriage, calmly smoking a cigar and most pleased that the whiskey flask was still intact[6]. Both cars were rescued and repaired, and neither was ever returned to passenger service. AN 413 finally became AL 4 in 1958, and AM 414 became an inspection car in 1973 before being written off in 1980. These cars replaced AN 206 and AM 261, the former being converted back into an AA class long distance car, and the latter into an AF second class suburban car, both in 1922.

The new AQ's also released some of the older AP class sleeping cars, and in 1920 two (AP 147 and 149) were converted into second class sleeping cars and redesignated APS. Another car (AP 146) was reclassified as an APC class composite sleeping car at the same time. Two more AP's were converted to composites and reclassified APC, AP 154 in 1923 and AP 151 in 1924. The type was then left alone till 1938.

Another class of coach became extinct on the WAGR in 1920 when the last of the original 6 wheeled "Cleminson" saloon cars was placed in storage. This car, No. 4, was rebuilt and placed on bogies around 1906-07, being redesignated second class at the same time. In 1927 it was converted into a Z class brakevan.

By 1921 the three old AG class "American" cars which had gone to Kalgoorlie as brake cars (9, 12 and 17) in 1905 had been returned to Perth from the goldfields, largely due to the inroads being made by the electric trams into the Kalgoorlie railway passenger traffic[7]. As there was no work anywhere else on the system for these ageing vehicles, all three entered the workshops where they were converted into buffet cars. These conversions involved the building of completely new bodies, similar in style to the AQ and AR class corridor coaches, on the old AG frames. They were classified AGB. The three cars entered service in 1921, and meals were provided for passengers in these cars on services which did not justify the provision of one of the larger AV class dining cars. Originally they operated on the Perth to Kellerberrin, Perth to Wyalkatchem, and Caron to Yalgoo trains.

In 1922 a hint of things to come arrived on the scene when the WAGR delved into the world of internal combustion railway vehicles for the first time by acquiring three petrol engined rail motor coaches. They were numbered 430-432, but were not given a classification, and they were joined soon afterwards by a lightweight trailer which was numbered 433. This tiny vehicle had started life as a P class brakevan before its conversion to a passenger car. They were used to replace locomotive hauled trains on some branch line services. Travel on the rail coaches was considered to be second class and they were used on country branch lines, mainly out of Merredin, Albany and Narrogin, at which places the cars were based[8]. The Merredin services were only short-lived, and eventually all three rail coaches were based at Albany. Car 432 was burnt out at Albany late in 1926, as was Car 430 in August, 1936, also at Albany. It is not known where the trailer went in its early days, or which of the three rail coaches it went with, but it finished up at Albany, and after the two rail coaches had been destroyed by fire, it ran behind rail coach No. 431.

As the Kalgoorlie tramway system continued to make inroads into the railway services and train numbers were reduced, the "Gilbert" cars became redundant and another foretaste of things to come was exhibited when AG 38 was removed from passenger service and converted into an exhibition car in 1922. This car was used to promote Western Australian industry and it carried the words "Westralian Industries League" above the windows, and "SUPPORT YOUR OWN INDUSTRIES" on the body sides below in large white letters. AG 38 was quite a success in this role and was used till 1927, being replaced the following year by the Reso (short for "resources") trains. It was then converted into an AL class inspection car.

In 1922 two more carriages joined the AF class, one a new car and the other a conversion, possibly as an attempt to upgrade the suburban cars at minimum cost. The new car was built on the frame of AC 59, with a new body similar in style to the AT class suburban cars, but only 42' (12.81m) long, being fitted. AF 59 looked like a shortened AT, with seven compartments. Like AF 13, AF 59 may also have been intended as a prototype for a large rebodying programmeme, but it seems that no money was available even for these conversions, for no further cars were given the same treatment. AF 59 also remained a unique vehicle in the class. The other carriage to enter the AF class was the old Ministerial car AM 261, in March, 1922. Its interior was stripped out and replaced with wooden tram car seats with throw over backs. The end windows were also filled in. AF 261 could accommodate 66 passengers in its passenger saloon, which was just over 47' (14.33m) long. The only new railway added to the WAGR's network at this time was the Lake Clifton line near Waroona, purchased in 1922 and closed in 1924 due to a lack of traffic. No new railways had been built since 1918.

In 1922 another Royal Commission was held to look into the WAGR's operations and this enquiry centred largely on cost saving measures such as locomotive improvements, automatic signalling, and improved track[9]. While none of these affected passenger cars directly in the short term, they all involved capital costs, so the shortage of funds for new carriages continued, and almost none were built. However, some changes were made. Between 1923 and 1925 all nineteen ACE's were converted to suburban cars by converting the lavatory compartment into a large passenger compartment with an unusual U shaped seat fitted in it. The cars were then classified AC, even though they differed slightly to the other 42' (8.12m) AC class cars. Thus the rather odd lavatory equipped ACE's ceased to exist and the nineteen carriages led a similar history to the other AC's. Some of the AJ class brakevans (AJ 263, 267, 269, 272, 367 and 368) were fitted with shelves for carrying milk at about this time and most of

the older ones were rebogied with the new long wheel base units which had first appeared in 1918, since these had proven to be satisfactory in service. In 1923 and 24 the older AV class dining cars were also fitted with these new bogies in place of the 6 wheel type in order to improve their riding qualities.

During the early 1920's the demand for first class rail travel began to decline and this resulted in six AA class cars being reclassified as composites and classed ACL. Three (AA 202, 204 and 211) were converted in 1923 and another three (AA 203, 209 and 210) in 1924. This conversion was accomplished by downgrading the appropriate compartments to accommodate 7 people each. These were the last of the ACL's, making a class total of fifty three cars. By this time the AA's had been displaced from the main line trains, but gave the WAGR good service for many years on country branch line passenger trains till these services were wound down during the 1950's and '60's.

In June, 1924 the AR Second Class sleeping cars were all reclassified ARS. In December another AR day car (282) was converted into a second class sleeping car and reclassified ARS, which class then consisted of the entire first group of AR class cars built (277-285), plus the six built as second class sleepers (419-424).

The three remaining six wheeled AH class passenger cars on the Eastern Railway (AH 26, 28 and 29) had been used to provide suburban services in Perth and were written off in 1924. AH 29 was re-issued to traffic in 1925 as a DW class workman's van, finishing up as a mobile school room before being written off in 1950. These were the last of the type on the main system, although two others still remained on the Ravensthorpe to Hopetoun line. These saw no use after 1930, and their bodies were removed from the frames and sold to private buyers later that decade. Both still exist.

A new class of suburban car arrived on the scene in 1924 with the introduction into service of a second class saloon, AY 26. This vehicle was, like AF 59, a prototype and although it seated 82 passengers, 8 less than an AT, it was seven tons (7.07t) lighter, making it considerably more efficient.

In 1926 a new design of passenger carrying brakevan, the ZB class, was introduced. The first batch of these consisted of five vans (10600-10604). The ZB's were similar to the ZA's in concept, but had only one second class compartment. They were shorter in length, and, like the early ZA's, had an end platform. As with all the WAGR's brakevans, a box was provided for the carriage of dogs, but in the ZB's this was located such that only a timber partition separated the dog box and the passenger compartment, and one can only feel sympathy for the passengers who, enduring a hot, dry and dusty compartment on a jolting and slow branch line goods train, may also have had to put up with a continually barking dog only a couple of feet away. The next ZB to be built was a conversion of the agricultural bank manager's van BC 1926 and this appeared in mid 1927 as ZB 1926. It was followed late in 1927 by another five vans (ZB 10605-10609) and still another five early in 1928 (ZB 10610-10614). These differed from the first batch in that they were fitted with longer wheel base bogies in place of the original bar frame type, and they were rated to carry a 10 ton (10.1t) load instead of the earlier van's 7 tons (7.07t). The ZB's were used on services where the patronage did not justify the use of a larger ZA class van.

Railway construction had stopped as a result of World War One and it did not recommence till 1923. Even then, things did not happen quickly, but an average of just over 80 miles (128 km) of track was laid every year for the next ten years. Much of this was lightly laid agricultural line, for the wheat harvest improved yearly during the latter half of the 1920's to reach a record in 1929. In 1926 the line from Holyoake to Narrogin was completed, so opening the full length of the railway between Pinjarra and Narrogin. In 1927 the Esperance line was completed through to Kalgoorlie, and the "American" car AG 15, which had been fitted with a lavatory in 1925 and sent to work the isolated railway, was returned to the main system. By 1929 the WAGR's route mileage was up to 4078 miles (6525 km)[10], with lines also completed to Lake Brown near Merredin, Bullfinch near Southern Cross, from Miling to Toodyay, Goomalling to Kalannie, Kattaning through Nyabing to Pingrup, Wagin through Lake Grace to Newdegate, Torbay through Denmark to Nornup, Busselton to Flinder's Bay, and Bridgetown through Manjimup to Pemberton.

In the late 1920's the Commonwealth Railways sleeping cars were somewhat better appointed than the existing WAGR cars, with twin berth compartments among other things, and the differences to a passenger changing from one system to the other at Kalgoorlie was obvious. As a result, a new type of sleeping car, classified AZ, was built by the WAGR. The AZ's were a first class car and were intended to be the first of a new generation of main line cars to replace the AQ's, AR's and AV's, but the old money problem reared its ugly head again and no comparable second class or dining cars were ever built. The AZ's replaced the AQ's on the Kalgoorlie trains, and these in turn displaced older cars from other services. Their design was identical to three sleeping cars built for the MRWA late in 1927 at the WAGR Midland Workshops, and four AZ's were built in 1928 (AZ 434-437). A second batch (438-443) was constructed in 1929, making a total of ten cars in the class. They were the first twin berth sleeping cars on the WAGR and were fitted with the new Stone's water raising apparatus located under the floor, which filled the main overhead water tanks. This equipment was also fitted to four older cars in 1929-30. An AZ body and running gear were used to build a new AM class Ministerial car (444) later in 1928, to work with AM 40 and AM 414. From the outside, this new car and an AZ were almost impossible to tell apart.

In 1929 six more AZ's (438-443) went into traffic, and Evans, the man responsible for these cars, was promoted to Commissioner in April[11]. He had been a progressive CME who had been hamstrung by a lack of funding, his AY and AZ classes giving excellent service to the WAGR much longer than he could have envisaged. The rail motors were a worthwhile experiment, but the concept was, perhaps, a little ahead of the technology available at the time. However, the experience gained with these little cars must have been invaluable. His proposal to build twelve country days cars was not proceeded with[12], despite the increasing age of the existing stock, and the backlog of new construction which built up during the 1920's was never caught up.

In 1928 the first of the Reso trains ran. These were tour trains which were run "to bring forcibly before the people the resources of Australia"[13], hence the name Reso. The Reso trains did not necessarily make a profit, but were considered worthwhile because of the publicity they gave to the development of the state. The first one conveyed "60 gentlemen from Victoria"[14] through the Eastern, Southwestern and Southern districts of Western Australia between 13 and 22 October, 1928, with ten vehicles in the consist - sleeping car AQ 418, buffet car AGB 9, dining car AV 426, which had been used on a Royal train during the visit to WA by the Prince of Wales in 1920, newly converted lounge car AY 26, new first class sleeping cars AZ 434, 435 and 436 which were successfully trialed on this train, newly converted "Gilbert" bath car AG 45, "Gilbert" inspection car AL 37, and brakevan AJ 366.[15] The suburban saloon AY 26 had proved a success on suburban trains so in 1927 two more AY's (28 and 29) were built at Midland Workshops, releasing AY 26 in 1928 for conversion into a lounge car for use on the new Reso trains. It retained its AY classification, and continued to run on these trains as the need arose. The old "Gilbert" car, AG 45 was converted into a bath car so that passengers travelling on the Reso trains could keep clean. Its career as a bath car came to an end in 1935 when it was replaced by the shower car AGS 17.

1911

Second Class Sleeping Car
AR class
ARS class (1924)

277-285
347-358
419-424

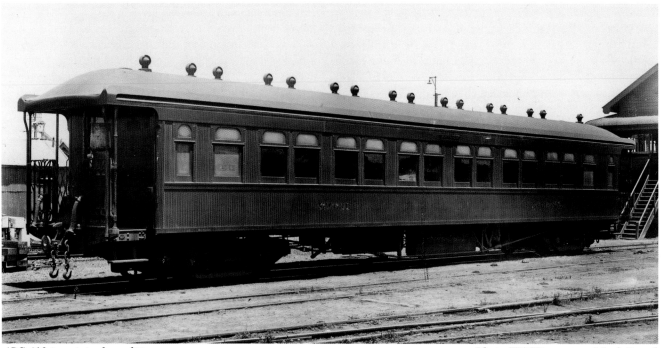

ARS 419 in original condition.   *Photo WAGR courtesy Mark Beard.*

In 1911 it was decided that sleeping facilities should be provided for second class passengers on overnight trains, so two AR class day time corridor cars (280 and 283) were taken into the workshops to have their seats replaced by six sleeping berths which converted into seating for day time travellers. Otherwise, the cars remained unaltered, although the second compartment along the corridor from the ladies' lavatory was reserved for ladies only. In this configuration there were berths for 36 sleeping passengers, while the sit up capacity remained unchanged at 48.

These cars proved so popular that the patronage of the first class sleeping cars began to suffer, and to meet the demand three more AR's (277-279) were converted in 1912, another (284) in 1913 and a final pair (281 and 285) in 1914.

The completion of the Trans Australia Railway in October, 1917 and the additional patronage generated as a result, saw the construction of seventeen new carriages in two sets, and included in these were six AR second class sleeping cars (419-424). These were 59' (17.99m) long, built on wooden underframes with long wheel base 4 wheeled bogies. They had their linen closets located across the corridor from the lavatory at each end, causing the corridor to have a short angled section just inside the entrances, and placing thr entry door closer to the centre of the end of the car. Otherwise, they were identical to the earlier AR class sleepers. These cars all went into service early in 1919.

By 1924 there was some confusion arising from the fact that the twenty seven AR class carriages were of two different types, thirteen day cars and fourteen sleeping cars, so in June that year the sleeping cars were all reclassified ARS. In December, 1924 AR 282 was also converted to a sleeping car and joined the ARS class, which then consisted of cars 277-285 and 419-424.

In the mid 1930's one of the steps taken to make train travel

a little more attractive was to limit the number of berths in second class sleeping cars to four, so six ARS's (277-279, 281, 283 and 285) were converted from six berth to four in 1936, and the rest (280, 282, 284 and 419-424) were dealt with in 1937. This reduced the sleeping capacity of these cars to 24 passengers, but made them a lot more comfortable.

The ARS class worked unmolested through the Second World War, and when the decision was made in 1951 to change the colour scheme of the WAGR's carriages to Larch green[16], all fifteen cars were repainted. This work took place between 1951 and 1956.

In 1955 two AR class day cars (AR 353 and 358) were converted into ARS sleeping cars and at the same time had their worn out wooden underframes replaced by steel underframes from two retired AT class suburban cars. This programme of rebuilding the wooden framed cars continued through 1956 when another six AR's (348-350, 352, 354 and 355) were similarly converted using AT and AU frames, and a final four cars (AR 347, 351, 356 and 357) were converted in 1957. All were repainted Larch green at the time of conversion. This rebuilding resulted in the last of the AR class day cars becoming ARS second class sleeping cars and it allowed, in 1957, the conversion of four ARS class cars (419, 420, 423 and 424) into AQZ first class sleeping cars. These cars were also placed on steel underframes, but when is not certain.

Some of the ARS's led only short lives as second class sleeping cars because, during the 1960's, the country carriage fleet underwent modernisation and rebuilding. In 1962 four ARS class cars (347, 351, 356 and 357) were rebuilt into first class twin berth sleepers and were reclassified ARM, bearing little resemblance to their AR ancestors. This refurbishment programme also involved another change of livery to Larch green and cream and all the ARS class cars were repainted, with the possible exception of ARS 282, written off in 1965.

In 1971 the last train ran over the old Eastern Goldfields Railway, which was promptly closed and torn up, having been replaced by the new standard gauge line between Kalgoorlie and Perth. The ARS's had no other services to go to and in 1973 the bulk of them were written off. These were ARS 278-281, 283, 285, 350, 352-355 and 422. Many were stored at Bellevue and Bassendean while awaiting disposal. In 1975 the "Midlander" and "Albany Weekender" both ran for the last time and the last six ARS's were written off the books (ARS 277, 284, 348, 349, 358 and 421). ARS 277 and 284 were both converted to workman's vans, followed by ARS 348 and 349 in 1979.

Some ARS class cars till survive. These include ARS 421, complete with wooden underframe, along with ARS 349 as a workman's van at the Bassendean Rail Transport Museum, the body of ARS 350 at the Whistlestop near Busselton, and the derelict remains of ARS 279 and 355, which lie together on a farm near Dwellingup, both having been cut in half.

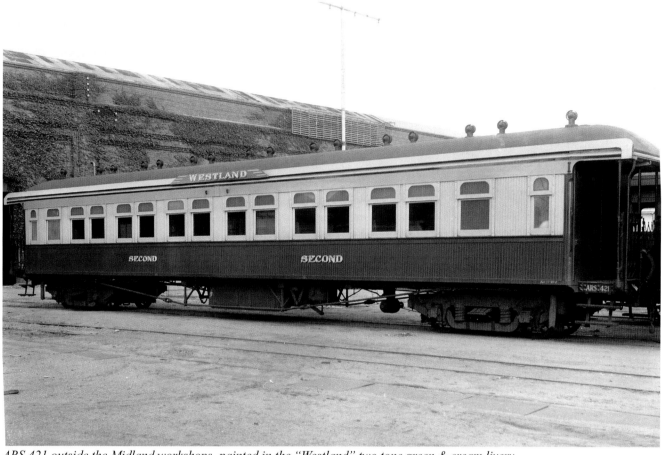

ARS 421 outside the Midland workshops, painted in the "Westland" two tone green & cream livery.

Photo WAGR, courtesy Lindsay Watson

ARS 283 in rebuilt condition.

Photo late Geoff Blee, courtesy Murray Rowe.

ARS 354 carrying a "Westland" name board in Perth Yard on a hot day, 13 December, 1967.

Photo Late Geoff Blee, courtesy Murray Rowe.

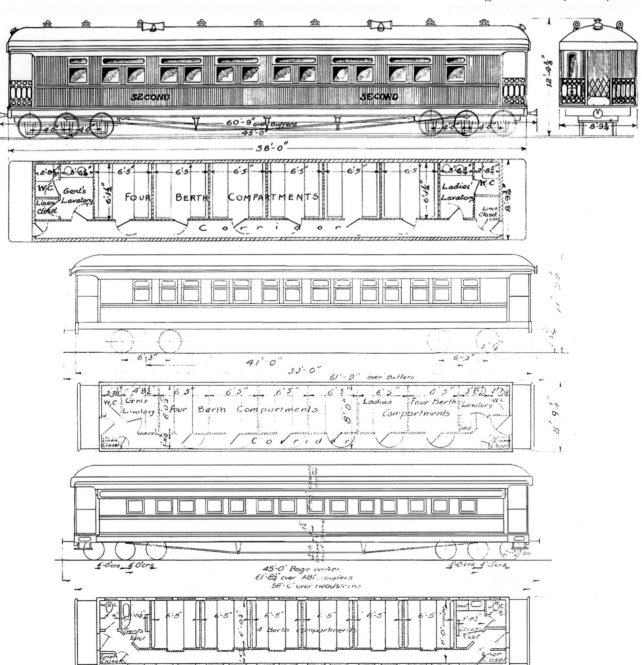

The ARS class cars, as originally built (top), as rebuilt with crown lights (centre) & without crown lights (bottom).

Drawings courtesy PTA.

*ARS compartment made up for night use.
Photo courtesy ARHS.*

Changing the linen in ARS 282. *Photo courtesy Battye Library Ref: 225684P*

With the number of miles ARS cars traveled, accidents were inevitable. In this case two ARS cars on the "Westland" have come to grief as the result of a wash away at Merredin on 21 July, 1960. *Photo courtesy ARHS Archives.*

After withdrawal, ARS cars were stored in large numbers at Bassendean & Bellevue. ARS 285 sits at the end of a line of stored cars at Bassendean, 4 December, 1972.   *Photo courtesy Jeff Austin.*

Lynton Englund's photograph of ARS 422 (closest to the camera) & ARS 281 derelict at Bellevue shows the differences between those cars which retained their crown lights after rebuilding.   *Photo courtesy Lynton Englund.*

AGB class

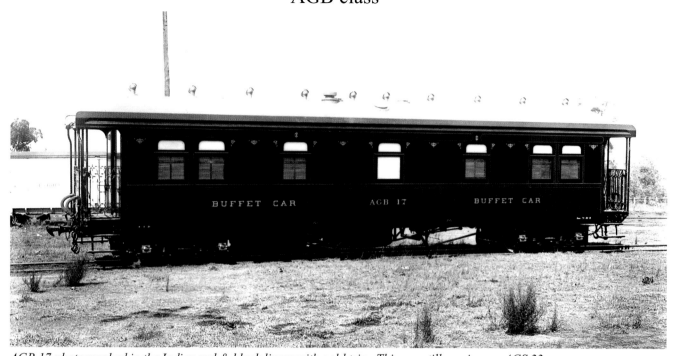

AGB 17 photographed in the Indian red & black livery with gold trim. This car still survives as AGS 22.

Photo WAGR courtesy Mark Beard.

By the beginning of the 1920's the train services in Kalgoorlie had lost a good many of their customers to the electric trams introduced in 1902[17]. Three AG class "American" cars (9, 12 and 17) had each been fitted with a brake compartment and sent to the goldfields capital in 1905, but late in 1920 there was no further use for them there and they were returned to Perth. Nor was there any work anywhere else on the system for these ageing vehicles, so all three were converted to buffet cars and reclassified AGB.

The conversions involved the building of completely new bodies, similar in style to the AQ and AR class corridor cars, on the old AG frames. Their matchboard bodies were painted Indian red, lined in black and gold with red and gold lettering. They had end platforms with gangways leading to adjacent cars, and entry was gained to the dining saloon through a door from each end platform. One end of the car was designated first class and the other second class, but both dining saloons were identical. Immediately inside the entry door was a cupboard, and down both sides of each saloon were tables and chairs. On one side were single tables of which there were two, able to seat two people each, and on the other side there were double tables (two), which seated 4 people each. Altogether, each AGB could accommodate 24 diners. The dining saloons were decorated in the same style of varnished woodwork found in the main line cars. The central section of the car contained a small kitchen (described as a "pantry")[18] which separated the first and second class dining saloons. It contained a fuel stove, wood box, sink, benches, drawers and cupboards, with an ice chest on one side. Doors into the dining saloon from the kitchen were located at either end with the ice chest placed

between them. There was no direct access into the kitchen from outside the car, and the lighting was electric.

Meals were provided for passengers in these cars on services which did not justify the provision of one of the larger AV class dining cars. Originally they operated on the Perth to Kellerberrin, Perth to Wyalkatchem, and Caron to Yalgoo trains.[19]

The three cars entered service in 1921, AGB 12 in January, AGB 9 in February, and AGB 17 in March, but their histories were only relatively short. AGB 17 was derailed in 1928 and damaged, but was soon repaired and returned to service.

The railways were by no means immune from the effects of the Great Depression in the early 1930's and many services were curtailed during this time due to the fall off of patronage. The buffet cars, like most of the WAGR's dining cars, continually lost money and by 1935 they had become redundant. In November, 1935 AGB 17 was converted into the one and only AGS class shower car for use on the Reso trains, where it replaced the "Gilbert" bath car, AG 45. AGB 9 was stored in 1936, but re-entered service two years later as a brakevan for suburban trains, while AGB 12 was converted to a survey car in 1938 and the following year was renumbered AGB 2.

All three of these carriages have survived, although not in their original form. AGB 9 is with the Hotham Valley Railway as Z.9, AGB 12 is also with the Hotham Valley Railway as a crew car, having finished its days as inspection car AL 2, and AGB 17 is preserved at the ARHS Rail Transport Museum as shower car AGS 22.

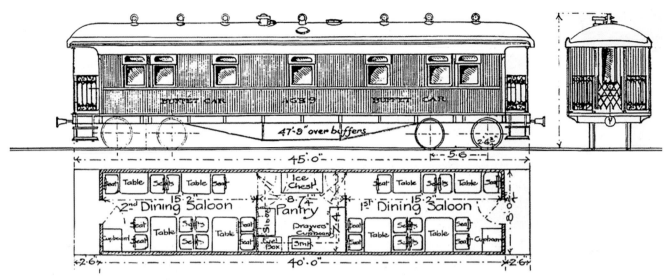

Drawing of Buffet Car AGB 9.

Drawing courtesy PTA.

AGB 9 later became Z 9, shown crossing a culvert, typical of those found in the Mt. Magnet area.

Photo late Geoff Blee, courtesy Murray Rowe

1922   Petrol Engined "Rail Coach"   430-432
AO class (1937)
Petrol Rail Coach Trailer   433
AOT class

Portrait shot of car 430 prior to it's classification as an AO.   *Photo WAGR, courtesy Mark Beard.*

In 1922 the WAGR purchased the first of its internal combustion railway vehicles when three petrol engined rail coaches were acquired. They were numbered 430-432, but were not classified.

Externally they looked like old fashioned 4 wheeled passenger cars, each with a wooden panelled body built on a steel underframe. However, they were also fitted with cow catchers at both ends, a feature not normally found on locomotive hauled passenger cars. They were 24'4" (7.42m) long with a 9' (2.74m) wheel base, leaving a considerable amount of overhang at each end. The window arrangement was rather odd, in that there were six doors on each side of the car, each with a space for a window, but they held neither window frame nor glass. Other sections were fitted with what appear to be window frames, but no glass, while still others were both framed and glazed. At each end of the car was a driver's cab, the driving position being on the left. Each cab had a door on either side, while access to the passenger saloon was gained via the aforementioned side doors, four on each side. Running boards were provided for use as steps at those places not having platforms. The saloon was made up of four "compartments", but the partitions between each "compartment" were only as high as the window sills. The seats in each "compartment" ran the full width and faced each other, giving accommodation for 38 passengers. There was no access provided between the "compartments", but by climbing over the seat backs it would have been possible to

move from one to another. Room in the passenger area was limited, so any parcels or mail were carried in the driver's cab. This had two separate windows in the ends of the car to enable the driver to see where he was going. Lighting was electric, with headlights fitted at both ends of the car, and the rail coaches were painted Indian red.

The engines in these vehicles were 40 h.p. units built by W.H. Dorman and Co. of Stafford in England, mounted on a chassis supplied by the Motor Rail and Tram Car Co., Simplex Works, at Bedford, England, but the origin of the bodies is uncertain. They had a fuel capacity of 30 gallons (136 litres).

In December the petrol coaches were joined by a lightweight trailer, numbered 433. This vehicle had started life as a P class brakevan before its conversion to a passenger car. It was a tiny vehicle, only 13'11" (4.24m) long, running on a 4 wheeled undercarriage, and it is thought to have had a steel underframe with a timber body. The sides were panelled and the ends were matchboard. It was able to carry 20 passengers in two compartments, and access to these was gained by side doors with steps mounted outside each door for those places where there were no platforms. The seats ran across the width of the compartments and faced each other. There was no access provided between the two compartments and it is not clear whether or not the partition dividing them was built to the ceiling, or only to window sill height as in the rail coaches. The seats could be removed to allow the vehicle to be used as a goods wagon and in this configuration it could carry a load of 4 tons (4.04t). The trailer appears not to have had glass in any of its windows and it was fitted with electric lights. It was only equipped with a handbrake, so it depended on the brakes mounted on the rail coach to stop it. It was painted Indian red.

Travel on the rail coaches was Second Class and they were used on country branch lines, mainly out of Merredin, Albany and Narrogin, at which places the cars were based. The Merredin services were only short-lived, and eventually all three rail coaches were based at Albany. Car 432 did not last long, being destroyed by fire at Albany late in 1926. Car 430 met a similar fate in August, 1936 when it, too, was burnt out, also at Albany. Its frame was later used to build a 4 wheeled flat top wagon, numbered Jetty 70. It is not known where the

trailer went in its early days, or which of the three rail coaches it went with, but it finished up at Albany, running behind rail coach No. 431.

In June, 1937 car 431 was classified AO and the trailer AOT. They were transferred to operate on the loop line between Kalgoorlie and Boulder, the patronage on this once busy railway having fallen off to such an extent that the two little vehicles could cope quite well with the available traffic.

In 1946 AOT 433 was renumbered 430 and it trailed around behind the petrol rail coach till 1950 when both vehicles were written off. What became of AO 431 is not known, but in 1951 AOT 430 was converted into a DW class workman's van and it continued to serve in this capacity till it was written off again in 1965, this time for good.

AO 433 in the Kalgoorlie area   *Photo courtesy ARHS Archives.*

An AO class car with the AOT trailer, crossing a bridge at Denmark.   *Photo courtesy Denmark Historical Society*

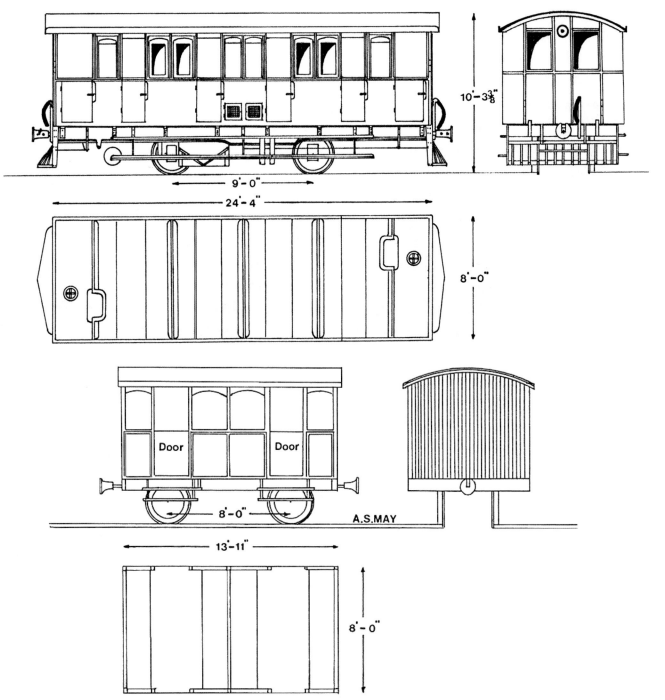

Drawings of the AO class railcar (top) & it's AOT class trailer (bottom).　　　　　　　*Drawings by Andrew May.*

AO 431 & the other known photograph of AOT 433, at Kalgoorlie.　　　　　　　*Photo courtesy ARHS Archives.*

Second Class Suburban Saloon
AY class

A brand new AY 26 poses for the camera.   *Photo WAGR courtesy Mark Beard.*

In 1924 a new type of suburban saloon was built at the Midland Workshops and classified AY, with the number 26. This 59' (17.99m) car seated 82 passengers, and had a steel underframe with timber body. Its tongue and groove sides and ends were painted Indian red. Entry to the car was gained via three sliding doors on each side, those in the centre being double doors, and the car was divided into three compartments, each with six rows of transverse seats and an aisle down the middle. The seats all faced the doorway nearest to them, and there was a fixed seat across the width of the car at each end. The AY was not fitted with gangways, so there was no access to other cars in the train. Interestingly, its military capacity was 132 men, which would have been a tight squeeze, especially if they were carrying their full equipment.

AY 26 proved to be a great success on suburban trains and it was joined by two more AY class cars, 28 and 29, late in 1927. Once these two vehicles had settled into service AY 26 was withdrawn in 1928 and converted into a lounge car for use on the new Reso trains. It retained its AY classification.

In June, 1938 the "Westland Express" was introduced to speed up and improve the service between Perth and Kalgoorlie. This train was to include lounge cars and, as there was no money for new carriages, two old ones were converted. These were AY 28 and 29, the latter appearing in June, 1938 and the former a month later. These cars also retained their AY classifications. Thus, the AY second class suburban cars, for the time being, ceased to exist.

At the end of World War Two much of the older carriage stock was worn out and in 1945 a set of six new suburban cars, including four AY's (452-455) and two AYB's, was built. Another set of four cars followed in 1946, made up of two AY's (460 and 461) and two more AYB's. All these cars were painted in a new Larch green, light green and cream colour scheme, but they did not run in this livery for long, being repainted in plain Larch green by 1955.

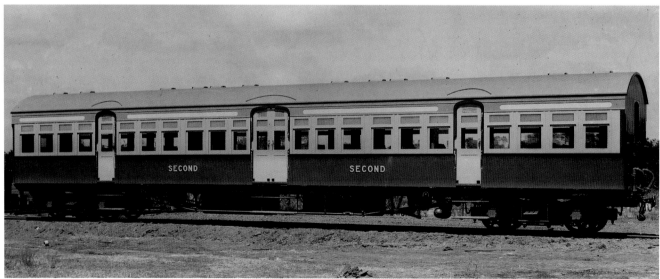

AY 452 in the two tone green & cream livery.   *Photo courtesy ARHS Archives.*

In 1958 AYL 26 was replaced on the "Westland" by an AVL class lounge car and was converted back to a suburban car again, making a total of seven AY class cars in service. It had also been painted Larch green and, having been fitted with end doors and gangways, it now seated 80 passengers.

In 1962, as part of the general carriage refurbishment programme, two "new" buffet-lounge cars were created by rebuilding AY 460 and 461, which were reclassified AYS and allocated to the "Westland" sets. The bodies of these cars were unrecognisable as AY's after this rebuild and even the bogies were changed in favour of the ride control type.

The remaining AY's (26, 452-455) continued to roam the suburbs, venturing out occasionally on tour trains, for another three decades. Two (AY 454 and 455) were painted in the mainline green and cream livery so they could be used as strengthening cars for the "Australind" when the demand warranted, but in 1963 all except AY 452 were repainted in the suburban livery of green, red and white, with 452 being done in 1966. In the 1970's all were put into the Westrail orange and blue livery, but were repainted green and cream during 1983-84.

In 1982 AY 454 was withdrawn from service and stored, but the re-opening of the Fremantle line in July, 1983 saw it returned to service for a short period of time. It was written off again in November, 1983 and its body sold privately in Stoneville. The other four AY class cars were withdrawn from service in January, 1991 and written off the following month. All four survive with the ARHS at Midland and Boyanup.

A D class loco hauls a train of new AY & AYB class cars.   *Photo late Alan Hamilton Collection, courtesy Joe Moir.*

AY 28 in suburban service before being converted to a lounge car.   *Photo Late LG Poole, courtesy ARHS Archives.*

AY 454 at Perth Station.   *Photo courtesy ARHS Archives.*

AY 452 in it's final condition at York, 2 September, 1989.   *Photo Bill Gray.*

An anonymous AY undergoing overhaul in the Midland Workshops   *Photo courtesy ARHS Archives.*

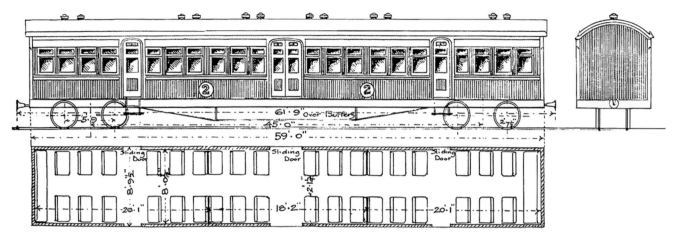

General arrangement drawing of the AY in original condition.   *Drawing courtesy PTA*

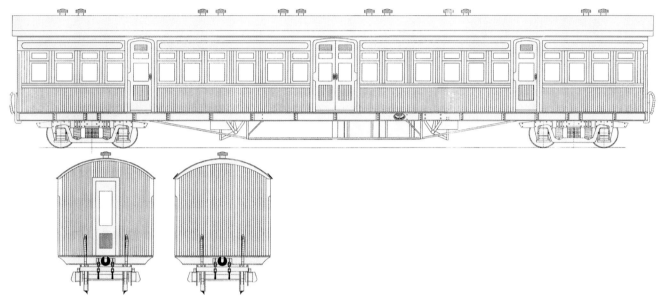

Drawing of the AY, showing the underfloor detail & end door.   *Drawing courtesy Roger Palmer.*

AY interiors, original (left) & AY 26 shortly before withdrawal (right)   *Photos WAGR courtesy ARHS & Bill Gray.*

DD 598 hauling a short train of AYB/AY class cars, the first two cars in the red, green & white livery & the trailing car in green & cream. *Photo late Geoff Blee, courtesy Murray Rowe.*

AY 452 on a suburban train at Perth station. These cars were allowed to become quite tatty before being repainted during the mid to late 1980's. *Photo Andrew May, courtesy ARHS Archives.*

C 1702 ready to depart Midland on an afternoon peak hour suburban train consisting of an AYB, two AYs & an AYF in late 1990. This was the condition of these cars in the last days of their operation. *Photo Bill Gray.*

ZB 202 at Narrogin.

Photo late Geoff Blee, courtesy Murray Rowe

The first five ZB class brakevans (10600-10604) were built in 1926, and were not dissimilar to the ZA's in their internal arrangements, but had only one passenger compartment and no lavatory. They were built on steel underframes with matchboard bodies painted Indian red and, like the early ZA's, they had an end platform and guard's compartment at one end, and the passenger compartment with three windows on each side at the other. Entry to the guard's compartment was by way of the platform and a door in the end of the car, and it held a pedestal mounted hand brake wheel, a seat at each lookout, and a small stove for warmth. A doorway from the compartment led into the central goods area, which was mostly empty space, save for some shelves on one side at the guard's end and a dog box at the other end. Loading was achieved through large, centrally located sliding doors, one on each side, and dogs were loaded via an external louvred hatch. Unlike other country car passenger compartments, the ZB's only had one entry door which was hinged to open outwards and was located on the right hand side facing the front of the train (the guard's compartment normally brought up the rear). The two seats in the compartment ran across the full width of it, facing each other, and 8 passengers could be accommodated. Lighting was by oil lamps, and the ZB's were used on services where the patronage did not justify the use of a larger ZA class van.

The next ZB to be built was a conversion of the agricultural bank manager's van BC 1926 (See App. 1) and this appeared in mid 1927 as ZB 1926. It was followed late in 1927 by another five vans (ZB 10605-10609) and still another five early in 1928 (ZB 10610-10614). These differed from the first batch in that they were fitted with longer wheel base bogies in place of the original bar frame type, and they were rated to carry a 10 ton (10.1t) load instead of the earlier van's 7 tons (7.07t).

A final group of three ZB's was turned out in 1933 to replace wagons destroyed by fire. The vans were allocated the numbers from three of the wagons (1160, 2532 and 3333) and were the last passenger carrying brakevans built by the WAGR.

Between 1938 and 1940 the WAGR's brakevans were reclassified and renumbered into their own separate group, the ZB's being renumbered about 1939, but retaining their classification. They became ZB 202-220 in order ZB 1160, 1926, 2532, 3333, and 10600-10614. In 1938 ZB 206 was sent to Port Hedland where it operated on the isolated railway to Marble Bar.

The rest of the class led a fairly mundane existence through World War Two, roaming the branch lines of the state. The first to be written off was ZB 204 in 1949 after being destroyed in a collision at Wooroloo, and this was followed in 1951 by ZB 206 at Port Hedland as a result of the closure of its railway.

All the remaining ZB's were painted Larch green during the 1950's and they ran in this livery till they were written off, although two vans, ZB 208 and 214 are understood to have been painted in the two tone green and cream livery in 1949. It is not known when they lost this colour scheme again.

The demise of the country branch line trains spelled the beginning of the end for the ZB class brakevans. ZB 203 was written off in 1961, followed by ZB 205 in 1965. In 1966

ZB 210 was converted into a VW class workman's van and in 1968 ZB 211 followed it. That same year, ZB 212 was written off and ZB 215 and 217 were converted into Z class brakevans. The remaining vans were written off or converted as follows:-

1969 - ZB 202 and 219 to Z class brakevans;
1970 - ZB 214 written off;
1971 - ZB 208 to VW class workman's van;
1972 - ZB 220 written off;
1973 - ZB 218 written off;

In 1977 ZB 207 and 213 were written off, and in addition to these, ZB 209 and 216 were both converted to Z class brakevans, but their dates of conversion are unknown.

At least two ZB's are known to have survived. The body of ZB 207 spent several years as part of the entry to Perth's "Underground" nightclub and is now part of "Crafty Marg's Carriage", a craft centre at Gidgegannup, outside Perth, and the body of ZB 213 was used as a store at Westrail's Kewdale freight terminal. At the time of writing it's remains were still there.

VW 5106, formerly ZB 210.   *Photo late Keith Douglas, via G. Watson*

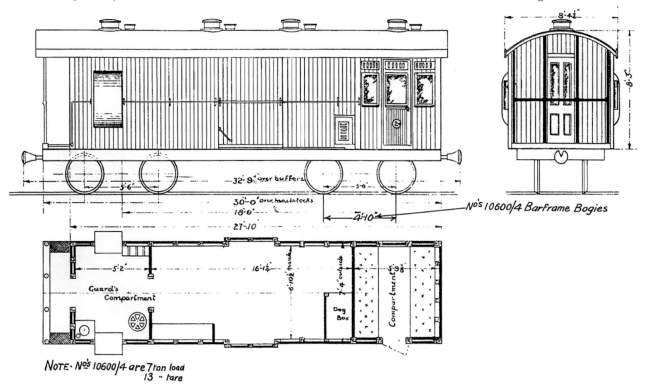

General arrangement drawing of the ZB brakevan.   *Photo courtesy PTA.*

Unidentified ZB brakevan at Armadale in 1944. Photo courtesy ARHS Archives.

The remains of ZB 213 at Kewdale on 17 April, 2003, having spent many years encased inside a brick shed.

Photo Bill Gray.

AZ 442 in new condition. This car was burnt out in 1966.   *Photo WAGR courtesy ARHS Archives.*

In order to bring the WAGR's sleeping car accommodation up to a standard similar to that of the Commonwealth Railways sleeping cars used on the Trans Australia Railway to Kalgoorlie, a new type of sleeping car, classified AZ, was built by the WAGR. The first Reso train of 1928 included in its consist three of these brand new cars, four of which were built in 1928 (AZ 434-437). They were identical to three sleeping cars built for the MRWA late in 1927 at the WAGR Midland Workshops, and a second batch (438-443) was constructed in 1929, making a total of ten cars in the class.

Visually, the AZ's resembled the AY class suburban cars. They rode on 4 wheeled bogies under a 59' (17.99m) steel underframe, with wooden bodies sheathed in tongue and groove timbers, painted in Indian red. Four doors were provided to gain entry to the car, one on each side at opposite ends and two directly opposite each other in the centre. This was because of a new (for the WAGR) internal arrangement in which the corridor ran half way down the car on one side, then changed sides in the centre of the coach to run down the other side in the other half. Opposite the entry doors at either end of the car were the lavatories, ladies at one end and men at the other. Each corridor led past five compartments, all twin berth, and the AZ's carried 30 passengers sitting up, or 20 when used as a sleeping car. Each compartment was fitted with berths which folded into full width seats for day use, a cupboard each for the upper and lower berth, and a fold down wash basin. The AZ's were fitted with the new Stone's water raising apparatus located under the floor, and used to fill the main overhead water tanks. Lighting was electric and end doors allowed access into adjacent carriages, the gangways being covered with canvas concertinas so that the passengers could pass from one carriage to the next under shelter. After the first three cars had successfully completed their trials on the first Reso train, they were put into traffic on the Kalgoorlie trains, replacing some of the AQ class sleeping cars.

By 1934 the riding qualities of the AZ's were giving cause for concern[20] and AZ 435 was fitted with new bogies of a different type to try and overcome the problem. These had a 6'3" (1.91m) wheel base instead of the shorter 5'9" (1.75m)

base of the originals and proved to be a success. The rest of the class were fitted with the same type of undercarriage over the next few years:-

> 1936 - AZ 438, 439, 441;
> 1937 - AZ 436;
> 1938 - AZ 434, 437, 440, 442;
> 1939 - AZ 443.

The Commonwealth Railways sleeping cars had shower compartments in them and the AZ's were further improved during 1936-37 by the provision of this amenity[21]. AZ 441 was the first to be altered and the rest quickly followed. They were also fitted with a conductor's compartment by the conversion of the passenger compartment adjacent to the men's lavatory. This reduced the passenger accommodation to 27 sit up passengers during day time use and 18 sleeping passengers at night. Sometime during the 1930's or '40's the AZ's also had their outer roofs removed.

An eleventh AZ was added to the carriage fleet in 1946 when the former Ministerial car, AM 444, was converted into a sleeping car, renumbered AZ 433. This vehicle had been built in 1928 using an AZ body shell and spent the last years of the war as an ambulance car. It had been fitted with the longer wheel base bogies in 1935.

In 1948 the AZ's were displaced from the "Westland" by the new AH class sleeping cars. The new cars on the "Westland" were painted in a new Larch green, light green and cream colour scheme, and although the AZ's were no longer the principal sleeping cars on the train, two also received this livery. These were AZ 433 and 442, repainted in October and June, 1948 respectively. Between 1951 and 1955 all eleven cars in the class were repainted all over Larch green, which was the new WAGR standard livery.

As part of the general carriage refurbishment programme during the early 1960's the AZ's were repanelled with plywood in place of their matchboard sides and were all repainted Larch green and cream. In 1964 AZ 434 was repainted again in the red and ivory livery for use on the

"Midlander" between Geraldton and Perth. It was also used on the "Albany Weekender", finally being returned to green and cream again in 1967.

On 23 March, 1966 the "Kalgoorlie" was travelling east when a fire broke out on the train[22] and two AZ's (441 and 442) were burnt out. Both had to be written off.

With the demise of the country passenger trains during the first half of the 1970's, and finally the "Albany Progress" (Western Australia's last overnight passenger train) in 1978, the AZ's became redundant. In 1979 eight of the remaining cars were leased to the Hotham Valley Railway, and AZ 443 was leased to the Great Southern Steam Association at Albany. In 1984 four of these cars (AZ 433, 437, 438 and 440) were returned to Westrail and converted to workman's vans, retaining their numbers. In late 1984 AZ 443 was leased to the Australian Railway Historical Society, and in 1985 it was transferred to the Rail Transport Museum at Bassendean to await restoration. Four AZ's (434, 435, 436 and 439) are still with the Hotham Valley Railway and all four AZ derived workman's vans still exist.

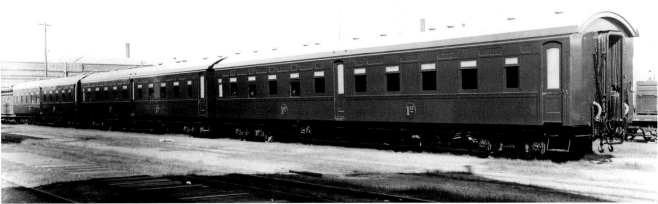

Four new AZ cars pose for the WAGR photographer at the Midland Workshops   *Photo courtesy ARHS Archives.*

AZ 443 at Perth about 1944.   *Photo late LG Poole, courtesy ARHS Archives.*

Double headed steam in the Darling Ranges. The second, third, fourth & sixth cars are AZs.
Photo late Alan Hamilton Collection, courtesy Joe Moir.

AZ 435 at Midland in green & cream, with its crown lights intact.
Photo late Geoff Blee, courtesy Murray Rowe.

AZ 440 at Perth, 7 January, 1967. This photo, by Geoff Blee, shows another colour scheme variation with the green band above the crown lights.
Photo courtesy Murray Rowe.

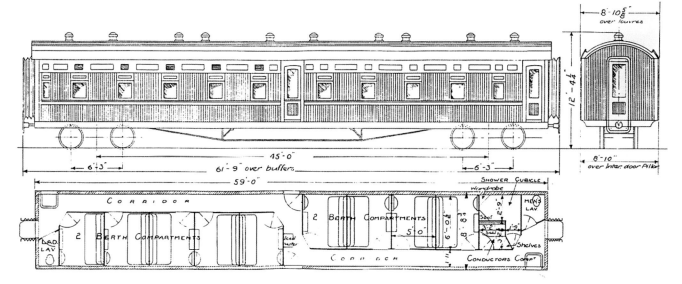

WAGR drawing of the AZ class cars.   *Drawing courtesy PTA.*

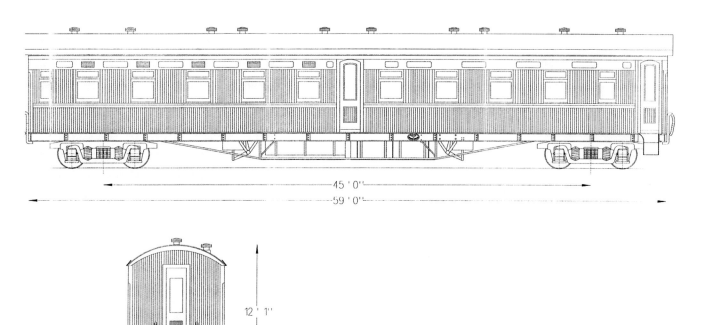

Class AZ

Roger Palmers drawing of the AZ showing bogie & underfloor detail.

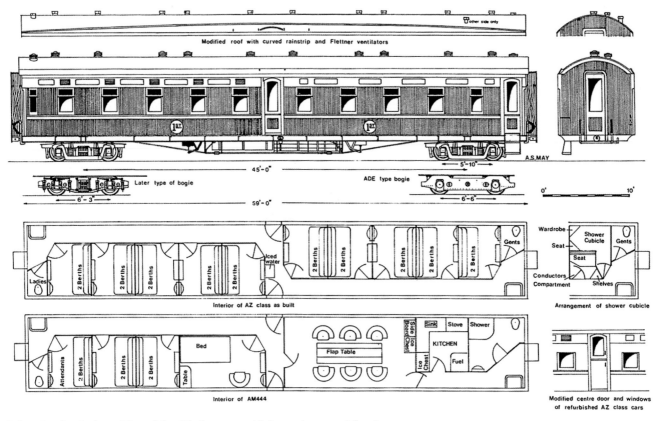

A drawing by Andrew May of the AZ class car with its various modifications.

AZ compartment interior made up for night use (left) & day use (right).

Photos WAGR courtesy ARHS Archives.

AZs in preservation. The Hotham Valleys AZ 434 at Forrestfield 13 April, 1991 (top), & AZ 443 at Bassendean 26 July, 1986 (bottom).   *Both photos Bill Gray.*

AM 444 in it's role as part of the Commonwealth Governments ambulance train.   *Photo courtesy Army Museum.*

When the AZ first class sleeping cars were built in 1928, a new Ministerial car was also built to work with AM 40 and AM 414. Its design was based on the AZ class and it was built using an AZ frame, bogies and body shell so, from the outside, it and an AZ were almost impossible to tell apart. The interior was, in some ways, also similar to the sleeping cars, with a toilet cubicle at each end opposite the entrance doors, and a split corridor. At one end of the car this corridor led past three AZ type two berth sleeping compartments and a small saloon with a bed, bedside table and an easy chair in it. Adjacent to the centre entrance doors was a partition with a doorway in it which opened into a large saloon containing a flap table and six easy chairs, a side board and an ice chest. A door in the corner of this saloon led to the other side corridor, from which entry was gained to a small kitchen and the other shower/lavatory

compartment. AM 444 was fitted with electric lighting.

Following the successful trials of the new 6'3" (1.91m) wheel base bogies on AZ 435, AM 444 was the next car to be fitted with them, but its life as a Ministerial car was only short. In 1942 it formed part of the ambulance train provided to the Commonwealth Government by the WAGR and it was painted white for this role, with red crosses on its sides and roof. It was returned to the WAGR after World War Two ended in 1945, but it did not immediately return to service, being converted into an AZ first class sleeping car and returning to traffic as AZ 433 in December, 1946.

The coach was converted into a VW class workman's van, VW 433, in March, 1984, and was written off in March, 1996. It still survives as VW 433, having been noted at Kulin in 1997.

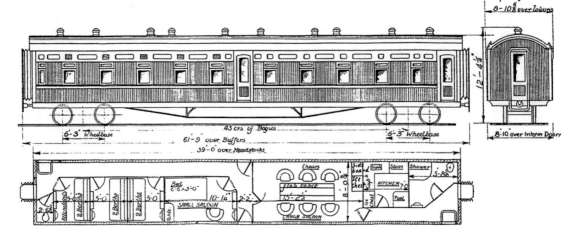

General arrangement drawing of Ministerial Car AM 444.   *Drawing courtesy PTA*

AYL 29 on a tour train in the 1970's.   *Photo courtesy Joe Moir.*

The AYL class lounge car resulted from a need to include such a vehicle in the consist of the new Reso trains and AY 26, built in 1924 as a suburban saloon, was chosen for the conversion. It retained its steel underframe and matchboard body, the major changes being the sealing up of the entry doors, and the addition of end doors and gangways allowing access from other coaches on the train. The gangways were covered by canvas concertinas.

The seats were removed, but the partitions breaking the car up into three sections were retained and in all three sections lounge chairs were placed along the walls, facing inwards. These were not fixed so that the passengers could move them around as far as the limited space would allow. The sections at either end of the car each contained a small table with four chairs, and one of these compartments had a two seater lounge in it. The section at the other end was designated as a smoking compartment. Thirty eight passengers could be accommodated in the car and the lighting was electric. AY 26 retained its classification and, like all the other WAGR cars, was painted Indian red. The first Reso train ran in 1928 and AY 26 was included in the consist, continuing to run on these trains as the need arose.

In 1938 the "Westland" was introduced as the WAGR's contribution to a faster rail service across Australia. This train ran between Perth and Kalgoorlie and, to further improve the service, two lounge cars were provided for it. These were also converted from AY class suburban cars, the two candidates being AY 28 and 29. After they entered service in mid 1938, AY 26 was regarded as a spare and spent its time on both the "Westland" and Reso trains.

In 1942 the WAGR supplied an ambulance train to the Commonwealth Government and all three AY class lounge cars were included. Their seats were removed and they were converted to ambulance ward cars, painted white all over with red crosses on the sides and roofs. By the end of 1945 the AY's were the only cars from the train still being used in their ambulance role. Two (AY 28 and 29) were returned to the WAGR early in 1946 and converted back into lounge cars, this time classed AYL. They went back into service in March, 1946, but their internal layout differed considerably to what it had been before the war. Precisely when the changes were made is uncertain, for although they would seem to have been done at the time of conversion, the cars are noted as being fitted with "ADU type seats"[23] at one end, and the ADU's were not introduced till 1949. In any case, externally they were much the same as they had been in their pre-war days, and they still retained their three internal sections. However, at one end they had the "ADU type seats" which faced fore and aft with an aisle down the middle. These seats were arranged in facing pairs with a drop table in between them. The centre section of the car contained a large race track shaped lounge seat which took up most of the section. It had two tables in it and an opening to allow passenger access. The other end section contained ten lounge chairs, five on each side with their backs towards the windows, and four similar arm chairs which could be moved around. Ash trays were provided in this section of the car for smokers and 29 first class passengers could be carried.

It was not until well into 1947 that AY 26 was also reconverted and reclassified as an AYL, but it seems to have been converted back into the original layout, perhaps suggesting that, initially at last, all three cars were returned to this configuration. The three AYL's were returned to service on the "Westland", particularly 28 and 29 which, in 1948, were repainted in the new Larch green, light green and cream livery for that train. This lasted till 1954 when AYL 28 was repainted plain Larch green, followed by AYL 26 and 29 in 1955.

In 1958 a new lounge car was produced by the rebuilding of one of the original dining cars (AV 314) for the "Westland" and, as a result, one of the three AYL class lounge cars was spare, so AYL 26 was converted, for the last time, back into its AY class suburban configuration.

In 1962, as part of the general carriage refurbishment programme, AYL 29 was fitted with new 7' (2.13m) wheel base ride control bogies, and AYL 28 received similar bogies the following year. At the same time their matchboard sides were covered with plywood panelling which was then painted Larch green and cream. The ride control bogies only spent a short time under these cars, being replaced in 1967 by 6'6" (1.99m) wheel base ADU type bogies.

The "Westland" ran for the last time in 1969 and the "Kalgoorlie" finished up in 1971, both victims of the new standard gauge line between Kalgoorlie and Perth. During the early 1970's the AYL's were sometimes used on the "Bunbury Belle" and "Shopper" services, along with an ADU, these cars being hauled by a Wildflower class unit, but their days in service were numbered. Most of the other named trains disappeared between 1974 and 1975, including the last Reso and, as a result, the lounge cars became redundant, both AYL's being written off by the end of 1975. All three cars which served as AYL's still exist, preserved by the ARHS. AYL 29 spent many years at the Pilbara Railway Historical Society Museum at Dampier in the north of the state, arriving at the Bassendean museum in February, 2002.

AYL 28 as an ambulance car at Mingenew, 28 November, 1942.   *Photo WRB Johnson, courtesy ARHS Archives*

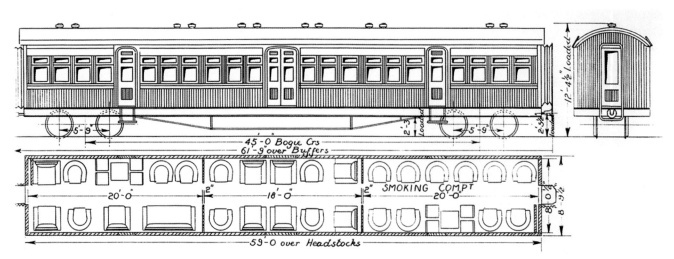

General arrangement drawing of an AYL in its original form.   *Drawing courtesy PTA.*

AYL interiors of the cars as first converted from AY suburban cars.
Photos courtesy ARHS (top) & Battye Library Ref. 284 739P(bottom).

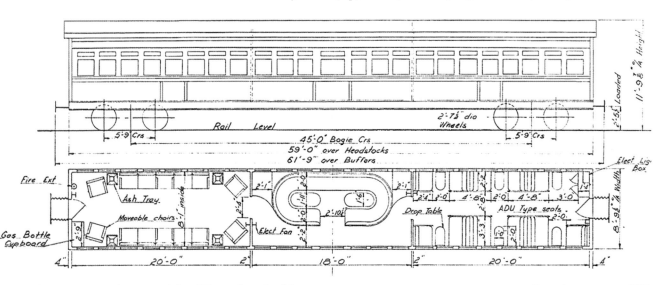

General arrangement drawing of the AYLs in their final form.   *Drawing courtesy PTA.*

Interior of an AYL,(probably 28) showing the colours used in the car.

Photos above courtesy ARHS Archives.
Photo late Geoff Blee, courtesy Murray Rowe (right).

AYL 28 carrying "The Kalgoorlie" nameboard at Perth.

Photo late Alan Hamilton, courtesy Joe Moir.

AYL 28 on a tour train consisting of "Australind" cars & a couple of AYUs.   *Photo late Alan Hamilton, courtesy Joe Moir.*

AYL 29 awaiting bogies at the ARHS Museum at Bassendean, photographed on 26 September, 2003 by Bill Gray

Bath car AG 45 poses for a photo, along with the passengers of an early RESO train.

Photo courtesy Battye Library Ref: 37001P

When the first Reso train was being organised in 1928 it was decided that bathing facilities were required for the comfort of the passengers and so the old AG class composite "Gilbert" car No. 45 was taken into the workshops and converted into a bath car.

Externally, as far as its body was concerned, AG 45 remained unaltered, but on the inside the seats were removed and in their place were fitted five bath cubicles with a corridor running along one side of the car, by which access was gained to the cubicles. The bath cubicles were about 4' (1.22m) square, although the end one was a little larger, and the cubicle walls were made of canvas. Entry to the car was by way of two end doors leading inside from the end platforms, and one end contained a waiting room, or "office". This area had a seat in each corner adjacent to the entry door, a table and two easy chairs. The other end of the car had a box for soiled linen and an iced water outlet in its corners. Although

AG 45 was not fitted with a dynamo, the lighting was electric, the car receiving its power from the adjoining carriage. It was painted Indian red with its number on the side in gold. It was completed in August, 1928 and issued to traffic in October the same year in time for the first Reso.

In 1929/1930 AG 45 was fitted with Stone's electric water raising apparatus, in which air was pumped into a water tank under pressure, so moving the water to the individual outlets. Two water tanks were fitted, each able to hold 107 gallons (486 litres).

AG 45 gave admirable service on the Reso trains till 1935 when it was replaced by the shower car AGS 17. It was then used as a "Governor" class railcar trailer, and during the Second World War worked on the RAAF recruiting train. It was finally converted to a workman's sleeping van, initially for use at Pinjarra, and it was demolished at Toodyay in 1963.

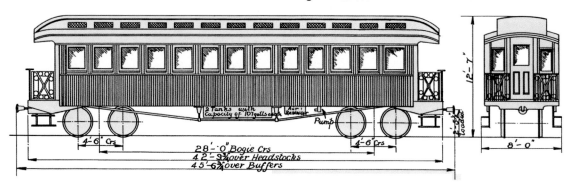

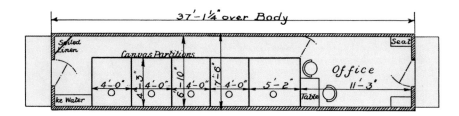

General arrangement drawing of bath car AG 45.

Drawing courtesy PTA

CHAPTER FIVE
DEPRESSION & WAR - 1931-1944

In 1929 the Depression began with the financial collapse of the Wall Street Stock Exchange in New York, the shock of which spread throughout the world, and Evan's successor, Mr. John Whiffing Richmond Broadfoot, was to be faced with even greater financial problems during the 1930's. The only new car to appear in 1930 was an AJ class brakevan, which went into traffic in February before the economic problems really took hold.

The Depression caused the 1930's to be a fairly quiet period in the railway's history. In 1931 the WAGR became responsible for the building of new railways when it took over the Railway Construction Branch of the Public Works Department, but there was precious little money available for new works and, by this time, the bulk of the WAGR's network of new track had been built. Railway construction was wound down, although the lines already started were slowly finished off. The Meekatharra to Wiluna line was completed in November, 1932 and twelve months later the railway between Pemberton and Northcliffe was opened. Lines from Lake Grace to Hyden, and Kulja to Bonnie Rock were also completed during the Depression.[1]

By 1931 the majority of the carriages had been fitted with electric lighting, the exceptions being classes AG, AJ, ZA and ZB, as well as the horse boxes. By the mid 1930's the AJ's (which had lost their electric lighting equipment to the passenger cars) were all electrically lit again, but the ZA's and ZB's were not converted to electricity till the 1950's and the horse boxes and most of the AG's weren't fitted with electric lighting equipment at all.

One of the second batch of ZA class brake vans (ZA 9346) was destroyed by fire in 1928, but the frame was salvaged, and in 1930 it was used for the construction of a "one off" AJ class express brakevan. This vehicle was, however, 7' (2.13m) shorter than the standard 49' (14.94m) long AJ's. It was numbered 260. Also in 1930 ZA 6281 on the Ravensthorpe to Hopetoun line was abandoned at Hopetoun, as passenger services had ceased. The frame was apparently sold for scrap, probably during the 1940's, but the body, written off in 1946, found use as a cabin in a holiday camp at Hopetoun. It was rescued sometime after 1966 and preserved in the Ravensthorpe Museum.

In the late 1920's one of the cost saving measures considered was the replacement of suburban steam trains during the quieter periods of the day with "self propelled coaches".[2] As a result, the Sentinal Cammell Co. of England was asked to provide a steam railcar, altered to suit Western Australia's conditions, and on 7 February, 1931 the WAGR's only Sentinal Steam railcar, ASA 445, was issued to traffic after being erected and fitted out at the Midland Workshops. ASA 445 went into service between Perth and Armadale on 10 February, 1931 and was used 7 days per week. When needed, the railcar could tow an AC class coach as a trailer. It suffered a big end failure in 1936, "under unfortunate circumstances for which the manufacturer was not responsible",[3] and in 1937 it was fitted with a new firebox, which did much to improve its ability to provide a more reliable service. Perhaps these problems, combined with a general lack of finance, are the

reasons why no more "self propelled coaches" appeared till the diesel railcars arrived in 1954.

The onset of the Depression caused a dramatic fall off in patronage on the railways, and demand for the "luxury" type of services, like dining cars, fell even more. First class travel, the demand for which had been falling during the 1920's anyway, was particularly reduced. The result was that many passenger cars, especially first class, became redundant, and a number of conversions took place to better utilise the stock. The dining cars were really only economical on the Kalgoorlie services and this, plus the onset of the Depression, had rendered AV 313 surplus to requirements. It had been stored since 1929, and was converted into an AM class Ministerial car in 1932, the corridor being the only vestige remaining of its dining car days.

Four AQ first class sleeping cars (342-345), displaced from the overnight Kalgoorlie trains by the AZ's, were converted into composite sleepers in 1932, to make them more versatile. They were classified AQC and replaced the even older sleeping cars on other overnight trains. They could seat 39 day passengers, 15 first class and 24 second, but they still slept only 20. Several AW first class suburban cars had been placed in storage, and to put them to some sort of use three were converted into AU first class brake cars by converting the passenger compartment at one end into a brake compartment. Two (218 & 326) were done in 1932 and the other (324) in 1933. Another two AW class cars (327 & 330) underwent more drastic surgery in 1933, emerging from the workshops as ACW class long distance composite cars, with side corridors leading to lavatory compartments located in the centre of the coach. Another four (AW 323, 325, 329 & 331) were similarly converted in 1934, leaving only five AW class cars in service. Four of the old AG "American" cars were stored in 1933, but two years later these vehicles, plus one other (AG 8, 10, 14, 16 & 18) were converted to AGV class brakevans for use on suburban goods trains. They were reclassified ZAG in 1936, and were joined by AG 11 and 15 as ZAG's in 1938. The external appearance of these cars was altered very little by this conversion, but it spelt the end of the "American" cars in passenger service. A final group of three new ZB class brakevans was turned out in 1933 to replace a number of wagons which had been destroyed by fire. The vans were allocated the numbers from three of the wagons (1160, 2532 & 3333) and were the last passenger carrying brakevans built by the WAGR.

In 1934, with the continuing fall off of traffic which had begun in the 1920's and fewer people travelling first class, four more AC class composite cars (99, 101, 105 & ex GSR 183) were converted to second class throughout, followed by another eleven (61, 63, 66, 69, 74, 75, 78, 79, 81, 85 & 94) in 1935, eight of these being former ACE's with the U shaped seat. They were all reclassified AF. This meant that by the end of 1935 there were only seven of the original AC class composite carriages left, and only one of the four ex GSR bogie composite cars, AC 182, the others having been converted to AF's. Six more AD class brake cars (52, 55, 125, 178, 180 & 187) became second class in 1935, and in 1937 all twelve of the second class AD's were reclassified ADS.

In 1935 a decision was made to convert all the ARS second class cars from six berths to four[4] and, to make up for the resulting loss of second class berths, four AQ's were reclassified as AQS second class cars. These were AQ 286, 291, 293 and 294. In this guise they could accommodate 44 day time passengers, but still only their original 22 sleeping passengers. No physical alteration (other than the class designators) was made to the AQ class cars to make them AQS.

In 1934 AZ 435 was fitted with a different type of bogie as a trial to try and overcome poor riding characteristics.[5] These had a 6'3" (1.91m) wheel base instead of the shorter 5'9" (1.75m) base of the originals. The success of the trial Ministerial car AM 444 was also fitted with them, followed by the rest of the AZ class cars between 1936 and 1939. The old bogies from the AZ's were used under other carriages. All six ACW class composite country cars were fitted with the old AZ bogies between 1935 and 1937, so replacing the 6 wheeled units with the 4 wheeled type, and four of the AJ class express brakevans not yet fitted with the long wheel base undercarriage received AZ bogies in 1938 (AJ 362, 363, 367) and 1939 (AJ 364). However, during the late 1940's these four vans were fitted with the same long wheel base bogies as the other AJ's to standardise the fleet.

Despite the economic deprivations of the early 1930's, the Reso trains continued to run and were even improved in 1935 with the addition of a shower car. This vehicle, classed AGS, was converted from one of the AGB class buffet cars (17) which had become redundant after making continuous losses during the 1930's. The new shower car replaced the old "Gilbert" bath car (AG 45). Of the other two buffet cars, AGB 9 was stored in 1936, but re-entered service two years later as a brakevan for suburban trains, while AGB 12 was converted to a survey car in 1938 and the following year was renumbered AGB 2.

In order to replace the platelayer's trolley which ran along the Port Hedland to Marble Bar line when the load did not justify a loco hauled train, a petrol driven rail motor was built at Midland in 1935.[6] The idea for this came from an inspection by Mr. T. Marsland from the CME's Department of a Millar's Timber & Trading REO road truck, converted for rail use at Yarloop. A Dodge truck chassis was used to build the WAGR's rail motor, numbered 432, which was somewhat different to the earlier internal combustion vehicles, with a 4 wheeled bogie at the front and a powered axle at the rear. It was sent to Port Hedland aboard the ship MV "Koolinda", being issued to traffic in October, 1935 and it was classed AI in 1937.

By 1936 steps were being taken to attract people back to rail travel as the world economic conditions were slowly beginning to improve. One of the problems the WAGR had to face was a notable difference between the facilities in the Commonwealth Railways cars and their own, particularly for those passengers who, after travelling across the country from Port Augusta and places east, had to transfer to the more basic and cramped WAGR trains. Having improved the ride on the AZ first class cars, shower compartments were added at one end of these coaches during 1936 and '37. AZ 441 was the first to be altered and the rest quickly followed. They were also fitted with a conductor's compartment by the conversion of the passenger compartment adjacent to the men's lavatory. This reduced the passenger accommodation to 27 sit up

passengers during day time use and 18 sleeping passengers at night.

Even the second class passengers had their travelling conditions improved. They had been introduced to the luxury of 4 berth compartments in 1932 with the AQC's, but in 1935 the decision was taken to convert all the ARS second class sleeping cars from 6 berths to 4. This took place in 1936 and '37, and reduced the sleeping capacity of these cars to 24 passengers, but made them a lot more comfortable. It also led to a shortage of second class berths on the WAGR, so four AQ class cars (286, 291, 293 & 294) were reclassified as second class sleepers (AQS) to keep up the number of second class berths available.

In August, 1937 a new line was opened from Cue to Big Bell,[7] this track proving to be the last piece of new railway in Western Australia for many years to come, and the Ravensthorpe to Hopetoun line was finally closed, having operated on a seasonal basis for some six years.[8] The passenger stock based there, two AH's and a ZA, had been abandoned in 1930.

Two of the petrol engined "rail coaches" had been destroyed by fire by 1936, both at Albany, leaving No. 431 and the trailer No. 433. In June, 1937 these vehicles were classified AO and AOT classes respectively, and were transferred to operate on the loop line between Kalgoorlie and Boulder. Patronage on the Kalgoorlie trains had fallen off to such an extent that these two little vehicles could cope quite well with the available traffic. AO 431 worked at Kalgoorlie till 1950 when, thoroughly worn out, it was retired and written off. What became of it is not known. AOT 433 was renumbered 430 in 1946 and it too was written off in 1950. In 1951 it was converted into a DW class workman's van and it continued to serve in this capacity till it was written off again in 1965, this time for good. The other rail motor, No. 432, was also classified in 1937, becoming an AI class vehicle and it worked at Port Hedland till 1949 when it was sold to the State Saw Mills.

Western Australia's first diesel electric railcars arrived late in 1937, these being the ADE class (446-451), also known as the "Governor" class because they were named after former state governors. These cars were regarded as a cost saving measure, as they were intended to reduce the need for mixed trains. They were given a new livery of Larch green, light green and cream which was quite different to the standard Indian red colour scheme used on all the other cars at this time. The new railcars were also substantially faster than the locomotive hauled trains which they replaced, and proved to be very popular with the general public, but their seating capacity was limited so they had to be used on the less well patronised daylight services.

The first ADE was numbered 446 and named "Governor Stirling". The other five cars, assembled at Midland, went into traffic in 1938. The name of each car was painted below the window line on each side of the entry doors, and as they entered traffic they were allocated to work specific services:-

ADE 446 - "Governor Stirling"   Perth to Merredin, via the mainline;
ADE 447 - "Governor Lawley"   Perth to Merredin, via Wyalkatchem;
ADE 448 - "Governor John Hutt"   Perth to Merredin, via Quairading;
ADE 449 - "Governor Weld"   Perth to Katanning,

via the mainline;
ADE 450 - "Governor Hampton" Bunbury to
Northcliffe, Busselton,
and Donnybrook;
ADE 451 "Governor Bedford" Geraldton to Mullewa
and Yuna.

They also ran services from the Darling Ranges to the coast during the summer, and in the opposite direction during the cooler winter months.

In 1938 five composite "Gilbert" cars (AG 41-45), two of which had been stored since their return from Kalgoorlie in 1933, were converted to operate as trailers to provide extra accommodation on the ADE railcar services. There were few external changes made to the AG's, but internally they had a guard's/luggage compartment and a lavatory compartment added. They were also fitted with electric lighting. Although the "Gilbert" cars, among the oldest of the WAGR's passenger cars, made an interesting contrast as they travelled along behind the latest state-of-the-art vehicles, they were not entirely satisfactory as railcar trailers. AG 43 was destroyed in an accident when it derailed and overturned at Wooroloo in October, 1938,[9] and the other four were coupled to ADE 446-449. ADE 450 and 451 ran alone. The "Gilbert" trailers were replaced by the purpose built ADT class trailers in 1939-40.

Towards the end of the 1930's, while no new lines were being built, a considerable amount of work was being done to upgrade and improve the existing ones, including regrading, deviations, laying of heavier rail, and duplicated track. Improvements in the service also continued with a new express, the "Westland", introduced in June, 1938 to coincide with a nationwide acceleration of the trans continental trains. The "Westland" cut the Perth to Kalgoorlie schedule by two hours, carrying only Kalgoorlie and eastern states passengers, and it was operated almost exclusively by "River" class locomotives (later Pr).[10] The dining cars saw much use on the "Westland", and it was on this train that they spent most of the rest of their working lives. The consist of the train also included a lounge car and, as there was no money for new carriages, two old ones were converted. These were suburban cars AY 28 and 29, which were altered along the same lines as the Reso lounge car AY 26. After they entered service in mid 1938, AY 26 was regarded as a spare and spent its time on both the "Westland" and Reso trains. Thus, the AY second class suburban cars, for the time being, ceased to exist. In addition, the first class cars on the WAGR were fitted with hot water facilities for the first time.[11]

Meanwhile, there was other activity in less important areas. In 1938 composite sleeping car APC 154 was sent north to operate on the isolated line between Port Hedland and Marble Bar. It had its electric lighting removed before it went and, after 1945, carried the load, such as it was, on its own due to the other passenger car, ACL 385, being withdrawn from service and sent back to the main system. APC 154 was written off in 1951 when the railway closed and never returned south.

In 1938 it was decided to completely renumber all brakevans into a separate number series and this was done in order of their existing numbers (which were not necessarily in order of construction).[12] The ZA's and ZB's retained their classifications, but were renumbered, while the AJ's were reclassified ZJ in 1940, but retained their existing numbers. ZA 5843-5857, and 6270-6284 became ZA 159-188, including the Hopetoun van, its allocation of ZA 185 being a book entry

only, ZA 4992 became ZA 158, and ZA 9336-9349 became ZA 189-201. The ZB's were renumbered in about 1939 and ZB 1160, 1926, 2532, 3333, and 10600-10614 became ZB 202-220. In 1938 ZB 206 was sent to Port Hedland where it operated to Marble Bar with APC 154. The ZAG's (formerly "American" cars) became ZG's without renumbering, and Z 9 (formerly AGB 9) retained its full identity. The AK class mail vans were also included, being renumbered and reclassified as wagon stock (P class). By the end of 1940 the renumbering and reclassifying process was complete.

A new type of screw adjustable coupling was introduced in 1939 to replace the old Jones type. This new coupling was a success and all main line cars were eventually fitted with it, but it was not fitted to any of the suburban cars.[13] Sometime during the 1930's or '40's the first class AZ sleeping cars had their outer roofs removed.

Very late in 1939 the first of six purpose built ADT class "Governor" railcar trailers arrived. These vehicles were similar in style to the ADE's and were painted two tone green and cream to match. The other trailers entered service in 1940, and the six cars were numbered 7-12. They led fairly simple lives as they trailed around behind the ADE's, each trailer being semi-permanently coupled to its own power car.

J.W.R. Broadfoot retired on 31 December, 1939,[14] not long after the outbreak of the Second World War in September, 1939, his main contribution having been the introduction of the ADE and ADT class railcars and trailers. Designs for new first class sleeping cars and articulated suburban sets had been prepared during the 1930's, but a lack of money ensured that these remained as paper projects. Broadfoot was succeeded by his Chief Draughtsman, Frederick Mills, who did not have an easy time as CME. With the finances reduced even further, a shortage of manpower, and the Midland Workshops building munitions for the war, the condition of locomotives and rolling stock steadily worsened, while the demands placed upon them increased dramatically. The demand for rail journeys increased sharply, mainly due to the wartime traffic and between 1940 and 1944 passenger journeys on the WAGR nearly doubled, creating a severe shortage of passenger cars. [15]This was exacerbated by the introduction of petrol rationing during 1940. Plans for the production of new coaches were shelved, but a bewildering series of reclassifications began in 1939 and continued into the 1940's. Five AE first class suburban cars (126, 128, 158, 160 & 163) were converted to AF second class cars in 1939 by altering the seating to fit more passengers in each compartment. Seven more AE's (156, 161, 192, 194 & 196-198) were reclassified as AF's in 1940, but war or no war, some people still wanted to travel first class, and the loss of twelve first class cars in such a short space of time produced a temporary shortage of this type of accommodation. Accordingly, three AF's (AF 128, 158 & 160) became AE's again later in the year.

In 1940 plans for a new steel bodied first class suburban car were put into effect. Four AF class cars (64, 69, 95 & 166) were written off and their bodies removed from the frames and scrapped. The underframes were then used to build four new first class suburban cars which retained the old AF numbers and took the AJ classification, recently vacated by the express brakevans. These cars were something of a departure from the normal suburban stock, with steel bodies and curved sides, a design based on the ADE and ADT class railcars and trailers. Like the railcars, they were painted in the Larch green, light green and cream colour scheme rather than the standard

Indian red.

To replace the AF class cars used to build the AJ's, four more AE first class cars (130, 157, 199 & 200) became AF's in 1941, and another two (AE 129 & 159) were reclassified AF in 1942. With these two cars the AF class reached its numerical peak of seventy eight carriages. Curiously, AF 161 became an AE again at about the same time. Why this swapping of carriages between first and second class took place is now hard to understand, but it was, perhaps, a case of reclassifying the best cars as AE's (first class) while those in poorer condition became AF's (second class).

In 1942 composite carriage AC 60 was taken into the workshops, its old wooden body was removed from the underframe and scrapped, a new steel body similar to the AJ class, but considerably longer, was built in its place. The old AC underframe was substantially lengthened to accommodate it and the resulting first class suburban saloon was classified AK, retaining the number 60. This conversion was such that it is doubtful if much more than the bogies and parts of the underframe were re-used. AK 60 was, for all intents and purposes, a stretched AJ. Another car, AF 66, (formerly an ACE) was written off in 1942 and the body removed and demolished in preparation for it to become the second AK class steel bodied suburban saloon, but a shortage of materials caused the project to be abandoned. AF 66 simply ceased to exist, and AK 60 remained the sole member of the class. Interestingly, the AK could carry 109 passengers (including standees), 27 more than an AY and 19 more than an AT, but it weighed a fraction over 19 tons (19.19t) tare, 6 tons (6.56t) lighter than an AY and 9 tons (9.09t) lighter than an AT. It had only a brief career as an AK, being fitted with a guard's compartment in 1950 and reclassified AKB.

The wartime carriage shortage was responsible for the splitting up of the remaining sets of suburban cars running as pairs, because the absence of two cars from traffic due to the failure of one of the pair was something that could not be tolerated in wartime. The five remaining AW First Class suburban cars were fitted with dynamos and downgraded to Second Class so that more people could be carried in them. They never returned to first class status because the demand for it never arose, and classed travel on the suburban system was cut out in the early 1950's.[16] AW 328, 333, and 334 were downgraded in 1940, followed by AW 20 and 332 in 1941.

Two AQS class sleeping cars were destroyed by fire, AQS 293 at Paroo in 1940 and AQS 291 at Pindar in 1941. That same year five AQ class cars (287-290 & 292) were "temporarily" reclassified as second class cars (AQS), this "temporary" reclassification becoming permanent in 1948. Late in 1941 two APS second class sleeping cars (147 & 149) were converted into APC composite cars.

This spate of alterations and reclassifications finally came to an end in 1943 when AE 160 became an AF for the second time, leaving only eight cars as AE's at the end of the war, and the second class brake car ADS 125 became an AD class composite car again.

The four remaining AG class cars being used as "Governor" railcar trailers (AG 41, 42, 44 & 45) were replaced by the ADT class, but the start of World War Two almost certainly gave these last passenger carrying "Gilbert" cars a reprieve from the scrap yards, as they were used from 1939 to provide a recruiting train for the RAAF.[17] In this role they toured around Western Australia enticing recruits to join the air force, but by 1941 the shortage of rolling stock was so acute that all four cars returned to passenger work. However, the age of the "Gilbert" cars was starting to catch up with them. Two (AG 41 & 44) were written off in 1944 after being wrecked in an accident at Robb's Jetty,[18] and by 1951 all four were out of regular service, although AG 45 survived as a workman's sleeping van till it was demolished at Toodyay in 1963.

The shortage of carriage stock during the war, combined with the military requirements to move large numbers of personnel quickly, resulted in at least two unusual conversions to the coaching stock. The first of these involved the survey car, AL 2. This vehicle had been built in 1921 as an AGB class buffet car on the underframe of "American" car AG 12. In 1938 it was converted to a survey car, but retained its AGB classification, being renumbered 2 in 1939. In 1941 it was converted back to a passenger carriage, classed AG, being fitted with the seats from the ex suburban car AY 26, which had been converted into a lounge car before the war.

An ambulance train was provided for the Commonwealth Government in 1942, consisting of fourteen cars (AQ's 339 & 340, AM 444, AV 314, AY's 26, 28 & 29, P 469, 658, 669, 718, 754 & 788 (mail vans), & ZJ 427) which were withdrawn from service stock for use on this train. They were all painted white with large red crosses on the sides and roofs, and the AY class lounge cars had their seats were removed and were converted to ambulance ward cars.[19] This train had a disastrous effect on the number of cars available for ordinary trains. The loss of cars for the ambulance train on a system already stretched to the limit caused the conversion of twenty five V class goods vans to carry passengers, by fitting them with seats. Each one could accommodate 40 passengers. and were temporarily classified VP. The VP's were among several goods vans in which it was envisaged that military personnel could be carried if necessary, but it is doubtful if all were used for the purpose.

Plans to produce a second ambulance train were shelved in 1944 as the situation started to ease, and planning for the construction of new cars started again, but wartime shortages prevented any work being done. The ambulance train vehicles returned to normal service in 1945, except for the former Ministerial car AM 444, which was converted into an AZ first class sleeping car and returned to traffic as AZ 433 in 1946. Former lounge cars AY 28 and 29 were returned to the WAGR early in 1946 and converted back into lounge cars, this time classed AYL. They went back into service in March, 1946, with a very different internal layout compared to that of the pre-war lounge cars. Externally, however, they were much the same as they had been in their pre-war days.

In 1945 and '46 several suburban brake cars in classes AS and AU were fitted with larger guard's compartments to enable them to take prams, presumably because of the post war baby boom. This was done by removing the partition between the luggage area and the adjoining passenger compartment and converting the former passenger area to carry luggage, thus reducing the number of passenger compartments. One AD class car (AD 124) was altered in a similar way in 1945.

Sentinal Steam Railcar
ASA class

ASA 445, apparently newly erected and undergoing trials before being painted.   *Photo courtesy ARHS*

In order to reduce the cost of providing a suburban service with near empty steam trains during the quieter periods of the day, the WAGR purchased a steam railcar from the Sentinal Cammell Co. of England. This vehicle was erected and fitted out at the Midland Workshops and issued to traffic on 7 February, 1931. It was of steel construction painted Indian red and its passenger capacity was 52, with another 12 allowed to stand, making a total capacity of 64 people.

The body was built by the Metropolitan Cammell Carriage, Wagon & Finance Co. of Nottingham, England, while the boiler, steam engine and associated equipment were constructed by the Sentinal Wagon Works at Shrewsbury. The boiler was superheated, with a working pressure of 300 psi (2068 kpa), the vehicle carried 400 gallons (1818 litres) of water in an under floor tank and 1 ton (1.01t) of coal in the bunker. The power plant was a six cylinder in-line steam engine, the cylinders arranged in pairs, and each cylinder had a 6" (152mm) bore and 7" (178mm) stroke. The valves were of the poppet type and the setting of these for the direction of travel and cut off adjustment was achieved by a system of sliding cam shafts by way of the control selectors in the cabs.[20]

ASA 445 went into service between Perth and Armadale on 10 February, 1931 and was used 7 days per week. The journey to Armadale took 47 minutes from Perth, while the return trip was 46 minutes. Other journeys terminated at Cannington, taking 22 minutes from the City and 23 minutes to get back again. When the demand warranted, as it often did, the railcar was capable of towing an AC class coach as a trailer. It suffered a big end failure in 1936, "under unfortunate circumstances for which the manufacturer was not responsible", and in 1937 it was fitted with a new firebox, which did much to improve its ability to provide a more reliable service.[21]

The steam railcar was overhauled for the last time in 1951 and in the process it was repainted in all over Larch green with yellow safety stripes on the ends. It was replaced by the ADG class railcars and was reportedly withdrawn from service after 1954, spending several years languishing at the Midland Workshops in storage, but this has not been confirmed. In 1959 it was taken into the workshops to have its seats, boiler, engine, and associated equipment removed and replaced with track recording equipment from ALT 88. It emerged in November that year as track recorder car ALT 5, and in this guise it spent several based at Forrestfield Marshalling Yards in Perth. In 1992 it was handed over to the Australian Railway Historical Society and sent to Boyanup Transport Museum for a cosmetic restoration.

ASA 445 in two tone green & cream, at Midland.   *Photo courtesy ARHS.*

ASA 445 displaying its yellow & black safety chevrons at East Perth, 26 November, 1953.

                                        Photo CC Singleton, courtesy ARHS Archives.

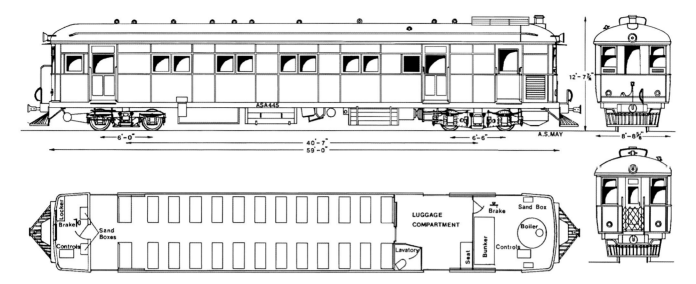

Andy May's drawing of the steam railcar.

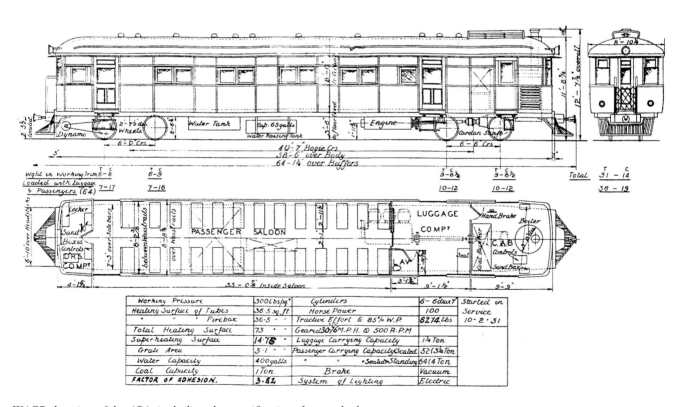

Working Pressure	300 Lbs/sq"	Cylinders	6 - 6 diam7"	Started in
Heating Surface of Tubes	36.5 sq.ft	Horse Power	100	Service
" " Firebox	36.5 " "	Tractive Effort @ 85% W.P	6274 Lbs	10.2.31
Total Heating Surface	73 " "	Geared 30.76 M.P.H. @ 500 R.P.M		
Superheating Surface	14.75 " "	Luggage Carrying Capacity	1¼ Ton	
Grate Area	5.1 " "	Passenger Carrying Capacity Seated	52 (3¼ Ton	
Water Capacity	400 galls	" " Seated & Standing	64 (4 Ton	
Coal Capacity	1 Ton	Brake	Vacuum	
FACTOR OF ADHESION.	3.82	System of Lighting	Electric	

WAGR drawing of the ASA, including the specifications box at the bottom.

The ASA at Armadale towing an AD class brake car.   *Photo courtesy ARHS.*

The ASA was converted to track recorder car ALT 5 in 1959.   *Photo late Geoff Blee, courtesy Murray Rowe.*

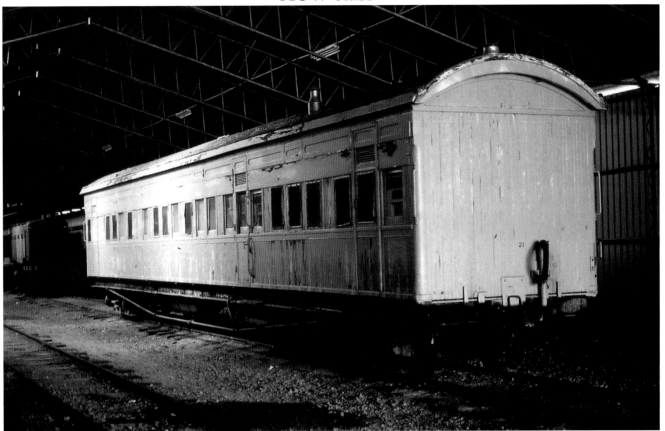

VC 2143, formerly ACW 330 (& AW 330 before that) at the Hotham Valley Railway depot at Dwellingup on 25 April, 1991. Even though this car was converted into a breakdown van in 1955 it retains most of it's external ACW identity.

Photo Bill Gray.

By 1933 the WAGR was experiencing a surplus of first class cars, partially due to a drop in demand during the 1920's, followed by the Depression in the early 1930's. Several AW class suburban cars were out of service and it was decided to convert them into something more useful. Two (AW 327 & 330) were converted into composite long distance carriages, classed ACW, in 1933, the first to emerge from the workshops being 330. From the outside there was little to tell the new ACW class carriage apart from its predecessors. Both were the same size, with steel frames and matchboard sides painted Indian red. There were three entry doors on each side instead of eight, this being the only major external difference, but the interiors were completely rebuilt. The ACW's could accommodate 19 first class passengers and 25 second class and were equipped with Stone's water raising apparatus for filling their water tanks.

ACW 327 was placed in service a few days after ACW 330, and another four cars (323, 325, 329 & 331) were converted to ACW's in 1934. When the AZ's were rebogied after 1934, their old bogies were used under the ACW's, so replacing the 6 wheeled units with the 4 wheeled type. They received their new bogies as follows:-

1935 - ACW 327, 331;
1936 - ACW 323, 329, 330;
1937 - ACW 325.

The ACW's survived the Second World War, but in 1947 the decision was taken to replace country branch line mixed trains with buses.[22] Three (ACW 323, 329 & 331) were withdrawn from service and, in late 1950, converted into VW class workman's vans. None of the remaining cars were repainted in Larch green because they did not last long enough. ACW 325 was written off in 1955 and ACW 330 was converted into a VC class breakdown van, leaving only one member of the class (ACW 327) in traffic. However, this car was also converted into a workman's van in 1957.

At least two ACW's can still be found, although not as ACW's. ACW 323 (later VW 2141, then AL 3) is preserved at Northampton, near Geraldton, and ACW 330 is with the Hotham Valley Railway as breakdown van VC 2143. In addition to these, ACW 325's frame was utilised in the construction of a new Vice Regal car, AN 413, in 1955, and is now preserved by the Australian Railway Historical Society.

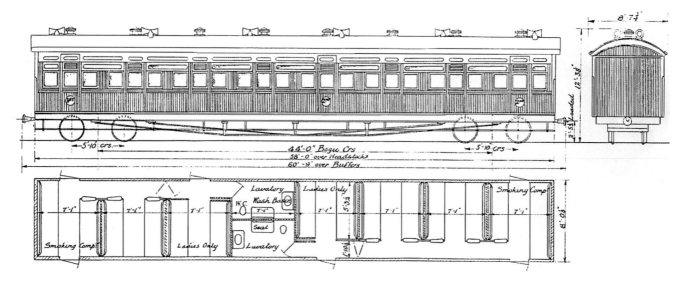

General arrangement drawing of the ACW class car.   *Drawing courtesy PTA.*

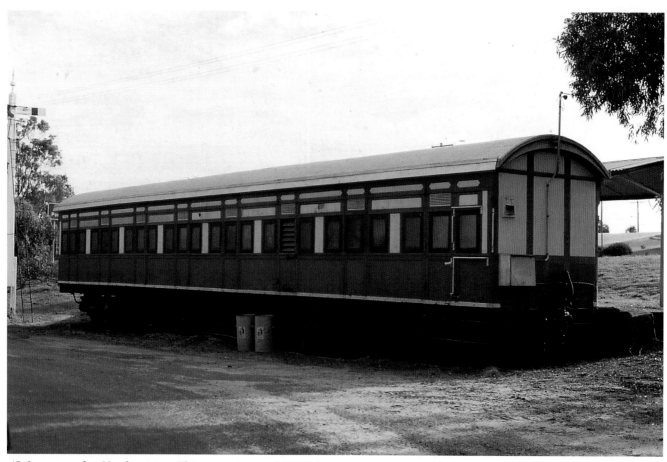

AL 3 preserved at Northampton. This car was once ACW 323.   *Photographed on 22 May, 1997 by Bill Gray.*

Shower Car
AGS class

AGS 22 being shunted out of the Rail Transport Museum at Bassendean for display at Perth Station, on 13 April, 1988.
Photo Bill Gray.

By the mid 1930's the Depression had rendered a number of cars redundant and some of these were removed from storage to be converted for other uses. This included the three AGB class buffet cars (see 1921) and the first to be altered was AGB 17, re-issued to traffic in November, 1935 as an AGS class shower car for use on the Reso trains. As with some of the other conversions at the time, the car retained its body and only minor external changes were made. Internally, some of the buffet car features were retained, despite the complete change of role for the car. The old first class dining saloon was largely unaltered and became an "office", or waiting area, able to seat 10 passengers. Lighting remained electric and the AGS was fitted with Stone's water raising apparatus to fill the over head water tanks. The AGS replaced the old "Gilbert" bath car (AG 45) on the Reso trains, and in 1941 it was renumbered AGS 22, but the reason for this is not now apparent.

In August, 1951 AGS 22 was withdrawn from service and stored, returning to traffic in February, 1954. During this time the WAGR's standard colour scheme was changed from Indian red to all over Larch green, and while it is not known precisely when AGS 22 received its new livery, it may well have been repainted in time for its return to service.

In October, 1964, during the carriage refurbishment programme, the AGS had its tongue and groove sides replaced with plywood panelling, losing much of its character in the process, and it was repainted in Larch green and cream.

The last Reso train ran in October, 1975 and after it, AGS 22 was retired and stored, being written off in October, 1976 when it became obvious that there was no further use for a shower car. Not long afterwards it was transferred to the Rail Transport Museum at Bassendean for preservation, and since that time it has been run again on two occasions. In April, 1988 the old car was hauled into Perth's City Station for display during Steamfest and, nearly a year later, it ran on the Australian Railway Historical Society's Great Southern Centenary tour from Perth to Albany and back between 3 and 7 March, 1989.

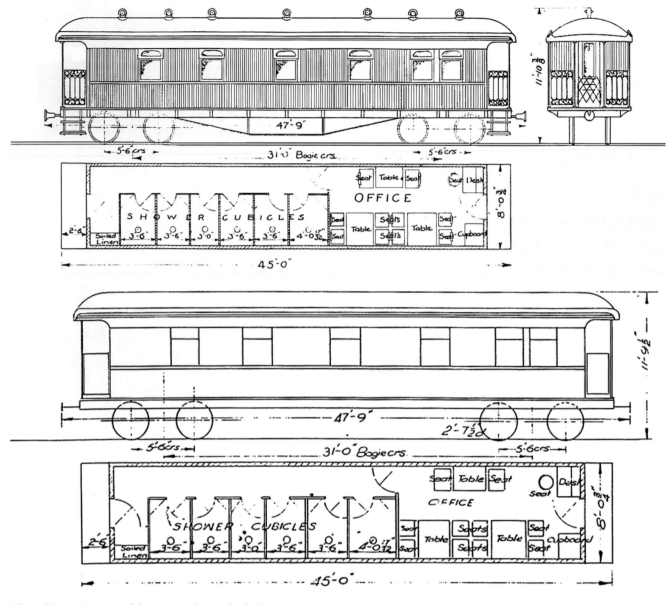

The AGS in it's original form (top) & as rebuilt (bottom).   *Drawings courtesy PTA.*

AGS 22 prior to being rebuilt.   *Photo late Geoff Blee, courtesy Murray Rowe.*

The WAGR photo of AI 432 when new.   *Photo courtesy ARHS.*

So as to provide a service on the Port Hedland to Marble Bar railway when train loads were very light, a petrol driven rail motor was built at Midland in 1935.

This rail motor (or petrol coach, as it was designated) was based on a Dodge K 32 truck chassis purchased from the Winterbottom Motor Co. in Perth. It was fitted with a 25 h.p. 6 cylinder in-line engine, and was a strange looking vehicle, to say the least, being supported by a 4 wheeled bogie at the front end, with a powered axle at the back in the normal set up of a road vehicle. It could seat 8 passengers, carried 1½ tons (1.51t) of freight, and had a fuel capacity of 15 gallons (68.2

litres). It was fitted with a special gearbox which allowed the use of all four gears in both forward and reverse, and it was capable of speeds of up to 50 mph (80 kph) in either direction. Numbered 432, it was sent to Port Hedland aboard the ship MV "Koolinda", being issued to traffic in October, 1935.

When the rail motors were placed in classes in 1937, 432 became an AI class vehicle and it worked through the Second World War at Port Hedland before being sold to the State Saw Mills in 1949 when no further use could be found for it. The Port Hedland to Marble Bar railway was closed only two years later. The final fate of this unusual vehicle is not known.

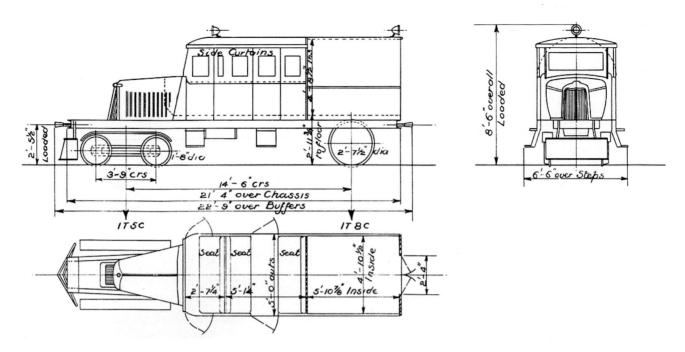

General arrangement drawing of AI 432.　　　　　　　　　　　　　　　　　　　　　*Drawing courtesy PTA*

AI 432 in service at Port Hedland　　　　　　　　　　　　　　　　　　　　　*Photo courtesy ARHS Archives.*

ADE 451 & ADT 7 pose for the WAGR camera at Midland.   *Photo courtesy ARHS.*

The first diesel electric rail vehicle in Australia went into service on the WAGR late in 1937. This was an ADE class railcar which had been built by Sir W.G. Armstrong Whitworth at Newcastle-on-Tyne in England, and delivered to Western Australia in assembled condition. The car had a steel underframe with a steel clad body and was painted in a new Larch green, light green and cream livery, being particularly distinguishable by the "hump" at the front end over the engine room. The car was able to accommodate 40 passengers in seats, with another 48 standing.

The power plant was a Saurer 6 cylinder in-line diesel engine, built by Armstrong Whitworth under licence to the Swiss Saurer company. It was placed across the engine room and developed 140 h.p. at 1400 rpm. A traction motor was hung on the underframe and drove the inner axle of the driving bogie. The fuel capacity was 128 gallons (582 litres).

The first ADE was numbered 446, and named "Governor Stirling". The other five cars, assembled at Midland, went into traffic in 1938, also named after former state governors, as follows:-

ADE 447 - "Governor Lawley"
ADE 448 - "Governor John Hutt"
ADE 449 - "Governor Weld"
ADE 450 - "Governor Hampton"
ADE 451   "Governor Bedford"

The name was painted below the window line on each side of the entry doors, and the railcars were known as the "Governor" class.

As each car entered service it was allocated to work specific services:-

ADE 446 - Perth to Merredin, via the mainline;
ADE 447 - Perth to Merredin, via Wyalkatchem;
ADE 448 - Perth to Merredin, via Quairading;
ADE 449 - Perth to Katanning, via the mainline;
ADE 450   Bunbury to Northcliffe; Busselton; Donnybrook;
ADE 451   Geraldton to Mullewa; Yuna.

They also ran services from the Darling Ranges to the coast during the summer, and in the opposite direction during the cooler winter months.

The ADE's were faster than the locomotive hauled trains and proved to be very popular with the general public. Soon after their entry into service five AG "Gilbert" cars (41-45) were converted to operate as trailers for them, but these were not entirely satisfactory. One was destroyed in an accident at Wooroloo in late 1938, and the other four were coupled to ADE 446-449, while 450 and 451 ran alone. It wasn't long before plans were prepared for six purpose built trailers for the railcars, and these were built at Midland Workshops, the first being ready for service late in 1939. They were classed ADT and were similar in design and appearance to the ADE's, but were shorter and lower than the power cars. The ADT's were painted to match the "Governors" in Larch green, light green and cream, and they seated 36 passengers.

ADT 11 in original condition.   *Photo courtesy ARHS.*

Five more ADT's entered service during 1940 and all six were numbered 7-12. They led fairly simple lives as they trailed around behind the ADE's, each trailer being semi-permanently coupled to its own power car.

Late in the 1940's the colour scheme on the cars and trailers was spoiled somewhat when the ends were painted in black and yellow zebra stripes to make them more visible at level crossings. One car had been trialled with black and white stripes, but it was decided that black and yellow would be more effective.[23] Between 1952 and 1954 all six ADE's and ADT's were repainted in the new all over Larch green colour scheme, the last of then being painted by 1956. They finally finished up in a modified suburban colour scheme of green lower body panels, a red stripe below the window line with silver upper panels and ends, and Stone roofs.

In 1949 the "Governors" and their trailers were displaced from their heavier work by the new ADF "Wildflower" class railcars, and they went to work some of the more remote areas of the state where loadings were relatively light. From 1950 the ADE's were also used on suburban services in Perth in place of loco hauled sets, usually on Sundays.

By 1961 all six power cars were thoroughly worn out. ADE's 446-448 had been retired during 1957 and ADE 450 was withdrawn in 1958, followed by ADE 449 in 1960. However, four of the old railcars (ADE 447, 449-451) were coupled together in 1961 and used as a suburban set, but they did not last long and all six ADE's, along with the six ADT's, were written off as a group in April, 1962. The "Governor" cars were placed in storage at Midland and were still there in 1974, but most were cut up for scrap soon after. However, ADE 447 "Governor Lawley" was sold to the Albany Harbour Board and sat at Albany for many years before being sold to the Wayback Tourist Railway in 1986. On 10 April, 1986 the old railcar was returned to Perth and stored at the outer suburb of Bushmead, but unfortunately the Wayback Tourist Railway did not survive and the historic railcar was left to rot, before finally being destroyed in 1991. It's frame has been stored at Willis Light Engineering in Rivervale in Perth, intended for eventual use under a tram. All but one ADT were later cut up, the body of that one car (ADT 9) was moved to a mining property at Mary Springs, north of Northampton. Late in 2002 it was moved to another property nearby.

ADE 446 climbs the Darling Range just East of National Park station.   *Photo courtesy ARHS.*

A new ADE (possibly ADE 449 "Governor Weld") departs Perth with a Gilbert car in tow.

Photo courtesy Don Finlayson.

ADE 448 "Governor Hutt" at Cunderdin with an ADE trailer, 2 August, 1946.

Photo MA Park, courtesy ARHS Archives.

An unidentified Governor car in the two tone green & cream livery displays the safety chevrons on the end to good effect.

Photo courtesy ARHS.

ADE 451 painted in a basically green colour scheme with white ends & a single red chevron.

Photo courtesy ARHS.

Rare colour photo of an ADE, in this case 448 "Governor John Hutt" showing the car in a green, red & silver livery.

Photo courtesy Bob Bruce.

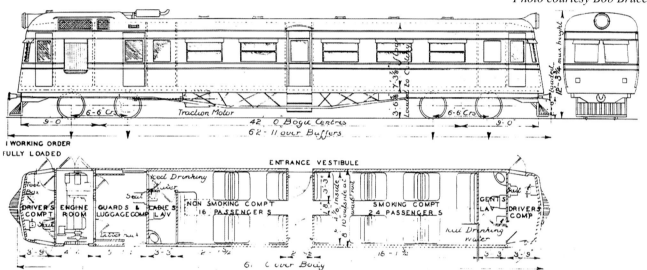

General arrangement drawing of the ADE Governor Car

Drawing courtesy PTA.

ADE 448 showing it's engine compartment (note the grease gun & tools on the ground), & interior.

Photos courtesy ARHS.

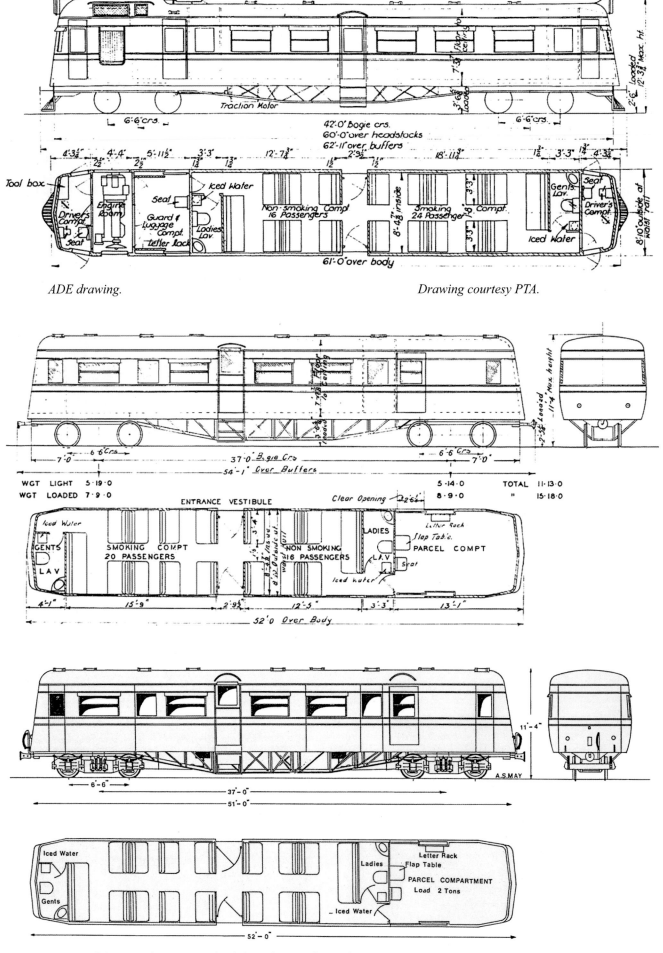

ADE drawing.

Drawing courtesy PTA.

Drawings of the ADT, from WAGR (top) & Andy May (bottom).

Courtesy Don Finlayson

Geoff Blee, courtesy Murray Rowe

Bill Gray

The end of the "Governors". (Top to bottom) ADE 449 & another await scrapping at Midland, ADE 447 at Albany 8 October, 1967 & again in it's final resting place at Bushmead, 15 April, 1989, & ADT 9 at Mary Springs, 22 May, 1997.

Photo: Bill Gray

AJ 64 in new condition.   *Photo WAGR courtesy Mark Beard.*

In 1940 four AF class suburban cars (64, 69, 95 & 166) were written off and demolished, but their underframes were retained to build four new first class suburban cars. These new cars retained the old AF numbers and were classified AJ. Their design was based on the ADE and ADT class railcars and trailers with steel bodies painted in the Larch green, light green and cream colour scheme rather than the standard Indian red. The AJ's could seat 50 passengers and their lighting was electric.

The class did not remain intact for long for, in 1947, AJ 69 was converted into a lounge car, painted Indian red and classified AJL. It was used on the "Kalgoorlie" with AYL 26 and in 1948 it worked on the Wiluna trains out of Meekatharra. In 1950 the lounge car service on the "Kalgoorlie" was discontinued, so AJL 69 was converted back to an AJ class suburban car, but retained its Indian red colour scheme.

In 1950 AJ 95 was withdrawn from use and shopped to have a small guard's compartment fitted at one end. It was reclassified AJB, but initially was not repainted, keeping its two tone green and cream livery. The three remaining cars were painted in the new all over Larch green livery, AJ 166 in 1953, and AJ 64 and 69 in 1955.

The first to be written off was AJ 69 in 1960. The AJB had gone the year before, and the early demise of these cars may well have been a result of corrosion in their steel bodies, a problem which was to plague all the steel bodied cars in their later years, but this is not certain.

The remaining two cars were painted in the suburban green and white livery with a red stripe below the window line in 1964 and '65, and spent their latter years in company with AKB 60 as a suburban set, with an AYF providing the brake car at the other end. Both were written off together in March, 1972 and both, AJ 64 and 166, went to Northam for preservation in 1974. Unfortunately 166 was burnt by the local fire brigade in a training excersize in the early 1980's, leaving AJ 4 as the sole survivor of the class. It is now located at the old Northam Station yard in derelict condition.

AJ 64 derelict at Northam 12 November, 1988.

Photo Bill Gray.

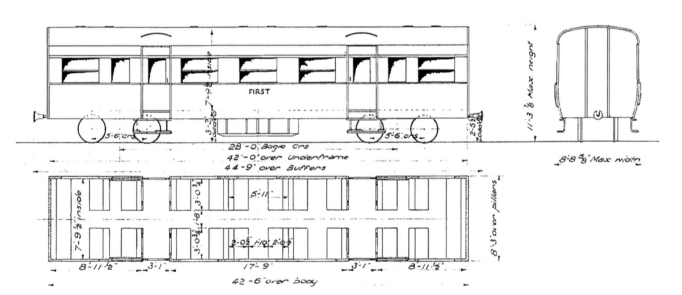

The WAGR general arrangement drawing of the AJ class car.

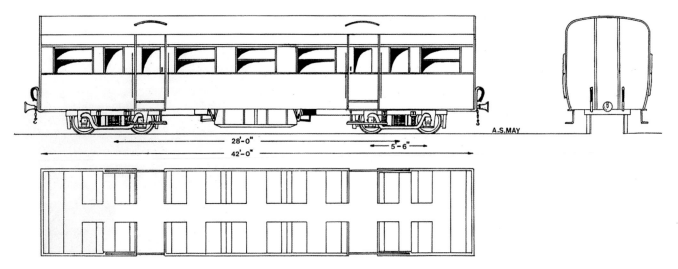

Andy May's drawing of the AJ class cars, showing bogie & underfloor detail.

Dd 600 hauling AKB 60, AJ 64 AJ 166 & an AYB class suburban brake car.   *Photo late Geoff Blee, courtesy Murray Rowe.*

AL 2.   *Photo courtesy Jeff Austin.*

The Second World War created an unprecedented increase in traffic and the WAGR found itself desperately short of passenger carriages. As a result, with the military requirements to move large numbers of personnel quickly, there were at least two unusual conversions made. The first of these involved the survey car, AL 2. This vehicle had been built in 1921 as an AGB class buffet car on the underframe of "American" car AG 12. In 1938 it was converted to a survey car, but retained its AGB classification, being renumbered 2 in

1939. In 1941 the shortage of cars saw it converted back to a passenger carriage, classed AG, by fitting it with the seats from the ex suburban car AY 26, which had been converted into a lounge car before the war. It carried 50 passengers and in 1943 was taken over by the army for its exclusive use, returning to normal service in 1944. It lasted as a passenger car till 1948 when it was converted into an AL class inspection car.

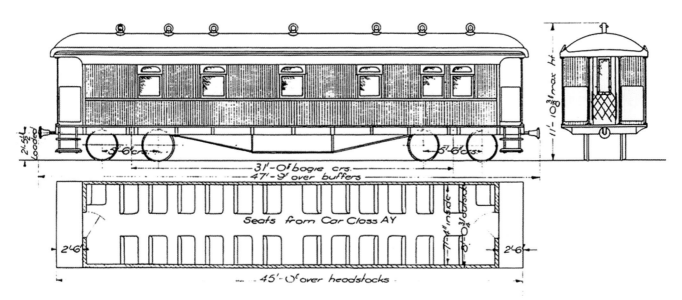

Drawing of AG 2 in it's wartime guise.   *Drawing courtesy PTA.*

Military Car
VP class

V 1885, the last survivor of the wartime VP class conversions. Sadly, it was not preserved.

Photo taken at Pinjarra 24 April, 1991 by Bill Gray.

The Second World War and the associated military requirements to move large numbers of personnel quickly, created an unprecedented increase in traffic and the WAGR found itself desperately short of passenger carriages. In addition, in 1942 fourteen passenger cars and mail vans were withdrawn from service and converted for use as an ambulance train, and to cover this loss of cars twenty five V class goods vans were converted to carry passengers, by fitting them with seats. This was a spartan arrangement, as anybody who had to travel in them would testify. The seats were simply two timber benches placed back to back in the middle of the floor, along the length of the van, able to accommodate 40 passengers. They were converted in two groups, one in July, 1942 and the other in April, 1943. The V vans converted to VP's were as follows:-

July, 1942 - 1865, 1870, 1873, 1887, 2201, 2241, 2863,
3264, 3297, 3303, 3314, 3383, 3386, 3414, & 3417;
April, 1943 - 1885, 2210, 2214, 2867, 3299, 3308, 3313, 3319, 3338, & 3344.

They were temporarily classified VP. The VP's were used on military trains over short distances, which was probably a good thing for those who had to ride in them. Ten were fitted with roof mounted oil lamps, but the rest had no such luxury, with night time travel being conducted in the gloom of hurricane lamps. After the war the VP's were converted to V class goods vans again, and at least one former VP (V 1885) survived with the Hotham Valley Railway. Unfortunately it's condition deteriorated and it was demolished in January, 2003. It's underframe was moved to Boddington and incorporated into a monument there.

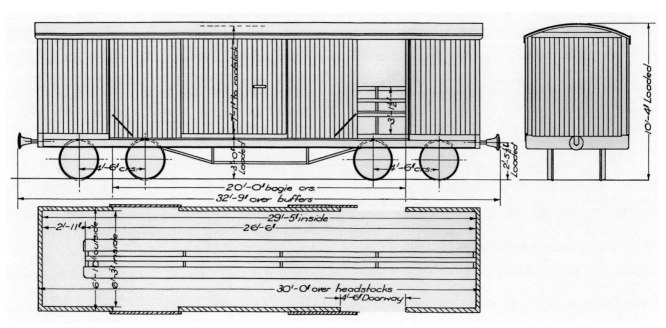

Drawing of VP class passenger van.

Drawing courtesy PTA.

First Class Suburban Saloon
AK class

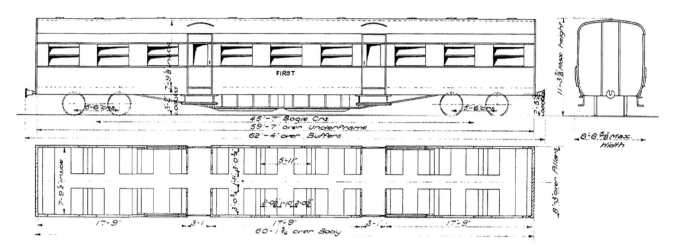

No photographs have been located of AK 60. Above is the WAGR general arrangement drawing.

Drawing courtesy PTA

In 1942 composite carriage AC 60 was taken into the workshops, its body removed and scrapped, and replaced by a new steel body similar to the AJ class, but considerably longer. The old AC underframe was substantially lengthened to accommodate it and the resulting first class saloon was classified AK, retaining the number 60. Another car, AF 66, was prepared for rebuilding to become the second AK, but the materials were not available and AK 60 remained the sole member of the class.

Being 60'1 " (18.34m) long over the body, AK 60 was, for all intents and purposes, a stretched AJ. It was painted in the same Larch green, light green and cream livery and was able to seat 74 passengers with standing room for 35 more.

AK 60 had only a brief career as an AK, being fitted with a guard's compartment in 1950 and reclassified AKB. It survives as part of a house at Gidgegannup, outside Perth.

By the end of the war in 1945 the WAGR was, like most other Australian railways, in a sorry state. The locomotives, carriage and wagon stock, track and equipment were either totally worn out or, at best, badly run down. As a result, a large reconstruction programme was begun which included new carriages, and the first of these was a set of six suburban cars. Surprisingly, these were another batch of AY's rather than a new design based on the AJ's or AK's. Four (AY 452-455) were second class saloons and two (AYB 456 & 457) were first class saloons with brake compartments. The AYB's were basically an AY with a guard's compartment at one end, and the new AY's were nearly identical to those built in the 1920's, the major difference being that the new cars had a different type of bogie. It is possible that these cars were built rather than a production batch of AJ's or AK's because they had wooden bodies, and steel was in short supply.

A second set of new AY and AYB class suburban cars was built in 1946. There were only four cars in this set, two second class saloons (AY 460 & 461), one first class brake car (AYB 458), and an identical second class brake car (AYB 459). The first class section of a suburban train was always at the Fremantle end, so the AYB on that end of a train was considered to be first class, while the AYB on the other end was second class. There was, however, no difference between the two classes of AYB, other than the fact that first class passengers rode in one and second class passengers rode in the other. All these post war AY/AYB class cars were painted in the two tone green and cream livery. Their entry into service resulted in the retirement of a dozen old carriages, including one AC class car (103), (leaving only five AC's in traffic), one "Gilbert" car (AG 45), and ten AF second class suburban cars. These losses in the AF ranks proved to be the beginning of the end of the class, and in 1947 AF 144 & 164 were written off after accidents. AF 144 was hit by a log truck at a level crossing at East Guildford,[1] and AF 164 was on a suburban train which collided head on with another head on in Fremantle yard.[2] AD 116, the first of the class to be written off, was also lost in this accident, as was an AE first class car (AE 193). To replace the first class car, AF 196 was reclassified AE again.

The 1947 WAGR Annual Report made some interesting comments about the provision of services to passengers which, today, would be taken for granted. It was reported that "A new departure which is unique in Australia and which has been developed by the initiative of the CME, is the provision of a hot water service to the compartment wash basins and shower compartments of the AZ....sleeping cars."

Further, "The provision of a morning cup of tea to 1st Class sleeping car passengers on the 'Westland Express' has worked very satisfactorily....and will be extended to 1st Class passengers on other services, notably Perth-Kalgoorlie, Perth-Albany, and Perth-Wiluna. Hot water will also be provided free to passengers on Perth-Wiluna trains".

Finally, "Arrangements for the provision of sheets in 2nd Class sleeping berths were initiated during the year and this service commenced on 7 July last (1946)." The WAGR purchased 5000 sheets in order to provide this service.

The ACL's had been going about their work over the previous two decades in an efficient and business like manner,

little affected by events like depressions and wars. In 1945 ACL 385 was returned south from Port Hedland, leaving an APC class sleeping car and ZB class brakevan there to carry the few passengers who would want to travel to Marble Bar. In 1948 the last of the APC class composite sleeping cars on the main system (APC 146 & 151) were converted back to first class AP's again and this left car number 154 at Port Hedland as the only surviving APC.

In 1946 the first of four Royal Commissions to take place in quick succession was convened, the other three all being held in 1947. The first one was an enquiry into the Australian Standard Garratt, produced by Mills during the war while he was seconded to the Commonwealth Land Transport Board, and the other three enquired into the supply of coal to the WAGR, the Midland Junction Workshops, and the Management, Workings & Control of the WAGR. This last enquiry was most interesting in that it was highly critical of the funding policies of previous governments for the railways over the years, which had allowed the rolling stock to become obsolete, and it supported the programme instituted in 1945 for the rebuilding of the WAGR.[3] It also made several suggestions intended to improve the overall efficiency of the railways, including the employment of road transport to replace uneconomic rail services, which meant that the country branch line mixed trains were to be phased out and replaced by buses. This process took quite a long time, but it was now not necessary to replace a lot of old cars in classes AA, AB, ACL, ACW, AP & APC. As they fell out of use these cars were stored, and many were not written off till several years after they were last used.

The major event of 1947 was the introduction of the "Australind" express for the Perth to Bunbury route.[4] The locomotives first used on the train were the newly imported oil burning U class engines and they hauled a set of six new carriages built especially for the "Australind". They were based on the existing AY class suburban cars, but differed considerably in detail. The train was made up of one first class saloon (AYC 500), three second class saloons (AYC 510-512), one first class buffet car (AYD 540), and one second class buffet car (AYD 550). The two types of AYC were similar, except that the seats along one side of the first class car were single instead of double. The AYD's were staffed by waitresses who served the passengers in their seats throughout the train, but as the service ran down during the 1950's, this practice ceased. For the first time on an Australian railway, fluorescent tubes provided the illumination in the new cars and proved to be a great success. The "Australind" cars were all turned out in the two tone green and cream colour scheme and brakevan ZJ 427 was chosen to be used on the train. It was refurbished for its new role, being fitted with end doors and gangways and repainted green and cream to match the other cars. The first "Australind" ran on 24 November, 1947,[5] hauled by U class engine 651, and then operated once a day six days per week. By January, 1948 the cars were running to Bunbury and back every day.

The AJ class of steel bodied suburban cars built during the war did not remain intact for long for, in 1947, AJ 69 was converted into a lounge car, painted Indian red and classified

U 651 at the head of the inaugural "Australind" at Perth station, 24 November, 1947.   *Photo WAGR, courtesy Joe Moir*

AJL. It was used on the "Kalgoorlie" with AYL 26 and in 1948 it worked on the Wiluna trains out of Meekatharra.[6] In 1950 the lounge car service on the "Kalgoorlie" was discontinued, and AJL 69 was converted back to an AJ class suburban car, but retained its Indian red colour scheme.

The "Westland" also underwent refurbishment during 1947 and 1948. Two of the AY's from the ambulance train (28 & 29) were converted to AYL's, repainted in the new Larch green, light green and cream livery, and placed in service on the "Westland", and the dining cars used on the "Kalgoorlie" and the "Westland" were refurbished and modernised, largely to increase their seating capacity to bring them closer into line with the Commonwealth Railways diners which could accommodate 48 passengers. After their refurbishment the AV's could accommodate 40 people at each meal sitting.[7] The kitchens were also modernised, and they operated with a crew of cook, kitchen hand, and four waitresses. The first three (AV 316, 425 & 426) were completed in 1947 and the other two (AV 314 & 315) in 1948. The cars done in 1947 emerged from the workshops in the standard Indian red livery, but the two cars turned out in 1948 were painted Larch green, light green and cream as part of the new look "Westland" consist. By this time "The Westland" was the only WAGR train still to provide a dining car service.

In 1941 approval had been given for the construction of six new steel bodied first class sleeping cars, but wartime shortages of materials and other resources caused them to be deferred. In 1948 all six were finally built for service on the newly refurbished "Westland", carrying the class letters AH and numbers 560-565. The design of these first class sleepers was similar to the AJ & AK class suburban cars, but the AH's were considerably larger. The first three cars (AH 560-562) were issued to traffic in March, 1948 after their construction at Midland Workshops, and the other three followed in June. They replaced the AZ first class sleeping cars on the "Westland" which were re-assigned to other overnight trains where they replaced the AQ's. Four more of the displaced AQ's (336, 338-340) were reclassified as AQC composite cars in 1949, themselves replacing four APC class composite sleeping cars. The end result of all this cascading

was that those AQ's which had been temporarily reclassified AQS during the war were now given permanent second class status. All the cars used on the "Westland", including the ARS sleeping cars, two of the AZ class sleeping cars (AZ 433 & 442) and the ZJ class brakevans, were painted Larch green and cream with a light green band above the windows.

In 1944 brakevan ZJ 272 had been equipped with a cool chamber for the carriage of perishable goods and in 1947 another five express brakevans (AJ 361, 363, 367, 368 & 428) were similarly treated. Two more (ZJ 359 & 364) received cool chambers in 1948 and the final conversion was ZJ 365 in 1949. One of these vans (ZJ 367) was fitted with end doors and gangways at the same time, allowing access from the vehicle into the rest of the train. In 1948 some of the other ZJ's were repainted in the green and cream livery for use on the "Westland" consist.

The first ZJ to disappear from the system went in 1948. This was ZJ 260 which was withdrawn from service in September that year and converted into a VY class gold bullion van, replacing VY 4999. ZJ 260, numbered VY 5000, was fitted with the safe from the old bullion van. That same month (September) ZJ 360 was damaged in a collision at Mt. Kokeby on the Great Southern Railway, south of Beverley, in which a goods train ran into the rear of the "Albany" express.[8] It was written off early in 1949. An ACL class long distance compartment car (ACL 393) was also wrecked in the same accident. This was one of a series of accidents which plagued the WAGR passenger fleet after the war, the first being the collision in Fremantle yard in 1947. In 1949 ZA 164 was written off after suffering a collision with locomotive G.46 at Geraldton, and the first AS second class suburban brake car to be written off was AS 370, which was on a suburban train being shunted across the main line at Midland Junction in February, 1949, when it derailed and was hit by "The Westland" express.[9] The ZB class brakevans had led a fairly mundane existence through World War Two, roaming the branch lines of the state, but the first of these to be written off was ZB 204 in 1949 after being destroyed in a collision at Wooroloo.[10]

One of the AF second class suburban cars (AF 87), originally an AP, was converted into an APT class blood transfusion car in 1948. It was painted in a distinctive white livery with red crosses on the sides and the interior was completely rebuilt with an office, theatre, processing room, rest room, kitchen, lavatory and shower compartment. APT 87 spent its time travelling the state giving country communities the chance to donate blood, and details of the car and its operations were sent to a number of countries overseas which had expressed interest in it.[11] However, road transport soon improved to the point where it was more versatile than rail, even if less economical, and in 1957 APT 87 was withdrawn from use and converted into a workman's van (VW 2145).

By 1949 the "Governor" class railcars had run almost 750,000 miles (1.2 million km) each and replacement was becoming necessary. Three diesel railcars, each with two trailers, were constructed at Midland Workshops and put into service to start replacing the high mileage "Governor" class cars. Another three sets were produced in 1950, with a power car and two trailers in each set. The railcars were classed ADF, numbered 490-495, and each was named after a Western Australian wildflower, as follows:-

ADF 490 - "Boronia"
ADF 491 - "Crowea"
ADF 492 - "Grevillea"
ADF 493 - "Hovea"
ADF 494 - "Leschanaultia"
ADF 495 - "Banksia"

This quickly resulted in the sets becoming known as the "Wildflower" class. The trailers were classed ADU and numbered 580-591.

The ADF's had a tare weight of 50 tons 15 cwt (51.26t), making them the heaviest vehicles in passenger stock ever to run on the WAGR's 3'6" (1067mm) gauge lines.

The first official run of a "Wildflower" class diesel set took place on 23 August, 1949, from Perth to Pinjarra, when the new train was put through its paces for the benefit of the press and VIP's.[12] Only six days later, ADF 490 "Boronia" headed the first service of the "Wildflowers" with a trip from Perth to Albany. Initially the ADF's and ADU's were permanently coupled in sets, and each set was run on its own specific route. ADF 491 "Crowea", for example, was used on a fast service from Perth to Geraldton, via Wongan Hills and Mullewa, and as the new railcars entered traffic, they replaced the ADE "Governor" class cars and many of the country daylight steam hauled trains. They were used between Perth and Merredin, Perth and Chidlows (an outer suburban service), Perth and Ongerup, and Kalgoorlie and Esperance, greatly improving running times. They were known in the country areas of the state as "The Diesel". The "Governor" class cars and their

ADT class trailers were removed from their heavier work and went to work some of the more remote areas of the state where loadings were relatively light. From 1950 the ADE's were also used on suburban services in Perth in place of loco hauled sets, usually on Sundays.[13]

The strain of the four Royal Commissions took its toll on Mill's health during the last years of the 1940's and he died suddenly on 22 June, 1949,[14] only a matter of weeks before his new ADF class railcars entered service. He had been responsible for two distinct types of passenger carriage while he was CME, the steel bodied cars derived from the ADE class railcar design (AJ, AK, AH, ADF & ADU) and the wooden bodied cars derived from the AY design (AYB, AYC & AYD) of the 1920's. The steel cars, while technologically up to date, suffered in the longer term with corrosion problems, while the tried and proven wooden bodied cars lasted considerably longer. The breaks in the number series between the post war cars arose because these cars were intended to be part of a large scale carriage building programme, and further vehicles of the same types were meant to fill the gaps. A proposal to build two new kitchen cars (AVK) and two new dining cars (AV) also fell through. Mills was succeeded as CME by Mr. Thomas Marsland, and at this time 75% of the WAGR's passenger carriages were more than 40 years old. A replacement programme was badly needed, but the neglect of the previous three decades meant that this would be a huge task.

Although doomed from the start due to the sheer enormity of the problem, the carriage rehabilitation programme continued, and during 1950 approval was finally given for the construction of 107 new country passenger cars. These were to consist of 31 first class cars, 60 second class cars and 16 composite cars,[15] but the proposal was still-born. A credit squeeze during 1951-52 saw the programme deferred and eventually abandoned altogether, so driving another nail into the coffin of the WAGR's country passenger services.

Since the Midland fire in 1909, the composite saloon AX 188 soldiered on as a unique vehicle till August, 1950, when it was written off and converted for use as an office and store at Collie, this being the end of the AX class.

In December, 1950 lounge car AJL 69 was converted back to a first class suburban saloon, so completing once again the set of four AJ class cars, plus the similar, but longer AK 60. In 1950 it was decided to marshall the steel bodied suburban cars of classes AJ and AK together to make up a set of five cars. This set required a brake car at each end and to avoid towing a heavy and, in suburban work, often useless brakevan on the steel bodied set, AJ 95 and AK 60 were withdrawn from use and shopped to have a small guard's compartment fitted at one end. They were reclassified AJB and AKB respectively, and returned to service in Perth's suburbs in late 1950.

ADF 490 on it's inaugural run, near Pinjarra, 23 August, 1949.   *Photo WAGR, courtesy ARHS.*

In October, 1951 it was decided to introduce a new standard livery for the carriage and brakevan stock to replace the Indian red and two tone green and cream colour schemes. The livery chosen was all over plain Larch green, and a new circular badge was devised which was applied to most cars at the same time.[16] In Western Australia a carriage could go up to seven years without receiving a repaint, and so it took a long time to put all the carriage stock into the new livery, the last cars being done towards the end of the 1950's. Two ZB class brakevans, ZB 208 and 214 are understood to have been painted in the two tone green and cream livery in 1949. It is not known when they lost this colour scheme again.

The isolated Port Hedland to Marble Bar railway was closed at the end of October, 1951[17] and most of the rolling stock, including the APC (154) and ZB brakevan (206) was written off on the spot. The only carriage to return from this line was ACL 385 which had come back to the main system in 1945.

The number of AF second class suburban cars in service had been slowly diminishing since the war and the slow trickle out of the class continued with the conversion of either AF 88 or 93 into a VT class track recorder car (VT 4998) in 1951. Which car was actually converted is not certain, but three months later the car was, for some unknown reason, renumbered ALT 88.

By 1952 a serious shortage of goods brake vans had developed and to help ease the situation five AF class cars (143, 102, 78, 157 & 34) were converted into temporary brake vans, numbered ZAF 430-434 respectively. They retained their bodies, but were repainted Larch green, and none ever returned to their passenger carrying role. In November that same year AF 59, the 42' (12.81m) car with the AT body, was converted into an AL class inspection car, also painted Larch green.

In 1952 the metal trades unions went on strike and during this time suburban trains did not run. The strike lasted six months and did a great deal of damage to the suburban services in that

many commuters who were forced to find alternative means of transport failed to return to rail travel after the dispute had ended. It also spelt the end of first and second class travel on the suburban system.[18]

After the ADE "Governor" class railcars were replaced by the ADF/ADU "Wildflower" sets, some of them were tried out in Perth's suburbs in 1950 to see how they would fare as suburban railcars. As it happened, they fared quite well and in September, 1951 orders were placed with the Cravens Railway Carriage & Wagon Co,. of Sheffield in England for twenty two new diesel railcars, eighteen for suburban work and four for country services. The previously mentioned credit squeeze caused the delivery of these cars to be delayed, but they finally arrived and went into traffic during 1954, 1955 and 1956. The introduction of the eighteen suburban cars, classed ADG and numbered 601-618, allowed a complete restructuring of the suburban timetables. The new service was faster, more frequent, and had more stops than the old steam service, and the railcars dealt with most of the off peak trains, although steam was still required during peak periods. The brakevan shortage still existed and some of the AD class brake cars displaced by the ADG's were released for use on suburban goods trains.

The steam railcar was overhauled for the last time in 1951 and in the process it was repainted in all over Larch green with yellow safety stripes on the ends. It was replaced by the ADG class railcars and was reportedly withdrawn from service after 1954. It finally had its mechanical parts removed and was fitted with the track recording equipment from ALT 88 to become track recorder car ALT 5 in November, 1959. In this guise it still exists, preserved at the Boyanup Transport Museum.

While plans were being prepared for new carriages which were destined never to be built, four AQ class cars with wooden underframes (415-418) were removed from service in 1954 to have their interiors rebuilt and upgraded to eight twin berth first class compartments, plus shower and conductor's compartments. Alterations to the exteriors of the cars were relatively few. They were classed AQZ.

Planning for the construction of a new eight car air conditioned set for the "Westland" also began in 1954. This set was to have consisted of three first class cars, three second class cars, a lounge-buffet car and a power car.[19] The carriages would have been fitted with Bradford-Kendall "Commonwealth" ride control bogies and AH 560 was experimentally fitted with a pair of these bogies in 1955. They were a success, but construction of the new cars was repeatedly delayed until the standard gauge project eventually rendered them unnecessary, and they were never built. The ride control bogies, which had already been bought, were used under other older cars.

From the mid 1950's, as if to prove that the old days had really gone forever, the WAGR administration started in earnest to do away with those parts of the system which were not making reasonable profits. This had to be done if only because the general prosperity of the population was increasing and people were turning more and more to private motor vehicles for their personal transport. The replacing of some mixed trains with road coaches was part of this process, as was the partial replacement of steam with diesel railcars in the suburbs, and from February, 1956 the sale of refreshments on the "Australind" stopped altogether,[20] causing the buffet sections of the AYD's to fall out of use while running on the train. Late in that decade "Australind" car AYC 500 was converted to a second class car with the addition of extra seating.

After the ADG's were all in service, delivery of four more diesel railcars began, the first three arriving in June, 1955 and the fourth in 1956. These railcars, classed ADH (651-654) had been ordered from the Cravens Railway Carriage & Wagon Co. of Sheffield in England at the same time as the ADG's, in September, 1951. They were similar in design to the ADG's and mechanically were identical, but were fitted out for low capacity country work with toilets, a freight compartment, a cool room, and hot and cold water facilities. They were used on regional services from Perth to Miling, Wyalkatchem, and Bunbury, and Geraldton to Cue[21] and, when the loadings warranted, were capable of towing an ACL class side door car as a trailer. The arrival of the fourth and last ADH in 1956 probably introduced a new livery for the railcars as it is believed that this car was delivered wearing white upper panels, Larch green lower panels, and a red stripe below the window line. The ends of the car were painted red and white, and this livery spread throughout the entire railcar fleet, eventually becoming the standard "suburban" colour scheme.

The ADG's quickly proved to be extremely popular in Perth's suburbs and created an upsurge in traffic which was quite unexpected, 160,000 extra single passenger journeys per month being recorded for the first four months.[22] As a stopgap measure extra passenger capacity was provided by having them tow an old suburban compartment car, but this arrangement was not satisfactory, partially due to the lack of access between the vehicles, which made life a bit difficult for the conductor whose job it was to check tickets and collect fares. As a result, nine old 42' (12.81m) suburban side door compartment cars (ADS 119, AC 73, AF 99, 140, 160, 167,

197, 200 & ZAF 433) were taken into the workshops at Midland Junction, their bodies demolished, and new saloon cars built on the old underframes. These carriages, classed AYE (701-709 respectively), had control cables running through them to allow the railcars to run in multiple with them, and were based on the AY design, but obviously were much shorter. They were used as railcar trailers and were all issued to traffic in 1955, after which the use of the old suburban cars as trailers stopped. The railcar sets normally consisted of ADG-AYE-ADG. The boxy, almost slab-like AYE's always looked slightly out of place with the curved sided railcars and this appearance of not fitting was accentuated when the railcars began to appear in the green, white and red livery, while the coaches remained green.

The improved services provided by the diesel railcars and their trailers spelt the end of many of the old suburban carriages. Thirty one cars were written off in 1955, including no fewer than twenty two AF's. Some had their chassis components used in the construction of ten new brakevans (Z 451-460) later in 1955, but the majority were demolished, except for AC 76 which was re-instated in 1956, and ACW 330 which was converted into a VC class breakdown van. Country car ACW 325 was also demolished, but had its frame fitted with AZ type bogies and used to build a new Vice Regal car (AN 413). From the outside this new VIP car looked like a normal passenger carriage, although its windows were quite widely spaced, and at one end it had a round cornered observation saloon to give those inside a panoramic view of the surrounding countryside. It took the number of the old AQ based Vice Regal car, 413, and was issued to traffic on 12 August, 1955. Some records indicate that the new Vice Regal car was a rebuild of the old one,[23] but this is almost certainly incorrect. AN 413 saw relatively little use and was handed over to the Australian Railway Historical Society for preservation at a special ceremony at the Rail Transport Museum on 13 May, 1990.

Another sixteen cars were written off in 1956, the majority being of the AT (seven cars) and AU (five cars) classes, but they did not entirely go to waste. The wooden chassis on several country cars, including AR second class day cars, and AQ and AQC class sleeping cars, were worn out by the mid 1950's, so rather than scrap these vehicles they were fitted with the steel underframes from the old suburban cars.[24] The AR class cars so converted were rebuilt as ARS second class sleeping cars and the conversion of the last of these cars (AR 356 on 24 June, 1957) spelled the end of the second class AR sit up cars. The programme took from 1955 to 1957 to finish, but it gave the country cars a new lease of life. In addition, the body from AT 305, recently written off, was placed on AW 20's frame, converting it to an AT with a subsequent increase in seating capacity. It was the only AW so treated, and it retained the number 20.

In 1957 four ARS second class sleeping cars (419, 420, 423 & 424) were rebuilt as AQZ first class sleeping cars to increase the number of first class berths available. The conversions were similar to the earlier AQZ's, but these cars were placed on steel underframes rather than retaining the original wooden ones. The first four AQZ's kept their wooden frames. The second batch of AQZ's was a legacy of the lack of money available for new carriages.

This staged shot from the WAGR shows two ADG-AYE-ADG sets crossing another at Mt. Lawley in 1957. The view illustrates the difference in appearance between the railcars & their trailers, especially with the AYE's painted in Larch Green. The photo is taken looking towards Maylands.

Photo courtesy ARHS.

The decision made in the late 1940's to replace the country branch line mixed trains with buses eventually caught up with the ACL class long distance side loading cars and as they became due for overhaul or repair they began, very slowly, to fall out of service and into storage, many not being written off till years later. The ACW class composite long distance cars had survived the Second World War, but were affected by the same decision. Three (ACW 323, 329 & 331) had been withdrawn from service and, in late 1950, converted into VW class workman's vans, ACW 325 was written off in 1955 and ACW 330 was converted into a VC class breakdown van, leaving only one member of the class (ACW 327) in traffic. However, this car was also converted into a workman's van in 1957.

During 1956 and 1957 the WAGR's track mileage dropped dramatically when 820 miles (1312 km) of railway was decommissioned.[25] This was nearly all expensive-to-maintain agricultural line, but three of these spur lines, totalling 172 miles (275 km), were recommissioned to carry wheat and superphosphate on a seasonal basis.

In 1958 another five AYE's were built, once again using the frames from old AF class suburban cars, these being AF 275, 57, 31, 32 & 273. Their frames went under AYE 710-714 respectively. It was permissible to marshall a second AYE between the two power cars, but it was rarely done because the weight of the extra trailer tended to degrade the train's performance too much. This second batch were identical to the earlier cars and their introduction allowed the use of AYE's on loco hauled sets, where they looked more like they belonged.

In 1958 dining car AV 314 was withdrawn from service and converted into a buffet/lounge car for continued use on "The Westland". It was reclassified AVL and retained its dining car body, end platforms, kitchen and corridor, but lost its crown light windows. As a result of the conversion, one of the three AYL class lounge cars was spare so AYL 26 was converted, for the last time, back into its AY class suburban configuration, making a total of seven AY class cars in service. It had been fitted with end doors and gangways, reducing its seating capacity to 80 passengers.

In June, 1958 Marsland was promoted to the position of Commissioner of Railways.[26] During his time as CME much had been done to rehabilitate the WAGR, but most of the money available had been spent on locomotives and wagons. The ADG railcars with their AYE trailers had improved the suburban services beyond recognition, but the very necessary replacement of the long distance stock had not been carried out, with only piecemeal repairs and rebuilding being done to keep the carriages operational.

Joshua Bradley was appointed CME in Marsland's place[27] and his department continued to plan for a new series of coaches, but ultimately this came to nothing, and the failure to build any new cars at this time brought about the demise of the overnight passenger train on the WAGR. The policy of rebuilding old cars continued under Bradley.

In 1957 the Midland Workshops had received an order for ten new diesel railcars, classed ADX (661-670). The design of these cars was based on the ADG class, but with several improvements, and when the first one entered service in 1959, it was difficult to distinguish it from its ADG class cousins. The main external differences were the double passenger entry doors and the provision of a curved rain strip above each door on the ADX's. Mechanically the ADX class was similar to its predecessors, but was fitted with a larger capacity engine. They were issued to traffic in the green, white and red colour scheme.

Another class of carriage, albeit a minor one, disappeared when the steel suburban brake car AJB 95 was written off in 1959. This car possibly suffered early from the corrosion problems which were to plague the first generation of steel bodied carriages in their later years. Half of AJB 95's body survived on a property at Greenmount till December, 1999, when it was demolished.

By the end of the 1950's nearly all Western Australia's country passenger trains were being hauled by the X and XA class diesels, the Midland Railway was dieselised, and the WAGR was ready to embark on its own full dieselisation programme. The steam locomotive was dying and with it, almost in sympathy, went Western Australia's country passenger trains.

Photo Bill Gray.

Suburban Brake Saloon
AYB class

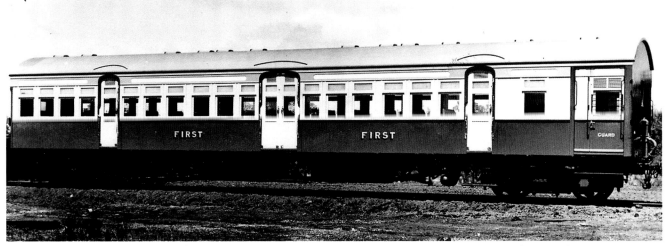

AYB 456 in new condition, painted two tone green & cream.   *Photo WAGR courtesy ARHS.*

As part of the rehabilitation programme of the WAGR's rolling stock after the Second World War, two new sets of AY and AYB class passenger cars were built for the Perth suburban services, one set of six carriages in 1945 and the other with four cars in 1946. Each set contained a pair of AYB class brake cars (456 & 457, & 458 & 459).

The AYB's were basically an AY with a guard's compartment at one end. They were built on steel underframes with matchboard sides painted in Larch green, light green and cream, and were able to accommodate 64 passengers. The first class section of a suburban train was always at the Fremantle end, so the AYB on that end of a train was considered to be first class, while the AYB on the other end was second class. There was, however, no difference between the cars, other than the fact that first class passengers rode in one and second class passengers rode in the other.

In 1952 AYB 456 and 457 lost their two tone green and cream livery in favour of the all over Larch green colour scheme, and AYB 458 and 459 followed in 1955. In 1963 AYB 459 was painted again, this time into the suburban railcar livery of white, green and red, and the two older AYB's were also repainted in 1966 and 1967. It is thought that AYB 458 stayed Larch green till as late as 1970, but by that time AYB 456 and 457 had been written off, both in 1969. The frame of AYB 456 was used to build a large shed at the Midland Workshops, while that of AYB 457 served as a workshops float till 1990. The remaining two carriages were repainted in the Westrail orange and blue livery during the 1970's, and they ran in this colour scheme till refurbished and repainted during 1986. Both cars were withdrawn from use in January, 1991 after spending their twilight years on Perth's peak hour suburban trains, and they were written off the following month. They were both preserved at the Greyhound Racing track at Cannington in Perth, before being sold to Mr. Ian Willis for passenger train work at Pemberton.

Dd 592 with a train of new AYB & AY class suburban cars.   *Photo WAGR courtesy ARHS.*

AYB 456 in green, showing signs of collision damage. The photo was taken at Midland on 28 May, 1967, however it is possible that the car was never repaired, but instead was written off in 1969.

Photo late Geoff Blee, courtesy Murray Rowe.

An AYB in the white, green & red suburban colour scheme

Photo late Geoff Blee, courtesy Murray Rowe.

Dm 588 with a train of mixed cars, the lead coach being an AYB.

Photo late Geoff Blee, courtesy Murray Rowe.

AYB 458, in tattered orange & blue, rests at Perth station.   *Photo Andrew May.*

AYB 458, freshly turned out in green & cream at Midland Workshops.   *Photo courtesy ARHS.*

AYB 459, also in green & cream, but considerably more weather worn, being shunted into Midland Station for the last ever morning peak hour service to be run by the wooden bodied cars, 11 January, 1991

Photo Bill Gray.

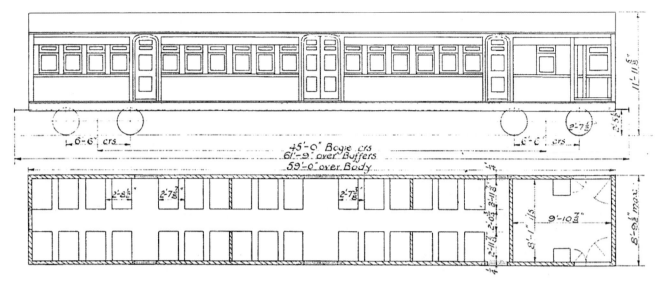

General arrangement drawing of the AYB.

Drawing courtesy PTA.

Joe Moir points out the frame of AYB 456, in use as part of a shed at the Midland Workshops, on a hot summers day, 22 January, 1994.

Photo Bill Gray.

AYC 510 in new condition poses at Perth station for the WAGR photographer.

Photo late Geoff Blee collection, courtesy Murray Rowe.

After World War Two the railways in Western Australia were in a very run down state and much was done to upgrade the system and improve the services. Part of this rebuilding programme included the introduction of a new train called the "Australind" to run between Perth and Bunbury.

The "Australind" set included four AYC class cars. One of these, AYC 500, was a first class car, while the other three, AYC 510-512, were second class, but the two types were similar, except that the seats along one side of the first class cars were single instead of double. The first class AYC's carried 44 passengers and the second class 56 passengers. Their design was based on the AY class suburban cars with timber bodies with matchboard sides and ends built on steel frames. They were issued to traffic in the two tone green and cream colour scheme. Lighting was electric and, for the first time on an Australian railway, fluorescent tubes provided the illumination, these proving to be a great success.

All four cars were issued to traffic on 22 November, 1947 and two days later they ran from Perth to Bunbury and back on the first ever "Australind".[28] The train ran once a day six days per week, but by January, 1948 the AYC's were running to Bunbury and back every day. In April, 1953 all four cars were painted plain Larch green. During the 1950's the WAGR's passenger services deteriorated and late in that decade AYC 500 was converted to a second class car with the addition of extra seating.

In 1960 the AYC's were withdrawn from service and sent to the workshops for a thorough refurbishment. They emerged in September that year with plywood panels painted Larch green and cream in place of the old matchboard, and newly painted and carpeted interiors.

All four AYC's were used on a special train from Perth to Avon Yard, near Northam, on 15 February, 1966 for the opening of that facility, and this was the first official 3'6" (1067mm) gauge train to run up the Avon Valley. Only six weeks later, on 30 March, 1966, AYC 512 was part of the consist on a Royal Train which carried the Queen Mother from Perth to Bunbury and return.

In November, 1982 AYC 500 was badly damaged in a collision at Claisebrook, near Perth. It was thought that the car would have to be written off, but Westrail was suffering from a shortage of suitable cars for the "Australind", so it was rebuilt and returned to service nearly a year later.

The AYC's ran on the last locomotive hauled "Australind" on 14 November, 1987. The cars were then retained by Westrail for hire to tour groups, especially the Hotham Valley Railway and the Australian Railway Historical Society, but they were badly run down and in need of work. The Hotham Valley Railway, believing that the cars were no longer capable of keeping up with the work planned in their tour schedules, purchased three sets of steel carriages from the South African Railways and, as the Australian Railway Historical Society were the only group still using the old cars, the four AYC's, along with the other "Australind" cars, were handed over to the Society on 30 August, 1990, for preservation in operating condition.

AYC 511 in the two tone green & cream livery at the Midland Workshops.   *Photo courtesy ARHS.*

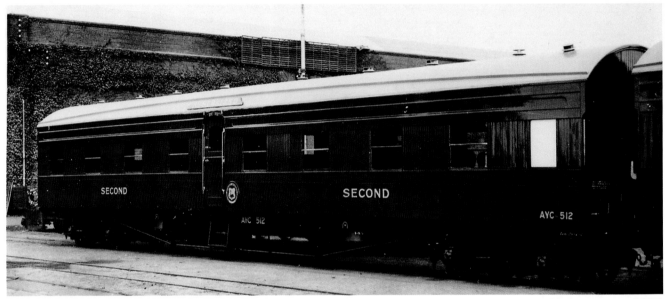

Also seen at the Midland Workshops is AYC 512 in the all over green livery of 1953.   *Photo courtesy ARHS.*

AYC 510 at the Midland Workshops, freshly painted in green & cream, & carrying the "Australind" name board, on 10 March, 1967. Note also the 2ND class plates & the "Mucky Duck" logo by the door.

Photo late Geoff Blee, courtesy Murray Rowe.

AYC 511 at Fremantle, also in green & cream, but much weathered. This shot was taken during an ARHS tour on 7 May,1988, at a time when the "Australind" cars were being retained by Westrail for hire to preservation groups.

Photo Bill Gray.

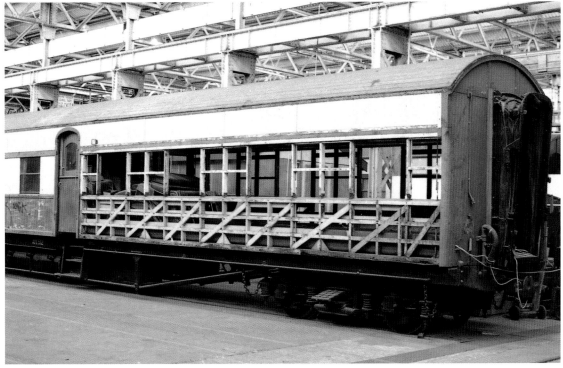

AYC 512 undergoing restoration in the Midland Workshops, shows off the construction of its body framework, 9 September, 2001.   *Photo Bill Gray.*

X.1010 at the head of the "Australind".   *Photo late Geoff Blee, courtesy Murray Rowe.*

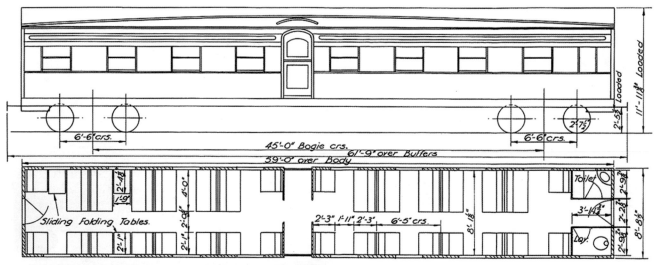

Drawing & photograph of the interior layout of AYC 500, the only AYC built as a First Class car.

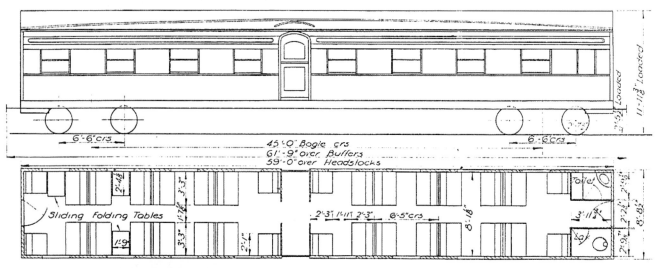

AYC general arrangement drawing & interior

Photos courtesy ARHS.
Drawings courtesy PTA.

A new AYD 540 poses for the WAGR photographer at Perth station.

Photo late Geoff Blee collection, courtesy Murray Rowe.

During the rebuilding of the WAGR after World War Two, a new train was introduced to run between Bunbury and Perth. This was the "Australind", designed to provide a faster and higher quality service than was previously available. Six new carriages were constructed at Midland for the train, including four AYC class saloon cars and two AYD class buffet cars, one first class and one second. These were numbered 540 and 550 respectively and, like the AYC's, their design was based on that of the AY class suburban cars. Externally there was little to tell them apart from the AYC's, except for an additional entry door on each side of the coach at one end. They were painted to match the rest of the train in the two tone green and cream colour scheme. AYD 540 seated 31 first class passengers and AYD 550 could carry 39 second class passengers. Lighting was electric with fluorescent tubes being used for the first time on an Australian railway.

Both buffet cars were issued to traffic on 22 November, 1947 and two days later they travelled from Perth to Bunbury and return on the first "Australind", hauled by the oil burning U class engine, 651.[29] When first issued to traffic the AYD's were staffed by waitresses who served the passengers in their seats throughout the train, but as the service ran down during the 1950's, this practice ceased. In April, 1953 the two buffet cars were repainted all over Larch green, and from February, 1956 the sale of refreshments on the train stopped altogether, causing the buffet sections of the AYD's to fall out of use while running on the "Australind".[30]

In 1960 the entire "Australind" set was taken out of service and refurbished. During this overhaul both AYD's were altered internally with AYD 550 being upgraded to first class. The alterations reduced the passenger capacity in the AYD's to 20, the seats in the buffet section not normally being booked. The buffet car exteriors were repanelled with plywood painted Larch green and cream, and they were trialed between Midland and Spencer's Brook on 8 September, 1960. AYD 550 caused the only minor problem on the trial with a hot axle box and the cars returned to service on 1 October, 1960, the first refurbished "Australind" being hauled by diesel locomotive X 1008.

AYD 550 was part of the consist on the first official train to run on the 3'6" (1067mm) gauge line up the Avon Valley when a special was organised to celebrate the opening of the new Avon Yard facility, near Northam, on 15 February, 1966.[31] The AYD's were first class cars, but in the early 1970's the "Australind" was deemed to be a one class train, so they lost their first class status.

As with the AYC's, the two buffet cars found themselves increasingly in demand for tour train work during the 1980's, being hired by Westrail to private tour operators, notably the Hotham Valley Railway and the Australian Railway Historical Society. The "Australind" was replaced by dedicated railcars in November, 1987, and the condition and age of the AYD's caused the Hotham Valley Railway some concern as to the ability of the cars to cope with the intensity of their proposed tour programmes, so buffet cars were included in the sets of steel cars purchased from South Africa in 1988. This left only the Australian Railway Historical Society as a regular user of the AYD's and on 30 August, 1990 they were handed over to that organisation for preservation in operating condition.

The "Australind" cars in two tone green & cream, that closest to the camera being AYD 540, December, 1947.

Photo courtesy ARHS.

AYD 540 yet again, this time in the all over green livery of April, 1953.

Photo courtesy ARHS.

AYD 550 at Midland Workshops, painted green & cream, 18 April, 1967.

Photo late Geoff Blee, courtesy Murray Rowe.

AYD 550 at Forrestfield Marshalling Yards, 10 June, 1989. The tatty condition of these cars at this time is evident.

Photo Bill Gray.

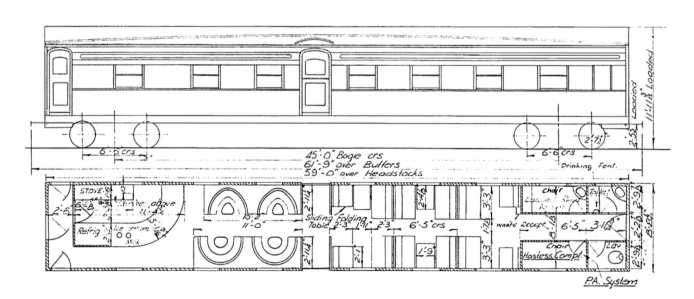

AYD drawings. The top drawings show AYD 540 (top) & 550 (centre) as built, while the bottom drawing shows the same cars after the 1960 refurbishment.
Drawings courtesy PTA.

Interior of the refurbished AYD buffet area.(above)

Interior of the passenger saloon, looking towards the buffet in an AYD. (left)

Photos courtesy ARHS.

Although clearly a posed publicity shot for the WAGR, this photograph represents an era when country rail travel was an adventure, for which people dressed in their best clothes.

Photo courtesy ARHS.

Lounge Car
AJL class

Unfortunately, no photographs or general arrangement drawings of the AJL have been found.

By 1947 the WAGR was well into the process of rebuilding after being severely run down during World War Two, and to improve the quality of some services, the steel bodied suburban car, AJ 69, was withdrawn from traffic and converted into a lounge car. It was classed AJL and initially used on the "Kalgoorlie" with AYL 26.

The car had been built in 1941 on the underframe of an old AF class carriage and during its conversion from AJ to AJL there were few, if any, changes made to the exterior, although the passenger entry doors may have been sealed over. It was repainted in Indian red rather than the two tone green and cream livery it previously carried. Details of the general arrangement of the car have yet to be discovered, but it carried 39 passengers in a First Class configuration of three compartments. It probably also had gangways and end doors added, with its normal passenger seats replaced by lounge chairs.

AJL 69 was used on the trains out of Wiluna, beyond Meekatharra during 1948, but its career as a lounge car proved to be fairly short lived. In 1950 the lounge car service on the "Kalgoorlie" was discontinued and AJL 69 was converted back to an AJ class suburban car. It returned to Perth's suburbs, still in Indian red, in December, 1950, finally being written off ten years later.

AH 564 in two tone green & cream livery as first carried by the class.   *Photo courtesy ARHS.*

In 1948 six new steel bodied cars were finally built for service on the newly refurbished "Westland", carrying the class letters AH and numbers 560-565. The design of these first class sleepers was along the lines of the other steel bodied cars like the AJ and AK classes, but the AH's were considerably larger. They contained eight two berth compartments, in which sixteen passengers could be accommodated at night, while daytime use saw 24 people carried, three per compartment. The AH's were painted in the two tone green and cream colour scheme.

The first three cars (AH 560-562) were issued to traffic in March, 1948 after their construction at Midland Workshops, and the other three followed in June. They replaced the AZ's on the "Westland", and during 1953 and '54 all six AH class cars were repainted in the new all over Larch green livery.

In 1954 it was decided to build a set of eight new air conditioned carriages for the "Westland", which were to have ridden on Bradford-Kendall "Commonwealth" ride control bogies. To test these new bogies a set were fitted to AH 560 in 1955. They were a great success, but the new cars were never built.

During the country car rehabilitation programme of the early 1960's there was little work done on the AH's by comparison with some of the older wooden cars, but they were repainted Larch green and cream in 1961, except AH 564 which was done the following year.

In 1969 the "Westland" stopped running and the AH's were relegated for use on other trains. The demise of the "Westland" was the beginning of the end for the main line country passenger trains and by the end of 1975 only the "Australind" and "Albany Progress" remained on the 3'6" (1067mm) gauge. The AH's were all written off as a group in December, 1975. AH 560 is thought to have been scrapped and AH 561 went to a farm at Dowerin for use as shearer's quarters,[32] while the body of AH 562 is on private property at Jandakot after spending many years at Wanneroo in Perth's northern suburbs. AH 563 was transferred to the Australian Railway Historical Society's Rail Transport Museum for preservation on 13 March, 1976 and AH 564 and 565 went to the Pilbara Railway Historical Society at Dampier, where they were fitted with standard gauge bogies, air conditioning and dark green paint. Both these cars were returned to Perth and were stored at the old Midland Workshops by the Australian Railway Historical Society.

Pr 522 in 1948 with a "Westland" set, the leading two cars being new AH class.   Photo courtesy ARHS.

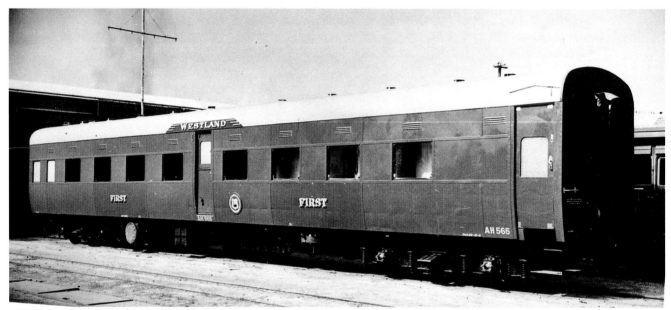

AH 565 in green.   Photo courtesy ARHS.

A favourite location for photographing the "Westland" was the curve just West of the Swan View tunnel. This shot depicts X.1011 leading The "Westland" around that curve, heading for Swan View. Behind the loco are two ARS, an AV, an AYL, two AH, an AZ, a cool van & a ZJ brake van.   Photo WAGR, courtesy ARHS

An anonymous AH car in green & cream, showing the thin green stripe painted above the window line.
Photo late Geoff Blee, courtesy Murray Rowe.

Three AH cars on a "Westland" set being shunted at Perth Station, 17 December, 1966.
Photo late Geoff Blee, courtesy Murray Rowe.

AH 561 showing the green & cream livery, but without the thin green strip above the window line.
Photo late Geoff Blee, courtesy Murray Rowe.

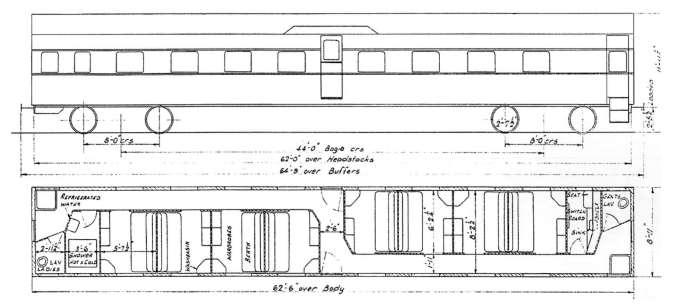

General arrangement drawing of the AH.

Drawing courtesy PTA

An AH compartment with the top bunk down.

Photos WAGR courtesy ARHS.

ADF 490 & two ADUs pose for the photographer near Pinjarra, August, 1949   *Photo courtesy ARHS.*

In 1949 three diesel railcars, each with two trailers, were constructed at Midland Workshops and put into service to start replacing the high mileage "Governor" class railcars. Another three sets were produced in 1950, with a power car and two trailers in each set.

The railcars were classed ADF, numbered 490-495, and each was named after a Western Australian wildflower, as follows:-

ADF 490 - "Boronia"
ADF 491 - "Crowea"
ADF 492 - "Grevillea"
ADF 493 - "Hovea"
ADF 494 - "Leschanaultia"
ADF 495 - "Banksia"

This quickly resulted in the sets becoming known as the "Wildflower" class. The trailers were classed ADU and numbered 580-591.

The design of the ADF's and their ADU trailers was based on the "Governor" class railcars, with steel clad bodies and curved sides. The ADF's had sloping ends and when issued to traffic, were painted Larch green on their lower panels and cream on their upper panels, with two bands of light green above and below the window line (or where the windows would have been, had they had them). The ends were painted in black and yellow diagonal safety stripes to make them more visible. With a tare weight of 50 tons 15 cwt (51.26t), they were the heaviest vehicles in passenger stock ever to run on the WAGR's 3'6" (1067mm) gauge lines.

Each car was powered by two 6H English Electric diesel engines, these having 6 cylinders, an 8" (203mm) stroke and a 6" (152mm) bore to develop 209 bhp at 1500 rpm. They drove two 130 kilowatt d.c. generators, which in turn powered four 75 hp traction motors slung on the outer axles of the 6 wheeled bogies.[33]

The colour scheme on the ADU's was two tone green and cream to match the ADF's, and they were almost the same size. Their bodies were also of steel construction and they had one sloped end, while the other was straight with an end door and concertina covered gangway. In this way, two ADU's could be marshalled "back to back", allowing passengers access between them, and initially this was how the "Wildflower" sets were marshalled. The ADU's had retractable, pneumatically operated steps at the passenger doors, which were interlocked with the braking system, and these were used at those places where there was no platform. They had accommodation for 64 passengers.

The first official run of a "Wildflower" class diesel set took place on 23 August, 1949, from Perth to Pinjarra, when the new train was put through its paces for the benefit of the press and VIP's. Only six days later, ADF 490 "Boronia" headed the first service of the "Wildflowers" with a trip from Perth to Albany. Initially the ADF's and ADU's were permanently coupled in sets, and each set was run on its own specific route. ADF 491 "Crowea", for example, was used on a fast service from Perth to Geraldton, via Wongan Hills and Mullewa, and as the new railcars entered traffic, they replaced the ADE "Governor" class cars and many of the country daylight steam hauled trains. They were used between Perth and Merredin, Perth and Chidlows (an outer suburban service), Perth and Ongerup, and Kalgoorlie and Esperance, greatly improving running times.[34] They were known in the country areas of the state as "The Diesel".

ADF 495 & two ADUs await departure from Perth station. Note the two tine green colour scheme with the safety chevrons on the end of the car.
Photo courtesy ARHS.

In 1952 the "Wildflower" sets began to receive the new WAGR Larch green colour scheme when two ADU's (584 & 585) were repainted, and the rest soon followed. Most were repainted by 1955, although the last two ADU's were possibly not completed till 1958.

By the early 1960's improved roads and greater use of private motor vehicles, combined with a general run down of the WAGR's passenger services, were causing the "Wildflower" sets to become uneconomic to operate on country services and plans were conceived to replace them. In 1959 ADF 490 was withdrawn and stowed at Midland, followed by ADF 494 in May, 1961, and ADF 491 in November, 1964. In 1961 a proposal was put forth to convert two of the ADF's into shunting units, but this idea was not proceeded with.[35] They were withdrawn from service one at a time, the final "Diesel" service being operated from Merredin to Perth on 9 September, 1963, with ADF 492 towing trailers ADU 589 and 591. The "Wildflower's's" work was taken over

by road coaches. Despite the demise of the daylight country passenger trains in the Northern, Eastern and Central areas of the state, the "Wildflower" sets still had plenty of life left in them. Another proposal in 1964 to convert two ADF's into brakevans came to nothing,[36] but one of the cars, ADF 490, was rebuilt as a VI class locomotive instruction van in November, 1964, apparently having been out of service since 1959.

As part of the overall improvement of the WAGR's passenger services under Commissioner Wayne, two new trains were introduced in 1964 utilising the ADF power cars and the ADU class trailers. These were the "Bunbury Belle" and the "Shopper", which operated between Perth and Bunbury. ADF 492, 493 and 495 were modified to allow multiple unit working and were repainted in the green, white and red railcar colour scheme from 1964. ADU 588-591 were refurbished for use on the "Shopper" and "Bunbury Belle", with two of these cars (ADU 588 &

A new ADU 580 Wildflower trailer with another.
Photo courtesy ARHS.

589) losing their sloping ends and guard's compartments. They remained the same length, but the passenger capacity was reduced to 56, and the area freed held vending machines for the sale of cigarettes, cool drinks, sandwiches and confectionary. ADU 590 and 591 were not altered in this way, for the normal consist on these trains was four ADU's with an ADF at each end. All four cars were repainted in the suburban livery of green, white and red to match the ADF's, and the first of the "Bunbury Belle/Shopper" services ran on 1 June, 1964.[37]

Two of the redundant ADU's (580 & 581) were converted for use on loco hauled trains in 1964 and were classified AYU, followed by another two cars (584 & 585) in 1966, while ADU 582 and 583 were written off that same year., It is doubtful that ADU 586 and 587 were much used after this time. The steel construction of these vars proved to be a weak point and corrosion was, towards the end of their lives, becoming a serious problem. ADF 494 was written off in 1970 after several years out of use and ADF 491 followed in 1971, in similar circumstances.

The "Bunbury Belle" and "Shopper" did not miss out during the dismantling of Western Australia's country passenger train services in the 1970's, and the last one ran on 1 August, 1975, being replaced by road coaches. The ADF's and ADU's had one final fling two weeks later when, on 16 August, 1975, the Australian railway historical Society ran a tour to Pinjarra and back. Appropriately, Pinjarra was the last country station visited by an ADF, because it was also the first, one week short of twenty six years earlier.

The three ADF's (492, 493 & 495) and the remaining ADU's (586-591) were written off as a group on 27 October, 1975. Due to their corrosion problems all but one of the ADU's were scrapped, as were ADF 492 and 493. However, ADF 495 was saved for preservation and was shunted into the Rail Transport Museum at Bassendean on 30 January, 1976. The bodies of ADF 490 (later VI 7980) and the four AYU's (converted from ADU's) were sold to Metana Minerals at Mount Magnet, where they were used as a generator room (the ADF) and accommodation cabins (the AYU's). Their remains are still there, although one of the AYU's has been placed in the Mount Magnet Museum. The body of an ADU is located near Seabird, north of Perth.

ADF 494 "Leschanaultia" at Perth station. The car is painted all over green with the yellow & black safety chevrons on the ends.   *Photo courtesy ARHS.*

ADF 494 & two ADU's roll out of Perth Station. The livery consisted of the all over green, but the front of the ADF was red & white.   *Photo courtesy Battye Library 284 737P.*

A portrait of ADF 492 in the green, white & red livery at East Perth, 4 July, 1966. There were a number of minor differences between the individual Wildflower cars in this livery, noteably in the position of the road number on the front.

Photo late Geoff Blee, courtesy Murray Rowe.

ADF 492 & two ADUs on a Shopper service.   *Photo late Geoff Blee, courtesy Murray Rowe.*

Portrait of an ADU at Midland, rebuilt with straight ends for the "Shopper" & "Bunbury Belle" services.

Photo late Geoff Blee, courtesy Murray Rowe.

ADU 588 at Perth station on 25 April, 1967. This was the first passenger car in Australia to carry a "Vendomatic" automatic vending machine.

Photo late Geoff Blee, courtesy Murray Rowe.

ADF 492 displaying the "Bunbury Belle" headboard. Note the position of the road number as compared to the previous photos of this car.
Photo late Geoff Blee, courtesy Murray Rowe.

An overhead view of ADF 495 at the head of two "Wildflower" sets at Perth station.
Photo late Geoff Blee, courtesy Murray Rowe.

ADF 492 showing the road number painted on twice. Taken at Perth station.   *Photo ARHS.*

ADF 493 with its train in the Darling Ranges.   *Photo late Geoff Blee, courtesy Murray Rowe.*

ADF 493 towing an AYE suburban car & an ADU.

Photo late Geoff Blee, courtesy Murray Rowe

ADF 494 with a four car set & carrying the "Bunbury Belle" headboard.   *Photo courtesy ARHS.*

ADF 492.   *Photo late Geoff Blee, courtesy Murray Rowe.*

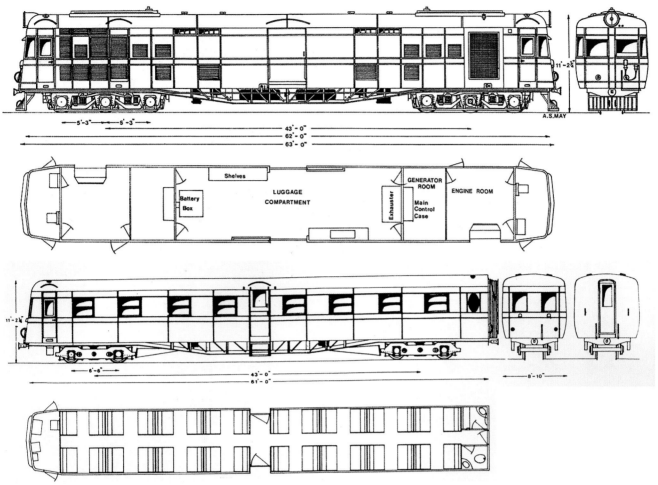

Andy May's drawings of the ADF, & the ADU as built.

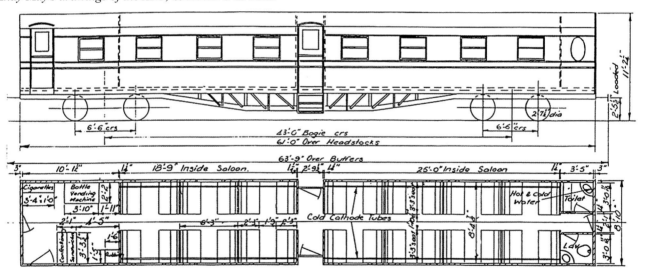

Drawing of ADU 588 & 589 as rebuilt for the "Shopper" & "Bunbury Belle".   Drawing courtesy PTA.

Interior of an ADU.

Photo courtesy ARHS.

Many railway modelers would say there is a prototype for everything, & these photos of ADFs towing a variety of coaches seem to prove it.

An ADF rolls down through the Darling Ranges towing two AD's & what appears to be an AE class car.

Photo courtesy Malcolm Searle.

ADF 492 sits at Perth station with an ADU & an AYL.   *Photo courtesy Don Finlayson.*

ADF 495 with an AYL & an ADU or AYU. The number painted on the ADFs nose has been painted in a smaller font over the previous number.

Photo late Alan Hamilton, courtesy Joe Moir.

AJB class

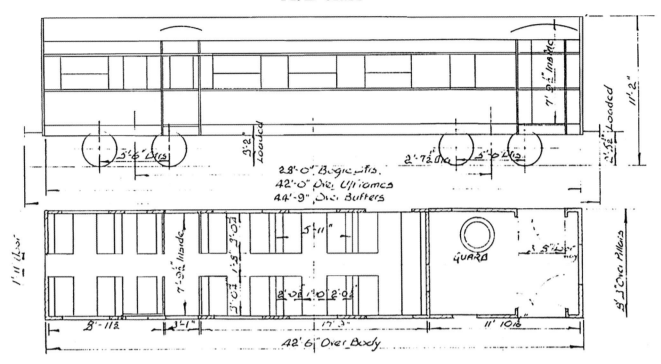

General arrangement drawing of AJB 95.   *Drawing courtesy PTA.*

In December, 1950 the set of four steel bodied AJ class cars, plus the similar, but longer AK 60, was complete again, and it was decided to use them as a suburban set. Such sets required brake cars, so one AJ and the AK were converted to brake cars. The AJ chosen was No. 95 and it was classed AJB. This was done by fitting a guard's compartment into one end of the car, and when complete the AJB could seat 37 passengers. The external dimensions of the car remained unchanged. It retained its two tone green and cream colour scheme. Apart from the resulting difference in door and window arrangement, the car remained similar in appearance to its AJ class brethren.

AJB 95 did not retain its green and cream livery for long, being repainted in all over Larch green in 1952, but its time as an AJB was only brief. It was written off in 1959, possibly suffering early from the corrosion problems which were to plague the first generation of steel bodied carriages in their later years. It was sold privately, and part of its body survived on a property at Greenmount till December, 1999, when the rusting remains were demolished and removed.

The wreck of AJB 95 wreck at Greenmount, 2 May, 1995. This historic relic was demolished at Christmas time, 1999.
Photo Bill Gray.

AKB class

AKB 60 crossing the timber trestle bridge at Clackline, 22 July, 1967.   *Photo late Geoff Blee, courtesy Murray Rowe.*

In 1950 it was decided to marshall the steel bodied suburban cars of classes AJ and AK together to make up a set of five cars. This set required a brake car at each end and one of the AJ's (95) and AK 60 were chosen for conversion.

AK 60 had been built eight years earlier on the lengthened underframe of the old wooden suburban car AF 60. It was of steel construction, and the addition of the guard's compartment was done in a similar fashion to that fitted to AJB 95. Passenger seating was reduced to 57 first class, and the car was reclassified AKB.

AKB 60 returned to service in Perth's suburbs in late 1950, and it retained its two tone green and cream colour scheme till 1953, when it was repainted plain Larch green. In 1959 AJB 95 was written off, followed by AJ 69 in 1960, and this left only AKB 60 and two AJ's.

In 1967 the car was repainted in the suburban railcar livery of green and white with a red stripe, being the last of the steel suburban cars to receive the new livery. About this time one of the newly converted AYF brake cars joined the set, and this consist ran till June, 1971, when AKB 60 was written off. It sat at Midland for many years and was offered to the Pinjarra Steam & Hills Railway Preservation Society (later the Hotham Valley Railway), but it was not taken up. About 1977 it was sold privately and is now part of a house on a rural property at Gidgegannup, outside Perth.

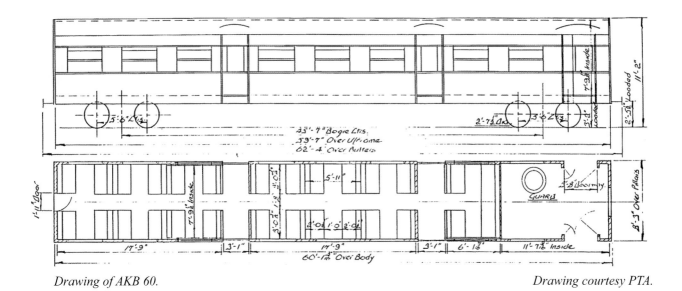

Drawing of AKB 60.   *Drawing courtesy PTA.*

Dd 599 with a suburban train consisting of AKB 60, two AJ class cars & an AS brake car, 26 September, 1967. The AKB had only just been repainted from all over Larch Green. *Photo late Geoff Blee, courtesy Murray Rowe.*

ADG class

ADG 601 as it entered service.   *Photo courtesy Battye Library 284 736P.*

Some of the surplus ADE "Governor" class railcars were trialed on Perth's suburban services in 1950 as suburban railcars.[38] The trial was declared a success and in September, 1951 orders were placed with the Cravens Railway Carriage & Wagon Co,. of Sheffield in England for twenty two new diesel railcars, eighteen for suburban work and four for country services. The eighteen suburban cars, classed ADG and numbered 601-618, arrived in 1954 and their introduction allowed a complete restructuring of the suburban timetables, in which steam was mainly required during peak periods, more stops were made, and there were more services with shorter journey times.

The ADG's were of steel construction, with a steel underframe and welded body, and they were painted Larch green, while the roof was coloured Stone. The ends carried black and yellow chevrons for safety. The seats supplied with the cars had throw over backs, but these were later replaced by fixed back seats. The ADG's had seating for 62 passengers with another 48 accommodated standing up.

Power was provided by two AEC 9.6 litre 6 cylinder diesel engines mounted horizontally under the floor of the car, each developing 125 bhp. The engine power was transmitted to the inner axle on each bogie via a fluid flywheel, a 4 speed pre-select epicyclic gearbox and a reduction gear.[39]

The ADG's quickly proved to be extremely popular and in the early days extra passenger capacity was provided by having them tow an old suburban compartment car, but this arrangement was not satisfactory, leading to the building of the AYE class trailers in 1955. This allowed the railcar sets to be run with an AYE in between the ADG's.

In the mid 1950's the black and yellow chevrons painted on

the ends of the cars were replaced with silver, trimmed in red, and by 1958 the suburban livery of green lower panels, white upper panels and a red waist band was beginning to appear on these cars. They had all been repainted in this livery by the mid 1960's. During the 1960's the cars were fitted with a destination box in the driver's cab above the gangway doors, and later they received a steel sun visor over the top of the driver's window, giving them a curious one-eyed look.

From 1963-64 the ADG's were fitted with superchargers to increase their power, as they were having trouble keeping up with the higher powered ADX class cars.[40] To further improve their performance they were fitted with Voith transmissions, the first being done in 1969. This was essentially an automatic gearbox and did much to make the driver's task simpler, but it also required modification to the control gear in the trailers. The ADG's with the Voith transmissions were temporarily reclassified ADG/V, a classification which became permanent in October, 1978. The cars were all converted between 1969 and 1973.

In 1975 the WAGR adopted the name "Westrail" as part of a new corporate image, and the ADG/V class cars were repainted in a new orange and blue livery, starting with ADG/V 605 in 1975. The last one was completed in 1979.

ADG/V 605 was withdrawn from service and stored in September, 1982, partially as a result of the closure of passenger services on the Fremantle line a couple of years earlier, but mainly because of the delivery of the new ADL/ADC railcar sets. However, suburban services resumed on the Fremantle line in July,1983,[41] and it was returned to traffic at that time.

In 1982 a bewildering series of car number changes took place within the class, the reason for which has been the subject of much discussion and debate. The "WAGR Register of Locomotive, Wagon, Carriage & Brakevan Stock" carries the following note:

"Between 1982 and 1984 the following ADG/V railcars were renumbered, utilising written off unit 616, to enable a more efficient turn around of cars undergoing general overhauls:-
616 to 612, 612 to 615, 615 to 603, 603 to 614, 614 to 602, 602 to 618, 618 to 606, 606 to 601."

Quite what this means is a bit uncertain and does little to explain why the renumbering was required. For a time it was believed that some cars had had their bodies and underframes separated, the best bodies placed on the best frames, and the new car taking on the number of the frame, but this is now thought to be unlikely. Another, possibly more plausible theory is that a small number of cars were stored and had had parts removed to keep others going. An instruction to return ADG/V 612 to traffic would have created something of a problem if that particular car had been badly cannibalized, so ADG/V 616, possibly in better condition, might have been renumbered 612 and returned to service. This would have left two ADG/V 612's in the system, so the "real" 612 was overhauled, renumbered 615, put back into traffic, and so on. One of the problems with this theory is that ADG/V 616 was not written off till November, 1983. Another problem is that both 616 and the real ADG/V 601 would need to have been written off. This may well have been done, since, some seven years later, sixteen of the original eighteen cars were still in service. Records indicate that the renumbered cars were returned to service as follows:

ADG/V 616 ceased to exist in December, 1982, and became ADG/V 612 in May, 1983,

The "real" ADG/V 612 to 615	
The "real" ADG/V 615 to 603	August, 1983
The "real" ADG/V 603 to 614	November, 1983
The "real" ADG/V 614 to 602	March, 1984
The "real" ADG/V 602 to 618	May, 1984
The "real" ADG/V 618 to 606	October, 1984
The "real" ADG/V 606 to 601	November, 1984

About this time the railcars also received a "bulged" front panel below the driver's cab window, presumably to give the driver more leg room.

In November, 1983 ADG/V 604 was written off and the body sold to the Ridolfo Brothers (Metana Minerals) at Mount Magnet, where it was used as employee accommodation. ADG/V 616 was also written off at the same time, having been used in the renumbering, and may have not been used for some time before this date.

In 1986 the 11.3 litre AEC engines from scrapped ADX class railcars were fitted to ADG/V 601, 603, 605, 606, 611, 612 and 617. These engines developed 150 bhp, 25 hp more than the smaller 9.6 litre units originally fitted, the idea being that lives of the old railcars would be extended till the Perth suburban network could be electrified. However, parts for the AEC engines were proving more and more difficult to find and later in 1986 ADG/V 617 was fitted with a pair of new Mercedes Benz engines, returning to service in February, 1987, followed later that month by ADG/V 602. Three others, ADG/V 614, 615 and 618 were fitted with these engines during the second half of 1987.

The next car to be written off, ADG/V 601, was the victim of a fire which was deliberately lit. It was burnt out at Kingsley on the Armadale line on 27 April, 1989 and was written off the following October/November.[42] The remaining fifteen ADG/V's were beginning to show their age, with increasing mechanical problems, such as overheating in the summer, but delays to the introduction of the electric railcars required their continued use, although they tended to be most used during peak hour services. To help them cope they often ran in sets of three power cars coupled together during their last months of service. The class was finally withdrawn in January, 1992 and written off the following month. ADG/V 610 seems to have been the last one to run in Westrail service when it operated a charter for the Australian Army from Forrestfield to Robb's Jetty and return over the 12 - 14 September, 1992.[43] It and ADG/V 614 were purchased by a member of the Hotham Valley railway, with 610 being delivered to Dwellingup on 19-10-1992. ADG/V 612 was set aside at Forrestfield for preservation by the Australian Railway Historical Society, but was also heavily vandalised before being moved to the vacated Midland Workshops on 7 July, 1994 for safe keeping. The remainder were stored at Robb's Jetty, but vandalism there was running rampant, culminating in two cars (607 & 608), which had been set aside for operation by a group at Kojonup, being deliberately burnt at Kwinana on 26 April, 1993. The rest of the cars were returned to Forrestfield early in May, 1993 and scrappings began on 10 June. Only three have survived.

Two ADG class cars (ADG 609 leading) in green with the safety chevrons on the ends.   *Photo courtesy ARHS.*

ADG 609 again with ADG 610 behind, at Perth station. The chevrons have been replaced with silver ends & a red stripe.
Photo courtesy ARHS.

ADG 614 leads an AYE & another ADG into a station on the Fremantle line.   *Photo courtesy ARHS.*

ADG 616 showing the all over green livery, with white & red ends.   *Photo courtesy Battye Library 284 735P*

ADG 602 in the suburban green, white & red livery, at East Perth on 22 January, 1968.

Photo late Geoff Blee, courtesy Murray Rowe.

ADG 610 rests at Perth station on 27 December, 1967. Note the black squares painted on the corners.

Photo late Geoff Blee, courtesy Murray Rowe.

ADG 610 rolling though East Perth in apparently new paint.   *Photo late Geoff Blee, courtesy Murray Rowe.*

ADG/V 606 in orange with an ADA in green, white & red.   *Photo courtesy Joe Moir.*

ADG/V 603 at Kwinana on the ARHS Farewell ADG Tour, 7 December, 1991   *Photo Bill Gray.*

ADG/V 608 ready to leave Midland for the City with a three car set. The "A" on the green plate at the front indicates the stopping pattern during peak periods, a sight often seen on the older railcar sets in their last days. The "A" pattern on the Midland line meant that the train would not be stopping at Meltham, & it would run express from Maylands to Claisebrook. This allowed the railcars to keep up with the faster electric railcar timetables.   *Photo Bill Gray.*

A fairly grubby ADG/V 617 with an ADA class trailer at Midland on 11 January, 1991. This was the most common consist for these cars.   *Photo Bill Gray.*

ADG 614 at Midland on 12 December, 1991, showing the state these old cars were allowed to deteriorate to towards the end of their lives.   *Photo Bill Gray.*

ADG/V 615 outside the Midland Workshops in brand new paint.   *Photo WAGR, courtesy ARHS.*

ADG/V 601 in the Midland Salvage area after being burnt out at Kingsley. It was removed to a scrap metal yard in Bayswater. Photo taken 12 April, 1990 by Bill Gray.

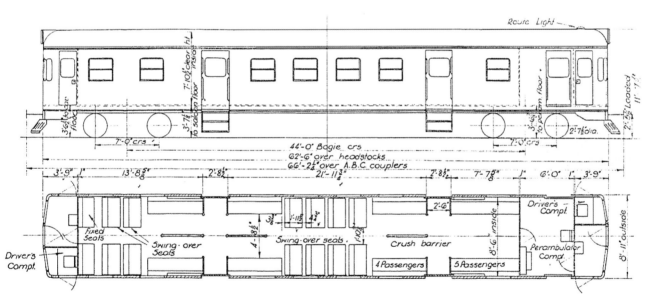

General arrangement drawing of the ADG class cars.   *Drawing courtesy PTA.*

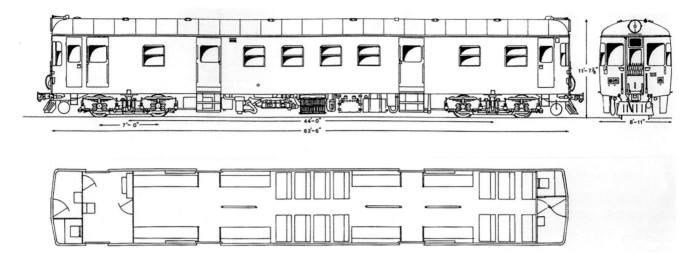

Andrew May's drawing of the ADGs, showing the bogie & underfloor detail.

Interior of ADG/V 615 at Forrestfield after it was withdrawn from service, 26 October, 1994. *Photo Bill Gray.*

One of the AEC engines under ADG/V 603, Kwinana, 7 December, 1991. *Photo Bill Gray.*

The following was written by Mr. H.J. Trower, a former rail car driver and a member of the Australian Railway Historical Society, and gives an interesting insight into both the workings & modification of the railcars over the years, as well as some of the ins and outs of the WAGR.

When the 18 ADG and the 4 ADH cars entered service in WA, and up to the second half of 1969 and 1970 they were Mechanical Railcars, but the two Wilson Gear Boxes were progressively removed and replaced with "Voith Torque Converter", making them Diesel Hydraulic Railcars. They had a fully fluid drive system with 2 ratios, hence the letter "V" which appears behind the stroke after the G, ADG/V.

The conversions commenced in the latter half of 1969 and into 1970, making these cars "automatics", the controls were completely changed, also the system for isolating final drives. These cars, of course, had some time previously been turbocharged, ADG 615 being the first one to be fitted with an exhaust driven turbocharger. This also reduced motor noise, so the exhaust mufflers were removed.

These Railcars ended their service nothing like they entered service, so many changes and modifications had taken place through the years. The horrible split windscreen on the driver's side, with the rubber weather strip was eventually swapped with the full one piece right hand side windscreen. There were a couple of drivers and myself who had repeatedly suggested the change on our running sheets. The concertina steel lattice gate beside the driver's seat to keep intruders away from the control panel vanished after a few years. The lousy little radiators that the class arrived here with would have made better hot water systems, and were eventually replaced by the larger type that can be seen on the remaining cars still existing and standing very dead and silent. ADG 605 was the first car to have the big radiator fitted and the windscreens swapped over. The latter was yet another greatly appreciated modification, for on hot days we could open the top half of the right hand windscreen and have a good air flow in the cab, but then as the class later went through the workshops, unfortunately the two piece right hand windscreens were replaced by a fixed one piece screen, so back to hot cabs.

The vacuum horns under the left hand side of the cab were eventually replaced by the louder and more effective Pneuphonic roof mounted horn. ADG 610 was the first one so fitted. I have memories of my first trip in 610 with the new loud horn. I was on 3A roster and had worked a trip from Armadale to Perth, left that set, then went to N°. 6 platform to take two ADG cars to Byford and return. 610 was the leading car. The platform had many people on it, as the "Westland" was on N°. 7 Platform. I bent down to get something from my Gladstone Bag and as I straightened up my foot accidentally pressed the foot control button for the horn. This was the loudest horn and people were not accustomed to hearing it. I am sure I could see daylight under everyone's feet on the platform then many pairs of eyes glared at me, however about 4 or 5 minutes later it was time to depart. The Guard rang the bell and my foot went smoothly to that button and once again as I departed there were very many nasty looks.

With the change to automatics the Box of Tricks under the driver's seat vanished along with the throttle lever on the LH side, also the N°. 1 and N°. 2 Motor Tachos were taken off the control panel, along with its change over switch. Sidelock fuses were replaced by Circuit Breakers, the Bell System was completely changed and Bell Cables done away with, also the bell key and switch box in the cab. This over came the bell problems we used to have. The Preselector for gear changes with the Wilson Gearbox became the throttle in the ADG/V, the Reverser was changed and the little actuating lever, often referred to as clutch lever by some drivers, disappeared also.

One of the early changes in the cab was the removal of the nice big speedos and these were replaced by speedos off Pm and Pmr engines, as Hasler Recorders were fitted to the steam locomotives. Also the Elliot Recorders in the cupboard in the N°. 1 cab of ADG cars were taken out early in the ADG & ADH life. They never worked satisfactorily. The Bell button up on the LH wall between the windscreen and side cab door was removed, as the Guard's Compartment originally only had one bell button on the wall in the centre of his compartment, which was dangerous, for if he wanted the driver to stop in a hurry he had to walk over to the bell button. So the bell button from the driver's cab made it possible to fit a bell button over each side door of the Guard's compartment, which was 100% safer as the guard could watch the passengers embarking or detraining and could instantly give the driver 3 bells to stop in an emergency.

Changes took place in the Saloon, crush bars were changed, the spring type knobs for standing passengers were taken out, the aluminium racks also, and the removable seats were replaced by fixed seats. Also the type of floor covering changed several times and other passenger improvements were made.

The original method of isolating the final drives was cumbersome and could be damned embarrassing. The driver had to go into the saloon with the reverser key and the vacuum brake handle. The reverser key had a flange end on it to be used as a screw driver, to undo 4 studs, lift a panel from the floor, then kneeling on the floor, reach down with the brake handle and lever the spring loaded pin into the isolating position, then replace the floor panel, go to the cab and operate the reverser to allow the spring loaded pin to do its job. This all took time, and N°. 1 end was bad enough, but at least the passengers were all in seats facing forward, but N°. 2 end with the long seats along the wall, was usually full of ladies with babies in prams. Of course some would have to be moved, then the driver would be down on his hands and knees at the passengers feet, just like a bloody slave begging for forgiveness. There used to be many times when motors cut out as the cars were operating on rubbish cheap fuel, not proper

Diesoline. In fact, 602, 606, and 611 were operating on crude oil, hence many failures. The fuel tanks were painted yellow on these cars.

I put in a suggestion that a 3/8 steel rod with a T piece handle on one end, and 2 prongs to grip the Isolating pin be placed in each car to save time and avoid the driver having to get down on his knees amongst the passengers. I was disgusted when I got a letter back stating that the present system of isolating final drives was considered to be quite satisfactory. The galah or galahs responsible for that knew very little about what a driver had to do to isolate a final drive in these circumstances, but the galah or galahs did "thank me for my interest". I was even more disgusted a few months later when the suggested Isolating Rods suddenly appeared in the ADG, ADH & ADX cabs and a gent in the Midland Workshops got all the credit for this wonderful invention.

Other changes to the ADG/ADH railcars were the interior lighting, fittings, and of course there were the exterior colour schemes. They looked awful when they first entered service as they were just larch green all over. I was informed by a very reliable source that Commissioner Hall requested the cars be so painted.

An interesting feature regarding the construction of the bodies of the ADG & DH cars was the fact that women welders did all the welding of all the roof panels in England. The welds were not ground off smooth as they were on roof panels on the ADX cars built in Midland Workshops.

The ADG and ADH cars had 2 underfloor AEC 125 hp motors, later they were turbocharged to increase their power for hauling driving trailers. The ADX cars had 2 underfloor British united Tractor Company motors of 150 hp each, they were slightly noisier motors.

I worked these cars for many years, also the much more sophisticated and stronger ADX and the Prospector Standard gauge cars. The ADK, the new Australind Railcars and Prospector cars are fully fluid drive with torque convertors.

Cab controls in ADH/V 651, 7 December, 1991, compared with a shot of that of the original ADG.
Photo Bill Gray.
                                                                    Photo courtesy Battye Library 284 740P

AQZ 415 at Albany on a tour. The car has a wooden underframe. Also of interest are the "sanitary" tins at each end, under the toilet outlets, presumably due to people staying overnight on the stationary train.

Photo courtesy Joe Moir.

In 1954 four AQ class cars with wooden underframes (415-418) were removed from service and were rebuilt internally with eight twin berth first class compartments, plus shower and conductor's compartments. Alterations to the exteriors of the cars were few, the main change being the deletion of the crown lights above the main window line, and the replacement of the matchboard sides with plywood panelling. They were classed AQZ and could carry 24 passengers as day cars and 16 passengers at night. The four cars were issued to traffic in the plain Larch green livery.

The AQZ's did their work well and in 1957 another four cars, this time ARS class sleeping cars (419, 420, 423 & 424) received a similar conversion, but they were placed on steel underframes rather than retaining the original wooden ones. When this took place is not certain, but it was probably at the time of conversion. The first four AQZ's kept their wooden frames, and AQZ 415 and AQZ 417 both survive with wooden frames.

In 1960 the four steel framed AQZ's were fitted with AZ type bogies. These were the same wheel base (6'3"/1.91m) as the old AQZ type, but were of an improved design.

The carriage refurbishment programme of the early 1960's brought few changes to the AQZ's, as they were still relatively "new" cars. In 1961 AQZ 420 was altered with the fitting of vestibule ends in place of the old end platforms, and the old timber framed windows were replaced with "Young" type windows, similar to those fitted in the suburban railcars. The top pane of these windows was fixed and only the bottom pane could be opened. The car was then allocated to the "Mullewa" set, the modifications having been done to minimise the entry of dust. AQZ 424 was also fitted with "Young" type windows in 1961, and was used on the Albany Progress.

In 1963 AQZ 419 was fitted with a small buffet. This was done by removing the sleeping compartment next to the conductor's compartment. The passenger capacity in this car

was reduced to 21 day passengers and 14 night passengers. It was used on the Meekatharra trains where the passenger loadings did not warrant a full sized buffet car and found favour in its later years on "coach attached" tours, due to its buffet. All eight AQZ's were painted Larch green and cream between 1961 and 1967.

As the overnight country passenger trains began to fall by the wayside during the 1970's, the requirement for sleeping cars also fell. The "Mullewa" stopped running in 1974, but AQZ 420 was retained in service, while AQZ 416 (probably with a wooden frame) was written off. The body of this car was sold to the Guildford Grammar School in Perth the following year, but has since been demolished. By the end of 1975 only the "Albany Progress" and "Australind" were left, and in 1976 AQZ 415, 417, 418 and 423 were all written off, followed by AQZ 419 in 1977. Of these cars AQZ 415 and 423 were sold to the Great Southern Steam Association for tour train work out of Albany, and the body of AQZ 419 went to the Midvale Primary School in Perth for use as a class room. This left only two AQZ's (420 & 424) in traffic and these were withdrawn from service following the demise of the "Albany Progress" in 1978.

A number of AQZ's have survived. AQZ 415, one of two survivors with wooden underframes, and AQZ 423 were sold to the Australian Railway Historical Society in late 1984. In September, 1985 AQZ 423 went back into service on that organisation's tour trains, and AQZ 415 spent several years stored at Bayswater before being transferred to the Rail Transport Museum at Bassendean in 1989. It was joined in January, 1990 by AQZ 419, which had been largely gutted for its role as a class room. At Bassendean it was used as a storage and amenities room before being sold in 2000. AQZ 415 was transferred from Bassendean to York in 1993(?). The other wooden framed AQZ which survived is 417, which spent some time located on a property at Mundaring before being moved to Sawyers Valley in mid 1991. It was put up at auction on 7 December, 1991, but was passed in. With white ant damage at one end, its future looked bleak. It was taken to Gwelup in Perth where it was cut in half, & was later sold in Byford. AQZ 420 and 424 were both leased to the Hotham Valley Railway in 1979 for tour train use, finally being purchased outright by that group in 1984.

AQZ 420 in the Larch green livery.   *Photo WAGR, courtesy Lindsay Watson.*

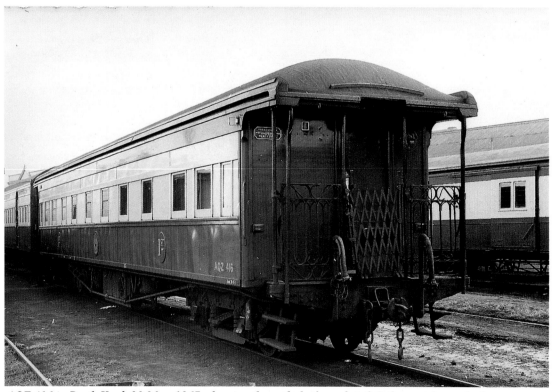

AQZ 416 in Perth Yard, 20 May, 1967, showing the end platform detail & the wooden underframe.
Photo late Geoff Blee, courtesy Murray Rowe.

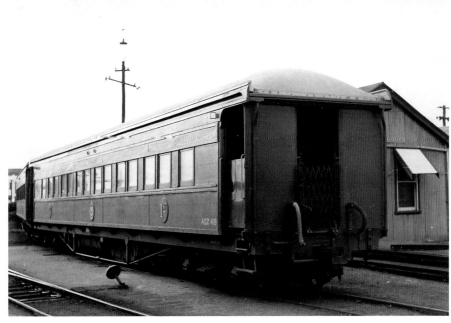

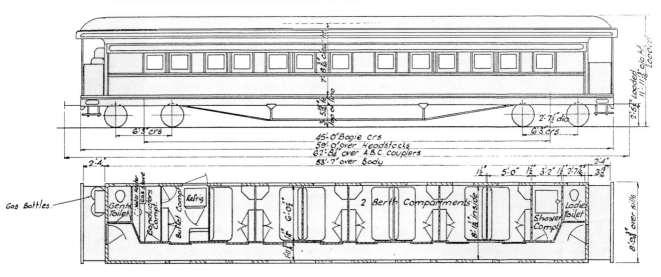

The photographs & drawing show AQZ 419, in green, after it had the buffet built into it. The lower shot shows the buffet service door & the buffet window with a flyscreen on it. The top photo shows the corridor side of the car. They were taken in Midland Marshalling Yard, 29 September, 1967.

Photos late Geoff Blee, courtesy Murray Rowe, drawing courtesy PTA.

AQZ 420 as modified for the "Mullewa" in Perth Yard on 4 December, 1966. Note the Young type windows & enclosed end platforms.   *Photo late Geoff Blee, courtesy Murray Rowe.*

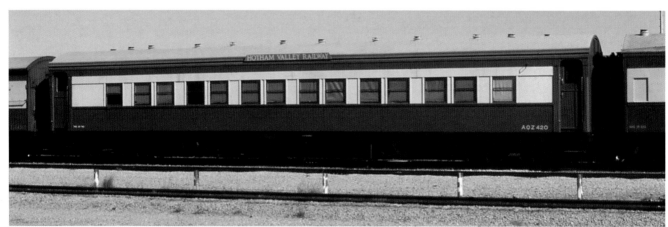

AQZ 420 again, showing the corridor side window layout. This differed between cars, depending on the origin of the car.   *Photo taken at Forrestfield Marshalling Yard, 13 April, 1991 by Bill Gray.*

AQZ 424, operated by the Hotham Valley Railway, showing the dust screens on the end platform.   *Photo taken at Forrestfield Marshalling Yard on 13 April, 1991 by Bill Gray.*

In their later years the masonite sides on the AQZs began to show some serious weathering, as is well illustrated in this shot of AQZ 415 taken at Perth. *Photo late Geoff Blee, courtesy Murray Rowe.*

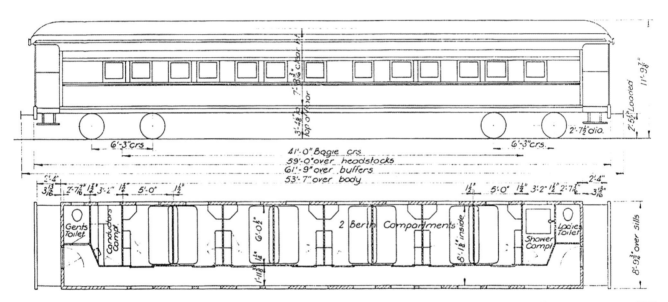

Drawing of the AQZ class on wooden underframes. *Drawing courtesy PTA.*

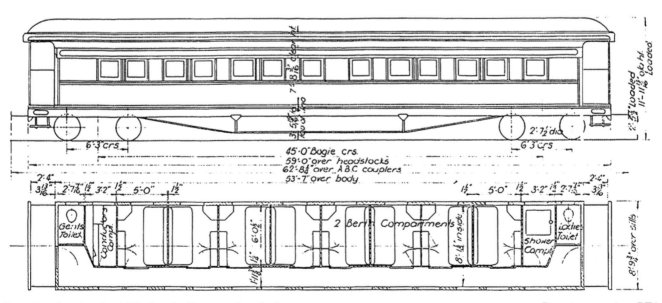

Drawing showing the AQZ class built on steel underframes. *Drawing courtesy PTA*

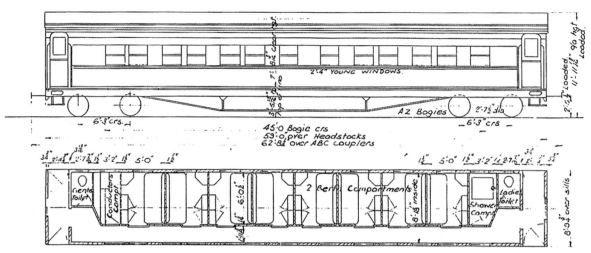

Drawing of AQZ 420.   Drawing courtesy PTA.

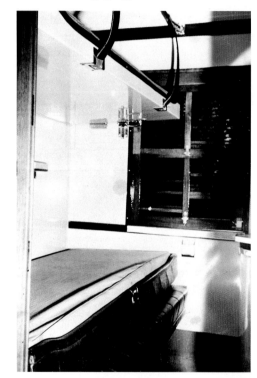

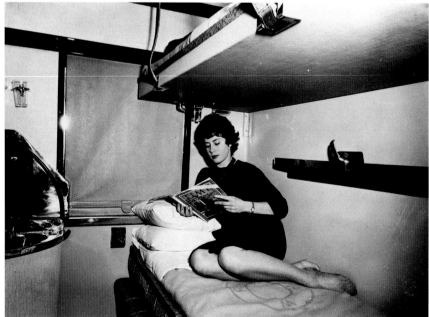

The WAGR shots of the AQZ compartments, complete with model showing the comforts of a WAGR first class compartment.
Photos courtesy ARHS.

ADH 653 in new condition.   *Photo courtesy ARHS.*

Ordered with the ADG class railcars from the Cravens Railway Carriage & Wagon Co. of Sheffield in England in September, 1951 were four ADH class diesel railcars, intended for low capacity country work. The first three arrived in June, 1955 and the fourth in 1956. They were the same as the ADG's in their basic design, and mechanically were identical, with two AEC 9.6 litre horizontally mounted diesel engines, each rated at 125 bhp at 1800 rpm. The engines drove the inner axle of each bogie through a fluid flywheel, a Wilson pre-select four speed gearbox, and reduction gearing.[44] The body was of welded steel construction and was the same size as the ADG's, but the ADH's were heavier. There were two passenger compartments, able to seat a total of 16 passengers. ADH 651-653 were turned out in Larch green with silver and red ends, while it is thought that ADH 654 entered service painted with green lower panels, white upper panels and a red band between them.

The ADH's were used on services from Perth to Miling, Wyalkatchem, and Bunbury, and Geraldton to Cue,[45] and when the loadings warranted they towed an ACL class compartment car as a trailer. However, their time as country railcars was only short because the policy of replacing country branch line trains with buses, or stopping services on them altogether, was beginning to bite. In 1960 most of the services operated by the ADH's were stopped, so they were brought to Perth and used on suburban trains, still in their country configuration. However, this was far from satisfactory and ADH 653 and 654 were taken out of service to be converted to proper suburban railcars, returning to traffic in January, 1962. The other two ADH's (651 & 652) were converted in mid 1963.

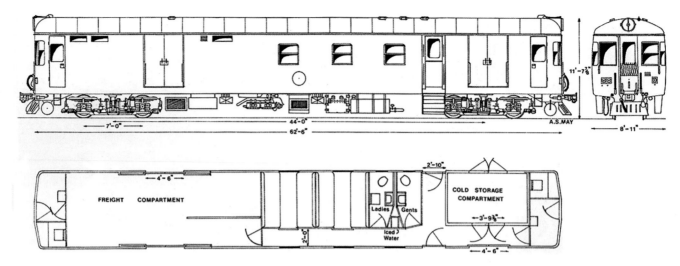

General arrangement drawing of the ADH country railcar.   *Drawing courtesy PTA.*

An ADH railcar at Dwarda on what appears to be a hot summers day. The car is towing ALT 88, the AP derived track recorder car, so is possibly on a trial of some sort, soon after delivery.   *Photo courtesy ARHS.*

AYE 703 in new condition & painted all over Larch green.   *Photo WAGR courtesy Lindsay Watson.*

The introduction to service of the ADG class railcars created an upsurge in traffic which was quite unexpected (160,000 extra single passenger journeys per month for the first four months) and it soon became obvious that the new railcars could not handle the increased patronage alone. As a stopgap measure the ADG's towed old suburban compartment cars around with them, but this was hardly satisfactory due to the lack of access into these carriages. To overcome the problem, nine old 42' (12.81m) suburban side door compartment cars were taken into the workshops at Midland Junction, their bodies demolished, and new saloon cars built on the old underframes. These carriages, classed AYE, had control cables running through them to allow the railcars to run in multiple with them. The suburban cars used were ADS 119, AC 73, AF 99, 140, 160, 167, 197, 200 and ZAF 433 formerly AF 157, and these became AYE 701-709, all issued to traffic in 1955.

The design of the AYE's was based on the AY class suburban cars, but obviously were shorter. They were built of timber on the old steel underframes, had plywood panelled sides, and were painted in Larch green with Stone coloured roofs. The windows were the half lift type, similar to those found in the railcars, and seating was provided for 48 passengers with room for another 44 standing in the central aisle.

After the AYE's were issued to traffic, use of the old suburban cars as railcar trailers stopped and the railcar sets normally consisted of ADG-AYE-ADG. It was permissible to marshall a second AYE between the two power cars, but this was rarely done because the weight of the extra trailer tended to degrade the train's performance too much.[46]

In 1958 another five AYE's were built, once again on the underframes of old suburban cars. In this batch AF 275, 57, 31, 32 and 273 gave up their frames to AYE 710-714, all of which entered service in June, 1958. They were identical to the earlier cars and their introduction allowed the use of AYE's on loco hauled sets.

Starting in 1960, the AYE class was painted in the "suburban" livery of green, white and red, with the last one, AYE 709 being completed in 1965, but without the red stripe.

In 1961 the dedicated ADA class railcar trailers were first placed in service, followed by a second batch of ADA's in 1964, and this allowed five AYE class cars to be transferred permanently for use behind locomotive hauled trains. In 1967 two cars (AYE 704 & 706) were fitted with a brake compartment and reclassified AYF, so allowing them to run at the rear of locomotive hauled suburban trains. AYE 705 was converted in a similar fashion in 1968.

When the ADG's and ADH's were fitted with the new Voith automatic transmission, modifications had to be made to the control gear in the trailers to allow them to run with the modified railcars. The AYE's were converted as follows:-

1969 - AYE 713, 714.
1970 - Nil.
1971 - AYE 708, 709.

These cars were unofficially known as the AYE/V class to

distinguish them from the unmodified carriages, a classification which became official in October, 1978. Meanwhile, in 1970, another two AYE's (702 & 707) were converted to AYF's and so were only used on locomotive hauled trains.

In the late 1970's the AYE's underwent another change of livery when they were painted in the Westrail orange and blue colour scheme. The first was AYE 711 in 1977 and all were running in the new livery by the end of 1979.

AYE 703 and 712 were the first to be written off, both going in May, 1980 after the closure of suburban passenger services on the Fremantle line the year before. When the first batch of ADL/ADC class railcars arrived in service in 1982, AYE 701 was one of several suburban cars to be placed in storage, but it was returned to traffic in July, 1983 when the Fremantle line was re-opened again. However, its time back in service was only brief, as it was written off again in November, 1983 and AYE 711 went with it. This left only five AYE's (708, 709, 710, 713 & 714) in traffic, all but AYE 710 being AYE/V's. In

1986 all five cars were painted in the Larch green and cream livery, and in May, 1990, AYE 710, the last car not converted for use with Voith transmissioned railcars, was written off after a minor fire on board. The remaining four AYE/V class cars continued in use on suburban trains till January, 1991, being written off as a group in February that year.

One of the cars written off in 1980 (AYE 703) was placed on the old Eastern Railway reserve at Glen Forrest in the hills near Perth, only to be so badly damaged by the local vandals that it was removed a short time later. AYE 701 was used as a farm shed before going to the Mandurah Airstrip, where it was used as clubrooms by the Royal Aero Club. It finished up in a paddock at Karnet, just off the Southwest Highway, but disappeared in 2000. Another (714) is preserved at Boyanup, AYE 708 is located at the Greyhound Racing track at Cannington before moving to Pemberton for further use, and AYE 710 went to York.

AYE 708 in the suburban green, white & red livery.   *Photo late Geoff Blee, courtesy Murray Rowe.*

AYE/V 714 on a train with another AYE/V & AYF 702. The cars have recently been repainted, but the road numbers were left, indicating the state of their weathering. Photo taken at Midland on 18 July, 1989. *Photo Bill Gray.*

Every weekday morning two loco hauled suburban sets were hauled from Forrestfield Marshalling yards to Bellevue, then shunted back to Midland station & split into two trains, ready to operate the morning peak hour services. Here AYE/V 709 is seen at Bellevue on 24 May, 1990. *Photo Bill Gray.*

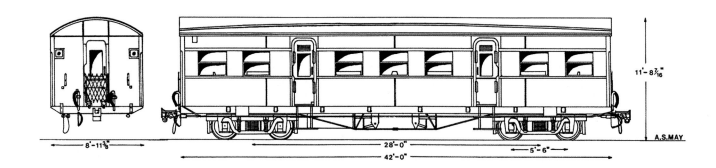

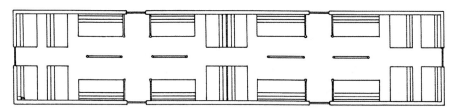

Andrew Mays drawing of an AYE/V, showing bogie & underfloor detail.

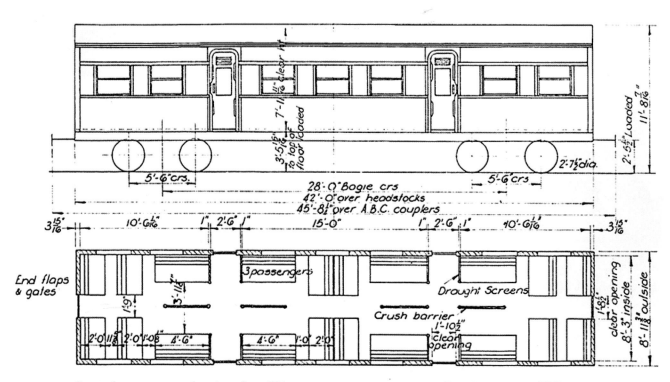

General arrangement drawing of an AYE.   *Drawing courtesy PTA.*

Interiors of two AYE cars, AYE 709 on the left, taken by the late Geoff Blee at Perth on 25 April, 1967, & above taken by Bill Gray of AYE/V 708 on 19 August, 1992, after the car had been withdrawn from service & taken to Cannington, a Perth suburb.

On 4 October, 1968 a Dm class locomotive hauled the last steam powered suburban train on the 5:04pm service from the City to Armadale. On 4 October, 1988 that service still existed, albeit diesel hauled, & to celebrate, restored locomotive Dd 592 hauled three AYEs, flanked by an AYF at each end, on the regular service. The Dd did its kind proud by keeping well to the timetable, despite the inclement weather. Many commuters were surprised to see their train being hauled by a steam engine, although it was reported that a few were not even aware of the change of motive power! The train is seen leaving Kingsley.

Photo Bill Gray.

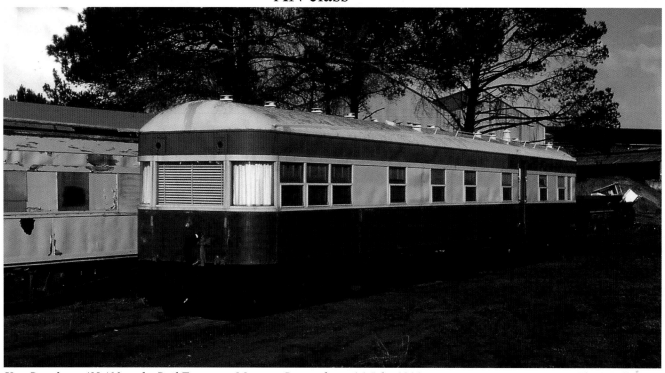

Vice Regal car AN 413 at the Rail Transport Museum, Bassendean, 16 July, 1990.   *Photo Bill Gray.*

In 1955 a new Vice Regal car was built to replace the old AQ based car AN 413. The new car was constructed on the steel underframe from ACW 325 and was fitted with AZ type bogies. The body was of timber construction with plywood side panels and the car was painted Larch green. From the outside it looked more or less like a normal passenger carriage, except that, at one end, it had a round cornered observation saloon to give those inside a panoramic view of the countryside through which they had just passed. The carriage, classed AN, took the number of the old AQ based Vice Regal car, 413, and was issued to traffic on 12 August, 1955. Some records indicate that the new Vice Regal car was a rebuild of the old one,[47] and this led to the story that AN 413 was the biggest "foreigner" (private job) the Midland Workshops ever had. The story goes that the car was built at the request of the then State Governor, Sir Charles Gardiner, but its construction appears never to have been officially sanctioned. Shortly before its completion the old AQ based AN 413 was pushed into the same shed as the new car and a few weeks later a new

AN 413 emerged and went into traffic. Three years later an inspection car bearing a remarkable resemblance to the old AN 413, but numbered AL 4, slipped quietly back into the system.

Once in service, AN 413 did not see a great deal of use due to the nature of its role. In March, 1966 it was repainted in the new Larch green and cream livery and it spent its later years housed at the Forrestfield Marshalling Yards. It was refurbished in August, 1985 after spending several years out of use, and it was finally handed over to the Australian Railway Historical Society at the Rail Transport Museum on 13 May, 1990.

AN 413, at Perth on 6 November, 1966, shows the other side of the car, & the non observation end.

Photo late Geoff Blee, courtesy Murray Rowe.

AN 413, carrying the Royal Crown plate on its side.

Photo late Geoff Blee, courtesy Murray Rowe.

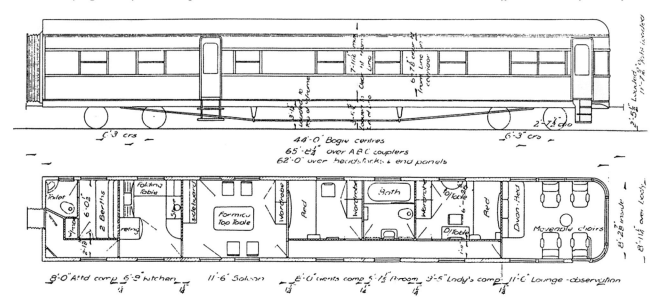

General arrangement drawing of AN 413.

Drawing courtesy PTA.

AN 413 brings up the rear of a train at Dwellingup on 23 August, 1987.

Photo Len Purcell, courtesy ARHS.

AVL class

AVL 314 as it was when it first arrived at the Rail transport Museum at Bassendean. Despite being used as a workmans van on a breakdown train it was, other than the colour, still in its AVL configuration.   *Photo taken 2 July, 1988 by Bill Gray.*

In 1958 one of the original dining cars, AV 314, was converted into a buffet/lounge car (AVL) for use on the "Westland" express. It retained its dining car body, end platforms, kitchen and corridor, but it lost its crown light windows. Reclassified AVL, the car was painted Larch green and entered service in its buffet/lounge car role in August, 1958, but it did not remain in that form for long. In 1962, as part of the carriage refurbishment programme, it was taken in hand and further modified to improve its facilities. The end platforms were both closed in and the old dining car kitchen was completely rebuilt. The AVL could seat 21 passengers in its new configuration and it was fitted with the Bradford-Kendall "Commonwealth" ride control bogies purchased for the never-to-materialise air conditioned "Westland" set. It was repainted Larch green and cream during these modifications and was returned to service in March, 1962. Interestingly, it retained its tongue and groove side timbers, rather than having them replaced with plywood panelling.

In August, 1964 the WAGR took over the MRWA and a new train, the "Midlander", was introduced to run between Perth and Geraldton. AVL 314 was part of a set of four cars chosen to operate this service, and all were painted in a special red and ivory livery. The "Midlander" only ran on weekdays, so on the weekends AVL 314 and the other red and ivory cars were used on the "Albany Weekender" trains. In December, 1967 the lounge car was returned to its Larch green and cream livery, although it continued to run on the "Midlander" till the demise of that train in July, 1975.[48]

AVL 314 was written off in December, 1975 and stored at the Midland Workshops till September, 1976 when it was painted yellow and re-issued to traffic as the workman's van for the 60 ton breakdown train. It retained its class and number. In mid 1988 it was leased by the Australian Railway Historical Society & arrived at their Rail Transport Museum at Bassendean in late June for restoration.

AVL 314 in its "Midlander" livery at Albany on 8 October, 1967.   *Photo late Geoff Blee, courtesy Murray Rowe.*

AVL 314, still in its Midlander colours, but this time on the "Midlander" consist at Perth on 25 April, 1967. This photo shows the other side of the car.   *Photo late Geoff Blee, courtesy Murray Rowe.*

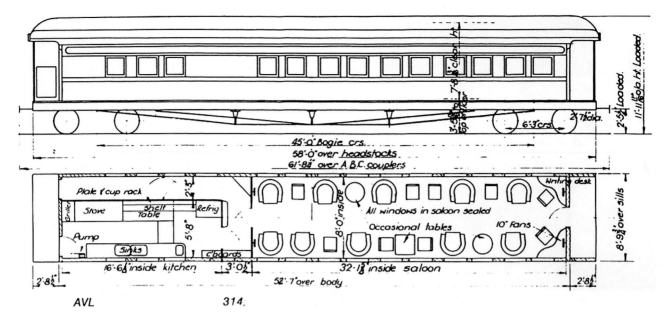

AVL 314 as originally built in 1958.   *Drawing WAGR courtesy Lindsay Watson.*

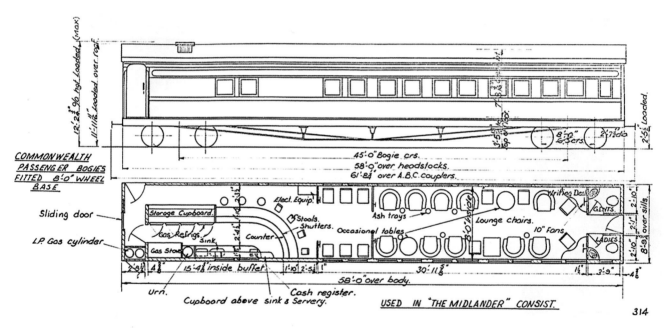

General arrangement drawing of the AVL class car.   *Drawing courtesy PTA.*

ADX 661 as built, with full pane windscreens both sides, flat front end & no sun visor over the drivers window.

Photo WAGR, courtesy ARHS.

In 1957 the Midland Workshops began the construction of ten new diesel railcars, classed ADX. The design of these cars was based on the ADG class, but with several improvements, and when the first one entered service in 1959, it was difficult to distinguish it from its ADG class cousins. The passenger entry doors were the double co-acting type, mechanically linked so that when one of the pair was opened, the other followed suit automatically. This arrangement "balanced" the doors and prevented them from sliding open and closed during starts and stops. The only other obvious difference between the ADX's and the ADG's was the provision of a curved rain strip above each door on the ADX's. They were issued to traffic in the green, white and red colour scheme.

Once on board an ADX, the internal layout was almost identical to the ADG's, but the longitudinal seats located between the ends of the saloon and the entry doors were shorter to allow for the co-acting doors. The passenger capacity of the ADX's was 58 seated and 52 standing. The car was built with swing over seat backs, but these were later replaced with fixed backs.

Mechanically the ADX class was similar to its predecessors, but was fitted with 11.3 litre AEC diesel engines rather than the 9.6 litre type in the ADG's. These engines were rated at 150 bhp, some 25 hp more than the smaller units. In every other way the mechanics were identical to the ADG's, with a fluid flywheel, 4 speed pre-select gearbox, and a reduction gear driving the inner axle on each bogie. The engines were mounted under the floor and the fuel capacity of these cars was 100 gallons (455 litres).[49]

In 1966 ADX 670 was taken into the workshops and modified with power operated doors, passenger seating in place of the perambulator compartment, stainless steel cowcatcher, steel sun visor over the driver's window, and a new Nanking blue and grey livery. It was able to seat 66 passengers in this configuration and was to have been a prototype for further conversions, but no more were done, even though ADX 670 seems to have been a success. In 1968 it was returned to its old green, white and red livery, although it retained its other modifications, including the stainless steel cowcatcher.

In 1969 work began on modifying the ADG and ADH class railcars with Voith automatic transmissions, but the ADX's were not done. The reason for this is not known, but it was ultimately to bring about the early demise of the class, and in the meantime they were restricted to running with each other and with those trailers not modified for the new equipment, these being ADA 765-770 and AYE 701, 703, and 710-712.

In 1975 the WAGR adopted the commercial name "Westrail" and, with it, a new orange and blue colour scheme. The ADX's were repainted in the new livery as follows:-

1975 - ADX 663;
1976 - ADX 664, 666;
1977 - ADX 662, 668, 669;
  ? - ADX 661, 665, 667, 670.

The Fremantle line was closed to suburban traffic in 1979 and this resulted in several suburban cars being withdrawn from use and stored. Among these were ADX 661 and 670, both of which were retired in 1982. The Fremantle line was re-opened to suburban services the following year, but the two ADX's never ran again. Both were written off in November, 1983 and transported to Mount Magnet to be used as staff accommodation on a mining site. In 1985 another three ADX's (665, 666 & 668) were also written off and the engines from them were fitted to some of the ADG/V class railcars in 1986. About this time the remaining ADX's were, like the ADG, ADH and ADA class cars, fitted with the "bulged" front lower driver's cab panel, presumably to improve the leg room.

The ADX's did not last much longer, but details of their disposal is not entirely clear. Reports indicate that during Royal Show Week in October, 1985, ADX 667 caught fire at Bassendean,[50] and another report about the same time indicates that ADX 669 was in the workshops for repair after suffering fire damage.[51] ADX 667 was back in service by February, 1986, but afterwards both cars were being used

as coaching stock on loco hauled peak hour trains, with their engines and other mechanical parts removed or disconnected. ADX 667 was written off in November, 1987, but ADX 669's date of write off has not yet come to light. ADX 663 was also written off in November, 1987, and by this time the ADX's were only seen during peak hours due to their poor mechanical condition. ADX 664 was withdrawn from service, but when is not known. It spent some considerable time stored at Forrestfield (noted there on 15 April, 1989).

ADX 662 soldiered on, the last survivor of the class, finally being withdrawn from service around September, 1988, its orange sides covered in blue and white graffiti, a legacy from the vandals who haunted the Claisebrook Carriage Depot during the hours of darkness. It was stored at Midland before being written off in August, 1989 and buried at the Gosnells tip with ADX 663 in December, 1989.

ADX 664 & ADA 767 at Rivervale, 30 October, 1967.   *Photo late Geoff Blee, courtesy Murray Rowe*

ADX 661 freshly painted at Midland Workshops 16 March, 1967.   *Photo late Geoff Blee, courtesy Murray Rowe.*

An anonymous ADX class car leads an ADA & an ADG past the East Perth Loco Depot, September, 1967.
Photo late Geoff Blee, courtesy Murray Rowe.

ADX 679 in the very attractive blue & grey colour scheme.   *Photo courtesy Don Finlayson.*

The cars start across the level crossing behind ADX 670 leading an ADA & ADG at Victoria Park on 17 October, 1966.
Photo late Geoff Blee, courtesy Murray Rowe.

The WAGR photographer captured ADX 666 with its attendant ADA at Perth station, freshly painted in the orange & blue livery.
Photo courtesy ARHS.

ADX 669 rests at Perth between tours of duty.
Photo Andy May, courtesy ARHS.

ADX 664 resting at Perth towards the end of its working life, & showing the weathering usually worn by these cars in regular service. *Photo Andy May, courtesy ARHS.*

A worn & tired looking ADX 662 with ADA 767, with only a few short months to go before it joins it's sisters in oblivion, stands quietly at the Claisebrook Railcar Depot, 19 March, 1988. *Photo Bill Gray.*

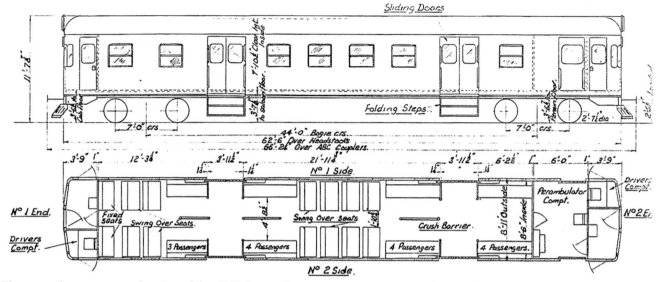

The general arrangement drawing of the ADX class railcar.   *Drawing courtesy PTA.*

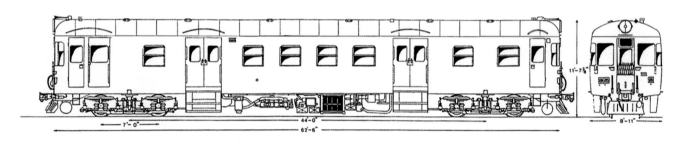

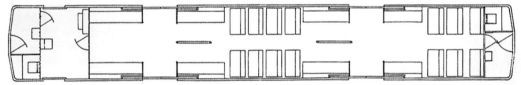

Andy May's detailed drawing of the ADX railcars.

The interior of a new ADX.
Photo courtesy Battye Library 284 741P

The interior of ADX 661, 15 November, 1967.
Photo late Geoff Blee, courtesy Murray Rowe.

CHAPTER SEVEN
AN INDIAN SUMMER & THE END - 1959-1975

During the late 1950's there was something of an upheaval in the upper administrative ranks of the WAGR with another Royal Commission being conducted and in 1959, as the dust settled, Mr. Cyril G.C. Wayne was appointed Commissioner.[1] The situation facing Wayne and his CME, Joshua Bradley, was not a pleasant one. The country branch line passenger services were fast disappearing, the mainline country passenger services were badly run down, and morale among the WAGR staff was at an all time low.

The branch line passenger services were beyond redemption, being uneconomic anyway, although some passenger accommodation was being provided on goods trains. In 1960 services were discontinued between Perth and Miling, Perth, Wyalkatchem and Merredin, Perth and Mukinbudin, Perth, Narrogin and Albany, Perth and Northam, and Geraldton and Mullewa.[2] Most of these services were operated by diesel railcars and as the last of them closed most of the railcars were retired and written off, or converted for other uses.

Lack of money was, as usual, a big problem in any attempt to improve passenger services, but there was enough available for the construction in 1960 of a batch of five new express brakevans to a design which differed little from the AJ's built in 1919. These were built as part of the carriage refurbishment programme and were classified ZJA (430-434).

In the absence of any money for major new construction the policy of rebuilding and refurbishing continued, and between 1960 and 1966 all the cars used on country passenger trains went through a modernising process. This involved work ranging from minor repairs to major rebuilds. Flat plywood or masonite panels replaced tongue and groove body sides on most cars, and the days of ornate varnished woodwork, moulded panelling and acid etched windows were well and truly over. Most of the refurbished cars were also rebogied.

The first carriages to be dealt with were the "Australind" cars which were taken out of service and sent to the workshops for a thorough refurbishment. During this overhaul both AYD's were altered internally with AYD 550 being upgraded to first class. The alterations reduced the passenger capacity in the AYD's to 20, the seats in the buffet section not normally being booked. The "Australind" cars emerged from the shops in September, 1960 with plywood panels painted Larch green and cream in place of the old matchboard, and newly painted and carpeted interiors, and were trialled between Midland and Spencer's Brook on 8 September, 1960.[3] AYD 550 caused the only minor problem on the trial with a hot axle box and the cars returned to service on 1 October, 1960, the first refurbished "Australind" being hauled by diesel locomotive X 1008.

The new Larch green and cream livery became standard for the mainline cars, while the suburban cars were painted in the railcar green, white and red. However, two AY class suburban cars (454 & 455) wore the mainline livery so they could be used as strengthening cars for the "Australind". The planning of new "Westland" cars was still in hand and the departure of the first refurbished "Australind" on 1 October, 1960 gave the Joint Railway Unions Committee the chance to publicize their desire to have the new cars built at Midland, when their members handed out leaflets at Perth station prior to the train's departure.[4]

In 1960 the four steel framed AQZ first class sleeping cars were fitted with AZ type bogies. These were the same wheel base (6'3"/1.91m) as the old AQZ type, but were of an improved design.

One of the oldest classes of car still in service became extinct in 1960 when side loading cars AC 96 & 97, the only members of the class to have been painted green, were written off, having been displaced from suburban services by the ADG and ADX classes of diesel railcar.

A new CME, Sidney Griffiths, was appointed in 1961 to replace Bradley,[5] and he was forced to continue the policy of rebuilding the old stock because of the lack of money for new cars. The small amount of money available to him for new carriages was spent on a batch of new lightweight steel bodied railcar trailers, similar in design to the ADG, ADH and ADX class railcars. They were classed ADA (751-760) and the first of them entered service in October, 1961. They had a driving cab at one end, and always faced east to simplify marshalling. The last of them went into service in August, 1962, having been delivered at an average rate of one per month. The building of these ten cars meant that steam hauled trains were only required at peak times.

X.1008 leads the refurbished "Australind" across the Bunbury Bridge.

Photo courtesy ARHS.

The country car refurbishment programme resulted in the production of several new classes of carriage. Two new buffet cars (AQL) were produced in 1961 by rebuilding AQS's 288 and 290, the latter car being fitted with vestibule ends and gangways, while 288 retained its old fashioned end platforms. They both rode on AZ bogies. Two more AQS class cars (287 & 292) were rebuilt as twin berth second class sleeping cars (AQM) and, like the AQL's, one (292) was rebuilt with vestibules, while the other (287) retained its end platforms. These, too, were fitted with AZ type bogies. The vestibuled cars were used on the "Mullewa" because of the dust problem in that area, and sleeping car AQZ 420 was altered in the same way for the same purpose. Its old timber framed windows were replaced with "Young" type windows, similar to those fitted in the suburban railcars. The other two cars, with their end platforms, were allocated to the "Albany Progress", where dust was not such a problem, although some of the cars used on this train (including AQM 287) were later fitted with dust shields. AQC 336 was written off in 1961 and AQC 343 was converted to an AQS to replace it. It was the only timber framed AQ to ever become an AQS and it was subsequently used on the "Albany Progress". Several other AQ's, AQC's, AQS's and ARS's were refurbished and had their new plywood sides repainted green and cream. Most were also rebogied at the same time. These included AQ 335, 341, AQC 339, 340, 342, 344 and AQS 289, 294 and 343.

While the mainline cars were being modernised, the branch line cars were quickly becoming redundant, including the railcars. By 1961 all six "Governor" cars and their ADT class trailers were thoroughly worn out. ADE's 446-448 had been retired during 1957 and ADE 450 was withdrawn in 1958, followed by ADE 449 in 1960. However, four of the old railcars (ADE 447, 449-451) were coupled together in 1961 and used as a suburban set,[6] but they did not last long and all six were written off as a group in April, 1962. They were placed in storage at Midland and were still there in 1974. However, most were cut up for scrap soon after, although ADE 447 "Governor Lawley" survived till broken up during 1991. The ADT's were also written off in April, 1962 and most were later cut up.

The ADH class country cars spent only a short time in that role. In 1960 most of the services operated by them were stopped, marking the end of the Perth to Merredin and Perth to Northam daylight trains, and the railcars were brought to Perth for use on suburban services, still in their country configuration. However, with a passenger capacity of only 16 they were hardly suitable for suburban service, and ADH 653 and 654 were converted to "proper" suburban railcars, returning to traffic in January, 1962. The other two (ADH 651 & 652) were converted in mid 1963. The converted ADH's were almost indistinguishable from the ADG and ADX class railcars. They differed from the ADG's by having double sliding entry doors, similar to the ADX class (the ADG's had single doors), and the main external difference between an ADH and an ADX was the full length rain strip on the roof of the former, while the latter had a curved rain strip above each door. Thus there were three different classes of suburban railcar on the Perth system, all almost identical in appearance.

In 1962 two more new classes of mainline car were created. The first was a pair of ARM second class twin berth sleeping cars, built from two old ARS class cars (354 & 357) and bearing little resemblance to their AR ancestors. The end

platforms were filled in with entry vestibules, the windows were replaced with the steel framed "Young" half lift type, the window spacing was changed and the matchboard sides were replaced with plywood panelling. Virtually new bodies were fitted to the steel frames acquired by these cars during the 1950's, and at first they retained their 6 wheeled bogies, being fitted with the Bradford-Kendall "Commonwealth" ride control type, purchased for the never-to-materialise air conditioned "Westland" set, in mid 1963. They also carried a conductor, which was unusual for a second class car, and were issued to traffic in April, 1962. Two other ARM's were built later in 1962 (351 & 356), entering service in October, and these were fitted with ride control bogies when issued to traffic. All four cars were allocated for use on the "Kalgoorlie".

The second new type of car built in 1962 was classified AYS, and consisted of two buffet-lounge cars built from AY suburban carriages 460 and 461. Like the other conversions of the time, the bodies of these cars were unrecognisable as AY's after this rebuild and even the bogies were changed in favour of the ride control type. The old tongue and groove sides were replaced with plywood panelling and the entry doors were removed. The windows were replaced with the steel framed half lift type, but the window spacing differed slightly between the two cars. End doors were the main means of entry for the passengers, so boarding the AYS's was generally done from other carriages. Unusually for the WAGR, both cars were named, AYS 460 "Colgoola" and AYS 461 "Boulder". They were allocated to the "Westland" sets, but were also used on the "Kalgoorlie".

A number of existing classes of car were upgraded during 1962, without being rebuilt. AVL 314 was further modified to improve its facilities. The end platforms were both closed in and the old dining car kitchen was completely rebuilt. It was fitted with the "Commonwealth" ride control bogies. It was repainted Larch green and cream during these modifications and returned to service in March, 1962. Interestingly, it retained its tongue and groove side timbers, rather than having them replaced with plywood panelling.

Lounge car AYL 29 was fitted with new 7' (2.13m) wheel base ride control bogies, and AYL 28 received similar bogies the following year. At the same time their matchboard sides were covered with plywood panelling which was then painted Larch green and cream. The ride control bogies only spent a short time under these cars, being replaced in 1967 by 6'6" (1.99m) wheel base ADU type bogies.

Even the relatively new AZ first class sleeping cars were repanelled with plywood over their matchboard sides and painted Larch green and cream. All the ZJ class brakevans still in service were similarly repainted, as were the ZJA's. These vans were ZJ 265-272, 359, 361-368, 427, 429 and ZJA 430-434.

The carriage refurbishment programme continued into 1963, but there were no more drastic rebuilds. AQZ 419 was fitted with a small buffet by removing the sleeping compartment next to the conductor's compartment. As a result the passenger capacity in this car was reduced to 21 day passengers and 14 night passengers. It was used on the Meekatharra trains where the passenger loadings did not warrant a full sized buffet car and found favour in its later years on "coach attached" tours, due to its buffet. All eight AQZ's were painted Larch green and cream between 1961 and 1966. The ARM's and AYS's were expected to last another twenty years, but the other non rebuilt cars of the AQ and AR types had a more limited life expectancy. On 5 November, 1962 construction began on the standard gauge railway between Perth and Kalgoorlie,[7] a project which would finally be instrumental in the demise of the "Westland" and the "Kalgoorlie".

By the early 1960's many of the branch line passenger trains no longer existed, having been replaced by bus services, and large numbers of carriages were in store, waiting patiently to carry passengers who were no longer there. The scrapping of the branch line cars began to gather pace in 1963, and further withdrawals that year included seventeen cars of the ACL, AP and ZA classes used on branch line passenger trains. In May, 1963 the remaining eight AP class sleeping cars (AP 91, 92, 146, 147, 149, 150, 152 & 155) were written off as a group, so causing the type, in its original form, to become extinct. Five (including two converted to AF and one to AA) served a little longer as workman's vans, as did AP 88/93 as an inspection car, and AP 86 as an instruction van. The frames of many of those written off survived a few more years as QS class flat wagons.

In the suburbs of Perth some of the AY and AYB class cars were repainted in 1963 in the suburban livery of green, red and white. These were AY 26, 453, 454, and 455, and AYB 459, and included the two AY's (454 and 455) which had been painted in the mainline green and cream livery for the "Australind", with AY 452 and AYB 457 being done in 1966 and AYB 456 in 1967. It is thought that AYB 458 stayed Larch green till as late as 1970, but by that time AYB 456 and 457 had been written off, both in 1969. In the 1970's all were put into the Westrail orange and blue livery, but were repainted green and cream during 1983-84.

By the early 1960's improved roads and greater use of private motor vehicles, combined with a general run down of the WAGR's passenger services, were causing the services run by the "Wildflower" sets to become uneconomic.[8] They were withdrawn from service one at a time, the final "Diesel" service being operated from Merredin to Perth on 9 September, 1963, with ADF 492 towing trailers ADU 589 and 591. The "Wildflower's" work was taken over by road coaches. Despite the demise of the daylight country passenger trains in the Northern, Eastern and Central areas of the state, the "Wildflower" sets still had plenty of life left in them. By 1964 three cars (ADF 490, 494 & 491) had been withdrawn from use and stowed at Midland. Two new services were introduced on the Bunbury line in 1964, the "Bunbury Belle" and the "Shopper", utilising refurbished ADF power cars and ADU class trailers. ADF 492, 493 and 495 were modified to allow multiple unit working and were repainted in the green, white and red suburban colour scheme from 1964. ADU 588-591 were refurbished for use on the "Shopper" and "Bunbury Belle", with two of these cars (ADU 588 & 589) losing their sloping ends and guard's compartments. ADU 590 and 591

were not altered in this way, for the normal consist on these trains was four ADU's with an ADF at each end (ADF-ADU-ADU-ADU-ADU-ADF), with the cars marshalled next to the ADF's retaining their sloping ends. The cars had automatic vending machines installed in them for the sale of refreshments, this feature being a first on any Australian train. The full train (four cars and two power units) ran the "Bunbury Belle" services on the weekends, while half the train (an ADF plus two ADUs) ran "The Shopper" during the week, with a single Bunbury - Perth service on Saturdays.[9] All four trailers were repainted in the suburban livery of green, white and red to match the ADF's, and the first of the "Bunbury Belle/ Shopper" services ran in June, 1964.[10]

Two more redundant ADU class "Wildflower" trailers (ADU 580 & 581) were converted for use on loco hauled long distance passenger trains in 1964 and were reclassified AYU, even though they looked nothing like the other AY series cars. However, they were not dissimilar in appearance to the modified ADU class cars. The slanted end and guard's compartment were removed, and the unusual oval window at each end indicated the location of the wash rooms and toilets, but in virtually every other way, on the outside at least, they retained their ADU characteristics. One (AYU 581) was allocated for use on the Mullewa to Meekatharra service, while the other (AYU 580) went into traffic on the "Midlander". Another two cars (ADU 584 & 585) were similarly converted in 1966, and they all seem to have led fairly uncomplicated lives, often being used on hired specials during the late 1960's and into the 1970's, where they looked completely out of place on a train of straight sided and slightly taller wooden country cars. Meanwhile ADU 582 and 583 were written off in 1966, and it is doubtful that ADU 586 and 587, the last of the original "Wildflower" trailers were much used after this time. The steel construction of these cars proved to be a weak point and corrosion was, towards the end of their lives, becoming a serious problem.

In August, 1964 the Midland Railway Company and its rolling stock were taken over by the WAGR. There were sixteen carriages of one kind or another still in Midland Railway service at the time, including seven sit up cars (J 4, Ja 5-8, 10 & 11), three sleeping cars (JV 31-33), four workman's vans (J 1, K 16 & KB 18 & 19), a tractor driver's van (KB 20) and the General Manager's saloon (KA 17). There were also two express brakevans (FA 51 & 52). The tractor driver's van was reclassified as a VW and transferred to wagon stock, while three cars in poor condition (Ja 7, 8 & 11) were written off immediately without being renumbered. They would have become ACL 34, 35 and 37. The other cars were all reclassified and renumbered. J 4 and Ja 5, 6 and 10 became ACL's (31-33, 36), while KA 17 became an AL, but retained its number.

The WAGR's "Midlander" publicity shot.   Photo courtesy Don Finlayson.

Two of the cars (J 1 & J 4) were originally composite carriages handed over to the MRWA in 1903. One, formerly AB 222 (MRWA J 1), had been converted to a workman's van in Midland Railway service, and was written off without entering service and stored. In 1970 it was re-instated as workman's van VW 5121 and it still exists. The other was formerly AB 250 which served the MRWA as J 4, and after the WAGR takeover it became ACL 31. The three JV's, while similar to the WAGR's AZ's, were still largely in original condition without shower or conductor's compartments, so they were repainted green and cream and had their old bogies replaced by those from the scrapped ADU class railcar trailers, before being downgraded to second class status and re-issued as AZS 444-446. They didn't enter service till August and September, 1965. This was the only new class of carriage to be created by the WAGR's takeover of the Midland Railway Co. The two express brakevans were reclassified as Z's and renumbered 40801 and 40802 amongst the Midland Railway wagons.

The MRWA's old service on the Perth to Geraldton route was replaced by a new WAGR train called the "Midlander". A set of four carriages was chosen for use on this train, including AVL 314, AYU 580, AZ 434 and ZJA 434, and to maintain a link with the old company they were painted in a special red and ivory colour scheme. The first "Midlander" service ran on 2 September, 1964.[11] At weekends, this set was used on the "Albany Weekender", often with reinforcing vehicles painted in the green and cream livery. In 1967 the coaches were returned to the Larch green and cream livery, to match the rest of the coaching stock, and this gave the train a neater appearance when strengthening cars were needed. Three of the cars were returned to general traffic, although the AVL continued to run on the "Midlander" till the demise of that train in July, 1975.[12]

The carriage refurbishment programme was starting to lose its momentum, but in October, 1964 the RESO shower car AGS 22 had its tongue and groove sides replaced with plywood panelling, losing much of its character in the process.

It was repainted in Larch green and cream.

Another batch of five ADA suburban railcar trailers was built in 1964 (761-765) and they entered service between 6 and 27 November that year, a complete contrast to the delivery rate of the first batch. This second batch may have been built on the underframes of the old ADT class cars which were written off in 1962, which could explain why they were delivered so quickly. The delivery of these cars allowed five AYE class suburban cars to be transferred permanently for use behind locomotive hauled trains.

Another class of pre-1900 cars vanished from the system in 1964 when AC 80, the last of the original ACE composite cars with the single lavatory compartment was written off, possibly still in Indian red, as no record of its repainting has come to light.

By 1965 a large number of branch line cars were in store and fifty three of these were included in the cars written off that year. Classes AA and AB became extinct, (although two cars, 202 & 210, survived as ACL's till 1968), while large numbers of cars from classes ACL, ZA and ZB were also written off. The last three of the old AE first class suburban cars disappeared one at a time, quietly and without fuss, AE 128 in September, 1962, AE 162 in April, 1964 after the placing in traffic of the second batch of ADA class railcar trailers, and AE 196 in June, 1965. This car had been out of use for some time before write off. Several ACL's which were still in good condition (31-33, 36, 210, 238, 386, 391, 392, 395, 404, 408, 409 & 412) were converted for suburban use by the simple method of having their lavatory doors screwed shut.[13] In every other way they retained their ACL characteristics, although some (386, 391, 392, 395, 404, 408, 409 & 412) were 58' (17.69m) long, with seven compartments, while the rest were 49' (14.95m), with six compartments, making two different types of car. The ACM's were no more than a stopgap measure at a time when passenger cars were badly needed. Most of the old AE and AF class compartment cars had gone by 1965, as had many of the post 1900 suburban cars of classes AS, AT, AU and AW. The

ADK/ADB class railcar sets had been ordered and the ACM's were intended to fill in till they arrived. This they did, but were dreadfully inefficient with a maximum load of 49 passengers, compared to 90 in an AT.

On 2 January, 1966 the last suburban passenger train ran between Bellevue, Chidlows and Northam[14] and from that time on outer suburban rail services beyond Midland were replaced by road buses, even though work had only just begun on the new bus/rail interchange station at Midland. The new station was only a short distance west of the old one, from where the buses ran till the interchange was opened in 1968. The original station then became known as "Workshops" and was the pick up and set down point for the WAGR worker's train, the "Rattler". The last train to use the old Eastern Railway between Bellvue and Spencer's Brook was the "Westland", running to Perth on the morning of 13 February, 1966, and the line up the Avon Valley was opened the same day, the Eastern Railway (with Western Australia's only tunnel) being abandoned.[15]

Griffiths had retired as CME in 1965 and was replaced in mid January, 1966 by Mr. William C. Blakeney-Britter.[16] All four AYC class cars and AYD 550 from the "Australind" were used on a special train from Perth to Avon Yard, near Northam, on 15 February, 1966 for the opening of that facility. This was the first official 3'6" (1067mm) gauge train to run up the Avon Valley. Only six weeks later, on 30 March, 1966, AYC 512 was part of the consist on a Royal Train which carried the Queen Mother from Perth to Bunbury and return.

On 17 March, 1966 the "Kalgoorlie" was near Woolundra, five miles east of Kellerberrin, enroute to Perth, when a fire broke out on board, destroying two AZ first class sleeping cars (441 & 442) and badly damaging an AYS class lounge-buffet car (461). The AZ's were written off, but the AYS was salvaged and returned to Midland Workshops for rebuilding. This work was completed by December, 1966, and AYS 461 was turned out virtually a new carriage, with a different interior layout to its sister, AYS 460. As a result of the fire the Board of Enquiry recommended that emergency communication cords be fitted to the WAGR's sixty sleeping cars.[17] The first car so fitted was used on the "Westland" on 30 June, 1966, and by November that year forty eight coaches had been done.[18]

In 1966 suburban railcar ADX 670 was taken into the workshops and modified with power operated doors, passenger seating in place of the perambulator compartment, stainless steel cowcatcher, steel sun visor over the driver's window, and a new Nanking blue and grey livery. It was able to seat 66 passengers in this configuration and was to have been a prototype for further conversions, but no more were done, even though ADX 670 seems to have been a success. In 1968 it was returned to its old green, white and red livery, although it retained its other modifications, including the stainless steel cowcatcher.

A final group of five ADA class suburban railcar trailers (ADA 766-770) was built in 1966, and joined their brethren on the Perth system. By comparison with the earlier batches of ADA's, these were delivered at a rate one every three weeks or so. During the 1960's each car was fitted with a steel sun visor over the driver's window.

Yet another class of old side loading cars disappeared when the last of the composite cars taken over from the Great Southern Railway seventy years earlier was written off. AC 182 was the last of the original four cars and it remained in service the longest, being written off in 1966. By the end of that year Commissioner Wayne's refurbishment programme was completed.

In 1967 two AYE class suburban saloons (704 & 706), several of which had been released for use on loco hauled trains after the delivery of the final batch of ADA class railcar trailers in 1966, were fitted with small brake compartments, so allowing them to run at the rear of locomotive hauled suburban trains. Another AYE (705) was converted to an AYF in 1968, followed by a final pair (702 & 707) in 1970.

One of the newly converted AYF brake cars joined the steel bodied suburban set, which consisted of two AJ's and the AKB class car. The steel carriages were repainted in the suburban railcar livery of green and white with a red stripe to match the AYF's, with AKB 60 being the last of the steel suburban cars to receive the new livery.

The ubiquitous AF class second class wooden suburban cars had been dwindling in numbers since the Second World War, but the introduction of the railcars sealed the fate of the class. Five (AF 63, 74, 85, 183 & 184) had been written off in 1960 after the Midland built ADX class diesel railcars were turned out, leaving only thirteen AF's still in existence and these slowly disappeared over the next seven years. In 1961 the ADA railcar trailers allowed the disposal of two more (AF 33 & 135), both of which were converted to workman's vans. In 1962 the conversion of two of the ADH country railcars for suburban work, combined with a drop in patronage, saw the demise of AF 35 and 175, followed by AF 181 in 1963 after the other two ADH class railcars were also converted for suburban use. In 1965, during the clearance of old carriages in storage, AF 168 and the unique AF 261 were among the forty one cars were written off. AF 261 was converted to a VC class car (VC 2100) for crew accommodation on break down trains. In 1966 AF 62, 142, 171, 172 and 274 were all written off, and in 1967 the class finally became extinct with the writing off of the unique AF 13. This vehicle was converted into a workman's van and lasted in service till 1979.

Express brakevan ZJ 363 was badly damaged in a collision in 1967. It was rebuilt with a new plywood body, but without the double roof, and three other ZJ's (269, 364 & 366) also lost their outer roofs at about the same time. However, the bodies of these three vans retained their matchboard sides.

The suburban railcar fleet received a boost early in 1968 with the arrival of the first of ten new railcar sets, each set consisting of an ADK class power car (681-690) with an ADB class trailer (771-780). The ADK's were built by Commonwealth Engineering (Comeng) in Sydney, NSW, and they introduced a number of new innovations into Perth's suburbs. Their design was based on the American Budd Co. monocoque constructed railcars in which the corrugated stainless steel body contributed significantly to the overall strength of the car, rather than relying entirely on the underframe. This produced a lighter vehicle which was able to make better use of its engine power. The ADK's were the WAGR's first stainless steel railcars, and the first to have a driving cab at one end only. They were also the first of the WAGR's passenger vehicles to have air brakes rather than vacuum, and it was this feature, along with a different type of control gear, which made them incompatible with other vehicles in the railcar fleet. They were also the first series of railcars with power operated doors. The ADB class trailers, the first of which entered service a few weeks after the ADK's in March, 1968, were built at Midland and were designed to operate specifically with the ADK's, those cars

Two ADK/ADB sets at Perth station, ADB 774 & ADK 684 on the left & ADB 780 & ADK 690 on the left.

Photo courtesy ARHS.

with the same last digit in their numbers normally being coupled together. Their arrival resulted in the immediate withdrawal from service of the ACM suburban cars and, a few months later in October, the running of the last suburban steam train. This meant the end of the line for most of the wooden bodied compartment cars, particularly the remaining pre-1900 stock. The AD and ADS classes of suburban brake cars largely finished their days on suburban and short distance trains, including suburban goods trains due to the brake van shortage during the early 1950's, and photographs of the day often show a diminutive AD type car bringing up the rear of a train of larger post 1900 suburban carriages. The class finally disappeared in 1968 when the last car, AD 108, was written off.

On 3 August, 1968 the standard gauge railway from Perth was connected to the Commonwealth Railways line at Kalgoorlie.[19] The "Westland" continued to run using the Avon Valley line and the Eastern Goldfields Railway, but the last train operated this service on 14 and 15 June, 1969,[20] replaced by the new standard gauge "Trans Australian" from South Australia, and the "Indian Pacific" from New South Wales after 1 March, 1970. These trains ended their journeys at Perth Terminal, built on the site of the old East Perth Locomotive Depot.

The final steam hauled suburban service took place on 4 October, 1968[21] and from then on the suburban services were handled by the ADG, ADH, ADX and ADA class railcars and trailers, along with the ADK/ADB sets, and supported by diesel hauled sets consisting of AY, AYB, AYE and AYF class cars. The ADG's had been modified in several ways during their life time. In the mid 1950's the black and yellow chevrons painted on the ends of the cars were replaced with silver, trimmed in red, and by 1958 the suburban livery of green lower panels, white upper panels and a red waist band was beginning to appear on them. They had all been repainted in this livery by the mid 1960's. During the 1960's the cars were fitted with a destination box in the driver's cab above the

gangway doors, and later they received a steel sun visor over the top of the driver's window. From 1963-64 the ADG's were fitted with superchargers to increase their power, as they were having trouble keeping up with the higher powered ADX class cars. To further improve their performance they were fitted with Voith transmissions, the first being done in 1969. This was essentially an automatic gearbox and did much to make the driver's task simpler. The cars were all converted between 1969 and 1973. After the successful conversion of the ADG class cars, the ADH's also received the Voith transmissions, the first in 1971 and the last in 1973. As this transmission also required modifications to be made to the control gear in the trailers, a number of ADA's (751-764) and AYE's (708, 709, 713, & 714) were also altered, the work taking five years to complete. The conversions were carried out between 1969 and 1973. All the modified cars were temporarily reclassified by having a "/V" added to their class letters, this classification becoming permanent in 1978. The ADX's, however, were not fitted with the new transmission. The reason for this is not known, but it was ultimately to bring about the early demise of the class, and in the meantime they were restricted to running with each other and with those trailers not modified for the new equipment, these being ADA 765-770 and AYE 701, 703, and 710-712.

During the late 1950's and right through the 1960's, as railcars took over the suburban services, the old passenger cars were quietly removed from traffic and written off. The last of the pre-1900 suburban cars (AD, AE & AF) had vanished into history with the passing of steam from the suburbs, and in 1970 most of the remaining 12 wheeled suburban cars went, with classes AS, AU and AW being eliminated from the system. AW 334 was written off in 1960 and AW 332 followed in 1961. However, it was discovered that AW 332 was in better condition than AW 333 which was still in service, so AW 332 was re-instated in 1962 as AW 333, and the original AW 333 went to the scrap yard in its place. The last two AW's, including 332 masquerading as 333, were written off in 1970.

Initially, the AS second class suburban brake cars had been little affected by the introduction of the diesel railcars. In 1960 AS 374 was converted into the WAGR Trade and Industries Display saloon, reclassified ASD. In concept it was very similar to the conversion of AG 38 almost forty years before. It was not until 1967 that the AS class began to disappear from Perth's suburban railway lines, following the delivery of the final batch of ADA class railcar trailers the year before, and the final AS class cars went quickly with the loss of AS 371 and 378 in 1969, followed by AS 369, 373, 377 and 379 in 1970. Twelve AT second class suburban cars were written off in 1970, having been out of regular use for two years, and in 1971 the last of the suburban 12 wheelers, AT 300, was also written off.

The steel car-plus-AYF suburban consist ran till June, 1971, when AKB 60 was written off. It sat at Midland for many years and was offered to the Pinjarra Steam and Hills Railway Preservation Society (later the Hotham Valley Railway), but it was not taken up. It was sold privately in 1975. The remaining two remaining AJ class suburban cars were written off together in March, 1972.

The opening of the standard gauge railway up the Avon Valley and onto Kalgoorlie in 1968 soon caused the demise of the WAGR's overnight passenger trains between Perth and the goldfields. The "Westland" stopped running in 1969, its passengers being accommodated on the Commonwealth Railways standard gauge "Trans Australian", and that same year orders were placed with Comeng in Sydney for five new standard gauge railcars (WCA class) and three trailers (WCE class) to operate high speed sit up services between Perth and Kalgoorlie. The demise of the "Westland" and the transfer of its rolling stock to other services brought about a cascading effect which caused the return of lounge cars to the "Kalgoorlie", and the ex "Westland" sleeping cars displaced five old AQ/AQC/AQS class end platform cars (AQ 335, 341, AQC 340, and AQS 343 & 344) from the "Kalgoorlie", which were written off in 1970. AQS 343 was retained and rebuilt as a hospital car to be used in the event of an accident in the relatively inaccessible Avon Valley. Reclassified AQA, it could carry 16 patients and spent a good deal of its time coupled to a flat wagon which was intended for use as a helipad. The coach was repainted white with a red cross on both sides, and thankfully, was never used in anger. AQ 335 and 341 were the last of the first class AQ's. The new railcars were the first standard gauge passenger cars to be wholly owned by the WAGR, and they presented some unique problems right from the start. Even though they were on standard gauge bogies, their size prevented them from being railed from the builder in Sydney to Western Australia, due to the tunnels and curves in the NSW Blue Mountains. As a result, they were trucked to Goobang Junction, near Parkes in NSW, and from there were towed to Perth behind goods trains. The first to arrive was a WCE class trailer in May, 1971, followed by another in June, and the first WCA class power car in August. The first power cars and trailer entered service on 20 November, 1971. Two days later the name "Prospector" was bestowed upon the new railcar service, and on 29 November the first train ran from Perth to Kalgoorlie.[22] Five WCA class power cars were purchased and numbered 901-905, along with three trailers, WCE 921-923, the last of the eight vehicles entering traffic in January, 1972.

Once the "Prospector" was in service, the "Kalgoorlie", having lived on borrowed time for two years, ran for the last time in 1971, and was the last train to travel over the old narrow gauge Eastern Goldfields Railway. The track on this line was then lifted, cutting the narrow gauge network in two, while the coaches from the "Kalgoorlie" sets were re-allocated to other overnight trains. In the early 1970's the "Australind" was deemed to be a one class train, so the cars used on that service lost their first and second class status.

The loss of the "Westland" and the "Kalgoorlie" left more carriages than were required and in 1973 a large number of redundant second class sleeping cars (ARS) were written off. In addition the four remaining AV class dining cars also became redundant, and AV 425 and 426 were withdrawn from use and stored, finally being written off in 1974. The other two dining cars saw occasional use on Reso trains and other specials, and the last one, (AV 286) ran in October, 1975 on an ARHS tour. AV 286 and 315 were both written off that year and in 1979 they were converted into workman's vans. By the end of 1973 it was becoming apparent that nothing could prevent the irreversible decline of the WAGR's passenger fleet. The newest passenger cars were over twenty years old and to replace them would have cost millions of dollars, money which was simply not available for the new CME, Mr. D.M. McCaskill, to spend. There was not even enough money for a refurbishment programme, and the only alternative left was to write off the remaining cars and get out of the passenger carrying business altogether.

The first service to go was the "Mullewa", which ran for the last time in 1974.[23] It was the most poorly patronised of the remaining trains and was an obvious candidate for early withdrawal. With this train went the last of the ACL class long distance side loading cars. They had been disappearing in ever increasing numbers since 1959, and in 1965 when large numbers of branch line cars, including ACL's, were in store, seventeen (ACL 1, 3, 6, 19, 21, 23, 27, 30, 189, 191, 204, 227-229, 234, 388 & 389) were written off in one go. Fourteen more became ACM's for suburban use, and by 1968 only four ACL's remained on the books. Two (ACL 232 & 405) were written off in 1973, and the other two (ACL 407 & 410) went to the Vintage Train at Bunbury, marking the end of the largest group or country cars to run in WAGR passenger service. "Mullewa" sleeping car AQZ 420 was retained in service, while AQZ 416 was written off, the body being sold to the Guildford Grammar School in Perth the following year, and finally being demolished. Buffet car AQL 290 was retained as a spare car on Bunbury or Albany trains, as the need arose, and former "Kalgoorlie" sleeping cars ARM 351 and 356, and sleeping car AQM 292 which had been used on the "Mullewa" did little work after its demise, but were retained on the books a little while longer. The "Midlander", "Albany Weekender", "Shopper" and "Bunbury Belle" were all withdrawn on 1 August, 1975,[24] followed by the last Reso train in October. The "Shopper" and "Bunbury Belle" were replaced by road coaches. The consequences for the carriage stock were serious. Thirty three vehicles, including some of the 1960's rebuilds, were written off by the end of that year. Second class sleeping car AQS 289 was written off in 1972, its body later destroyed in civil defence exercises, and in 1975 AQC 339, the last of the breed, was written off, being converted to a workman's van four years later. When the trains to the goldfields finished up the ARS class sleeping cars had no other services to go to and in 1973 the bulk of them were written off. These were ARS 278-281, 283, 285, 350, 352-355 and 422. After the demise of the "Midlander" and "Albany Weekender" in 1975 the last six ARS's were written off the books (ARS 277, 284, 348, 349, 358 & 421), and a number of these were stored in deteriorating condition at Bellevue. Lounge car AVL 314, sleeping car AZS 446 and the AQM class sleeping cars (287 & 292) were written off in December, 1975. The AVL was stored at the Midland Workshops till September, 1976 when it was painted yellow and re-issued to traffic as the workman's van for the 60 ton breakdown train, and the AZS and AQM's found their way into the hands of preservation groups. The relatively new AH first class sleeping cars were also no longer required and they were all written off as a group in December, 1975. The running of the last Reso train also meant that the AYL class lounge cars and the AGS shower car became redundant. Both AYL's (28 & 29) were written off by the end of 1975, and AGS 22 was retired and stored, being written off in October, 1976 when it became obvious that there was no further use for a shower car. The ADF's and ADU's had one final fling two weeks after their last regular Bunbury services when, on 16 August, 1975, the Australian Railway Historical Society ran a tour to Pinjarra and back. Appropriately, Pinjarra was the last country station visited by an ADF, because it was also the first, one week short of twenty six years earlier. The three ADF's (492, 493 & 495) and the remaining ADU's (586-591)

were written off as a group on 27 October, 1975, and due to their corrosion problems all but one ADU and one ADF were scrapped. Thus, during 1975, mainline classes AQ, AQC, AQS, ARS, AV, AVL, AZS, AQM, AH, AYL, AGS, ADF and ADU, and branchline class ACL all disappeared from the WAGR. In addition, the wind down of the country branchline passenger services two decades earlier had caused the demise of the ZA class brakevans, and in 1975 the last one, ZA 177, was written out of WAGR service. Several ZA's served another two decades as workman's vans. At the end of 1975 the only narrow gauge country passenger trains left were the "Albany Progress" and the "Australind".

In September, 1975 the WAGR decided to adopt the name "Westrail" as part of a new corporate image and a new livery was chosen.[25] Wagons and brakevans were painted yellow, while locomotives and suburban carriages became orange with a blue band at waist level. The suburban railcars and their trailers also had their roofs painted brown. Eventually it was decided to retain the Larch green and cream livery for the remaining country passenger stock and only one country passenger car (ARM 351) was ever repainted orange and blue, while the suburban stock and some inspection cars had all been repainted by the end of 1980.

ARS cars stored at Bellevue. ARS 354 is closest to the camera.   *Photo courtesy Joe Moir.*

Suburban Railcar Trailer
ADA class

ADA 751, fresh out of the workshops, poses for the WAGR photographer. *Photo courtesy ARHS.*

In October, 1961 the first of a batch of steel bodied railcar trailers, built to run with the ADG, H and X class railcars, entered service. There were ten cars in this first batch, classed ADA and numbered 751-760, the last of them going into service in August, 1962. Externally they were similar to the ADG, H and X class power cars, but shorter, and they had a driver's cab at one end only, passenger entry doors in the centre, and external beading on the body panel joins. They were relatively light cars and their underframes were identical to those under the ADT class "Governor" railcar trailers. The ADA's bogies were, however, fitted with roller bearings in the axle boxes. Interestingly, they had spoked wheels rather than the solid type found on the other railcars, this giving them a vaguely antique look. The passenger entry had double sliding doors, mechanically operated and interlocked so that opening one of the pair caused the other to open as well. The ADA's seated 62 passengers and a further 32 people could be carried standing up. They were issued to traffic in the green, white and red livery.

Another batch of five ADA's was built in 1964 (761-765) and they entered service between 6 and 27 November that year, a complete contrast to the delivery rate of the first batch. This second batch may have been built on the underframes of the old ADT class cars which were written off in 1962, which could explain why they were delivered so quickly. A final group of five cars (ADA 766-770) was built in 1966, and these were delivered at a rate one every three weeks or so.

To prevent problems with marshalling, the ADA's always faced east, and they generally led fairly quiet lives as they carried Perth's commuters around the suburban network. During the 1960's each car was fitted with a steel sun visor over the driver's window.

With the introduction of the Voith transmissions in the ADG and ADH class railcars, a number of ADA's were fitted with new control gear so they could operate with the modified vehicles. ADA 751-764 were converted, the work taking five years to complete. The conversions were carried out between 1969 and 1973, and the cars converted were temporarily reclassified ADA/V. This left ADA 765-770 to run with the unmodified ADX railcars, and the ADA/V classification became permanent in October, 1978.

During the latter half of the 1970's, after the WAGR had adopted the corporate name "Westrail", the ADA's and ADA/V's were repainted in the new orange and blue livery, a colour scheme they carried to the ends of their working lives. About this time they were also fitted with an enlarged cab front lower panel to allow more room for the driver's legs.

When the Fremantle line was closed to suburban traffic in 1979 several of the older suburban cars were removed from service and stored. ADA/V 755 was written off in November, 1980, followed by ADA 768 in August, 1981. The demise of the ADX's during the mid 1980's saw the writing off of more of the unmodified ADA's, although three were used in a locomotive hauled set of ADA's and engineless ADX's, known as the "Tin Can" set. ADA 765 and 766 were also both noted in this consist in mid 1986. However, their lightweight construction did not allow heavy loads to be marshalled behind them, so their efficiency in this role was limited. The set was withdrawn from use after the arrival of the Queensland cars in 1986. In 1985 ADA 770 was written off, followed by ADA 767 and 769, the remains of which were still at Midland in April, 1991. ADA 765 and 766 were both converted to ADA/

V in April, 1989, a move deemed to be more economical than encapsulating the asbestos in ADA/V 752 and 758. These two cars were written off in August, 1989, having been out of service for nearly nine months, and in December, 1989 they were both buried at the Gosnells rubbish tip. The remaining fourteen ADA/V class cars were progressively withdrawn during the last half of 1991, most being out of service by 25 October that year. The class was kept at Claisebrook Railcar Depot till 16 December, 1991, when nine of them (751, 753, 754, 759, 760, 763, 764, 765 and 760(?) were towed to Forrestfield, enroute to Robb's Jetty for storage. They were

written off in February, 1992. At Robb's Jetty they were being wrecked by vandals, so early in May the now derelict cars were returned to Forrestfield. Their time here was only brief, as they were sold for scrap, being hauled away and cut up during June, 1992. Only three are known to have survived. ADA 763 was preserved by the Australian Railway Historical Society, coupled to ADG 612. It was stored at Forrestfield, but was the subject of some considerable vandalism, so was moved to the closed Midland Workshops on 7 July, 1994. One has been preserved at the Bluegum Railway, near Karridale, and another near Lake Leschanaultia, outside Perth.

A batch of new ADAs at the Midland Workshops.   *Photo courtesy ARHS.*

ADA 765, looking a little weathered, on a siding near the East Perth locomotive depot on 16 September, 1967.
Photo late Geoff Blee, courtesy Murray Rowe.

ADA/V 756 is carried along between two ADG/V class cars between Bassendean & Ashfield stations, 8 November, 1991.
Photo Bill Gray.

ADA/V 759 at Midland station, 4 November, 1990.
Photo Bill Gray.

ADA/V 762 leads a four car suburban set out of the City, 25 September, 1988. *Photo Bill Gray.*

ADA/V 760, having been heavily vandalised at Robb's Jetty, sits at Forrestfield with several of its sisters, to await its fate, 1 June, 1992. *Photo Bill Gray.*

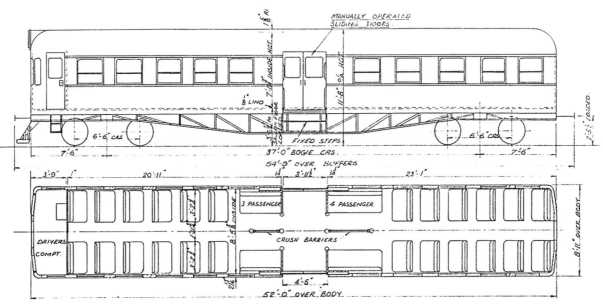

The general arrangement drawing if the ADA class railcars.   Drawing courtesy PTA.

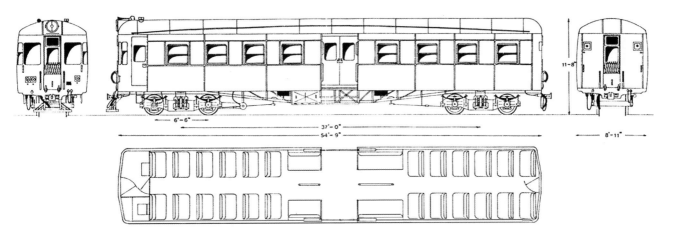

Andy May's drawing of the ADAs.

A couple of young travellers enjoy a journey between Perth & Midland in an ADA class car, October, 1991.   Photo Bill Gray.

AQL 288 upon its arrival at Bassendean for restoration, 14 January, 1986.   *Photo Bill Gray.*

The AQL class, consisting of two cars (288 & 290) was born of the upgrading of the WAGR's mainline rail services during the early 1960's. They were based on AQS second class sleeping cars originally built in 1904, and were issued to traffic as AQL class buffet cars in 1961, AQL 288 in May and AQL 290 in October.

Although of the same class, there were some major external differences between the two cars. AQL 288 retained its end platforms and, according to the WAGR drawings, its original windows, complete with crown lights, while AQL 290 had its end platforms enclosed and converted into entry vestibules with stable type entry doors. It was fitted with steel framed "Young" windows of the half lift variety, in which only the bottom pane could be raised. The matchboard sides on both cars were replaced with plywood sheeting painted Larch green and cream, and they rode on AZ bogies.

The basic interior layout of the two cars was similar, but again there were differences. AQL 288 was fitted with a fairly small buffet, but had a passenger compartment at one end, while AQL 290's large buffet precluded the inclusion of a separate passenger compartment. AQL 288 accommodated 19 first class passengers in the main saloon, and another 6 in the compartment, while AQL 290 had seating for 18 passengers. AQL 288 was allocated to the "Albany Progress", while AQL 290, with its vestibule ends, went to work on the "Mullewa".

If AQL 288 did, in fact retain its timber windows at conversion, it was at some stage modified when it was fitted with "Young" windows similar to those in AQL 290, and dust shields on the end platforms, replacing the scrolled metal work. Precisely when these changes took place is uncertain. The window spacing on the car also appears to have been altered at this time, but the interior was not changed.

Both cars gave good service on their respective trains, but the end of country passenger express trains in the mid 1970's put them out of work. The "Mullewa" stopped running in 1974[26] and AQL 290 was retained as a spare car on Bunbury or Albany trains, as the need arose. In December, 1975 AQL 288 was written off and replaced on the "Albany Progress" by AQL 290, but with the running of the final "Albany Progress" in December, 1978,[27] AQL 290 was withdrawn from use and leased to the Hotham Valley Railway, later being purchased outright. Meanwhile, in May, 1976 AQL 288 had been sold to the Great Southern Steam Association at Albany, but it only saw limited use there, finally being sold to the Australian Railway Historical Society in Perth late in 1984. It was stored at Forrestfield for a short time and restoration began in January, 1986. After a number of lengthy delays, AQL 288 was outshopped on 28 May, 1991 and returned to service on ARHS tour trains a few days later.

AQL 290 parked in the Hotham Valley Railway compound at Dwellingup, 28 May, 2001.   *Photo Bill Gray.*

AQL 288 after it's restoration is seen on a train heading into Forrestfield Marshalling Yard, 1 June, 1991.   *Photo Bill Gray.*

AQL 290 rests in the late afternoon sun, carrying a "Mullewa" nameboard.

Photo late Geoff Blee, courtesy Murray Rowe.

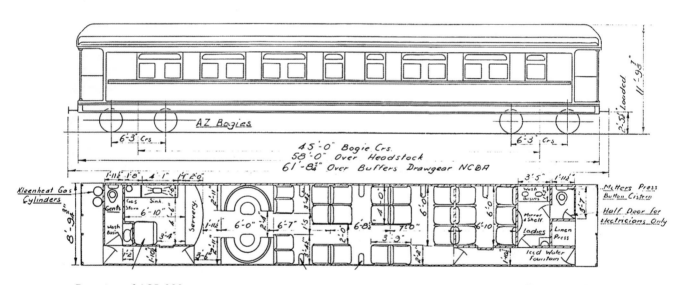

Drawing of AQL 288   Courtesy PTA.

Inside AQL 288 before its restoration, 14 January, 1986.   Photos Bill Gray.

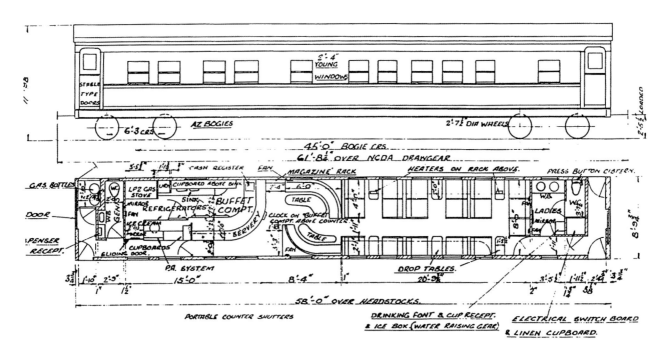

Drawings of AQL class buffet car, AQL 290

Drawings courtesy PTA

Inside a new AQL 290

Photo courtesy ARHS.

Second Class Sleeping Car
AQM class

AQM 292 at Forrestfield on 11 April, 1992.

Photo Bill Gray.

To operate with the two AQL class buffet cars, another pair of AQS class cars (287 & 292) were converted into AQM second class sleeping cars. The first in traffic was AQM 287 which left the Midland Workshops in May, 1961 with AQL 288. AQM 287 retained its end platforms and, according to the WAGR drawings, its timber framed windows, but lost its tongue and groove body timbers in favour of plywood panelling. It was painted Larch green and cream and fitted with AZ type bogies, making it very similar in appearance to AQL 288. If AQM 287 did retain its timber framed windows at conversion (no photographs have come to light of it with timber windows) they were later replaced by "Young" steel framed half lift windows, and the old crown lights above were boarded over.

Inside the AQM all the ornate woodwork was removed, flat ceilings were fitted in the corridor, and paint, laminex and vinyl replaced varnish, timber and leather. The car contained nine twin berth passenger compartments similar to those found in the AQZ's, but smaller, and these could accommodate 36 passengers during the day and 18 people at night.

AQM 292 was issued to traffic in October, 1961 along with buffet car AQL 290 and looking very much like it. Its end platforms and bull nosed roof were replaced by entry vestibules, plywood panelling replaced the tongue and groove side timbers and "Young" steel framed half lift windows were fitted. The crown lights were boarded over and the car was fitted with AZ bogies. Externally it was the same size as AQM 287, and it, too, was turned out in Larch green and cream. The interior, apart from the entry vestibules, was the same as AQM

287, as was the passenger capacity, but it was fitted with end doors and concertinas over the gangways.

AQM 287 went to work on the "Albany Progress", while AQM 292 with its "dust proofing" went to the "Mullewa". In company with their buffet car cousins, the two sleeping cars worked well, those on the "Mullewa" also running with a vestibule ended AQZ first class sleeping car. The AQM's were written off in December, 1975 after most of Western Australia's overnight country passenger express trains had passed into history.

AQM 287 was sold to the Pinjarra Lion's Club in May, 1976 and loaned to the Hotham Valley Railway where it was used on works trains or as sleeping quarters for that organisation's volunteer workers. AQM 292 was sold to the Great Southern Steam Association at Albany in May, 1976 and ran on the occasional tour train, but generally saw very little use. At one stage a fire was lit in one of its compartments, causing some damage to the car, and in late 1984 it was purchased by the Australian Railway Historical Society. The AQM was towed to Perth, spending some time in storage at Forrestfield, and in 1986 it was transferred to the Rail Transport Museum at Bassendean where restoration began. In March that year, with most of the basic work done, a fire broke out in the same compartment previously burnt[28] and, although it was brought under control after a sharp eyed passing railcar driver saw it and called the fire brigade, considerable damage was sustained to the compartment and roof above it. It was, however, repaired, the restoration completed, and AQM 292 returned to service on 1 June, 1990.

AQM 287 at the Hotham Valley Railway depot at Dwellingup, 28 May, 2001.   *Photo Bill Gray.*

AQM 292 after a tour working passes through High Wycombe on 1 June, 1991. This shot shows the other side of the car to that shown in the heading photo.   *Photo Bill Gray.*

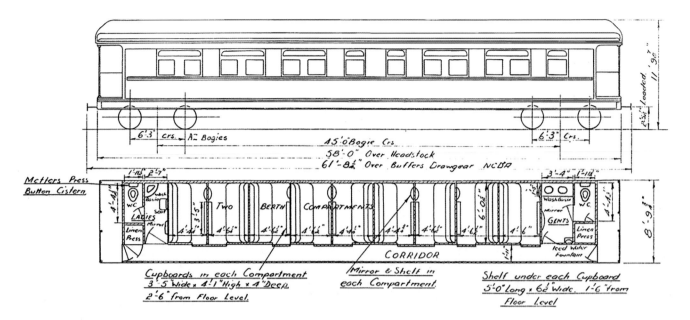

The general arrangement drawing of AQM 287 shows it with timber framed windows & crown lights.

Drawing courtesy PTA.

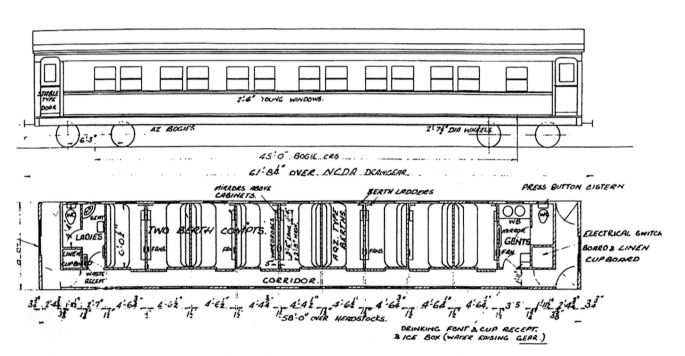

General arrangement drawing of AQM 292 showing it with modified end platforms & Young type windows.

Drawing courtesy PTA.

Suburban Railcar
ADH class

ADH 651 soon after its conversion from a country car.   *Photo late Geoff Blee, courtesy Murray Rowe.*

With the cutting back of the country branch line rail services, the relatively new ADH class country railcars were put out of work, so they were employed on the Perth suburban network. Since they could only carry 16 passengers, they were converted to proper suburban railcars, ADH 653 and 654 returning to traffic in January, 1962. ADH 651 and 653 were similarly converted in mid 1963.

The converted ADH's were almost indistinguishable from the ADG and ADX class railcars. They were fitted with double sliding entry doors, similar to the ADX class (the ADG's had single doors), which were mechanically interlocked so that if one was opened its other half would also automatically open. This system tended to stop the annoying problem of the doors sliding open or closed as the train accelerated or decelerated. The swing over seats were later replaced with fixed back seating to carry 104 passengers, 52 seated and 52 standing, and the ADH's had a bit more room in them than the ADG's or ADX's. The only obvious difference between an ADH and an ADX was the full length rain strip on the roof of the former, while the latter had a curved rain strip above each door. At some stage the ADH's were repainted in the green, white and red livery, probably at the time of conversion, although it is thought that ADH 654 had carried this livery since new. They were fitted with destination boxes above the end gangway doors, and later received a fixed steel sun visor over the driver's window.

After the successful conversion of several ADG class cars with Voith automatic transmissions, the ADH's also received this equipment, the first in 1971 and the last in 1973. They were then known as ADH/V, but this classification did not become official till October, 1978.

In 1975 the WAGR changed its name to Westrail and a new orange and blue livery was introduced. This eventually caught up with the railcars and the ADH/V's were repainted between 1976 and 1978.

In 1981 ADH/V 653 was involved in a rear end collision with a goods train near Perth terminal, resulting in a bent frame. The car was considered to be beyond economic repair, so it was withdrawn from service and its body taken to the Belmont rubbish tip in Perth and buried, presumably because it obtained asbestos. It had travelled 1,013,908 miles (1,689,847 km). About this time the other three cars were fitted with a new bulged lower panel on the front of the cab at the driver's side, apparently to improve the driver's leg room.

The remaining ADH/V's soldiered on, their ageing AEC engines being replaced by new Mercedes Benz units, ADH 651 in 1987, and ADH 652 and 654 in 1988, to keep them going till the Perth suburban network could be electrified. Towards the end of their lives, following the withdrawal of most of the ADA class trailers in October, 1991, the ADH's were coupled together with the ADG's in sets of three power cars. In this way, if one car failed the set could continue the service. The ADH's were withdrawn from use in January, 1992 and written off the following month. They were stored at Robb's Jetty, but were badly vandalised, so were returned to Forrestfield early in May, 1993. Scrapping of the withdrawn suburban railcars began on 10 June, 1993 and by the end of it all one ADH/V 651 was with the Fire Brigade at Forrestfield, 652 was at Mt. Helena, preserved by a former driver, and the third, ADH/V 654 had been scrapped.

ADH 653 in the green, white & red suburban livery. *Photo late Geoff Blee, courtesy Murray Rowe.*

ADH/V 652 leads an ADA & an ADG up the hill near Lathlain, 16 March, 1988. *Photo Bill Gray.*

ADH/V 652 at Midland station, showing a destination sign & a lot more dirt on 4 December, 1990. The ADH/Vs were well & truly on borrowed time by this time.   *Photo Bill Gray.*

ADH/V 651 with ADG/V 603 on the "Farewell Tour" at Kwinana on 7 December, 1991, with only a couple of weeks left. Gone were the days of cleaning passenger cars used on tours, the white on the ADH/V apparently being the result of recently removed graffiti.   *Photo Bill Gray.*

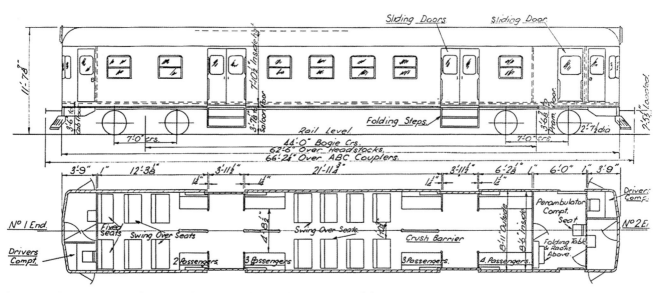

The general arrangement drawing of the ADH class railcar, converted from a country car.   *Drawing courtesy PTA*

Second Class Sleeping Car
ARM class

ARM 357 in new condition. *Photo courtesy ARHS.*

In the early 1960's four ARS class cars (347, 351, 356 & 357) were rebuilt as ARM second class sleeping cars. These carriages had started out as AR second class sit up cars in 1908, built on wooden underfames, and they had been rebuilt as ARS class sleeping cars on ex suburban car steel underframes only five years earlier. The first pair (347 & 357) were issued to traffic in April, 1962 and the second pair (351 & 356) the following October.

From the outside the ARM's were barely recognisable as having come from AR's, but they did bear a strong resemblance to some of the other cars which were modified at the same time. The end platforms were filled in with entry vestibules, the windows were replaced with the steel framed "Young" half lift type, the window spacing was changed and the matchboard sides were replaced with plywood panelling. The cars were turned out in Larch green and cream, and the first two (347 & 357) were issued to traffic with their old 6 wheel bogies, while ARM 351 and 356 were placed on ride

control bogies. This type of undercarriage was fitted to 347 and 357 in 1963.

The ARM's carried 36 passengers by day and slept 18 at night in nine twin berth passenger compartments which were very much like those in the AQM class cars. They also carried a conductor, which was unusual for a second class car.

The ARM's went to work on the "Kalgoorlie" but after that train stopped running in 1971 they were allocated to other overnight trains. ARM 351 and 356 were used on the "Mullewa" till it was stopped in 1974. After 1975 none of the class saw much use, the only overnight train still running being the "Albany Progress", and this ran for the last time in 1978, after which all four ARM's were retired and stored.

ARM 347 and 357 were written off in November, 1979 and sold to the Hotham Valley Railway, while ARM 351 and 356 were rebuilt yet again in 1980 as ARA class brake sitting cars for the "Australind". All four cars are preserved.

ARM 356 carrying "Kalgoorlie" nameboards at Midland on 16 March, 1967.

Photo late Geoff Blee, courtesy Murray Rowe.

ARM 347 at Pinjarra on 2 December, 1989, in the care of the Hotham Valley Railway.

Photo Bill Gray.

ARM 357 at the Midland Workshops, carrying the "Kalgoorlie" nameboards & showing its ride control bogies off to good effect on 13 April, 1967.
Photo late Geoff Blee, courtesy Murray Rowe.

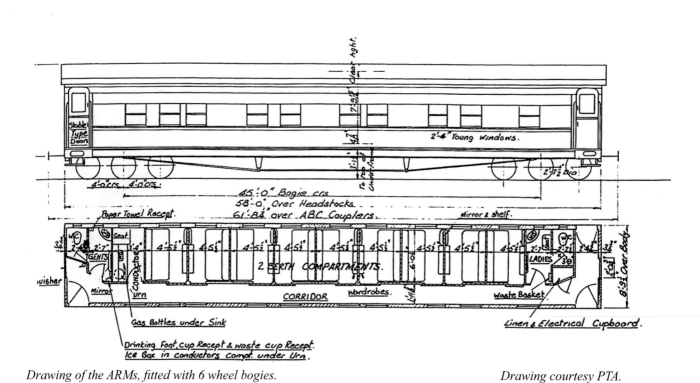

Drawing of the ARMs, fitted with 6 wheel bogies.
Drawing courtesy PTA.

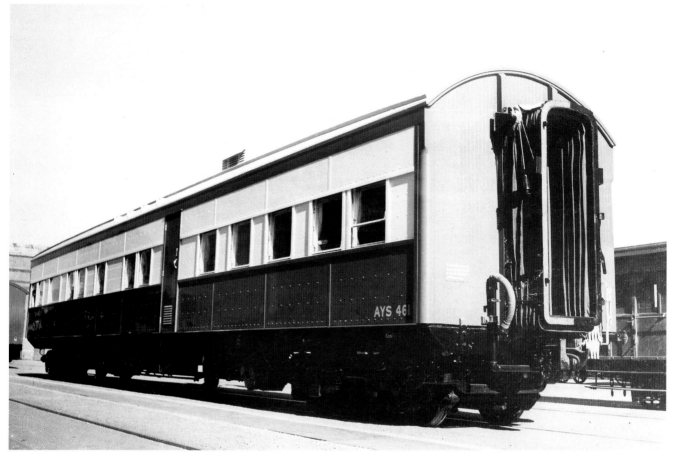

AYS 461 in original condition, before the fire in 1966 saw it rebuilt.

Photo late Geoff Blee, courtesy Murray Rowe.

The next "new" cars to appear during the 1960's rebuilding programme were two lounge-buffet cars, classed AYS. They were built from a pair of 1946 vintage AY class suburban cars, 460 and 461, but when the conversions were complete there was little to tell that they had ever been AY's. The old tongue and groove sides were replaced with plywood panelling and the entry doors were removed. The windows were replaced with the steel framed half lift type, but the window spacing differed slightly between the two cars. End doors were the main means of entry for the passengers, so boarding the AYS's was generally done from other carriages. They rode on ride control bogies and were issued to traffic in Larch green and cream. Unusually for the WAGR, both cars were named, AYS 460 "Colgoola" and AYS 461 "Boulder". AYS 461 could seat 17 passengers, and AYS 460 accommodated 20. They were both regarded as first class cars.

AYS class cars were built for use on the "Kalgoorlie" between Perth and Kalgoorlie, and it was on a service being operated by this train that AYS 461 was gutted by fire on 23 March, 1966 while travelling to Perth. Two AZ class sleeping cars were destroyed in the fire, but the AYS was saved and returned to Midland Workshops for repair and rebuilding.

AYS 461 emerged from the workshops by December, 1966,

virtually a new carriage. The windows, all single pane, had been re-arranged so there were more of them, and plywood panelling on the tops gave them a round cornered appearance. Inside, the car was unrecognisable to anyone familiar with the old layout. The buffet had been relocated to the centre of the vehicle (a blessing to anyone who had to work in it, not being over the wheels) and it now had first and second class sections. The first class section could accommodate 12 passengers and the second class section seated 9. It was the first WAGR carriage to be fitted with air conditioning.[29]

The WAGR's country passenger trains stopped running during the 1970's, the AYS's fell into disuse and were leased to preservation groups. AYS 460 went to the Kalgoorlie-Boulder Loopline Preservation Society where it is on static display, and AYS 461 went to the Great Southern Steam Association at Albany, where it saw occasional use behind steam locomotive W 947. In late 1984 the lease was transferred to the Australian Railway Historical Society and the AYS arrived at the Bassendean Rail Transport Museum at the end of that year for restoration. It was later purchased outright by the Society and was the first carriage to be returned to service by that organisation, making its debut in April, 1985.

AYS 460 photographed at Kalgoorlie on 30 December, 1967.

AYS 461 at Perth, after rebuilding. *Both photos late Geoff Blee, courtesy Murray Rowe.*

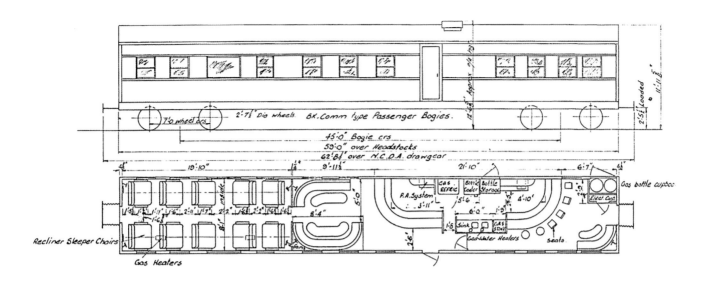

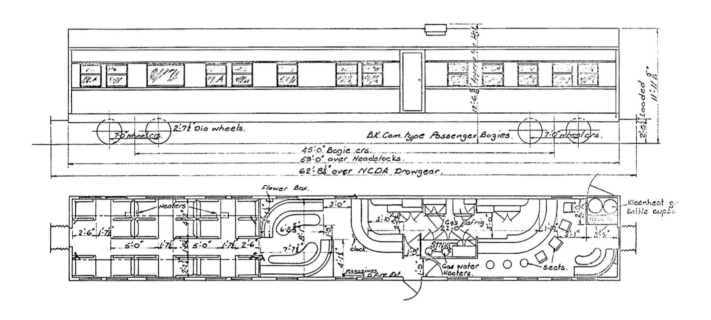

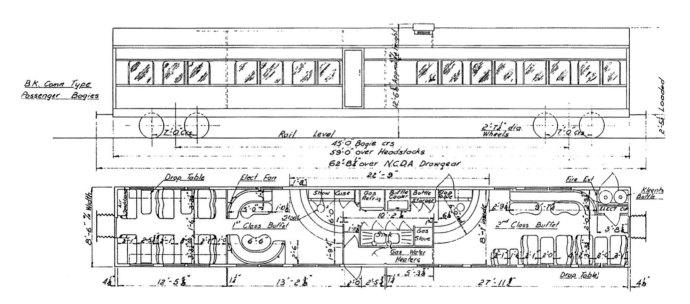

From top to bottom are the AYS cars in their various forms, AYS 460 at the top, AYS 461 as originally built in the centre, & AYS 461 in its final form at the bottom.
Drawings courtesy PTA.

AYS 461 in preservation, taken at Forrestfield on 11 April, 1992.   *Photo Bill Gray.*

AYS 461 outside the Rail Transport Museum at Bassendean on 9 March, 1987. his view shows the other side of the coach.
Photo Bill Gray.

AYU 580 rests at Perth station 25 April, 1967.   *Photo late Geoff Blee, courtesy Murray Rowe.*

By 1964 some of the steel bodied ADU class railcar trailers had become redundant with the retirement of their ADF power cars from country rail services. Four found employment on the "Shopper" and "Bunbury Belle" services, while two others (580 & 581) were converted to loco hauled cars for long distance passenger trains. Classed AYU, they were not dissimilar to the modified ADU class cars. They were fitted with layback seats and gas heating,[30] the slanted end and guard's compartment were removed, and the unusual oval window at each end indicated the location of the wash rooms and toilets, but in virtually every other way, on the outside at least, they retained their ADU characteristics. They could carry 55 passengers and were painted Larch green and cream.

Upon completion in August, 1964 AYU 580 was painted red and ivory, and issued to traffic as part of the new "Midlander"

set, while AYU 581, in its green and cream, worked between Mullewa and Meekatharra.

In 1966 two more ADU's (584 & 585) were converted into AYU's, and both went into service in green and cream. They all seem to have led fairly uncomplicated lives, often being used on hired specials during the late 1960's and into the 1970's, where they looked completely out of place on a train of straight sided and slightly taller wooden country cars.

All four AYU's were written off as a group in May, 1980, their bodies being sold to the Ridolfo Brothers and transported to the Metana Minerals mining site at Mount Magnet for use as cabin accommodation. At least one has been removed to the Mount Magnet museum, while the remains of the others are believed to have been sold for use at other mine sites in the area.

AYU 580 again, in the "Midlander" livery at Perth, 1 August, 1965.

Photo late Geoff Blee, courtesy Murray Rowe

AYU 584 at Perth, 1967.

Both photos late Geoff Blee, courtesy Murray Rowe.

AYU 584 & one of its sisters looking a little forlorn as they wait for motive power.

Photo courtesy Joe Moir.

An AYU loads its passengers at Perth station, ready for a" Midlander" service.   *Photo courtesy Don Finlayson.*

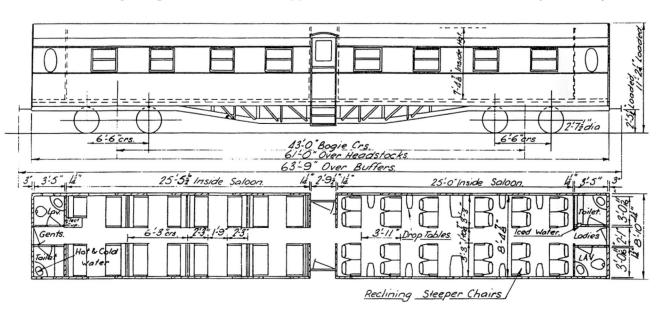

General arrangement of the AYU.   *Drawing courtesy PTA.*

Interior of an AYU class car, taken on 5 May, 1964.
Photo WAGR, courtesy ARHS.

AZS 444 at the Midland Workshops. This car was later destroyed in "Operation Neva".

Photo late Geoff Blee, courtesy Murray Rowe.

The AZS class was created by the WAGR's takeover of the Midland Railway Co. in August, 1964, and then, only by default. The class consisted of three sleeping cars, which had served the Midland Railway as the JV class. They were built late in 1927 at the Midland Workshops.[31] The WAGR's AZ class followed the same design, but the JV's had not been subjected to many, if any, modifications over the years. When taken into WAGR ownership they were still largely in original condition with their tongue and groove side timbers, no shower compartment and no conductor's compartment.

Upon arriving in WAGR ownership the three cars (formerly JV 31-33) were repainted green and cream and had their old bogies replaced by those from the scrapped ADU class railcar trailers. Without facilities like shower and conductor's

compartments, they could hardly have remained as first class cars, so they were down graded to second class, hence the classification AZS. They were renumbered 444-446 and entered service in August and September, 1965.

The AZS class did not last long, especially as the overnight trains began to disappear during the 1970's. AZS 444 was written off in 1971 and burnt in an exercise called "operation Neva" at Millendon in July, 1972. AZS 445 was written off in 1974. This car was rebuilt as a workman's van and still survives. AZS 446 lasted till December, 1975, after which it was transferred to the Rail Transport Museum at Bassendean for preservation, where it has been returned to its original identity of JV 33.

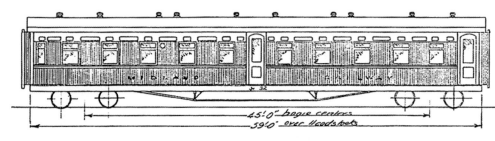

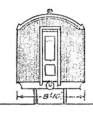

The WAGR didn't bother producing new drawings of the AZS, but simply relabeled the Midland Railways JV class drawing.

Drawing courtesy PTA.

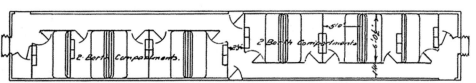

Suburban Compartment Car
ACM class

ACM 32, a former MRWA Jv class car & ACL at Boyanup, 30 January, 1967. This car spent a mere two years in WAGR service.
Photo late Geoff Blee, courtesy Murray Rowe.

The ACM class was one of those classes of carriage which, by rights, should never have existed. It consisted of fourteen cars, all ACL's which were found to be in reasonable condition in 1965 when large numbers of old branch line cars were being demolished. These carriages (ACL 31-33, 36, 210, 238, 386, 391, 392, 395, 404, 408, 409 & 412) were converted to ACM's by the simple method of having their lavatory doors screwed shut, before going to work on Perth's suburban trains. In every other way they retained their ACL characteristics, although some (386, 391, 392, 395, 404, 408, 409 and 412) were 58' (17.69m) long, with seven compartments, while the rest were 49' (14.95m), with six compartments, making two different types of car. Each compartment carried 7 passengers, and the cars were painted plain Larch green.

The ACM's were no more than a stopgap measure at a time when passenger cars were badly needed. Most of the old AE and AF class compartment cars had gone by 1965, as had many of the post 1900 suburban cars of classes AS, AT, AU and AW. The ADK/ADB class railcar sets had been ordered and the ACM's were intended to fill in till they arrived. This they did, but were not very efficient, with a maximum load of 49 passengers, compared to 90 in an AT.

ACM 32 was written off in 1966, followed by the other cars in 1968 when the new railcars were in service. Three (ACM 31, 404 & 409) were converted to workman's vans and four (33, 210, 238 & 391) are preserved by the Leschanault Railway Preservation Society at Boyanup, for use on the Vintage Train.

ACM 412, converted from a seven compartment ACL.

Photo late Geoff Blee, courtesy Murray Rowe.

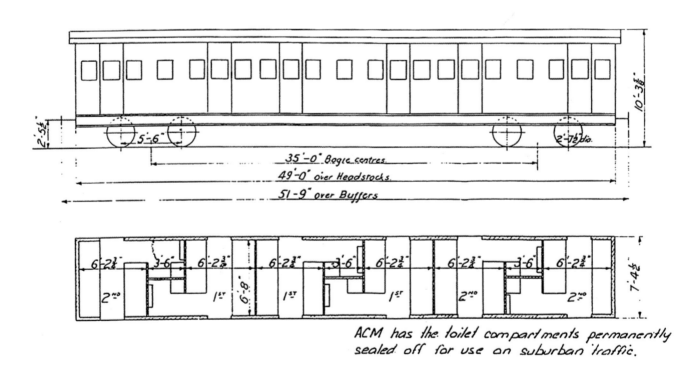

ACM has the toilet compartments permanently sealed off for use on suburban traffic.

Rather than produce a new drawing for a car which was only a stop gap, the ACM drawing was that of an ACL with the note added underneath, explaining the difference between the two types.
Drawing courtesy PTA.

ACM 391, another seven compartment car, as preserved by the Leschanault Railway Preservation Society, photographed at Boyanup on 12 May, 1991.   *Photo Bill Gray.*

ACM 210 as preserved at Boyanup.   *Photo courtesy Jack Parker.*

Suburban Brake Saloon
AYF class

AYF 704 at Midland, 11 September, 1967.

Photo late Geoff Blee, courtesy Murray Rowe.

By 1967 the last of the ADA class trailers had been delivered to run with the ADG, H and X classes of railcar, and their arrival released a few of the 1955 vintage AYE class saloon cars from railcar trailer duties. It was felt that better use might be made of these cars if some of them were converted to brake cars, so two (704 & 706) were taken into the workshops and had small brake compartments fitted to them. It would appear from the WAGR drawings that these cars, classified AYF, remained unaltered on the outside, the guard having to enter and leave his compartment via the passenger saloon. However, soon afterwards a door was let into each side of the car to allow him direct access. The brake compartment reduced the passenger capacity to 42 seated and 40 standing, and the conversion of AYE's to AYF's meant that they ran exclusively on locomotive hauled trains.

Another AYE (705) was converted to an AYF in 1968, followed by a final pair (702 & 707) in 1970. After conversion all five had been returned to traffic wearing the green, white and red livery, but between 1976 and 1979 they were repainted orange and blue.

In 1981 AYF 702 was stored, partially due to the cessation two years earlier of passenger services on the Fremantle line, but also because of the delivery of the new ADL/ADC class railcars. When the Perth to Fremantle line opened again in July, 1983, AYF 702 was returned to service, but three of its sisters were not so lucky. In November, 1983 AYF 704, 705 and 707 were all written off, and the following year were sold. Two (704 & 705) went to Kalgoorlie to be preserved in operating order by the Kalgoorlie-Boulder Loopline Preservation Society on their tourist railway. AYF 707 is recorded as having gone to Anaco Ltd., a heavy freight haulage company, and it was hauled to the Metana Minerals mine at Mt. Magnet, and later, to Menzies.

The remaining two AYF's (702 & 706) were repainted green and cream during the latter part of the 1980's and employed on locomotive hauled suburban trains in Perth till withdrawn from service in January, 1991. They were written off the following month, one going to Carnarvon and the other to a farm at North Dandalup.

AYF 706 at Midland.

Photo late Geoff Blee, courtesy Murray Rowe.

AYF 706 at Perth station at the rear of a long train which includes two AYE's, one without the red stripe & moulding which would have been at the bottom of that stripe, an AYL in green & cream, an AY, another AYE & three AYC's.

Photo late Geoff Blee, courtesy Murray Rowe.

AYF 706 in the orange & blue livery at Perth station.   *Photo Andy May, courtesy ARHS.*

AYF 702 at York on 2 September, 1989. The car has been partially repainted.   *Photo Bill Gray.*

AYF 706 on a suburban train at Bassendean on a warm day on 27 December, 1990, only two weeks before its withdrawal from service. The weathered state of the car is evident.   *Photo Bill Gray.*

G 50 rumbles past the Rail Transport Museum between Bassendean & Ashfield stations, on 19 April, 1989. Trailing along behind the locomotive are an AYF, a freshly painted AY, two AYE's & another AYF bringing up the rear.   *Photo Bill Gray.*

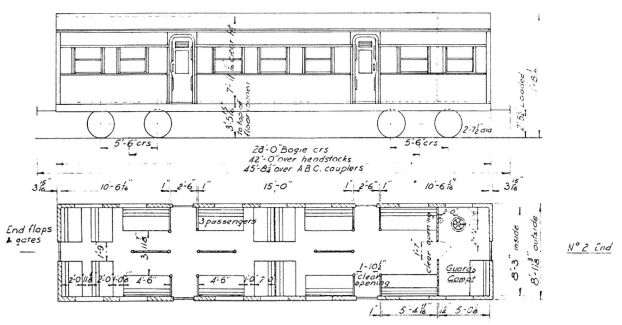

This WAGR drawing shows an AYF without the guards compartment access doors. It is not known if the original cars were built this way at conversion, or if the drawing was simply a proof of concept drawing, based on the AYE drawings.

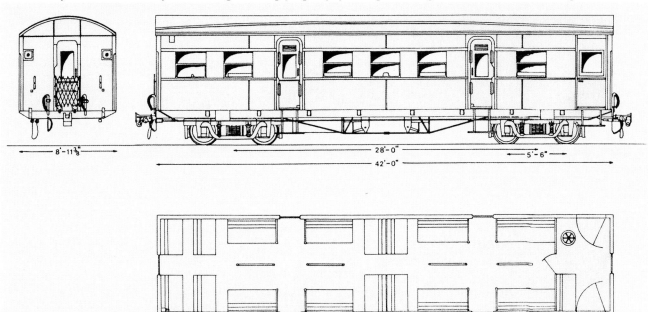

Andy May's drawing of the AYF shows the cars as they were better known with the guard compartment doors.

Inside the passenger compartment & guards compartment of AYF 702. The photos were taken at Midland on 8 January, 1990.

Photos Bill Gray.

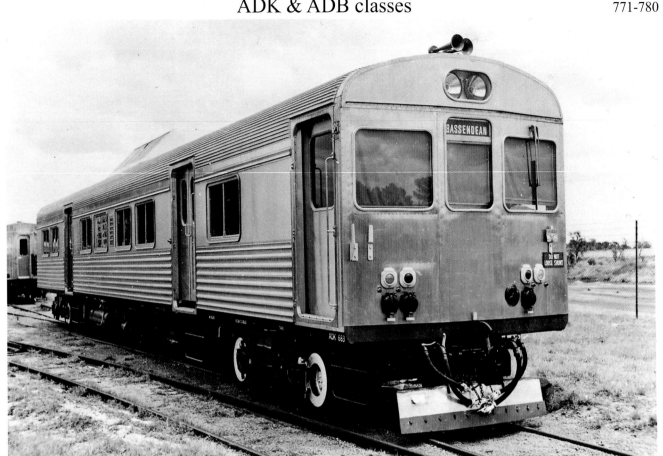

ADK 683 in new condition soon after delivery.   *Photo courtesy ARHS.*

Early in 1968 the first of ten new suburban railcar sets arrived, each set consisting of an ADK class diesel railcar and an ADB class trailer. The ADK's were built by Commonwealth Engineering (Comeng) in Sydney, NSW, and they introduced a number of new innovations into Perth's suburbs. Their design was based on the American Budd Co. monocoque constructed railcars in which the corrugated stainless steel body contributed significantly to the overall strength of the car, rather than relying entirely on the underframe. This produced a lighter vehicle which was able to make better use of its engine power. The ADK's were the WAGR's first stainless steel railcars, and the first to have a driving cab at one end only. They were also the first of the WAGR's passenger vehicles to have air brakes rather than vacuum, and it was this feature, along with a different type of control gear, which made them incompatible with other vehicles in the railcar fleet. The ADB class trailers, the first of which entered service a few weeks after the ADK's in March, 1968, were built at Midland and were designed to operate specifically with the ADK's, those cars with the same last digit in their numbers normally being coupled together. The ADBs were not Budd cars, but were carried on a full underframe.

Being built of stainless steel, the ADK's and ADB's were never painted, although the buffer beams were coloured red, and in later years the driver's cab end panels received a coat of orange in an attempt to make them more obvious at level crossings. In 1990 the orange ends on most cars were repainted red and white as part of the Transperth livery. The passengers boarded the car through double air operated sliding doors and the ADK's could accommodate 76 passengers with room for another 58 people standing up, while the ADB's could seat 64 passengers with another 32 standing. The windows in the ADK's were unusual in that the dividers were mounted vertically rather than horizontally, but the ADB's were fitted with the more usual half lift type in which only the bottom pane could be raised. The ADK's rode on Pioneer III air sprung bogies and were fitted with externally mounted disc brakes, the polished discs being obvious in the gloom underneath the cars. The ADB's had their corrugated stainless steel bodies mounted on the same type of underframe as the ADT and ADA classes of trailer fitted with ADA type bogies, and they were shorter and lower than the power cars, not having any roof mounted cooling equipment. To simplify marshalling, the ADB's always faced east.

The ADK's were fitted with two 180 bhp Cummins 6 cylinder diesel engines mounted under the floor. Each of these drove a Voith Diwadus hydro mechanical transmission, which drove the inner axle on each bogie, and the engine radiators were mounted on the roof, so avoiding the problem of them being clogged up by trackside debris, as happened with the earlier railcars. Each car could carry 180 gallons (818 litres) of fuel, giving it a range of 500 miles (800 km), and they were fitted with a governor to limit their speed to 50 mph (80 kph). They were capable of multiple unit operation.[32]

The ADK's (681-690) with their ADB class trailers (771-780) did their work well as they roamed the suburbs, suffering the occasional failure, as does any machine. By the end of 1991, with electrification of the suburban system completed and the problems with the electric railcars being solved, the days of the ADK's and ADB's were numbered. They were progressively withdrawn from service in early 1992. Five sets were in storage at Forrestfield by the end of March, and all but ADK 690 and ADB 774 had been retired by early April. These vehicles were retained at Claisebrook Railcar Depot for shunting and emergency use, and were later used to demonstrate the class to representatives from the New Zealand Railways, being noted on a run to Jumperkine on 21 May, 1992.[33] By October, 1992 ADK 687 and 690 had been coupled together back to back and were at Claisebrook for shunting and emergency use. At least one of these cars was used for driver familiarisation on the new Joondalup line during December, 1992. About February, 1993 ADK 689 was taken into the Midland Workshops for conversion into a track recorder car, but the work was never finished and the old railcar was still at the Midland Workshops when they closed in March, 1993. The remainder of the fleet, including the Claisebrook shunting cars were sold to the New Zealand Railways for service in Auckland. The ten ADB's were delivered to Fremantle on 23 March, 1993, and the nine ADK's followed then next day. They were loaded onto the motor vessel "Envoyager" along with the ADL/ADC class railcars and departed Fremantle on 26 March, 1993.[34] The uncompleted and heavily graffitied ADK 689 was moved to Forrestfield at the end of April, 1995, from where it disappeared. Its fate is unknown.

ADK 681, 682 & 687 at Rivervale on 20 March, 1968. The ADKs were run in sets before the arrival of the ADB class trailers. *Photo late Geoff Blee, courtesy Murray Rowe.*

ADK 685 & 686 on standard gauge bogies rest at Parkeston, near Kalgoorlie, on 5 January, 1968, during their delivery run to Perth. *Photo late Geoff Blee, courtesy Murray Rowe.*

A near new four car ADB & ADK set roll out of Perth.   *Photo late Geoff Blee, courtesy Murray Rowe.*

ADK 681 at Midland advertises trains for the annual Christmas Pageant in Perth.   *Photo courtesy ARHS.*

ADK 690 & ADB 780 climbing the grade near Lathlain, 16 March, 1988. *Photo Bill Gray.*

ADK 689 & ADB 779 cross the Bunbury Bridge at East Perth on 30 March, 1988. The orange ends were suffering badly from the chemicals used to wash the cars. *Photo Bill Gray.*

ADB 777 & ADK 687 at Midland station on 16 June, 1992, during trials held prior to sale to the New Zealand Railways.
Photo Bill Gray.

ADK at the head of a seven ADK/ADB railcar sets stored at Forrestfield, 1 June, 1992.
Photo Bill Gray.

ADK 689 in the Midland Workshops undergoing conversion to a self propelled track recorder car. When the workshops were closed in March, 1993 it was effectively abandoned. *Photo Bill Gray.*

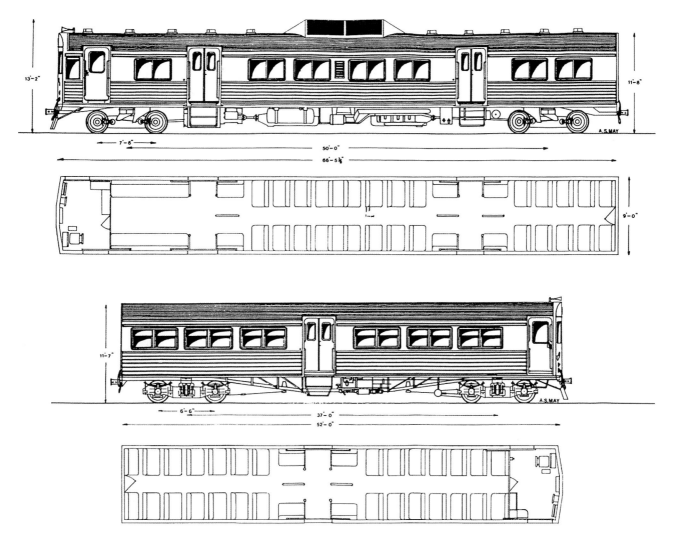

Andy Mays drawing of the ADK railcar & its ADB trailer.

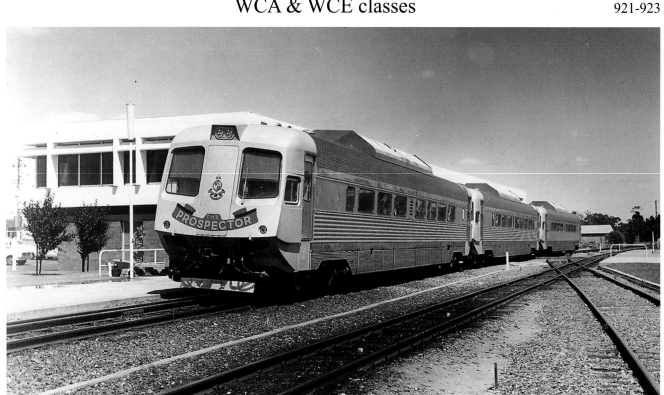

WCA 902 leads a three car set through Northam on the dual gauge line.   *Photo courtesy PTA.*

The opening of the standard gauge railway up the Avon Valley and onto Kalgoorlie in 1968 soon caused the demise of the WAGR's overnight passenger trains between Perth and the goldfields. The "Westland" stopped running in 1969, its passengers being accommodated on the Commonwealth Railways standard gauge "Trans Australian", and that same year orders were placed with Comeng in Sydney for five new railcars (WCA class) and three trailers (WCE class) to operate high speed sit up services between Perth and Kalgoorlie. These were the only standard gauge passenger cars to be wholly owned by the WAGR. The new cars were delivered in 1971, and when they entered service the "Kalgoorlie" ran for the last time, being replaced by the new train which was named the "Prospector".

Like the ADK class railcars, the new vehicles were built to the American Budd design of stressed skin integral construction (monocoque), and by WAGR standards, they were unlike anything ever seen before in their levels of passenger comfort. The power cars were 88' (27.074m) long, with a tare weight of 69 tons 18 cwt (70.6t), making them the biggest and heaviest passenger vehicles to be used by the WAGR. The WCE's were the same size, but not being fitted with engines, other than for air conditioning and auxiliary power, were considerably lighter at 50 tons 17 cwt (51.36t). Externally, the power cars and trailers were almost identical. The driver's cabs and entry vestibules at each end were of a streamlined futuristic design, but looked as though they had been bolted on as an afterthought rather than being part of the steel body of the car, and their fibreglass construction and different colouring accentuated this effect. The WCE's had an extra passenger window in them, and the cab windows at

one end were opaque, these being the only obvious differences between them and the power cars. The "Prospector" cars were fully air conditioned, this equipment being mounted in the hump on the roofs along with the engine cooling radiators in the WCA's. Inside, the two cars were similar, but there were some differences. The WCE's had a driving cab at one end only, the other end being employed as a luggage compartment, hence its opaque windows. As a result, there was more room in them, so they had an extra row of seats, enabling them to carry 64 passengers, while a total of 60 passengers could be carried in the WCA's. When designed, passenger comfort was high on the list of priorities and the interiors were not unlike those of modern airliners. Each passenger had a personal reading light, the seats could be reclined as well as rotated to face the direction of travel, curtains were fitted to the windows, the floor was carpeted, and the cars were heavily insulated against dust and noise. Refrigerative air conditioning took care of the inside temperatures, and hostess service provided passengers with airline style meals in their seats.[35]

The "Prospector" cars normally ran at speeds of 70 mph (116 kph) and were capable of travelling even faster. Power was provided by two M.A.N. D.3 650 H.M.6.U. diesel engines, each with twelve cylinders and able to produce 360 bhp at 1850 rpm. These each drove a Voith T.113R turbo transmission, with a Voith final drive at each bogie. These were the air sprung Pioneer III type, not dissimilar to those under the ADK class suburban railcars, and they were fitted with Westinghouse air brakes. Leyland Model 401 6 cylinder diesel engines provided the power for the air conditioning, as well as the standby electrical power.[36]

The "Prospector" cars presented some unique problems right from the start. Even though they were on standard gauge bogies, their size prevented them from being railed from the builder in Sydney to Western Australia, due to the tunnels and curves in the NSW Blue Mountains. As a result, they were trucked to Goobang Junction, near Parkes in NSW, and from there were towed to Perth behind goods trains. The first to arrive was a WCE class trailer in May, 1971, followed by another in June, and the first WCA class power car in August. The first power cars and trailer entered service on 20 November, 1971. Two days later the name "Prospector" was bestowed upon the new railcar service, and the new train successfully completed a trial run from East Perth to Toodyay. On 29 November the first Prospector ran from Perth to Kalgoorlie. Five WCA class power cars were purchased and numbered 901-905, along with three trailers, WCE 921-923, the last of the eight vehicles entering traffic in January, 1972.

Being stainless steel, there was little need of paint on the cars, and their liveries were fairly basic. Initially, the fibreglass nose sections were plain grey, with the name "Prospector" painted on the ends in gold lettering over a green background, and the WAGR crest applied above it on the intercommunicating door. Experiments were conducted to try and make the cars easier to see and this involved painting one car, WCA 904, with black and yellow chevrons on the ends. It was outshopped in this livery on 1 December, 1972. In the late 1970's all eight cars were painted with orange ends. In 1984 WCA 905 was issued to traffic in a new livery which made use of the Westrail orange and blue, in which the ends were white, a blue stripe ran along the window line, and the whole lot was trimmed in orange. This livery was also adopted for all eight cars.

The final livery was similar, but consisted of the cab windows being surrounded in blue, while the orange and blue stripes on the sides of the car were made of reflective tape. The name "Prospector" was placed above the window line in the upper blue stripe. This was a similar livery adopted for the ADP/ADQ "Australind" railcars. There were, of course any number of minor variations over the years. A photograph tells the story in a thousand words.

Over the 30 and 31 March, 1987 a special "Prospector" was run to see how much time could be taken off the normal Perth to Kalgoorlie run of about eight hours. Sometimes achieving speeds of 90 mph (150 kph), the special chopped approximately two hours off the journey time.

Age began to catch up with the "Prospector" cars, and their heavy utilisation caused them to suffer an increasing number of failures. Every now and then a set could be seen behind a locomotive after suffering some sort of mechanical problem, and a result a re-engining and refurbishing program began in 1991 with WCA 905. The new engines fitted to this car were Cummins KTA 19R 6 cylinder diesels which produced 541 bhp (406Kw) at 2100 rpm, considerably more then the old M.A.N. engines, which produced 360 bhp (284Kw) at 1850 rpm. These engines were the same as those powering the new "Australind" cars. Following successful trials with WCA 905, the other four "Prospector" power cars were also re-engined during 1992.

In late June, 2004 the new "Prospector" cars began to enter service, but the fate of the WCA/WCE sets was a little uncertain. The Western Australian Government had announced that the new cars would not be available for private charters, but they would be prepared to have discussions with tour operators regarding the old cars.[37] Some of the cars were stored at Kewdale, but the WCE's were used occasionally on locomotive hauled tour trains, and the WCA's were used as stand by cars while the new Prospector cars suffered several teething problems. They were also used regularly on Avon Link services between Northam and Perth, running their last journeys on 29 July, 2005 and being officially withdrawn on 1 August.

WCE 921 as delivered to Western Australia in 1971.

Photo courtesy PTA.

A Prospector set in the Avon Valley, shown in the original livery.   *Photo courtesy PTA.*

Thought to be an experimental livery, it is not known whether the Prospector ever carried this colour scheme, or whether this Westrail photo has been touched up.

An unidentified Prospector car at Perth terminal with the orange cab front & full state crest.   *Photo courtesy PTA.*

A four car set in the Avon Valley, showing the Westrail crest   *Photo courtesy PTA.*

The WAGR photographer seems to have spent a good deal of his time in the Avon Valley. Here we see a Prospector set in the orange livery, showing the WAGR crest.

Photo courtesy ARHS.

WCA 904 on the Montreal Rd level crossing at Midland in March, 1973, showing the safety chevrons painted on the ends.
Photo courtesy ARHS.

An unidentified Prospector set speeds towards Bayswater, July, 1988. *Photo Bill Gray.*

WCA 903 closest to the camera, with WCE 923 behind, stand quietly on the curve at Greenmount on 21 August, 1994, after vandals had placed a sheet of galvanized iron across the track. *Photo Bill Gray.*

Single car WCA 904 heads out of Midland in 11 January, 1991. For most of the 33 years these cars were in service Midland sported a dedicated Prospector stopping place on the standard gauge line, just west of the station. This prevented the Prospector services being disrupted by suburban traffic to & from Midland station. Photo Bill Gray.

WCE 922 & WCA 902 roll through Greenmount on a sunny summers day, adorned in the final livery carried by the WCA/WCE Prospector sets, 30 December, 1997. Photo Bill Gray.

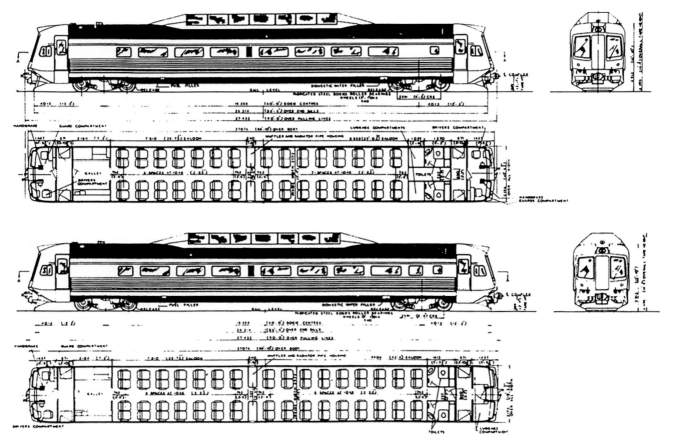

Drawings of the WCA (top) & WCE classes (bottom).   *Drawings courtesy PTA.*

Interior of WCA 904 at Kalgoorlie on 7 April, 2003.

Photos Bill Gray.

CHAPTER EIGHT
THE FINAL YEARS - 1976 & BEYOND

By 1976 the days of being able to catch a train to, or in, the country in Western Australia were virtually over, and the majority of the carriages which once ran on these trains were gone, their bodies sold or broken up and burnt, and their frames cut up for scrap.

Mr. L. Pritsikas replaced McCaskill as CME in 1976,[1] the "Australind" became a one class service after 1977, and the last of the former passenger carrying branchline vehicles disappeared in 1977 when brakevans ZB 207 and 213 were written off. The last overnight passenger train, the "Albany Progress", ran for the final time on 1 December, 1978,[2] fittingly hauled by steam locomotive W 947 during its final departure from Albany. The carriages from this train (AZ, AQZ and ARM sleeping cars, AYS buffet cars and an AYU sit up car) were not immediately scrapped, however, and many of the cars found their way into the hands of preservation groups. Eight of the remaining AZ first class sleeping cars were leased to the Hotham Valley Railway, and AZ 443 was leased to the Great Southern Steam Association at Albany in 1979. The last two AQZ first class sleeping cars (420 & 424) still in traffic were withdrawn from service and were leased to the Hotham Valley Railway in 1979 for tour train use, finally being purchased outright by that group in 1984. Buffet car AQL 288 had been written off and replaced on the "Albany Progress" by AQL 290 in December, 1975, but with the running of the final "Albany Progress", AQL 290 was withdrawn from use and also leased to the Hotham Valley Railway, later being purchased outright. After 1975 the four ARM class sleeping cars saw little use, and all four were retired and stored. The two AYS class buffet cars (460 & 461) ran on the last "Albany Progress" and were leased to preservation groups in 1979. AYS 460 went to the

Kalgoorlie-Boulder Loopline Preservation Society, and AYS 461 went to the Great Southern Steam Association at Albany. The demise of the "Albany Progress" left the "Australind" as Western Australia's last locomotive hauled country passenger train, a final fragment of 100 years of country train travel. It lingered another nine years, like a dinosaur out of its time, a misfit in an age of air conditioning and stainless steel.

It is something of an irony that after the destruction of the WAGR's once extensive network of country passenger trains, two 'new' country cars were built. In 1980 all four AYU's were written off and this produced a shortage of loco hauled stock suitable for use on the "Australind". As a result, two ARM's which had been in store since the demise of the "Albany Progress", were resurrected and rebuilt with saloon type seating and guard's compartments as ARA class long distance brake sitting cars. They were issued to traffic in December, 1980, and their presence on the "Australind" meant that a brakevan was not always needed. The train normally ran with an ARA at each end, and their passenger capacity and ability to be marshalled this way meant that they quickly found favour on hired specials. As a consequence, both cars were often seen on ARHS or HVR tour trains.

Country trains were not the only victims of political short sightedness, for all was not well in the suburbs, either. Passenger services on the Perth to Fremantle line ceased in 1979, this controversial decision turning the suburban services into a political football. One of the strongest opponents of the closure was the former CME, D.M. McCaskill, and after a long struggle and general election, the line was opened again for passenger traffic in July, 1983. However, closure of the line had contributed to the retirement of several cars in classes

ARM 356 in orange on the "Albany Progress", preparing to depart for Perth for the final time.   *Photo courtesy Mike Fry.*

ADG, ADH, ADA and AYE, and some of these did not return to service when the line was re-opened. Saloon cars AYE 703 and 712 were written off in May, 1980, and railcar trailer ADA/V 755 was written off in November, 1980, followed by ADA 768 in August, 1981. Railcar ADH/V 653 also went in 1981 after an accident, its body being taken to the Belmont rubbish tip in Perth and buried. It had traveled 1,013,908 miles (1,689,847 km) during its time in service.

By the beginning of 1980 some of the older suburban railcars were starting to show their age, and purchase of replacements was approved, resulting in orders being placed with Goninans in Newcastle, NSW, for five new two car suburban diesel railcar sets. Each set consisted of a power car (ADL) and a trailer (ADC), numbered 801-805 and 851-855 respectively, and the policy of coupling power cars and trailers carrying the same last digit in their numbers continued with them. They were delivered during late 1981 and early 1982, but suffered from some teething problems, particularly with the auxiliary equipment, noise and vibration, so the first did not enter service till May, 1982.[3] The ADL power cars were, in some ways, similar to the ADK class with the corrugated stainless steel monocoque construction, but they had a more modern appearance about them. The ADL's were a similar size to the ADK's, but looked bigger because their Sigma air conditioning units and engine radiators were mounted inside the roof line. The ADC class trailers were virtually identical to the power cars, but without the mechanical equipment. The ADL/ADC sets were the first suburban cars to be air conditioned.

The new railcars replaced a number of older suburban vehicles which were rapidly wearing out. Suburban saloon AYE 701 had been placed in storage, but it was returned to traffic in July, 1983 when the Fremantle line was re-opened. However, its time back in service was only brief, as it was written off again in November, 1983 and AYE 711 went with it. This left only five AYE's (708, 709, 710, 713 & 714) in traffic, all but AYE 710 being AYE/V's. Suburban brake car AYF 702 was stored in 1981, and was returned to service in July, 1983, but three of its sisters (AYF 704, 705 & 707) were all written off in November, 1983, and sold the following year. In 1982 suburban car AY 454 was withdrawn from service and stored, but the re-opening of the Fremantle line in July, 1983 saw it returned to service for a short period of time. It was written off again in November, 1983 and sold privately in Stoneville. Diesel railcars ADX 661 and 670 were retired in 1982 and never ran again. Both were written off in November, 1983 and transported to Mount Magnet to be used as staff accommodation on a mining site. ADG/V 605 was withdrawn from service and stored in September, 1982, but it was returned to traffic for the re-opening of the Fremantle line in July,1983.

As the "Australind" was WA's only locomotive hauled country passenger train, the demise of the ZJ class express brakevans began to gather momentum, and the writing off of ZJ 427 in 1982 left that train without a brakevan. It was replaced by the ARA class brake cars and, when required, ZJA 431, which emerged from the workshops late in 1982 sporting a fresh coat of paint, plywood sides, and gangways. In November, 1982 "Australind" car AYC 500 was badly damaged in a collision at Claisebrook, near Perth. It was thought that the car would have to be written off, but Westrail was suffering from a shortage of suitable cars for the "Australind", so it was rebuilt and returned to service nearly a year later.

Apart from the initial problems with the air conditioning systems, noise, and vibration, the ADL/ADC railcars were satisfactory so orders were placed with Goninans for another five sets. These entered service during the early months of 1985 and sported some differences to the earlier batch. Externally, the door grab handles were relocated, and the air horns were mounted in a different place on the cab roof, while inside, the seats were fabric covered rather than vinyl. In all other ways, they were the same. In fact, it was easier to pick the difference between a 1981 car and a 1985 car than it was to differentiate between an ADL and an ADC, although the give away was that the ADC's, in common with the other suburban railcar trailers, always faced east.

The introduction of the second batch of new railcars heralded the demise of the aging ADX's. In 1985 another three ADX's (665, 666 & 668) were written off and the engines from them were fitted to some of the ADG/V class railcars in 1986. About this time the remaining ADX's were, like the ADG, ADH and ADA class cars, fitted with the "bulged" front lower driver's cab panel, presumably to improve the leg room. The demise of these ADX's during the mid 1980's saw the writing off of more of the unmodified ADA's, although three were used in a locomotive hauled set of ADA's and engineless ADX's. However, their lightweight construction did not allow heavy loads to be marshalled behind them, so their efficiency in this role was limited. The set was withdrawn from use after the arrival of the Queensland cars in 1986.

The end of an era passed when, from July, 1985 Westrail stopped using brakevans on most of its trains.[4] In 1984 ZJ 267 was written off and the following year most of the remaining express brakevans were removed from service. These were ZJ 270, 362, 429, ZJA 430 and 432-434. Most were stored for a while before being disposed of, but two express brakevans (ZJ 266 & ZJA 431) remained in service till 1992.

In order to cope with the predicted increase in railway patronage in Perth during the America's Cup Yacht Race Challenge towards the end of 1986, fourteen stainless steel SX and SXV class saloon cars were leased from the Queensland Railways to boost passenger accommodation on the suburban network. The leased cars included ten SX class suburban saloons (SX 1664-1668 & 1727-1731) and four SXV (SXV 1663, 1669, 1726 & 1732) class suburban brake saloons. The Queensland cars were railed from Acacia Ridge in Brisbane on standard gauge bogies. The first set of six cars (SXV-SX-SX-SX-SX-SXV) entered service on 22 September, 1986, and by 7 October all fourteen had arrived. The placing in traffic of the Queensland cars finally permitted the withdrawal of most of the remaining ADX class railcars, although one lingered on for two more years. The Queensland cars worked well through the America's Cup, and were kept in Westrail service till the electric railcars arrived.

In 1986 the name "Transperth" was adopted for the suburban transport system of buses and trains. ADL 809 and ADC 859 were painted in a new Transperth livery, which featured a red stripe along the window line and black ends outlined in white. This was later changed so that the ends of the cars were painted white on the top half and red on the bottom. At the same time a number of the wooden suburban cars were refurbished and repainted green and cream, particularly those being used on hired specials, as they were beginning to look very run down. During this time the 11.3 litre AEC engines from scrapped ADX class railcars were fitted to ADG/V 601, 603, 605, 606, 611, 612 and 617. These engines developed 150 bhp, 25 hp more than the smaller 9.6 litre units originally fitted, the idea being that lives of the old railcars would be extended till the Perth suburban network could be electrified. However, parts for the AEC engines were proving more and more difficult to find and later in 1986 ADG/V 617 was fitted with a pair of new Mercedes Benz engines, returning to service in February, 1987, followed later that month by ADG/V 602. Three others, ADG/V 614, 615 and 618 were fitted with these engines during the second half of 1987. The three remaining ADH/V class railcars also had their ageing AEC engines being replaced by new Mercedes Benz units, ADH 651 in 1987 and ADH 652 and 654 in 1988.

The final Western Australian locomotive hauled country passenger train, the "Australind", outlasted most of its contemporaries by more than ten years, almost becoming a relic in its own time. On 14 November, 1987 the last locomotive hauled "Australind" ran from Perth to Bunbury and back, and as preserved diesel XA 1405 eased its train into Perth's City Station, the Western Australian locomotive hauled country passenger train became extinct. However, the "Australind"

persevered in the form of a fast diesel railcar service. In mid 1985 orders had been placed with Comeng at Bassendean for three new diesel hydraulic railcars and two trailers to replace the old train. The first of the new cars, a driving power car (ADP 101) made its appearance on trials in June, 1987, and the other two driving cars (102 & 103) and the non driving cars (ADQ 121 & 122) appeared soon afterwards. They introduced another variation in railcar design into Western Australia in that both were power cars, but only the ADP's had driving cabs. Thus the "Australind" railcar consists had no trailers. The first regular "Australind" service using the new railcars ran two days after the demise of the loco hauled train. Some of the remaining ADX class diesel mechanical railcars were included in a suburban coaching stock set early in 1986, and one car (662), with an ADA, was finally withdrawn from service around September, 1988. It was stored at Midland before being written off in August, 1989 and buried at the Gosnells tip with ADX 663 in December, 1989.

The last of the wooden country cars left Westrail service in August, 1990. After the running of the last locomotive hauled "Australind" the AYC, AYD and ARA class cars from the train were retained by Westrail for hire to tour groups, especially the Hotham Valley Railway and the Australian Railway Historical Society, but they were badly run down and in need of work. The Hotham Valley Railway, believing that the cars were no longer capable of keeping up with the work planned in their tour schedules, purchased three sets of steel carriages from the South African Railways and, as the Australian Railway Historical Society were the only group still using the old cars, the four AYC's, two AYD's and two ARA's were handed over to the Society on 30 August, 1990 for preservation in operating condition.

Diesel locomotives XA 1405 (then in preservation) & 1402 rest briefly at Harvey with the last loco hauled "Australind" on 14 November, 1987.

Photo Bill Gray.

The WCA and WCE "Prospector" cars were heavily utilised, and their age began to catch up with them, so the entire WCA fleet was re-engined and refurbished during 1991 and 1992. The cars were withdrawn one at a time and fitted with new Cummins diesels of the same type as those powering the new "Australind" railcars. A number of other systems were overhauled at the same time. WCA 905 was the first car done and its success led to the other four being completed by the end of 1992.

The issue of the electrification of the Perth suburban network had raised its head at regular intervals, especially as the Sydney and Melbourne networks had been electrified since the early 1900's, and the Brisbane suburban network was changed over during the 1980's. However, the governments over the years were reluctant to commit the money needed for such a project. Electrification of the suburban network had been on the minds of some administrators for a long time, and in 1984 serious investigations began into the feasibility of this enormous task.[5] The decision was finally made to electrify the Perth suburban network, an announcement being made in April, 1987 and forty three new electric railcar sets (later increased to forty eight), were ordered in February, 1988 from Walkers/ASEA Ltd. of Maryborough, in Queensland, the builders of the modern Queensland Railways electric trains. The design of the Western Australian cars was based on these, but with changes in width, cab front, brakes, and bogies. In January, 1989 work began on the electrification of Perth's railways. Big changes in signalling, station platforms and track, along with more obvious additions of masts, overhead wiring, lineside fences and the EMU depot at Claisebrook, changed the face of Perth's suburban railway lines in a very short space of time. In addition, the decision to build the new northern suburbs railway from Perth to Joondalup was announced in November, 1988.

The electric "power" cars were classed AEA (201-243) and the "trailers" AEB (301-343) and, after trials in Queensland the first set (AEA 201 & AEB 301) arrived at Forrest field in Perth on 1 September, 1990. However, several serious problems were encountered which delayed their introduction into service for some time. These included two industrial disputes over pay and the manning of the cars, and trouble with the bogies, brakes and excessive vibration. One by one the problems were largely resolved and the EMU's finally entered limited service on 28 September, 1991, operating between Perth and the Claremont Showgrounds during the annual Royal Show. Another five sets (AEA 244-248 & AEB 344-348) went into service in late 1998 and early 1999.

Even though the EMU's were not ready for service as early as had been anticipated, the retention of the Queensland cars allowed yet another era in the history of Western Australia's railways to come to an end on 11 January, 1991 when the last suburban services to be run by locomotive hauled wooden bodied AY/AYB/AYE and AYF sets were operated. The last service saw diesel locomotive C.1702 haul a train consisting of an AYF, two AY's and an AYB from Midland into Perth. The remaining suburban cars, and the last wooden cars on the Westrail system (AY 26, 452,453 & 455, AYB 458 & 459, AYE/V 708, 709, 713 & 714, & AYF 702 & 706) were written off the following month.

The diesel railcars and two sets of Queensland cars soldiered on for the next 12 months, and the long awaited introduction of the electric railcars finally allowed their withdrawal from service. The Queensland cars were the first to go, having outlived the cars they were sent to assist. Four had been placed on standard gauge bogies and returned East during April, 1991, and the last eight cars ran the final official services in Perth on Friday 13 December, 1991. They were retained at Midland on standby for another week and it is believed

The end of an era captured on film.... C 1702 backs onto the final locomotive hauled suburban train of wooden carriages at Midland on the afternoon of 11 January, 1991.
Photo Bill Gray.

that one set ran a single service Midland-Perth-Midland on Monday 16 December, for the school holidays, so bringing an end to regular locomotive hauled passenger trains in Western Australia. They were then stored at Midland and the last of them returned to Queensland on 9 June, 1992. The railcars did not last much longer. Most of the ADA/V class trailers had been withdrawn from use on 25 October, 1991, and the ADG and ADH class railcars were often seen marshalled together, so allowing them to keep up with the timetables being operated by the newer and faster cars. However, their days were numbered, and they were withdrawn from service during January, 1992. Classes ADA, ADG and ADH were written off the following month. In something of a surprise move the other diesel railcars were also withdrawn from service soon afterwards. The ADK class and their ADB trailers were becoming a rare sight by March, 1992, with five sets out of service by the 20th of that month. The 5 April, 1992 was the first time that the suburban services were run exclusively by the electric railcars, although the last evening service on each of the three suburban lines was run by an ADL/ADC set, and occasional ADL/ADC sets were being used to temporarily relieve overcrowding. These cars were not written off, but instead were stored at Forrestfield, with an ADL/ADC set being maintained at Claisebrook in case of emergencies. This set was joined later in the year by ADK 690 and ADB 774. The railcars, which had been used for shunting, were replaced in late 1992 by an MA class diesel shunting locomotive. The diesel railcars could still be seen occasionally due to the interest being shown in them by the New Zealand Railways and members from both classes were used on the Northern Suburbs Railway to assist in checking clearances and for driver familiarisation. All but one ADK class car were sold to the New Zealand Railways during 1993.

The increasing unreliability of the WCA and WCE Prospector cars saw a consultant employed by the state government to determine the best way to deal with the problem of providing a reliable service between Perth and the goldfields capital. This resulted in three new Prospector sets being purchased, made up of two sets of two cars, and one set of three cars. One of the two car sets was dedicated to the Avon Link services between Northam and Perth, this set being given a different livery to the others two. The new cars were classed WDA and WDB, while the third car in the three car set was classified WDC. The first set arrived from Goninans at Broadmeadow in New South Wales, and was put on display at East Perth Terminal for a media promotion on 28 May, 2003. The new marketing name "Transwa" was also launched at the same time, along with a new, colourful livery for the Prospector, the Australind and the WAGR's bus fleet. WDA 001 and WDB 011 entered revenue service on 28 June, 2004 and the other two sets soon afterwards. The old WCA and WCE cars mostly remained in service providing a back up role, largely on the Avon Link.

Back in the suburbs, the government had approved a rapid transit corridor linking Perth and Mandurah, and a large number of new electric railcars were going to be required to operate these services. The contract for the construction of the new cars was given to Adtranz in Queensland, the big difference between the new cars and the AEA/AEB sets being that the new ones would be built as three car sets. The first set, No. 49, consisting of cars, BEA 449, BEB 549 and BET 649, arrived in Perth on 1 June, 2004. As with all new rail cars it then began trials from the new railcar depot at Nowergup on the northern suburbs railway.

Thus, Western Australia's once proud passenger train network has been reduced to two modern country railcar services and the four Perth suburban lines, the latter being operated by the AEA/AEB and BEA/BEB/BET electric railcar sets. What the future holds for passenger trains in Western Australia is difficult to tell, although the suburban system seems set to expand even further as Perth's population grows, and the EMU sets have attracted record numbers of passengers back to rail travel. Country passenger services will never be what they once were but, as personal transport becomes more expensive and the world's fossil fuel reserves run low, the possibility always exists that the efficiency of railways as a form of travel will see some sort of revival.

Three different eras of suburban rail travel are represented at Midland station on 13 December, 1991, with an EMU set, an ADL/ADC set & a loco hauled set in the form of Queensland set No. 39. The loco, A 1504 is running around its cars & will shortly back onto them before making another run into the City & on to Fremantle.　　　　*Photo Bill Gray.*

ARA rests at Fremantle during an Australian Railway Historical Society tour of Perth's suburbs on 7 May, 1988. The guard can be seen waiting for the locomotive (Dd 592) to back onto the train.   *Photo Bill Gray.*

In 1980 two "new" country cars were built. These were ARA class long distance sit up cars for the "Australind", the last surviving loco hauled country passenger train in Western Australia, and they both entered service in December, 1980. The cars were converted from ARM second class sleeping cars (351 & 356) and were fitted with brake compartments so there would no longer be a requirement to trail a brakevan on the "Australind".

Externally, the ARA's were of identical dimensions to the ARM's from which they were derived, as no major changes were made to their bodies, although the windows arrangement was altered to allow for their new role as sit up cars and for the brake compartment. They were painted Larch green and cream and could carry 48 passengers.

The ARA's went into service on the "Australind", normally with one at each end of the train, and their passenger capacity and ability to be marshalled this way meant that they quickly found favour on hired specials. As a consequence, both cars were often seen on ARHS or HVR tour trains.

On 14 November, 1987 the last locomotive hauled "Australind" ran, but the ARA's, as part of the "Australind" set, were retained by Westrail for hire to rail tour groups. However, by 1988 the Hotham Valley Railway was planning to embark on an intense tour programme and, believing that the old wooden cars would be unable to carry out such an itinerary, they imported a number of steel bodied carriages from the South African Railways. This left the ARHS as the main user of the "Australind" cars, and on 30 August, 1990 the entire set, including the ARA's, was handed over to that organisation for preservation in working order.

Bunbury bound passengers wait patiently in ARA 351 at Perth station prior to departure.

Photo Andrew May, courtesy ARHS.

ARA 356, freshly painted, after arriving at Mundijong on an ARHS excursion on 19 September, 1994.   Photo Bill Gray.

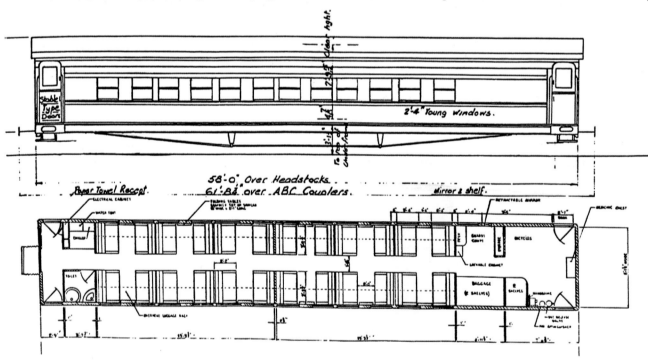

The general arrangement drawing of the ARA class cars.   Drawing courtesy PTA.

Inside the ARA saloon (left) & the conductors compartment (right)

Photos courtesy David Gray

A four car ADL/ADC set, with ADL 802 in the lead, rounds the curve between Ashfield & Bayswater stations. Tonkin Highway now crosses the railway at this point, the siding has gone & the overhead wiring for the electric railcars is now prominent.

Photo courtesy ARHS.

Just as the ADG and ADK/ADB class railcars represented big improvements in suburban services in their turn, so did the ADL/ADC class railcars. The first ADL's and ADC's were delivered in 1981, and while they were, in some ways, similar to the ADK class with the corrugated stainless steel monocoque construction, they had a more modern appearance about them. The ADL's were a similar size to the ADK's, but looked bigger because their Sigma air conditioning units and engine radiators were mounted inside the roof line, and the ADC's were virtually identical to the power cars, but without the mechanical equipment.

The ADL/ADC sets were the first suburban cars to be air conditioned, the power unit for the air conditioning and auxiliary power being a General Motors Detroit 4-71T turbocharged diesel engine which was carried under the floor of the ADC class trailers.[6] Both the ADL's and the ADC's could carry 68 seated passengers and another 62 standing and, apart from the upper portions of the fibreglass ends which were coloured orange, they went into traffic in unpainted stainless steel.

The power plants in the ADL's were two Cummins NT855 R4 turbo charged diesel engines, which were able to develop 325 bhp (212kw) at 2100 rpm. These powered the driving axle on each bogie via a Voith turbo transmission and Voith final drives.[7] The cars were fitted with air brakes.

The first batch of five cars (ADL 801-805 & ADC 851-855) were built by A. Goninan & Co. of Newcastle in NSW, and the first of these went into service very late in 1981. Apart from some problems with the air conditioning systems, and excessive noise and vibration, the ADL/ADC railcars gave good service, so orders were placed with Goninans for another five sets. These entered service during the early months of 1985 and were slightly different to the earlier batch. Externally, the door grab handles were different, and the air horns were mounted in a different place on the cab roof, while inside, the seats were fabric covered rather than vinyl. In all other ways, they were the same. In fact, it was easier to pick

the difference between a 1981 car and a 1985 car than it was to differentiate between an ADL and an ADC, although the give away was that the ADC's, in common with the other suburban railcar trailers, always faced east.

The earlier cars were later modified to match the second series, with their horns placed above the cab roof, and all the cars later still, received horn & headlight guards.

In 1986 ADL 809 and ADC 859 were painted in a new Transperth livery, which featured a red stripe along the window line and black ends outlined in white. This treatment of the ends made the cars difficult to see head-on, so another set was repainted with the ends all white. The livery eventually adopted saw the ends painted white on the top half and red on the bottom.

The policy of coupling power cars and trailers carrying the same last digit in their numbers continued with the ADL's and ADC's, and the ten sets gave relatively trouble free service. They were scheduled for replacement by the electric trains during 1993-94, but in a surprise move the majority of the class was suddenly withdrawn from service in January, 1992, after the electric railcars were satisfactorily established. They were stored at Forrestfield Marshalling Yards, although at least one set saw limited service till late April, 1992. ADL 810 and ADC 860 was also retained at Claisebrook Railcar Depot early in 1992 in case of emergencies, and for shunting. This set was used to demonstrate the class to the New Zealand Railways and was also employed between the City and Leederville Station on the new Northern Suburbs Railway on 26 September, 1992, to conduct speed limit tests on that section of the line. It was still at Claisebrook in January, 1993. The entire class was sold to the New Zealand Railways for use in Auckland's suburbs, and was towed to Fremantle on 22 March, 1993 for loading on board the motor vessel "Envoyager". In company with the ADK and ADB class railcars, the ADL's/ADC's departed Fremantle on 26 March, 1993.[8]

ADC 854 at the front of a 4 car set pauses at West Perth to allow a small number of passengers to detrain. The train carries the plain metal cars body with the cab front painted orange.   *Photo courtesy ARHS.*

ADL 803 & ADC 853 climb the bank at Lathlain on 16 March, 1988. The set is carrying the first of the Transperth liveries, which was no more than the addition of the red stripe along the windows, with the "T" logo painted at each end.

Photo Bill Gray.

ADC 859 & ADL 809, a second series set, display the short lived black & red livery as they approach Ashfield station, heading for Midland, 14 May, 1988.   *Photo Bill Gray.*

ADL 810 & ADC 860 rumble over the old Bunbury Bridge, the timber trestle which crossed the Swan River between Rivervale & East Perth on 30 March, 1988. The bridge, like the railcar, has long since been replaced by a much more modern structure, & the set carries the final livery worn by these cars.   *Photo Bill Gray.*

ADC 860 sits at Midland with ADL 810 & an ADK/ADB set during trials for the New Zealand Railways, 16 June, 1992.

Photo Bill Gray.

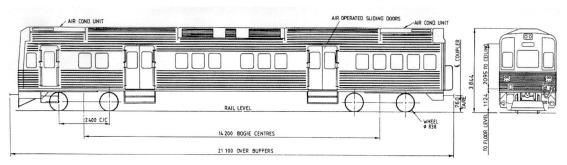

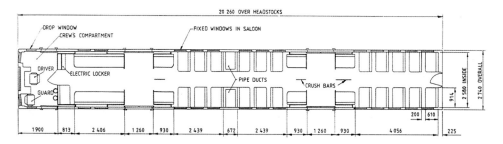

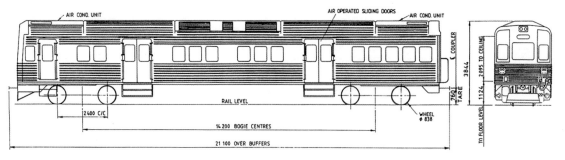

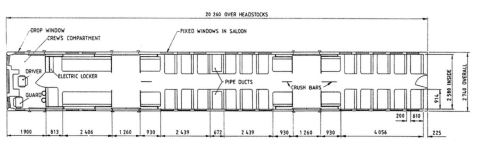

The general arrangement drawings of the ADL (top) & ADC (bottom), well illustrate the similarities between the power car & its trailer.   *Drawings courtesy PTA.*

Inside ADL 805 at Perth station, 27 April, 1991.   *Photo Bill Gray.*

Diesel shunter T 1815 was used to move ADL 810 & ADC 860 around Forrestfield during demonstration trails for the New Zealand Railways. The set was photographed on 30 May, 1992.   *Photo Bill Gray.*

Suburban Saloon & Brake Car (The Queensland Cars)
SX & SXV classes

SX 1664-1668,
1727-1731.
SXV 1663, 1669, 1726, 1732.

SX 1666 at Bellevue on 20 October, 1991 after the afternoon peak hour.   *Photo Bill Gray.*

The America's Cup yacht race challenge was to be held off Fremantle at the end of 1986, and large numbers of tourists were expected to visit Perth at that time. The existing suburban railcar and coach fleet was sometimes hard pressed to meet its commitments on a normal working day if things did not run smoothly, let alone cope with thousands of tourists, plus the people of Perth, who might avail themselves of the railways to journey to Fremantle to enjoy the proceedings. Accordingly, arrangements were made with the Queensland Railways to lease fourteen of their SX and SXV class cars to help handle the traffic during this very busy time. The leased cars included ten SX class suburban saloons and four SXV class suburban brake saloons.

The SX and SXV class carriages had been built by Commonwealth Engineering in Sydney, being finally fitted out at that company's works at Rocklea in Brisbane. They were introduced into northside Brisbane suburban service in August, 1961 where they replaced many of the older wooden side door compartment cars. Eventually, ninety one of the carriages were built, only to be replaced themselves during the 1980's by the electrification of that city's suburban network.[9]

The cars were made of corrugated stainless steel, built in the Budd system of monocoque construction. Both classes of car rode on Bradford-Kendall "Commonwealth" bogies, fitted with roller bearings, and they were equipped with air brakes. The cars were originally intended to be converted to electric traction and as a result they were virtually electric trains without the motors and other equipment. The SXV's would have been the driving cars and so one end of them was fitted with a blanked off headlight, a destination box and end windows. What would have been the driving cab and luggage compartment became a large guard's compartment,[10] giving the SXV's a slightly ungainly look, while the SX's had a neater and more balanced appearance.

The passenger entry doors were air operated, and side facing seats were fitted in each corner adjacent to the entry ways, while fore and aft facing seats with swing over backs were

fitted in the rest of the car. These had fixed timber arm rests. Lighting was fluorescent and overhead luggage racks were fitted. The SX's could accommodate 64 passengers sitting and 87 standing, while the SXV's were able to seat 46 and had standing room for another 74. Tubular hand rails were fitted which, when looking along the interior of the car were prolific enough to be reminiscent of the "monkey bars" in a children's playground.

The first Queensland car to arrive in Perth was SX 1664, which had been despatched from Acacia Ridge in Brisbane on 14 July, 1986 on standard gauge bogies. On 4 August, having had its narrow gauge bogies refitted, it was towed around the Perth suburban network behind diesel locomotive XA 1402 to confirm that the cars would be suitable for Perth operations, and once this exersize was successfully completed, the other thirteen cars were sent across the country. The first set of six Queensland cars (SXV-SX-SX-SX-SX-SXV) went into service on 22 September, 1986, and by 7 October all fourteen had arrived. They were unpainted apart from the QR logo on their body sides, which was retained. Not all the cars ran in regular service, but a number were kept as spares.

The placing in traffic of the Queensland cars finally permitted the withdrawal of most of the remaining ADX class railcars, although one lingered on for two more years. The cars worked well through the America's Cup, so well in fact, that when the supposed time came in February, 1987 for their return to Queensland, none of them went.

Their retention allowed Westrail to withdraw the last of the wooden bodied AY/AYB/AYE/AYF class cars in January, 1991, and having outlived some of the carriages they came to assist, four cars (SX 1667, 1728, 1729, & 1731) which were used as spares, were placed on standard gauge bogies in mid April, 1991 and returned to Queensland. The two sets in regular service (sets 39 & 48) continued to operate till the withdrawal of the cars in December, 1991. They then left Perth in small groups, and the last of them was returned to Queensland on 9 June, 1992.

SXV 1732 at Bellevue on 22 November, 1990. Following the afternoon peak periods the empty set was propelled from Midland back to Bellevue, where they waited till the road was clear for them to cross over the standard gauge & return to Forrestfield for the night. *Photo Bill Gray.*

SX 1730 at Bellevue on 20 October, 1991. *Photo Bill Gray.*

SX 1730 & SXV 1732 roll gently into Midland station behind an A class diesel loco, ready for the morning peak hour on 22 October, 1991.

Photo Bill Gray.

Queensland car SX 1729 at Forrestfield on 13 April, 1991. The car is resting on standard gauge bogies prior to its return to the "Sunshine State".

Photo Bill Gray.

Diesel loco A. 1512 with Queensland Set 48 at Bellevue after peak hour, late on the afternoon of 23 November, 1990.

Photo Bill Gray.

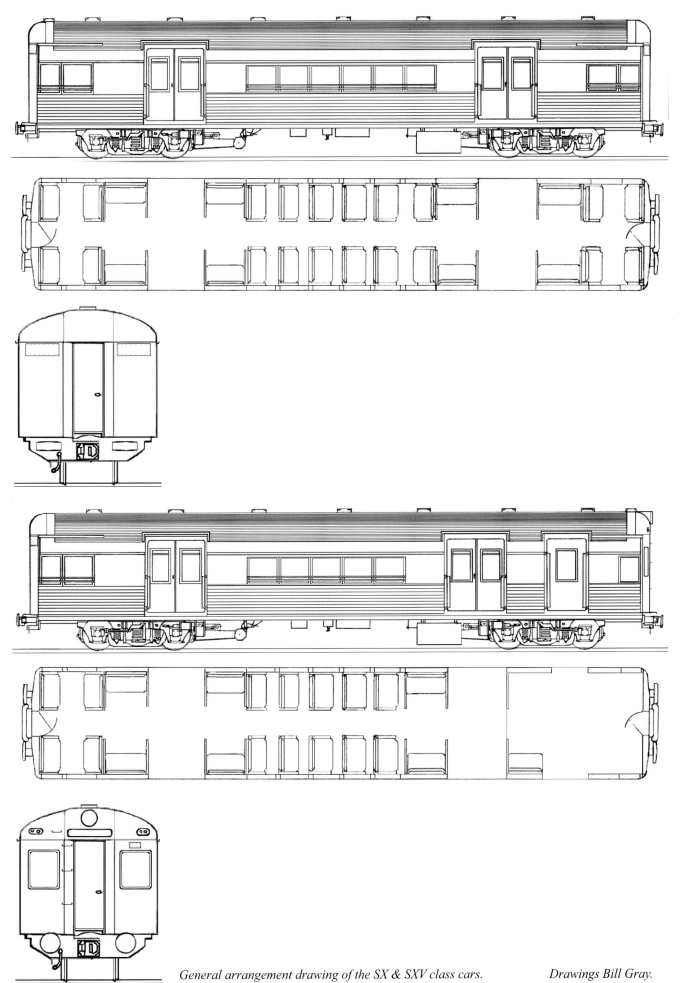

General arrangement drawing of the SX & SXV class cars.   *Drawings Bill Gray.*

Interior of SX 1664 at Midland, 8 January, 1991, showing the full length of the car (left) & the central saloon (right).

Inside SXV 1669 looking towards the guards compartment, Midland, 10 January, 1991.   Photos Bill Gray.

Queensland brake car SXV 1663 & an A class diesel wait to depart Midland station for the City on the afternoon of 7 January, 1991.   Photo Bill Gray.

An unidentified near new "Australind" set climbing the bank at Lathlain in mid March, 1988, on the final stage of its journey from Bunbury.   *Photo Bill Gray.*

The final Western Australian locomotive hauled country passenger train, the "Australind", ran for the last time on 14 November, 1987, but was replaced by a small fleet of modern railcars, also named "Australind". In mid 1985 orders were placed with Comeng at Bassendean for three new diesel hydraulic railcars and two trailers to replace the old train.[11] The first of the new cars, a driving power car (ADP 101) made its appearance on trials in June, 1987, and the other two driving cars (102 & 103) and the non driving cars (ADQ 121 & 122) appeared soon afterwards.

The ADP and ADQ class "Australind" railcars were built in the now normal manner of stressed skin construction used for most of Australia's modern trains. They introduced another variation in railcar design into Western Australia in that both were power cars, but only the ADP's had driving cabs. Thus the "Australind" railcar consists had no trailers. They were constructed of corrugated stainless steel, the front of the driver's cab in the ADP's being of moulded fibreglass with a single large windscreen, and raked back to give a streamlined effect, but, unlike the "Prospector" cars, the cab was part of the body and looked like it belonged. Air conditioning and engine radiators were mounted inside the roof line in the same fashion as the ADL class suburban railcars. The ADP's could seat 40 passengers in reclining seats which could be rotated to face the direction of travel if desired, and in the last row two seats could be removed to make way for a wheel chair. The ADQ's were virtually identical to the ADP's, but without

a driving cab or galley, and they could accommodate 60 passengers.

Each car was fitted with a Cummins KTA 19 diesel engine as its main power source, these engines providing 709 bhp (406 k/w) at 2100 rpm. They drove a Voith T 311r + KB 260/2 hydrodynamic transmission, which then powered one bogie on each car through Voith final drives. The transmissions were also fitted with hydrodynamic brakes and the bogies were Comeng-built with air suspension. The auxiliary power unit in each car was a Detroit V8 diesel engine with a Stanford SC234 generator set, and this engine drove the Sigma refrigerative air conditioning unit.[12]

Being stainless steel, the "Australind" cars were largely left in their natural metal finish, but they were given a blue line along the windows with the word "Australind" above it in orange, which merged into an orange stripe running the length of the car. The fibreglass ends on the ADP's were painted white, the driver's window surround blue, and the lower panels on the front of the car orange.

Having a driving cab at only one end of the ADP's meant that two driving cars were normally marshalled back to back, with a non driving car in between them when bookings warranted.

The "Australind" railcars have given excellent service to date and there is no reason to believe that they will not run as long as their locomotive hauled predecessor, if not longer.

Australind railcars ADP 103, ADQ 122, ADQ 121, & ADP 102 hurry through Roelands on their way to Perth from Bunbury on 25 January, 2002. The cars carry the second livery to be worn by the "Australind" sets.

Photo Bill Gray.

ADP 101 in the TransWA livery leads an Australind set into Armadale on 10 August, 2005.   *Photo Bill Gray.*

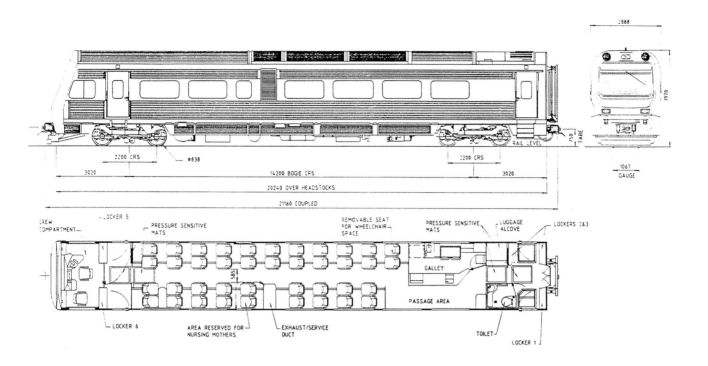

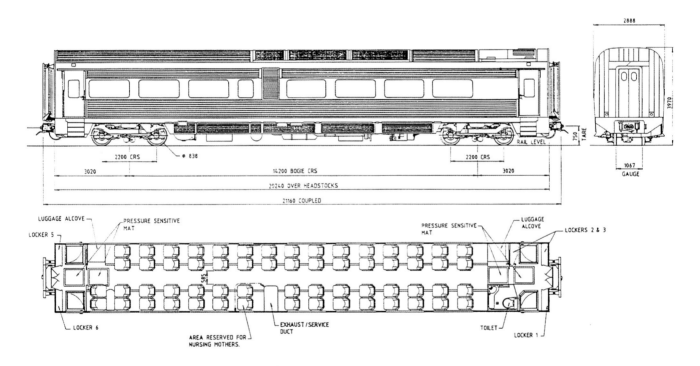

The general arrangement drawings showing the ADP class driving cars (top) & ADQ class trailers (bottom).

Drawings courtesy PTA.

EMU set 19 at Perth station on 13 April, 1992. The landscaping at the newly revamped station had not been completed.
Photo Bill Gray.

In 1984 studies began on the electrification of Perth's suburban railways, and when the decision was made to go ahead with the project forty three new electric railcar sets were ordered in February, 1988. The builders of the modern Queensland Railways electric trains, Walkers/ASEA Ltd. of Maryborough, in Queensland, were chosen to construct them, with the design of the Western Australian cars being based on the Queensland railcars, but with changes in width, cab front, brakes, and bogies.

The electrical multiple unit railcars (EMU's for short) were semi-permanently coupled in pairs, and a total of three pairs were able to run together. As originally designed, one of the pair was a power car and the other a trailer, but to achieve better acceleration and higher speeds the trailer was fitted with traction motors powering one of its bogies. The bodies of the EMU's were built of corrugated stainless steel, using the semi-monocoque construction technique, and only the "power" car was fitted with a pantograph to collect the current from the overhead wiring. This supplied both cars and was the main external difference between them, although the under floor equipment was also different. They were painted in the white, black and red livery as carried by the ADL/ADC class diesel railcars.

The interior seating was for 72 passengers with room for another 82 standing, and each car had a space specifically for a wheel chair. They had power operated sliding passenger entry and end doors with a covered gangway to allow access through the train, and a public address system was fitted to allow messages and information to be passed onto the passengers, either from the driver or from a recording.

In the technical department, the "power" car pantograph collected a.c. electrical power of 25 kv and 50 Hz frequency from the overhead wiring and passed it through a transformer before converting it to d.c. The current was then fed to traction motors, mounted in pairs on each bogie under the "power" cars and on one bogie under the "trailers". The bogies were designed and built by Westrail, and were fitted with outside disc brakes in the same manner to the ADK class railcars. The cars used a combination of air and dynamic brakes. The latter worked by the traction motors effectively becoming generators, converting the speed of the car back into electricity and thereby slowing down the train. Compressed air also operated the passenger and end doors, the air suspension, automatic couplers and other minor equipment.

The "power" cars were classed AEA (201-243) and the "trailers" AEB (301-343), and the first of them was trialed in Queensland during late June and early July, 1990. The first EMU set, AEA 201 and AEB 301 was towed across Australia on standard gauge bogies and arrived at Forrestfield in Perth on 1 September, 1990, where it promptly became the centre of two work bans and a picket over a pay dispute and one man train operation. Two more sets arrived during the month, and by early December, 1990, six sets of EMU's were in Perth. However, several problems, including teething trouble with the bogies which set up a harmonic vibration which brought on nausea in otherwise well people, caused the introduction of the new cars to be delayed even further. After several months of trials, mainly on the Armadale line, the EMU's entered revenue service on 28 September, 1991, carrying passengers between Perth and the Showgrounds at Claremont for the annual Royal Show. The new railcars were then progressively placed in traffic with very little fanfare due to the adverse publicity created by the delays. Finally, on 5 April, 1992, they officially ran the suburban network on their own, with only the last evening service on each of the three suburban lines being operated with diesel railcars. On 11 April, 1992 the first four EMU sets were named in ceremonies at Perth, Fremantle, Armadale and Midland, as follows:

> Set 201/301 "City of Perth"
> Set 202/302 "City of Armadale"
> Set 203/303 "Shire of Swan"
> Set 204/304 "City of Fremantle"

Set 205/305 was named "City of Wanneroo" on 21 March, 1993, after the opening of the Northern Suburbs Railway. The last set (Set 43) was named "City of Maryborough"[13], after the Queensland town in which the cars were built, and it entered service on 30-9-1993.

Even after they were in service the new railcars suffered a number of problems. Within the first twelve months, two sets, 24 and 25, and AEB 305 had all suffered collision damage after major altercations with motor vehicles at level crossings. Sadly, at least three people had died in these accidents, which were partly attributed to the electric railcars being faster and quieter than the diesel cars they had replaced.[14] The cars also suffered a series of braking problems in which they would slide through stations, unable to stop at the appropriate place at the platforms. Set 24 was badly damaged at Armadale station during trials in September, 1992 when it slid into the buffer stop at the end of the line.[15] This resulted in trains having to stop before entering terminating station platforms, then slowly move into the platform at a snails pace. Set 24 was returned to service around July, 1994.

Sets 17, 26 and 39 were damaged in a shunting accident at Claisebrook on 18 March, 1993 resulting in AEA 226 and AEB 339, and AEA 217 and AEB 326 running together as matched pairs[16] for several months till their stable mates had been repaired.

On the 29 November, 1992 the EMU's appeared with the name "Fastrak" applied on the front of each car, in place of the "TransPerth" sign, "Fastrak" being the marketing name adopted by TransPerth for the railcar fleet. The new name lasted a little over two years and by February, 1995, was disappearing off the cars again.

In early 1994 a shortage of parts saw Set 20 out of service and being used for spares, an unusual occurrence for a near new EMU set. Happily, it was back in service around March, 1994.

Despite the problems encountered by the EMU fleet the cars began to settle down to their job well. Demand on the suburban system quickly increased beyond all expectations and even before the first order for 43 sets had been filled it had become apparent that there were not going to be enough railcar sets to meet the demand. Early in 1994 a consultant had been commissioned by Fastrak to evaluate the future requirements for more railcar sets. As a result, the 1996 WA State Budget included the necessary funds for another five EMU sets.

Walkers/Adtranz won the contract for the construction of these cars. Externally they were identical to the earlier vehicles, but consideration was given to fitting them with longitudinal seating. To this end Set 16 had its seating changed to longitudinal, first being noted in this configuration on 14 August, 1997.[17] The idea of this was that more people could be carried in the cars, albeit the majority of them standing. The first of the new EMUs, Set 44 was rolled out at the Maryborough Works in June, 1998 and was tested between Maryborough West and Isis Junction in Queensland in early August, before being railed to Perth in September. It was noted at Morandoo (Port Waratah) on 14 September, 1998, and at Paterson on 28 September. At the end of that month Set 44 was delivered to Forrestfield where the standard gauge bogies were replaced with its normal EMU undercarriage, and it was then towed to Claisebrook Railcar depot to receive its internal fittings. This process took about eight weeks, followed by trials, and Set 44 entered service in December, 1998.

The other cars were noted at Morandoo during delivery as follows:[18]

Set 45	28 September, 1998
Set 46	13 October, 1998
Set 47	2 November, 1998
Set 48	9 November, 1998

Set 45 entered service in December, 1998, Sets 46 and 47 in January, 1999, and Set 48 in March, 1999. These cars introduced a change in livery for the EMU fleet, with the reflective red stripe above the window line being changed to green. The rest of the EMU fleet was altered in a similar manner soon afterwards.

Set 16 had been converted to longitudinal seating, and one of the new sets may have been delivered in this configuration, but it was not a popular concept with commuters. Despite the negative publicity, at the time of writing, Sets 1 through to 19, and Sets 47 and 48 have had their seating reconfigured to the longitudinal arrangement.

All 48 sets, known as the "A" series after the new cars started to arrive in 2004, have settled down to provide the people of Perth with an efficient and rapid suburban service.

EMU set 09 at Forrestfield on 16 February, 1991. The cars are still on the standard gauge bogies which carried them across Australia on their delivery run from Queensland. Photo Bill Gray.

Set 31 rests at Claisebrook railcar depot over the weekend on 27 April, 1996, in the Transperth livery. Photo Bill Gray.

AEB 324 under repair at the Midland Workshops on 22 January, 1994, following its altercation with a buffer stop at Armadale. The workshops had been closed by this time, so this was probably the last official job carried out there by Westrail.

Photo Bill Gray.

AEA 205 leads its AEB class trailer into Mt. Lawley station on 16 April, 1993. The cars are wearing the relatively shortlived "Fastrak" livery.

Photo Bill Gray.

EMU set 06 accelerates out of Claisebrook, heading for McIver on its way to the City. This set has been given the green stripe above the window line, but still carries the Transperth livery, with the titling on the cab front next to the logo rather than above it, or on the other side of the car.						*Photo Bill Gray.*

The suburban timetables are structured so that several sets arrive at Perth station at about the same time, allowing passengers to transfer from one line to another. During a busy school holiday period on 20 April, 2001, Sets 36 & 12 rest briefly at Perth station before setting out on their next services.						*Photo Bill Gray.*

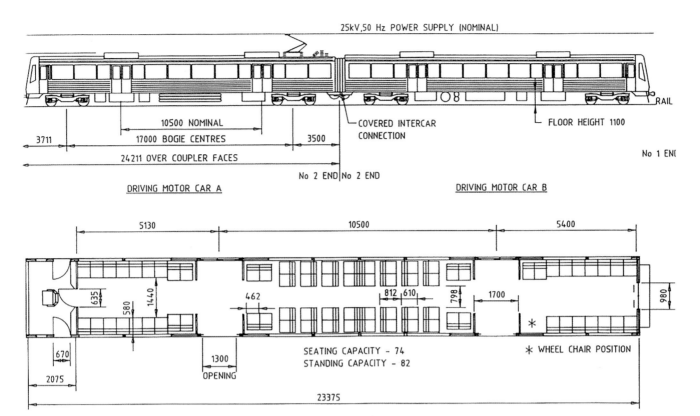

25kV,50 Hz POWER SUPPLY (NOMINAL)

COVERED INTERCAR CONNECTION

FLOOR HEIGHT 1100

RAIL

No 1 ENI

3711

10500 NOMINAL

17000 BOGIE CENTRES

3500

24211 OVER COUPLER FACES

No 2 END|No 2 END

DRIVING MOTOR CAR A

DRIVING MOTOR CAR B

5130

10500

5400

635

580

1440

462

812 610

798

1700

980

670

1300

OPENING

SEATING CAPACITY – 74
STANDING CAPACITY – 82

✳ WHEEL CHAIR POSITION

2075

23375

General arrangement drawing of Western Australia's first EMU sets.   *Drawing courtesy PTA.*

The interiors of the EMU sets. The more traditional seating arrangement inside Set 42 at Midland on 24 September, 2003, & the later, & less popular, longitudinal arrangement inside AEB 318 at Midland on 20 January, 2005.   *Photos Bill Gray.*

When the EMU sets needed to be moved to Forrestfield for maintenance work, the Claisebrook shunter MA 1862 was used to tow the sets over the route. This was a regular movement early on Saturday afternoons, & here we see the MA taking EMU set 38 through Hazelmere on such a movement on 28 January, 2003.

Photo Bill Gray.

WDA 002 & WDB012 round the curve at Greenmount on the morning service to Kalgoorlie, 17 January, 2005.

Photo Bill Gray.

By mid 1996 the old WCA & WCE Prospector cars were beginning to show their age, and even though they had been re-engined during 1991 and 1992 they were becoming less and less reliable, suffering continual mechanical problems. As a result a consultant was called in to investigate the problem and look at the best way of replacing the ageing railcars. The consultant's report suggested the purchase of eight standard gauge tilting cars, permanently coupled into four sets, each of two cars.[19] These did not quite eventuate, but seven cars were ordered instead, these being two sets of two cars, and one set of three cars.

The order for the new railcars was given to United Goninans at Broadmeadow, near Newcastle in New South Wales. They were classified WDA and WDB, with the sole "trailer" (or centre car in the three car set) being classed WDC. The cars were designed to be capable of some very fast speeds and were planned to reduce the travelling time between Perth and Kalgoorlie to six hours, nearly two hours faster than the old timetable. Unlike the original Prospector, the new cars were rail hauled to Western Australia, despite a few problems with their being out of gauge for some of the NSW platform roads.

In a departure from previous practice, all 7 cars were powered, each being fitted with two 500 hp Cummins diesel engines. The WDA class contained a buffet as well as space for wheel chairs, and a disabled persons toilet. These cars could seat 36 passengers, plus two wheel chairs. The WDB's had a slightly smaller toilet, no buffet, and were able to seat 60 passengers. Likewise, the WDC could seat 60 people and had a toilet at one end, but no driving cab. These cars were also powered to ensure the three car set could match the speeds of the two car sets.

The first set, WDA 001 and WDB 011 were delivered to

United Goninans at Bassendean in Perth about 4 April, 2003, ready to begin trials. The new cars were put on display at East Perth Terminal on 28 May, 2003 for a media promotion which included the launch of the WAGR's new marketing name, "Transwa". In another departure from tradition, the cars appeared in a radical new Transwa livery of bright yellow ends with a slate blue "cheat" line along the windows and yellow, orange and light blue "waves" painted on the body sides.

The first mainline trial took place on 8 September 2003,[20] the media reporting that the trials had to be carried out in secret due to the propensity for over excited rail enthusiasts to throw themselves in the way of the speeding train while trying to take photographs of it! At the successful conclusion of the trials, WDA 001 and WDB 011 ran an inaugural VIP special from East Perth to Kalgoorlie on 27 June, 2004, the train departing Perth on a very low key note, with little fanfare. The arrival at Kalgoorlie was reportedly a much more enthusiastic affair. Regular services with the new railcars began the next day.[21]

The Prospector cars were based at Midland Workshops from 8 December, 2003, but all was not well with the new railcars. The second set, WDA 002 and WDB 012, had arrived in Western Australia by December, 2003, and entered service on 28 June, 2004, running empty to Kalgoorlie, then successfully carrying a load of passengers back to Perth,[22] but problems were beginning to appear. The third set consisting of WDA 003, WDB 013 and WDC 023 was delivered to Kewdale on 25 May, 2004 and was being trialed by September, 2004, but the trials on this set, and the two sets already delivered, were showing problems with failures caused by the electrical systems, especially the inverters, and with dust in the controlling computer systems on board. In addition, toilet retention tanks leaked, there were overheating problems, and the auxiliary power supply, which controlled the air-conditioning, lighting, entertainment systems and other ancillary equipment, was not operating as expected, in some cases shutting everything down so that the various systems had to be reset again.[23] The problems became so bad that the WAGR initially refused to accept the third set, and for a while it looked like the whole lot would have to go back to the manufacturer. To make matters worse, the underperforming electrical systems in the cars had been built in Germany, parts had to come from there, and by early 2005 the manufacturer of those systems was said to be facing bankruptcy. Delays were also caused by the inability of the cars to use the old refueling system in Perth, leading to a requirement for a new one, unusual noises in the axle bearings, and difficulties arose with the multiple unit controls when attempts were made to multi couple Sets 1 and 2.[24] By early 2005, the first two sets had been withdrawn from service 12 times while these various problems were attended to.[25]

Despite these issues, and its initial reluctance to do so, the Sate Government finally accepted the three car set on 24 December, 2004, based on United Goninans putting up an additional $7 million security against further problems with the cars. Thus the new Prospector cars were finally all in traffic, and settled down to provide a comfortable, high speed rail service between Perth and the Goldfields.

The three car Prospector set approaches the Great eastern Highway overpass on the morning of 19 January, 2005.

Photo Bill Gray.

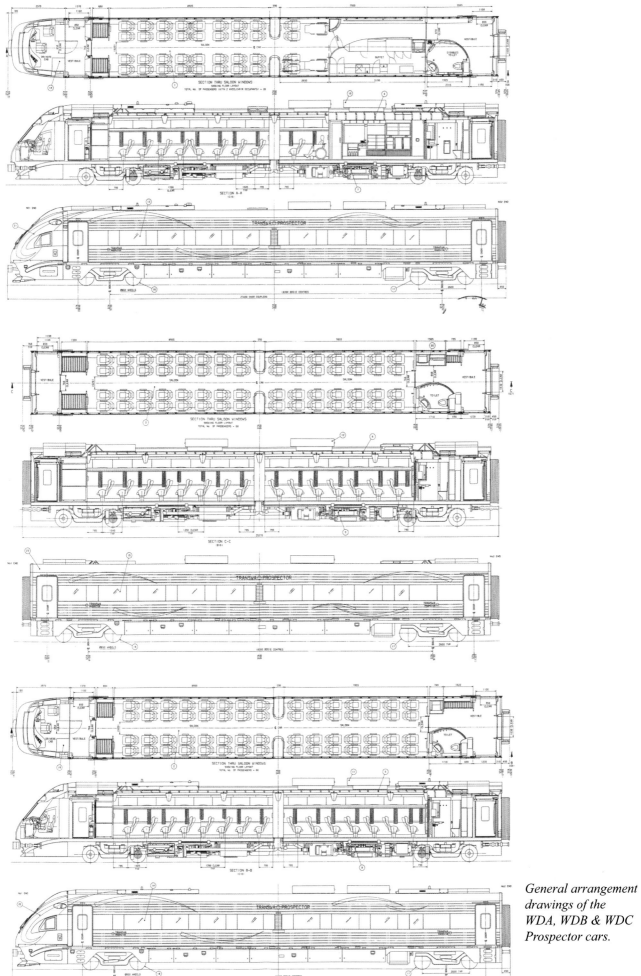

General arrangement drawings of the WDA, WDB & WDC Prospector cars.

Courtesy PTA.

The Avon Link set sits outside the old Midland Workshops site during acceptance trials, 4 February, 2005.   *Photo Bill Gray.*

On 24 September, 1995 Westrail announced a new service for commuters from Northam to Perth, using the old WCA/WCE Prospector cars. This was known as the AvonLink service, and once under way it was extended as far as Merredin. When the new Prospector cars were ordered, a similar two car set was also purchased, specifically for this service. These cars were classified WEA and WEB, 031 and 041 respectively. For all intents and purposes the new cars were identical to the WDA and WDB class cars ordered for the Prospector services, although there were some internal differences, notably to do with the buffet. Externally, the most notable difference was the livery for these cars, being slate blue and green as opposed to slate blue and yellow on the Prospector cars.

The AvonLink set arrived in Western Australia in company with the three car Prospector set on 25 May, 2004 and was being trialed in December, 2004. Unfortunately the cars suffered many of the same teething problems as their brethren.

The set had still not been accepted by early February, although it was thought the acceptance date would not be far away. The new cars finally entered service on 1 August, 2005.

The AvonLink set glides through Bellevue towards Midland on the afternoon of 1 September, 2005.   *Photo Bill Gray.*

2004

Electric Railcars & Trailers
BEA, BEB & BET Classes

449-479
549-579
649-679

B series EMU set 56 sits on standard gauge transfer bogies at the Midland Workshops on 20 September, 2004, soon after delivery. The graffiti vandals have already been at work.   *Photo Bill Gray.*

As early as 1993, the state government had approved a rapid transit corridor linking Perth and Mandurah, and Westrail's designers were considering further extensions to the suburban rail system, including electric lines from Armadale to Mundijong, Currumbine to Yanchep, and Bassendean to Ellenbrook.[26] It was considered that the Perth to Mandurah railway alone would require a substantial number of new electric railcars, 117 to be exact, capable of 130 kph, and these were first planned to be in service by Winter 2003.[27] Not surprisingly, this date turned out to be a little optimistic, however eventually the details were worked out and in May, 2002 the State Government announced that a contract for the new cars would be given to EDI Rail-Bombardier.

The new suburban car fleet was to consist if 31 sets of three cars, making 93 cars in all. In a departure from 104 years of tradition the new cars were classified BEA and BEB for the end cars and BET for the centre car. Some cynics have suggested that the "BE" classification traditionally belonged to sheep vans and perhaps there is some correlation in that! However, the new cars were anything but sheep truck-like and have been shown to be an improvement in comfort and passenger ride over the first series. As a result of the classification, the older EMUs became officially known as the "A" series cars and the new ones as "B" series.

All bogies on the BEA and BEB class cars were powered, while the centre car (BET class) was not. However, the only pantograph on the train was located on the roof of this car and,

like the A series cars, this collected a.c. electrical power of 25 kv and 50 Hz frequency from the overhead wiring. Unlike the A series the current was not converted to d.c., but remained a.c. and as fed to the traction motors as such. As a result, the new cars cannot be multi coupled with the older EMUs.

The end cars each had seating for 76 passengers, while the centre car seated 84, making a total of 236 seated passengers, with enough room for another 321 standing. (These figures make an interesting comparison with the AT second class suburban cars of 100 years earlier, each of which carried 90 passengers seated, and, officially, at least, none standing). In addition, there was room for six wheelchairs, two in each car. Interestingly, the seats were placed transversely rather than longitudinally, despite the conversions to the seating arrangements carried out in the A series cars. Internally, there were no doors between the cars, giving the passenger the impression of sitting in a long, rather disjointed tube. The cars were very quiet to travel in, but in most other respects of construction and facilities, were similar to, but improved upon, the A series cars. They were built of corrugated stainless steel, using the semi-monocoque construction technique, with power operated sliding passenger entry doors, a public address system which allowed messages and other information to be passed onto the passengers, either from the driver or from a recording, a combination of air and dynamic brakes, air operated suspension, and automatic couplers.

The first set, No. 49, consisting of three cars, BEA 449, BEB

549 and BET 649, arrived at Acacia Ridge in Brisbane, from Maryborough on 26 May, 2004. Here it was placed on the standard gauge bogies which would carry it across the country to Perth. The next day it set out on that journey, arriving on 1 June, 2004. It was taken to the Midland Workshops where it's narrow gauge bogies were restored to it, and was transferred to the new railcar depot at Nowergup on 9 June. Nine days later the new railcar ran its first trial down the Northern suburbs line to Perth, then on to Armadale.

By 12 August 2004 four new EMUs had been delivered and by 20 September, another four had arrived. Sets 49 to 56 all entered service together on 4 October, 2004 for the opening of the new Clarkson station on the Northern suburbs line. Initially the cars were used exclusively on the Perth to Whitfords services, also on the Northern suburbs line, where the stations are some distance apart. This was due to their traction motors being designed for high speed running as is found on this line and on the Mandurah railway when it is complete, as opposed to the shorter distance stop-start requirements on the other suburban lines.

By Christmas 2004, set 61 had been delivered and was still on transfer bogies at Midland over the Christmas period. Its own bogies arrived at Midland on 14 January, 2005. Deliveries continued at a steady pace during 2005, with set 69 transferring from Midland to Nowergup on 15 August.

EMU set 54 speeds down the railway reserve on the Mitchell Freeway towards Perth on a morning service on 11 August, 2005.
Photo Bill Gray.

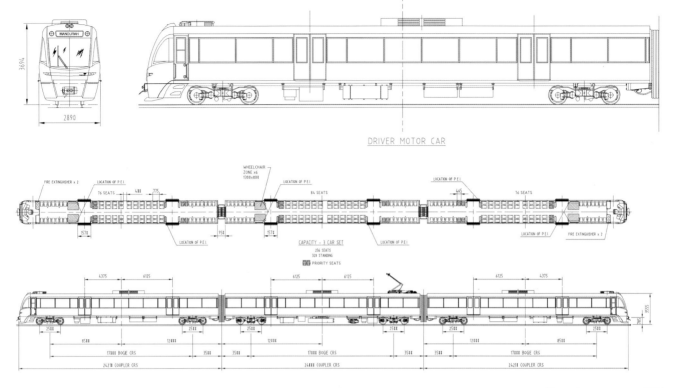

DRIVER MOTOR CAR

CAPACITY - 3 CAR SET

236 SEATS
329 STANDING
PRIORITY SEATS

Drawing courtesy PTA.

The interior of B series EMU set 49 at Whitfords station on 19 January, 2005.

Photo Bill Gray.

THE FINAL WORD....

And so, the last regular locomotive hauled passenger train has run. The placing in service of Perth's electric trains spelled the end in Western Australia of WAGR owned "real" trains - an engine at the front and a string of carriages trailing obediently behind.

In thirty short years the WAGR built up a remarkable rail passenger network across sparsely populated and hostile country, but years of subsequent neglect allowed that system to die. During the 1950's the branch line services were mostly discontinued, and the main line services deteriorated. Under Commissioner Wayne the main line trains enjoyed a brief revival during the 1960's, but by then it was too late. The money should have been spent years before on newer stock. During the 1970's country passenger trains in Western Australia all but ceased to exist. Perhaps this was inevitable as society became wealthier, increasingly mobile and more independent, but, with growing awareness of both the environment and the price we pay for private transport, history may well judge harshly the almost complete lack of foresight by government after government since 1910 as to the importance of their railways.

There can be no doubt that modern trains, such as we have, are faster and more comfortable than their predecessors, but there is a measure of sterility about riding in an acrylic and stainless steel box, looking through double glazed windows and breathing processed air, this being common to most forms of modern day transport. Gone are the days of travelling in an ornately decorated, varnished timber passenger compartment with leather seats, and windows that open, allowing the smell of the countryside, punctuated by the occasional waft of coal smoke, to tantalise the nostrils, of listening to the engine in the distance at the head of the train as, with great sense of purpose, it thunders towards its destination, or of that unique background sound of wheels under a wooden bodied carriage passing over points and rail joints.

To many people these things are not considered as loss, but as ever increasing progress carries us relentlessly towards an uncertain future, and men rush from place to place, not having the time to show genuine concern for one another, there are those who quietly mourn the passing of days when things were just a little slower and travelling by train, despite some of the discomforts, was an adventure.

Photo courtesy ARHS.

APPENDIX ONE
OTHER PASSENGER CARRYING VEHICLES

Horse Boxes

A class 5105-5142

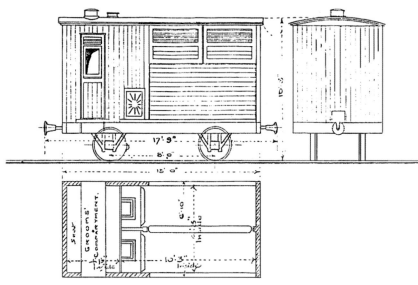

In 1882 two vehicles were built by the Metropolitan Railway Carriage & Wagon Co., both 4 wheelers able to carry two horses and three grooms. Two more were placed in traffic in 1891, followed by another six in 1893. In 1896 ten horse boxes were built by the Bristol Carriage & Wagon Co. to a new design, although they were still 4 wheelers, and still carried two horses and three grooms. Another fourteen came from the Lancaster Wagon Co. in 1897. Four more similar vehicles were taken over with the Great Southern Railway in December, 1896. By 1900 all had been classed E, numbers 1-38, and in 1900 all were reclassified A class 5105-5142, but in three groups, A 5105-5114 (ten cars from the Metropolitan Railway Carriage & Wagon Co.), A 5115-5138 (twenty four cars from the Bristol Carriage & Wagon Co. and the Lancaster Wagon Co.) and A 5139-5142 (four cars ex the Great Southern Railway).

In 1908 work began on rebodying the A class horse boxes, as follows:-
1908/1909 - 5109, 5112-5115, 5118-5121, 5127, 5129-5131, 5133, 5135, 5136, 5138, 5141.
Second half of 1909 - 5105, 5106, 5110, 5111, 5124, 5126, 5128, 5137, 5140, 5142.
1910 - 5117.
1911 - 5134.
1912 - 5107, 5108, 5116, 5122, 5123, 5125, 5132, 5139.

The increased use of motor transport, then the Depression, saw demand for horse boxes fall, and in 1936 and '37 A 5105, 5108-5110, 5112, 5114, 5122-5124, 5127, 5131, 5133, 5134, 5138 and 5142 were converted into Bs class cattle vans. During the Second World War, A 5107, 5111, 5113, 5116, 5119-5121, 5126, 5128-5130, 5132, 5139 and 5141 were converted into D class vans in 1943, and in 1951 A 5115, 5117 & 5136 were also converted to D class vans. In 1954 A 5135 was written off, followed by A 5106, 5125, 5137 the next year. The final horse boxes, A 5118 and 5140 were written off in 1958.

The photo depicts A 5120, courtesy ARHS, & the drawing of the A class horsebox is courtesy PTA.

Ba class 1000-1005,

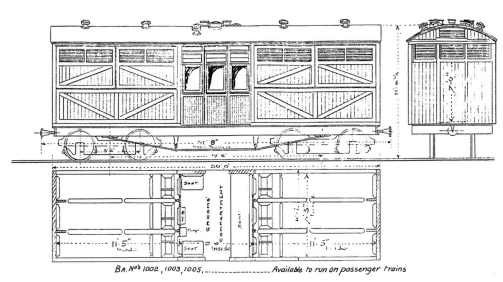

BA. Nᵒˢ 1002, 1003, 1005. _____ *Available to run on passenger trains*

Drawing courtesy PTA.

Early in 1903, six new horse boxes (Ba 1000-1005) were supplied by the Metropolitan Railway Carriage & Wagon Co. They ran on 5'6" (1.68m) wheel base plate frame bogies. Three (Ba 1002, 1003, & 1005) were able to run on passenger trains. The Ba's carried six horses and five grooms.

In 1952 Ba 1000-1002, 1004 and 1005 were rebuilt as brakevans ZBA 435-439, and in 1954 Ba 1003 was written off.

A train of horseboxes unloads at Helenavale racecourse. The first van behind the loco is Ba 1003.
Photo courtesy Mrs. N. Easther, via Mundaring & Hills Historical Society

Bb class 1-5, 1074, 1892, 1896, 2718, 4259, 4265, 5893.

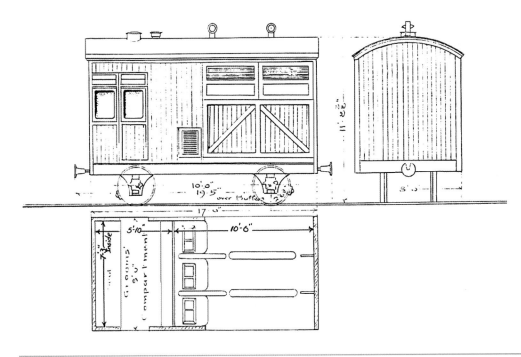

In 1907 ten Bb class horse boxes able to carry three horses plus three grooms appeared. They were 4 wheeled vehicles, and were numbered 1, 2, 4, 5, 1074, 1892, 1896, 2718, 4259 & 4265. The last Bb class horse box to enter service was rebuilt from DY class bullion van 5893, in 1920. It retained it's number.

In 1954 Bb 4, 1074, 2718 and 5893 were written off and in 1955 Bb 1, 2, 5, 1892, 1896, 4259 and 4265 were also written off.

Bb class horsebox drawing, courtesy PTA.

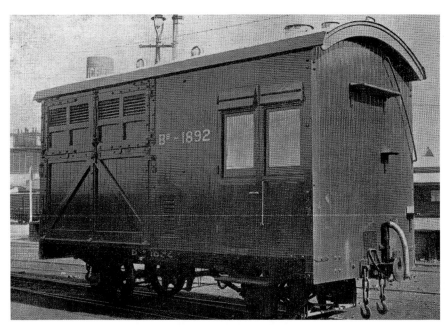

Horsebox Bb 1892.

Photo from Rail Gazette.

Mail Vans

In 1889 a small van was built at the WAGR workshops at Fremantle to carry the mail up the Great Southern Railway from Albany to Fremantle, so cutting a considerable amount of time off the sea journey. It was the only vehicle at that time to travel on both the government owned Eastern Railway and the privately owned Great Southern line, and it is thought to have been a 4 wheeler. It spent its last years as a mail tender, possibly being relegated to that status with the arrival of the 6 wheeled TB class mail vans from 1892, and it disappeared from the records in 1895. It was probably scrapped.

In 1891 a 6 wheeled post office sorting van entered service on the Eastern Railway. This van was built on a Cleminson underframe, possibly from passenger car AC 5 or BC 6and had a panelled timber body with an iron underframe. It is believed to have been written off in 1899.

TB class (pre 1900
AK class (1900) 250, 251(1st), 251(2nd), 252-257.

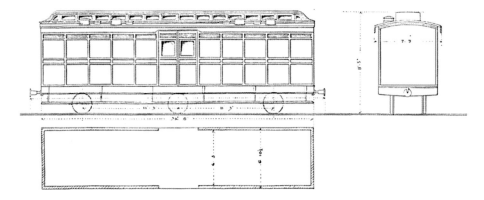

Drawing courtesy PTA.

In 1892 a 6 wheeled "Cleminson" mail van, fitted with a clerestory roof was built at the Fremantle Workshops. It was classified TB. About 1899 all the mail vans were renumbered, this van becoming 251 as part of the passenger stock list, and as a result of the 1900 Royal Commission, it was reclassified AK.

In 1904 AK 251, along with the other two Cleminson mail vans, was converted to an AS class luggage vans.

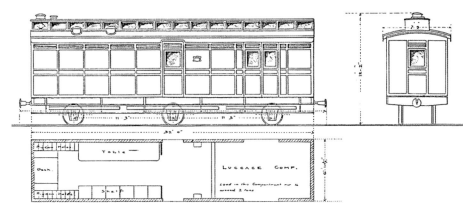

Drawing courtesy PTA.

In 1895/96 two "Cleminson" mail vans were built at Fremantle, using imported ironwork. These vehicles were similar, but not identical, to the Cleminson van previously built in 1892. All three "Cleminson" vans were classified TB. About 1899 these vans were renumbered 252 and 253 in order of construction as part of the passenger stock list. As a result of the 1900 Royal Commission, they were reclassified AK. In 1904 both vans were converted into AS class luggage vans.

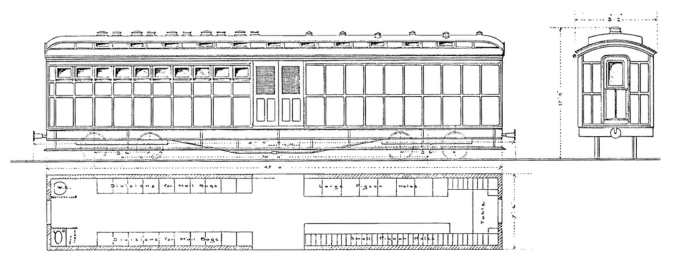

The first of the bogie mailvans. Four of these were built & became AK 254 - 257.   *Drawing courtesy PTA.*

In 1896 two large bogie mail vans were built by the Ashbury Railway Carriage & Iron Co. in England, followed by two more identical vans from the same builder in 1898. These four vans also joined the TB class. About 1899 the seven mail vans were renumbered 251-257 in order of construction as part of the passenger stock list, and as a result of the 1900 Royal Commission, they were reclassified AK. Thus the Ashbury vans became AK 254-257

In 1940 the AK class mail vans were reclassified as wagon stock:-

    AK 254 - P 669
    AK 255 - P 718
    AK 256 - P 754
    AK 257 - P 788

All six former mail vans were used on the Commonwealth Government's ambulance train during World War Two, and they returned to WAGR service as covered vans, with at least two being altered to carry milk, and one other to carry fish. They were written off between 1950 and 1960.

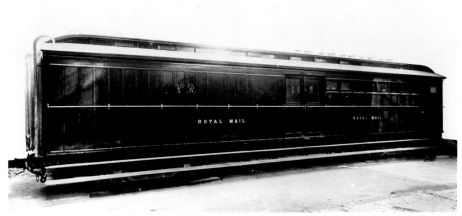

Ashbury Railway Carriage & Iron Co. photo of the AK class mail van.
Photo courtesy ARHS.

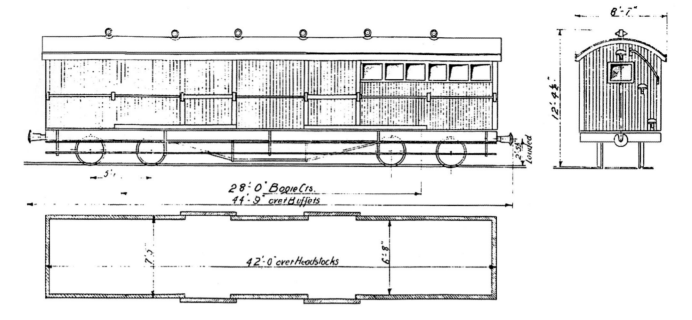

The final bogie mail vans took the first two numbers of the 250 series, ie. AK 250 & 251.   *Drawing courtesy PTA.*

In 1911 two completely new bogie mail vans (AK 250 & 251) were built at Midland, joining the four Ashbury vans. In 1940 they were reclassified as wagon stock:-

    AK 250 - P 469
    AK 251 - P 658

All six vans were used on the Commonwealth Government's ambulance train during World War Two, and they returned to WAGR service as covered vans, with at least two being altered to carry milk, and one other to carry fish. They were written off in 1965 and 1969. The last to go was P 658, (formerly AK 251) and it was preserved at the ARHS Rail Transport Museum at Bassendean, while the body of P 469 (formerly AK 250) was relocated to a car racing track at Meekatharra, near the airport.

P 658, preserved, at Bassendean Rail Transport Museum, 29 October, 1994.   *Photo Bill Gray.*

Bullion Vans
VY & DY classes

4999, 5893, 5000.

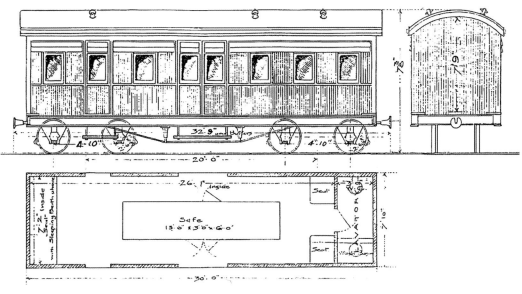

In 1898 a bogie bullion van was built at the Fremantle Workshops to carry bullion down from the Eastern goldfields. It later became VY 4999. In 1948 VY 4999 was withdrawn from service and its safe fitted into brakevan ZJ 260, which became the new bullion van. In November, 1948, VY 4999 re-entered service as workman's van (VW 4999). In the late 1980's VW 4999 was stored at Northam and moved to Midland in December, 1990 for disposal. It survives with the ARHS at Midland.

The original bullion van, Vy 4999. The photograph shows it as a workmans van, out of service at the back of the Midland Workshops on 23 April, 1991.

Photo Bill Gray.

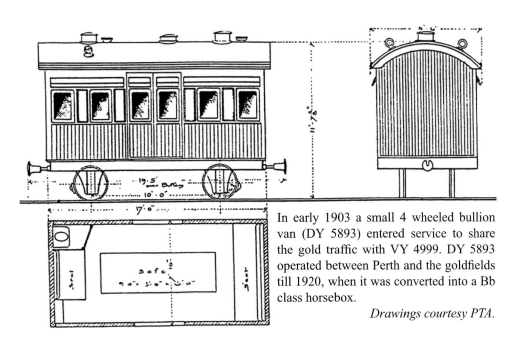

In early 1903 a small 4 wheeled bullion van (DY 5893) entered service to share the gold traffic with VY 4999. DY 5893 operated between Perth and the goldfields till 1920, when it was converted into a Bb class horsebox.

Drawings courtesy PTA.

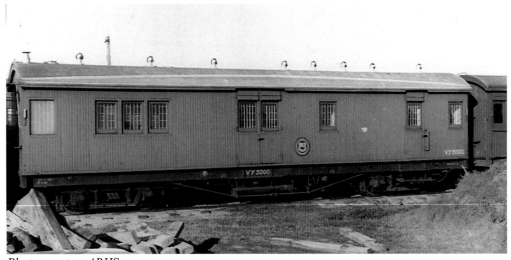

In 1948 the safe from VY 4999 was fitted into the "short" brakevan ZJ 260, which was then renumbered VY 5000, and re-entered traffic as the new bullion van in September, 1948.

VY 5000 was converted to a workman's van in July, 1968, and in 1972 was converted to an inspection car AL 1. It was written off in 1980 and is now preserved with Bellarine Peninsular Railway in Victoria.

Country Inspector's & Agricultural Bank Manager's Vans
Bc class 185, 186, & 1926

Agricultural Bank Managers van Bc 185 in original condition. Note the tarpaulin to cover the buggy & afford it some protection from the elements & cinders from the locomotives. This end of the van were later covered.

Photo WAGR, courtesy Mark Beard.

In 1898 the frame and chassis from an R class bogie wagon were used to build a country inspector's van, numbered 1926, which, iIn 1900, was classified in the freight stock as Bc class.

In 1907 two more similar vans (Bc 185 & 186), known as agricultural bank manager's vans. were built. About 1912 the flat top end of the three vans was covered over in the style of a normal goods van.

In 1927 Bc 1926 was converted into a ZB class brakevan, and Bc 185 was rebuilt as a Z class brakevan, while Bc 186 lasted till 1934 when it was also converted into a Z class brakevan.

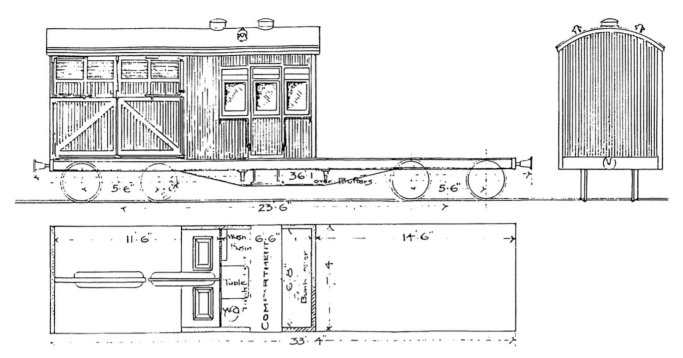

Drawing of a Bc class van with the open deck.   *Photo courtesy PTA.*

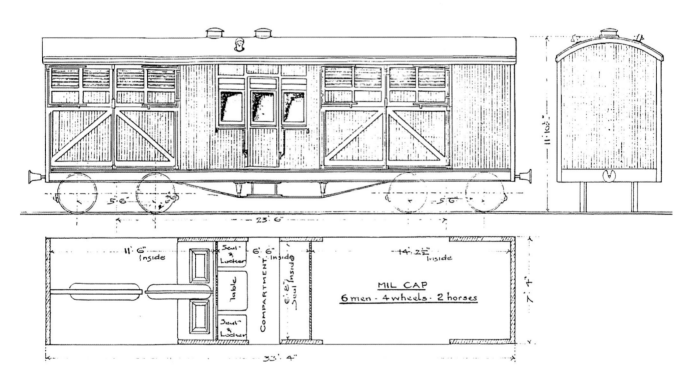

Drawing of the Bc class van, as modified with the end covered in.   *Drawing courtesy PTA.*

Luggage Vans
AS class 251-253

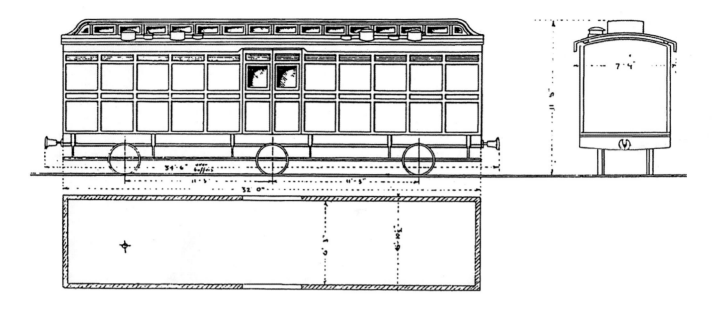

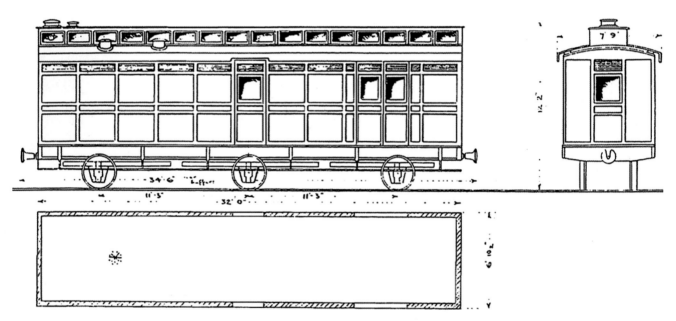

Drawings of the AS class luggage vans, AS 251 at the top & AS 252 & 253 at the bottom.   *Drawings courtesy PTA.*

In 1904 the 6 wheeled mail vans AK 251, 252 and 253 were converted into luggage vans and reclassified AS. Thet only lasted two years and in 1906 all three were rebuilt as Z class brakevans on bogie underframes, with new bodies. AS 251 became Z 6790, AS 252 was numbered Z 6789 and AS 253 became Z 6785. None have survived.

Eye Sight Testing Van
VA class
VX class (1936)
VU class (1967)

9700

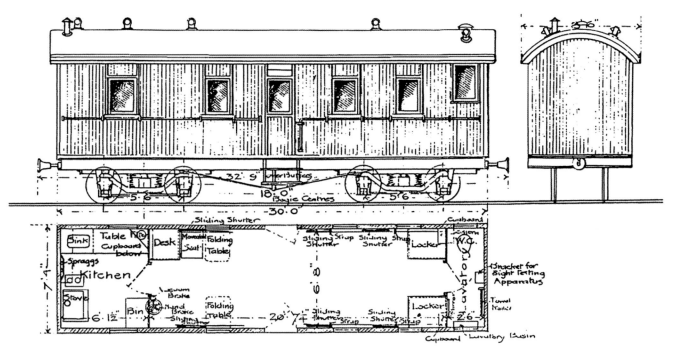

Eye sight testing van Vx 9700.   *Drawing courtesy PTA.*

VW 9700 as a workmans van at Forrestfield, 16 February, 1991.   *Photo Bill Gray.*

In 1912 an eye sight testing van, VA 9700, was built at Midland. It travelled around the rail network of the state carrying staff with it, who performed the periodic eye tests which all train crews and signalmen were subjected to in the interests of safety.

In 1936 it was reclassified VX, then VU in 1967. It was finally converted into a VW class workman's van in 1970. In 1989 it was stowed Forrestfield for storage prior to disposal and the historic little van was demolished in the early 1990's.

APPENDIX TWO
PASSENGER CARRIAGES CONVERTED FOR OTHER USES

Commissioner, Governor, and State Saloons
Ministerial & Vice Regal Cars
A class A 1, 5, 6
AM & AN classes AM 40, 261, 313, 414, 444 AN 206, 413 (1st and 2nd)

Car No. 1. In 1885 Car No. 1, a 4 wheeler, was withdrawn from service and converted into a State Saloon. It received a clerestory roof and had its compartment partitions removed to allow it to be fitted with comfortable furnishings. It was classified A class about 1885 and in 1889 A 1 returned to passenger service, finally ending its days with Millar's Karri and Jarrah Co. at Jarrahdale.

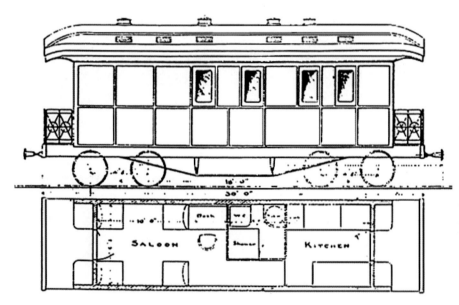

A.5. In 1889 6 wheeler AC 5 underwent some fairly major reconstruction to become State Saloon A 5. Its 6 wheeled Cleminson underframe was replaced by a 30' (9.15m) bogie underframe (possibly from a goods wagon), and it was fitted with end platforms. A 5 was redesignated as the Commissioner's Saloon in 1890. In 1895 it was redesignated again, this time as a Ministerial Saloon, the title of "Commissioner's Saloon" no longer being used. A5 was replaced by the purpose built A 261, and became an AL class inspection car.

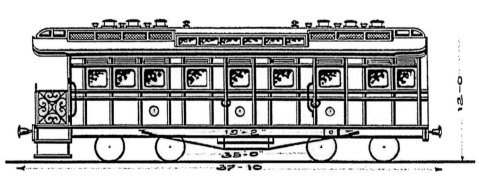

A 6. Another old 6 wheeler, BC 6, replaced A 5 as the new State Saloon in 1890. It was fitted with a bogie underframe, a platform at one end and, presumably, upgraded furnishings inside to become A 6. It remained in VIP service till 1901 when it was replaced by AN 206 and was converted into a Z class brakevan in 1899.

Drawings courtesy PTA

A 261 was the first car to be built for the WAGR specifically as a VIP coach (see 1895). It was reclassified AM in 1900, & replaced by AM 414 in 1920. It was converted to an AF second class suburban car. It survives in that form at the Bassendean Rail Transport Museum.

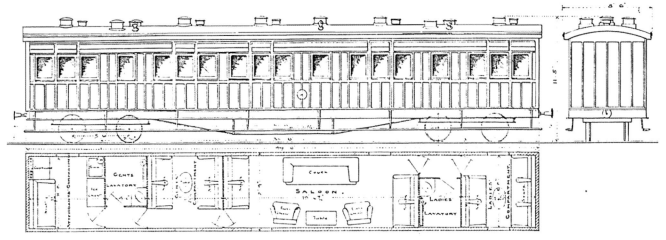

AN 206 joined AM 261 in the VIP fleet in 1901. It was a Vice Regal Saloon rebuilt from the first class long distance car AA 206. Externally, this carriage was not altered a great deal, the main change being the sealing of some of the compartment doors, but inside the car the compartments were all removed and a new interior fitted. AN 206 was replaced by AN 413 and was converted back into an AA class long distance car in 1922.

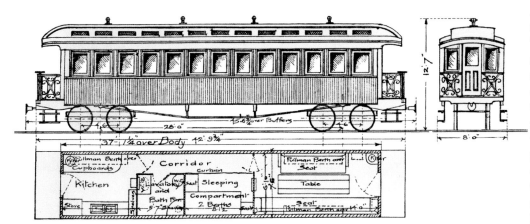

AM 40. In 1907, apparently as a back up, the old "Gilbert" car AG 40 was converted into a Ministerial car and reclassified AM 40. It was not dissimilar to the AL class in its internal arrangements with a kitchen, conference room, two berth sleeping compartment with a curtain to provide privacy from the corridor, and a lavatory and bath compartment. AM 40 was reclassified as an AL class inspection car in 1961. It is preserved at the Bassendean Rail Transport Museum.

AL 40 soon after its reclassification from AM.   *Photo late Geoff Blee, courtesy Murray Rowe.*

Drawings courtesy PTA

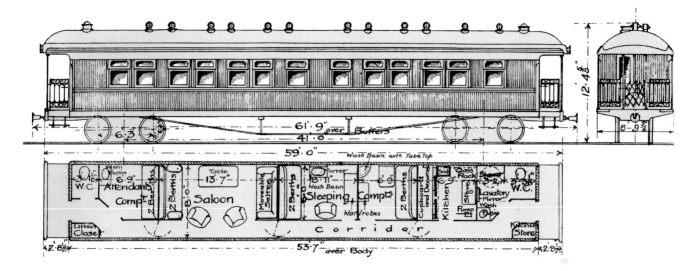

WAGR drawing of AN 413 (top) and as AL 4 at Forrestfield on   *Photo Bill Gray.*

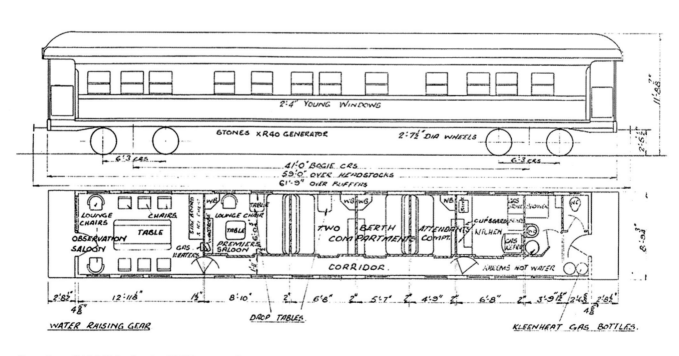

Drawing of AM 414 after its 1960's upgrade.   *Courtesy PTA*

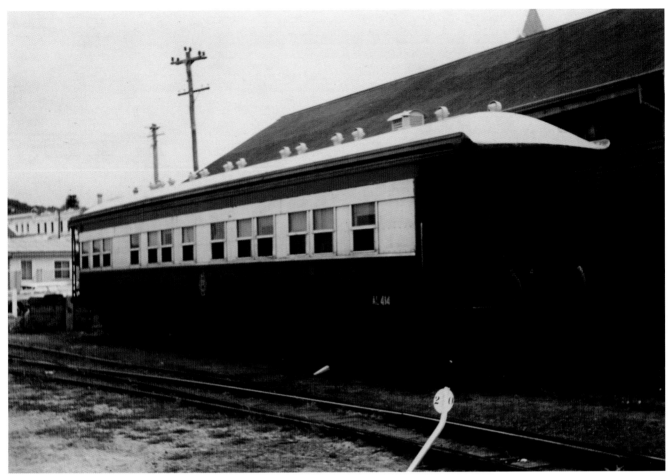

AM 414, as an AL at Albany (bottom)   *Photo courtesy Jeff Austin.*

AN 413 & AM 414 were converted from AQ first class sleeping cars in 1920 to become the new Vice Regal car, and Ministerial car respectively. AN 413 replaced AN 206, and AM 414 replaced AM 261. Few, if any, external changes were made, while inside AN 413 the corridor was retained, as were the lavatory compartments at each end. The rest was rebuilt with bigger compartments, a well furnished saloon, and a small kitchen. The interior in AM 414 was similar, but the furnishings were not as luxurious.

Both the new VIP carriages were issued to traffic on 28 June, 1920, in time for the visit to Western Australia of the Prince of Wales and his entourage. Exactly one week after the cars entered service they were being used to carry the Prince and his party on a tour through the south of the state, near Jardanup, between Pemberton and Bridgetown, when AM 414 and AN 413, which were at the rear of the seven car train, derailed and toppled over onto their sides. The accident was caused by heavy rain which washed away a low embankment, so allowing the track to spread. Fortunately, the train was crossing the embankment at low speed due to the inclement weather and no-one was badly hurt. Reports of the day
indicated that the Prince was found in the overturned carriage, calmly smoking a cigar and most pleased that the whiskey flask was still intact. Both cars were rescued and repaired.

AN 413 was replaced by a new AN 413 and became AL 4 in 1958. It was handed over to the Australian Railway Historical Society for preservation.

At some stage, probably during the early 1960's, AM 414 was upgraded in a similar fashion to the AQL and AQM class country cars. Externally it was fitted with Young type half lift windows and panelled body sides, while inside it was fitted with an observation saloon/conference room, a Premier's saloon, two twin berth sleeping compartments, a new attendant's compartment, and upgraded kitchen and lavatory compartments. It was reclassified as an AL in 1973 and was written off in 1980.

AM 444. In 1928 the AZ based Ministerial car AM 444 joined the fleet, built new, but it had only a short VIP career, being allocated to the ambulance train for the Commonwealth government in 1942 (see 1928). I t was converted into an AZ class sleeping car, then a workman's van. AM 444 still survives as former workman's van VW 433.

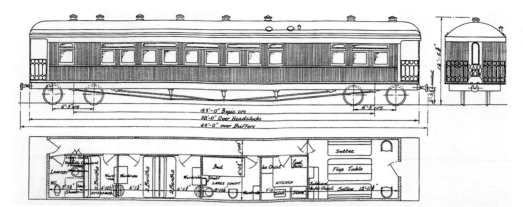

Drawing of AM 313, courtesy PTA.

AM 313 outside the Midland Workshops, 15 August, 1996.

Photo Bill Gray.

This view shows the other side of AM 313 at a very wet Kattanning on 5 March, 1989, the occasion being the Centenary of the Great Southern Railway.

Photo Bill Gray.

AM 313. In 1932 a fourth Ministerial car was apparently required and surplus dining car AV 313 was chosen for conversion. It was fitted with a conference room, a kitchen, a large compartment with a proper bed in it, a twin berth attendant's compartment, and a lavatory compartment with toilet and shower. AM 313 was handed into the care of the WA Division of the ARHS.

AM 313 in service, showing the observation saloon.

Late Geoff Blee, courtesy Murray Rowe.

AN 413 (2nd) A new Vice Regal car was built in 1955 (See 1955), replacing AN 413 and taking its number. AN 413 was, handed over to the Australian Railway Historical Society for preservation during a special ceremony at the Rail Transport Museum on 13 May, 1990.

Inspection and Survey,
A class
AL class (1900) Cars AL 1-5, AG 12, AL 17, 36-40 AG 41 & 43, AL 59, AL 88, 190, & 414.

Former GSR General Managers Saloon. The first inspection car on the WAGR was the ex Great Southern Railway General Manager's saloon, taken over with the GSR in 1896. It spent its last years at Geraldton and was also the first deletion from the inspection car stock when it was destroyed in an accident. June, 1916.

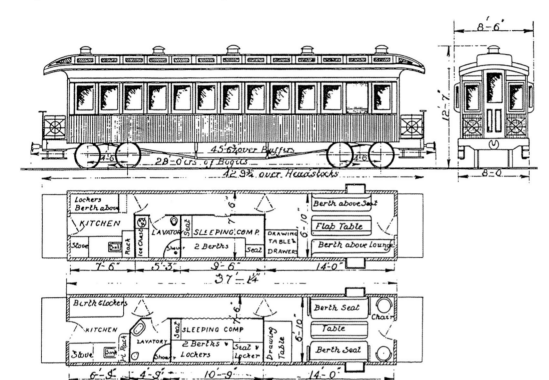

Drawing depicting the Inspection car conversion of the Gilbert cars, specifically AL 36 (top) & AL 37 & 38 (bottom). The other Gilbert car conversions were of a similar internal layout, with only minor detail changes, & AL 40, having been converted from a Ministerial car in 1961, was not fitted with a lookout.

Drawing courtesy WAGR.

AL 39 at Midland 4 July, 1966. Photo late Geoff Blee, courtesy Murray Rowe

Gilbert cars. In 1898 two American built "Gilbert" carriages were converted to inspection cars and classed A. These cars, 37 and 39, were fitted with a kitchen, a bath compartment containing a lavatory as well as the bath, a sleeping compartment, and an observation compartment. Over the years slight modifications took place in both cars, the main one being the alteration of the observation compartment into a conference compartment with a central table and longitudinal seats. Externally the "Gilbert" cars remained unchanged at the time of conversion, but in later years the second window from one end on each side was removed and the hole fitted with a small lookout. The."Gilbert" cars turned out to be something of a favourite for inspection car work. In 1903 AG 36 was withdrawn from passenger service and converted into an AL, its internal arrangements being much the same as those in the earlier "Gilbert" car conversions. Sometime prior to the 1930's AG 41 and 43 were both converted to similar survey cars. In 1938 another "Gilbert" car, AG 38, was converted to an AL in a similar fashion to those which had gone before it. In 1937 the two survey cars (AG 41 & 43) were converted to trailers for the "Governor" class railcars.

By the late 1950's the "Gilbert" cars were starting to show their age, and this fact, coupled with a shrinking need for the railway administrators to do their inspections by rail, saw the beginning of the end for these cars. AL 36 was written off in 1959, followed by AL 37 in 1961 and AL 38 in 1962, this latter vehicle being converted into a workman's van.

One final "Gilbert" car became an inspection car in 1961, this being the former Ministerial Car, AM 40. However, its career as an AL was brief and it was written off in 1971. It was transferred to the ARHS Rail Transport Museum at Bassendean.

In 1967 AL 38 was written off and found a new home at the old Castledare Boys Home in the Perth suburb of Ferndale, where it was used by the Castledare Miniature Live Steam Railway as a ticket office-cum-kiosk. Unfortunately, it was burnt by vandals and totally destroyed.

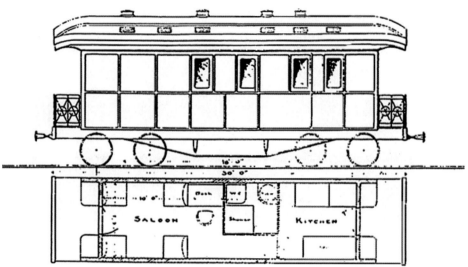

A5 In 1901 the old Ministerial Saloon A 5 was converted into an inspection car, probably by nothing more than a designation change on its record card and a change of role. It is doubtful that any major physical alterations took place. It was transferred to Geraldton as a survey car in 1940. In 1953 AL 5 was written off. It was seventy one years old and lasted another three years before being demolished.

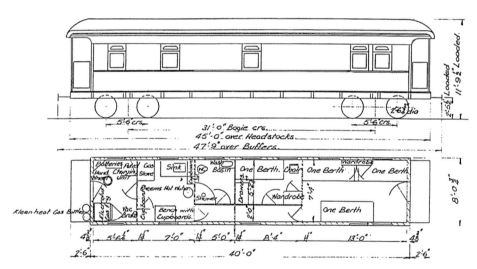

Buffet car AGB 12., The redundant buffet car AGB 12 (see 1921) was converted into a survey car in 1938 and renumbered AGB 2 the following year. This car turned out to be the next retirement from the fleet when it was returned to passenger service as AG 2 during World War Two (see 1941), but in 1948 it was converted into an inspection car and reclassified AL 2. This conversion did not follow the layout of the earlier cars, and AL 2 was designated as the MPE's car. It was written off in 1980 and survives with the Hotham Valley railway.

AL 2 at the Hotham Valley Railway depot at Dwellingup, 25 April, 1991.

Photo Bill Gray.

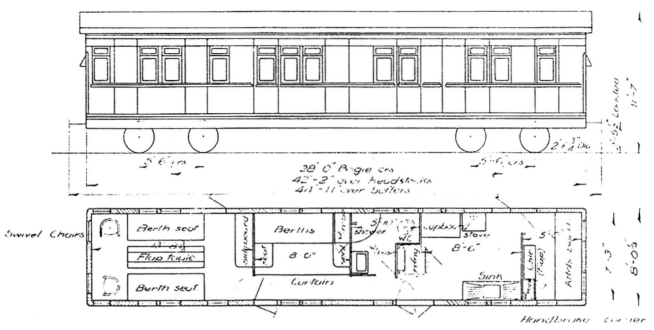

General arrangement drawing of AL 59. Drawings courtesy PTA.

Inspection car AL 59 in Avon Yard. *Photo late Geoff Blee, courtesy Murray Rowe.*

Suburban car AF 59. In 1952 the former second class suburban car AF 59 was converted to an AL. It retained its basic body, although some of the side doors were sealed, and windows were cut into the end walls. Its internal layout followed that of the "Gilbert" cars, but in addition, AL 59 was fitted with a small compartment off the kitchen, containing a berth for an attendant. It was written off in 1980 and is preserved at Northam.

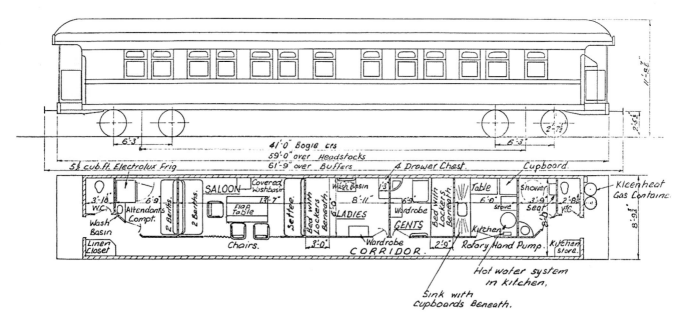

General arrangement drawing of Commissioners car AL 4.   *Drawing courtesy PTA.*

AL 4 at the Bassendean Rail Transport Museum on 17 June, 1995.   *Photo Bill Gray.*

Vice Regal car AN 413, which had been replaced by the new AN 413, was renumbered AL 4 in 1958 and returned to service as an inspection car. It was not altered internally, and was reserved for inspection tours by WAGR Commissioners and branch heads. When the other remaining inspection cars were written off in 1980, AL 4 was retained as the District Engineer's car. It is preserved now by the Australian Railway Historical Society

Track recorder car ALT 88 was added to the stock in 1960 as AL 88 and was written off in 1980. It is preserved at Boulder.

Al 17.   *Photo late Geoff Blee, courtesy Murray Rowe.*

AL 17. In 1964 the WAGR took over the Midland Railway Co. and with it acquired the General Manager's Saloon, KA 17. In June, 1965 this carriage went into WAGR service as inspection car AL 17. It was replaced by AL 414, was written off in June, 1973 and preserved at the Bassendean Rail Transport Museum.

Ministerial car AM 414 became an inspection car in May, 1973, being numbered AL 414. It largely remained unaltered in its new role and it replaced the old Midland Railway car AL 17. It was based at Albany and was written off in 1980.

AL 414 at Albany.   *Photo courtesy Joe Moir.*

Workman's van VW 2141 was the final conversion of a passenger car to an inspection car. This car was formerly ACW 323 and was renumbered AL 3. It's conversion took place in 1979, but it was written off in 1980 and is preserved at Northampton.

Workman's & Breakdown Vans

P class   P 4914 & 5182,

DW class   DW 652,

VW & VC classes VW 28, 277, 284, 286, AVL 314, VW 315, 339, 348, 349, 433, 435, 437, 438, 440, VC 2100, VW 2139-2142, VC 2143, VW 2144-2146, 4999, 5000, 5062-5075, 5078-5087, VC 5088-5090, VW 5089 & 5100, VC 5103 & 5105, VW 5105-5115, 5117-5119, 5121-5125, 5127-5129, 5131-5143, 5145, 5146, 5149, VC 5156, VW 9700, 40761-40764.

During the early days of the railways in Western Australia covered vans were employed to store the equipment used by the workmen who toiled at the building and maintenance of the tracks and lineside equipment, often in remote and uncivilised locations. The men were usually accommodated in camps, some of them quite large, where they slept in tents and used ganger's trolleys to get to the various worksites if they were any distance from the camp. However, dismantling and re-erecting the camps was a laborious and time consuming task, so by the late 1800's a number of classes of goods van had been converted for use as workmen's accommodation. These vehicles had the obvious advantage of being able to be hauled to the worksite with a minimum of disruption, and moved again easily when the work was completed. They were usually fitted with bunks or beds, and a kitchen containing a table, cupboards and a stove, but they were fairly utilitarian. It is thought that, at first, they retained their original classifications.

In 1901 the first passenger carriage to become a workman's van appeared when the obsolete 4 wheeler, AI 3 was converted, this car being renumbered P 4914. It was followed by a second 4 wheeler, AI 259 in 1902. It became P 5182, but in 1903 the P class vans were reclassified DW. Passenger cars were still much in demand as passenger cars, so no more were converted to workman's vans till 1925 when the Cleminson car AH 29 was altered into DW 652. Compartment cars lent themselves very well to becoming workman's vans and DW 652 simply had berths placed above the seats in the old passenger compartments, while two compartments at one end were combined to make a kitchen containing lockers, stove, table, and two bench seats.

Over the years, some vans and passenger cars were converted into breakdown vans, these vehicles usually being attached to a breakdown train to provide accommodation for the crews whose task it was to clean up after accidents and derailments. They were similar to the workman's vans, but generally carried jacks and other rerailing equipment needed for their more specialised tasks. They were later classified VC, while the standard workman's van became class VW. Among the VC class in the early years were several bogie vans, built on 42' frames, with side windows and large sliding doors at each end, behind which was stored the rerailing equipment.

In 1945 "Gilbert" car AG 45 was written off and converted to a sleeping van, but it never returned to the WAGR's books under any classification. Several other cars were apparently treated in the same way, but not being on the books meant that they did not officially exist, and most quietly faded away, being broken up or burnt when their condition rendered them uninhabitable. In 1948 the old bullion van VY 4999 was converted to a VW, but passenger car conversions did not really come into their own till the 1950's, when increasing numbers of old carriages became redundant. During this decade cars from classes ACW, AP, AF, AB and AA were converted into workman's vans, while the 1960's contributed cars from classes AE, AD, AU, ZA, AT, ZB, AS and ACM, as well as more AF's, AP's and ACL's, plus a single AQ. Conversions of more carriages from some of these classes, notably ACL and the AS/T/U/W suburban cars took place during the 1970's, but as more modern cars became available during that decade, the older ones were replaced. Conversion from the AQ and AR classes were the most common at this time, but a few ZA's, an AY, an AVL, and an AZS also underwent conversion. The final batch of cars was added to the workman's van stock in 1984 when four AZ class sleeping cars, most of which had been on hire to the Hotham Valley Railway, were converted.

The alterations made to all these carriages varied from almost total internal rebuilds, to simply placing the old car back in service with little more than a repaint. Many were gutted to be fitted with kitchen and sleeping areas, and some had significant external alterations made to them as well.

During 1989 the policy regarding workman's vans was reviewed and the decision made to do away with them. They began to assemble at Forrestfield and the Midland workshops during 1989 and 1990, and large numbers of them were stored there, and at Northam, awaiting disposal. Many were sold, a number demolished and burnt, and a few found their way into the hands of preservation groups.

Cars known to have been used as workman's vans are listed below, and those known to still survive are marked accordingly.

1901	P 4914	(AI 3)	w/o	1949	VW 6790	(Frame from AG 18)	To VS 6790 in 1950.
1902	P 5182	(AI 259)	w/o	1950	VW 2139	(ACW 331)	w/o 1990, sold (?)
1925	DW 652	(AH 29)	w/o 1950		VW 2140	(ACW 329)	w/o 1991. Preserved
1946	-	(AG 45)	Demolished 1963.				Wanneroo
1947	VC 1441	(AG 14)	w/o 1972, preserved		VW 2141	(ACW 323)	To AL 3 in 1980, &
			Bassendean.				preserved Northampton.
1948	VW 4999	(VY 4999)	To ARHS, stowed Midland	1951	VW 2142	(AP 90)	w/o 1973
			Workshops.	1952	VW 5062	(AF 199)	w/o 1961

	VW 5063 (AF 173)	w/o 1976
	VW 5064 (AF 194)	w/o 1977
	VW 5065 (AF 88)	w/o 1976
1955	VC 2143 (ACW 330)	w/o 1987, pres. by HVR.
1957	VW 2144 (ACW 327)	w/o 1990.
	VW 2145 (APT 87)	w/o 1976 & to ARHS 1990
1958	VW 2146 (AB 244)	w/o 1975
	VW 5066 (AP 89)	w/o 1976 & preserved Esperance.
1959	VW 5067 (ACL 211)	w/o 1982
	VW 5068 (AB 245)	w/o 1982
1961	(VW 5069 [Z 5065(Z 83)])	w/o 1976)
	VW 5070 (AP 151)	w/o 1976
	VW 5071 (ZA 175)	w/o 1996
	VW 5072 (ZA 179)	w/o 1985
	VW 5073 (AE 195)	w/o 1987.
	VW 5074 (AU 324)	w/o 1996
	VW 5075 (AF 135)	w/o 1963
	(VS 5076)	
(1962	VS 5077)	
	VW 5078 (AF 33)	w/o 1976
	VW 5079 (AD 107)	w/o 1976
1962	VW 5080 (AL 38)	w/o 1967
1964	VW 5081 (AT 382)	w/o 1996
	VW 5082 (AQ 338)	w/o 1975. Remains at Bushmead.
1965	VW 5083 (ZA 158)	w/o 1983
	VW 5084 (ZA 168)	w/o 1991, sold
	VW 5085 (ZA 170)	w/o 1985
	VW 5086 (ZA 171)	w/o 1996
	VW 5087 (ZA 181)	w/o 1992, preserved Wyalkatchem.
	VC 2100 (AF 261)	w/o 1974, preserved Bassendean.
	VC 5088 (ZA 191)	w/o 1985, to ARHS, then Cannington.
	VW 40761 (KB 18)	w/o 1981.
	VW 40764 (K 16)	w/o 1975
1966	VC 5105 (ZA 176)	w/o 1976, preserved Collie
	VW 5106 (ZB 210)	w/o 1973
	VW 5107(1st) (ZA 194)	w/o 1971
	VW 5108 (ZA 174)	
	VW 5109 (ZA 186)	
	VW 5110 (ZA 193)	
	VW 40762 (K 19)	w/o 1985
	VW 40763 (K 20)	Preserved Pemberton.
1967	VW 5100 (ZA 189)	w/o c.1985, preserved Whiteman Park.
	VW 5112 (AF 13)	w/o 1979, preserved at Bellarine Peninsular Railway, Victoria.
	VW 5131 (AT 134)	Probably burnt 1994
	VW 5132 (AU 318)	w/o 1981 & sold. Preserved at Chidlow
	VW 5133 (ZA 188)	w/o 1986/1987.
	VW 5134 (ZA 180)	w/o 1986.
	VW 5138 (AU 307)	w/o 1982.Preserved Northam
1968	VW 5111 (AS 375)	w/o 1991, preserved Balcatta
	VW 5113 (ACL 403)	w/o 1991, sold in Toodyay
	VW 5114 (AS 372)	w/o 1991, preserved Capel
	VW 5115 (ZA 201)	
	VW 5117 (ZA 196)	w/o 1978. Preserved as a coffee shop at Fremantle.

	VW 5118 (ASD 374)	w/o 1996
	VW 5119 (ZB 211)	w/o 1991
	VW 5137 (AT 302)	w/o 1992, preserved Wyalkatchem
	VW 5139 (ZA 163)	w/o 1990.
	VW 5140 (ZA 160)	w/o 1987
	VW 5000 (VY 5000)	To AL 1 in 1972, preserved Bellarine Peninsular Railway, Victoria.
1969	VC 5089 (ZA 161)	w/o 1976.
	VC 5090 (ZA 183)	to Vintage Train as ZA 183, 1980. W/o Westrail books 1985.
	VW 5135 (AF 168)	w/o
	VW 5136 (AE 162)	w/o
1970	VW 5121 (J 1)	Preserved ARHS Bassendean.
	VW 5122 (ACL 409)	w/o 1992, preserved Wyalkatchem.
	VW 5123 (ACL 404)	w/o 1991
	VW 5124 (AU 317)	w/o 1974.
	VW 5125 (AU 326)	w/o 1970.
	(VW 5127 [Y 6798]	w/o 1976)
	VW 5128 (ACL 236)	w/o 1980.
	(VW 5129 [Z 28]	w/o 1976)
	VW 9700 (VA 9700)	Demolished.
1971	VW 5141 (AT 303)	w/o 1984.
	VW 5142 (AU 308)	w/o?
	VW 5143 (AW 328)	
	VW 5145 (ZB 208)	w/o 1977.
1973	VW 5146 (AQ 344)	w/o 1996, preserved Collie
	(VW 5147 [VA 10152]	w/o 1976).
1974	VC 5103 (AZS 445)	To ARHS & sold privately 2004. Preserved Lake Clifton
c.1974?	VC 5104 ?	w/o 1983.
	VW 5149 (ACM 31)	(mobile ablutions van) Preserved Kojonup
	(VW 5150 [VA 10200])	
1975	(VC 5106 [Z 225])	
	(VC 5107(2nd) [Z 227])	
1976	AVL 314 (AVL 314)	w/o 1988, preserved Bassendean.
	(VC 5154 [Z 23]	To ZD 23, 1976).
	(VC 5155 [Z 226]	To ZD 226, 1976.
	VW 5156 (ZA 159)	w/o 1991, sold Mt. Helena
1979	VW 28 (AYL 28)	To ARHS Bassendean.
	VW 277 (ARS 277)	To Dongara, in use as back packers accommodation.
	VW 284 (ARS 284)	Preserved Midland Workshops
	VW 286 (AV 286)	Preserved Midland Workshops
	VW 315 (AV 315)	Preserved Cunderdin
	VW 339 (AQC 339)	Preserved Northam.
	VW 348 (ARS 348)	Preserved Midland Workshops)
	VW 349 (ARS 349)	Preserved Midland Workshops.
1984	VW 433 (AZ 433)	Preserved
	VW 437 (AZ 437)	Preserved
	VW 438 (AZ 438)	Preserved
	VW 440 (AZ 440)	Preserved Clackline.

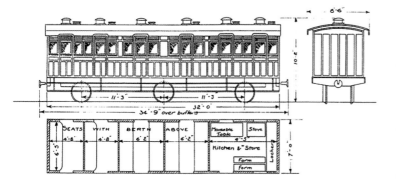

An entire book could be devoted to the workmans & breakdown vans alone, such were the number & variety of them. Pictured is the general arrangement drawing of DW 652, converted from Cleminson car AH 29 in 1925.

Drawing courtesy PTA.

VW 5080, formerly Gilbert car AG 38 & Inspection car AL 38. The first Gilbert car conversion to a workmans van took place in 1946. AL 38 was converted in 1961.

Photo courtesy Malcolm Searle.

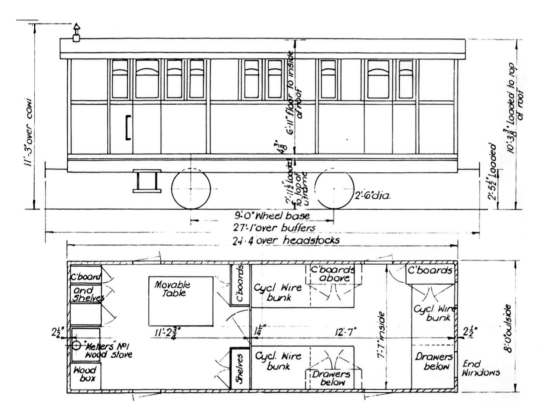

DW 5092 was converted to a workmans van from the old rail motor AO 430 in 1952. It lasted till 1965.

Drawing courtesy PTA.

VW 5135, formerly AF 168. It was converted in 1969.

Photo courtesy Joe Moir.

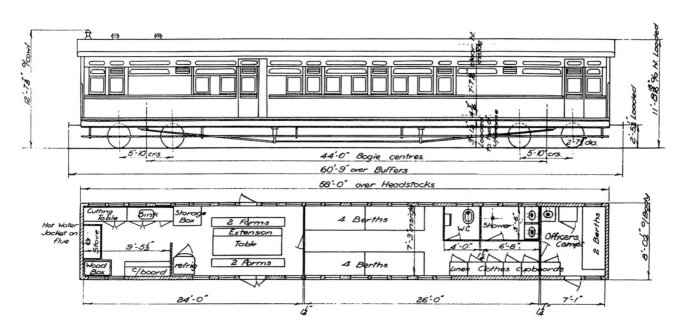

The earliest "big car" conversions were from ACWs, the first being VW 2139 (ex ACW 331) - (top) & VW 2140 (ex ACW 329), (centre) both in 1950. The drawing shows VC 2143. A photo of this car appears in the ACW section.
All 5 VWs converted from ACW lasted till the end.   *Photos Bill Gray, drawing courtesy PTA.*

The first AP conversion was 1951, while VW 2145 was converted from the blood transfusion car APT 87 in 1957. It is seen here at Midland on 3 September, 1990. *Photo Bill Gray.*

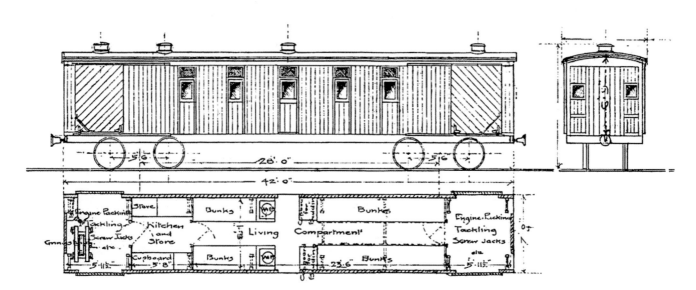

Despite appearances, this VC is not a converted carriage. The WAGR built 9 of these breakdown vans.

Photo late Geoff Blee, courtesy Murray Rowe, drawing courtesy PTA.

More than half the ZAs built were converted to workmans vans. The following illustrate the variety of types to be found in these vehicles.

VW 5083 (ZA 158) out of service at the rear of the Midland Workshops, 23 June, 1990.
This car was one of only two VWs to be painted in Westrail orange & blue (the other was VW 5100, formerly ZA 189), & both were used on the Weedex Train.

Photo Bill Gray.

VW 5084 (ZA 168), also out of service at Northam on 21 July, 1989

Photo Bill Gray.

VW 5086 (ZA 171), heavily modified.

Photo courtesy ARHS.

VC 5088 (ZA 191) was the Deutschland re-railing equipment van. It was photographed at Midland, 23 November, 1990.

Photo Bill Gray.

VW 5110 (ZA 193)(top) & VW 5115 (ZA 201) both at Forrestfield, 10 June, 1989.
Photos Bill Gray.

VW 5139 (ZA 163) was resident at Pinjarra for many years.   Photo courtesy ARHS.

VW 5140, formerly ZA 160, a 1968 conversion, at Forrestfield, 9 February, 1985.
Photo courtesy ARHS.

The first of the second generation suburban cars became a VW in 1961, & conversions began in earnest in 1967. VW 5131 (top) was AT 134, photographed at Forrestfield, 16 February, 1991, & VW 5143 (below), captured at Avon Yard on 21 July, 1989, was once AW 328.

The first of the long ACL's was converted to a workmans van 1n 1968, & ACL 404 followed two years later, becoming VW 5123. Here it is out of service at the rear of the Midland Workshops on 23 April, 1991.

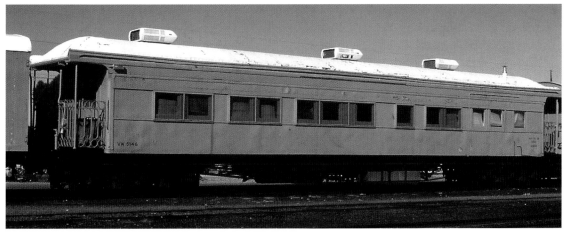

VW 5146 (AQ 344) was the second end platform car converted (the first was AQC 338 in 1964), being done in 1973. It is seen here at Picton on 12 May, 1991.

Photos Bill Gray.

AYL 28 was the only car of its kind to be converted to a VW, & it kept its road number. It was photographed at Midland Workshops on 23 April, 1991.   *Photos Bill Gray.*

Four years elapsed after AQ 344 was converted before any more end platform cars were done. In 1979 AQC 339 (top) & AV 315 (below) were both converted. VW 339 was photographed at Midland on 22 November, 1990, & VW 315 at Forrestfield on 10 June, 1989.   *Photos Bill Gray.*

The AZ's were the last cars to be converted, in 1984, some of them having served with the Hotham Valley Railway. VW 440 is seen preserved at Clackline on a very hot 2 February, 1999.

The unusual VW 40763 at Forrestfield, 10 June, 1989. The van was originally built on an AP underframe by the Midland Railway Co. That frame was later replaced before the WAGR inherited the vehicle in 1964.

Almost certainly the last time ACL 403 will ever be on wheels. As VW 5113 it has had most of its metal parts removed & has been sold. Photographed at Midland 13 December, 1991.   *Photos Bill Gray.*

Brakevans
AD, AGV/ZAG/ZG, ZAF, ZBA & Z classes

AGV/ZAG ZG 8, AGV/ZG/Z 9, AGV/ZAG/ZG 10, ZAG/ZG 11, AGV/ZAG/ZG 14, ZAG/ZG 15, AGV/ZAG/ZG 16, & 18, Z 26, 29, 107, 108, 109, AD 176, 202, 209, 215-217, 219, ZAF 430-434, ZBA 435-439, Z 4993, 5006, 6785, 6789, 6790, 10615, ? (ex BC x 2).

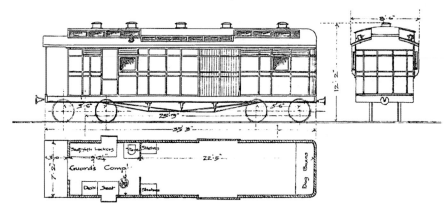

AN 6. The first former passenger car to be converted to a brakevan was the old Vice Regal car AN 6 in 1902. This vehicle retained its basic body shape, although most of the windows were filled in, side loading doors were added and the interior was removed to allow the fitting of the brake compartment and dog boxes. It was numbered Z 4993, then Z 26 about 1940, finally being rebuilt in 1952. It was still in service in 1972.

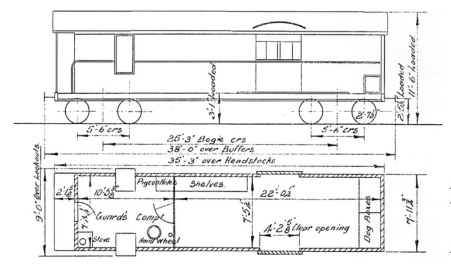

Z.4993 (later Z 26) as built from AN 6 (top) & as rebuilt in 1952 (bottom)

Drawings courtesy PTA.

AS Luggage vans. In 1906 the three short-lived AS class luggage vans (251-253) were converted to Z class brakevans. AS 251 was fitted with a bogie underframe and new roof, a brake compartment was fitted and dog boxes were added. It became Z 6790. AS 252 and 253 had their innards refitted in a similar fashion and were also put on bogies, but apart from the addition of lookouts and the relocation of the doors, their bodies were left alone. These vans became Z 6789 and 6785 respectively, In 1938-1940 the three vans became Z 109, 108 and 107. Z 109 was run into by a goods train at Bakers Hill in 1949 and the other two lasted till the late 1960's.

AH 4 became Z 10615 in 1927.

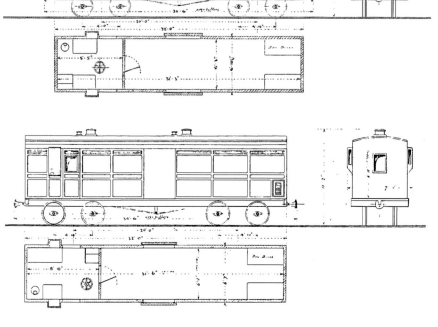

Brakevans Z 6789 (top) & 6790 (bottom), both converted from an AS luggage vans, 6790 displaying the wider panel spacing.

Drawings courtesy PTA.

Agricultural Bank Manager's & Country Inspector's vans, Bc 185 and Bc 1926 were converted to a Z van and ZB brakevan respectively in 1927. The second agricultural bank manager's van, Bc 186, was converted into a Z van in 1934, its former passenger compartment being converted into the brake compartment. It was also fitted with bars and hooks to carry meat.

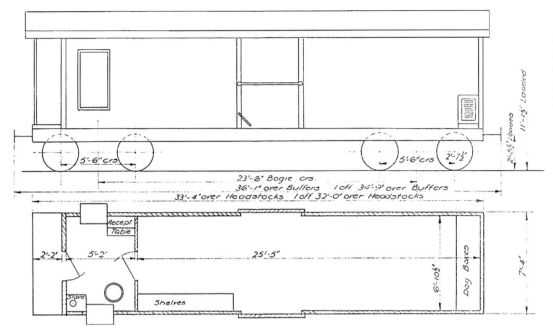

Funeral car AO 7 had its underframe used to build a new brakevan (Z 5006, later Z 29) in 1930.

Brakevan built using the underframe from the AO funeral car & Bc vans.

Drawing courtesy PTA.

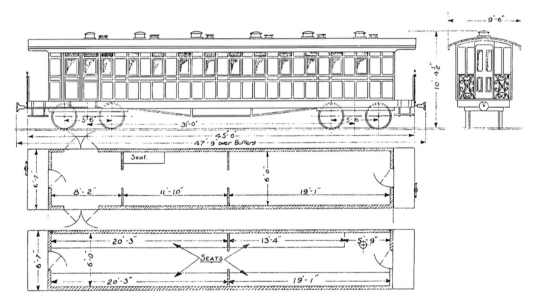

ZAG/ZG brakevan. The drawing depicts Nos. 10 & 14 (upper), & No. 18 (lower) Cars 8 & 16 were similar to 18, but without the long seats.   Courtesy PTA

AG "American" cars. In 1935 five of the old AG "American" cars (8, 10, 14, 16 and 18) were converted into AGV class brakevans, four of the five cars coming out of store. Externally, these cars remained the same, while the changes inside were few. Cars 10 and 14 already had brake compartments in them, having worked at Kalgoorlie as brake cars, while cars 8, 16 and 18 had a pedestal mounted hand brake fitted at one end of the saloon. Car 18 even retained its longitudinal seats. All five were reclassified ZAG in 1936, andthe last two AG's (11 & 15) were converted into ZAG's in 1938. These vans did not last very long and started to disappear as early as 1941, all them having been demolished or converted for other uses by 1960.

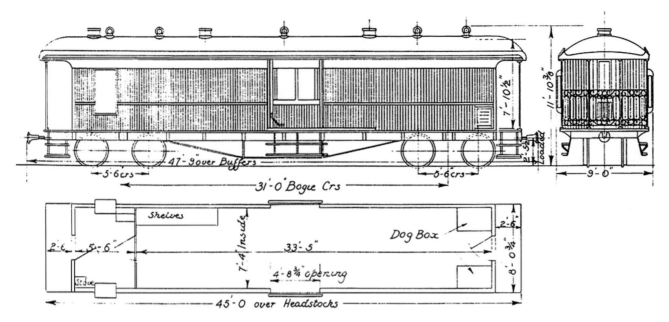

Z 9 general arrangement.   *Drawing courtesy PTA.*

Z 9 at Pinjarra on 2 December, 1989.   *Photo Bill Gray.*

Buffet car, AGB 9 became a suburban brakevan in 1938, retaining its body style, but losing all its side windows. In addition, it had lookouts and centrally located sliding doors fitted. It also received a brake compartment and two dog boxes. It was classified AGV for three months (presumably a mistake, as it did not resemble the other AGV's), but it was then reclassified Z and transferred to wagon stock.

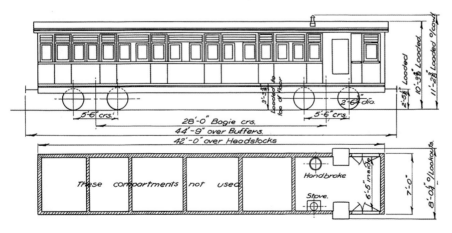

Drawing of the ZAF brakevan, converted from AF Second class cars.

Courtesy PTA.

AF second class suburban cars. Five cars (AF 143, 102, 78, 157, & 34) were converted into ZAF class brakevans (ZAF 430-434) in 1952. These were regarded as temporary conversions and involved the removal of the seats and sealing of the compartment doors, while two compartments at one end of the car were combined to make a brake compartments. In 1955 ten new brakevans (Z 451-460) were built on the frames of scrapped 42' (12.81m) long suburban cars, and these allowed the writing off of the ZAF's. ZAF 431 donated its frame to ADS 52, and ZAF AYE 709.

Ba class horse boxes. Five vehicles (Ba 1000-1002, 1004 & 1005) were converted to brakevans in 1952, being classed ZBA (435-439). These vehicles had the brake compartment located in the centre of the body, with two sliding loading doors on each side.

ADS 176. In 1965 ADS 176 had its seats removed and its compartment doors screwed shut for use on suburban goods trains, but rather like the ZAF's before it, its career was brief and it was written off in 1967 without being reclassified.

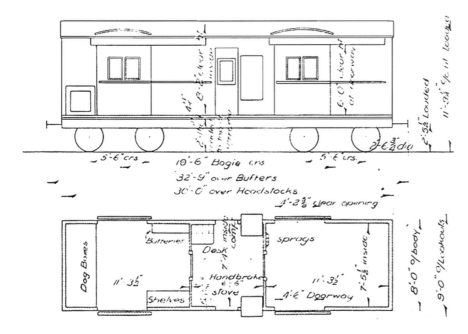

ZB class brakevans. The last conversions of passenger carrying vehicles were a group of ZB class vans. These cars had their passenger compartments removed, so converting them into Z class vans. This took place between 1968 and 1970 and involved ZB 202, 209, 215-217 and 219, all of which retained their numbers. At least one (ZB 217) was rebuilt with a steel body and pitched roof. These vans mostly lasted till mid 1985 when the WAGR finally stopped using brakevans on the majority of its trains.

ZBA brakevan drawing, converted from ZB class brakevans.
Courtesy PTA

Z 209, converted from ZB 209.

Photo Andrew May, courtesy ARHS.

Steel bodied brakevan Z 217 converted from ZB 217. Photographed by the WAGR photographer at Forrestfield.

Photo courtesy ARHS

Exhibition Cars
AG & ASD classes AG 38 & ASD 374

AG 38. In 1922 "Gilbert" car AG 38 was converted into an exhibition car. It carried the words "Westralian Industries League" above the windows, and "SUPPORT YOUR OWN INDUSTRIES" along the sides in large, white letters. The end platforms were enclosed and the interior of the car was fitted out with display stands, but otherwise it remained unaltered. AG 38 proved to be highly successful in this role and did not return to normal service till 1927, its work being taken over by the Reso trains. It returned to service as an inspection car (AL 38), and finished its career as a workman's van.

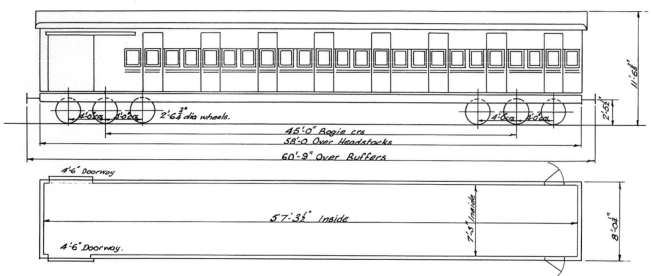

ASD 374, with the photo showing the car during conversion from an AS class suburban car.
Drawing courtesy PTA, photo late Geoff Blee, courtesy Murray Rowe.

ASD 374. In 1960 second class suburban brake car AS 374 became the second exhibition car when it was converted into the WAGR Trade and Industries Exhibition coach. It was reclassified ASD and had its interior gutted and a large sliding door fitted on each side at one end. Visitors to the car gained access via the original compartment doors at the other end. ASD 374 lasted eight years before being converted into a workman's van (VW 5118) and it spent its final years in this role located at West Toodyay.

Locomotive Instruction Vans
VI class 7979 & 7980

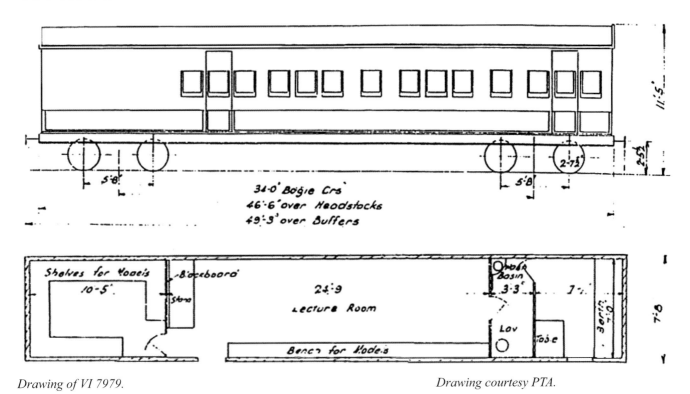

Drawing of VI 7979.   *Drawing courtesy PTA.*

AF 86. In 1946 second class suburban car, AF 86, which began life in 1896 as an AP class sleeping car, was re-issued to traffic as a locomotive instruction van, VI 7979. In this role the old coach was virtually a mobile class room, towed from depot to depot to allow the instruction and examination of enginemen. VI 7979 was written off in September, 1971.

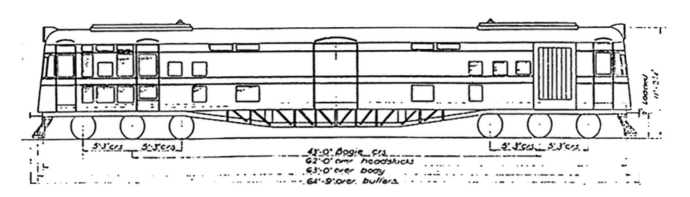

Drawing of VI 7980.   *Drawing courtesy PTA.*

ADF 490. In 1964 former "Wildflower" class railcar ADF 490 (see 1949) was converted into Locomotive Instruction van VI 7980. This vehicle was a complete contrast to the earlier one and was considerably larger. VI 7980 was written off in September, 1980. This latter vehicle was sold to Metana Minerals at Mount Magnet, where its body was used to house a diesel generating set. Although now out of use, its remains are still there.

Blood Transfusion Car
APT class 87

APT 87. Drawing courtesy PTA. Photo late Geoff Blee collection, courtesy Murray Rowe.

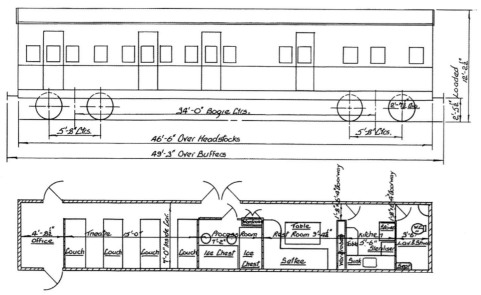

One of the more interesting passenger car conversions was that of AF 87, a second class suburban carriage which was converted into an APT class blood transfusion car in 1948. APT 87 had been built in 1896 as an AP first class sleeping car, and it was converted into an AF in 1903. The post war introduction of the AY and AYB class suburban cars caused it to become redundant, and it was re-issued to traffic as the WAGR's sole APT class car in October, 1948.

Externally, AF 87 had few changes made to it, mostly in the alteration of doors and windows. Inside, it was completely rebuilt with an office, theatre, processing room, rest room, and kitchen. A lavatory and shower compartment took up the end of the car.

APT 87 was painted in a distinctive white livery with red crosses on the sides, and it spent its time travelling the state giving country communities the chance to donate blood. Details of the car and its operations were sent to a number of countries overseas which had expressed interest in it. However, road transport soon improved to the point where it was more versatile than rail, even if less economical, and in 1957 APT 87 was withdrawn from use and converted into a workman's van (VW 2145).

Although officially written off in 1976, the old car avoided detection till 1990, when it was sent to Midland for disposal, but later that year it was rescued by the Australian Railway Historical Society for preservation at their Rail Transport Museum at Bassendean.

Track Recorder Car
ALT class   5 & 88

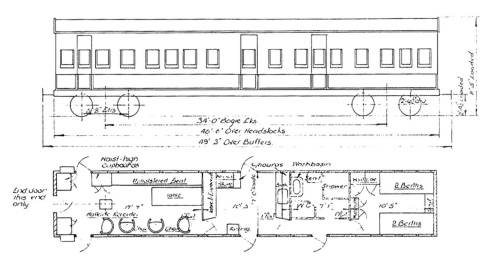

AF 93. In 1951 an AF second class suburban car was placed in traffic as a Track Recorder car. Records indicate that the car concerned was AF 93, formerly an AP class sleeping car, but this may be incorrect. After the work was completed, the car was numbered VT 4998, but only three months later it was renumbered ALT 88, leading to the possibility that it was the almost identical AF 88 which was actually converted, and not 93. Both cars had been stored out of service together, and a workman's van, supposedly converted from AF 88, was issued to traffic carrying "Car No. 93" number plates. Therefore, the evidence would indicate that AF 88 was converted to a track recorder car by mistake, when the conversion should have been carried out on AF 93. The car had most of its side doors sealed up, and it was fitted with a recording compartment which contained a Hallade recorder. It had a kitchen, toilet and shower compartment, and four berth sleeping compartment. ALT 88 became an inspection car, AL 88, in 1960, with its recording equipment being placed in the new Track recorder car ALT 5. It has survived, having been written off in 1980 and preserved by the Kalgoorlie Boulder Loop Line Preservation Society.

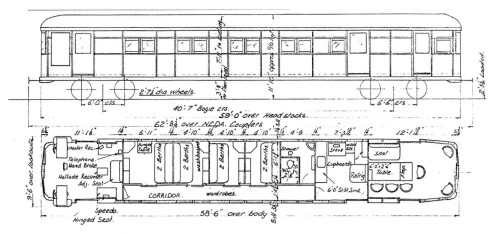

ASA 445. In 1959 the old steam railcar ASA 445 (see 1931) was converted into a track recorder car, using the equipment from ALT 88. The new car was numbered ALT 5. The external changes made to ASA 445 during its conversion were fairly minor, and it retained its appearance. Inside, the original driving cab at one end was lengthened and became the recording compartment, which was somewhat better equipped than that in the old car. ALT 5 was also self sufficient, being fitted with a rest room, kitchen, shower and toilet compartment, and three AQZ style twin berth sleeping compartments. A fourth, bigger, sleeping compartment was also fitted. ALT 5 was issued to traffic in plain Larch green, but in May, 1977 it was repainted in Westrail orange and blue. It was housed at Forrestfield Marshalling Yards, although it was not used for some time. It was handed over to the Australian Railway Historical Society for preservation and was taken to the Boyanup Transport Museum for display.

Photo Bill Gray

Hospital Car
AQA class 343

AQA 343. The completion of the new dual gauge railway up the Avon Valley out of Perth marked the end of two well known WAGR passenger trains, the "Westland" and the "Kalgoorlie", which were replaced by the "Prospector" and the Commonwealth Railways standard gauge "Trans Australian" and "Indian Pacific". The Avon Valley was relatively inaccessible, and there was some concern that, should there be a major derailment or accident there, then there would be some considerable problems getting anyone who was injured to a hospital. It was decided that the best means of transport out was by rail, so the old second class sleeping car, AQS 343, was converted into a hospital car and reclassified AQA.

The car remained largely unchanged on the outside, although a pair of hinged double doors were cut into the sides in the centre of the body and the vehicle was painted white with a small red cross on each side, adjacent to the double doors. It was stripped internally except for the ladies lavatory compartment, and it was fitted with stretchers and emergency and communications equipment. AQA 343 was able to carry sixteen patients and was often coupled to a flat wagon which was intended for use as a helipad.

Thankfully, the hospital car was never used in anger, but spent most of its time stowed at the Forrestfield Marshalling Yards. After its retirement it had it is interior equipment stripped out and went to the Rail Transport Museum at Bassendean for preservation.

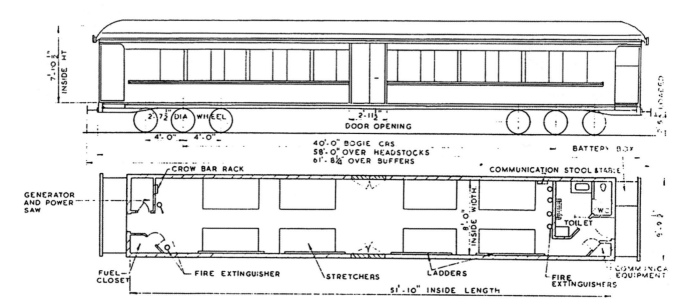

Courtesy PTA.

AQA 343, photographed at Bassendean by Bill Gray on 25 October, 1992.

APPENDIX THREE
OTHER CARRIAGES

While the WAGR operated the vast majority of passenger carriages in the state, a number of other operators also hauled passengers by rail in purpose built cars. Unfortunately, many of the records of some of these (usually) private operations, even if they were kept, have disappeared over the years. Thus, the following précis of other operators of passengers cars is almost certainly not complete, but rather gives a run down of the bigger, or better known operations.

THE MIDLAND RAILWAY COMPANY

The Midland Railway Company of Western Australia (MRWA) was one of three land grant railways to come to fruition in the late nineteenth century, and it proved to be the longest lived, lasting from 1894 till 1964 when it was taken over by the WAGR. During that time a total of thirty three coaches passed through the companies hands.

The first group of cars ordered were ten bogie composite carriages, each with a guard's and luggage compartment. The Great Southern Railway, Western Australia's other major land grant railway, started out with ten similar carriages (later WAGR AD class), and it appears that the MRWA cars were completed **without** the guard's compartment. The specifications were probably altered following experience on the GSR. The two companies had the same consulting engineer and the early goods rolling stock on the two railways seems to have been similar, if not identical, in design.

The ten carriages (1-10) were delivered from the Lancaster Wagon Co. of England in 1892, but the MRWA, rarely in a sound financial state throughout its existence, wasn't ready for them. Five were sold to the WAGR without ever entering MRWA service. They were replaced by a second batch of five identical cars (11-15) in 1894.

The ten bogie composite cars (1-5 & 11-15) were used on all the MRWA passenger services until a Parliamentary Select Committee enquiry was held into the company in 1902. It was decided that these cars were really quite unsuitable for the Midland's operations as they had no lavatory facilities, but were being used on trains which ran the full 277 mile (443 km) length of the railway. As a result, it was recommended that the company immediately acquire lavatory coaches. Plans were prepared for new carriages, but these were not built. Instead, a swap was arranged with the WAGR in which four MRWA bogie composite cars were exchanged for four AB class long distance cars equipped with lavatories. The lavatory cars were classed J and numbered 1-4, and the four Midland cars came from the batch 1-5, but which four were handed over is not known. They became AC 273-276 on the WAGR, and the survivor from the original ten cars was renumbered K 16.

In 1904 the service operated by the ten Midland carriages (four J's & six K's) consisted of a daily mixed train in each direction. The down train left Midland Junction at 8.25am and reached Walkaway at 11.36pm, while the up train left Walkaway at 7.16am to arrive at Midland Junction at 10.30pm. The two trains crossed at Watheroo in mid afternoon and ran at an average speed of only 18.25 mph (29.2 kph). There was also a down mail train which left Midland Junction at 6.10pm on Thursday nights, arriving at 7.15am the following morning. This returned as the corresponding up mail train from Walkaway at 9.25pm Fridays, to arrive at Midland at 10.50am Saturdays. The WAGR provided the mail vans (AK class) and a sleeping car (AP class) for this train. The up mail was slightly faster than the down with an average speed of 21.2 mph (33.9 kph). The maximum permitted speed on the line was only 28 mph (44.8 kph).

A second group of six lavatory composite cars similar to those acquired from the WAGR were built for the MRWA in 1911, classed Ja, and a final batch of four more came from the Metropolitan Railway Carriage & Wagon Co. in 1913 to handle an on-going increase in traffic, previously coped with by hiring stock from the WAGR. The first batch were numbered 5-10, but the last four in this group were renumbered 18-21 in 1913, (order uncertain) and the second batch were allocated the numbers 22-25.

In 1912 one of the K class bogie composite cars (11) was converted into a brake composite car and reclassified Kb. The altered car was not unlike the WAGR's AD class and K 15 was also converted to a Kb in 1914. These conversions were presumably intended to increase the usefulness of the cars after their displacement by the new JA class lavatory cars. In 1915 the MRWA arranged another swap with the WAGR, this time gaining an AP class sleeping car and losing one of the near new Ja class cars (22) in the process.

The Midland Railway trains all terminated at Midland Junction because the MRWA locomotives were not permitted to operate over the government system. The problem of transporting the passengers into Perth without having them change trains at Midland was overcome by using WAGR locomotives to haul the Midland Railway coaches into the city.

The MRWA acquired three new corridor sleeping cars in 1927, built by the WAGR at their Midland Workshops. The WAGR's AZ first class cars, which first appeared in 1928, were an identical design. The new sleeping cars numbered Jv 31-33, were the last new carriages bought by the MRWA. None of the other Midland carriages had corridors so it was decided to rebuild the three remaining K class cars still in original condition (K 16 was converted into a saloon for the general manager in 1920 and reclassified Ka) to run with the new sleepers and in 1928 K 12 was rebuilt into a second class car for this purpose. Despite being heavily modified during this conversion, it retained its K classification, as did K 13 which followed in 1929/30. K 14, the last bogie composite car in original condition, was rebuilt in a similar fashion in 1930 as a first class car, classified Jk.

In the early 1930's a start was made on renumbering the carriages into a more logical sequence, as follows:-

About 1932	Ja 20 to Ja 7/8
	Ja 23 to Ja 7/8
1932-1934	Ja 24 to Ja 9
	Ka 16 to Ka 17
1934-1936	Ja 19 to Ja 10
	Ja 21 to Ja 11
1936	Kb 11 to Kb 19 (book number only)
	Kb 15 to Kb 18 (book number only)
1936-1938	K 12 to K 15
	Ja 18 to Ja 12
1940-1944	Ja 25 to Ja 13
	K 13 to K 16

Jb 22, the ex WAGR sleeping car, was never renumbered, as it was written off between 1938 and 1940, and Kb 11 and 15 were out of use by 1936 because of their lack of lavatory facilities, so their renumbering was essentially an academic exercise. The end result of this process was a number sequence which ran:-

J 1-4, Ja 5-13	-	composite long distance lavatory cars.
Jk 14	-	first class lavatory car.
K 15 & 16	-	second class lavatory car.
Ka 17	-	General Manager's saloon.
Kb 18 & 19	-	Brake composite car (out of use).
Jv 31-33	-	First class sleeping cars.

After hard use during World War Two, most of the older stock was worn out and the introduction of the MRWA road bus service in 1946 resulted in a reduction in the number of mixed trains on which these older carriages were used. In 1948-50 Ja 13 was written off and Ja 12 was possibly written off at the same time, but might only have been withdrawn from use, as it is also reported as being written off in 1955. In 1950 Jk 14, K 15 and 16 were withdrawn, although K 16 was returned to service as a crew van.

The metal trades strike of 1952 resulted in the cancellation of all passenger services between June and December, 1952, and when it was over, a limited service of only one train per week was introduced from January, 1953. This service sufficed for the rest of the company's existence.

More withdrawals took place during the 1950's, with J 1 converted to a crew van in 1953, and two years later J 2, Ja 9, and possibly Ja 12 all being written off, followed by J 3 in 1957. This was the last coach to be written off by the company.

In August, 1964 the MRWA and its operations were taken over by the WAGR, including the locomotives and rolling stock. Although some merging had taken place before the actual take over, some of the stock was not placed in WAGR service till 1965. Coaches taken over were J 4, Ja 5-8, 10, 11, Ka 17, and Jv 31-33. In addition to these a number of crew and workman's vans built from passenger cars were also taken over. Some cars did not enter WAGR service, the worst ones being written off and demolished. The cars which did enter service were:-

J 4, Ja 5, 6 & 10	became ACL 31-33 & 36
Ka 17	became AL 17
Jv 31-33	became AZS 444-446

Service vehicles taken on strength by the WAGR included:-

K 16	became VW 40764
Kb 18 & 19	became VW 40761 & 40762
Kb 20	became VW 40763
J 1	became VW 5121.

A number of these vehicles till survive, including Ka 17, J 1, Ja 6, and Jv 33 at the Bassendean Rail Transport Museum, Jv 32 as VC 5103 sold to a private owner, and the tractor driver's van VW 40763 at Pemberton.

1892 Bogie Composite Cars (K class)

The specifications for the first ten bogie composite cars at the time they were ordered is described in Chapter Two (1892 Bogie Composite Cars - AB/AC class), and the specification document indicates that no expense was spared. They were built by the Lancaster Wagon Co. in England and had been delivered to Fremantle by 1892. These would have been numbered 1-10, but five (6-10) were sold to the WAGR and became AB (later AC) 31-35.

Five more identical cars were bought to replace those sold to the WAGR and they were numbered 11-15. The ten cars entered service when the MRWA was opened in November, 1894. Whether by chance or design is uncertain, but the seat cushion frames were adjustable so that a large bed could be made covering the entire floor of the compartment. Thus the train traveller on the MRWA, able to stretch out and sleep, arrived at his destination far more refreshed than did his counterpart on the government system, who had to spend a night time journey sitting up in an equivalent WAGR coach.

These cars were classified K in 1903. At this time, four more bogie composite cars from the batch numbered 1-5 went to the WAGR in exchange for four of their AB class lavatory equipped long distance cars, but which four is not known. The last surviving car from this batch was renumbered K 16.

Two of the remaining six K class cars (K 11 & 15) were converted into brake composites in 1912 and 1914 respectively, and in 1920 K 16 was converted into the general manager's saloon, being reclassified Ka 16. In 1928 the first of the three K class cars left was converted to run with the new Jv class sleeping cars. This car, K 12, had its roof height raised and was rebuilt internally as a second class car with semi-open seating and a lavatory at each end. K 13 was similarly converted in 1929/30, and K 14 was rebuilt in 1930, but as a first class car classified Jk 14.

This, in effect, spelt the end of the K class cars in their original condition and role, and the only survivor from the group is the much modified K 5, preserved as AL 17.

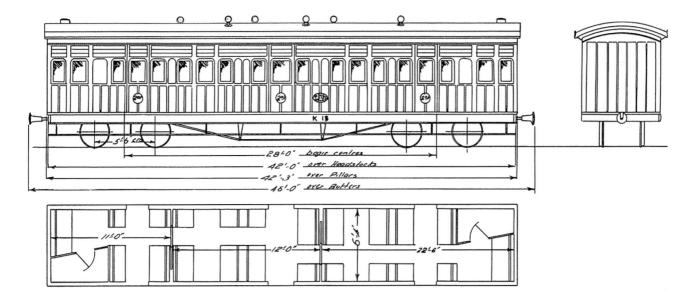

MRWA drawing of the K class coach. *Drawing courtesy PTA.*

1903 Long Distance Lavatory Cars (J & Ja classes)

Ja 6, as preserved at the Rail transport Museum at Bassendean, 27 November, 1994. *Photo Bill Gray.*

After the Parliamentary Select committee enquiry in 1902, the MRWA had to find some lavatory cars, and drawings were prepared for a car, which looked something like a WAGR AT class car on the outside, but had an interior not unlike the cars which later became ACL's. However, these were not built, and instead an arrangement was made with the WAGR to swap four bogie composite cars for four long distance lavatory cars. The official exchange took place in June, 1903, and the WAGR's AB 222, 242, 249, and 250 went to the MRWA as J 1-4.

In 1911 five similar cars were purchased new, these being numbered Ja 5-10, but in 1913 the last four of these vehicles were renumbered Ja 18-21 (not necessarily in that order), so fitting in with the next batch of cars delivered from the Metropolitan Railway carriage & Wagon Co. in 1913, Ja 22-25.

Ja 22 did not last long, however, being handed over to the WAGR in 1915 in exchange for one of their AP class sleeping cars, so leaving twelve cars in the J/Ja class.

During the 1930 renumberings, several members of the class were affected, these being Ja 18-21 and 23-25, which became Ja 12, 10, 7/8, 11, 7/8, 9 and 13 respectively, while J 1-4 and Ja 5 and 6 all retained their numbers.

After the Second World War, many of the cars were worn

out and in 1948-50 Ja 12 and 13 were withdrawn from use. By 1953, with only one passenger train per week, even fewer cars were required. J 1 was converted into a crew van in 1953, and J 2, Ja 9 and possibly Ja 12 were all written off in 1955. In 1957 J 3 was also written off, and the frames of these cars (2, 3, 9, 12 & 13) were used to build bogie bolster wagons. The bodies of J 2 and 3 were sold and sat in derelict condition at Hazelmere near Perth for many years before being burnt to make way for a housing development.

When the WAGR took the company over in 1964 J 4, and Ja 5-8, 10 and 11 passed on to their new owner. J 4, Ja 5, 6 and 10 entered service with the WAGR as ACL 31-33 and 36, all four being converted to ACM class suburban cars in 1965. ACM 33 is the only one to survive, being used occasionally on the Vintage Train at Bunbury before being restored as Ja 6 and moved to Bassendean in Perth. Meanwhile Ja 7, 8 and 11 were not return to service by the WAGR and were written off in 1965.

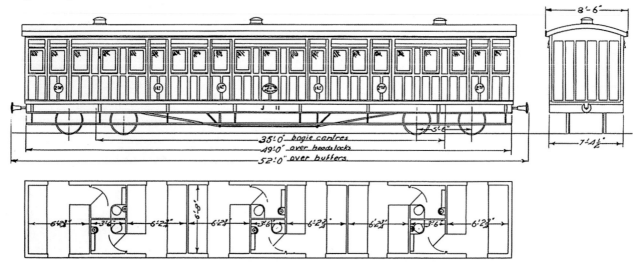

General arrangement drawing of a J class coach, J 11 being represented.   *Drawing courtesy PTA..*

1912 Brake Composite Cars (KB class converted from K class)

In 1912 the K class cars had been partially displaced by the J/Ja classes, so K 11 was converted into a brake composite car, not unlike the WAGR's AD class. This vehicle was a success and was followed by K 15 in 1914. Both cars retained their numbers, but were reclassified Kb. They led apparently useful lives, but were out of service by 1936, about which time they were renumbered Kb 19 and 18 respectively. These were only book numbers and were never carried by the carriages.

After many years in storage the cars were converted to crew vans. Kb 18 was rebuilt in 1944 and Kb 19 followed in 1949. Both vehicles were still in service when taken over by the WAGR in 1964, and Kb 18 entered service in 1965 as workman's van VW 40761, followed by Kb 19 in 1966 as VW 40762. They were finally written off in 1981 and 1985 respectively.

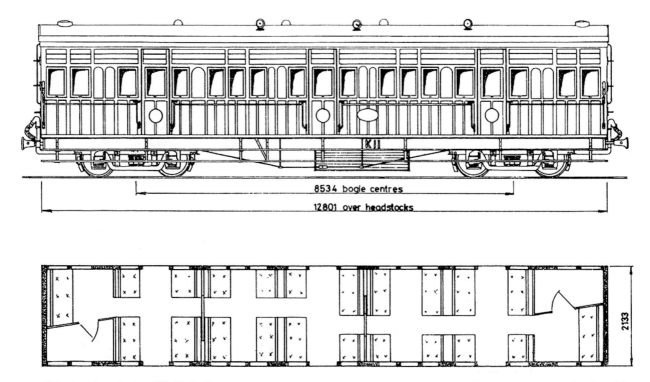

This drawing depicts KB 11 & 15.   *Drawing courtesy Lindsay Watson.*

1915 First Class Sleeping Car (Jb class)

The opening of the WAGR line between Midland Junction and Geraldton, via Wongan Hills, in 1915 provided some competition for the MRWA and another swap was arranged, in which the MRWA received an ex WAGR AP class sleeping car (AP 148) in exchange for one of their new composite cars (Ja 22). The Ja became ACL 258 on the WAGR, while the AP was numbered Jb 22 on the MRWA.

This car was something of an oddity in the MRWA fleet, especially after the Jv class sleeping cars arrived in 1927, and it was written off sometime between 1938 and 1940. The old coach lay stored for more than ten years and in 1950 its body was removed and the frames used to build a vehicle for transporting the MRWA caterpillar tractor and its driver. This vehicle, numbered Kb 20, was reminiscent of the old WAGR agricultural bank manager's vans, with a van body on one half of the vehicle and an open deck on the other.

The old AP sleeping car frames did not last long on Kb 20, a new set of frames being built for it in 1955. It entered WAGR service in 1965 as VW 40763 and is currently at Pemberton.

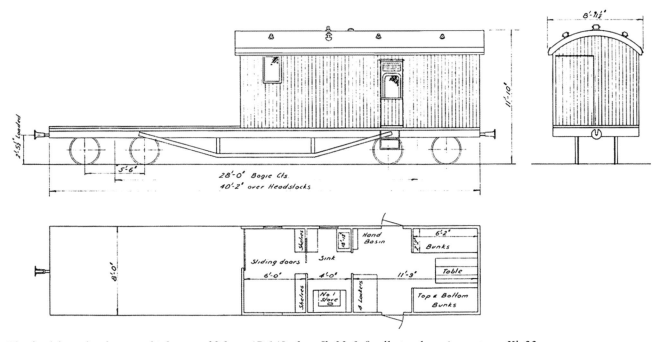

The final form for the car which started life as AP 148, then Jb 22 & finally track equipment van Kb 22.

Drawing courtesy PTA.

A WAGR loco hauls an MRWA train through suburban Perth. The cars nearest the camera are J 6 & Jv 32.

Photo courtesy ARHS.

1920 General Manager's Saloon (KA class converted from K)

Ka 17 after it's restoration to MRWA colours, at the rail Transport Museum at Bassendean, 27 November, 1994

Photo Bill Gray.

The last survivor of the first ten Midland Railway passenger cars (K16) was converted into a saloon for the general manager in 1920. This conversion was quite extensive and involved fitting one end platform and raising the height of the roof. Internally the car was fitted out in much the same way as the WAGR's inspection cars and it was reclassified Ka. Between 1932 and 1934 it was renumbered Ka 17 and

served till its takeover by the WAGR in 1964. It was fitted with the stove, hot water system and fridge from inspection car AL 39, and in June, 1965 it returned to service at Narrogin as AL 17. In 1973 this rather unique coach was written off, and is now preserved at the ARHS Rail Transport Museum at Bassendean, restored as Ka 17.

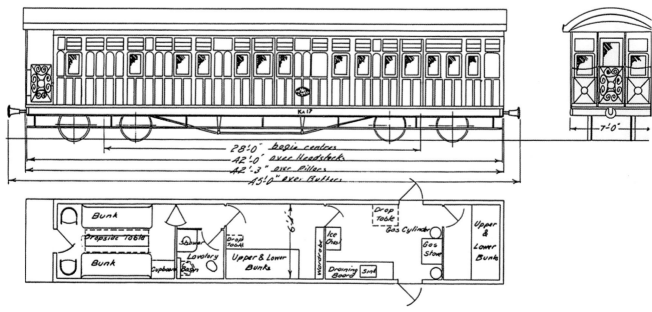

Ka 17.

Drawing courtesy PTA.

1927 First Class Sleeping Car (Jv class)

Jv 33 on display during a Midland Workshops open day on 28 October, 1995.   *Photo Bill Gray.*

The Jv class sleeping cars were the last carriages to be purchased new by the MRWA and the first of them entered service in 1927. The WAGR's AZ class was based on the design of these cars, and were identical to them when built (see 1928). The Jv's remained in almost original condition throughout their working lives and were the only corridor cars owned by the MRWA. Their existance caused the conversion of three of the old K class cars to run with them, two of these being converted to second class cars and one to a first class car.

In 1964 the Jv's were taken over by the WAGR and entered service in the second half of 1965 as their AZS class, riding on old ADU bogies and numbered 444-446 (see 1965). Because they lacked shower compartments and other modifications which had been carried out on the WAGR's AZ class cars, the AZS's were used as second class carriages, and the first one (AZS 444) was written off in 1971and destroyed in a civil defence excersize the following year. AZS 445 went in 1974, being converted into a breakdown van, VC 5103, and was sold privately after being stored at Midland by the ARHS for a number of years. AZS 446 was written off in 1975 and preserved at the ARHS Rail Transport Museum at Bassendean as Jv 33.

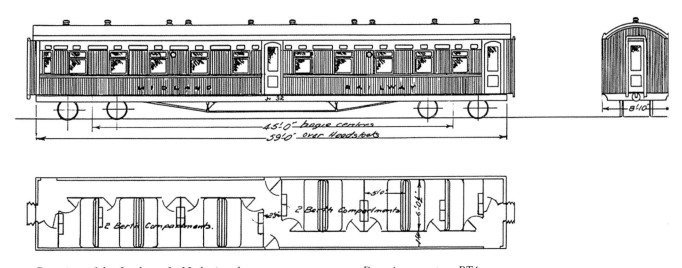

Drawing of the Jv class, Jv 32 depicted.   *Drawing courtesy PTA.*

1928 Second Class Cars (K class)

K 16 in its final role as the WAGR's VW 40764. The raised roof line can be clearly seen.

Photo late Geoff Blee, courtesy Murray Rowe.

When the Jv class sleeping cars arrived in 1927, it was decided to convert the last three K class bogie composite cars to run with the new sleepers. The first to be converted was K 12 in 1928, its rather "flat roofed" appearance being altered by raising the roof closer to the height of that of the sleeping cars, while its innards were rebuilt with semi-open seating and a lavatory at each end. K 13 was rebuilt in a similar fashion in 1929/30.

During the 1930's renumberings K 12 became K 15 and K 13 became K 16, and both cars were withdrawn from use in 1950. K 15 had its body removed and the frame was converted into an Nb class bogie bolster wagon, while K 16 re-entered service as a crew van. Both were taken over by the WAGR in 1964 and K 16 became a workman's van, VW 40764, the following year. It was written off in 1975.

1930 First Class Car (JK class)

The rebuilding of the two K class cars as second class carriages to run with the new Jv class sleeping cars left only one K class car in original condition, and this vehicle, K 14, was rebuilt in 1930 in a similar fashion to the two second class cars, but was fitted with more comfortable furnishings and so became a first class car. As such it was reclassified Jk, retaining the number 14.

Jk 14 kept its identity during the 1930's renumberings and was retired from service in 1950. It was stored till 1960, when its frame was used to build a bogie bolster wagon of the Nb class. This vehicle was part of the stock taken over by the WAGR in 1964.

Timber Company Railways

Ex AI 1 with several other Millars vehicles, two of which appear to be passenger cars. Photo courtesy Len Purcell.

There can be no doubt that passengers were carried over the maze of timber company railways which spread web like over the Southwest of Western Australia. There can also be no doubt that there must have been a variety of vehicles in which people traveled, which included some purpose built cars. None are known to still exist, and records of those used are scanty, at best.

Three known operators of passenger cars were Millars, who ran at least two ex WAGR 4 wheel AI class cars, and possibly four, the State Saw Mills who got one AI car which lasted just over a week in their service before being burnt, & the Canning Jarrah Timber Co., which also used one former AI class carriage. This latter company also hired a former Bunbury Tramway car from the WAGR. Other carriages are known to have been purpose built. A photograph of one of these appears in Chapter One.

Public Works Department

The Public Works Department was responsible for the construction and operation of a number of jetties at the various ports along the coast line of Western Australia. Many of these jetties carried railways, primarily operated by small shunting type locomotives to haul wagon loads to and from the ships which berthed there. Some of the ports also had vehicles used to carry passengers. These were sometimes open wagons, possibly fitted with bench seats and a tarpaulin for protection from the elements, through to small tram like vehicles. Carnarvon was one of the better equipped ports as far as passenger cars went, its jetty being some distance from the town. To provide services there the Public Works Department acquired two former WAGR 4 wheel AI class carriages. About 1928 a new car was built by the WAGR at Midland for the Carnarvon Jetty services. The body was similar to the AT class suburban cars then in service with the WAGR, but on a short wheel base 4 wheel chassis.

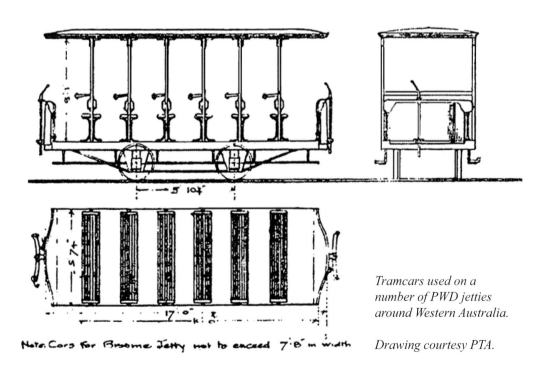

Note. Cars for Broome Jetty not to exceed 7'8" m width

Tramcars used on a number of PWD jetties around Western Australia.

Drawing courtesy PTA.

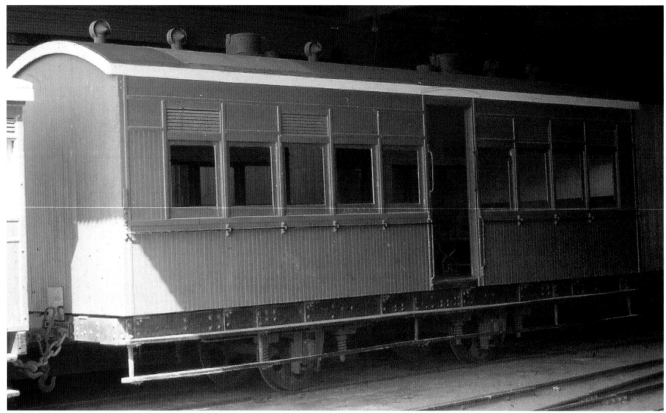

The one off car built at Midland for the PWD at Carnarvon in 1965. *Photo courtesy Ian Cutter.*

Preservation Groups

Hotham Valley Railway

W 903 & a restored C class diesel lead an HVR tour train onto mainline at Bellevue, 11 October, 1997. *Photo Bill Gray.*

The Hotham Valley Railway was formed in 1974 to operate steam locomotives on the branch line between Pinjarra and Dwellingup, to the south of Perth, after the WAGR decided that steam locomotives should no longer be allowed to run in the Perth metropolitan area. In many ways they were a preservation group, using retired WAGR carriages, including AZ, AQZ, ARM, AQL and AQM class cars. Eventually, steam was once again permitted into the metropolitan area, allowing steam hauled tours to be run from Perth. The HVR, along with the ARHS, often hired coaching stock from Westrail, particularly suburban cars and the "Australind" sets. As Westrail moved away from the last of their locomotive hauled cars during the mid 1980's, and the remaining carriages needed maintenance, the HVR ramped up its tour operations and decided that the old wooden stock probably would not be able to keep up with their proposed services. The railway had already bought six former Tasmanian Government Railways cars from Australia National Railways, these being four SS, an SSD and an SSS class car, to operate short services into the forest from Dwellingup, and then went to South Africa where they purchased three sets of ex South African Railways 3rd class cars, a total of 25 carriages. These cars were steel bodied and were refurbished before being brought to Australia. The cars gave good service, although several spent long periods of time out of use. The Hotham Valley Railway, teetering on the brink of collapse during the late 1990's, put one set of South African cars on the market, but none were sold. The railway did survive after effectively undergoing a total reorganization, and all the ex Tasmanian cars, 24 of the South African cars (one was destroyed by fire) and four RA class open wagons converted to carry passengers (classified RAP) are still in Hotham Valley ownership.

Tasmanian cars.

SSD 1 at Dwellingup prior to an Etmylin Forest trip, 25 April, 1991.   *Photo Bill Gray.*

The Hotham Valley Railway purchased six carriages from Australia National Railways in 1979. These were former Tasmanian Government Railways cars, consisting of four SS class cars, a single SSD and an SSS. The SS class cars were part of a batch of nine, built by the Tasmanian Government Railways for their Hobart suburban services. These cars entered traffic between 1956 and 1964 and carried 48 passengers. The SSD was one of two constructed in 1964 and was essentially an SS with a guards compartment, which reduced its passenger capacity to 40. The SSS was a larger car, built in Hobart in 1966 and able to carry 72 passengers.

These cars were withdrawn from service when Hobart suburban services ceased at the end of 1974, and five years later were delivered to Fremantle from Burnie aboard the ship "Townsville Trader". In late November, 1979 the six cars arrived at Pinjarra, but little work was carried out on them till 1982 when they were taken to Dwellingup. Restoration commenced two years later and the cars entered service in time for the busy America's Cup during 1986 and 87. They are mostly operated on the Etmylin Forest services.

The cars are numbered as follows:-

SSD 1	"Jarrah" ex SSD 1	
SSD 2	"Marri"	ex SS 9
SS 3	"Wandoo"	ex SS 1
SS 4	"Blackbutt"	ex SS 4
SS 5	"Tuart"	ex SS 8
SSS 6	"Karri"	ex SSS 1

SS4 at a damp Dwellingup on 7 June, 2002.   *Photo Bill Gray.*

South African cars.

Twenty five cars were purchased from the South African Railways at a time when the Hotham Valley Railway was rapidly expanding its tour operations, and the old Westrail wooden bodied stock was reaching the end of its useful life. The cars were part of a very large number of carriages built by Union Carriage & Wagon at Nigel in South Africa and Linke Hoffman Busch in Satzgitter, West Germany, totaling 1,317 units (more than have operated over the WAGR since its inception!). Twenty four of the Hotham Valley cars were converted from third class cars which had previously been sleeping cars, while one car was converted direct from a sleeping car into a guards/luggage van. All twenty five cars were refurbished in South Africa at the South African Railways Bloemfontein Workshops, and arrived in Western Australia in three batches, the first eight being shipped on the "MV Pietergracht"and arriving on 10 October, 1988, the second batch came on the "MV Looiersgacht" on 11 November, 1988, and the last nine on the "MV Carliner" on 2 February, 1989. The first eight cars entered service on 17 December, 1988.

The cars were 19.96 metres over the body, 2.85 metres wide, 3.96 metres high, with the bogie centres set at 14.48 metres. They were fitted with Commonwealth ride control bogies, the wheel base of these being 2.06 metres. The cars were of steel construction, painted in the WAGR colour scheme of green and cream and were classified according to the old WAGR conventions, A for passenger carriage, H for Hotham, and the third letter denoting the type of car, as follows:-

AHA 301-303:-
First class cars with guards compartment. (56 seats)
AHB 304-306:-
First class cars with buffet (28 seats)
AHD 307:-
Dining car (not fitted out in South Africa)
AHE 308-310:-
Tourist class with guards compartment (64 seats)
AHF 311, 312, 314-317:-
First class cars (56 seats)
AHG 318:-
Guards/luggage van
AHL 319:-
Lounge car (not fitted out in South Africa)

AHT 320-326:-
Tourist class cars (64 seats)

The cars (except one) were all named after Western Australian rivers, as follows:-

301	Ashburton
302	Murray
303	Fitzroy
304	Greenough
305	Gascoyne
306	Fortescue
307	Serpentine
308	Kalgan
309	Coongan
310	Chapman
311	Bloemfontein
312	Avon
314	Brunswick
315	Denmark
316	Murchison
317	Lunenberg
318	Frankland
319	Hotham
320	Harvey
321	Irwin
322	Preston
323	Blackwood
324	Mortlock (Built by Union Carriage & Wagon late 1970's, 24 volt electrics & high ceilings.)
325	Canning
326	Dale

AHF 314 was built by Linke Hoffmann Busch, AHG 318 was converted from an E1 class sleeping car, and AHT 323 and 324 were built by the Union Carriage & Wagon in the late 1970's, fitted with 24 volt electrics & high ceilings.

As a result of the namings, the cars were marketed as the "Riverland" cars. They were put into service on the longer distance services, although several spent long periods out of use.

AHA 303 "Fitzroy" at Pinjarra on 26 April, 1998.The AHE class were identical externally.   *Photo Bill Gray.*

AHB 304 "Greenough" on a tour train at Midland, 16 July, 1998.   *Photo Bill Gray.*

The only member of the AHD class, 307 "Serpentine" sits at Pinjarra on 2 December, 1989.   *Photo Bill Gray.*

AHF 316 "Murchison" hides behind the wild oats at Pinjarra on 17 January, 1998 The AHT class was externally identical.
Photo Bill Gray.

Sole guard's/luggage van in the Hotham Valley fleet, AHG 318 "Frankland" sits at Pinjarra, 17 January, 1998.

Photo Bill Gray.

AHL 319 "Hotham" brings up the rear of a train at Pinjarra, 26 April, 1998.

Photo Bill Gray.

Pilbara Railway Historical Society

Although primarily formed in 1975, with the blessing of Hammersley Iron to preserve locomotives from the massive iron ore mining operations in the Pilbara, the Pilbara Railway Historical Society also needed to run tours to try to generate the necessary income to keep their museum open and the exhibits, both working and static, in good order. Hammersley Iron assisted with the importation of the famous English steam locomotive "Pendennis Castle" for the Society in 1977, much to the chagrin of some British rail enthusiasts. Having a working steam engine to operate tours also required passenger carriages, and a small number of cars were sourced from various sources. Initially, an AYL and three AH class cars were acquired from the retired WAGR fleet. All three cars were placed on standard gauge bogies, the two AHs being placed on a camp train by Hammersley Iron which was on permanent

standby in case of a derailment or accident. It appears they were never needed in that role and eventually found their way into the care of the Pilbara Railway Historiocal Society for tour train use. The AYL never got beyond being shunted around the yard at Seven Mile.

Hammersley Iron also purchased three passenger cars from the New South Wales Government Railways in 1975, these being FS class 2010, 2138, and 2141. These cars had been built at Granville by Clyde Engineering, 2010 entering service on the NSW Government Railways in September, 1935, 2138 in November, 1937, and the other two a month later. The three cars were condemned in September, 1975 and sold to Hamersley Iron, FS 2010 being used as an inspection car, while the other two were used by the Pilbara Railway Historical Society. In 1986 a fourth FS was purchased for the Society, FS 2143. This car had entered service on the NSWGR in December, 1937 and was condemned and sold to the Pilbara based mining company in April, 1986. in company with the sole KBY class parcels van it was railed across Australia, then shipped from Fremantle to Dampier aboard the "Freeway Express".

These cars ran a number of tours over the years, behind "Pendennis Castle", or behind company diesel locomotives.

Eventually, the steam loco was returned to the United Kingdom, the ex WAGR cars returned to the South of the state into the care of the Australian Railway Historical Society, and the Museum was disbanded. The former NSW cars remain stored at the company's depot near Karratha, however at the time of writing it is thought that moves are afoot to return them to service.

With thanks to Ian Rourke for much of the information on the PRHS & it passenger carriages. Information on the FS class cars gleaned from "The Coaching Stock of the NSW Railways" by David Cooke, Don Estelle, Keith Seckold & John Beckhaus, published by Eveleigh Press, is also acknowledged.

Bennett Brook Railway

The Western Australian Light Railway Preservation Association (WALRPA) was originally formed at Whiteman Park on the north eastern side of Perth to preserve a small number of locomotives which had been discarded from various 2' gauge industrial railways in Western Australia. During the early 1980's it was decided to form the Bennett Brook Railway within the park in order to operate some of these machines, and as a result there was a need for 2' gauge passenger cars. These were built using components from former WAGR vehicles, including QBB and QPS class flat wagons, and R class open wagons. The frames of these vehicles were completely stripped and narrowed, worn or damaged parts were replaced and they were placed on regauged former WAGR bogies. The bodies were mostly scratch built, although some WAGR parts were used, including 6' radius roof beams, and seats from retired ADG and ADA class railcars. The resulting carriages were classified using WAGR classification letters, although the type of vehicle did not necessarily bear any resemblance to its WAGR classed brother.

The first cars were rolled out of the Mussel Pool workshops at Whiteman Park in 1985, these being two AQ saloon cars and an AQB brake saloon. These were followed by a buffet car (classed AV) in 1987, two open wagons (classed AR) in 1988, an open wagon with a saloon (ARP), another open wagon in 1989, and finally a Z class passenger brake van converted from a WAGR V van in 1994.

Details of these cars are as follows:-

1985	AQB 2970	Built from QBB wagon
	AQ 4745	Built from QBB wagon
	AQ 1788	Built from QBB wagon
1987	AV 3273	Built from V class van
1988	AR 1783	Built from R class wagon
	AR 4461	Built from R class wagon
1989	ARP 1638	Built from R class wagon
	R 3644	Built from R class wagon
1994	Z 3251	Built from V class van

A four car train arrives at Whiteman Park's Central Station on 13 September, 1997.   *Photo Bill Gray.*

With thanks to Lindsay Watson for the information of the Bennett Brook Railway.

APPENDIX FOUR
SURVIVORS

Preservation of passenger cars began in Western Australia in 1969 when the Australian Railway Historical Society began work to establish the Rail Transport Museum at Bassendean. Inspection car AL 40, second class sleeper AQS 294, and passenger brakevan ZA 173 were the first carriages on the site, and this museum now holds the largest single collection of preserved Western Australian passenger cars, both operational and static.

The other major collection of passenger cars is held by the Hotham Valley Railway at Dwellingup. This organisation was set up in 1974 to run preserved steam locomotives and carriages up the winding Dwellingup branch, from Pinjarra. The following year they obtained their first carriage, dining car AV 426, a vehicle which is still in regular service on their trains. This organisation also owns twenty four steel bodied cars purchased from the South African Railways, and five ex Tasmanian steel bodied coaches.

Several other preservation groups hold small collections of coaches, or have done so in the past and sold them to larger organisations. Notable among these are the Great Southern Steam Association, formerly of Albany, whose collection of seven cars was acquired by the ARHS in late 1984. The Boyanup Transport Museum is home to the Vintage Train which includes eight old compartment cars, and the Pilbara Railways Historical Society at Dampier in the north of the state which had preserved two AH class steel bodied sleeping cars (on standard gauge bogies), and an AYL class lounge car. These cars are now with the ARHS in Perth. The Kalgoorlie-Boulder Loopline Preservation Society has six cars preserved, four running and two on static display. A number of static carriages can be found in museums around the state, the main ones being at Northam, Coolgardie, Collie, Esperance, Wyalkatchem and Kojonup.

One car, still held by the WAGR, and worthy of mention, is Western Australia's first railway carriage, AI 258, which was "discovered" in 1988 by a member of the ARHS who was told of a "tram body" lying in a nursery at Carnarvon. In an action which was nothing short of miraculous, the old car was rescued and restored to its original glory at the Midland workshops. Many cars have been sold as farm sheds over the years and there can be no doubt that a large number of these have simply rotted away or been otherwise destroyed, but the discovery of AI 258 raises hopes that any number of these historic cars might still be found and eventually recovered.

The following is a list of known surviving passenger cars, and any reader who might know of any others not mentioned, in any condition, is urged to contact the Australian Railway Historical Society about them, and hopefully a little more of Western Australia's railway heritage might be saved.

Balcatta

AS 375	as VW 5111

Bassendean/Midland (ARHS)

Ja 6	(formerly ACM 33)
AG 14	
Ka 17	
AGS 22	
AY 26	
AYL 28	as VW 28
AYL 29	
Jv 33	
AL 40	formerly AG 40
AP 87	as VW 2145
ZA 173	
AB 222	as VW 5121
AK 251	as P 658
AT 259	
AM 261	as AF 261
ZJ 266	
ZJ 270	
ARS 284	as VW 284
AV 286	as VW 286
AQL 288	
AQM 292	
AQS 294	
AM 313	
AVL 314	
AQA 343	
ARS 348	as VW 348
ARA 351	
ARA 356	
AN 413 (1st)	as AL 4
AN 413	
ARS 421	
AQZ 423	
AV 425	
ZJA 431	
AZ 443	
AY 452	
AY 453	
AYS 461	
ADF 495	
AYC 500	
AYC 510	
AYC 511	
AYC 512	
AYD 540	
AYD 550	
AH 563	
AH 564	
AH 565	
ADG/V 612	
ADA/V 763	
VY 4999	as VW 4999

Boddington

VP 1885	Frame only.

Boyanup (Transport Museum)

AC/AF 181-184	End section of one of these cars.
ZA 183	
ACM 210	
AU 218	
ACM 238	
ACM 391	
ACL 406	
ACL 407	
ACL 410	
ZJA 432	
ZJA 434	
ASA 445	as ALT 5
AY 455	
ADG/V 602	
ADG/V 610	
AYE/V 709	

Bullsbrook

ZJ 368	

Busselton (The Whistle Stop site)

ARS 350	

Cannington

ZA 191	as VC 5088

Capel

AS 372	as VW 5114

Chidlows

AU 318	as VW 5132

Clackline

AZ 440	as VW 440

Collie (Rail Museum)

ZA 176	as VW 5105
AQZ 415	formerly at York & Bassendean
AQC 344	as VW 5146

Coolgardie (Old Station)

ACL 232	
ZJ 359	
ACL 405	

Cranbrook

ARS 354	

Cunderdin

AV 315	

Dongara

ARS 277	as VW 277

Dowerin

AH 561	

Dwellingup/Pinjarra (Hotham Valley Railway)

AGB 9　　　　　　as Z 9
AGB 12　　　　　as AL 2
ZB 202　　　　　as Z 202
AQM 287
AQL 290
ACW 330　as VC 2143
ARM 347
ARM 357
ZJ 367
AQZ 420
AQZ 424
AV 426
AZ 434
AZ 435
AZ 436
AZ 439
ADG/V 605
ADG/V 614
ADG/V 603

Dwellingup (Private)
ARS 279　　　　　derelict body cut in half
ARS 355　　　　　derelict body cut in half

East Perth Terminal.
AI 258　　　　　　formerly NR 1

Esperance (Museum)
AP 89　　　　　　as VW 5066

Esperance (At Live Steam Railway)
ZJ 429

Forrestfield (WAGR)
WCA 901-905　　(stowed pending sale)
WCE 921-923　　(stowed pending sale)

Forrestfield (Fire Brigade)
ADG/V 615
ADH/V 651

Fremantle (Carriage Coffee Shop)
ZA 196　　　　　as VW 5117

Fremantle (Hubble St)
ZJ ???

Gidgegannup (Crafty Marg's Carriage)
ZB 207

Gidgegannup
AKB 60

Hazelmere
ZJ 268

Hopetoun (private)
AH 25　　　　　　(body)

Jandakot, Perth (private)
AH 562　　　　　(body)
ADG/V 606　　　(rumoured, to be
　　　　　　　　　confirmed)

Kalamunda
ZJ 427

Kalgoorlie-Boulder (Loopline)
AP 88/93　　　　as AL 88
AYS 460
AYF 704
AYF 705
AYE/V 713
AYE/V 714

Karnet
AYE 701　(has been moved/demolished?)

Kewdale
ZB 213

Kojonup
AZ 438　　　　　as VW 438
ARS 349　　　　as VW 349
VW 5149　　　　formerly J 4

Kulin
AM 444　　　　　as VW 433
AZ 437　　　　　as VW 437

Lake Clifton
AZS 445　　　　　as VC 5103

Lake Leschanaultia
ADA ???

Ledge Point (Private)
AP ???　　　　　body

Mary Springs
ADT 9　　　　　　body

Menzies
AYF 707

Mt. Helena (private)
ADH/V 652
ADA/V 756

ZA 159　　　　　　as VC 5156

Mount Magnet (Metana Minerals)
ADF 490　　　　　(remains of body)
AYU 580　(　　　　body) (One of these
AYU 581　　　　　(body) is in the Mount
AYU 584　　　　　(body) Magnet
　　　　　　　　　　　Museum)
AYU 585　　　　　(body)
ADG/V 604　　　　(remains of body)
ADX 661　　　　　(remains of body)
ADX 670　　　　　(remains of body)

Mundijong
AQZ 417

Narrogin
ZA 160

Northam (Old Station Museum)
AL 59　　　　　　formerly AF 59
AJ 64
AU 307　　　　　as VW 5138
AQC 339　　　　　as VW 339

Northampton
ACW 323　as AL 3

Blue Gum Park, Karridale
ADA ???

Pemberton
AYB 458
AYB 459
AYE/V 708
VW 40763 Originally built from AP
　　　　　　　　　　　148
AYF 706

Queenscliffe, Victoria (Bellarine Peninsular
Railway)
AF 13　　　　　　as VW 5112
ZA 200
ZJ 260　　　　　as AL 1
AS 376

Ravensthorpe (Museum)
AH 24

ZA 6281 (ZA 185)

Seabird (private)
ADU ???　　　　　(body)

Stoneville
AY 454　　　　　sold?

Toodyay
ZJ 269　　　　　Formerly at Guildford
ACW 327　　　　as VW 2144
(probably
　　　　　　　　　since sold)
AS 372　　　　　as VW 5114 (probably
　　　　　　　　　since sold)
ACL 403　　　　as VW 5113
ZJA 433　　　　(probably since sold)

Wanneroo
ACW 329　as VW 2140

Wattle Grove
AQZ 419

Whiteman Park (WALRPA)
ZA 159　　　　　as VW 5100
Ex MRWA coach frame

Wyalkatchem
ZA 181　　　　　as VW 5087
AT 302　　　　　as VW 5137
ACL 409　　　　asVW 5122

York
AYE 710

Location Uncertain
ZA 158　　　　　as VW 5083, (at
　　　　　　　　　Midland 1-11-90
ZA 163　　　　　as VW 5139
ZA 168　　　　　as VW 5084, Body sold
ZA 174　　　　　as VW 5108
ZA 193　　　　　as VW 5110
ZA 201　　　　　as VW 5115
ACL 209　　　　To salvage for sale.
ZB 210　　　　　as VC 5106
ZB 211　　　　　as VW 5119
AT 306　　　　　(ex Sawyers Valley &
　　　　　　　　　Broughtons)
AU 308　　　　　as VW 5142
ACW 328　as VW 5143
ACW 331　as VW 2139
AQ 342　　　　　("Sold to John Tyler")
ASD 374　　　　as VW 5118
AT 382　　　　　as VW 5081
ACL 404　　　　as VW 5123
ZJA 430
AYF 702

Auckland, New Zealand.
ADK 681-690　　(in service)
ADB 771-780　　(in service)
ADL 801-810　　(in service)
ADC 851-860　　(in service)

Queensland
SXV 1663
SX 1664
SXV 1665
SX 1666-1669
SXV 1726
SX 1727-1731
SXV 1732

Cars in regular service
Picton
ADP 101-103
ADQ 121 & 122

Claisebrook (WAGR)	Nowergup	Midland
AEA 201-249	BEA 549-579	WDA 001 - 003
AEB 301-349	BEB 649-679	WDB 011 - 013
	BET 349-379	WDC 023.
		WEA 031
		WEB 041

Steam loco Dd 592 thunders across the old Bunbury Bridge with a tour train in tow, 15 October, 1988. The bridge has gone, the loco is static at Bassendean & the carriages, an ARA-AYC-AY-AYS-AYE-ARA have been preserved. *Photo Bill Gray*

An excellent candidate for preservation. VW 5121, looking a little dilapidated, stands at Forrestfield, 10 June, 1989. The historic car was preserved & can be found at the ARHS Museum at Bassendean.

Photo Bill Gray.

Half of ARS 355 rests near Dwellingup, along with a similar half of ARS 279, 26 April,1991.

Photo Bill Gray.

The body of an unidentified AP being used as a holiday shack near Ledge Point.

Photo courtesy Clive Woodward.

Despite being withdrawn from service & abandoned at Hopetoun about 1930, ZA 6281 has survived, first as a holiday house, then a little more securely on a museum at Ravensthorpe. Photographed at Ravensthorpe on 3 January, 2000 by Bill Gray.

The Northern Districts Model Railway Club have made use of VW 5111, formerly suburban car AS 375 by using it as part of their club rooms at Balcatta, seen here on 17 April, 1992, soon after it was placed on site.

Photo Bill Gray.

Giving it a better chance of surviving, ZA 196 is located in a park at South Beach, Fremantle, where it is used as a coffee shop & is regularly maintained. Seen here 25 July, 1989.

Photo Bill Gray.

One of the more colourful applications to be applied to a railway van is that on ZJ 429, the last ZJ built. It is located at Esperance & is used to house live steam railway equipment. The van is quite well maintained. Photographed on 27 December, 1999.

Photo Bill Gray.

As the last of the workman's vans were sold & old railway carriages became harder to get, they appreciated rapidly in value. As a result, a few in private hands are being extremely well looked after, such as AU 318, located on a property at Chidlows. The old carriages has been restored inside, & has had a roof built over it to protect it from the elements. Photographed on 28 December, 1998.

Photo Bill Gray.

Another car under a roof is VW (ARS) 277, in use at Dongara as back packer accommodation, photographed on 24 May, 1997.

Photo Bill Gray.

Apart from insurance issues, one of the greatest problems facing rail museums is vandalism, from graffiti such as that seen on AQZ 415 & ARS 421 at Bassendean on 19 April, 1989, to arson. Sadly, such problems are on-going

Photo Bill Gray.

A group of surviving carriages at the Bassendean Rail transport Museum, about to get a drenching from an approaching storm, July, 1995.

Photo Bill Gray.

ACL 232 preserved at the old Coolgardie railway station, 16 January, 1986. *Photo Bill Gray.*

Despite debilitating insurance problems for many rail tour operators & preserved railways, those cars which have survived into the hands of such operators are often in the best condition, being maintained for tour train use. Here, in happier days, Dd 592 & XA 1405 lead an ARHS tour train under the old wheat loader at Bellevue on 29 August, 1992.

Photo Bill Gray.

Three That Got Away

Ex MRWA cars J2 & J3 at Hazelmere, 9 June, 1989. Both cars were burnt early, 1994.

VW 5082, formerly AQC 338 in its final resting place at Bushmead, 15 April, 1989.   *Photos Bill Gray.*

APPENDIX FIVE

BOGIES

Unlike some other Australian Railways, the WAGR does not appear to have had any classification system for the bogies used under it's carriages. To complicate matters further, a number of different bogies actually looked very similar, sometimes the only differences being the wheel base. In order to describe the different bogie types used by the WAGR, Andrew May came up with an alphabetical classification system, while Graham Watson employs a system of describing the bogies by their wheel base, followed by the first car they were used under. Both systems have merit, and therefore a combination of the two has been used in this book.

A. Standard 5' 6" AG "American."

First used under the AG class "American" cars in 1884. It was still in service at the end of the suburban cars in 1991.

It was used under the following classes, and derivatives thereof:-

AC, AD, ACE, AC (ex GSR), AE, AF (including AF 13 & 59), AA, AB, AO, AJ (ZJ) brakevans 263-272 & 359-368), ZA, AX, ACL, AGB, ZB, AGS, AJ, AK, AJL, AJB, AKB, AYE, ACM & AYF.

-.   4' 8" AG "Gilbert."

A "one off" bogie, used under the AG class "Gilbert" cars.

-.   5' 8" AM.

Very similar to the AP bogie (below), only ever used under AM 261 from 1895.

-.   5' 8" AP.

Only ever used under the AP class sleeping cars from 1896, although it was very similar to the bogie used under AM 261, the primary difference being a different style of coil spring..

B.   4' 0" + 4' 0" 6 wheel bogie.

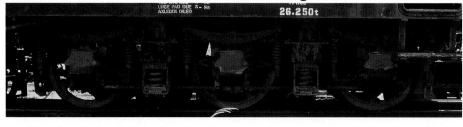

Only one type of 6 wheeled bogie was used under passengers cars on the WAGR, the first being seen under the AR class cars (and subsequently ARS 277-285 & 347-358) in 1903.

It was also used under classes AQ (286-294 & 335-346), AT, AW, AU, AS, AV (313-316 till fitted with 6' 3" AQ type (C) in 1924, & AV 286 which was fitted with the 8'AH type (H) in 1953, before reverting to the shorter 6' 3" AQ type (C) at an unknown date later).

ACW (till the mid 1930's when it was replaced by 5' 9" AY bogies (D)).

ARM (347 & 357 only, till 1963).

C.　　6' 3" AQ.

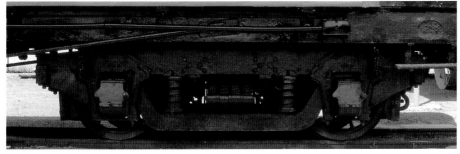

First used under AQ 413-418 in 1918 (the earlier AQ's had 6 wheel bogies (B)).

These bogies were also used under ZJ 263-272, 359-361, 365, 366 & 368 in the early 1920's to replace the Standard 5' 6" bogies (A) originally placed under these vans. ZJ 362-364 also received these bogies in 1938/39 to replace the 5' 9" AY type (D) which had been fitted to them in place of the 5' 6" standard bogies (A). Other cars fitted were AV 313-316, and AV 425 till 1967 when it got 7' Commonwealth "Ride Control" bogies (J), & AV 426.

ARS 419-424.

AQZ 419, 420, 423 & 424 till 1960 when they were replaced with 6' 3" AZ type (E).

AVL 314 (converted from AV 314 in 1958) till 1964 when it got the 7' Commonwealth "Ride Control" type (J).

D.　　5' 9" AY.

First used under AY 26 in 1924, and under the new AZ class cars till the mid to late 1930's when they were replaced by new 6' 3" bogies (E) built for these cars.

AM 444 was likewise built with the 5' 9" AY type (D), but got new AZ type bogies (E) in 1935.

After these bogies were removed from the AZ's they cascaded to ZJ 362-364 & 367 and seem to have been subsequently replaced on these four vans by the 6' 3" AQ type (C) in the 1940's, so standardizing the ZJ fleet with the same type of bogie.

AYL 28 & 29 (converted from AY) had these bogies till 1963 & 1962 respectively when they were replaced by 7' Commonwealth "Ride Control" bogies (J), which were themselves replaced in 1967 by 6' 6" ADU type bogies (G).

E.　　6' 3" AZ.

First used in the mid to late 1930's under the AZ class cars and AM 444 to replace the 5'9" bogies (D) these cars were built with.

They were also used under AN 413, & the AQL and AQM classes.

-.　　6' 6" ADT.

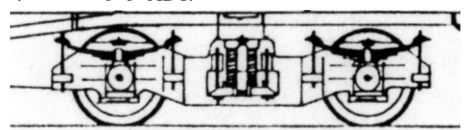

First used under the ADT class "Governor" trailers in 1939.

Also used under ADA & ADB class railcar trailers.

F.　　6' 6" AYB.

First used under AYB class suburban brake cars in 1945.

Also used under AYC, AYD classes, and AY 452-455, 460 and 461. (The earlier AY's were fitted with 5' 9" AY bogies (D).

G. 6' 6" ADU.

This type seems to have been first employed under the ADE "Governor" class cars.

They were then used under the ADU class "Wildflower" trailers, and subsequently under the AYU's.

They cascaded onto the AZS class cars after 1964, replacing their original 5' 9" AY (D), and the AYL class after 1967, replacing the 7' Commonwealth "Ride Control" bogies (J).

H. 8' AH.

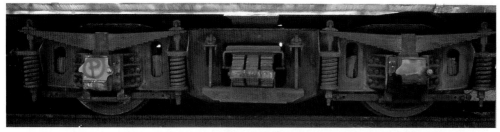

Built specially for the AH class steel bodied cars in 1948. AH 560 was fitted with the 7' Commonwealth type (J) in 1955, but was refitted with it's own bogies again 1n 1957.

J. 7' Commonwealth "Ride Control" bogies (J).

Purchased for a new eight car air conditioned "Westland" set which was never built. One set first saw service under AH 560 between 1955 and 1957.

Other classes fitted with them were ARM, AYS, ARA, AYL, AV 315 & 425, AVL 314, AM 313 and AM 414.

In addition, the SX & SXV class cars leased from the Queensland Railways were fitted with the same type of bogie.

The bogies under AM 313 (centre) are stamped "QGR". These were the bogies first fitted under AH 560 in February, 1955 & were apparently destined for Queensland, but appear to have been delivered direct from Bradford Kendall to the WAGR, explaining why they are different to the bogies under AYS 461 (top). The bottom photo shows the ride control bogies under an SXV class car.

Photos Bill Gray.

Railcar Bogies.
ASA Steam Railcar

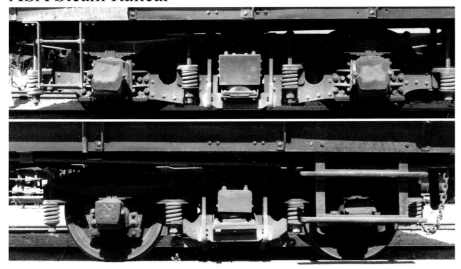

ASA Steam railcar had a 6' 6" wheel base bogie at the powered end (top) & a 6' wheel base bogie at the non powered end..

ADG, ADH & ADX

ADG, ADH, & ADX railcars all shared a 7' wheel base bogie.

ADK & WCA/WCE.

The ADK & Prospector cars shared the Pioneer III 7' 6" wheel base bogies, those under the Prospector being standard gauge.

ADL/ADC
The ADLs & ADCs ran on 2400mm wheel base bogies.

ADP/ADQ

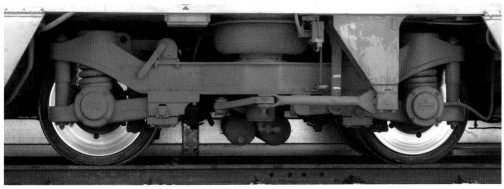

The Australind cars ran on 2200 mm wheel base bogies.

"A" Series EMU

These bogies were approximately 2400 mm wheel base.

WDA/WDB/WDC/WEA/WEB

These cars ran on 2600mm wheel centre bogies.

BEB/BET/BEC

The bogie under a "B" series EMU, BEA & BEB (top), & BET (bottom). Although of different designs, both bogies were 2500mm wheel base

6'3" AZ type (E) bogie

A "Standard" (A) bogie from under a ZA class passenger brakevan.

All photos Bill Gray.

INDIVIDUAL CARRIAGE HISTORIES

1876 4 wheeled composite,   MRC&WCo.   [AI class]
(NR) 1   Built 1875, & ready for service 4-1876;
            To AB 258, 1899;
            Reclassified AI, 9,-1900;
            To GWSA, 1903/04;
            Returned WAGR 15-9-1909;
            Probably out of use;
            Sold to PWD 9-3-1912 as tramcar, to Carnarvon, 6-1912;
            Wfu 1960's & still there 1965;
            Body & frame separated, body to Bougainvillea Nursery, &
            frame to recreation ground;
            "Discovered" 1988;
            To Gascoyne Historical Society, 5-1988;
            To Midland Workshops 20-10-1989 & restored;
            Placed on display, Westrail Centre, East Perth, 19-10-1993.

(NR) 2   Built 1875, & ready for service 4-1876;
            To AB 259, 1899;
            Reclassified AI, 9-1900
            Conv. to travelling workman's van P 5182, 1902;
            Renumbered DW 5182, 1903/04;
            W/o, 1936.

1881 4 wheeled composite MRWC&Co.   [AI class]
AB 1   Built 1880 for Eastern Railway;
            Arrived Fremantle on the "Fitzroy", 11-1-1881;
            Ready for traffic, 2-1881;
            In service by 3-1881;
            Conv. to State saloon A 1 (fitted with clerestory roof), 6-1885;
            Rolled over Albany, 23-5-1889
            Conv. to First class saloon, AB 1, 1889;
            Conv. to composite saloon, 1890;
            Reclassified AI 9-1900
            Sold Millar's Karri & Jarrah Co., 1903;
            Demolished Jarrahdale, c.1960.

(ACL 1   See 1909)
(AL 1   See 1930)
(NR 1   See 1876)

AB 2   Built 1880 for Eastern Railway;
            Arrived Fremantle on the "Fitzroy", 11-1-1881;
            Ready for traffic, 2-1881;
            In service by 3-1881;
            Reclass. AI, 9-1900;
            To WAGR Sawmill line at Banksiadale, 20-6-1914;
            Destroyed by fire, 30-6-1914.

(AG 2   See 1894)
(AGB 2   See 1894)
(AL 2   See 1894)
(NR 2   See 1876)

AB 3   Built 1880 for Eastern Railway;
            Arrived Fremantle on the "Fitzroy", 11-1-1881;
            Ready for traffic, 2-1881;
            In service by 3-1881;
            Reclass. AI, 9-1900;
            Converted to travelling workman's van P 4914, 1901;
            Renumbered DW 4914, 1903/04;
            W/o, 1960.

(ACL 3   See 1909)
(NR 3   See 1891)

1881 6 wheel composite saloon MRC&WCo.   [AH Class.]
AC 4   Probably arrived Fremantle on the "Daylight", 22-4-1881;
            In service by May, 1881;
            Classified AC, first class c.1885;
            Fitted with clerestory roof by 1900;
            Reclassified AH, 9-1900;
            Rebuilt with bogies 1906/07;
            Redesignated second class, seating for 30;
            Probably stored 4-10-1920;
            Conv. to Z 10615, 23-4-1927;
            Renumbered Z.154, c.1938;
            Run into by goods train & destroyed, Spencer's Brook, 2-8-1950.

(AL 4   See 1918)
(NR 4   See 1891)

1882 6 wheel composite saloon MRC&WCo.   [AH Class.]
AC 5   Probably arrived Fremantle on the "Daylight", 22-4-1881;
            Entered service after 7-1881;
            Reclass. AC, first class c.1885;
            Possibly rebuilt 1886;
            Put on bogies & converted to A class State saloon, 1889;
            Reclass. Commissioner's saloon, 1890;
            Reclass. Ministerial saloon, 1895;
            Reclass. AL, 9-1900;
            Conv. to inspection car, 1901;
            To Geraldton as survey van 10-7-1940;
            Fitted with electric lights during overhaul, 6-4-1945;
            W/o 11-2-1953;
            Scrapped 10-10-1956.

(ALT 5   See 1931)
(NR 5   See 1894)

1883 6 wheel second class saloon MRC&WCo.   [AH Class]
BC 6   Arrived Fremantle on the "West Australian", 28-2-1883;
            Entered service, 3-1883;
            Conv. to A class State saloon (bogies, end platform & clerestory
            roof), 29-5-1889;
            Reclass. AN, 9-1900;
            Conv. to Z 4993, 1902;
            Reno'd. Z 26, 1938-1940;
            Rebodied, 1952.

(ACL 6   See 1909)

BC 7   Arrived Fremantle on the "West Australian", 28-2-1883;
            Entered service, 3-1883;
            Conv. to AC class brake composite 13-2-1889;
            Conv. to funeral car, 1899;
            Reclass. AO, 9-1900;
            Fitted with bogies prior to World War 1;
            W/o 1930;
            Frame used to build Z 5006, 17-5-1930;
            To Z 29, & w/o 7-11-1973.

(ADT 7   See 1939)

1884 Bogie composite "American" saloon   MRC&WCo. [AG Class.]
AB 8   Delivered to Fremantle on the "SS Kennett", 9-2-1884;
            Entered service, 3-1884;
            Reclass. ABA;
            Reclassified AG, 9-1900;
            Stored 1933 (?);
            Conv. to AGV suburban goods brakevan, 19-12-1935;
            Reclass. ZAG, 23-6-1936;
            Reclass ZG, 31-5-1940;
            Demolished, 2-12-1950;
            W/o, 11-1 1951.

(ADT 8   See 1939)

AB 9   Delivered to Fremantle on the "SS Kennett", 9-2-1884;
            Entered service, 3-1884;
            Reclass. ABA;
            Reclassified AG, 9-1900;
            Fitted with guard's comp't. for Kalgoorlie, 1905;
AGB 9   Rebuilt as AGB class buffet car, 22-2-1921.
            Stored 1936;
            Conv. to suburban brakevan AGV 9, 22-7-1938;
            Reclass. Z 9, 1-10-1938;
            Painted Larch green & cream, ?/196?;
            Wfu, 7-1985;
            To HVTR, c.9.1985.

(ADT 9   See 1939)

AB 10   Delivered to Fremantle on the "SS Kennett", 9-2-1884;
            Entered service, 3-1884;

Reclass. ABA;
Reclassified AG, 9-1900;
Stored 1933 (?);
Conv. AGV suburban goods brakevan, 1935;
Reclass. ZAG, 1936;
Reclass. ZG, 1940;
W/o, 1947.

(ADT 10 See 1939)

AB 11   Delivered to Fremantle on the "SS Kennett", 9-2-1884;
         Entered service, 3-1884;
         Reclass. ABA;
         Reclassified AG, 9-1900;
         Conv. ZAG suburban goods brakevan, 1938;
         Reclass. ZG, 1940;
         W/o, 1960.

(ADT 11 See 1939)

AB 12   Delivered to Fremantle on the "SS Delconyn", 13-6-1885;
         Entered service, c.7-1885;
         Built 1885;
         Reclass. ABA;
         Reclassified AG, 9-1900;
         Fitted with guard's comp't. for Kalgoorlie, 1905;
AGB 12   Rebuilt as buffet car AGB 12, 22-1-1921;
         Conv. to survey car, 1938;
         Reno'd. AGB 2, 13-4-1939;
         Conv. to AG 2 using seats from an AY, 10-12-1941;
         Used by the army 1943-1944;
         Conv. to inspection car AL 2, 30-10-1948;
         Painted two tone green & cream, 5-1951;
         Repainted Larch green during the 1950's;
         Repainted in the green, white & red livery during the 1970's;
         Repainted orange & blue during the 1970's;
         Last used Geraldton & wfu 1980;
         Leased to HVTR.

(ADT 12 See 1939)

1885 4 wheeled composite car   MRC&WCo.   [AI Class]
AB 13   Delivered to Fremantle on the "SS Delconyn", 13-6-1885;
         In service about July, 1885;
         Reclass. AI, 9-1900;
         Sold to Millar's Wellington Mill at Dardanup, 29-10-1907.

(AF 13 See 1909)

1885 Bogie composite "American" saloon MRC&WCo. [AG Class]
AB 14   Delivered to Fremantle on the "SS Glenmorven", 12-9-1885;
         Reclass ABA;
         Reclassified AG, 9-1900;
         Stored 1933(?);
         Conv. to AGV suburban goods brakevan, 31-5-1935;
         Reclass. ZAG, 23-6-1936;
         Reclass. ZG, 27-4-1940;
         Conv. to break down van VC 1441, 26-11-1947;
         Last used Geraldton & w/o, 13-12-1972;
         To ARHS Rail Transport Museum.

AB 15   Delivered to Fremantle on the "SS Glenmorven", 12-9-1885;
         Reclass. ABA;
         Reclassified AG, 9-1900;
         Fitted with toilet & to isolated Esperance line, 1925;
         Returned to main system, 1927;
         Conv. to ZAG suburban brakevan, 11-3-1938;
         Reclass. ZG, 31-5-1940;
         Scrapped, 1941.

AB 16   Delivered to Fremantle on the "SS Glenmorven", 12-9-1885;
         Reclass. ABA;
         Reclassified AG, 9-1900;
         Stored 1933 (?);
         Conv. AGV suburban goods brakevan, 1935;
         Reclass. ZAG, 1936;
         Reclass. ZG, 1940;
         W/o, 1947.

AB 17   Delivered to Fremantle on the "SS Glenmorven", 12-9-1885;
         Reclass. ABA;
         Reclassified AG, 9-1900;
         Fitted with guard's comp't. for Kalgoorlie, 1905;
AGB 17   Rebuilt as AGB class buffet car, 7-3-1921.
         Derailed & damaged, 1928, repaired;
         Conv. to AGS shower car, 23-11-1935;
AGS 22   Reno'd AGS 22, 7-4-1941;
         Stored 15-8-1951;
         Returned to traffic, 16-2-1954;
         Painted Larch green during the 1950's;
         Painted green & cream, 10-1964;
         Wfu 1975 & stored, 9-1976;
         W/o, 8-10-1976;
         To ARHS Rail Transport Museum.

(AL 17 See 1964)

AB 18   Delivered to Fremantle on the "SS Glenmorven", 12-9-1885;
         Reclass. ABA;
         Reclassified AG, 9-1900;
         Stored 1933 (?);
         Conv. AGV suburban goods brakevan, 19-9-1935;
         Reclass. ZAG, 23-6-1936;
         Reclass. ZG, 31-5-1940;
         Rebuilt with new body to workman's van VW 6790, 30-9-1949;
         Became scale adjustor's van VS 6790, 20-2-1950;
         W/o, 15-1-1980 & scrapped.

1886 4 wheel composite cars   MRC&WCo.   [AI Class]
AB 19   Built 1885;
         In service about 3-1886;
         Reclass. AI, 9-1900;
         Possibly sold Millar's Karri & Jarrah Co., 1903, or cond. 1904.

(ACL 19 See 1909)

AB 20   Built 1885;
         In service about 3-1886;
         Reclass. AI, 9-1900;
         Trsferred Kalgoorlie to Perth 11-1903 (at Coolgardie 15-11-
1903)
         Possibly sold Millar's Karri & Jarrah Co., 1903, or cond. 1904.

AB 21   Built 1885;
         In service about 3-1886;
         Conv. louvred meat van F 4555, 10-1899.

(ACL 21 See 1909)

AB 22   Built 1885;
         In service about 3-1886;
         Reclass. AI, 9-1900;
         Sold to Dept. of Northwest for PWD at Carnarvon as a tramcar,
         30-5-1925;
         Body demolished c.1965.

(AGS 22 See 1884)

AB 23   Built 1885;
         In service about 3-1886;
         Conv. louvred meat van F 4556, 10-1899.

(ACL 23 See 1909)
(ACL 23 See 1911)

1887 Bunbury Tram Cars
         Arrived Bunbury aboard the iron barque "Rewa", 24-12-1887.

??   Second class car shipped Fremantle 12-4-1891
         Damaged in transit & stowed.

30   Composite car shipped to Fremantle for use on Eastern Railway,
         24-4-1891 (Also referred to by WAGR as a "small carriage")

(NR) 5   Composite car shipped to Northern railway 1894;
         Became AB 262, 1899;
         Reclass. AI, 9-1900;

Sold to Canning Jarrah Timber Co., 24-3-1902;
Fate unknown.

1888 6 wheeled composite cars with compartments MRC&WCo.
[AH Class]
ABC 24   Reclassified AH, 9-1900;
           To Hopetoun, 4-1909;
           Abandoned Hopetoun, 1930;
           Sold to Mr. F.E. Daw, 2-1940;
           W/o as abandoned, 31-3-1943;
           Body at Ravensthorpe Museum.

ABC 25   Reclassified AH, 9-1900;
           To Hopetoun, 4-1909;
           Abandoned Hopetoun, 1930;
           Body sold to buyer in Newdegate, 29-9-1939;
           W/o as abandoned, 31-3-1943;
           Body still exists in private house in Hopetoun.

ABC 26   Reclassified AH, 9-1900;
           W/o 30-6-1924.

(AY 26   See 1924)

ABC 27   Reclassified AH, 9-1900;
           Damaged in accident;
           W/o 11-2-1904.

(ACL 27 See 1909)
(ACL 27 See 1911)

1889 Mail Van WAGR Fremantle Workshops
  ?   Built to operate between Albany & Perth;
           Probably scrapped c.1895.

1891 6 wheeled composite cars   MRC&WCo.   [AH Class]
ABC 28   Reclassified AH, 9-1900;
           W/o, 30-6-1924.

(AY 28   See 1924)

ABC 29   Reclassified AH, 9-1900;
           W/o 30-6-1924;
           Conv. to workman's van DW 652, 17-1-1925;
           Used as mobile classroom at Lakeside, late 1940's;
           W/o, 14-3-1950;
           Demolished c.1964.

(AY 29   See 1924)

1891 4 wheel composite cars   MRC&WCo.   [AI Class]
NR 3   Built 1890;
           Delivered Geraldton aboard the "SS Flinders", 29-4-1891;
           Entered service, 14-5-1891;
           Renumbered AB 260, 1899;
           Reclass. AI, 9-1900;
           Sold GWSA, 17-6-1906;
           Returned WAGR, 15-9-1909;
           Probably stored at Midland;
           To WAGR Sawmills, 20-6-1925;
           Later demolished.

NR 4   Built 1890;
           Delivered Geraldton aboard the "SS Flinders", 29-4-1891;
           Entered service, 14-5-1891;
           Transferred to Eastern Railway 1895, but not numbered.
           Allocated AB 261, 1899;
           (A 4 wheel car was burnt at Mingenew about 15-8-1898. It
           was probably NR 4)
           W/o, 1899.

(30 See Bunbury Cars 1887)
(ACL 30 See 1909)
(ACL 30 See 1911)

1892 Ex MRWA 42' bogie composite cars   LWCo. [42' AC Class]
AB 31   Ex MRWA K 6;
           To WAGR as AB 31;
           Reclassified AC, 9-1900;

Conv. to AF, 8-10-1910;
Frame used for AYE 712, 7-6-1958.

(ACL 31 See AB 250, 1899)
(ACM 31 See AB 250, 1899)

AB 32   Ex MRWA K 7;
           To WAGR AB 32;
           Reclassified AC, 9-1900;
           Conv. to AF, 7-3-1913;
           Coupled to AF 165 from 12-2-1919 till ???
           Frame used for AYE 713, 7-6-1958.

AB 33   Ex MRWA K 8;
           To WAGR as AB 33;
           Reclassified AC, 9-1900;
           Conv. to AF, 23-12-1911;
           Coupled to AF 135 from 4-1919 till ???;
           Painted Larch green, 8-1956;
           Conv. to VW 5078, 23-12-1961
           W/o, 28-6-1976.

AB 34   Ex MRWA K 9;
           To WAGR as AB 34;
           Reclassified AC, 9-1900;
           Conv. to AF, 1910;
           Conv. to ZAF 434, & painted Larch green, 1952.

AB 35   Ex MRWA K 10;
           To WAGR as AB 35; Reclassified AC, 9-1900;
           Conv. to AF, 30-9-1911;
           Coupled to AF 171 from 30-5-1919 till ???;
           Painted Larch green, ?-195?;
           W/o, 26-7-1962.

1892 6 wheeled mail van.   [AK Class]
T ???   Numbered 251, 1899;
           Reclass. AK 9-1900;
           Conv. to AS class luggage van, 11-1904;
           Conv. to Z 6790, 19-5-1906/7-1906;
           To Z 109, 8-1939;
           Destroyed when run into by goods train, Bakers Hill, 4-2-1949;
           W/o, 13-6-1949.

1893 First class "Gilbert" cars   Gilbert Car Mfg. Co.   [AG Class]
AB 36   Delivered Fremantle aboard "SS Nairnshire", 13-12-1892;
           Reclass. AG, 9-1900;
           Conv. to AL, 1903;
           Painted Larch green, 6-1954;
           Last used at Narrogin;
           W/o, 15-6-1959.

AB 37   Delivered Fremantle aboard "SS Nairnshire", 13-12-1892;
           Conv. A class inspection car, 17-5-1898;
           Reclass. AL, 9-1900;
           Painted Larch green, 3-1954;
           Last used at Kalgoorlie;
           W/o, 13-6-1961.

AB 38   Delivered Fremantle aboard "SS Nairnshire", 13-12-1892;
           Reclass. AG, 9-1900;
           Conv. to Exhibition car, c.1922;
           Conv. to AL, 1928;
           Painted Larch green, ?-195?;
           Conv. to VW 5080, 17-12-1962;
           W/o, 19-6-1967;
           To Castledare Live Steam Railway Club, Ferndale, 29-9-1967;
           Burnt by vandals.

AB 39   Delivered Fremantle aboard "SS Nairnshire", 13-12-1892;
           Conv. to A class inspection car, 20-12-1898;
           Reclass. AL, 9-1900;
           Painted Larch green, 9-1952;
           Last used at Perth;
           W/o, 18-5-1965;

AB 40   Delivered Fremantle aboard "SS Nairnshire", 13-12-1892;
           Reclass. AG, 9-1900;
           Conv. to AM Ministerial car, 10-8-1907;

Painted Larch green, 5-1952;
Reclass. AL, 13-1-1961 (conv. at Bunbury);
W/o, 12-7-1971;
Preserved ARHS Rail Transport Museum, Bassendean.

1893 Composite "Gilbert" cars   Gilbert Car Mfg. Co.   [AG Class]
AB 41   Delivered Fremantle aboard "SS Nairnshire", 13-12-1892;
Reclassified AG, 9-1900;
Conv. to survey car;
Conv. to trailer for "Governor" railcars, 21-2-1938 till 30-4-
1940;
Used on recruiting train for RAAF till 1941;
Damaged in accident at Robb's Jetty, 6-7-1944;
W/o, 30-9-1944.

AB 42   Delivered Fremantle aboard "SS Nairnshire", 13-12-1892;
Reclassified AG, 9-1900;
Conv. to trailer for "Governor" railcars, 27-11-1938 till 1939;
Used on recruiting train for RAAF till 1941:
W/o, 2-10-1951;
Sold to Albany Harbour Board as mobile office;
Burnt.

AB 43   Delivered Fremantle aboard "SS Nairnshire", 13-12-1892;
Reclassified AG, 9-1900;
Conv. to survey car;
Conv. to trailer for "Governor" railcars, 13-4-1938;
Destroyed in accident at Wooroloo when it derailed & turned
over, 26-10-1938;
W/o, 31-12-1938.

AB 44   Delivered Fremantle aboard "SS Nairnshire", 13-12-1892;
Reclassified AG, 9-1900;
Conv. to trailer for "Governor" railcars, 9-2-1938 till 1939;
Used on recruiting train for RAAF till 1941;
Destroyed in derailment at Robb's Jetty, 6-7-1944;
W/o, 30-9-1944.

AB 45   Delivered Fremantle aboard "SS Nairnshire", 13-12-1892;
Reclassified AG, 9-1900;
Conv. to bath car for RESO trains, 3-10-1928;
Replaced by AGS 17, 1935;
Bath fittings removed 21-12-1935 & car to District Engineer,
Geraldton;
Conv. to trailer for "Governor" railcars, 1-3-1938 till 30-4-1940;
Used on recruiting train for RAAF till 1941;
W/o, 22-12-1945;
Fitted out as sleeping van, & to Pinjarra, 7-9-1946;
To Northam, 28-6-1949;
Demolished at Toodyay, 4-7-1963.

1895 Composite bogie brake cars   MRC&WCo.   [AD Class]
AB 46   Reclassified AD, 9-1900;
W/o 22-3-1955 & scrapped.

AB 47   Reclassified AD, 9-1900;
Painted Larch green, 5-1953;
W/o, 5-1959.

AB 48   Reclassified AD, 9-1900;
Painted Larch green, 7-1956?;
Suffered side damage & entered shops for repair, 27-6-1966,
but work never done;
W/o 8-8-1966 & demolished.

AB 49   Reclassified AD, 9-1900;
Damaged in paintshop fire, Midland, 10-12-1909;
Rebuilt as AD, so presumably damaged & not destroyed;
Re-issued to traffic, 3-2-1912;
Painted Larch green, 7-1955;
Collided with ADG 606, at Perth Carriage Sheds(?), 23 -5-1962
W/o, 26-7-1962.

AB 50   Reclassified AD, 9-1900;
Painted Larch green, 4-1954;
W/o, 4-5-1967.

AB 51   Reclassified AD, 9-1900;
Painted Larch green, 9-1955;

W/o, 31-5-1967.

AB 52   Reclassified AD, 9-1900;
Conv. to second class, 1935;
Reclass. ADS, 23-4-1937;
Painted Larch green, 6-1955;
Fitted with underframe from ZAF 431, 9-11-1956;
W/o, 25-7-1960.

AB 53   Reclassified AD, 9-1900;
Painted Larch green, 10-1953;
W/o, 11-10-1956.

AB 54   Reclassified AD, 9-1900;
Painted Larch green, 2-1952;
W/o, 21-5-1959.

AB 55   Reclassified AD, 9-1900;
Conv. to second class, 1935;
Reclass. ADS, 23-4-1937;
Painted Larch green, 4-1955;
W/o, 21-5-1959.

1895 Composite bogie cars   OC&WCo.   [AC Class]
AB56   Reclassified AC, 9-1900;
Conv. to second class & reclass. AF, 13-4-1911;
Coupled to AF 167, 30-6-1919 till ???;
W/o, 17-8-1955;
Demolished, 20-8-1955.

AB 57   Reclassified AC, 9-1900
Conv. to second class & reclass. AF, 21-12-1912;
Coupled to AF 144, 5-1919 to ???;
Painted Larch green, 9-1953;
Frame used for AYE 711, 7-6-1958.

AB 58   Reclassified AC, 9-1900
Conv. to second class & reclass. AF, 8-4-1911;
Coupled to AF 132, 30-5-1919 till ???;
W/o, 17-8-1955;
Demolished, 20-8-1955.

AB 59   Reclassified AC, 9-1900
Frame used to build AF class car, 1-12-1922.
(AF 59 see 1922)

AB 60   Reclassified AC, 9-1900
Rebuilt as AK class, 25-7-1942.

(AK 60 See 1942)

AB 61   Built 1896
Reclassified AC, 9-1900;
Conv. to second class & reclass. AF, 8-11-1935;
W/o, 3-8-1946.

AB 62   Built 1896;
Reclassified AC, 9-1900
Conv. to second class & reclass. AF, 7-12-1912;
Painted Larch green, 2-1958;
W/o, 15-12-1966.

AB 63   Built 1896;
Reclassified AC, 9-1900;
Conv. to second class & reclass. AF, 3-5-1935;
Painted Larch green, 10-1956;
W/o, 30-11-1960.

AB 64   Built 1896;
Reclassified AC, 9-1900
Conv. to second class & reclass. AF, 4-10-1913;
W/o, 31-3-1940;
Frame used to build AJ class steel bodied car.

(AJ 64 See 1940)

AB 65   Built 1896;
Reclassified AC, 9-1900;
W/o, 17-8-1955.

1895/96 6 wheel mail vans   WAGR Fremantle.   [Class. AK 9-1900]

T ???   Renumbered 252, 1899;
             Reclassified AK, 9-1900
             Conv. to AS class luggage van, 8-1904;
             Conv. to Z 6789, 7-1906;
             Renumbered Z 108, 11-1938;
             W/o, 4-12-1968.

T ???   Renumbered 253, 1899;
             Reclassified AK, 9-1900;
             Conv. to AS class luggage van, 11-1904;
             Rebuilt as Z 6785, 7-1906;
             To Z.107 (?), 1-1940.

1895/96 4 wheeled car WAGR Fremantle?

AB(?)201   Built 1888 as P class breakdown van;
             Entered service 1-8-1888;
             Conv. to passenger car, 1895/96;
             Conv. back to P class breakdown van, c.1899;
             Reclass. As D 201;
             W/o, 7-3-1954.

1895 Bogie cars fitted with lavatories   BM&Co.   [AC Class, later ACE]

AB 66   Reclassified AC (composite car), 9-1900
             Reclass. ACE 6-1-1906;
             Conv. to AC by altering the lavatory compartment to a
             passenger compartment, 10-8-1923;
             Conv. to AF, 8-11-1935;
             Was to have been rebuilt as AK class steel bodied car, but no
             materials available;
             W/o, 30-11-1942.

AB 67   Reclassified AC (composite car), 9-1900;
             Reclass. ACE, 1-11-1906;
             Conv. to AC by altering the lavatory compartment to a
             passenger compartment, 8-5-1925;
             Demolished, 30-9-1955;
             W/o, 10-10-1955.

AB 68   Reclassified AC (composite car), 9-1900;
             Reclass. ACE, 3-5-1907;
             Conv. to AC by altering the lavatory compartment to a
             passenger compartment, 24-8-1923;
             Painted Larch green, 8-1953;
             W/o, 30-11-1960.

AB 69   Reclassified AC (composite car), 9-1900;
             Reclass. ACE, 1-11-1906;
             Conv. to AC by altering the lavatory compartment to a
             passenger compartment, 20-6-1924;
             Conv. to AF, 2-10-1935;
             W/o, 31-5-1940;
             Frame used for steel bodied AJ class car.

(AJ 69   See 1940)

AB 70   Destroyed in accident at Stoneville, 30-6-1896.

(ACL 70 See 1909)
(ACL 70 See 1911)

AB 71   Reclassified AC (composite car), 9-1900:
             Reclass. ACE, 13-7-1908;
             Conv. to AC by altering the lavatory compartment to a
             passenger compartment, 3-1-1925;
             W/o, 17-8-1955.

AB 72   Reclassified AC (composite car), 9-1900;
             Reclass. ACE, 1-11-1906;
             Conv. to AC by altering the lavatory compartment to a
             passenger compartment, 9-4-1925;
             Demolished 3-9-1955;
             W/o, 14-9-1955.

AB 73   Reclassified AC (composite car), 9-1900;
             Reclass. ACE, 1-11-1906;
             Conv. to AC by altering the lavatory compartment to
             a passenger compartment, 1-12-1924;
             Conv. to AYE 702, 18-6-1955.

AB 74   Reclassified AC (composite car), 9-1900;
             Reclass. ACE, 3-5-1907;
             Conv. to AC by altering the lavatory compartment to a
             Passenger compartment, 7-12-1923;
             Conv. to AF, 8-10-1935;
             Repainted Larch green, 5-1955;
             W/o, 25-7-1960.

AB 75   Reclassified AC (composite car), 9-1900;
             Reclass. ACE, 7-1-1907;
             Conv. to AC by altering the lavatory compartment to a
             passenger compartment, 19-12-1924;
             Conv. to AF 3-7-1935;
             W/o 22-3-1955.
             Frame to brakevan Z.452, 18-6-1955;
             W/o, 19-11-1985.

AB 76   Reclassified AC (composite car), 9-1900;
             Reclass. ACE, 6-1-1906;
             Conv. to AC by altering the lavatory compartment to a
             passenger compartment, 10-7-1925;
             Painted Larch green, 5-1956;
             W/o, 17-8-1955;
             Returned to traffic 18-5-1956;
             W/o again, 21-9-1962.

AB 77   Reclassified AC (composite car), 9-1900;
             Reclass. ACE, 1-11-1906;
             Conv. to AC by altering the lavatory compartment to a
             passenger compartment, 8-8-1924;
             W/o, 17-8-1955.

AB 78   Reclassified AC (composite car), 9-1900;
             Reclass. ACE,   -1906;
             Conv. to AC by altering the lavatory compartment to a
             passenger compartment, 24-12-1925;
             Conv. to AF 8-11-1935;
             Conv. to brakevan ZAF 432,   -10-1952;
             W/o 11-10-1956.

AB 79   Reclassified AC (composite car), 9-1900;
             Reclass. ACE, 1-11-1906;
             Conv. to AC by altering the lavatory compartment to a
             passenger compartment, 10-8-1923;
             Conv. to AF, 23-8-1935;
             W/o, 22-3-1955.

AB 80   Reclassified AC (composite car), 9-1900;
             Reclass. ACE, 6-1-1906;
             Conv. to AC by altering the lavatory compartment to a
             passenger compartment, 5-10-1923;
             W/o, 14-8-1964.

AB 81   Reclassified AC (composite car), 9-1900;
             Reclass. ACE, 6-1-1906;
             Conv. to AC by altering the lavatory compartment to a
             passenger compartment, 24-12-1925;
             Conv. to AF 6-9-1935;
             Repainted Larch green, 1-1956;
             W/o, 21-5-1959.

AB 82   Reclassified AC (composite car), 9-1900;
             Reclass. ACE, 1-11-1906;
             Conv. to AC by altering the lavatory compartment to a
             passenger compartment, 24-12-1925;
             W/o, 17-8-1955.

AB 83   Reclassified AC (composite car), 9-1900;
             Reclass. ACE, 6-1-1906;
             Conv. to AC by altering the lavatory compartment to a
             passenger compartment, 19-9-1924;
             Painted Larch green, 12-1954;
             W/o, 4-4-1960.

AB 84   Reclassified AC (composite car), 9-1900;
             Reclass. ACE, 1-11-1906;

Conv. to AC by altering the lavatory compartment to a
passenger compartment, 6-3-1925;
W/o, 22-3-1955.

AB 85   Reclassified AC (composite car), 9-1900;
Reclass. ACE, 6-1-1906;
Conv. to AC by altering the lavatory compartment to a
passenger compartment, 15-8-1924;
Conv. to AF 30-7-1935;
Repainted Larch green, 8-1954;
W/o, 4-4-1960.

1895 Ministerial Saloon   BRC&WCo.   [AM Class]
-    Originally unclassed & not numbered;
Delivered aboard the "SS Gulf of Lions", 30-1-1895;
AM 261   Classified AM & numbered 261, 9-1900
Conv. to AF, 15-3-1922;
Painted Larch green 2-1958;
Conv. to breakdown van VC 2100, painted yellow, 10-9-1965;
W/o, 21-8-1974;
Pres. at ARHS Rail Transport Museum, Bassendean, 10-1974.

1896 Bogie mail vans   ARC&WCo.   [AK Class]
T ???   Numbered T 254;
Reclassified AK, 9-1900;
Reclass. P 669, 30-6-1940;
Used on ambulance train for Commonwealth Govt, 1942;
W/o, 27-8-1952.

T ???   Numbered T 255;
Reclassified AK, 9-1900;
Reclass. P 718, 30-6-1940;
Used on ambulance train for Commonwealth Govt, 1942;
W/o, 4-11-1960.

1896 First class sleeping cars   MRC&WCo.   [AP Class]
A 86   Entered service, 9-3-1896;
Reclassified AP, 9-1900;
Conv. to AF, 29-8-1903;
W/o 22-12-1946;
Conv. to locomotive instruction van VI 7979, 6-4-1946;
W/o 24-9-1971

A 87   Entered service, 9-3-1896;
Reclassified AP, 9-1900;
Conv. to AF, 23-1-1903;
Conv. to APT blood transfusion car, 23-10-1948;
Conv. to VW 2145, 12-11-1957
W/o, 28-6-1976;
To ARHS, 9-1990.

A 88   Entered service, 9-3-1896;
Reclassified AP, 9-1900;
Conv. to AF, 22-8-1903;
W/o 1-8-1950;
Conv. to VW 5065, 30-6-1952;
W/o, 28-6-1976.

(ALT 88 See A 93)

A 89   Entered service, 9-3-1896;
Reclassified AP, 9-1900;
Conv. to AA, 6-5-1905;
Conv. to VW 5066, 27-10-1958;
W/o, 10-3-1976;
Preserved at Esperance Museum.

A 90   Entered service, 15-4-1896;
Reclassified AP, 9-1900;
Conv. to VW 2142, 22-12-1951;
W/o, 7-11-1973.

A 91   Entered service, 15-4-1896;
Reclassified AP, 9-1900;
Repainted Larch green, 11-1954;
W/o 3-5-1963;
Frame used for QS class wagon.

A 92   Entered service, 15-4-1896;

Reclassified AP, 9-1900;
Repainted Larch green, 4-1952;
W/o, 3-5-1963;
Frame used for QS class wagon.

A 93   Entered service, 15-4-1896;
Reclassified AP, 9-1900;
Conv. to AF, 30-6-1903;
Conv. to track recorder car VT 4998, 9-6-1951;
ALT 88   Reclass. ALT 88, 1-9-1951;
Painted Larch green during the 1950's;
Reclass. AL 88, 24-12-1960;
W/o   -1980;
To Kalgoorlie-Boulder Loopline Preservation Society, 6-1980.

1896 Bogie composite cars   MRC&WCo.   [AC Class]
AB 94   Reclassified AC, 9-1900;
Conv. to AF, 17-5-1935;
W/o, 3-8-1946.

AB 95   Reclassified AC, 9-1900;
Conv. to AF, 11-2-1911;
W/o, 31-3-1940;
Frame used for AJ class steel bodied car.

(AJ 95 See 1940)

AB 96   Reclassified AC, 9-1900;
Painted Larch green, 1-1953;
W/o, 30-11-1960.

AB 97   Reclassified AC, 9-1900;
Painted Larch green, 10-1956?;
W/o, 30-11-1960.

AB 98   Reclassified AC, 9-1900;
W/o, 22-3-1955.

AB 99   Reclassified AC, 9-1900;
Conv. to AF 15-6-1934;
Demolished & frame used for AYE 703, 24-5-1955

AB 100   Reclassified AC, 9-1900;
Conv. to AF, 12-12-1913;
Coupled to AF 131/132 (?) from 20-3-1919 till ???;
W/o, 17-8-1955;
Demolished 20-8-1955.

AB 101   Reclassified AC, 9-1900;
Conv. to AF, 1-6-1934;
W/o, 22-12-1945.

AB 102   Reclassified AC, 9-1900;
Conv. to AF, 29-11-1913;
Conv. to brakevan ZAF 431, 18-10-1952;
W/o, 11-10-1956;
Frame to ADS 52, 9-11-1956.

AB 103   Reclassified AC, 9-1900;
W/o, 22-12-1945.

AB 104   Reclassified AC, 9-1900;
W/o, 17-8-1955;
Demolished 3-9-1955.

AB 105   Reclassified AC, 9-1900;
Conv. to AF, 29-3-1934;
W/o 22-12-1945.

1897 Brake Composite cars 106-117 BC&WCo. 118-125 BM&Co.
[AD Class]
AB 106   Reclassified AD, 9-1900;
Painted Larch green, 5-1953;
W/o, 30-6-1958.

AB 107   Reclassified AD, 9-1900;
Painted Larch green, 2-1952;

To VW 5079, 23-12-1961;
      W/o, 28-6-1976.

AB 108   Reclassified AD, 9-1900;
          Painted Larch green, 3-1952;
          W/o, 19-4-1968.

AB 109   Reclassified AD, 9-1900;
          Painted Larch green, 7-1954;
          W/o, 25-7-1960.

AB 110   Reclassified AD, 9-1900;
          Painted Larch green, 3-1953;
          Wrecked in collision with Pmr 728, 28-12-1962;
          W/o, 5-4-1963.

AB 111   Reclassified AD, 9-1900;
          Painted Larch green, 10-1951;
          W/o, 25-7-1960.

AB 112   Reclassified AD, 9-1900;
          Painted Larch green, 10-1955;
          W/o, 23-9-1966.

AB 113   Reclassified AD, 9-1900;
          W/o, 22-3-1955.
          Frame to brakevan Z.456, 18-6-1955;
          W/o, 19-11-1985.

AB 114   Reclassified AD, 9-1900;
          Conv. to second class brake car, 1905;
          Reclass. ADS 18-6-1937;
          Painted Larch green, 12-1953;
          Damaged in collision, 16-6-1967;
          W/o, 30-10-1967.

AB 115   Reclassified AD, 9-1900;
          Coupled to AE 156 from c.1919 till ???;
          Painted Larch green, 5-1953;
          Fitted with underframe from AF 57, 20-12-1956;
          W/o, 25-7-1960.

AB 116   Reclassified AD, 9-1900;
          Destroyed in head on collision at Fremantle Yard, 31-7-1947;
          W/o, 7-10-1947.

AB 117   Reclassified AD, 9-1900;
          Damaged in paint shop fire at Midland, 10-12-1909;
          Rebuilt as AD & re-entered service, 3-2-1912;
          Painted Larch green, 8-1952;
          W/o, 8-2-1967.

AB 118   Reclassified AD, 9-1900;
          Conv. to second class brake car, 1905;
          Reclass. ADS, 18-6-1937;
          Painted Larch green, 12-1952;
          W/o, 30-11-1960.

AB 119   Reclassified AD, 9-1900;
          Conv. second class brake car, 1905;
          Reclass. ADS, 21-5-1937;
          Used as temporary diesel railcar trailer;
          Frame used for AYE 701, 11-6-1955.

AB 120   Reclassified AD, 9-1900;
          W/o, 17-8-1955;
          Demolished 27-8-1955.

AB 121   Reclassified AD, 9-1900;
          Conv. to second class brake car, 1905;
          Fitted with electric lighting 30-6-1914;
          Reclass. ADS, 18-6-1937;
          Painted Larch green, 8-1953;
          W/o, 30-8-1962.

AB 122   Reclassified AD, 9-1900;
          Used as diesel railcar trailer at Bunbury;
          Painted Larch green, 7-1952;
          W/o, 21-1-1963.

AB 123   Reclassified AD, 9-1900;
          Painted Larch green, 7-1953;
          W/o, 12-5-1964.

AB 124   Reclassified AD, 9-1900;
          Fitted with enlarged brake compartment, 1945;
          Painted Larch green, 9-1954;
          W/o, 25-7-1960.

AB 125   Reclassified AD, 9-1900;
          Conv. to second class car, 1935;
          Reclass. ADS, 23-4-1937;
          Reconv. to AD, 14-9-1943;
          Painted Larch green, 2-1954;
          W/o, 26-7-1962.

__1897 First class car with lavatory   GRC&WCo.   [AE Class]__
AB 126   Reclassified AE, 9-1900;
          Conv. to AF, 9-9-1939;
          W/o, 17-8-1955;
          Demolished 3-9-1955.

AB 127   Reclassified AE, 9-1900;
          Coupled to AE 199 from 8-1917 till ???;
          W/o, 16-2-1951.

AB 128   Reclassified AE, 9-1900;
          Coupled to AE 160 from 8-1917 till ???;
          Conv. to AF, 1939;
          Reconv. to AE, 1940;
          Repainted Larch green, 7-1953;
          W/o, 21-9-1962.

AB 129   Reclassified AE, 9-1900;
          Coupled to AE 159 from 8-1917 till ???;
          Conv. to AF, 9-10-1942;
          W/o, 17-8-1955;
          Demolished 30-9-1955.

AB 130   Reclassified AE, 9-1900;
          Conv. to AF, 7-11-1941;
          W/o, 22-12-1945.

__1897 Second class car with lavatory   GRC&WCo.   [AF Class]__
AB 131   Built 1896;
          Reclassified AF, 9-1900;
          Coupled to AF 100 from 3-1919 till ???;
          W/o, 22-3-1955;
          Frame to brakevan Z 457, 18-6-1955;
          W/o, 29-4-1985.

AB 132   Built 1896;
          Reclassified AF, 9-1900;
          Coupled to AF 58 from 30-5-1919 till ???;
          W/o, 22-3-1955.

AB 133   Reclassified AF, 9-1900;
          W/o 17-8-1955;
          Demolished 27-8-1955.

AB 134   Reclassified AF, 9-1900;
          Burnt in paint shop fire, Midland, 10-12-1909.

(AT 134 See 1911)

AB 135   Reclassified AF, 9-1900;
          Coupled to AF 33 from 4-1919 till ???;
          Conv. to workman's van VW 5075, 28-10-1961;
          W/o, 16-10-1963.

AB 136   Reclassified AF, 9-1900;
          W/o, 22-3-1955.
          Frame to brakevan Z 459, 18-6-1955;
          W/o, 28-8-1985.

AB 137   Reclassified AF, 9-1900;
          Coupled to AF 172 from 20-3-1919 till ???;
          W/o, 16-2-1950.

AB 138   Reclassified AF, 9-1900;
            Coupled to AF 62 from 30-6-1919 till ???;
            W/o, 17-8-1955.

AB 139   Reclassified AF, 9-1900;
            Burnt in paint shop fire, Midland, 10-12-1909.

(AT 139 See 1911)

AB 140   Reclassified AF, 9-1900;
            Frame used to build AYE 704, 28-5-1955.

AB 141   Reclassified AF, 9-1900;
            Fitted with electric lighting 12-2-1919;
            Coupled to AF 174 from 12-2-1919 till ???;
            W/o, 18-5-1956;
            Frame used to build Z van.

AB 142   Reclassified AF, 9-1900;
            Repainted Larch green, 3-1955;
            W/o, 15-12-1966.

AB 143   Reclassified AF, 9-1900;
            Conv. to brakevan ZAF 430, 18-10-1952;
            W/o, 11-10-1956.

AB 144   Reclassified AF, 9-1900;
            Fitted with electric lighting 6-12-1913;
            Coupled to AF 57 from 5-1919 till ???;
            Involved in collision with a log truck at the East St. level
            crossing, East Guildford, 24-10-1947;
            W/o, 30-10-1947.

AB 145   Reclassified AF, 9-1900;
            Burnt in paint shop fire, Midland, 10-12-1909.

(AT 145 See 1911)

1898 First class sleeping cars   MRC&WCo.   [AP Class]
A 146   Reclassified AP, 9-1900;
            Conv. APC class composite car, 4-9-1920;
            Reconv. to AP, 1949;
            Repainted Larch green, 6-1953;
            W/o, 3-5-1963;
            Frame used to build QS class wagon.

A 147   Reclassified AP, 9-1900;
            Conv. APS second class car, 15-3-1920;
            Conv. to APC composite car, 13-11-1941;
            Reconv. to AP by removal of top bunks, 29-10-1948;
            Repainted Larch green, 8-1953;
            W/o, 3-5-1963;
            Frame used to build QS class wagon.

A 148   Reclassified AP, 9-1900;
            MRWA in exchange for JA 22, 3-5-1915;
            To WAGR as tractor driver's van, 8-1964;
            Entered service as VW 40763, 7-10-1966;
            Stowed Midland & w/o;
            To York Railway station for display;
            To Pemberton.

A 149   Reclassified AP, 9-1900;
            Conv. to APS second class car, 15-3-1920;
            Conv. APC class composite car, 13-11-1941;
            Reconv. to AP, 27-11-1948;
            Repainted Larch green, 6-1952;
            W/o, 3-5-1963.

A 150   Reclassified AP, 9-1900;
            Repainted Larch green, 6-1952;
            W/o, 3-5-1963;
            Frame used to build QS class wagon.

A 151   Reclassified AP, 9-1900;
            Conv. APC class composite car, 21-3-1924;
            Reconv. to AP, 4-12-1948;
            Repainted Larch green, 8-1955;
            Conv. to workman's van VW 5070, 7-8-1961;

W/o, 28-6-1976.

A 152   Reclassified AP, 9-1900;
            Repainted Larch green, 6-1952;
            W/o, 3-5-1963;
            Frame used to build QS class wagon.

A 153   Reclassified AP, 9-1900;
            Repainted Larch green, 3-1952;
            W/o, 26-7-1962;
            Frame used to build QS class wagon.

A 154   Reclassified AP, 9-1900;
            Conv. APC class composite car, 21-12-1923;
            Reconv. to oil lighting, 6-9-1938;
            To Port Hedland, 7-9-1938;
            W/o in Port Hedland, 1-11-1951;
            Believed to have been burnt.

A 155   Reclassified AP, 9-1900;
            Fitted with electric lighting 6-12-1924;
            Repainted Larch green, 11-1954;
            W/o, 3-5-1963;
            Frame used to build QS class wagon.

1898 First class car with lavatory   GRC&WCo.   [AE Class]
AB 156   Reclassified AE, 9-1900;
            Coupled to AD 115, c.1919 till ???;
            Conv. to AF, 15-2-1940;
            W/o, 22-3-1955.
            Frame to brakevan Z 460, 18-6-1955;
            W/o, 29-4-1985.

AB 157   Reclassified AE, 9-1900;
            Conv. to AF, 8-12-1941;
            Conv. to brakevan ZAF 433, 8-10-1952;
            Frame used to build AYE 709, 18-6-1955.

AB 158   Reclassified AE, 9-1900;
            Conv. to AF, 23-8-1939;
            Reconv. to AE, 19-4-1940;
            Repainted Larch green, 12-1953;
            W/o, 21-5-1959.

AB 159   Reclassified AE, 9-1900;
            Coupled to AE 129 from 8-1917 till ???;
            Conv. to AF, 20-4-1942;
            W/o, 17-8-1955;
            Demolished, 30-9-1955.

(ZA 159 – 173 see 1902)

AB 160   Reclassified AE, 9-1900;
            Coupled to AE 128 from 8-1917 till ???;
            Conv. to AF, 29-9-1939;
            Reconv. to AE, 15-2-1940;
            Reconv. to AF 29-1-1943;
            Frame used to build AYE 705, 11-6-1955.

AB 161   Reclassified AE, 9-1900;
            Conv. to AF, 25-5-1940;
            Reconv. to AE, 18-9-1942;
            Repainted Larch green, 3-1954;
            W/o, 4-4-1960.

AB 162   Reclassified AE, 9-1900;
            Repainted Larch green, 4-1953;
            W/o, 22-4-1964;
            Conv. to workman's van VW 5136, 4-1969.

AB 163   Reclassified AE, 9-1900;
             Conv. to AF, 25-8-1939;
            Repainted Larch green, 3-1954;
            W/o, 21-5-1959.

1898 Bogie Mail Van   ARC&ICo.   [AK Class]
T ???   Numbered T.256;
            Reclassified AK, 9-1900;

Reclass. P 754, 30-6-1940;
Used on ambulance train for Commonwealth Govt, 1942;
Returned, 1945;
Involved in collision;
W/o, 11-10-1950.

T ???   Numbered T.257;
Reclassified AK, 9-1900;
Reclass. P 788, 30-6-1940;
Used on ambulance train for Commonwealth Govt, 1942;
Returned, 1945;
W/o 29-5-1959.

1898 Second class cars   GRC&WCo.   [AF Class]
AB 164 Reclassified AF, 9-1900;
Coupled to AF 169, 4-1917 till ???;
Destroyed in head on collision at Fremantle Yard, 31-7-1947;
W/o, 7-10-1947.

AB 165 Reclassified AF, 9-1900;
Coupled to AF 32, 12-2-1919 till ???;
W/o, 17-8-1955;
Demolished, 21-10-1955.

AB 166 Reclassified AF, 9-1900;
W/o 30-4-1940;
Frame used to build AJ class steel bodied car.

(AJ 166 See 1940)
(ZA 166 see 1902)

AB 167 Reclassified AF, 9-1900;
Coupled to AF 56, 30-6-1919 till ???;
Frame used for AYE 705, 11-6-1955.

AB 168 Reclassified AF, 9-1900;
Repainted Larch green, 12-1951;
W/o, 30-8-1965;
Conv. to workman's van VW 5135, 5-1969.

AB 169 Reclassified AF, 9-1900;
Coupled to AF 164, 4-1917 till ???;
W/o, 17-8-1955;
Demolished, 3-9-1955.

AB 170 Reclassified AF, 9-1900;
W/o, 8-12-1950.

AB 171 Reclassified AF, 9-1900;
Coupled to AF 35 from 30-5-1919 till ???;
Repainted Larch green, 8-1954;
W/o, 15-12-1966.

AB 172 Reclassified AF, 9-1900;
Fitted with electric lighting, 19??;
Coupled to AF 132/137(?) from 20-3-1919 till ???;
Repainted Larch green, 4-1956;
W/o, 15-12-1966.

AB 173 Reclassified AF, 9-1900;
W/o, -1950;
Conv. to workman's van VW 5063, 30-6-1952;
W/o 1976.

AB 174 Reclassified AF, 9-1900;
Fitted with electric lighting, 19-12-1914;
Coupled to AF 141 from 12-2-1919 till ???;
W/o, 22-12-1945.

AB 175 Reclassified AF, 9-1900;
Repainted Larch green, 12-1954;
W/o, 21-9-1962.

1896 Ex GSR Brake composite cars   MRC&WCo.   [AD Class]
AB 176 Built 1887 for the GSR, no. unknown;
To WAGR, 1-12-1896;
Numbered AB 176;
Reclassified AD, 9-1900;
Reclassified AD, 9-1900;

Painted Larch green, 2-1953;
Doors screwed shut & seats removed for use on suburban goods trains (stencilled "Suburban Goods Traffic Only"), 21-12-1965;
W/o, 5-4-1967.

AB 177 Built 1887 for the GSR, no. unknown;
To WAGR, 1-12-1896;
Numbered AB 177;
Reclassified AD, 9-1900;
Conv. to second class brake car, 1905:
Reclass. ADS, 18-6-1937;
Repainted Larch green, 5-1953;
W/o, 21-5-1959.

AB 178 Built 1887 for the GSR, no. unknown;
To WAGR, 1-12-1896;
Numbered AB 178;
Reclassified AD, 9-1900;
Conv. to second class brake car, 21-12-1934;
Reclass. ADS, 23-4-1937;
W/o, 16-2-1951.

AB 179 Built 1887 for the GSR, no. unknown;
To WAGR, 1-12-1896;
Numbered AB 179;
Reclassified AD, 9-1900;
Painted Larch green, 12-1952;
W/o, 6-2-1966.

AB 180 Built 1887 for the GSR, no. unknown;
To WAGR, 1-12-1896;
Numbered AB 180;
Reclassified AD, 9-1900;
Conv. to second class brake car, 1935;
Reclass. ADS, 23-4-1937;
Repainted Larch green, 2-1954;
W/o, 29-4-1965.

1896 Ex GSR Bogie composite cars   MRC&WCo.   [AC Class]
AB 181 Built in 1888 for the GSR, no. unknown;
Arrived Albany on the "Morialta", 2-10-1888;
To WAGR, 1-12-1896;
Renumbered AB 181;
Reclassified AC, 9-1900;
Conv. to AF second class car, 29-6-1907;
Painted Larch green, 5-1954;
Wrecked in collision with Pmr 728, 28-12-1962;
W/o 5-4-1963.

AB 182 Built in 1888 for the GSR, no. unknown;
Arrived Albany on the "Morialta", 2-10-1888;
To WAGR, 1-12-1896;
Renumbered AB 182;
Reclassified AC, 9-1900;
Painted Larch green, 12-1953;
W/o, 15-12-1966.

AB 183 Built in 1888 for the GSR, no. unknown;
Arrived Albany on the "Morialta", 2-10-1888;
To WAGR, 1-12-1896;
Renumbered AB 183;
Reclassified AC, 9-1900;
Fitted with electric lighting, 1-11-1930;
Conv. to AF second class car, 11-5-1934;
Painted Larch green, 11-1953;
W/o, 30-11-1960.

AB 184 Built in 1888 for the GSR, no. unknown;
Arrived Albany on the "Morialta", 2-10-1888;
To WAGR, 1-12-1896;
Renumbered AB 184;
Reclassified AC, 9-1900;
Conv. to AF second class car, 4-10-1912;
Painted Larch green, 8-1954;
W/o 30-11-1960.

1896 Ex GSR brake composite car   MRC&WCo.   [AD Class]
AB 185 Built 1887 for the GSR, no. unknown;
To WAGR, 1-12-1896;

Numbered AB 185;
Reclassified AD, 9-1900;
Fitted with electric lighting, 29-5-1914;
Painted Larch green, 7-1953;
W/o, 25-7-1960.

AB 186   Built 1887 for the GSR, no. unknown;
To WAGR, 1-12-1896;
Numbered AB 186;
Reclassified AD, 9-1900;
Conv. to second class brake car, 1905;
Fitted with acetylene lighting as a trial from 1907 to 1930
Reclass. ADS, 18-6-1937;
Repainted Larch green, 2-1952;
W/o, 3-8-1961.

AB 187   Built 1887 for the GSR, no. unknown;
To WAGR, 1-12-1896;
Numbered AB 187;
Reclassified AD, 9-1900;
Fitted with electric lighting 11-4-1914;
Conv. to second class brake car, 1935;
Reclass. ADS, 21-5-1937;
Repainted Larch green, 2-1952;
W/o, 31-5-1967;
Frame possibly to Jetty 336.

AB 188   Built 1887 for the GSR, no. unknown;
To WAGR, 1-12-1896;
Numbered AB 188;
Reclassified AD, 9-1900;
AX 188   Rebuilt as AX class composite saloon, 28-3-1906;
W/o, 18-8-1950;
Conv. for use as office & store at Collie.

AB 189   Built 1887 for the GSR, no. unknown;
To WAGR, 1-12-1896;
Numbered AB 189;
Reclassified AD, 9-1900;
AX 189   Rebuilt as AX class composite saloon, 6-10-1906;
Destroyed in paint shop fire, Midland, 10-12-1909.

(ACL 189 See 1911)

1896 Ex GSR 4 wheeled inspection car   Craven Bros.   [AL Class]
A 190   Built 1888 for the GSR, no. unknown;
Entered service, 22-11-1888;
Rebuilt on 6 wheeled frame in early 1890's as General
Manager's saloon;
To WAGR, 1-12-1896;
Renumbered A 190;
Reclassified AL, 9-1900;
Destroyed in accident, 6-6-1916.

1898 First class cars   GRC&WCo.   [AE Class]
AB 191   Delivered 10-1897
Entered service 3-1898
Reclassified AE, 9-1900;
Destroyed in paintshop fire, Midland, 10-12-1909.

(ACL 191 See 1911)

AB 192   Delivered 10-1897
Entered service 3-1898
Reclassified AE, 9-1900;
Conv. to AF, 15-2-1940;
W/o, 3-8-1946.

AB 193   Delivered 10-1897
Entered service 3-1898
Reclassified AE, 9-1900;
Damaged in collision at Fremantle, 31-7-1947;
W/o 7-10-1947.

AB 194   Delivered 10-1897
Entered service 3-1898
Reclassified AE, 9-1900;
Conv. to AF, 31-5-1940;
W/o, 1-8-1950;

Conv. to workman's van VW 5064, 30-6-1952;
W/o, 2-12-1977.

AB 195   Delivered 10-1897
Entered service 3-1898
Reclassified AE, 9-1900;
Painted Larch green, 18-9-1953;
Conv. to workman's van VW 5073, 28-10-1961;
W/o, 3-1987.

AB 196   Delivered 10-1897
Entered service 3-1898
Reclassified AE, 9-1900;
Conv. to AF, 25-5-1940;
Reclass. AE, 1947;
Repainted Larch green, 5-1956;
W/o, 21-1-1965.

AB 197   Delivered 10-1897
Entered service 3-1898
Reclassified AE, 9-1900;
Conv. to AF, 31-5-1940;
Frame used for AYE 707, 11-6-1955.

AB 198   Delivered 10-1897
Entered service 3-1898
Reclassified AE, 9-1900;
Conv. to AF, 25-5-1940;
W/o, 22-12-1945.

AB 199   Delivered 10-1897
Entered service 3-1898
Reclassified AE, 9-1900;
Coupled to AE 127 from 8-1917 till ???;
Conv. to AF, 7-11-1941;
W/o, 1-8-1950;
Conv. to workman's van VW 5062, 30-6-1952;
W/o, 23-1-1961.

AB 200   Delivered 10-1897
Entered service 3-1898
Reclassified AE, 9-1900;
Conv. to AF, 9-5-1941;
Frame used for AYE 708, 18-6-1955.

1898 Country Inspector's Van   Midland Workshops.   [BC class]
BC 1926 Conv. from R class wagon, 1898;
Conv. to ZB class brakevan, 1927;
ZB 203   Renumbered ZB 203, 1938;
W/o 24-7-1961.

1899 First class long distance cars   OC&WCo.   [AA Class]
AB 201   Reclassified AA, 9-1900;
Painted Larch green, 9-1952;
W/o 4-3-1965.

(AB 201 See 1895)

AB 202   Reclassified AA, 9-1900;
Reclass. ACL, 17-9-1923;
Painted Larch green, 11-1956;
Painted Larch green & cream, 6-1963;
W/o, 2-7-1968.

AB 203   Reclassified AA, 9-1900;
Reclass. ACL, 27-6-1924;
Painted Larch green, 3-1954;
W/o, 19-8-1963.

(ZB 203 see 1898)

AB 204   Reclassified AA, 9-1900;
Reclass. ACL, 7-9-1923;
Painted Larch green, 3-1957;
W/o, 9-3-1965;
Frame to QS 16113, 20-6-1967.

(ZB 204 see 1933)

AB 205 Reclassified AA, 9-1900;
Painted Larch green, 3-1954;
W/o, 4-3-1965;
Frame to QS class wagon.

AB 206 Reclassified AA, 9-1900;
Rebuilt as AN class Vice Regal car, 20-7-1901;
Reconv. to AA, 8-9-1922;
Painted Larch green, 12-1952;
W/o, 4-3-1965;
Frame to QS 16119, 30-6-1967.

AB 207 Reclassified AA, 9-1900;
Painted Larch green, 10-1955;
W/o, 4-3-1965;
Frame to QS 16108, 3-6-1965;
W/o, 28-2-1978.

AB 208 Reclassified AA, 9-1900;
Painted Larch green, 7-1954;
W/o, 4-3-1965;
Frame to QS 16116, 26-6-1967.

AB 209 Reclassified AA, 9-1900;
Reclass. ACL, 17-4-1924;
Painted Larch green, 6-1955;
W/o, 24-5-1962;
Shopped for repair, 9-11-1966, but not completed;
To Salvage for sale.

AB 210 Reclassified AA, 9-1900;
Reclass. ACL, 16-4-1924;
Painted Larch green, 6-1956;
Conv. to ACM class suburban car, 17-9-1965;
W/o, 31-5-1968;
To Vintage Train at Bunbury, 11-3-1976;
Preserved at Boyanup Transport Museum.

AB 211 Reclassified AA, 9-1900;
Reclass. ACL 14-12-1923;
Painted Larch green, 5-1955;
Conv. to workman's van VW 5067, 8-12-1959;
W/o, 4-3-1982.

AB 212 Reclassified AA, 9-1900;
Painted Larch green, 12-1956;
W/o, 4-3-1965;
Frame to QS 16095, 17-5-1965;
W/o, 31-3-1977.

AB 213 Reclassified AA, 9-1900;
Painted Larch green, 11-1956;
W/o, 4-3-1965;
Frame to QS 16092, 15-5-1965.

AB 214 Reclassified AA, 9-1900;
Painted Larch green, 9-1955?;
W/o, 4-3-1965;
Frame to QS 16104, 25-5-1965.

AB 215 Reclassified AA, 9-1900;
Painted Larch green, 3-1957;
W/o, 4-3-1965;
Frame to QS 16105, 25-5-1965.

AB 216 Reclassified AA, 9-1900;
Painted Larch green, 9-1953?;
W/o, 25-7-1960.

AB 217 Reclassified AA, 9-1900;
Painted Larch green, ?-195?;
W/o, 4-3-1965;
Frame to QS 16109, 3-6-1965.

AB 218 Reclassified AA, 9-1900;
Destroyed in paintshop fire, Midland, 10-12-1909.

(AW 218 See 1911)

AB 219 Reclassified AA, 9-1900;
W/o 2-3-1956.

AB 220 Reclassified AA, 9-1900;
Painted Larch green, ?-195?;
W/o, 4-3-1965;
Frame to QS 16101, 25-5-1965.

1899 Second class long distance cars OC&WCo. [AB Class]

A 221 Reclassified AB, 9-1900;
Painted Larch green, 9-1953;
W/o, 3-8-1956.

A 222 Reclassified AB, 9-1900;
Conv. to composite car, & to MRWA in exchange for a K class car, 30-6-1903;
Numbered J 1;
Converted to crew van, 1953;
Returned to WAGR 1-8-1964, but w/o;
Re-instated as workman's van VW 5121, 4-1970;
W/o
Del. Bassendean 10-1992 for preservation.

(ACL 222 See 1909)
(ACL 222 See 1911)

A 223 Reclassified AB, 9-1900;
Painted Larch green, 10-1952;
W/o, 4-3-1965;
Frame to QS 16110, 1-6-1965.

A 224 Reclassified AB, 9-1900;
Painted Larch green, 9-1956;
W/o, 4-3-1965.

A 225 Reclassified AB, 9-1900;
Conv. to AC class composite car, 2-11-1901;
Reclass. ACL, 1-11-1906;
W/o, 14-3-1957.

A 226 Reclassified AB, 9-1900;
Conv. to AC class composite car, 27-4-1901;
Reclass. ACL, 3-5-1907;
Painted Larch green, 2-1959?;
W/o, 2-7-1968.

A 227 Reclassified AB, 9-1900;
Conv. to AC class composite car, 31-8-1901;
Reclass. ACL, 6-1-1906;
Painted Larch green, 7-1955;
W/o, 9-3-1965.

A 228 Reclassified AB, 9-1900;
Conv. to AC class composite car, 7-9-1901;
Reclass. ACL, 6-1-1906;
Painted Larch green, 9-1955;
W/o, 9-3-1965.

A 229 Reclassified AB, 9-1900;
Conv. to AC class composite car, 27-4-1901;
Reclass. ACL, 13-11-1907;
Painted Larch green, 1-1957;
W/o, 9-3-1965.

A 230 Reclassified AB, 9-1900;
Conv. to AC class composite car, 9-9-1901;
Reclass. ACL, 1-11-1906;
Painted Larch green, 6-1953;
W/o, 23-3-1961.

A 231 Possibly reclass. AB, 9-1900;
Conv. to AC class composite car by 1901;
Reclass. ACL, 1-11-1906;
Painted Larch green, 8-1957;
W/o 17-5-1963.

A 232 Possibly reclass. AB, 9-1900;
Conv. to AC class composite car by 1901;
Reclass. ACL, 1906;
Painted Larch green, 4-1957;

NOTE: Four cars in the batch 231-240 were conv. to composite before 1900 & were reclass. AC rather than AB in 1900, but which four is not known.

Painted Larch green & cream, 11-1965;
W/o, 1-8-1973;
Preserved at Old Coolgardie Station Museum.

A 233   Possibly reclass. AB, 9-1900;
Conv. to AC class composite car by 1901;
Reclass. ACL, 7-1-1907;
Painted Larch green, 12-1957;
W/o, 2-7-1968.

A 234   Possibly reclass. AB, 9-1900;
Conv. to AC class composite car by 1901;
Reclass. ACL, 1906;
Painted Larch green 10-1955;
W/o, 9-3-1965.

A 235   Possibly reclass. AB, 9-1900;
Conv. to AC class composite car by 1901;
Reclass. ACL, 7-1-1907;
Painted Larch green 10-1952;
W/o, 2-7-1963.

A 236   Possibly reclass. AB, 9-1900;
Conv. to AC class composite car by 1901;
Reclass. ACL, 1-11-1906;
Painted Larch green 2-1952;
W/o, 2-7-1968;
Conv. to workman's van VW 5128, 6-1970;
W/o, 22-9-1980.

A 237   Possibly reclass. AB, 9-1900;
Conv. to AC class composite car by 1901;
Reclass. ACL, 1906;
Painted Larch green 8-1955;
W/o, 1-11-1963.

A 238   Possibly reclass. AB, 9-1900;
Conv. to AC class composite car by 1901;
Reclass. ACL, 6-10-1908;
Painted Larch green 7-1957;
Conv. to ACM class suburban car, 19-10-1965;
W/o, 31-5-1968;
To Vintage Train, at Bunbury, 11-3-1976;
Preserved at Boyanup Transport Museum.

A 239   Possibly reclass. AB, 9-1900;
Conv. to AC class composite car by 1901;
Reclass. ACL, 13-11-1907;
Painted Larch green 5-1952;
W/o, 1-11-1963.

A 240   Possibly reclass. AB, 9-1900;
Conv. to AC class composite car by 1901;
Reclass. ACL, 1906-1908;
Painted Larch green 11-1958?;
W/o., 1-11-1963.

A 241   Reclassified AB, 9-1900;
Painted Larch green 4-1957;
W/o, 4-3-1965;
Frame to QS 16117, 30-6-1967.

A 242   Reclassified AB, 9-1900;
Conv. to composite car, & to MRWA in exchange for a K class
car, 30-6-1903;
Numbered J 2;
W/o 1955, & body sold, while frame used for bogie bolster
wagon NB 336, 1959;
NB 336 to WAGR as Q 40742, 1965;
Body sold & became derelict at Hazelmere;
Burnt c.1995.

(AT 242 See 1911)

A 243   Reclassified AB, 9-1900;
Rolled over Broad Arrow after splitting points, 1-8-1903
Painted Larch green 12-1956;
W/o, 4-3-1965;
Frame to QS 16118, 30-6-1967;

W/o, 7-1990.

A 244   Reclassified AB, 9-1900;
Conv. to workman's van VW 2146, 30-8-1958;
W/o, 4-12-1975.

A 245   Reclassified AB, 9-1900;
Conv. to workman's van VW 5068, 8-12-1959;
W/o, 4-3-1982.

A 246   Reclassified AB, 9-1900;
Painted Larch green 11-1952;
W/o, 4-3-1965;
Frame to QS 16103, 27-5-1965.

A 247   Reclassified AB, 9-1900;
Painted Larch green 4-1957;
W/o, 4-3-1965;
Frame to QS 16115, 26-6-1967.

A 248   Reclassified AB, 9-1900;
Painted Larch green 4-1952;
W/o, 4-3-1965;

A 249   Reclassified AB, 9-1900;
Conv. to composite car & to MRWA in exchange for a K class
car, 30-6-1903;
Numbered J 3;
W/o 1957 & body sold, while frame used for bogie bolster
wagon NB 335, 1959;
NB 335 to WAGR as Q 40741, 1964;
Body sold & became derelict at Hazelmere
Burnt c.1995.

(AT 249 See 1911)

A 250   Reclassified AB, 9-1900;
Conv. to composite car & to MRWA in exchange for a K class
car, 30-6-1903;
Numbered J 4.
To WAGR 1-8-1964;
Re-entered service as ACL 31 in Larch green, 11-12-1964;
Conv. to ACM class suburban car, 1965;
W/o, 5-1968;
Conv. to workman's van VW 5149, 2-1974
Preserved Kojonup.

(AK 250 See 1911)
(AK 251(1st) See 1892)
(AK 251(2nd) See 1911
(AS 251 See 1892)
(AK 252 See 1895/96)
(AS 252 See 1895/96)
(AT 252 See 1912)
(AK 253 See 1895/96)
(AS 253 See 1895/96)
(AT 253 See 1912)
(AK 254 See 1896)
(AK 255 See 1896)
(AK 256 See 1898)
(AK 257 See 1898)
(ACL 258 See 1915)
(AI 258 See 1879)
(AI 259 See 1879)
(AT 259 See 1912)
(AI 260 See 1891)
(ZJ 260 See 1930)
(AI 261 See 1891)
(AM 261 See 1895)
(AI 262 See 1894)
(AT 262 See 1912)

1902 Express Brakevans   ARC&ICo.   [ZJ Class]
AJ 263   Entered service 3-5-1902;
Possibly fitted with long wheel base (6'3") bogies, c.early
1920's;
Fitted with shelves for milk, mid 1920's;
Reclassified ZJ, 30-6-1940;

Painted Larch green, 1950's;
W/o, 10-10-1957.

AJ 264   Entered service 10-5-1902;
         Possibly fitted with long wheel base (6'3") bogies, c.early
1920's;
         Reclassified ZJ, 30-6-1940;
         W/o, 13-12-1954.

AJ 265   Entered service 10-5-1902;
         Fitted with long wheel base (6'3") bogies, 4-1923;
         Reclassified ZJ, 30-6-1940;
         Painted Larch green, 10-1955?;
         Painted green & cream, 12-1963;
         W/o, 13-4-1978.

AJ 266   Entered service 10-5-1902;
         Fitted with long wheel base (6'3") bogies, 5-1922
         Reclassified ZJ, 30-6-1940;
         Painted Larch green, 12-1956;
         Painted green & cream, 2-1963;
         W/o, 3-1992;
         Delivered to ARHS Bassendean, 8-1992.

AJ 267   Entered service 24-5-1902;
         Fitted with long wheel base (6'3") bogies, 5-1921;
         Fitted with shelves for milk, mid 1920's;
         Reclassified ZJ, 30-6-1940;
         Painted Larch green, 10-1955;
         Painted green & cream, 10-1966;
         W/o 3-1984.

AJ 268   Entered service 2-8-1902;
         Possibly fitted with long wheel base (6'3") bogies, c.early
1920's;
         Painted Larch green, 8-1956;
         Painted green & cream, 5-1962;
         W/o, 13-4-1978
         Body at Hazelmere.

AJ 269   Entered service 16-8-1902;
         Fitted with long wheel base (6'3") bogies, 6-1923;
         Fitted with shelves for milk, mid 1920's;
         Reclassified ZJ, 30-6-1940;
         Painted Larch green, 6-1952;
         Painted green & cream, 5-1964?;
         Fitted with single roof, 1967;
         W/o, 23-1-1980;
         Body preserved at Guildford, Perth;
         Moved to Toodyay, 2000.

AJ 270   Entered service 16-8-1902;
         Fitted with long wheel base (6'3") bogies, 6-1923;
         Reclassified ZJ, 30-6-1940;
         Painted Larch green, 8-1957;
         Painted green & cream, 5-1962;
         W/o, 19-11-1985;
         To ARHS, 1987;
         Converted to mobile Museum van;
         Recommissioned, 9-10-1988.

AJ 271   Entered service 27-9-1902;
         Fitted with long wheel base (6'3") bogies, 3-1922;
         Reclassified ZJ, 30-6-1940;
         Painted Larch green, 7-1958;
         Painted green & cream, 5-1962;
         W/o, 1-7-1981.

AJ 272   Entered service 27-9-1902;
         Fitted with long wheel base (6'3") bogies, 5-1923
         Reclassified ZJ, 30-6-1940;
         Fitted with cool chamber, 1944;
         Painted Larch green, 10-1958;
         Fitted with gangways, 1960;
         Painted green & cream, 12-1960;
         W/o, 22-8-1979.

1902 Second class compartment brakevans OC&WCo.(5843-5857)
                                        [ZA class]

ZA 5843   Renumbered ZA 159, 1938;
ZA 159   W/o 1965/1976?;
          Conv. to breakdown van VC 5156, 5-1976;
          W/o 7-1991;
          Sold to private owner, Alice Rd, Mt. Helena.

ZA 5844   Renumbered ZA 160, 1938;
ZA 160   W/o 1968;
          Conv. to workman's van VW 5140, 19-7-1968;
          W/o, 9-1987;
          Preserved Narrogin

ZA 5845   Entered service, 2-8-1902;
ZA 161   Renumbered ZA 161, 1938;
          W/o, 1969;
          Conv. to breakdown van VC 5089, 12-1969;
          To VW 5089, 3-1976;
          W/o 24-8-1976.

ZA 5846   Burnt in paint shop fire, Midland, 10-12-1909;
          Extent of damage unknown, but rebuilt, 1912;
ZA 162   Renumbered ZA 162, 1938;
          W/o, 1967.

ZA 5847   Renumbered ZA 163, 1938;
ZA 163   W/o 1966;
          Conv. to workman's van VW 5139, 10-1968;
          W/o, 7-1990.

ZA 5848   Entered service 23-8-1902;
ZA 164   Renumbered ZA 164, 24-12-1938;
          Involved in collision with engine G 46 at Geraldton, 1-2-1947;
          W/o, 19-12-1949.

ZA 5849   Renumbered ZA 165, 1938;
ZA 165   W/o 1965.

ZA 5850   Renumbered ZA 166, 1938;
ZA 166   Destroyed in collision at Spencer's Brook, 22-8-1956;
          W/o 1956.

ZA 5851   Renumbered ZA 167, 1938;
ZA 167   W/o 1962;
          Frame to QS 12-1963

ZA 5852   Renumbered ZA 168, 1938;
ZA 168   W/o 1965;
          Conv. to workman's van VW 5084, 21-4-1965;
          W/o 5-1991, body sold.

ZA 5853   Renumbered ZA 169, 1938;
ZA 169   W/o 1963;
          Frame to QS, 12-1963.

ZA 5854   Renumbered ZA 170, 1938;
ZA 170   W/o 1965;
          Conv. to workman's van VW 5085, 21-4-1965;
          W/o 1-1985.

ZA 5855   Renumbered ZA 171, 1938;
ZA 171   W/o 1965;
          Conv. to workman's van VW 5086, 21-4-1965;
          W/o, 3-1996.

ZA 5856   Renumbered ZA 172, 1938;
ZA 172   W/o 1965.

ZA 5857   Entered service, 20-2-1904;
          Renumbered ZA 173, 1938;
ZA 173   W/o 6-11-1970;
          Preserved ARHS Rail Transport Museum, Bassendean

1903 Second class compartment brakevans   ARC&ICo.(6270-6284)
                                        [ZA class]

ZA 6270   Renumbered ZA 174, 1938;
ZA 174   W/o 1965;
          Conv. to workman's van VW 5108, 19-7-1966.

ZA 6271   Renumbered ZA 175, 1938;
ZA 175   Conv. to workman's van VW 5071, 28-10-1961;
        W/o, 3-1996;
        To Bridgetown;
        At Collie by 1999..

ZA 6272   Entered service, 30-6-1903;
ZA 176   Renumbered ZA 176, 25-2-1939;
        W/o 1966;
        Conv. to breakdown van VC 5105, 2-8-1966/5-1966;
        To VW 5105, 3-1976;
        W/o, 24-8-1976;
        Preserved at Collie.

ZA 6273   Renumbered ZA 177, 1938;
ZA 177   W/o 1975.

ZA 6274   Renumbered ZA 178, 1938;
ZA 178   W/o 1965.

ZA 6275   Renumbered ZA 179, 1938;
ZA 179   Conv. to workman's van VW 5072, 28-10-1961;
        W/o 1-1985.

ZA 6276   Renumbered ZA 180, 1938;
ZA 180   W/o 1967;
        Conv. to workman's van VW 5134, 3-1967;
        W/o 3-1986.

ZA 6277   Renumbered ZA 181, 1938;
ZA 181   W/o 1965;
        Conv. to workman's van VW 5087, 21-4-1965;
        W/o 6/7-1992;
        Pres. at Wyalkatchem.

ZA 6278   Renumbered ZA 182, 1938;
ZA 182   W/o 1964.

ZA 6279   Renumbered ZA 183, 1938;
ZA 183   W/o 1969;
        Conv. to breakdown van VC 5090, 12-1969;
ZA 183   Restored to ZA 183 for the Vintage Train, 3-1980;
        W/o to Vintage Train, Bunbury, 11-1985.

ZA 6280   Renumbered ZA 184, 1938;
ZA 184   W/o 1963;
        Frame to QS, 12-1963.

ZA 6281   Entered service 30-9-1903;
        To Hopetoun, 18-6-1910;
        Abandoned there, 1930;
ZA 185   Book entry of ZA 185, 1938;
        W/o 30-11-1946;
        Used as holiday accommodation;
        Preserved at the Ravensthorpe Museum.

ZA 6282   Renumbered ZA 186, 1938;
ZA 186   W/o 1966;
        Conv. to workman's van VW 5109, 19-7-1966.

ZA 6283   Burnt in paint shop fire, midland, 10-12-1909;
        Extent of damage unknown, but rebuilt, 1912;
ZA 187   Renumbered ZA 187, 1938;
        W/o 1963.

ZA 6284   Entered service, 10-10-1903;
        Renumbered ZA 188, 1938;
ZA 188   Fitted with electric lights, 16-5-1958;
        Conv. to workman's van VW 5133, 3-1967;
        W/o 22-1-1986 & again 3-1987.

1903 Ex MRWA K class 42' bogie composite cars LWCo. [AC class]
AC 273   Built in 1892 for MRWA;
        Numbered between K 1 & K 5;
        To WAGR in exchange for long distance car, 30-6-1903.
        Numbered AC 273;
        Conv. to AF, 20-3-1913;
        Frame used for AYE 714, 7-6-1958.

AC 274   Built in 1892 for MRWA;
        Numbered between K 1 & K 5;
        To WAGR in exchange for long distance car, 30-6-1903.
        Numbered AC 274;
        Conv. to AF, 4-11-1911;
        Painted Larch green, 10-1954;
        W/o, 15-12-1966.

AC 275   Built in 1892 for MRWA;
        Numbered between K 1 & K 5;
        To WAGR in exchange for long distance car, 30-6-1903.
        Numbered AC 275;
        Conv. to AF, 9-3-1912;
        Coupled to AF 276 from c.1920 till ???;
        Frame used for AYE 710, 7-6-1958.

AC 276   Built in 1892 for MRWA;
        Numbered between K 1 & K 5;
        To WAGR in exchange for long distance car, 30-6-1903.
        Numbered AC 276;
        Conv. to AF, 13-4-1911;
        Coupled to AF 275 from c.1920 till ???;
        W/o, 22-12-1945.

1903 Second class corridor day cars GRC&WCo. [AR class]
AR 277   Entered service, 5-12-1903;
        Conv. to second class sleeping car,8-10-1912;
        Reclass. ARS, 1924/25;
        Conv. to four berth from six, 23-9-1936;
        Painted Larch green, 7-1954;
        Painted green & cream, 2-1964;
        W/o, 9-12-1975;
        Conv. to workman's van VW 277, 11-1979;
        W/o
        Stowed at Midland
        Sold in Dongara, 1994;
        To Youth Hostel, Dongara.

AR 278   Entered service, 5-12-1903;
        Conv. to second class sleeping car,10-12-1912;
        Reclass. ARS, 1924/25;
        Conv. to four berth from six, 16-10-1936;
        Painted Larch green, 10-1952;
        Painted green & cream, 4-1965;
        W/o 12-11-1973.

AR 279   Entered service, 12-12-1903;
        Conv. to second class sleeping car,8-10-1912;
        Reclass. ARS, 1924/25;
        Conv. to four berth from six, 14-2-1936;
        Painted Larch green, 10-1951;
        Painted green & cream, 9-1968;
        W/o 12-11-1973;
        Sold, & ½ the body located on private property near Dwellingup.

AR 280   Entered service, 12-12-1903;
        Conv. to second class sleeping car,23-12-1911;
        Reclass. ARS, 1924/25;
        Conv. to four berth from six, 24-4-1937;
        Painted Larch green, 12-1952;
        Painted green & cream, 4-1965;
        W/o, 12-11-1973.

AR 281   Entered service, 12-12-1903;
        Conv. to second class sleeping car,9-4-1914;
        Reclass. ARS, 1924/25;
        Conv. to four berth from six, 20-11-1936;
        Painted two tone green & cream for the "Westland", 6-1948;
        Repainted Larch green, 12-1953;
        Painted green & cream, 12-1964;
        W/o, 12-11-1973.

AR 282   Entered service, 12-12-1903;
        Conv. to ARS second class sleeping car, 27-12-1924;
        Conv. to four berth from six, 7-5-1937;
        Painted Larch green, 2-1953;
        Possibly painted green & cream, 7-1962?;
        W/o, 29-7-1965.

AR 283   Entered service, 19-12-1903;
          Fitted with door for consumptives, 13-10-1909;
          Conv. to second class sleeping car, 23-12-1911;
          Reclass. ARS, 1924/25;
          Conv. to four berth from six, 6-11-1936;
          Painted two tone green & cream for the "Westland", 6-1948;
          Repainted Larch green, 9-1954;
          Painted green & cream, 10-1962?;
          W/o, 12-11-1973.

AR 284   Entered service, 19-12-1903;
          Fitted with door for consumptives, 24-3-1910;
          Conv. to second class sleeping car, 19-12-1913;
          Reclass. ARS, 1924/25;
          Conv. to four berth from six, 19-2-1937;
          Painted Larch green, 12-1954;
          Painted green & cream, 12-1964;
          W/o, 19-12-1975;
          Conv. to workman's van VW 284, 11-1979;
          Purchased by I. Studham for ARHS, 5-1995.

AR 285   Entered service, 19-12-1903;
          Fitted with door for consumptives, 6-8-1910;
          Conv. to second class sleeping car, 8-4-1914;
          Reclass. ARS, 1924/25;
          Conv. to four berth from six, 4-12-1936;
          Painted Larch green, ?-195?;
          Painted green & cream, 7-1965?;
          W/o, 12-11-1973.

1904 First class sleeping cars   GRC&WCo.   [AQ class]
AQ 286   Entered service, 23-7-1904;
          Reclass. AQS second class sleeping car, 20-11-1935;
          Rebuilt as AV class dining car, 23-10-1950;
          Fitted with 8' wheel base AH type bogies, 11-1953;
          Painted Larch green, 11-1953;
          Painted green & cream, 5-1964;
          Fitted with 6'3" wheel base AQZ type bogies;
          W/o,19-12-1975;
          Conv. to workman's van VW 286, 11-1979;
          Purchased by I. Carne for ARHS, 5-1995.

AQ 287   Entered service, 30-7-1904;
          Redesignated second class sleeping car, 1941;
          Reclass. AQS, 30-6-1948;
          Painted Larch green, 11-1956;
AQM 287 Conv. to AQM second class sleeping car, with 6'3" AZ type
          bogies & painted green & cream, 5-5-1961;
          W/o, 19-12-1975;
          Purchased by Lion's Club of Pinjarra, 5-1976;
          Donated to HVTR, painted & outshopped 1-1979.

AQ 288   Entered service, 30-7-1904;
          Redesignated second class sleeping car, 1941;
          Reclass. AQS, 30-6-1948;
          Painted Larch green, 6-1952;
AQL 288 Conv. to AQL second class buffet car, with 6'3" AZ type bogies
          & painted green & cream, 5-5-1961;
          W/o, 19-12-1975;
          To Great Southern Steam Train Tours, 5-1976;
          To ARHS, 12-1984;
          Restoration completed, 28-5-1991;
          Returned to service, 1-6-1991.

AQ 289   Entered service, 10-9-1904;
          Fitted with Stone's water raising apparatus, 1929/30;
          Redesignated second class sleeping car, 1941;
          Reclass. AQS, 30-6-1948;
          Painted Larch green, 11-1956;
          Painted green & cream, 6-1963;
          W/o, 27-10-1972;
          Destroyed in Civil Defence practice.

AQ 290   Entered service, 27-8-1904;
          Fitted with Stone's water raising apparatus, 1929/30;
          Redesignated second class sleeping car, 1941;
          Reclass. AQS, 30-6-1948;
          Painted Larch green, 11-1956;
AQL 290 Conv. to AQL second class buffet car, with 6'3" AZ type bogies

& painted green & cream, 5-10-1961;
          (In traffic 6-4-1961?);
          Used on the "Mullewa" till 1974;
          Used on the "Albany Progress", 12-1975 till 12-1978;
          Leased to Hotham Valley Railway; into HVR shops for
          overhaul (mainly painting), 8-3-1980.

AQ 291   Entered service, 27-8-1904;
          Redesignated AQS second class sleeping car, 22-11-1935;
          Destroyed by fire between Pindar & Wurarga, 27-2-1941;
          W/o, 30-6-1941.

AQ 292   Entered service, 22-10-1904;
          Fitted with Stone's water raising apparatus, 1929/30;
          Redesignated second class sleeping car, 1941;
          Reclass. AQS, 30-6-1948;
          Painted Larch green, 8-1956;
AQM 292 Conv. to AQM second class sleeping car, with 6'3" AZ type
          bogies & painted green & cream, 25-10-1961;
          Used on the "Mullewa";
          W/o, 19-12-1975;
          To GSSA, Albany, 5-1976;
          To ARHS, 12-1984;
          Damaged by fire, 20-3-1987;
          Restoration completed, 28-5-1990.
          Returned to service, 1-6-1990.

AQ 293   Entered service, 22-10-1904;
          Redesignated AQS second class sleeping car, 20-11-1935;
          Destroyed by fire between Paroo & Wiluna, 9-1-1940;
          W/o, 30-6-1940.

AQ 294   Entered service, 22-10-1904;
          Redesignated AQS second class sleeping car, 22-11-1935;
          Painted Larch green, 11-1954;
          Painted green & cream, 8-1964;
          W/o, 7-10-1968;
          Preserved ARHS Rail Transport Museum, Bassendean.

1904 Second class suburban cars   GRC&WCo.   [AT class]
AT 295   Entered service 24-12-1904;
          Coupled to AT 302 from c.1920 till ???;
          W/o, 3-5-1956;
          Frame re-used under ARS 350, 26-3-1956.

AT 296   Entered service 24-12-1904;
          Coupled to AT 304 from c.1920 till ???;
          Painted Larch green, 11-1954;
          W/o, 26-4-1961.

AT 297   Entered service 24-12-1904;
          Coupled to AT 306 from 11-1921 till ???;
          W/o, 13-12-1954.

AT 298   Entered service 24-12-1904;
          Painted Larch green, 11-1956;
          Painted in the green, white & red livery, 2-1964;
          W/o, 18-9-1970.

AT 299   Entered service 24-12-1904;
          Destroyed in paint shop fire, Midland, 10-12-1909.

(AT 299 See 1912)

AT 300   Entered service 24-12-1904;
          Coupled to AT 303 from 11-1921 till ???;
          Painted Larch green, 2-1956;
          Painted in the green, white & red livery, 8-1966;
          W/o, 30-6-1971.

AT 301   Entered service 24-12-1904;
          Coupled to AT 305 from c.1920 till ???;
          Painted Larch green, 3-1956;
          Painted in the green, white & red livery, 5-1964;
          W/o, 18-9-1970.

AT 302   Entered service 24-12-1904;
          Coupled to AT 295 from c.1920 till ???;
          Painted Larch green, 3-1956;

W/o, 25-2-1965;
Conv. to workman's van VW 5137, 10-1968;
W/o, 6/7-1992;
Preserved at Wyalkatchem.

AT 303   Entered service 14-8-1905;
Coupled to AT 300 from 11-1921 till ???;
Painted Larch green, 3-1956;
Painted in the green, white & red livery, 9-1963;
W/o, 18-9-1970;
Conv. to workman's van VW 5141, 6/7(?)-1971;
W/o, 1-1984.

AT 304   Entered service 14-8-1905;
Coupled to AT 296 from c.1920 till ???;
Painted Larch green, 5-1956;
Painted in the green, white & red livery, 12-1964;
W/o, 18-9-1970.

AT 305   Entered service 14-8-1905;
Coupled to AT 301 from c.1921 till ???;
W/o, 3-5-1956;
Body used for conversion of AW 20 to AT 20, 19-10-1956.

AT 306   Entered service, 14-8-1905;
Destroyed in paint shop fire, Midland, 10-12-1909.

(AT 306 See 1912)

1905 First class suburban brake cars   GRC&WCo.   [AU class]
AU 307   Entered service, 20-4-1905;
Coupled to AW 327, c.1921 till 12-1933?;
Fitted with enlarged brake compartment, 1946;
Painted Larch green, ?-195?;
Painted in the green, white & red livery, 3-1965;
Conv. to workman's van VW 5138, 30-6-1967;
W/o 31-8-1982;
Preserved at Old Station Museum, Northam.

AU 308   Entered service, 20-4-1905;
Coupled to AW 331, 6-1918 till 5-1934?;
Fitted with enlarged brake compartment, 1946;
Painted Larch green, 11-1956;
Painted in the green, white & red livery, 2-1964;
W/o, 26-3-1970;
Conv. to workman's van VW 5142, 6/7-1971;

AU 309   Entered service, 20-4-1905;
Destroyed in paint shop fire, Midland, 10-12-1909.

(AU 309 See 1911)

AU 310   Entered service, 20-4-1905;
Coupled to AW 334, c.1921 till 1941;
Fitted with enlarged brake compartment, 1946;
W/o, 3-5-1956;
Frame re-used under AQ 339, 18-5-1956.

AU 311   Entered service, 20-4-1905;
Coupled to AW 329, c.1920 till 5-1934?;
Fitted with enlarged brake compartment, 1946;
Painted Larch green, 3-1957;
W/o, 18-9-1970.

AU 312   Entered service, 26-5-1906;
Coupled to AW 20, 30-6-1921 till 1941;
Fitted with enlarged brake compartment, 1945;
Painted Larch green, 9-1953;
W/o, 18-7-1956.
Frame re-used under AQ 335, 3-8-1956.

1905 Dining cars   GRC&WCo.   [AV class]
AV 313   Entered service, 18-3-1905;
Fitted with AQZ type (6'3" wheel base) bogies, 6-1924;
Stored, 1929;
AM 313   Conv. to AM class Ministerial car, 15-11-1932;
Painted Larch green, ?-195?;
Fitted with 7' wheel base ride control bogies, 11-1957;
Painted green & cream, 2-1966;

W/o 11-1991;
Used on ARHS "Arts Train", October, 1992;
To ARHS 31-1-1993.

AV 314   Entered service, 18-3-1905;
Fitted with AQZ type (6'3" wheel base) bogies, 12-1923;
Used on ambulance train for Commonwealth Govt., 1942;
Returned to normal service, 1945;
Refurbished for the "Westland", & painted two tone green & cream, 6-1948;
Painted Larch green, 7-1953;
AVL 314   Conv. to AVL class lounge car for the "Westland", 2-8-1958;
End platforms enclosed & painted green & cream, 16-3-1962;
Painted red & ivory, fitted with 7' wheel base ride control bogies, & used on the "Midlander", 21-8-1964;
Repainted green & cream, 12-1967;
W/o, 19-12-1975;
Written back & attached to break down train, 9-1976;
Leased to ARHS, 11-1987;
Arrived at Rail Transport Museum, Bassendean, 30-6-1988.

AV 315   Entered service, 17-6-1905;
Fitted with AQZ type (6'3" wheel base) bogies, 11-1924;
Refurbished for the "Westland", & painted two tone green & cream, 3-1948;
Painted Larch green, 10-1951;
Fitted with 7' wheel base ride control bogies, 4-1965;
Painted green & cream, 3-1966;
W/o, 19-12-1975;
Conv. to workman's van VW 315, 11-1979;
W/o 2-1992 & stowed Midland;
To Cunderdin for preservation, c. 5-1993

AV 316   Entered service, 7-8-1905;
Fitted with AQZ type (6'3" wheel base) bogies, 8-1924;
Used on the "Kalgoorlie" & the "Westland";
Refurbished in 1947;
Destroyed by fire at Yellowdine, 3-9-1950;
W/o, 31-10-1950.

1905 First Class suburban brake cars   WIW.   [AU class]
AU 317   Entered service, 8-7-1905;
Fitted with enlarged brake compartment, 1945;
Painted Larch green, ?-195?;
Painted in the green, white & red livery, 7-1964;
W/o, 1968;
Conv. to workman's van VW 5124, 3-1970;
W/o, 21-8-1974.

AU 318   Entered service, 8-7-1905;
Coupled to AW 323, c.1920 till 6.1934?;
Fitted with enlarged brake compartment, 1945;
Painted Larch green, 9-1956;
W/o, 15-12-1966;
Conv. to workman's van VW 5132, 3-1967;
W/o, 7-12-1981;
Sold to Tully Stud, Auburn Park, Chidlow (on Gt. Eastern Hwy);
Moved to 880 Progress Drive, Chidlow, c.1995.

AU 319   Entered service, 8-7-1905;
Destroyed in paint shop fire, Midland, 10-12-1909;

(AU 319 See 1911)

AU 320   Entered service, 8-7-1905;
Coupled to AW 330, c.1920 till 12-1933;
Fitted with enlarged brake compartment, 1946;
Painted Larch green, 4-1956;
Painted in the green, white & red livery, 5-1964;
W/o, 16-12-1965.

AU 321   Entered service, 13-7-1905;
Coupled to AW 328, 9-1921 till 1941;
Fitted with enlarged brake compartment, 1945;
W/o, 18-7-1956;
Frame re-used under AQ 341, 7-8-1956.

AU 322   Entered service, 13-7-1905;
Coupled to AW 325, 5-1921 till 3.1934?;

Fitted with enlarged brake compartment, 1946;
W/o, 18-7-1956;
Frame re-used under AR 354.

1905 First class suburban cars   WIW.   [AW class]
AW 323   Entered service, 15-3-1905;
           Coupled to AU 318 from c.1920 till 6-1934?;
ACW 323 Conv. to ACW class long distance composite car, 29-6-1934;
           Fitted with 6'3" wheel base bogies from AZ 439, 4-7-1936;
           Conv. to workman's van VW 2141, 25-11-1950;
           Conv. to inspection car, 10-1979;
           Reclass. AL 3, 3-1980;
           Used at Collie as sleeping quarters;
           Written off 2-9-1980;
           Sold to Shire of Northampton, 1980.

AW 324   Entered service, 15-3-1905;
           Conv. to AU first class brake car, 14-2-1933;
           Fitted with enlarged brake compartment, 1945;
           Painted Larch green, 10-1954;
           W/o, 26-4-1961;
           Conv. to workman's van VW 5074, 28-10-1961;
           W/o, 3-1996.

AW 325   Entered service, 25-3-1905;
           Coupled to AU 322 from 5-1921 till 3-1934?;
ACW 325 Conv. to ACW class long distance composite car, 2-3-1934;
           Fitted with 6'3" wheel base bogies from AZ 436, 20-2-1937;
           W/o, 6-5-1955;
           Frame used to build Vice Regal car AN 413, 12-8-1955.

AW 326   Entered service, 25-3-1905;
           Destroyed in paint shop fire, Midland, 10-12-1909.

(AW 326 See 1911)

AW 327   Entered service, 1-4-1905;
           Coupled to AU 307 from c.1921 till 12-1933?;
ACW 327 Conv. to ACW class long distance composite car, 31-12-1933;
           Fitted with 6'3" wheel base bogies from AZ 435, 2-3-1935;
           Conv. to workman's van VW 2144, 12-11-1957;
           W/o, 7-1990.

AW 328   Entered service, 1-4-1905;
           Coupled to AU 321 from 9-1921 till 1941;
           Fitted with AZ bogies, 1936;
           Reclass. second class, 24-10-1940;
           Painted Larch green, 3-1952;
           Painted in the green, white & red livery, 11-1963;
           W/o, 26-3-1970;
           Conv. to workman's van VW 5143, 6/7?-1971.

AW 329   Entered service, 19-4-1905;
           Coupled to AU 311 from c.1920 till 5-1934?;
ACW 329 Conv. to ACW class long distance composite car, 18-5-1934;
           Fitted with 6'3" wheel base bogies from AZ 438, 13-11-1936;
           Conv. to workman's van VW 2140, 25-11-1950;
           At Midland for disposal by 23-4-1991;
           W/o, 5-1991;
           Sold to Joe Shaw, Toodyay;
           Offered for sale, 10-1994;
           To Wanneroo.

AW 330   Entered service, 19-4-1905;
           Coupled to AU 320 from c.1920 till 12-1933;
ACW 330 Conv. to ACW class long distance composite car, 13-12-1933;
           Fitted with 6'3" wheel base bogies from AZ 441, 12-12-1936;
           Conv. to breakdown van VC 2143, 28-5-1955;
           W/o, 9-1987;
           To Hotham Valley Railway.

AW 331   Entered service, 4-5-1905;
           Coupled to AU 308 from 6-1918 till 5-1934?;
ACW 331 Conv. to ACW class long distance composite car, 18-5-1934;
           Fitted with 6'3" wheel base bogies from AM 444, 21-12-1935;
           Conv. to workman's van VW 2139, 2-12-1950;
           W/o, 7-1990.

AW 332   Entered service, 4-5-1905;

Destroyed in paint shop fire, Midland, 10-12-1909.

(AW 332 See 1911)

AW 333   Entered service, 15-5-1905;
           Coupled to AU 319 from c.1920 till 1940;
           Reclass. second class, 19-12-1940;
           Painted Larch green, 5-1957;
           W/o, 26-4-1961;
           Scrapped 1961, & AW 332, which had been w/o, was re-instated
           as AW 333 - see 1911.

AW 334   Entered service, 15-5-1905;
           Coupled to AU 310 from c.1920 till 1940;
           Reclass. second class, 24-10-1940;
           Painted Larch green, 2-1956;
           W/o, 30-11-1960.

AW 20   Built Midland Workshops;
           Entered service, 29-7-1905;
           Coupled to AU 312 from 30-6-1921 till 1941;
           Reclass. second class, 1941;
           Fitted with body from AT 305, 19-10-1956 & reclass. AT 20;
           Painted Larch green, 10-1956;
           Painted in the green, white & red livery, 11-1963;
           W/o, 18-9-1970;
           Demolished, 12-1970, but frame retained.

c.1906 Second class compartment brakevan.   [ZA class]
ZA 4992 Renumbered ZA 158, 1938;
ZA 158   Conv. to workman's van VW 5083, 21-4-1965;
           W/o, 6-1983;
           At Midland, 1-11-1990.

1908 First class sleeping cars   WIW.   [AQ class]
AQ 335   Entered service - - 1908;
           Fitted with frame from AU 318 & painted Larch
           green, 3-8-1956;
           Painted green & cream, 3-1964;
           W/o, - -1970.

AQ 336   Entered service 14-4-1908;
           Reclass. AQC class composite car, 9-4-1949;
           Painted Larch green, 10-1953;
           W/o, 24-2-1961.

AQ 337   Entered service 16-5-1908;
           Painted Larch green, 5-1954;
           W/o 3-6-1958.

AQ 338   Entered service 16-5-1908;
           Reclass. AQC class composite car, 18-6-1949;
           Painted Larch green, 3-1953;
           Conv. to workman's van VW 5082, 12-6-1964;
           Used as the Bunbury District Engineer's car;
           W/o 11-3-1975;
           Remains at Bushmead.

AQ 339   Entered service 16-5-1908;
           Used on ambulance train for the Commonwealth Govt, 1942;
           Returned to normal service, 1945;
           Reclass. AQC class composite car, 26-3-1949;
           Fitted with frame from AU 310 & painted Larch
           green, 18-5-1956;
           Painted green & cream, 10-1965;
           W/o, 19-12-1975;
           Conv. to workman's van VW 339, 11-1979;
           Arr. Midland for disposal, 22-11-1990;
           W/o, 5-1991;
           Preserved at the Old Station Museum, Northam.

AQ 340   Entered service 23-5-1908;
           Arrived Kalgoorlie on fire, 28-1-1933;
           Used on ambulance train for the Commonwealth Govt, 1942;
           Returned to normal service, 1945;
           Reclass. AQC class composite car, 22-7-1949;
           Painted Larch green, 1-1954;
           Painted green & cream, 7-1964;

W/o, 26-3-1970;
Remains demolished at Bushmead, 1992.

AQ 341   Entered service 23-5-1908;
Fitted with frame from AU 321 & painted Larch
green, 7-8-1956;
Painted green & cream, 5-1964;
W/o, 26-3-1970.

342-346 built at Midland Workshops
AQ 342   Entered service 29-8-1908;
Reclass. AQC class composite car, 16-12-1932;
Painted Larch green, 11-1953;
Painted green & cream, 9-1964;
W/o 7-10-1968 (after accident at Gin Gin?);
Sold to John Tyler.

AQ 343   Entered service 29-8-1908;
Reclass. AQC class composite car, 18-12-1932;
Painted Larch green, 3-1953;
Conv. to AQS second class sleeping car, 29-5-1961;
Painted green & cream, 5-1961;
Used on the "Albany Progress";
AQA 343   Rebuilt as AQA class hospital car, outshopped 23-5-1970;
Returned to service, 26-5-1970;
W/o, 6/7-1992;
To ARHS Bassendean, 10-1992.

AQ 344   Entered service 4-9-1908;
Reclass. AQC class composite car, 25-7-1932;
Fitted with suburban car frame & painted Larch green, 11-1955;
Painted green & cream, 7-1966;
W/o, 26-3-1970;
Conv. to workman's van VW 5146, 9-1973;
Last used as the Bunbury Shop car;
W/o, 3-1996;
Preserved Collie.

AQ 345   Entered service 29-8-1908;
Reclass. AQC class composite car, 29-7-1932;
Painted Larch green, 10-1952;
Destroyed by fire between Murrin Murrin & Malcolm, 13-2-1957;
W/o, 11-6-1957.

AQ 346   Entered service 4-9-1908;
Possibly painted Larch green during 1950's;
W/o, 10-10-1957.

1908 Second class corridor day cars   WIW.   [AR class]
AR 347   Entered service 22-2-1908;
Painted Larch green, 6-1952;
Conv. to ARS second class sleeping car using ex suburban car frame, 20-6-1957;
ARM 347   Rebuilt as ARM second class twin berth sleeping car, painted green & cream, for the "Kalgoorlie", 13-4-1962;
Fitted with ride control bogies, 6-1963;
W/o, 11-1979;
To Hotham Valley Railway.

AR 348   Entered service, 22-2-1908;
Conv. to ARS second class sleeping car using frame from AT 299 & painted Larch green, 26-3-1956;
Painted green & cream, 8-1965;
W/o, 19-12-1975;
Conv. to workman's van VW 348, 11-1979;
Purchased by P. Hufner for ARHS, 5-1995.

AR 349   Entered service, 4-4-1908;
Conv. to ARS second class sleeping car using frame from AT 252/355? & painted Larch green, 26-3-1956;
Painted green & cream, 8-1963;
W/o, 19-12-1975;
Conv. to workman's van VW 349, 11-1979;
Stowed Forrestfield;
Transferred to ARHS Bassendean 10-1992.
Transferred to Midland Workshops, 7-7-1994;
To Kojonup.

AR 350   Entered service, 4-4-1908;
Conv. to ARS second class sleeping car using frame from AT 295 & painted Larch green, 26-3-1956;
Painted green & cream, 11-1963;
W/o, 12-11-1973;
Sold to The Deer Park, Donnybrook, 5-1976;
To the Whistlestop, Busselton, 6-4-1987.

AR 351   Entered service, 4-4-1908;
Painted Larch green, 9-1952;
Conv. to ARS second class sleeping car using frame from suburban car, 20-6-1957;
ARM 351   Conv. to ARM second class twin berth sleeping car, painted green & cream, with ride control bogies for the "Kalgoorlie", 30-10-1962;
Used on the "Mullewa";
Painted orange & blue after 1975;
ARA 351   Conv. to ARA long distance day brake car for the "Australind", 16-12-1980;
To ARHS, 30-8-1990;
W/o, 18-9-1990.

AR 352   Entered service, 23-5-1908;
Painted Larch green, 2-1952;
Conv. to ARS second class sleeping car using frame from AU 309, 9-10-1956;
Painted green & cream, 12-1963;
W/o, 12-11-1973.

AR 353   Entered service, 23-5-1908;
Conv. to ARS second class sleeping car using frame from AT 242 & painted Larch green, 16-12-1955;
Painted green & cream, 8-1963;
W/o, 12-11-1973.

354-358 built at Midland Workshops.
AR 354   Entered service, 6-6-1908;
Painted Larch green, 4-1955;
Conv. to ARS second class sleeping car using frame from AU 322, 9-10-1956;
Painted green & cream, 2-1965;
W/o, 12-11-1973;
Preserved at Ellecker;
Moved to Cranbrook, March, 2003.

AR 355   Entered service, 6-6-1908;
Caught fire on No. 7 Passenger "Albany Express" near Narrogin, 15-1-1919;
Painted Larch green, 9-1953;
Conv. to ARS second class sleeping car using frame from AT 252?, 7-12-1955;
Painted green & cream, 8-1963;
W/o, 12-11-1973;
Sold, & ½ the body located on private property near Dwellingup.

AR 356   Entered service, 6-6-1908;
Painted Larch green, 3-1954;
Conv. to ARS second class sleeping car using frame from suburban car, 24-6-1957;
ARM 356   Conv. to ARM second class twin berth sleeping car, painted green & cream, with ride control bogies for the "Kalgoorlie", 30-10-62;
Used on the "Mullewa";
ARA 356   Conv. to ARA long distance day brake car for the "Australind", 16-12-1980;
To ARHS, 30-8-1990;
W/o, 18-9-1990.

AR 357   Entered service, 6-6-1908;
Painted Larch green, 3-1957;
Conv. to ARS second class sleeping car using frame from suburban car, 21-6-1957;
ARM 357   Rebuilt as ARM second class twin berth sleeping car, painted green & cream, for the "Kalgoorlie", 13-4-1962;
Fitted with ride control bogies, 3-1963;
W/o, 11-1979;
To Hotham Valley Railway.

AR 358   Entered service, 6-6-1908;
          Conv. to ARS second class sleeping car using frame from
          AT 139 & painted Larch green, 7-12-1955;
          Painted green & cream, 11-1963;
          W/o, 19-12-1975;
          Dam. by fire during conversion to VW & sent to Salvage, 1979.

1907 Express Brakevan   WIW.   [ZJ class]
AJ 359   Entered service, 15-2-1907;
          Fitted with long wheel base (6'3") bogies, 12-1923;
          Reclass. ZJ, 30-6-1940;
          Fitted with cool chamber, 1948;
          Painted Larch green, 12-1951;
          Painted green & cream, 25-6-1965;
          W/o, 1-8-1973;
          Sold to Mr. CJ Free;
          Preserved Old Coolgardie Station.

AJ 360   Entered service, 15-2-1907;
          Possibly fitted with long wheel base (6'3") bogies, early 1920's;
          Reclass. ZJ, 30-6-1940;
          Damaged in collision at Mt. Kokeby when goods train ran into
          rear of "Albany Express", 29-9-1948;
          W/o, 24-1-1949.

AJ 361   Entered service, 15-2-1907;
          Fitted with long wheel base (6'3") bogies, 5-1924;
          Reclass. ZJ, 30-6-1940;
          Fitted with cool chamber, 18-1947;
          Painted Larch green, 12-1956;
          Painted green & cream, 10-1967;
          W/o, 1-7-1981.

AJ 362   Entered service, 15-2-1907;
          Fitted with old AZ bogies, 12-1938;
          Reclass. ZJ, 30-6-1940;
          Possibly fitted with long wheel base (6'3") bogies, 7-1940;
          Painted green & cream for the "Westland", 6-1948;
          Painted Larch green, 5-1956;
          Painted green & cream, 6-1964;
          W/o, 29-4-1985.

AJ 363   Entered service, 15-2-1907;
          Fitted with old AZ bogies, 3-1938;
          Reclass. ZJ, 30-6-1940;
          Fitted with cool chamber, 7-3-1947;
          Possibly fitted with long wheel base (6'3") bogies, 9-1948;
          Painted Larch green, 12-1957;
          Painted green & cream, 6-1965;
          Damaged in collision, 1967;
          Rebuilt with plywood body & single roof;
          W/o, 13-4-1978;
          To Hotham Valley Railway;
          Demolished, 12-2003

1906 Express Brakevans   Midland Workshops.   [ZJ class]
AJ 364   Entered service, 22-12-1906;
          Fitted with old AZ bogies, 4-1939;
          Reclass. ZJ 30-6-1940;
          Possibly fitted with long wheel base (6'3") bogies, 6-1941;
          Fitted with cool chamber, 1948;
          Painted Larch green, 12-1954;
          Painted green & cream, 4-1965;
          Fitted with single roof, 1967;
          W/o, 1-7-1981.

AJ 365   Entered service, 22-12-1906;
          Fitted with long wheel base (6'3") bogies, 5-1924;
          Reclass. ZJ 30-6-1940;
          Fitted with cool chamber, 1949;
          Painted Larch green, 6-1952;
          Painted green & cream, 9-1964;
          W/o, 1-7-1981.

AJ 366   Entered service, 22-1-1907;
          Fitted with long wheel base (6'3") bogies, 12-1921;
          Reclass. ZJ 30-6-1940;
          Painted Larch green, 7-1952;
          Painted green & cream, 6-1964;

Fitted with single roof, 1967;
W/o, 13-4-1978.

AJ 367   Entered service, 26-1-1907;
          Fitted with shelves for milk, mid 1920's;
          Fitted with old AZ bogies, 7-1938;
          Reclass. ZJ 30-6-1940;
          Possibly fitted with long wheel base (6'3") bogies, 11-1947;
          Fitted with cool chamber, 1947;
          Painted green & cream for the "Westland", 6-1948;
          Painted Larch green, 5-1957;
          Painted green & cream, 5-1961;
          Fitted with gangways;
          W/o, 1-7-1981;
          To Hotham Valley Railway, 11-9-1981.

AJ 368   Entered service, 26-1-1907;
          Fitted with shelves for milk, mid 1920's;
          Fitted with (6'3") wheel base AQZ type bogies, 9-1923;
          Reclass. ZJ 30-6-1940;
          Fitted with cool chamber, 12-9-1947;
          Painted Larch green, 11-1953;
          Painted green & cream, 2-1964;
          W/o, 31-10-1974;
          To Rodeo ground at Bullsbrook.

1908 Suburban second class brake cars   WIW.   [AS class]
AS 369   Entered service, 22-8-1908;
          Fitted with enlarged brake compartment, 1945;
          Painted Larch green, 11-1956;
          Painted in the green, white & red livery, 10-1964;
          W/o, 20-10-1970.

AS 370   Entered service, 22-8-1908;
          Fitted with enlarged brake compartment, 1946;
          Damaged in collision at Midland Junction while being shunted
          across the main line & was run into by the "Westland", 28-2-49;
          W/o, 21-4-1949.

AS 371   Entered service, 12-9-1908;
          Fitted with enlarged brake compartment, 1946;
          Painted Larch green, 7-1957;
          Painted in the green, white & red livery, 9-1964;
          W/o, 16-4-1969.

AS 372   Entered service, 12-9-1908;
          Fitted with enlarged brake compartment, 1945;
          Painted Larch green, 4-1956;
          Painted in the green, white & red livery, 9-1963;
          W/o, 15-6-1967;
          Conv. to workman's van VW 5114, 5-1968;
          W/o, 5-1991;
          Sold to Joe Shaw, Toodyay;
          Sold to Ron Hobson, Garden City Nursery, Ankatell;
          Offered for sale, August, 1996;
          Sold to Alice Norton, 18-6-1996;
          Moved to Capel, August, 1997.
(25 km Sth. Bunbury, R. Hall Rd. (gravel), 1 km, 1st left McCormack,
vineyard on right. Ref: Alice 9448-2907)

AS 373   Entered service, 10-10-1908;
          Fitted with enlarged brake compartment, 1946;
          Painted Larch green, 9-1957;
          Painted in the green, white & red livery, 9-1963;
          W/o, 20-10-1970.

AS 374   Entered service, 3-10-1908;
          Fitted with enlarged brake compartment, 1946;
          Painted Larch green, 2-1956;
          Conv. to ASD class trade & industry display saloon, 11-11-1960;
          Conv. to workman's van VW 5118, 28-11-1968;
          Based West Toodyay;
          W/o, 3-1996.

AS 375   Entered service, 24-10-1908;
          Fitted with enlarged brake compartment, 1946;
          Painted Larch green, 2-1956;
          Painted in the green, white & red livery, 11-1963;
          W/o, 7-10-1968;

Conv. to workman's van VW 5111, 25-10-1968;
W/o 5-1991, & stowed Midland;
Body to Nthn. Suburbs Model R'way Ass., Balcatta.

AS 376   Entered service, 24-10-1908;
            Fitted with enlarged brake compartment, 1946;
            Painted Larch green, 10-1956;
            Painted in the green, white & red livery, 4-1964;
            W/o, 7-10-1968;

AS 377   Entered service, 14-11-1908;
            Fitted with enlarged brake compartment, 1945;
            Painted Larch green, 9-1956;
            Painted in the green, white & red livery, 9-1963?;
            W/o, 18-9-1970.

AS 378   Entered service, 14-11-1908;
            Fitted with enlarged brake compartment, 1946;
            Painted Larch green, 3-1955;
            Painted in the green, white & red livery, 2-1964;
            W/o, 16-4-1969.

AS 379   Entered service, 25-11-1908;
            Fitted with enlarged brake compartment, 1946;
            Painted Larch green, 5-1956;
            Painted in the green, white & red livery, 8-1964;
            W/o, 26-3-1970.

AS 380   Entered service, 25-11-1908;
            Fitted with enlarged brake compartment, 1946;
            Painted Larch green, 8-1956;
            Painted in the green, white & red livery, 10-1963;
            W/o, 8-2-1967.

1909 Second class suburban car   Midland Workshops.   [AF class]
AF 13   Short car (37');
            Entered service 20-2-1909;
            Painted Larch green, 12-1956;
            Conv. to workman's van VW 5112, 3-7-1967;
            W/o, 9-5-1979;
            To Bellarine Peninsular Railway, Vic.

1909 Long distance composite car with lavs Midland Shops. [ACL class]
ACL 1   Entered service 18-12-1909;
            Painted Larch green, 1-1956;
            W/o, 4-3-1965.

ACL 3   Entered service 18-12-1909;
            Painted Larch green, 9-1955;
            W/o, 4-3-1965.

ACL 6   Entered service 24-12-1909;
            Painted Larch green, 10-1955;
            W/o, 9-3-1965.

ACL 19   Entered service 24-12-1909;
            Painted Larch green, 3-1954;
            W/o, 9-3-1965.

ACL 21   Entered service 24-12-1909;
            Painted Larch green, 5-1954;
            W/o, 9-3-1965.

ACL 23   Never completed, destroyed in paintshop fire, Midland, 10-12-09

ACL 27   Never completed, destroyed in paintshop fire, Midland, 10-12-09

ACL 30   Never completed, destroyed in paintshop fire, Midland, 10-12-09

ACL 70   Never completed, destroyed in paintshop fire, Midland, 10-12-09

ACL 222   Never completed, destroyed in paintshop fire, Midland, 10-12-09

1912 Second class suburban car   WIW.   [AT class]
AT 381   Entered service 3-4-1912;
            Coupled to AT 382 from c.1920 till ???;
            Painted Larch green, 7-1957;
            Painted in the white, green & red livery, 12-1963;
            W/o, 18-9-1970.

AT 382   Entered service 3-4-1912;
            Coupled to AT 381 from c.1920 till ???;
            Painted Larch green, 7-1956;
            W/o, 17-12-1963;
            Conv. to workman's van VW 5081, 28-2-1964;
            W/o, 3-1996.

AT 383   Entered service 19-4-1912;
            Coupled to AT 384 from 2-9-1921 till ???;
            Painted Larch green, 2-1956;
            Painted in the white, green & red livery, 5-1964;
            W/o, 18-9-1970.

AT 384   Entered service 19-4-1912;
            Coupled to AT 383 from 2-9-1921 till ???;
            Painted Larch green, 2-1956;
            Stowed 29-4-1966;
            W/o, 15-6-1967.

1911 & 12 Long distance composite car with lavs.   Midland Shops.
                                                      [ACL class]
ACL 385   Entered service 9-9-1911;
            To Port Hedland, 13-4-1912;
            Returned to main system 23-1-1945;
            Painted Larch green, 8-1955;
            Possibly painted green & cream, 11-1964;
            W/o, 2-7-1968.

ACL 386   Entered service 9-9-1911;
            Painted Larch green, 6-1952;
            Conv. to ACM class suburban car, 25-6-1965;
            W/o, 31-5-1968.

ACL 387   Entered service 9-9-1911;
            Painted Larch green, 6-1952;
            W/o, 17-4-1962.

ACL 388   Entered service 29-6-1912;
            Painted Larch green, 3-1954;
            W/o, 9-3-1965.

ACL 389   Entered service 4-9-1912;
            Painted Larch green, 3-1954;
            W/o, 9-3-1965.

ACL 390   Entered service 4-9-1912;
            Painted Larch green, 3-1955;
            W/o, 10-8-1967.

ACL 391   Entered service 12-9-1912;
            Painted Larch green, 4-1952;
            Conv. to ACM suburban car, 13-8-1965;
            W/o, 31-5-1968;
            To Vintage Train, Bunbury, 11-3-1976.

ACL 392   Entered service 12-9-1912;
            Painted Larch green, 12-1951;
            Conv. to ACM suburban car, 7-9-1965;
            W/o, 31-5-1968.

ACL 393   Entered service 4-10-1912;
            Damaged in accident at Mt. Kokeby when goods train ran into
            rear of "Albany Express";
            W/o, 29-9-1948.

ACL 394   Entered service 4-10-1912;
            Painted Larch green, 7-1955;
            W/o, 2-7-1968.

ACL 395   Entered service 4-10-1912;
            Painted Larch green, 2-1952;
            Conv. to ACM suburban car, 17-9-1965;
            W/o, 31-5-1968.

ACL 23   Entered service 9-12-1911, replacing burnt car;
Painted Larch green, 10-1952;
W/o, 9-3-1965.

ACL 27   Entered service 9-12-1911, replacing burnt car;
Painted Larch green, ?-195?;
W/o, 9-3-1965.

ACL 30   Entered service 9-12-1911, replacing burnt car;
Painted Larch green, ?-195?;
W/o, 9-3-1965.

ACL 70   Entered service 9-12-1911, replacing burnt car;
Painted Larch green, 9-1955;
W/o, 15-12-1966.

ACL 189   Entered service 16-12-1911;
Painted Larch green, 7-1954;
W/o, 4-3-1965.

ACL 191   Entered service 16-12-1911;
Painted Larch green, 7-1955;
W/o, 9-3-1965.

ACL 222   Entered service 16-12-1911, replacing burnt car;
Painted Larch green, 12-1955;
W/o, 27-8-1964.

1911 First class suburban brake car   WIW.   [AU class]
AU 309   Entered service, 2-9-1911, replacing burnt car;
Coupled to AW 332 from 8-1921 till 1941;
Fitted with enlarged brake compartment, 1945;
Possibly painted Larch green, 12-1955;
W/o, 18-7-1956;
Frame re-used under ARS 352, 9-10-1956.

AU 319   Entered service, 2-9-1911, replacing burnt car;
Coupled to AW 333 from c.1920 till 1941;
Painted Larch green, 9-1952;
W/o, 2-11-1965.

1911 First class suburban car   WIW.   [AW class]
AW 218   Entered service 1911;
AU 218   Conv. to AU first class brake car, 22-12-1932;
Fitted with enlarged brake compartment, 1945;
Painted Larch green, 10-1951;
Painted in the green, white & red livery, 12-1964;
W/o, 1970;
To Vintage Train, Bunbury.

AW 326   Entered service 19-9-1911;
AU 326   Conv. to AU first class brake car, 22-12-1932;
Fitted with enlarged brake compartment, 1946;
Painted Larch green, 3-1956;
Painted in the green, white & red livery, 11-1963;
Conv. to workman's van VW 5125, 23-4-1970/5-1970?;
W/o, 18-9-1970.

AW 332   Entered service 21-10-1911;
Coupled to AU 309 from 8-1921 till 1941;
Reclass. second class, 23-5-1941;
Painted Larch green, 2-1957;
W/o, 26-4-1961;
AW 333   Re-instated as AW 333, 13-7-1962;
Painted in the green, white & red livery, 1-1966?;
W/o, 18-9-1970.

1911 Second class suburban cars   WIW.   [AT class]
AT 134   Entered service 11-11-1911;
Coupled to AT 252 from c.1919 till ???;
Painted Larch green, 7-1956;
W/o, 15-12-1966;
Conv. to workman's van VW 5131, 13-2-1967;
Stowed Forrestfield;
To Midland, burnt?, 1994.

AT 139   Entered service 4-12-1911;
Coupled to AT 145 from c.1919 till ???;
W/o, 3-5-1956;

Frame re-used under ARS 358.

AT 145   Entered service 4-12-1911;
Coupled to AT 139 from c.1919 till ???;
Painted Larch green, 10-1955;
W/o, 21-1-1963.

AT 242   Entered service 19-12-1911;
Coupled to AT 249 from c.1919 till ???;
Frame re-used under ARS 353 16-12-1955;
W/o, 3-5-1956.

AT 249   Entered service 19-12-1911;
Coupled to AT 242 from c.1919 till ???;
Painted Larch green, 4-1957;
Painted in the green, white & red livery, 1-1964;
Stored 1-5-1970;
W/o, 18-9-1970.
Demolished 12-1970 & frame retained.

AT 252   Entered service 5-2-1912;
Coupled to AT 134 from c.1919 till ???;
W/o, -1956;
Frame re-used under ARS 349.

AT 253   Entered service 5-2-1912;
Coupled to AT 299 from 10-1921 till ???;
Painted Larch green, 19-10-1956;
Painted in the green, white & red livery, 3-7-1964;
Stored 1-5-1970;
W/o, 18-9-1970.
Demolished 12-1970 & frame retained.

AT 259   Entered service 23-2-1912;
Coupled to AT 262 from c.1920 till ???;
Painted Larch green, 10-1951?;
Painted in the green, white & red livery, 7-1964;
W/o, 18-9-1970;
To ARHS, Rail Transport Museum, Bassendean, 8-10-1971.

AT 262   Entered service 23-2-1912;
Coupled to AT 259 from c.1920 till ???;
Painted Larch green, 9-1958;
Painted in the green, white & red livery, 10-1964;
W/o, 18-9-1970.
Demolished 12-1970, & frame retained.

AT 299   Entered service 20-3-1912, replacing burnt car;
Coupled to AT 253 from 10-1921 till ???;
Painted Larch green, 3-1952;
W/o, 3-5-1956;
Frame re-used under ARS 348, 26-3-1956.

AT 306   Entered service 1912, replacement for burnt one;
Coupled to AT 297 from 11-1921 till ???;
Painted Larch green, 4-1956;
Painted in the green, white & red livery, 2-1964;
W/o, 26-3-1970;
Sold & body converted to house, Sawyer's Valley;
Sold 7-12-1991?
Moved to Broughtons Auction site, Bellevue;
Sold.

1911 Mail Vans   Midland Workshops.   [AK class]
AK 250   Entered service 30-6-1911;
Reclass. P 469, 30-6-1940;
Used on ambulance train for Commonwealth Govt., 1942;
W/o, 18-5-1965.
Body at Meekatharra.

AK 251   Entered service 30-6-1911;
Reclass. P 658, 30-6-1940;
Used on ambulance train for Commonwealth Govt., 1942;
W/o, 17-3-1969;
To ARHS Rail Transport Museum, Bassendean, 11-1972.

1912 Second class compartment brakevans   Midland Shops.   [ZA class]
ZA 9336   Renumbered ZA 189, 1938;
ZA 189   W/o 1966;
          Conv. to workman's van VW 5100, 15-3-1967;
          W/o c.1985;
          Preserved at Whiteman Park.

ZA 9337   Renumbered ZA 190, 1938;
ZA 190   W/o, 5-1964.

ZA 9338   Renumbered ZA 191, 1938;
ZA 191   W/o 1965;
          Conv. to breakdown van VC 5088, 10-1965;
          W/o, 9-1985;
          To ARHS, then Cannington Greyhound Track.

ZA 9339   Renumbered ZA 192, 1938;
ZA 192   W/o 1969;
          Converted to Z 192, 5-3-1969;
          W/o 28-11-1977.

ZA 9340   Renumbered ZA 193, 1938;
ZA 193   W/o 1965;
          Conv. to workman's van VW 5110, 19-7-1966;
          Stowed Forrestfield.

ZA 9341   Renumbered ZA 194, 1938;
ZA 194   W/o 1966;
          Conv. to workman's van VW 5107(1st), 15-6-1966;
          W/o, 13-9-1971;
          Cut in half along its length & half preserved by Otto Walkameyer
          3-1972;
          To Whiteman Park, 3-2005.

ZA 9342   Renumbered ZA 195, 1938;
ZA 195   W/o 1962;
          .Frame to QS, 12-1963.

ZA 9343   Entered service 21-12-1912;
ZA 196   Renumbered ZA 196, 27-1-1940;
          Noted painted all over brown, June, 1966;
          W/o 1966/10-11-1968?;
          Conv. to workman's van VW 5117, 11-1968;
          W/o, 13-4-1978;
          To the Esplanade, Fremantle, as The Carriage Coffee Shop.

ZA 9344   Renumbered ZA 197, 1938;
ZA 197   W/o 1965;

ZA 9345   Renumbered ZA 198, 1938;
ZA 198   W/o 1962;
          Frame to QS, 12-1963..

ZA 9346   Destroyed by fire, 1928;
          Frame used to build brakevan AJ 260, 1930.

ZA 9347   Renumbered ZA 199, 1938;
ZA 199   W/o 6-12-1973;
          Body put on standard gauge flat top WSD 30614 as workmans
          van, 2-1974;
          Frame to Jetty 988, 10-1976;
          Body removed & demolished, 4-1979

ZA 9348   Renumbered ZA 200, 1938;
ZA 200   W/o 6-1970;
          To Bellarine Peninsular Railway, Victoria.

ZA 9349   Renumbered ZA 201, 1938;
ZA 201   W/o 1967;
          Conv. to workman's van VW 5115, 5-1968;
          Stowed Forrestfield.

1912 Second class long distance car   WIW.   [AB class]
AB 396   Entered service 13-12-1912;
          Painted Larch green, 9-1955;
          W/o, 4-3-1965;
          Frame to QS 16106, 28-5-1965.

AB 397   Entered service 13-12-1912;

          Painted Larch green, 4-1954;
          W/o, 4-3-1965.

AB 398   Entered service 17-12-1912;
          Painted Larch green, 8-1955;
          W/o, 12-5-1964;
          Frame to QS.

AB 399   Entered service 17-12-1912;
          Painted Larch green, 3-1956;
          W/o, 4-3-1965;
          Frame to QS 16107, 1-6-1965.

1913 400-402 built Midland.
AB 400   Entered service 21-1-1913;
          Painted Larch green, 1-1958;
          W/o, 4-3-1965;
          Frame to QS 16100, 21-5-1965.

AB 401   Entered service 21-1-1913;
          Painted Larch green, 9-1955?;
          W/o, 12-5-1964;
          Frame to QS 16096, 15-5-1965.

AB 402   Entered service 21-1-1913;
          Painted Larch green, 9-1955;
          W/o, 4-3-1965;
          Frame to QS 16097, 17-5-1965;
          W/o, 28-2-1978.

1915 Long distance composite lav. car (ex MRWA).   [ACL class]
ACL 258   Entered MRWA service as JA 22, 29-6-1913;
          To WAGR 3-5-1915 in exchange for AP 148;
          Entered service as ACL 258, 15-5-1915;
          Painted Larch green, 12-1951;
          W/o, 30-10-1967.

1915 Long distance composite lav. car Midland.   [ACL class]
ACL 403   Entered service 25-3-1916;
          Painted Larch green, 7-1955;
          W/o, 1968;
          Conv. to workman's van VW 5113, 5-1968;
          W/o, 5-1991;
          Body sold in Toodyay, del. 14-12-1991.

ACL 404   Entered service 25-3-1916;
          Painted Larch green, 6-1952;
          Conv. to ACM suburban car, 27-8-1965;
          W/o, 31-5-1968;
          Conv. to workman's van VW 5123, 16-4-1970;
          W/o, 5-1991.

ACL 405   Entered service 25-12-1915;
          Painted Larch green, 8-1953;
          At Kalgoorlie, 5-1973
          W/o, 1-8-1973;
          Sold to Mr. C.J. Tree;
          Preserved at Old Coolgardie Station.

ACL 406   Entered service 25-12-1915;
          Painted Larch green, 8-1957;
          W/o, 2-7-1968;
          To Vintage Train at Bunbury, 11-3-1976.

ACL 407   Entered service 25-12-1915;
          Painted Larch green, 8-1955;
          Painted green & cream, 5-1961;
          To Vintage Train, Bunbury, 12-1975.

ACL 408   Entered service 30-6-1916;
          Painted Larch green, 4-1952;
          Conv. to ACM class suburban car, 17-9-1965;
          W/o, 31-5-1968.

ACL 409   Entered service 30-6-1916;
          Painted Larch green, 9-1956;
          Conv. to ACM class suburban car, 24-9-1965;
          W/o, 31-5-1968;

Conv. to workman's van VW 5122, 29-5-1970;
W/o, 5-1992;
Pres. Wyalkatchem.

ACL 410   Entered service 22-4-1916;
Painted Larch green, 8-1956;
Painted green & cream, 10-1961;
To Vintage Train, Bunbury, 12-1975.

ACL 411   Entered service 8-4-1916;
Painted Larch green, 6-1953;
W/o, 30-10-1967.

ACL 412   Entered service 15-4-1916;
Painted Larch green, 7-1954;
Conv. to ACM class suburban car, 13-8-1965;
W/o, 31-5-1968.

1918 First class sleeping car   WIW.   [AQ class]
AQ 413   Entered service 6-11-1918;
Conv. to AN class Vice Regal car, 28-6-1920;
Renumbered AL 4, 1958/6-6-1959? (New Vice Regal car
became AN 413, built on frame of ACW 325);
Painted Larch green, 6-1959;
Painted green & cream, 2-1966;
W/o, 11-1991:
Used on ARHS "Arts Train", 10-1992;
To ARHS 31-1-1993.

AQ 414   Entered service 6-11-1918;
Conv. to AM class Ministerial car, 28-6-1920;
Painted Larch green, 2-1954;
Painted green & cream, 10-1961;
Fitted with 6'3" AZ type bogies, 12-1961;
Fitted with 7' wheel base ride control bogies, 8-1967;
Conv. to AL class inspection car, 5-1973;
W/o, 11-6-1980.

AQ 415   Entered service 29-11-1918;
AQZ 415   Conv. to AQZ first class sleeping car, painted Larch green,
28-10-1954;
Painted green & cream, 9-1965;
W/o, 8-10-1976;
To GSSA, Albany;
Sold to ARHS, 12-1984;
Stored at Cresco's in Bayswater;
To RTM, Bassendean, 17-4-1989;
To York station;
To Collie, 2004.

AQ 416   Entered service 29-11-1918;
AQZ 416   Conv. to AQZ first class sleeping car, painted Larch green,
28-10-1954;
Painted green & cream, 6-1965;
W/o, 4-9-1974;
Sold to Guildford Grammar School for use as change rooms at
Hazelmere;
Demolished, c.1978.

AQ 417   Entered service 13-12-1918;
AQZ 417   Conv. to AQZ first class sleeping car, painted Larch green,
28-10-1954;
Painted green & cream, 3-1964;
W/o, 8-10-1976;
Sold & stored at Mundaring;
Moved to Sawyers Valley mid 1991, noted 6-12-1991;
Sold to Joe Shaw, Toodyay;
To Gwelup & cut in half;
To Byford.

AQ 418   Entered service 13-12-1918;
AQZ 418   Conv. to AQZ first class sleeping car, painted Larch green,
28-10-1954;
Painted green & cream, 4-1966;
W/o, 8-10-1976.

1919 Second class sleeping car   WIW.   [AR class]
AR 419   Entered service 3-1-1919;
Reclass. ARS, 30-6-1924;

Conv. to 4 berth 27-3-1937/47?;
Painted two tone green & cream for the "Westland", 6-1948;
Painted Larch green 7-1955;
AQZ 419   Conv. to AQZ first class sleeping car, 14-12-1957;
Fitted with 6'3" AZ type bogies, 5-1960;
Fitted with mini buffet & painted green & cream, 27-9-1963;
W/o, 31-5-1977;
Body to Midvale Primary school;
To ARHS Rail Transport Museum, Bassendean, 30-1-1990;
Sold in Wattle Grove for $6000;
Left Bassendean, 1-11-2001.

AR 420   Entered service 3-1-1919;
Reclass. ARS, 30-6-1924;
Conv. to 4 berth 16-12-1937/47?;
Painted two tone green & cream for the "Westland", 3-1948;
Painted Larch green ?-195?;
AQZ 420   Conv. to AQZ first class sleeping car, 14-12-1957;
Fitted with 6'3" AZ type bogies, 5-1960;
Fitted with vestibule ends for the "Mullewa" & painted green &
cream, 10-1961;
Leased to Hotham Valley Railway, 1979;
Into HVR shops for repairs 26-10-1980;
Sold to Hotham Valley Railway, 1984.

AR 421   Entered service 4-2-1919;
Reclass. ARS, 30-6-1924;
Conv. to 4 berth 1-10-1937;
Painted two tone green & cream for the "Westland", 3-1948;
Painted Larch green 9-1956;
Painted green & cream, 11-1965;
W/o, 19-12-1975;
To GSSA, Albany;
Sold to ARHS, 12-1984;
Stored at Cresco's in Bayswater;
To Rail Transport Museum, Bassendean, 17-4-1989.

AR 422   Entered service 4-2-1919;
Reclass. ARS, 30-6-1924;
Conv. to 4 berth 11-6-1937;
Painted two tone green & cream for the "Westland", 3-1948;
Painted Larch green 6-1956;
Painted green & cream, 10-1964;
W/o, 12-11-1973.

AR 423   Entered service 11-2-1919;
Reclass. ARS, 30-6-1924;
Conv. to 4 berth 14-12-1937;
Painted Larch green, 1-1954;
AQZ 423   Conv. to AQZ first class sleeping car, 14-12-1957;
Fitted with 6'3" AZ type bogies, 5-1960;
Painted green & cream, 7-1963;
W/o, 8-10-1976;
To GSSA, Albany;
To ARHS, 12-1984;
Returned to service 7-9-1985.

AR 424   Entered service 11-2-1919;
Reclass. ARS, 30-6-1924;
Conv. to 4 berth, 23-7-1937;
Painted two tone green & cream for the "Westland", 6-1948;
Painted Larch green, 8-1955;
AQZ 424   Conv. to AQZ first class sleeping car, 14-12-1957;
Fitted with 6'3" AZ type bogies, 5-1960;
Painted green & cream, 5-1961;
Leased to HVR, 1979;
Sold to HVR, 1984.

1918 Dining Cars   Midland.   [AV class]
AV 425   Entered service 24-4-1919;
Refurbished, 5-1947;
Painted Larch green, 12-1951;
Painted green & cream, 12-1966;
Fitted with 7' wheel base ride control bogies, 7-1967;
Stored 1969;
W/o, 6-9-1974;
To ARHS Rail Transport Museum, Bassendean, 11-1974;
Restored & returned to service, 1-6-1991.

AV 426   Entered service 24-4-1919;
           Refurbished, 1947;
           Painted Larch green, 9-1953;
           Painted green & cream, 8-1966;
           Stored 1969;
           W/o, 6-9-1974;
           To Hotham Valley Railway, 28-7-1975.

1919 Express brakevans   Midland.   [ZJ class]
AJ 427   Entered service 12-7-1919;
           Used on Royal train, 1927;
           Reclass. ZJ, 30-6-1940;
           Used on ambulance train for Commonwealth Govt, 2-1942;
           Returned to normal service, 4-1945;
           Fitted with gangways for the "Australind", 1947;
           Painted green & cream, 6-1948;
           Painted Larch green, 4-1953;
           Painted green & cream, 9-1960;
           W/o, 7-9-1982;
           To Kalamunda Arts & Crafts Group, 11-1982;
           Preserved at Kalamunda, 10-1983.

AJ 428   Entered service 25-7-1919;
           Reclass. ZJ, 30-6-1940;
           Fitted with cool chamber, 1947;
           Destroyed by fire between Malcolm & Murrin Murrin, 13-2-
1957.

AJ 429   Entered service 3-10-1919;
           Reclass. ZJ, 30-6-1940;
           Painted green & cream, 11-1947;
           Painted Larch green, 7-1956;
           Painted green & cream, 1-1963;
           W/o, 29-4-1985;
           At Esperance in use as carriage shed for model live steam railway

1922 Petrol Engined 4 wheel railmotor W.H. Dorman (engine), Simplex
(chassis)   [AO class]
430   Entered service, 16-7-1922;
           Destroyed by fire at Albany, 30-8-1936;
           Frame to Jetty 70, 25-4-1945.

(AOT 430 See 1922)
(ZJA 430 See 1960)

431   Entered service, 9-8-1922;
           Class. AO, 30-6-1937;
           To Kalgoorlie to operate on Boulder Loopline, c.1937;
           W/o, 27-6-1950.

(ZJA 431 See 1960)

432   Entered service, 29-8-1922;
           Destroyed by fire, 1926;
           W/o, 31-12-1926.

(AI 432 See 1935)
(ZJA 432 See 1960)

1922 Railmotor Trailer.   .Midland.   [AOT class]
433   Conv. from P class brakevan;
           Entered service, 16-12-1922;
           Class. AOT, 30-6-1937;
           To Kalgoorlie to operate on Boulder Loopline, c.1937;

AOT 430   Renumbered AOT 430, 16-9-1946;
           W/o, 27-6-1950;
           Conv. to workman's van DW 5092, 7-9-1951;
           W/o, 27-9-1965.

AF 59   Built using underframe from AC 59 (see 1895);
           Entered service 1-12-1922;
           Conv. to AL, painted Larch green, 7-11-1952;
           Used at Northam;
           To Northam Railway Preservation Society, 8-1980.

(AZ 433 See 1928)
(ZJA 433 See 1960)

1924 Suburban saloon cars   Midland.   [AY class]
AY 26   Conv. to lounge car for RESO & "Westland", 1928;
           Used on ambulance train for Commonwealth Govt., 1942;
           Conv. to ambulance ward car;
           Conv. to AYL lounge car for the "Kalgoorlie", 1947;
           Painted Larch green, 7-1955;
           Conv. to AY suburban car, 10-1958;
           Painted in the green, white & red livery, 10-1963;
           Painted orange & blue after 1975;
           Repainted green & cream, c.9-1986;
           Wfu, 11-1-1991;
           W/o, 2-1991;
           To ARHS, 1991/92;

Built 1927.
AY 28   Entered service 3-12-1927;
           Conv. to lounge car for "Westland", 29-7-1938;
           Used on ambulance train for Commonwealth Govt., 1942;
           Conv. to ambulance ward car;
           Conv. to AYL lounge car for the "Westland", 5-3-1946;
           Painted two tone green & cream, 3-1948;
           Painted Larch green, 7-1953/54?;
           Painted green & cream, 9-1962;
           Fitted with 7' wheel base ride control bogies, 5-1963;
           Fitted with 6'6" ADU type bogies, 5-1967;
           W/o, 19-12-1975;
           Conv. to workman's van VW 28, 11-1979;
           W/o, 5-1991;
           To ARHS 9-1991.

AY 29   Entered service 3-12-1927;
           Conv. to lounge car for "Westland", 30-6-1938;
           Used on ambulance train for Commonwealth Govt., 1942;
           Conv. to ambulance ward car;
           Conv. to AYL lounge car for the "Westland", 5-3-1946;
           Painted two tone green & cream, 6-1948;
           Painted Larch green, 8-1955;
           Fitted with 7' wheel base ride control bogies & painted green
           & cream, 6-1962;
           Fitted with 6'6" ADU type bogies, 5-1967;
           W/o, 19-12-1975;
           To PRHS, Dampier, 6-1976
           To ARHS Bassendean, 2-2002.

1926 Single compartment brakevans   Midland.   [ZB class]
ZB 10600   Renumbered ZB 206, 1938;
ZB 206   To Port Hedland;
           W/o, 1951.

ZB 10601   Renumbered ZB 207, 1938;
ZB 207   W/o 28-11-1977;
           Sold to Underground Nightclub;
           Sold to Marg's Crafty Carriage, Gidgegannup.

ZB 10602   Renumbered ZB 208, 1938;
ZB 208   Painted two tone green & cream, 6-1949;
           Conv. to workman's van VW 5145, 9-1971;
           W/o, 22-11-1977.

ZB 10603   Renumbered ZB 209, 1938;
ZB 209   Conv. to Z 209, 4-1970;
           W/o, 7-1985.

ZB 10604   Entered service, 25-12-1926;
ZB 210   Renumbered ZB 210, 22-7-1939;
           Conv. to workmans van VW 5106, 15-6-1966;
           W/o, 21-8-1973.

Built 1927.
ZB 10605   Renumbered ZB 211, 1938;
ZB 211   W/o, 6-2-1968;
           Conv. to workman's van VW 5119, 9-1968;
           Noted at Midland, 1-11-1990;
           W/o, 5-1991.

ZB 10606   Renumbered ZB 212, 1938;
ZB 212   W/o 6-2-1968.

ZB 10607 Entered service 24-12-1927;
ZB 213   Renumbered ZB 213, 1938;
          Received at workshops in 1968 & submitted for w/o;
          W/o not approved, stored sometime after 1968;
          W/o, 21-6-1977
          Body used as a store at Kewdale Marshalling Yard.

ZB 10608 Renumbered ZB 214, 1938;
ZB 214   Painted two tone green & cream, 5-1949;
          W/o, 2-6-1970.

ZB 10609 Entered service 24-12-1927;
ZB 215   Renumbered ZB 215, 1938;
          Conv. to brakevan Z 215, 8-12-1968;
          W/o, 31-1-1985.

Built 1928.
ZB 10610 Entered service 27-1-1928;
ZB 216   Renumbered ZB 216, 1938;
          Conv. to brakevan Z 216, 7-1970;
          W/o, 28-8-1985;

ZB 10611 Renumbered ZB 217, 1938;
ZB 217   Conv. to Z class brakevan with steel body & pitched roof,
          10-1968;
          W/o 20-4-1982.

ZB 10612 Renumbered ZB 218, 1938;
ZB 218   W/o, 18-1-1973.

ZB 10613 Renumbered ZB 219, 1938;
ZB 219   Conv. to Z class brakevan, 9-1969;
          W/o, 21-8-1974.

ZB 10614 Renumbered ZB 220, 1938;
ZB 220   W/o 22-3-1972.

1928 First class sleeping car   Midland.   [AZ class]
AZ 434   Entered service 29-9-1928;
          Rebogied with 6'3" wheel base bogies, 12-1934;
          Fitted with shower compartment 1936/37;
          Painted Larch green, 7-1954;
          Painted green & cream, 10-1962;
          Painted red & ivory & used on the "Midlander", 1964;
          Painted green & cream, 12-1967;
          Leased to HVR.

(ZJA 434 see 1960)

AZ 435   Entered service 29-9-1928;
          Fitted with shower compartment 1936/37;
          Rebogied with 6'3" wheel base bogies, 2-1937;
          Painted Larch green, 4-1955;
          Painted green & cream, 7-1962;
          Leased to HVR, c. 8-1979;
          W/o 3-1984, & to C. Taylor of Pinjarra for use by HVR in
          exchange for AZ 437.

AZ 436   Entered service 29-9-1928;
          Fitted with shower compartment 1936/37;
          Rebogied with 6'3" wheel base bogies, 7-1938;
          Painted Larch green, 6-1955;
          Painted green & cream, 8-1962;
          Leased to HVR.

AZ 437   Entered service 6-10-1928;
          Rebogied with 6'3" wheel base bogies, 11-1936;
          Fitted with shower compartment 1936/37;
          Painted Larch green, 8-1955;
          Painted green & cream, 8-1962;
          W/o, 11-1979;
          Sold to C. Taylor of Pinjarra for use by HVR, 1980;
          Returned to Westrail in exchange for AZ 435 & conv. to
          workman's van VW 437, 3-1984;
          W/o;
          Preserved at Kulin.

AZ 438   Entered service 30-3-1929;
          Rebogied with 6'3" wheel base bogies, 7-1936;

Fitted with shower compartment 1936/37;
Painted Larch green, 7-1953;
Painted green & cream, 12-1962;
Conv. to workman's van VW 438, 3-1984;
W/o, 3-1996;
Preserved at Kojonup.

AZ 439   Entered service 30-3-1929;
          Fitted with shower compartment 1936/37;
          Rebogied with 6'3" wheel base bogies, 3-1938;
          Painted Larch green, 12-1951;
          Painted green & cream, 7-1963;
          Leased to HVR.

AZ 440   Entered service 20-4-1929;
          Rebogied with 6'3" wheel base bogies, 12-1936;
          Fitted with shower compartment 1936/37;
          Painted Larch green, 12-1954;
          Painted green & cream, 4-1963;
          Conv. to workman's van VW 440, 3-1984;
          W/o;
          Preserved at Clackline, 1997.

AZ 441   Entered service 29-6-1929;
          Fitted with shower compartment 1936;
          Rebogied with 6'3" wheel base bogies, 9-1938;
          Painted Larch green, 9-1953;
          Painted green & cream, 9-1963;
          Destroyed by fire on the "Kalgoorlie", 23-3-1966;
          W/o, 26-5-1966.

AZ 442   Entered service 29-6-1929;
          Fitted with shower compartment 1936/37;
          Rebogied with 6'3" wheel base bogies, 3-1939;
          Painted two tone green & cream for the "Westland", 6-1948;
          Painted Larch green 2-1954;
          Painted green & cream, 2-1964;
          Destroyed by fire on the "Kalgoorlie", 23-3-1966;
          W/o, 26-5-1966.

AZ 443   Entered service 29-6-1929;
          Rebogied with 6'3" wheel base bogies, 12-1935;
          Fitted with shower compartment 1936/37;
          Painted Larch green, 8-1953;
          Painted green & cream, 4-1963;
          Leased to GSSA, Albany;
          To ARHS on lease, 12-1984;
          Sold to ARHS.

1928 Ministerial car using AZ body shell   Midland.   [AM class]
AM 444   Entered service 10-11-1928;
          Rebogied with 6'3" wheel base bogies, 10-1938;
          Used on ambulance train for Commonwealth Govt., 1942;
          Conv. to AZ 433, 21-12-1946;
          Painted two tone green & cream for the "Westland", 10-1948;
          Painted Larch green 11-1953;
          Painted green & cream, 7-1963?;
          Leased to HVR;
          Returned to Westrail & conv. to workman's van VW 433, 3-1984
          W/o, 3-1996;
          Preserved at Kulin.

1930 Express brakevan   Midland.   [ZJ class]
AJ 260   Built on the underframe of ZA 9346;
          Entered service 1-2-1930;
          Reclass. ZJ, 30-6-1940;
          Conv. bullion van VY 5000, 18-9-1948;
          Conv. to workman's van VW 5000, 3-7-1968;
          Conv. to inspection car AL 1 at Bunbury, 3-1972;
          Based at Manjimup as overnight accommodation for railway
          officers;
          W/o, 2-9-1980.
          To Bellarine Peninsular Railway, Victoria.

1931 Sentinal Steam Car   Midland, from imported parts.   [ASA class]
ASA 445   Entered service 7-2-1931;
          Used on Perth to Armadale line;
          Painted two tone green & cream, 4-1940;

Painted Larch green -195?;
Conv. to track recorder car ALT 5, using equipment from
ALT 88, 7-11-1959;
Painted orange & blue 5-1977;
W/o, 9-1991;
To ARHS at Boyanup, 1992.

1933   Single compartment brakevans   Midland.   [ZB class]
ZB 1160   Renumbered ZB 202, 1938;
ZB 202   Conv. to brakevan Z 202, 10-1969;
W/o, 7-1985;
To HVTR, Dwellingup.

ZB 2532   Entered service 23-12-1933;
ZB 204   Renumbered ZB 204, 1938;
Destroyed in collision at Wooroloo when hit by goods train,
24-11-1949.

ZB 3333   Renumbered ZB 205, 1938;
ZB 205   W/o 1965.

1935 Railmotor on Dodge chassis, 6 cyl. 25 hp.   Midland.   [AI class]
432(2nd)   Entered service 19-10-1935;
Delivered to Port Hedland aboard "MV Koolinda", ex Perth,
21-10-1935;
Used Port Hedland to Marble Bar line;
Class. AI, 30-6-1937;
Sold to State Saw Mills, 21-4-1949;
Fate unknown.

1937 Governor class railcars   Armstrong Whitworth.   [ADE class]
(These cars entered service in the 2 tone green & cream livery, & were all
repainted in the green, white & red livery during the 1950's).
ADE 446   "Governor Stirling". Entered service 27-11-1937;
Worked Perth to Merredin (mainline);
Painted Larch green, 12-1953;
W/o, 9-4-1962;
Still at Salvage, 1974.

ADE 447   "Governor Lawley". Entered service 7-2-1938;
Worked Perth to Merredin (via Wyalkatchem);
Painted Larch green, 12-1953;
Coupled to ADE's 449, 450, & 451 as suburban set, 1961;
W/o, 9-4-1962;
Sold to Albany Harbour Board;
Sold to Wayback Tourist Railway;
Arrived at Bushmead for storage 10-4-1986;
Demolished early 1992.

ADE 448   "Governor John Hutt". Entered service 2-2-1938;
Worked Perth to Merredin (via Quairading);
Painted Larch green, 3-1954;
W/o, 9-4-1962;
Still at Salvage, 1974.

ADE 449   "Governor Weld". Entered service 9-2-1938;
Worked Perth to Katanning;
Painted Larch green, 5-1953;
Coupled to ADE's 447, 450, & 451 as suburban set, 1961;
W/o, 9-4-1962;
Still in store at Old Midland Loco, 16-10-1973.

ADE 450   "Governor Hampton". Entered service 12-3-1938;
Worked Bunbury branches;
Painted Larch green, 10-1952;
Coupled to ADE's 447, 449, & 451 as suburban set, 1961;
W/o, 9-4-1962;
Still at Salvage, 1974.

ADE 451   "Governor Bedford". Entered service 25-4-1938;
Worked Geraldton branches;
Painted Larch green, 12-1952;
Coupled to ADE's 447, 449, & 450 as suburban set, 1961;
W/o, 9-4-1962.

1939 Governor railcar trailers   Midland.   [ADT class]
These cars entered service in the 2 tone green & cream livery).
ADT 7   Entered service 14-12-1939;
Painted Larch green, 12-1953;

W/o, 17-4-1962.

ADT 8   Entered service 1-2-1940;
Painted Larch green, 5-1956;
W/o, 17-4-1962.

ADT 9   Entered service 29-2-1940;
Painted Larch green, 6-1953;
W/o, 17-4-1962;
Body at Mary Springs;
Moved to a different property at Mary Springs, late 2002.

ADT 10   Entered service 21-3-1940;
Painted Larch green, 4-1952;
W/o, 17-4-1962.

ADT 11   Entered service 20-4-1940;
Painted Larch green, ?-195?;
W/o, 17-4-1962.

ADT 12   Entered service 27-7-1940;
Painted Larch green, 8-1956;
W/o, 17-4-1962.

1941 Steel bodied suburban car Midland (frames from AF class cars).
[AJ class]
(These cars entered service in the 2 tone green & cream livery).
AJ 64   Entered service 1-9-1941;
Painted Larch green, 1-1955;
Painted in the green, white & red livery, 5-1965;
W/o, 3-3-1972;
To Northam, 11-1974;
Remains at Northam.

AJ 69   Entered service 31-10-1941;
Conv. to AJL class lounge car for Kalgoorlie & Wiluna trains,
20-12-1947;
Conv. back to AJ 2-12-1950;
Painted Larch green, 1-1955;
W/o, 5-9-1960.

AJ 95   Entered service 11-12-1941;
Fitted with guard's compt. & reclass. AJB, 2-12-1950;
Painted Larch green, 3-1952;
W/o 21-5-1959;
Remains noted at Greenmount, 4-95;
Demolished 12-1999.

AJ 166   Entered service 2-10-1941;
Painted Larch green, 12-1953;
Painted in the green, white & red livery, 11-1964;
W/o 3-3-1972;
To Northam, burnt.

1942 First class suburban saloon   Midland.   [AK class]
(This car entered service in the 2 tone green & cream livery).
AK 60   Entered service 25-7-1942;
Fitted with guard's compt. & reclass. AKB, 2-12-1950;
Painted Larch green, 10-1953;
Painted in the green, white & red livery, 3-1967;
W/o, 9-6-1971;
Located behind apprentice's school, 10-1973;
To salvage for disposal, 10-1977;
Offered to HVR, but not taken up;
To Gidgegannup & incorporated into a house,.

1945 Second class suburban saloon   Midland.   [AY class]
(These cars entered service in the 2 tone green & cream livery).
AY 452   Entered service 22-12-1945;
Painted Larch green, 11-1955;
Painted in the green, white & red livery, 4-1966;
Painted orange & blue after 1975;
Repainted green & cream, c.9-1986;
Wfu, 11-1-1991
W/o, 2-1991;
To ARHS, 1991/92;
To Boyanup, 1992/93;
To Bassendean, 5-1995.

AY 453   Entered service 22-12-1945;
          Painted Larch green, 11-1955;
          Painted in the green, white & red livery, 9-1963;
          Painted orange & blue after 1975;
          Repainted green & cream, c.5-7-1986;
          Wfu, 11-1-1991;
          W/o, 2-1991;
          To ARHS, 1991/92..

AY 454   Entered service 22-12-1945;
          Painted Larch green, 12-1952;
          Painted in the green, white & red livery, 10-1963;
          Painted green & cream, 12-1960;
          Painted orange & blue after 1975;
          Stored 1982;
          Returned to service 7-1983;
          W/o, 11-1983;
          Sold, 1984 in Stoneville;

AY 455   Entered service 22-12-1945;
          Painted Larch green, 3-1953;
          Painted green & cream, 12-1960;
          Painted in the green, white & red livery, 11-1963;
          Painted orange & blue after 1975;
          Repainted green & cream, c.9-1986;
          Wfu, 11-1-1991;
          W/o, 2-1991;
          To ARHS, 1991/92;
          To Boyanup, 1992/93..

1945 First/second class suburban brake saloon   Midland.   [AYB class]
(These cars entered service in the 2 tone green & cream livery).
AYB 456   Entered service 22-12-1945;
          Painted Larch green, 12-1952;
          Painted in the green, white & red livery, 10-1967;
          W/o, 22-7-1969;
          Frame used to build shed at Midland Workshops.

AYB 457   Entered service 22-12-1945;
          Painted Larch green, 12-1952;
          Painted in the green, white & red livery, 1-1966;
          W/o 22-7-1969
          Frame used as workshop float at Midland till 1990.

Built 1946.
AYB 458   Entered service 3-8-1946;
          Painted Larch green, 12-1955;
          Painted in the green, white & red livery, 7-1970?;
          Painted orange & blue after 1975;
          Repainted green & cream, 11-4-1986;
          Wfu, 11-1-1991;
          W/o, 2-1991;
          To Cannington Greyhound Track;
          Purchased by Ian Willis & to Pemberton.

AYB 459   Entered service 3-8-1946;
          Painted Larch green, 12-1955;
          Painted in the green, white & red livery, 11-1963;
          Painted orange & blue after 1975;
          Repainted green & cream, 26-3-1986;
          Wfu, 11-1-1991;
          W/o, 2-1991;
          To Cannington Greyhound Track;
          Purchased by Ian Willis & to Pemberton.

1946 Second class suburban saloon   Midland.   [AY class]
(These cars entered service in the 2 tone green & cream livery).
AY 460   Entered service 3-8-1946;
          Painted Larch green, 12-1955;
          Conv. to AYS buffet car "Colgoola", on 7' wheel base ride
          control bogies, & painted green & cream, 30-10-1962;
          To KBLLPS, 1984(?).

AY 461   Entered service 3-8-1946;
          Painted Larch green, 11-1955;
          Conv. to AYS buffet car "Boulder", on 7' wheel base ride
          control bogies, & painted green & cream, 22-9-1962;
          Gutted in fire on "Kalgoorlie" 23-3-1966;
          Rebuilt by 12-1966;

          First WAGR car fitted with air conditioning;
          Leased to GSSA, Albany;
          To ARHS, 12-1984;
          To Midland, 7-7-1994.

1947 First class "Australind" saloon   Midland.   [AYC class]
(This car entered service in the 2 tone green & cream livery).
AYC 500   Entered service 22-11-1947;
          Painted Larch green, 4-1953;
          Painted green & cream, 9-1960;
          Damaged in collision at Claisebrook, 11-1982;
          Rebuilt;
          To ARHS 30-8-1990
          W/o, 18-9-1990.

1947 Second class "Australind" saloon   Midland.   [AYC class]
(These cars entered service in the 2 tone green & cream livery).
AYC 510   Entered service 22-11-1947;
          Painted Larch green, 4-1953;
          Painted green & cream, 9-1960;
          To ARHS, 30-8-1990
          W/o, 18-9-1990.

AYC 511   Entered service 22-11-1947;
          Painted Larch green, 4-1953;
          Painted green & cream, 9-1960;
          To ARHS, 30-8-1990
          W/o, 18-9-1990.

AYC 512   Entered service 22-11-1947;
          Painted Larch green, 4-1953;
          Painted green & cream, 9-1960;
          To ARHS, 30-8-1990;
          W/o, 18-9-1990;
          To Midland, 7-7-1994..

1947 First class "Australind" buffet car   Midland.   [AYD class]
(This car entered service in the 2 tone green & cream livery).
AYD 540   Entered service 22-11-1947;
          Painted Larch green, 4-1953;
          Painted green & cream, 9-1960;
          To ARHS, 30-8-1990
          W/o, 18-9-1990;
          To Midland, 7-7-1994.

1947 Second class "Australind" buffet car   Midland.   [AYD class]
(This car entered service in the 2 tone green & cream livery).
AYD 550   Entered service 22-11-1947;
          Painted Larch green, 4-1953;
          Painted green & cream, 9-1960;
          To ARHS, 30-8-1990
          W/o, 18-9-1990.

1948 First class steel bodied sleeping car   Midland.   [AH class]
(These cars entered service in the 2 tone green & cream livery).
AH 560   Entered service 22-3-1948;
          Painted Larch green, 4-1954;
          Experimentally fitted with Bradford-Kendall "Commonwealth"
          ride control bogies, 1955;
          Painted green & cream, 12-1961;
          W/o, 19-12-1975;
          Scrapped Midland.

AH 561   Entered service 22-3-1948;
          Painted Larch green, 6-1953;
          Painted green & cream, 6-1961;
          W/o, 19-12-1975;
          Sold to farmer at Dowerin for use as shearers quarters.

AH 562   Entered service 22-3-1948;
          Painted Larch green, 10-1953;
          Painted green & cream, 11-1961;
          W/o, 19-12-1975;
          Body at Jandakot.

AH 563   Entered service 4-6-1948;
          Painted Larch green, 11-1953;
          Painted green & cream, 7-1961;

W/o, 19-12-1975;
To ARHS Rail Transport Museum, 13-3-1976.

AH 564   Entered service 4-6-1948;
Painted Larch green, 6-1954;
Painted green & cream, 4-1962;
W/o, 19-12-1975;
To PRHS at Dampier, 1-1977;
Placed on standard gauge bogies;
To ARHS at Midland,.

AH 565   Entered service 4-6-1948;
Painted Larch green, 8-1953;
Painted green & cream, 10-1961;
W/o, 19-12-1975;
To PRHS at Dampier, 1-1977;
Placed on standard gauge bogies;
To ARHS at Midland,.

1949 "Wildflower" class railcars   Midland.   [ADF class]
(These cars entered service in the 2 tone green & cream livery & were all repainted in the green, white & red livery during the 1950's).
ADF 490   "Boronia". Entered service 29-8-1949;
Painted Larch green, ?-195?;
Stored 3-1959;
Conv. to instruction van VI 7980, 6-11-1964;
W/o, 22-9-1980;
Sold to Metana Minerals, Mt. Magnet to house generating set.

ADF 491   "Crowea". Entered service 5-11-1949;
Painted Larch green, 3-1953;
Stored 20-11-1964 at Midland.

ADF 492   "Grevillea". Entered service 14-12-1949;
Painted Larch green, 9-1953;
Used on the "Bunbury Belle" & "Shopper", 1964;
W/o, 27-10-1975.

ADF 493   "Hovea". Entered service 18-3-1950;
Painted Larch green, 4-1954;
W/o, 27-10-1975.

ADF 494   "Leschanaultia". Entered service 6-4-1950;
Painted Larch green, 7-1953;
Used on the "Bunbury Belle" & "Shopper", 1964?;
Wfu, 5-1961;
W/o, 20-2-1970.

ADF 495   "Banksia". Entered service 24-6-1950;
Painted Larch green, 3-1954;
Used on the "Bunbury Belle" & "Shopper", 1964;
W/o, 27-10-1975.
To ARHS Rail Transport Museum, Bassendean, 30-1-1976.

1949 "Wildflower" railcar trailers.   Midland.   [ADU class]
(These cars entered service in the 2 tone green & cream livery).
ADU 580   Entered service 29-8-1949;
Painted Larch green, 11-1953;
Conv. to AYU & painted red & ivory for use on the
  "Midlander", 21-8-1964;
Painted green & cream, 2-1967;
W/o, 23-5-1980;
Body to Metana Minerals, Mt. Magnet.

ADU 581   Entered service 29-8-1949;
Painted Larch green, 11-1953;
Painted green & cream, 6-1963;
Conv. to AYU & painted red & ivory for use on the
  "Midlander", 14-9-1964;
Used between Mullewa & Meekatharra;
Repainted green & cream, 1967;
W/o, 23-5-1980;
Body to Metana Minerals, Mt. Magnet.

ADU 582   Entered service 29-8-1949;
Painted Larch green, 9-1953;
W/o, 14-10-1966.

ADU 583   Entered service 5-11-1949;

Painted Larch green, 9-1953;
W/o, 14-10-1966.

ADU 584   Entered service 14-12-1949;
Painted Larch green, 2-1952;
Conv. to AYU for use on loco hauled trains & painted green & cream, 8-7-1966;
W/o, 23-5-1980;
Body to Metana Minerals, Mt. Magnet.

ADU 585   Entered service 14-12-1949;
Painted Larch green, 2-1952;
Conv. to AYU for use on loco hauled trains, & painted green & cream, 8-7-1966;
W/o, 23-5-1980;
Body to Metana Minerals, Mt. Magnet.

ADU 586   Entered service 18-3-1950;
Painted Larch green, 12-1955;
Painted in the green, white & red livery, 3-1960?;
W/o, 27-10-1975.

ADU 587   Entered service 18-3-1950;
Painted Larch green, 12-1955;
Painted in the green, white & red livery, 3-1960?;
W/o, 27-10-1975.

ADU 588   Entered service 26-5-1950;
Painted Larch green, 8-1958?;
Sloping ends removed for "Bunbury Belle" & "Shopper", & painted in the green, white & red livery 5-1964;
W/o, 27-10-1975.

ADU 589   Entered service 26-5-1950;
Painted Larch green, 8-1958?;
Sloping ends removed for "Bunbury Belle" & "Shopper", & painted in the green, white & red livery 5-1964;
W/o, 27-10-1975.

ADU 590   Entered service 1-7-1950;
Painted Larch green, 3-1953;
Used on "Bunbury Belle" & "Shopper", but sloping ends retained, & painted in the green, white & red livery, 5-1964;
W/o, 27-10-1975.

ADU 591   Entered service 1-7-1950;
Painted Larch green, 3-1953;
Used on "Bunbury Belle" & "Shopper", but sloping ends retained, & painted in the green, white & red livery, 5-1964;
W/o, 27-10-1975.

1954 Suburban railcars   Cravens.   [ADG class]
(These cars entered service in plain Larch green, & all were repainted in the green, white & red livery during the 1950's.)
ADG 601   Entered service 28-5-1954;
Fitted with Voith Transmission, trialed to Muchea with;
ADA 751 3-9-1969;
Returned to service, 22-9-1969;
Painted orange & blue, 5-1978;
Reclass. ADG/V 10-1978;
Scrapped/dumped c.1984.

ADG 602   Entered service 28-5-1954;
Fitted with Voith Transmission 6-5-1971;
Painted orange & blue, 7-1978;
Reclass. ADG/V 10-1978;
ADG/V 618 Car renumbered ADG/V 618, 28-5-1984;
Fitted with Mercedes Benz engines, 24-10-1987;
To Forrestfield for storage, 1-1992;
W/o, 3-1992.

ADG 603   Entered service 18-6-1954;
Fitted with Voith Transmission 4-11-1971;
Painted orange & blue, ?-197?;
Reclass. ADG/V 10-1978;
ADG/V 614 Car renumbered ADG/V 614, 8-11-1983;
Fitted with Mercedes Benz engines, 18-7-1987;
To Forrestfield for storage, 12-2-1992;

W/o, 3-1992;
To Colin Taylor for HVTR, noted at Forrestfield 11-1992, still
there 4-1994;
To Pinjarra.

ADG 604   Entered service 18-6-1954;
Fitted with Voith Transmission 15-8-1972;
Painted orange & blue, 9-1977;
Reclass. ADG/V 10-1978;
W/o, 14-11-1983;
Body to Metana Minerals, Mt. Magnet, 1984.

ADG 605   Entered service 7-7-1954;
Fitted with Voith Transmission 27-10-1972;
Painted orange & blue, 12-1975;
Reclass. ADG/V 10-1978;
Stored 9-1982;
Returned to traffic, 7-1983;
Fitted with ADX engines, 1986;
Caught fire on Armadale line 8-4-1987;
Returned to service 25-7-1987;
Withdrawn from use, 12-1991;
To Forrestfield for storage, 12-1991;
W/o, 3-1992;
Still at Forrestfield, 9-1994;
To Colin Taylor for HVTR.

ADG 606   Entered service 18-6-1954;
Collided with AD 49, Pert Carriage Sheds(?), 23-5-1962;
Fitted with Voith Transmission 12-5-1972;
Painted orange & blue, 7-1977;
Reclass. ADG/V 10-1978;
ADG/V 601 Car renumbered ADG/V 601, 23-11-1984;
Fitted with ADX engines, 1986;
Set alight by vandals at Challis on Armadale line & burnt out,
27-4-1989;
W/o, 9-8-1989 (Westland 62)/8-12-1989 (Westland 64)
/Oct/Nov. 1989 (W/N 49/89);
Remains scrapped 1-1991.

ADG 607   Entered service 5-8-1954;
Fitted with Voith Transmission 9-1-1970;
Painted orange & blue, ?-197?;
Reclass. ADG/V 10-1978;
To Forrestfield for storage, 1-1992;
W/o, 3-1992;
Sold to Kojonup Tourist Railway, 12-1992;
Stored at Kwinana;
Burnt by vandals, 26-4-1993.

ADG 608   Entered service 20-10-1954;
Fitted with Voith Transmission 23-9-1969;
Painted orange & blue, 9-1978?;
Reclass. ADG/V 10-1978;
Fitted with ADX engines, 1986;
To Forrestfield for storage, 1-1992;
W/o, 3-1992;
Sold to Kojonup Tourist Railway, 12-1992;
Stored at Kwinana;
Burnt by vandals, 26-4-1993.

ADG 609   Entered service 9-7-1954;
Fitted with Voith Transmission 15-5-1970;
Painted orange & blue, ?-197?;
Reclass. ADG/V 10-1978;
Withdrawn from use by 12-1991;
W/o, 3-1992;
Scrapped 6-1992.

ADG 610   Entered service 5-8-1954;
Fitted with Voith Transmission 8-3-1972;
Painted orange & blue, 5-1977;
Reclass. ADG/V 10-1978;
To Forrestfield for storage, 1-1992;
W/o, 3-1992;
To Dave Hockey, del. Dwellingup 19-10-1992.

ADG 611   Entered service 5-8-1954;
Fitted with Voith Transmission 4-8-1970;

Painted orange & blue, ?-197?;
Reclass. ADG/V 10-1978;
Fitted with ADX engines, 1986;
Withdrawn from use, 9-1991;
W/o, 3-1992;
Scrapped 6-1992.

ADG 612   Entered service 13-8-1954;
Fitted with Voith Transmission 2-8-1971;
Painted orange & blue, ?-197?;
Reclass. ADG/V 10-1978;
ADG/V 615 Car renumbered ADG/V 615, 3-5-1983;
Fitted with Mercedes Benz engines, 5-9-1987;
W/o, 3-1992;
To WA Fire Brigade at Forrestfield.

ADG 613   Entered service 13-8-1954;
Fitted with Voith Transmission 18-8-1970;
Painted orange & blue, ?-197?;
Reclass. ADG/V 10-1978;
To Forrestfield for storage, 1-1992;
W/o, 3-1992.

ADG 614   Entered service 14-10-1954;
Fitted with Voith Transmission 22-12-1970;
Painted orange & blue, ?-197?;
Reclass. ADG/V 10-1978;
ADG/V 602 Car renumbered ADG/V 602, 22-3-1984;
Fitted with Mercedes Benz engines, 14-2-1987;
To Forrestfield for storage, 1-1992;
W/o, 3-1992;
To Dave Hockey at Pinjarra.

ADG 615   Entered service 10-9-1954;
Fitted with Voith Transmission 6-11-1972;
Painted orange & blue, 5-1976;
Reclass. ADG/V 10-1978;
ADG/V 603 Car renumbered ADG/V 603, 16-8-1983;
Fitted with ADX engines, 1986;
Withdrawn from use, 12-1991;
To Forrestfield for storage, 12-1991;
W/o, 3-1992;
Still at Forrestfield, 9-1994;
To HVTR.

ADG 616   Entered service 28-9-1954;
Fitted with Voith Transmission 10-3-1971;
Reclass. ADG/V 10-1978;
ADG/V 612 Car renumbered ADG/V 612, 15-12-1982;
Fitted with ADX engines, 1986;
To Forrestfield for storage, 1-1992;
W/o, 3-1992;
To ARHS, stowed Forrestfield;
To Midland, 7-7-1994.

ADG 617   Entered service 28-9-1954;
Fitted with Voith Transmission 16-12-1969;
Painted orange & blue, ?-197?;
Reclass. ADG/V 10-1978;
Fitted with ADX engines, 1986;
To Midland for fitting of Mercedes Benz engines, 10-1986;
Outshopped, 2-1987;
Withdrawn from use, 12-1991;
To Forrestfield for storage, 12-1991;
W/o, 3-1992;
To WA Fire Brigade at Forrestfield;
Burnt by mistake, & scrapped.

ADG 618   Entered service 28-9-1954;
Fitted with Voith Transmission 22-1-1973;
Painted orange & blue, 4-1977;
Reclass. ADG/V 10-1978;
ADG/V 606 Car renumbered ADG/V 606, 4-10-1984;
Fitted with ADX engines, 1986;
Withdrawn from use, 10-1991;
W/o, 3-1992;
Reported at Jandakot?

1955 Country Railcars   Cravens.   [ADH class]
(All cars painted in the green, white & red livery, when converted for
suburban use, except ADH 654, which may have been delivered in that
colour scheme).
ADH 651 Entered service 18-6-1955;
            Conv. to suburban railcar, 2-7-1963;
            Fitted with Voith transmission, 16-6-1972;
            Painted orange & blue, 8-1977;
            Reclass. ADH/V, 10-1978;
            Fitted with Mercedes Benz engines, 5-12-1987;
            To Forrestfield for storage, 12-2-1992;
            W/o, 3-1992;
            To WA Fire Brigade at Forrestfield.

ADH 652 Entered service 22-6-1955;
            Conv. to suburban railcar, 4-6-1963;
            Fitted with Voith transmission, 9-5-1973;
            Painted orange & blue, 1-1978;
            Reclass. ADH/V, 10-1978;
            Fitted with Mercedes Benz engines, 27-2-1988;
            To Forrestfield for storage, 12-2-1992;
            W/o, 3-1992;
            Preserved at Mt. Helena by driver J.C. Wright, by 12-3-1993.

ADH 653 Entered service 29-6-1955;
            Conv. to suburban railcar, 12-1-1962;
            Fitted with Voith transmission, 22-12-1971;
            Painted orange & blue, 1-1977;
            Reclass. ADH/V, 10-1978;
            Damaged in collision with goods train near Perth Terminal;
            W/o, 1-7-1981.

ADH 654 Entered service 12-7-1956;
            Conv. to suburban railcar, 23-1-1962;
            Fitted with Voith transmission, 22-9-1971;
            Painted orange & blue, 9-1976?;
            Reclass. ADH/V, 10-1978;
            Fitted with Mercedes Benz engines, 28-5-1988;
            To Forrestfield for storage, 1-1992;
            W/o, 3-1992;
            Scrapped.

1955 Suburban saloon cars   Midland.   [AYE class]
AYE 701 Built using frame from ADS 119;
            Entered service 11-6-1955;
            Painted in the green, white & red livery, 12-1960;
            Painted orange & blue, ?-197?;
            Stored 1982;
            Returned to service, 7-1983;
            W/o, 11-1983.
            Sold;
            At Murray Field (Royal Aero Club), Mandurah, c.1991;
            At Karnet.

AYE 702 Built using frame from AC 73;
            Entered service 18-6-1955;
            Painted in the green, white & red livery, 9-1960;
            Fitted with guard's compartment & reclass. AYF, 6-7-1970;
            Painted orange & blue, ?-197?;
            Stored 1982;
            Returned to service, 7-1983;
            Painted green & cream, c.9-1986;
            Wfu, 11-1-1991;
            W/o, 2-1991.

AYE 703 Built using frame from AF 99;
            Entered service 24-5-1955;
            Painted in the green, white & red livery, 8-1962;
            Painted orange & blue, ?-197?;
            W/o, 23-5-1980;
            To Eastern Hills Apex Club (Shire of Mundaring);
            Placed in railway reserve at Glen Forrest;
            Gone by 7-1982.

AYE 704 Built using frame from AF 140;
            Entered service 28-5-1955;
            Painted in the green, white & red livery, 11-1962?;
            Fitted with guard's compartment & reclass. AYF, 11-9-1967;
            Painted orange & blue, ?-197?;

W/o, 11-1983;
            To KBLLPS, 1984/85.

AYE 705 Built using frame from AF 160;
            Entered service 11-6-1955;
            Painted in the green, white & red livery, 9-1961;
            Fitted with guard's compartment & reclass. AYF, 12-2-1968;
            Painted orange & blue, ?-197?;
            W/o, 11-1983;
            To KBLLPS, 1984/85.

AYE 706 Built using frame from AF 167;
            Entered service 11-6-1955;
            Painted in the green, white & red livery, 12-1961;
            Fitted with guard's compartment & reclass. AYF, 21-4-1967;
            Painted orange & blue, ?-197?;
            Painted green & cream, c.9-1986;
            Wfu 11-1-1991;
            W/o, 2-1991;
            To Carnarvon:
            To Pemberton.

AYE 707 Built using frame from AF 197;
            Entered service 11-6-1955;
            Painted in the green, white & red livery, 3-1961;
            Fitted with guard's compartment & reclass. AYF, 26-3-1970;
            Painted orange & blue, ?-197?;
            W/o, 11-1983;
            To Anaco Ltd. (Freight company), for Mt. Magnet;
            To Menzies.

AYE 708 Built using frame from AF 200;
            Entered service 18-6-1955;
            Painted in the green, white & red livery, 11-1962?;
            Fitted with modified control gear, 5-5-1971;
            Painted orange & blue, 3-1978;
            Reclass. AYE/V, 10-1978;
            Painted green & cream, c.9-1986;
            Wfu, 11-1-1991;
            W/o, 2-1991;
            To Cannington Greyhound Track;
            Purchased by Ian Willis, & to Pemberton.

AYE 709 Built using frame from ZAF 433 (AF 157);
            Entered service 18-6-1955;
            Painted in the green, white & red livery, 10-1965;
            Fitted with modified control gear, 17-5-1971;
            Painted orange & blue, 7-1978;
            Reclass. AYE/V, 10-1978;
            Painted green & cream, c.9-1986;
            Wfu, 11-1-1991;
            W/o, 2-1991;
            To ARHS Boyanup.

710-718 built 1958.
AYE 710 Built using frame from AF 275;
            Entered service 7-6-1958;
            Painted in white, green & red livery, 11-1961;
            Painted orange & blue, 23-2-1979;
            Was to have been withdrawn from normal service after the
            1984/85 ADL's arrived & retained for hired specials;
            Painted green & cream, c.9-1986;
            Damaged by fire, 25-10-1989;
            W/o, 24-5-1990:
            To York Station.

AYE 711 Built using frame from AF 57;
            Entered service 7-6-1958;
            Painted in white, green & red livery, 3-11-1961;
            Painted orange & blue, 16-9-1977;
            W/o, 14-11-1983.

AYE 712 Built using frame from AF 31;
            Entered service 7-6-1958;
            Painted in the green, white & red livery, 6-1961?;
            Painted orange & blue, ?-197?;
            W/o, 5-1980.

AYE 713 Built using frame from AF 32;
Entered service 7-6-1958;
Painted in the green, white & red livery, 7-1961;
Fitted with modified control gear, 31-10-1969;
Painted orange & blue, 10-1978;
Reclass. AYE/V, 10-1978;
Painted green & cream, c.9-1986;
Used with ADG/V/ADH/V set from 22-11-1988;
Wfu 11-1-1991;
W/o, 2-1991;
To Kalgoorlie Boulder Loopline Preservation Society.

AYE 714 Built using frame from AF 273;
Entered service 7-6-1958;
Painted in the green, white & red livery, 7-1961;
Fitted with modified control gear, 31-10-1969;
Painted orange & blue, 5-1979;
Reclass. AYE/V, 10-1978;
Painted green & cream, 8-1986;
Wfu, 11-1-1991;
W/o, 2-1991;
To Kalgoorlie Boulder Loopline Preservation Society.

1955 Vice Regal Car   Midland.   [AN class]
AN 413   Built on frame of ACW 325, with AZ bogies;
Entered service 12-8-1955;
Painted Larch green, 6-1959;
Painted green & cream, 3-1966;
To ARHS for preservation;
Arrived Bassendean, 13-5-1990.

1959 Suburban diesel railcars   Midland.   [ADX class]
(Delivered in the green, white & red livery).
ADX 661 Entered service 17-8-1959;
Painted orange & blue, ?5-197?;
Stored, 9-1982;
W/o, 14-11-1983;
To Metana Minerals, Mt. Magnet, 1984.

ADX 662 Entered service 16-9-1959;
Painted orange & blue, 22-2-1977;
Stored, 9-1988;
W/o, 9-8-1989;
Buried Gosnells Tip, 8-12-1989.

ADX 663 Entered service 2-10-1959;
Painted orange & blue, 22-12-1975;
W/o, 25-11-1987;
Buried Gosnells Tip, 8-12-1989.

ADX 664 Entered service 7-11-1959;
Painted orange & blue, 7-1976;
Engines removed & used in loco hauled suburban set;
Noted stored at Forrestfield, 15-4-1989;
W/o, 13-9-1990.

ADX 665 Entered service 27-11-1959;
Last railcar in green, painted orange & blue at Perth Carriage
sheds, c. 5-1980;
W/o, 30-7-1985.

ADX 666 Entered service 17-12-1959;
Painted orange & blue, 15-4-1976;
W/o, 30-7-1985.

ADX 667 Entered service 3-2-1960;
Painted orange & blue ?-197?;
Engines removed & car used in loco hauled suburban set;
Wfu, 14-4-1986?;
W/o, 25-11-1987.

ADX 668 Entered service 10-3-1960;
Painted orange & blue, 15-3-1977;
Wfu, 30-4-1985;
W/o, 30-7-1985.

ADX 669 Entered service 1-4-1960;
Painted orange & blue, 6-1977;
Engines removed & used in loco hauled suburban set;
W/o, 13-9-1990.

ADX 670 Entered service 14-5-1960;
Modified with powered double doors, no guard's compt.,
stainless steel cowcatcher & blue & grey livery, outshopped 7-7-1966;
Entered service, 11-7-1966;
Repainted green, white & red, & doors to mechanical operation,
22-10-1968;
Painted orange & blue, ?-197?;
Wfu, 2-4-1982;
W/o, 14-11-1983;
To Metana Minerals, Mt. Magnet, 1984.

1960 Express brakevans   Midland.   [ZJA class]
ZJA 430 Entered service 4-6-1960;
Painted green & cream, 10-1961;
W/o, 7-1985;
Sold 1988.

ZJA 431 Entered service 4-6-1960;
Painted green & cream, 3-1964;
Rebuilt with plywood sides & gangways, 1982;
W/o, 10-1991;
To ARHS, Bassendean.

ZJA 432 Entered service 11-6-1960;
Painted green & cream, 3-1964;
W/o, 7-1985;
To Leschanault Preservation Society, Boyanup.

ZJA 433 Entered service 18-6-1960;
Painted green & cream, 5-1964;
Painted red & ivory for use on the "Midlander", 8-1964;
Painted green & cream, 8-1967;
W/o, 7-1985;
Stowed Midland, & still there 11-1990;
Sold to Joe Shaw at Toodyay;
Preserved privately at York.

ZJA 434 Entered service 25-6-1960;
Painted green & cream, 5-1964;
W/o, 11-1985.
To Leschanault Preservation Society, Boyanup.

1961 Suburban railcar trailers   Midland.   [ADA class]
(Delivered in the green, white & red livery).
ADA 751 Entered service 21-10-1961;
Fitted with modified control gear, & trialled to Muchea with
ADG 601, 3-9-1969;
Returned to service, 22-9-1969;
Painted orange & blue, ?-197?;
Reclass. ADA/V, 10-1978;
Wfu, 25-10-1991;
Towed from Claisebrook to Forrestfield, enroute to Robbs Jetty
for storage, 16-12-1991;
W/o, 3-1992;
Moved to Forrestfield, 5-1992;
Scrapped, 6-1992.

ADA 752 Entered service 3-11-1961;
Fitted with modified control gear, 4-8-1970;
Painted orange & blue, 7-1977;
Reclass. ADA/V, 10-1978;
Wfu, 18-11-1988;
W/o, 9-8-1989;
Buried at Gosnells Tip, 8-12-1989.

ADA 753 Entered service 24-11-1961;
Fitted with modified control gear, 18-8-1970;
Painted orange & blue, ?-197?;
Reclass. ADA/V, 10-1978;
Wfu, 25-10-1991;
Towed from Claisebrook to Forrestfield, enroute to Robbs Jetty
for storage, 16-12-1991;
W/o, 3-1992;
Moved to Forrestfield, 5-1992;
Scrapped, 6-1992.

ADA 754   Entered service 22-12-1961;
          Fitted with modified control gear, 23-9-1969;
          Last railcar to be repainted green, mid 1976;
          Painted orange & blue, ?-197?;
          Reclass. ADA/V, 10-1978;
          Wfu, 25-10-1991;
          Towed from Claisebrook to Forrestfield, enroute to Robbs Jetty
          for storage, 16-12-1991;
          W/o, 3-1992;
          Moved to Forrestfield, 5-1992;
          Scrapped, 6-1992.

ADA 755   Entered service 23-2-1962;
          Fitted with modified control gear, 22-9-1971;
          Painted orange & blue, ?-197?;
          Reclass. ADA/V, 10-1978;
          W/o, 7-11-1980.

ADA 756   Entered service 13-4-1962;
          Fitted with modified control gear, 15-5-1970;
          Painted orange & blue, ?-197?;
          Reclass. ADA/V, 10-1978;
          W/o, 3-1992;
          Preserved at Mt. Helena by driver J.C. Wright, by 12-3-1993.

ADA 757   Entered service 25-5-1962;
          Fitted with modified control gear, 24-12-1969;
          Painted orange & blue, ?-197?;
          Reclass. ADA/V, 10-1978;
          W/o, 3-1992.

ADA 758   Entered service 20-6-1962;
          Fitted with modified control gear, 22-12-1970;
          Painted orange & blue, ?-197?;
          Reclass. ADA/V, 10-1978;
          Wfu, 18-11-1988;
          W/o, 9-8-1989;
          Buried at Gosnells Tip, 8-12-1989.

ADA 759   Entered service 24-7-1962;
          Fitted with modified control gear, 2-8-1971;
          Painted orange & blue, ?-197?;
          Reclass. ADA/V, 10-1978;
          Wfu, 25-10-1991;
          Towed from Claisebrook to Forrestfield, enroute to Robbs Jetty
          for storage, 16-12-1991;
          W/o, 3-1992;
          Moved to Forrestfield, 5-1992;
          Scrapped, 6-1992.

ADA 760   Entered service 6-8-1962;
          Fitted with modified control gear, 16-12-1969;
          Painted orange & blue, 3-1977;
          Reclass. ADA/V, 10-1978;
          Wfu, 25-10-1991;
          Towed from Claisebrook to Forrestfield, enroute to Robbs Jetty
          for storage, 16-12-1991;
          W/o, 3-1992;
          Moved to Forrestfield, 5-1992;
          Scrapped, 6-1992.

761 to 765 built 1964.
ADA 761   Entered service 10-11-1964;
          Fitted with modified control gear, 20-10-1972;
          Painted orange & blue, ?-197?;
          Reclass. ADA/V, 10-1978;
          W/o, 3-1992.

ADA 762   Entered service 10-11-1964;
          Fitted with modified control gear, 7-7-1972;
          Painted orange & blue, 4-1978;
          Reclass. ADA/V, 10-1978;
          W/o 3-1992.

ADA 763   Entered service 6-11-1964;
          Fitted with modified control gear, 9-5-1973;
          Painted orange & blue, ?-197?;
          Reclass. ADA/V, 10-1978;
          Wfu, 25-10-1991;

          Towed from Claisebrook to Forrestfield, enroute to Robbs Jetty
          for storage, 16-12-1991;
          W/o, 3-1992;
          To ARHS, stowed Forrestfield;
          To Midland, 7-7-1994.

ADA 764   Entered service 10-11-1964;
          Fitted with modified control gear, 22-12-1971;
          Painted orange & blue, 6-1977;
          Reclass. ADA/V, 10-1978;
          Wfu, 25-10-1991;
          Towed from Claisebrook to Forrestfield, enroute to Robbs Jetty
          for storage, 16-12-1991;
          W/o, 3-1992;
          Moved to Forrestfield, 5-1992;
          Scrapped, 6-1992.

ADA 765   Entered service 27-11-1964;
          Fitted with modified control gear, & reclass. ADA/V;
          Painted orange & blue, 7-1978;
          Conv. to ADA/V, 28-4-1989;
          Wfu, 25-10-1992;
          Towed from Claisebrook to Forrestfield, enroute to Robbs Jetty
          for storage, 16-12-1991;
          W/o, 3-1992;
          Moved to Forrestfield, 5-1992;
          Scrapped, 6-1992.

766 to 770 built 1966.
ADA 766   Entered service 4-5-1966;
          Fitted with modified control gear, & reclass. ADA/V;
          Painted orange & blue, ?-197?;
          Conv. to ADA/V, 28-4-1989;
          Wfu, 25-10-1992;
          W/o, 3-1992;
          Scrapped, 6-1992.

ADA 767   Entered service 8-6-1966;
          Painted orange & blue, ?-197?;
          Withdrawn from use, 9-1988;
          W/o, 8-1990;
          Noted in salvage, Midland, 11-1990.

ADA 768   Entered service 17-6-1966;
          Painted orange & blue, ?-197?;
          Damaged in collision, 26-5-1981;
          W/o, 22-7-1981.

ADA 769   Entered service 12-7-1966;
          Painted orange & blue, 4-1977;
          W/o, 8-1990;
          Scrapped?

ADA 770   Entered service 1-8-1966;
          Painted orange & blue, 4-1976;
          W/o, 30-7-1985.

1964 MRWA stock into WAGR service.
Workman's vans.
VW 5121   Ex WAGR AB 222 (see 1899);
          To MRWA as J 1, 30-6-1903;
          Conv. to crew van, 1953;
          To WAGR 1-8-1964 & w/o 1965;
          Re-instated as VW 5121, 4-1970;
          Stowed Forrestfield;
          To ARHS Bassendean, 10-1992.

VW 40761 Entered MRWA service as bogie composite car K 15, 1894;
          Rebuilt as KB class brake composite car, 1914;
          Out of use by 1936;
          Renumbered KB 18, c.1936 (book no. only);
          Conv. to crew van, 1944;
          To WAGR 1-8-1964;
          Entered service as VW 40761, 31-12-1965;
          W/o, 17-9-1981.

VW 40762 Entered MRWA service as bogie composite car K 11, 1894;
          Rebuilt as KB class brake composite car, 1912;
          Out of use by 1936;

Renumbered KB 19, c.1936 (book no. only);
Conv. to crew van, 1949;
To WAGR 1-8-1964;
Entered service as VW 40762, 7-10-1966;
W/o, 1-1985.

VW 40763 Ex WAGR AP 148 (see 1898);
Entered MRWA service as sleeping car JB 22, 1915;
W/o, 1938-40;
Conv. to vehicle for tractor & driver, & reclass. KB 20, 1950;
Fitted with new chassis, 1955;
To WAGR 1-8-1964;
Entered service as VW 40763, 7-10-1966;
Stowed Forrestfield;
Stowed Midland, still there 1-1-1993;
To York station:
To Pemberton.

VW 40764 Entered MRWA service as bogie composite car K 13, 1894;
Rebuilt as second class car, 1929/30;
Renumbered K 16, 1940-1944;
W/o, 1950;
Conv. to crew van;
To WAGR 1-8-1964;
Entered service as VW 40764, 31-12-1965;
W/o, 7-1975.

Long Distance composite cars.
ACL 31   Ex WAGR AB 250 (see 1899);
To MRWA as J 4, 30-6-1903;
To WAGR 1-8-1964;
Entered service as ACL 31, painted Larch green, 11-12-1964;
Conv. to ACM suburban car, 1965;
W/o, 5-1968;
Conv. to workman's van VW 5149, 2-1974.

ACL 32   Entered MRWA service as JA 5, 1911;
To WAGR 1-8-1964;
Entered service as ACL 32, painted Larch green, 17-12-1964;
Conv. to ACM suburban car, 28-7-1965;
W/o, 31-5-1968.

ACL 33   Entered MRWA service as JA 6, 1911;
To WAGR, 1-8-1964;
Entered service as ACL 33, painted Larch green, 17-12-1964;
Conv. to ACM suburban car, 1965;
W/o, 1968;
To Vintage Train, Bunbury;
Restored to MRWA livery as Ja 6 & to Bassendean.

ACL 36   Entered MRWA service as one of JA 7-10, 1911;
Renumbered JA 19, 1913;
Renumbered JA 10, 1934-1936;
To WAGR 1-8-1964;
Entered service as ACL 36, painted Larch green, 11-12-1964;
Conv. to ACM suburban car, 28-7-1965;
W/o, 31-5-1968.

    -      Entered MRWA service as one of JA 7-10, 1911/, or
Entered MRWA service as JA 23, 1913;
One of the coaches numbered 7-10 renumbered JA 20, 1913;
JA 20 or 23 renumbered JA 7, 1932;
To WAGR 1-8-1964;
Never used, w/o 4-3-1965.

    -      Entered MRWA service as one of JA 7-10, 1911/, or
Entered MRWA service as JA 23, 1913;
One of the coaches numbered 7-10 renumbered JA 20, 1913;
JA 20 or 23 renumbered JA 8, 1932;
To WAGR 1-8-1964;
Never used, w/o 4-3-1965.

    -      Entered MRWA service as one of JA 7-10, 1911;
Renumbered JA 21, 1913;
Renumbered JA 11, 1934-1936;
To WAGR 1-8-1964;
Never used, w/o 4-3-1965.

Sleeping cars.
AZS 444   Entered MRWA service as JV 31, 1927;
To WAGR, 1-8-1964;
Fitted with unpowered Governor railcar bogies;
Entered service, painted green & cream, as AZS 444, 13-8-1965;
Damaged by fire & wfu, 1971;
W/o, 9-6-1971;
Burnt during fire brigade excersize, Operation Nova, at
Millendon, 7-1972.

AZS 445   Entered MRWA service as JV 32, 1927;
To WAGR, 1-8-1964;
Fitted with unpowered Governor railcar bogies;
Entered service, painted green & cream, as AZS 445, 3-9-1965;
W/o, 29-5-1974;
Conv. to breakdown van VC 5103, 29-5-1974;
Wfu & stored at Northam;
W/o, 6-1991;
Stowed Midland for ARHS;
Sold 2004 in Lake Clifton.

AZS 446   Entered MRWA service as JV 33, 1927;
To WAGR, 1-8-1964;
Fitted with unpowered Governor railcar bogies
Entered service, painted green & cream, as AZS 446, 17-8-1965;
W/o, 19-12-1975;
Preserved ARHS Rail Transport Museum, Bassendean, 1976;
Restored, & returned to service, 11-1994;
At Midland.

Inspection car.
AL 17   Delivered to the MRWA 1892;
One of the first ten MRWA bogie composite cars 1-5;
Numbered K 16, 1903;
Conv. to General manager's saloon & renumbered KA 16,1920;
Renumbered KA 17, 1932-1934;
To WAGR, 1-8-1964;
Entered service as AL 17, using stove, hot water system &
fridge from AL 39, & painted Larch green, 4-6-1965;
Based at Narrogin;
W/o, 28-6-1973;
Preserved at ARHS Rail Transport Museum, Bassendean;
Restored to MRWA livery as Ka 17.

Express Brakevans.
Z 40801   Ex MRWA FA 51;
Entered service c.1965 as Z 40801;
W/o, 1975.

Z 40802   Ex MRWA FA 52;
Entered service c.1965 as Z 40802;
W/o, 1975.

1968 Suburban diesel railcars Commonwealth Engineering [ADK class]
ADK 681   Left Clyde for WA 11-11-1967;
Entered service 19-2-1968;
Withdrawn from use 3-1992;
Sold to NZ Railways;
Delivered Fremantle, 24-3-1993;
Departed on board "MV Envoyager", 26-3-1993.

ADK 682   Left Clyde for WA 11-11-1967;
Entered service 19-2-1968;
Withdrawn from use 3-1992;
Sold to NZ Railways;
Delivered Fremantle, 24-3-1993;
Departed on board "MV Envoyager", 26-3-1993.

ADK 683   Entered service 15-3-1968;
Withdrawn from use 3-1992;
Sold to NZ Railways;
Delivered Fremantle, 24-3-1993;
Departed on board "MV Envoyager", 26-3-1993.

ADK 684   Entered service 2-4-1968;
Withdrawn from use 3-1992;
Sold to NZ Railways;
Delivered Fremantle, 24-3-1993;
Departed on board "MV Envoyager", 26-3-1993.

ADK 685   Entered service 3-3-1968;
          Withdrawn from use 3-1992;
          Sold to NZ Railways;
          Delivered Fremantle, 24-3-1993;
.   Departed on board "MV Envoyager", 26-3-1993.

ADK 686   Entered service 3-3-1968;
          Withdrawn from use 3-1992;
          Sold to NZ Railways;
          Delivered Fremantle, 24-3-1993;
.   Departed on board "MV Envoyager", 26-3-1993.

ADK 687   Entered service 13-2-1968;
          Withdrawn from use 3-1992;
          Coupled back to back with ADK 690 for shunting at
          Claisebrook, noted 10-1992
          Sold to NZ Railways;
          Delivered Fremantle, 24-3-1993;
.   Departed on board "MV Envoyager", 26-3-1993.

ADK 688   Entered service 13-2-1968;
          Withdrawn from use 3-1992;
          Sold to NZ Railways;
          Delivered Fremantle, 24-3-1993;
.   Departed on board "MV Envoyager", 26-3-1993.

ADK 689   Entered service 9-4-1968;
          Withdrawn from use 3-1992;
          Into Midland Workshops for conversion to track recording
          vehicle, 2/3-1993;
          Conversion not completed;
          To Forrestfield for storage;
          W/o, 9-1997.

ADK 690   Entered service 31-5-1968;
          Withdrawn from use 3-1992;
          Demonstrated to New Zealand Railways to Jumperkine,
          21-5-1992;
          Based at Claisebrook during 1992 on standby;
          Coupled back to back with ADK 687 for shunting at
          Claisebrook, noted 10-1992
          Sold to NZ Railways;
          Delivered Fremantle, 24-3-1993;
.   Departed on board "MV Envoyager", 26-3-1993.

1968 Suburban railcar trailers   Midland.   [ADB class]
ADB 771   Entered service 27-3-1968;
          Withdrawn from use 3-1992;
.   Sold to NZ Railways;
          Delivered Fremantle, 23-3-1993;
.   Departed on board "MV Envoyager", 26-3-1993.

ADB 772   Entered service 1-4-1968;
          Withdrawn from use 3-1992;
.   Sold to NZ Railways;
          Delivered Fremantle, 23-3-1993;
.   Departed on board "MV Envoyager", 26-3-1993.

ADB 773   Entered service 10-4-1968;
          Withdrawn from use 3-1992;
.   Sold to NZ Railways;
          Delivered Fremantle, 23-3-1993;
.   Departed on board "MV Envoyager", 26-3-1993.

ADB 774   Entered service 24-4-1968;
          Withdrawn from use 3-1992;
          Demonstrated to New Zealand Railways to Jumperkine,
          21-5-1992;
          Based at Claisebrook during 1992 on standby;
.   Sold to NZ Railways;
          Delivered Fremantle, 23-3-1993;
.   Departed on board "MV Envoyager", 26-3-1993.

ADB 775   Entered service 10-5-1968;
          Withdrawn from use 3-1992;
.   Sold to NZ Railways;
          Delivered Fremantle, 23-3-1993;
.   Departed on board "MV Envoyager", 26-3-1993.

ADB 776   Entered service 24-5-1968;
          Withdrawn from use 3-1992;
.   Sold to NZ Railways;
          Delivered Fremantle, 23-3-1993;
.   Departed on board "MV Envoyager", 26-3-1993.

ADB 777   Entered service 17-6-1968;
          Withdrawn from use 3-1992;
.   Sold to NZ Railways;
          Delivered Fremantle, 23-3-1993;
.   Departed on board "MV Envoyager", 26-3-1993.

ADB 778   Entered service 24-6-1968;
          Withdrawn from use 3-1992;
.   Sold to NZ Railways;
          Delivered Fremantle, 23-3-1993;
.   Departed on board "MV Envoyager", 26-3-1993.

ADB 779   Entered service 15-7-1968;
          Withdrawn from use 3-1992;
.   Sold to NZ Railways;
          Delivered Fremantle, 23-3-1993;
.   Departed on board "MV Envoyager", 26-3-1993.

ADB 780   Entered service 26-7-1968;
          Withdrawn from use 3-1992;
.   Sold to NZ Railways;
          Delivered Fremantle, 23-3-1993;
.   Departed on board "MV Envoyager", 26-3-1993.

1971 Long distance diesel railcars "Prospector" Comeng.   [WCA class]
WCA 901   Entered service 20-11-1971;
          Re-engined 22-12-1992.

WCA 902   Entered service 20-11-1971;
          Re-engined -8?-1992.

WCA 903   Entered service 20-11-1971;
          Re-engined 18-9-1992.

WCA 904   Entered service 20-11-1971;
          Outshopped from Midland with black & yellow stripes on ends,
          1-12-1972;
          Re-engined 3-4-1992.

WCA 905   Entered service 10-1-1972;
          Re-engined 24-12-1988;
          Fitted with Cummins KTA 19R 6 cylinder inline diesel engine
          541 hp (406kw) at 2100rpm, & generally refurbished, 1991.

1971 Long distance railcar trailers "Prospector" Comeng.   [WCE class]
WCE 921   Entered service 20-11-1971.

WCE 922   Entered service 16-11-1971.

WCE 923   Entered service 1-12-1971.

1981 Suburban diesel railcars   Goninans.   [ADL class]
ADL 801   Trialled 3 & 4-11-1981;
          Handed over to Westrail, 17-11-1981;
          Entered service 23-12-1981;
          Withdrawn from use 3/4-1992;
.   Sold to NZ Railways;
          Delivered Fremantle, 22-3-1993;
.   Departed on board "MV Envoyager", 26-3-1993.

ADL 802   Trialled to Pinjarra 16-12-1981;
          Withdrawn from use 3/4-1992;
.   Sold to NZ Railways;
          Delivered Fremantle, 22-3-1993;
.   Departed on board "MV Envoyager", 26-3-1993.

ADL 803   Delivered 3-12-1981;
          Entered service 22-2-1982;
          Withdrawn from use 3/4-1992;
.   Sold to NZ Railways;
          Delivered Fremantle, 22-3-1993;
.   Departed on board "MV Envoyager", 26-3-1993.

ADL 804   Withdrawn from use 3/4-1992;
.   Sold to NZ Railways;
            Delivered Fremantle, 22-3-1993;
.   Departed on board "MV Envoyager", 26-3-1993.

ADL 805   Delivered 10-2-1982;
            Withdrawn from use 3/4-1992;
.   Sold to NZ Railways;
            Delivered Fremantle, 22-3-1993;
.   Departed on board "MV Envoyager", 26-3-1993.

806 to 810 built 1984.
ADL 806   Delivered 17-9-1984;
            Entered service 13-3-1985;
            Withdrawn from use 3/4-1992;
.   Sold to NZ Railways;
            Delivered Fremantle, 22-3-1993;
.   Departed on board "MV Envoyager", 26-3-1993.

ADL 807   Entered service 6-3-1985;
            Withdrawn from use 3/4-1992;
.   Sold to NZ Railways;
            Delivered Fremantle, 22-3-1993;
.   Departed on board "MV Envoyager", 26-3-1993.

ADL 808   Delivered 5-11-1984;
            Entered service 6-3-1985;
            Withdrawn from use 3/4-1992;
.   Sold to NZ Railways;
            Delivered Fremantle, 22-3-1993;
.   Departed on board "MV Envoyager", 26-3-1993.

ADL 809   Delivered 27-12-1984;
            Entered service, 18-3-1985;
            Withdrawn from use 3/4-1992;
.   Sold to NZ Railways;
            Delivered Fremantle, 22-3-1993;
.   Departed on board "MV Envoyager", 26-3-1993.

ADL 810   Withdrawn from use 3/4-1992;
            Used to conduct speed limit tests to Leederville, 26-9-1992;
.   Sold to NZ Railways;
            Delivered Fremantle, 22-3-1993;
.   Departed on board "MV Envoyager", 26-3-1993.

1982 Suburban railcar trailers   Goninans.   [ADC class]
ADC 851   Trialled 3 & 4-11-1981;
            Handed over to Westrail, 17-11-1981;
            Entered service 23-12-1981;
            Withdrawn from use 3/4-1992;
.   Sold to NZ Railways;
            Delivered Fremantle, 22-3-1993;
.   Departed on board "MV Envoyager", 26-3-1993.

ADC 852   Trialled to Pinjarra 16-12-1981;
            Withdrawn from use 3/4-1992;
.   Sold to NZ Railways;
            Delivered Fremantle, 22-3-1993;
.   Departed on board "MV Envoyager", 26-3-1993.

ADC 853   Delivered 3-12-1981;
            Entered service 22-2-1981;
            Withdrawn from use 3/4-1992;
.   Sold to NZ Railways;
            Delivered Fremantle, 22-3-1993;
.   Departed on board "MV Envoyager", 26-3-1993.

ADC 854   Withdrawn from use 3/4-1992;
.   Sold to NZ Railways;
            Delivered Fremantle, 22-3-1993;
.   Departed on board "MV Envoyager", 26-3-1993.

ADC 855   Delivered 10-2-1982;
            Withdrawn from use 3/4-1992;
.   Sold to NZ Railways;
            Delivered Fremantle, 22-3-1993;
.   Departed on board "MV Envoyager", 26-3-1993.

856 to 860 built 1984.
ADC 856   Delivered 17-9-1984;
            Entered service 13-3-1985;
            Withdrawn from use 3/4-1992;
.   Sold to NZ Railways;
            Delivered Fremantle, 22-3-1993;
.   Departed on board "MV Envoyager", 26-3-1993.

ADC 857   Entered service 6-3-1985;
            Withdrawn from use 3/4-1992;
.   Sold to NZ Railways;
            Delivered Fremantle, 22-3-1993;
.   Departed on board "MV Envoyager", 26-3-1993.

ADC 858   Delivered 5-11-1984;
            Entered service 6-3-1985;
            Withdrawn from use 3/4-1992;
.   Sold to NZ Railways;
            Delivered Fremantle, 22-3-1993;
.   Departed on board "MV Envoyager", 26-3-1993.

ADC 859   Delivered 27-12-1984;
            Entered service 18-3-1985;
            Withdrawn from use 3/4-1992;
.   Sold to NZ Railways;
            Delivered Fremantle, 22-3-1993;
.   Departed on board "MV Envoyager", 26-3-1993.

ADC 860   Withdrawn from use 3/4-1992;
            Used to conduct speed limit tests to Leederville, 26-9-1992;
.   Sold to NZ Railways;
            Delivered Fremantle, 22-3-1993;
.   Departed on board "MV Envoyager", 26-3-1993.

1986 Suburban Saloon cars, ex QR   Comeng.   [SX class]
SX 1664   Ex Acacia Ridge, Brisbane, 14-7-1986;
            Arrived Perth, 27-7-1986;
            Trialed Perth 4-8-1986;
            Withdrawn from use, 12-1991;
            Returned to Queensland, 5/6-1992.

SX 1666   Arrived Perth 5-9-1986;
            Withdrawn from use, 12-1991;
            Returned to Queensland, 5/6-1992.

SX 1667   Arrived Perth 5-9-1986;
            Spare car, not often used;
            Returned to Queensland, 5-1991.

SX 1668   Arrived Perth 3-9-1986;
            Spare car, not often used;
            Returned to Queensland, 5-6-1991.

SX 1669   Arrived Perth 3-9-1986;
            Withdrawn from use, 12-1991;
            Returned to Queensland, 5/6-1992.

SX 1727   Arrived Perth 1-10-1986;
            Spare car, not often used;
            Returned to Queensland, 5/6-1991.

SX 1728   Arrived Perth 5-10-1986;
            Spare car, not often used;
            Withdrawn from use, 12-1991;
            Returned to Queensland, 5-1991.

SX 1729   Arrived Perth 5-10-1986;
            Spare car, not often used;
            Returned to Queensland, 5-1991.

SX 1730   Arrived Perth 7-10-1986;
            Returned to Queensland, 5/6-1992.

SX 1731   Arrived Perth 30-9-1986;
            Spare car, not often used;
            Returned to Queensland, 5-1991.

1986 Suburban brake cars ex QR   Comeng.   [SXV class]
SXV 1663 Arrived Perth 9-1986?

Withdrawn from use, 12-1991;
Returned to Queensland, 5/6-1992.

SXV 1665 Arrived Perth 9-1986?
Withdrawn from use, 12-1991;
Returned to Queensland, 5/6-1992.

SXV 1726 Arrived Perth 1-10-1986;
Withdrawn from use, 12-1991;
Returned to Queensland, 5/6-1992.

SXV 1732 Arrived Perth 30-9-1986;
Withdrawn from use, 12-1991;
Returned to Queensland, 5/6-1992.

1987 Long distance diesel railcars "Australind" Comeng.   [ADP class]
ADP 101   First trial 5-6-1987;
Entered service 16-11-1987.

ADP 102   Entered service 16-11-1987.

ADP 103   Entered service 16-11-1987.

1987 Long distance railcar trailers "Australind" Comeng.   [ADQ class]
ADQ 121   Entered service 16-11-1987.

ADQ 122   Entered service 16-11-1987.

1990 Electric Motorised Units "A" series Walkers/ASEA. [AEA & AEB classes]

AEA 201/AEB 301   Delivered 1-9-1990;
Entered service 28-9-1991;
Named "City of Perth", 11-4-1992.

AEA 202/AEB 302   Delivered 9-1990?
Entered service 28-9-1991;
Named "City of Armadale", 11-4-1992;
Hit car on level crossing at Kelmscott, 16-7-1992.

AEA 203/AEB 303   Delivered 1-10-1990?
Entered service 28-9-1991;
Named "Shire of Swan", 11-4-1992

AEA 204/AEB 304   Delivered - -1990?;
Entered service 28-10-1991;
Named "City of Fremantle", 11-4-1992.

AEA 205/AEB 305   Delivered 22-7-1991;
Entered service 28-9-1991;
Named "City of Wanneroo", 21-3-1993.

AEA 206/AEB 306   Delivered - -199 ?;
Entered service 17-10-1991.

AEA 207AEB 307   Delivered - -199 ?;
Entered service 22-10-1991.

AEA 208/AEB 308   Delivered - -1991?;
Entered service 28-10-1991.

AEA 209/AEB 309   Delivered -2-1991?;
Entered service 29-11-1991.

AEA 210/AEB 310   Delivered - -1991?;
Entered service 19-11-1991.

AEA 211/AEB 311   Delivered c. 4-1991;
Entered service 2-12-1991.

AEA 212/AEB 312   Delivered - -1991?;
Entered service 19-12-1991.

AEA 213/AEB 313   Delivered - -1991?;
Entered service 2-12-1991.

AEA 214/AEB 314   Delivered 5-1991;
Entered service 14-11-1991.

AEA 215/AEB 315   Delivered - -1991?

Entered service 30-12-1991.

AEA 216/AEB 316   Delivered - -1991?
Entered service 16-1-1992.

AEA 217/AEB 317   Entered service 14-2-1992;
AEB 317 damaged in shunting accident at
Claisebrook, 18-3-1993;
AEA 217 used with AEB 326 3-1993 till c.11-1993.
AEB 317 returned to service, 11-1993.

AEA 218/AEB 318   Entered service 28-2-1992.

AEA 219/AEB 319   Entered service 10-3-1992.

AEA 220/AEB 320   Entered service 25-3-1992;
AEA 220 used for spares from 1-1994 till 3-1994.

AEA 221/AEB321   Entered service 2-4-1992.

AEA 222/AEB 322   Entered service by 20-12-1992.

AEA 223/AEB 323   Entered service - -1992.

AEA 224/AEB 324   Delivered, but not placed in service due to collision
damage when it slid into the buffer stop at Armadale
during trials, 9-1992;
Entered service c.7-1994.

AEA 225/AEB 325   Hit car on level crossing at Beckenham during trial
run, 5-7-1992;
Repaired & entered service - -1992.

AEA 226/AEB 326   Entered service - -1992;
AEA 226 coupled to AEB 339, & AEB 326 coupled
to AEA 217 from 3-1993 till c.11-1993.

AEA 227/AEB 327   In service by 31-8-1992.

AEA 228/AEB 328   Entered service - -1992.

AEA 229/AEB 329   Entered service - -1992.

AEA 230/AEB 330   Entered service - -1992.

AEA 231/AEB 331   Trialled 28-8-1992;
Entered service by 22-1-1993

AEA 232/AEB 332   Entered service 1992

AEA 233/AEB 333   Entered service 1992

AEA 234/AEB 334   Entered service 1992

AEA 235/AEB 335   Delivered 10-1992

AEA 236/AEB 336   Delivered 10-1992

AEA 237/AEB 337   Delivered 10-1992

AEA 238/AEB 338   Entered service by 26-2-1993.

AEA 239/AEB 339   Entered service
Damaged in shunting accident, Claisebrook,
18-3-1993;
AEB 339 coupled to AEA 226 from 3-1993 till
c.11-1993.

AEA 240/AEB 340   At Claisebrook for trials, 4-1993.
Entered service, 1993.

AEA 241/AEB 341   Entered service, 1993.

AEA 242/AEB 342   Moved from Midland to Forrestfield on its own bogies
for trials, 25-6-1993;
In service by 9-1993

AEA243/AEB 343   Entered service 30-9-1993;
                  Named "City of Maryborough".

AEA 244/AEB 344   Delivered 9-1998;
                  Entered service, 12-1998

AEA 245/AEB 345   Delivered 10-1998;
                  Entered service, 12-1998

AEA 246/AEB 346   Delivered 10-1998;
                  Entered service, 1-1999.

AEA 247/AEB 347   Delivered 11-1998;
                  Entered service, 1-1999.

AEA 248/AEB 348   Delivered 11-1998;
                  Entered service, 3-1999.

2004 Long distance diesel railcars & trailer s"Prospector"   United
Gonionans.   [WDA, WDB & WDC classes]
WDA 001/WDB 011   Arrived Perth about 4-4-2003;
                  Entered Transwa service 27-6-2004;

WDA 002/WDB 012   Arrived in Perth by 12-2003
                  Entered service 28-6-2004

WDA 003/WDB 013/WDC 023   Arrived Perth by 9-2004
        Entered service 23-12-2004
2004 Long distance diesel railcars & trailer s"Avon Link"   United
Gonionans.   [WEA & WEB classes]
WEA 031/WEB 041   Arrived Perth by December, 2004

2004 Electric Motorised Units "B" series EDI Rail-Bombardier.   [BEA,
BEB & BET classes]
Set 49   Arrived Perth 1-6-2004
           Entered service, 4-10-2004.

Set 50   Arrived Perth by 12-8-2004;
           Entered service 4-10-2004

Set 51   Arrived Perth by 12-8-2004;
           Entered service 4-10-2004

Set 52   Arrived Perth by 12-8-2004;
           Entered service 4-10-2004

Set 53   Arrived Perth by 20-9-2004;
           Entered service 4-10-2004

Set 54   Arrived Perth by 20-9-2004;
           Entered service 4-10-2004

Set 55   Arrived Perth by 20-9-2004;
           Entered service 4-10-2004

Set 56   Arrived Perth by 20-9-2004;
           Entered service 4-10-2004

Set 57

Set 58

Set 59

Set 60

Set 61   Arrived Perth 12-2004

Set 62 to Set 79 due for delivery 2005/2006

REFERENCES

Chapter 1.

1. WA Times, 28 September, 1875
2. Annual Report of the Commissioner of Public Works & Railways, Parliamentary Paper No. 18 of 1882
3. The Inquirer, 19 January, 1881
4. The Inquirer, 16 February, 1881
5. The Inquirer, 22 June, 1881
6. ARHS Bulletin 406, August, 1971 & ARHS Bulletin 438, April, 1974
7. The Morning Herald, 1 March, 1883
8. The Inquirer, 20 February, 1884
9. WAR Annual Report, 1886, Paper No. 24 of 1887
10. Ibid
11. WAR Annual Report, 1187, Paper No. 5 of 1888
12. Article "The Four Wheeled Passenger Coaches of the WAGR" by J. Austin & A. May, The Westland No. 64, April,1990, ARHS (WA Division)
13. Unpublished notes A. May
14. WA Times, 21 April, 1876
15. Report on the Works in Progress on Geraldton & Northampton Railway, Parliamentary paper No. 5 of 1876
16. The Morning Herald, 18 June, 1885
17. The Inquirer, 17 June, 1885
18. Unpublished notes A. May
19. Victorian Express, 2 & 16 May, 1891
20. Conference Minutes, 1899. Copy held in ARHS (WA Division) Archives
21. WAGR drawing No. 896, signed by TF Rotheram 12 January, 1903
22. Minutes of General Managers Conference, 23 June, 1898, & Commissioners Conference 29 July, 1898.
23. Item 917, Locomotive Engineers Conference, 21 September, 1899
24. The Morning Herald, 18 August, 1898
25. Article "Northern Railways 1C" by J. Austin, ARHS Bulletin 642, April, 1991
26. The Inquirer, 22 June, 1881.
27. The West Australian, 28 January, 1881
28. Builder's drawing No. 3082
29. Parliamentary Paper No. 25, dated 28 May, 1886
30. WAR Annual Report, 1887, Paper No. 5 of 1888
31. The Inquirer, 4 October, 1882
32. Parliamentary Paper No. 4 of 1887
33. The Inquirer, 11 August, 1886
34. WAR Annual Report, 1888, Paper No. 8 of 1889
35. Ibid
36. CME Branch correspondence, 21 July, 1898 & 13 August, 1898.
37. WAR Annual Report, Parliamentary Paper No. 14 of 1883
38. The Inquirer, 20 February, 1884
39. The Inquirer, 17 June, 1885 & 2 September, 1885
40. WAR Annual Report, 1886
41. The Western Mail, 31 December, 1887
42. Annual Report, 1893, Parliamentary paper No. 24 of 31 December, 1891
43. "A History of WAGR Steam Locomotives" by A. Gunzberg, ARHS 1984.
44. Minutes of Commissioners Conference 4 February, 1898.
45. CME Branch Correspondence, 16 February, 1898
46. Minutes of Commissioners Conference 25 February, 1898.
47. Minutes of General Managers Conference, 29 September, 1898
48. Minutes of Commissioners Conference 27 October, 1898.
49. Minutes of Locomotive Department meeting, 10 November, 1898.
50. WAR Annual Report, 1893, Parliamentary Paper No. 24
51. Article "The Hopetoun - Ravensthorpe Railway" by P. Nugent, ARHS Bulletin 349, November, 1966

Chapter 2.

1. "A History of WAGR Steam Locomotives" by A. Gunzberg, ARHS 1984.
2. Correspondence with reference to the Midland Railway with proposals for its Final Completion, Paper No. 22, 1892
3. Report of Proposals Submitted to the Government by the Midland Railway Co., Paper No. A10 of 1892
4. Paper A23 of 1893, Parliamentary Proceedings
5. "Broken Journeys Vol 2" by Kenn Pearce, Railmac Publications, 1988
6. "A History of WAGR Steam Locomotives" by A. Gunzberg, ARHS 1984.
7. Comparative Statement of New Stock Erected 1894 to 1897
8. "One Hundred Years of the Great Southern Railway of Western Australia", edited by AR Bollans, ARHS 1989, & photographic evidence
10. WAGR Annual Report, 1897
11. WAGR General managers Conference Minutes, 26 August, 1897
12. Article "Early Railways in the Kalgoorlie Area" ARHS Bulletin 337, November, 1965
13. WAGR Annual Report, 1901, Paper 41
14. Minutes of Commissioners Conference 29 June, 1898, & The Morning Herald, 9 February, 1900.
15. Unpublished notes A. May
16. WAGR drawing No. 896, signed by TF Rotheram 12 January, 1903
17. Minutes of Commissioners Conference 1904
18. The Morning Herald, 16 January, 1900, & Annual Report, 1900, Paper No.35
19. The Morning Herald, 24 August, 1901
20. The Morning Herald, 27 February, 1902
21. WAGR Annual Report, 1900

22. WAGR Annual Report, 1900, referred to as complete in 1901 Annual report, page 29

23. WAGR Weekly Notice No. 37, page 12, week ending 14 September, 1900

25. Unpublished notes A. May

26. Ibid

27. Ibid

28. ARHS Bulletin No. 555, Page 11, January, 1984

29. Paper A23 of 1893, Parliamentary Proceeding 4 September, 1893

30. WAGR drawing 9c/173

31. "Troops, Trains & Trades" by P. Rogers, Chapter 6, published by P. Rogers, 1999

32. WAGR Annual Report, 1952

33. CME Branch Correspondence, 13 January, 1898, to 15 December, 1898.

34. Unpublished notes A. May

35. Ibid

36. WAGR Annual Report, 1908

37. WAGR Annual Report, 1910

38. WAGR Annual Report, 1952

39. ARHS Bulletin No. 345, Supplement Page 9, July, 1966

40. "A History of WAGR Steam Locomotives" by A. Gunzberg, ARHS 1984.

41. Carriage record cards

42. WAGR wagon record card, via J. Austin

43. Ibid

44. Unpublished notes A. May

45. Notation on WAGR Ministerial Car drawing No. 1

46. Ibid

47. Article "100 Years of Sleeping Cars" by J. Austin, The Westland No. 135, April,1995, ARHS (WA Division)

48. CME Branch Correspondence, 29 march, 1898

49. WAGR Annual Report, 1939

50. Article "The Port hedland - Marble Bar Railway" by EW Woodland, ARHS Bulletin 447, January, 1975

51. WAGR Annual Report, 1952

52. Comparative Statement of New Stock Erected 1894 to 1897

53. CME Branch Correspondence, 8 November, 1898

54. Unpublished notes A. May

55. CME Branch Correspondence, 2 August, 1898

56. Unpublished notes A. May

57. The West Australian, 25 October, 1947

58. The daily News, 1 August, 1947

59. WAGR Annual Report, 1962 & 1964

Chapter 3.

1. Article "Early Railways in the Kalgoorlie Area" by W.H. Shepley. ARHS Bulletin No. 337, November, 1965, Page 209.

2. Ibid. Page 210.

3. Article "A Short History of the Midland Railway" by M.J. Searle. ARHS Bulletin 555, January, 1984. Page 11

4. WAGR Annual Report, 1903.

5. WAGR Annual Report, 1902.

6. "West Australian", 12 September, 1903.

7. WAGR Annual Report, 1903.

8. "A History of WAGR Steam Locomotives" by A. Gunzberg. ARHS 1984.

9. WAGR Annual Report, 1905.

10. Ibid.

11. WAGR drawings unnumbered.

12. WAGR drawings 1a/1734 & 1/1798.

13. WAGR Annual Report, 1908.

14. Article "The Hopetoun to Ravensthorpe Railway" by P.W. Nugent. ARHS Bulletin 349, November, 1966

15. Carriage record cards.

16. Article by J. Austin, Westland No. 60. ARHS (WA Division).

17. WAGR Annual Report, 1910.

18. WAGR drawings 1a/1734 & 1/1798.

19. "West Australian" 30 September, 1948.

20. Article "Brakevans - End of an Era" by A. May, Westland No. 9, September, 1985. ARHS (WA Division)

21. A. May unpublished notes.

22. WAGR Annual Report, 1919.

23. WAGR Annual Report, 1929.

24. WAGR Annual Report, 1935.

25. "Trains, Troops & Trades" by P. Rogers, published P. Rogers 1999.

26. Article by J. Austin, Westland No. 60. ARHS (WA Division).

27. Ibid.

28. WAGR Annual Report, 1953.

29. Article by J. Austin, Westland No. 60. ARHS (WA Division).

30. WAGR Annual Report, 1934.

31. WAGR Annual Report, 1921.

32. WAGR Annual Report, 1929.

33. Article "Notes on WAGR's Dining Cars" by LG Watson. ARHS Bulletin 539, September, 1982.

34. Ibid.

35. Ibid.

36. WAGR drawings 2/1374, plus another unnumbered.
37. Article by J. Austin, Westland No. 60. ARHS (WA Division).
38. West Australian, 30 September, 1948. The accident occurred at 5.15am on 29 September, 1948.
39. WAGR Annual Report, 1949.
40. Daily News, 1 March,1949.

Chapter 4.

1. Article "The Port Hedland – Marble Bar Railway" by EW Woodlands, ARHS Bulletin 447.
2. WAGR Annual Report, 1915.
3. Ibid.
4. "A History of WAGR Steam Locomotives" by A. Gunzberg, ARHS (WA) 1984.
5. Article "Notes on WAGR Dining Cars" by LG Watson, ARHS Bulletin 539, September, 1982.
6. "Broken Journeys Vol. II" by Ken Pearce, Railmac Publications, 1989.
7. Article "Early Railways in the Kalgoorlie Area" by WH Shepley, ARHS Bulletin 337, November, 1985.
8. WAGR Annual Report 1923.
9. "A History of WAGR Steam Locomotives" by A. Gunzberg, ARHS (WA) 1984.
10. WAGR Annual Report 1929.
11. "A History of WAGR Steam Locomotives" by A. Gunzberg, ARHS (WA) 1984.
12. WAGR Annual Report 1928, Pages 8 & 16.
13. WAGR Annual Report 1929.
14. Ibid.
15. Working Timetable October, 1928.
16. WAGR Annual Report, 1952, Page 18.
17. Article "Early Railways in the Kalgoorlie Area" by WH Shepley, ARHS Bulletin 337, November, 1985.
18. WAGR drawing 10/1734.
19. A. May unpublished notes.
20. WAGR Annual Report 1936.
21. WAGR Annual Report 1938.
22. ARHS Bulletin 343 Supplement, page6.
23. WAGR drawing 27/1734.

Chapter 5.

1. WAGR Annual Report 1935.
2. WAGR Annual Report, 1929.
3. WAGR Annual Report, 1936.
4. WAGR Annual Reports 1935 & 1936.
5. WAGR Annual Report, 1936.
6. Ibid.
7. WAGR Annual Report, 1938.
8. Article "The Hopetoun – Ravensthorpe Railway" by P. Nugent, ARHS Bulletin 349, November, 1966.
9. The West Australian, 27 October, 1938.
10. "A History of WAGR Steam Locomotives" by Adrian Gunzberg, ARHS 1984.
11. WAGR Annual Report, 1936.
12. A. May unpublished notes.
13. WAGR Annual Reports, 1938, 1939, & 1940.
14. "A History of WAGR Steam Locomotives" by Adrian Gunzberg, ARHS 1984.
15. WAGR Annual Report, 1944.
16. WAGR Annual Report, 1953, Page 11.
17. WAGR Annual Report, 1940.
18. A. May unpublished notes.
19. "Troops, Trains & Trades" by P. Rogers, published P. Rogers 1999
20. G. Watson unpublished article.
21. WAGR Annual Report, 1937.
22. WAGR Annual Report, 1947.
23. WAGR Annual Report, 1948.

Chapter 6.

1. West Australian 25 October, 1947.
2. Daily News 1 August, 1947.
3. WAGR Annual Report, 1948.
4. Ibid
5. "The Australind" by Bob Taylor, ARHS WA Division, 1987./ WAGR Annual Report, 1948.
6. WAGR Annual Report, 1947.
7. Ibid.
8. West Australian, 30 September, 1948.
9. West Australian, 1 March, 1949.
10. Daily News, 24 November, 1949.
11 WAGR Annual Report, 1949.
12. WAGR Annual Report, 1950.
13. WAGR Annual Report, 1951.
14. WAGR Annual Report, 1949.
15. WAGR Annual Report, 1950.
16. WAGR Annual Report, 1952
17. Ibid.
18. WAGR Annual Report, 1953.
19. A. May unpublished notes

20. "The Australind" by Bob Taylor, ARHS WA Division, 1987.
21. "Diesel Mechanical Railcars of WAGR" by A. May & D. Merrin, ARHS WA Division 1996.
22. Ibid. In the first year of operation more than 2 million extra passenger journeys were made - WAGR Annual Report, 1955.
23. Carriage record card, ARHS Archives
24. WAGR Annual report, 1956.
25. WAGR Annual Report, 1957.
26. WAGR Annual Report, 1958.
27. WAGR Annual Report, 1959.
28. WAGR Annual Report, 1948.
29. "The Australind" by Bob Taylor, ARHS WA Division, 1987.
30. Ibid.
31. Ibid.
32. The Westland No. 126, July, 1995, ARHS WA Division.
33. "WAGR Railcars" by AJ Tilley, ARHS 1975.
34. Article "Here's Your Train - The ADF's" by A. May & D. Finlayson, Westland No.20, September, 1986, ARHS WA Division.
35. Ibid
36. Ibid.
37. "The Australind" by Bob Taylor, ARHS WA Division, 1987.
38. WAGR Annual Report, 1951.
39. WAGR Annual Report, 1954, & "Diesel Mechanical Railcars of the WAGR" by A. May & D. Merrin, ARHS 1996.
40. WAGR Annual Report, 1964.
41. "Diesel Mechanical Railcars of the WAGR" by A. May & D. Merrin, ARHS 1996.
42. Westrail Weekly Notice W/N 49/89 Ref CME 66/2922, Oct./Nov/ 1989.
43. Westland No. 93, October, 1992, ARHS WA Division.
44. "Diesel Mechanical Railcars of the WAGR" by A. May & D. Merrin, ARHS 1996.
45. Ibid.
46. Ibid.
47. Carriage record card.
48. Westrail Annual Report, 1976.
49. "Diesel Mechanical Railcars of the WAGR" by A. May & D. Merrin, ARHS 1996.
50. Ibid.
51. Westland No. 11, November, 1985, ARHS WA Division.

Chapter 7.
1. WAGR Annual Report, 1959
2. WAGR Annual Report, 1960.
3. "The Australind" by Bob Taylor, ARHS WA Division, 1987.
4. Ibid.
5. WAGR Annual Report, 1961.
6. Ibid.
7. WAGR Annual Report, 1968.
8. Article "Here's Your Train! - The ADFs" by A. May & D. Finlayson, ARHS WA Division Westland No. 20, September, 1986.
9. "Here & There" Page 8, Supplement to ARHS Bulletin 321, July, 1964.
10. "The Australind" by Bob Taylor, ARHS WA Division, 1987.
11. WAGR Annual Report, 1965
12. Westrail Annual report, 1976.
13. "Here & There" Page 8, Supplement to ARHS Bulletin 344, June, 1966.
14. WAGR Annual Report, 1966.
15. Ibid
16. Ibid
17. "Here & There" Page 7, Supplement to ARHS Bulletin 344, June, 1966.
18. "Here & There" Page 5, Supplement to ARHS Bulletin 349, November, 1966.
19. WAGR Annual Report, 1968.
20. WAGR Annual Report, 1969.
21. Westland No. 47, November, 1985, ARHS WA Division.
22. WAGR Annual report, 1972.
23. WAGR Annual Report, 1974.
24. Westrail Annual Report, 1976.
25. Ibid.
26. WAGR Annual report, 1974.
27. Westrail Annual report, 1979.
28. Correspondence with P. Uhe, 1986.
29. "Here & There" Page 5, Supplement to ARHS Bulletin 532.
30. "Here & There" Page 7, Supplement to ARHS Bulletin 347, September, 1966.
31. WAGR Annual Report, 1928.
32. Article "Here's Your Train! - The ADKs" by A. May & D. Finlayson, ARHS WA Division Westland No. 27, March, 1987.
33. Westland No. 90, July, 1992, ARHS WA Division.
34. Westland No. 99, April, 1993, ARHS WA Division.
35. Article "The Prospector 20 Years On" by D. Finlayson, Westland No. 82, November, 1991, ARHS WA Division.
36. Article "Here's Your Train! - The Prospector" by D. Finlayson, ARHS WA Division Westland No. 29, May, 1987.
37. Here & There, ARHS Bulletin 791, September, 2003.

Chapter 8.
1. Westrail Annual Report, 1976
2. Westrail Annual Report, 1979
3. Article "Here's Your Train! - The ADLs" by Andrew May & Don Finlayson, ARHS Westland No. 28, April, 1987.
4. Article "Brakevan- End of an Era" by Andrew May, ARHS Westland No. 9, September, 1985.

5. ARHS Westlander No. 9, September, 1984.

6. Article "Here's Your Train! - The ADLs" by Andrew May & Don Finlayson, ARHS Westland No. 28, April, 1987.

7. Ibid.

8. ARHS Westland No. 99, April, 1993.

9. Railway Transportation Magazine, June, 1962.

10. Ibid.

11. ARHS Westland No. 9, September, 1985

12. Westrail drawing dated 12-10-1987.

13. ARHS Westland No. 156, January, 1998

14. ARHS Westland No.   May, 1992.

15. ARHS Westland No. 102, July, 1993

16. ARHS Westlands No. 100, May, 1993 & No. 106 November, 1993.

17. ARHS Westland No. 153, October, 1997.

18. ARHS Bulletin No. 735, January, 1999.

19. ARHS Westland No. 165, October, 1998.

20. Article "The New Prospector" by Dr. Paul Collin, ARHS Westland No. 229, February, 2004.

21. ARHS Westland No. 235, August, 2004.

22. Ibid.

23. Personal correspondence P. Collin, & Railway Digest, February, 2005.

24. Personal correspondence P. Collin, & Railway Digest December, 2004, May 2005.

25. Railway Digest, February, 2005

26 ARHS Westland 110, March, 1994.

27. ARHS Westland No. 191, December, 2000.

Most of the Conference Minutes & other former WAGR files are held in the ARHS Archives at the Bassendean Rail Transport Museum, or at the Battye Library in Perth.

Information not referenced in the text has been derived from three main sources:-
1. Carriage record cards, held in the Archives of the Australian Railway Historical Society, WA Division;
2. Carriage diagrams, CME Dept., Midland.
3. WAGR Annual Reports.

Abbreviations.

ARC&ICo - Ashbury Railway Carriage & Iron Co., Manchester, England
ARHS   - Australian Railway Historical Society.
BM&Co.   - Brown, Marshall & Co., Birmingham, England
BRC&WCo.- Birmingham Railway Carriage & Wagon Co., Smethwick, Birmingham, England
Compt.   - Compartment
Conv.   - Converted
Gilbert   - Gilbert Manufacturing Co., Troy, New York, USA
Govt.   - Government
GRC&WCo. - Gloucester Railway Carriage & Wagon Co., Gloucester, England
GSSA   - Great Southern Steam Association.
GWSA   - Goldfields Water Supply Administration
HVR   - Hotham Valley Railway
KBLLPS   - Kalgoorlie-Boulder Loop Line Preservation Society
LWCo.   - Lancaster Wagon Co., Lancaster, England
MRC&WCo.- Metropolitan Railway Carriage & Wagon Co., Birmingham, England
MRWA   - Midland Railway Co. of Western Australia
OC&WCo. - Oldbury Railway Carriage & Wagon Co., Oldbury, England
Oou   - Out of use
PTA   - Public Transport Authority of Western Australia
PWD   - Public Works Department
Reclass   - Reclassified
Reno'd.   - Renumbered
RTM   - Rail Transport Museum
WAGR   - West Australian Government Railways
Wfu   - Withdrawn from use
WIW   - Westralia Iron Works, Rocky Bay, North Fremantle, WA
W/o   - Written off.

The term "Written off" indicates that the vehicle concerned had it's number removed or "written off" the WAGR's records.
"Condemned" has the same meaning as "written off".
"Demolished" indicates that the vehicle was physically destroyed.

Dates
Dates of conversions, etc. are the dates the car re-entered service.
Some dates of repainting or bogie exchanges are estimates based on the known dates of general overhauls.

The End